COM+

Richard Leinecker

SAMS

A Division of Macmillan USA
201 West 103rd Street
Indianapolis, Indiana 46290

Unleashed

COM+ Unleashed

Copyright © 2000 by Sams Publishing

International Standard Book Number: 0-672-31887-3

Library of Congress Catalog Card Number: 99-067859

Printed in the United States of America

First Printing: July 2000

03   02   01   00   4   3   2   1

Trademarks

Warning and Disclaimer

ASSOCIATE PUBLISHER
Bradley L. Jones

EXECUTIVE EDITOR
Chris Webb

ACQUISITIONS EDITOR
Danielle Bird

DEVELOPMENT EDITOR
Steve Rowe

MANAGING EDITOR
Charlotte Clapp

PROJECT EDITOR
Carol Bowers

COPY EDITOR
Rhonda Tinch-Mize

INDEXER
Eric Schroeder

PROOFREADERS
Tony Reitz
Maryann Steinhart

TECHNICAL EDITORS
Tom Archer
Christophe Nasarre

MEDIA DEVELOPER
Jason Haines

INTERIOR DESIGNER
Gary Adair

COVER DESIGNER
Aren Howell

PRODUCTION
Darin Crone

Contents at a Glance

Contents

About the Author

Rick Leinecker is a veteran software developer and author with more than 15 years of experience. Among his current book titles are *The Visual C++ 6 Bible* and *Sams Teach Yourself Visual J++ in 21 Days*. He's written hundreds of magazine articles, and now writes for developer Web sites such as www.developer.com and www.sourceDNA.com.

You might find some of his software such as *Perfect Checkmate* and *Bicycle Bridge* when you visit retail stores. He's written dozens of entertainment titles over the years including *Trump Castle* and *Miami Vice*.

He's held a number of lead positions in major companies including Senior Software Engineer at MCI's digital imaging division and Senior Software Engineer at Landmark Communications.

You can find Rick's hot-off-the-press work by visiting www.developer.com and www.sourceDNA.com, where he writes weekly articles on DNA technology. He also moderates the Windows 2000 forums on www.CodeGuru.com. You can find his well-developed imaging library named *ImageObject* at www.infinitevision.net.

When he's not writing books and software, Rick can be found participating in theater guild productions such as *Bye Bye Birdie* and *Camelot*. He also sings, plays the guitar and French horn, and writes music.

Dedication

This book is dedicated to my girls: Tammy, Jane, Judy, and Beth.

Acknowledgments

Any book is difficult and time consuming to write. But a book that covers emerging technology is even more so because there isn't always a lot of existing information to go on. That's why I'm especially thankful for Danielle Bird, who knew when to be patient and when to push. To her I extend my sincerest gratitude.

Steve Rowe was a fantastic help in the process. He has a well-tuned sense of when to suggest refinement and additions, and when to leave material alone. My hat's off to him for a job well done.

Tom Archer was a help to me personally because he was always there to answer my questions and act as a sounding board. He also turned out to be a very capable technical editor when called upon. Thanks, Tom; the book's quality has been lifted by your efforts.

Tell Us What You Think!

As the reader of this book, *you* are our most important critic and commentator. We value your opinion and want to know what we're doing right, what we could do better, what areas you'd like to see us publish in, and any other words of wisdom you're willing to pass our way.

As an Associate Publisher for Sams Publishing, I welcome your comments. You can fax, email, or write me directly to let me know what you did or didn't like about this book—as well as what we can do to make our books stronger.

Please note that I cannot help you with technical problems related to the topic of this book, and that due to the high volume of mail I receive, I might not be able to reply to every message.

When you write, please be sure to include this book's title and author as well as your name and phone or fax number. I will carefully review your comments and share them with the author and editors who worked on the book.

Fax:	317-581-4770
Email:	adv_prog@mcp.com
Mail:	Bradley L. Jones
	Associate Publisher
	Sams Publishing
	201 West 103rd Street
	Indianapolis, IN 46290 USA

Introduction

This book achieves several objectives:

- Unleashes the power of COM+ in the context of practical, advanced solutions.
- Uncovers ways in which COM+ can be used that perhaps the reader never imagined possible.
- Removes the magic curtains that surround Windows DNA and its framework of powerful server-side products such as the COM+ catalog.
- Points out common pitfalls and subtle inconsistencies encountered in real-world COM+/DNA projects.

Intended Audience

This book is by no means a reference text or theoretical survey on COM+. It is intended for intermediate- to advanced-level COM+ programmers to take COM+ to the next level. It is assumed that the reader has a working knowledge of C++ and is comfortable working with points and the Windows environment.

What This Book Covers

COM+ is a huge topic, and its thorough examination would require several large volumes of text. This book places emphasis on programming advanced COM+ applications using the Microsoft DNA framework as a roadmap. Server-side DNA products such as MTS and MSMQ are discussed at length because of their importance and convergence with COM+. Although DNA focuses on n-tier distributed Internet applications, the programming techniques discussed apply to COM+ programming and interoperability in general.

Many powerful features in COM+ are often overlooked by the novice programmer because they are complex or have inadequate documentation. This book minimizes the learning curve surrounding the more esoteric, but powerful, facets of COM+. Although opaque on the surface, some of these features, such as monikers, custom marshaling, and persistent storage, are essential for the COM+ developer ready to make applications as scalable, reliable, and efficient as possible.

Although I do not cover COM+ from a theoretical perspective, I cannot dismiss the topic altogether, either. There are some fascinating algorithms and protocols in COM+ that I will survey throughout the book in order to help the reader grasp an understanding of the limitations and capabilities of this technology.

What It Doesn't Cover

It is assumed that you are aware and convinced of the benefits of COM+ and how it works at a low level. The fundamental building blocks of COM+ aren't explained. You should be familiar with the IUnknown interface, for example, and its role in COM+.

Comparisons between COM+ and other component technologies (such as CORBA) aren't discussed.

IIS is an integral part of DNA. It is beyond the scope of this book because it sits at the boundary of Web technology, and COM+ is generally programmed through scripts and other higher-level languages. If you are targeting Internet Web-enabled applications, you can try some of the reference texts mentioned in Chapters 1 and 2.

Contacting the Author

One of my primary motivating factors in writing books and contributing my personal time to newsgroups and developing Web sites is that I enjoy helping my fellow developers. To that extent and also as my way of saying "Thank you" for purchasing this book, don't hesitate to contact me with any questions regarding this book or DNA/Web development in general. I can be reached at a Web site I've created specifically for Web developers like you at www.sourceDNA.com.

Downloading the Examples

The examples presented throughout the book are located on the CD-ROM, along with an installation utility to make it easier to find just what you're looking for.

For some reason, although many developers have no problem telling their managers that bugs in software are just a fact of life, these same developers find it incomprehensible that the software found in a book can be anything less than perfect. Although the editors of this book have done a tremendous job in testing the examples, unfortunately, as with any other software project, bugs do in fact exist in everyone's code. Therefore, I would strongly recommend always checking the MCP Web site at ftp://www.mcp.com/product_support or http://www.sourceDNA.com for the latest versions of the source code.

Software Requirements

The following sections discuss the software requirements for *COM+ Unleashed*. Several different technologies and programming tools are used in this book.

COM

COM does not specify any particular development language or tool as long as it can produce a binary vtable preamble and register components. Although it certainly is possible to use very low-level languages, such as Assembly, to produce COM components, it would require a Herculean effort to accomplish that in a team environment. Microsoft has produced dozens of tools and development kits to help developers avoid as many implementation details as possible to focus on application design and logic.

I will embrace this vision and use what Microsoft has to offer to help you get the job done faster and with fewer bugs. Specifically, the code segments in this book use Visual C++ 6.0 with Service Pack 3, along with the Active Template Library. For a few of the code examples, Visual Basic 6.0 and VB Script will be used to demonstrate alternative methods of implementing COM.

The COM Library is standard in Windows NT, 95/98, and 2000.

COM+

While COM is supported on Windows NT and 95/98, only Windows 2000 has support for COM+. In order to develop, test, and use many of the examples in this book, you must have a computer with Windows 2000 installed.

MTS/MSMQ

MTS and MSMQ are freely available from the Microsoft Web site and come as part of the Option Pack 4.0. MSMQ requires at least one NT Server 4.0 machine to serve as a Primary Enterprise Controller. MTS will work on Windows NT and 95/98.

How This Book Is Organized

This book consists of four parts, each building on the previous one. An effort has been made to give each part a self-contained look and feel, but you can also easily follow them in progression.

The parts of this book are previewed in the following sections.

Windows DNA and COM+

This part examines the Component Object Model and its relationship with the Microsoft DNA framework. The main server-side products and development tools are covered in the context of DNA. You also learn the sound design principles of multitiered architectures (ideal for component-based programming).

Advanced COM+ Programming Techniques

With the assumption that the reader is at an intermediate-to-advanced level of COM+ programming, the more powerful, but sometimes cryptic features of COM/COM+ are explained here. Topics like component persistence, events, monikers, threading, and other advanced issues are covered in detail.

Component Management and Transactions

Microsoft Transaction Server and COM+ Services are covered in this section. These powerful resources and component management services do much more than broker transactions.

Asynchronous Component Programming

MSMQ and COM+ queued components provide asynchronous communications in today's mobile and disconnected computing world. These technologies provide fault-tolerant and scalable solutions for application-to-application communication.

Windows DNA
and COM+

PART
I

IN THIS PART

COM+: The Glue for Windows DNA

CHAPTER 1

Windows DNA

DNA, or Distributed InterNet Applications Architecture, is a current hot buzzword many software developers are using. It's about creating scalable and robust applications that run within a distributed Microsoft environment, or more often, within a browser via the Internet (or intranet). The Internet is expected to grow exponentially without a plateau in sight. Microsoft is anticipating this growth and wants to be a market leader not only on the user or client side with its Internet Explorer browser, but also on the development side. This is where DNA comes in.

Convergence

The Internet is rapidly becoming the platform of choice for much of the new development. But what about all existing programming models, skills, and software code? Convergence with the Internet is imminent. By encapsulating legacy code in components and using DNA to guide new development, it is possible to take the best of the client-server world (multiple tiers, distributed work, transaction processing, queuing) and add Internet elements (scripting, a ubiquitous platform, and reusable components) to create a robust framework that can accommodate virtually all existing technologies. This enables an enterprise to gradually build out legacy systems and replace them with scalable, reusable, and reliable ones (see Chapter 19, "The COM Transaction Integrator," for details on legacy systems and DNA).

DNA is an abstraction. There is no specification for building DNA applications such as there is for COM/DCOM/COM+, and there are no DNA-logo requirements or rules for regulating DNA compliance.

Microsoft does promote DNA as a robust framework, however, for building scalable, multitiered Internet applications. (The design of multitiered architectures is covered in Chapter 2, "Multitiered Component Architectures.")

To developers, this framework is more like a road map of the Microsoft tools and products to use and where they fit in a multitiered design. For example, DNA services like MSMQ and MTS greatly reduce the implementation effort of an Internet-ready application and increase its reliability. What's even more important is that a lot of the services provided by the DNA architecture are practically free to the developer, especially with the introduction of COM+. In some cases (like MTS), it is sufficient to drag and drop a component into a service's operating environment and automatically and transparently receive all the service's benefits. You can implement dynamic load balancing by changing a setting in the Component Manager.

As a matter of fact, COM+ has become an integral part of the DNA strategy. It gives developers the infrastructure necessary to easily develop multitiered applications without having to write the infrastructure code. They can simply focus on the business problems that they're trying to solve.

Tip

Whether you are building a simple online catalog of retail merchandise or a full-blown, enterprisewide secure intranet with user-interaction control, DNA can significantly reduce the development time of your Web applications.

In the eyes of information technology executives, DNA minimizes the total cost of ownership of a system and leverages existing investments in skill sets and legacy technology. DNA provides services to handle the more complex low-level communication details associated with scalable Internet applications. This greatly reduces the cost of developing a system.

Leading the charge in the DNA front are HTML and XML. HTML is the platform-independent language that allows virtually all personal and business computers to communicate with each other. XML is an extension of HTML that allows you great flexibility, including the ability to create COM+ objects.

Tip

Your applications do not require a Web or Internet element to take full advantage of the DNA services discussed in this chapter. Products like MTS and MSMQ can be used for standalone, local applications as easily as they are for distributed environments. In fact, with COM's location transparency feature, your DNA application doesn't know whether it's running in a standalone or distributed environment, and it shouldn't care.

Internet Spoken Here: HTML and XML

Plain vanilla HTML (the language of the Internet) does not provide control-flow mechanisms or variables. After an HTML page is created, it's static in time and cannot change its outcome based on user input. Fortunately, with the help of Dynamic HTML, XML, and Active Server Pages, you can augment HTML and create an illusion of a rich and stateful Web environment. Depending on the application, state (the capability to persist a program's variables) might not be necessary.

A Stateless Environment

Browsers, with all their cosmetic multimedia glory, are for all practical purposes dumb read-only viewers. They are stateless and nonlinear; that is, they can jump from one page to another randomly, without following any predefined paths.

Without the help of DNA technologies like IIS Sessions or DHTML variables or XML scriptlets, browser-based applications can't keep state from one page to the next. This represents a significant challenge to software developers (COM or otherwise) who use browsers as interactive deployment platforms.

Keeping state has never been an issue with traditional Windows applications that are event-driven or follow a finite state machine pattern. HTML, XML, and DNA, for that matter, change the Windows programming paradigm (a controlled GUI environment) and force developers to think about statelessness. To complicate matters, DNA application users (Web browsers) have fewer constraints placed on their working environment and are free to roam about unchecked.

The client or browser can jump randomly through a server's Web without going through any predefined steps or states. If you are familiar with automata theory, the browser is like a nondeterministic finite automaton with every state a starting and final state.

It is possible to carry information around from one page to the next by embedding data into URLs, but this is clumsy to program (it requires lots of parsing), discloses intellectual property, and doesn't scale well. Cookies are a good alternative because they can persist server-side information on the client, but this capability can be absent from older browsers or turned off by the user for security and privacy reasons.

COM+ can act as a bridge to solve this problem. It can easily persist information on the client machine, solving much of the problem with keeping state.

The server, on the other hand, is faced with the problem of tracking a seemingly anonymous connection as it randomly hops about from one page to another. By mapping a client's IP address and using timers, sessions can be created and state maintained for each browser accessing the server. This is one way that Microsoft's Internet Server (IIS) can keep state for a client. You learn about this and other methods in more detail in the following sections, but first you must learn about the Windows DNA Services.

The Windows DNA Services

You begin your examination of DNA from a high level by covering the various abstractions in Figure 1.1, from right to left. This figure highlights the association of services and technologies within the DNA framework. Again, DNA is not a specification, and this illustration is only a representation of DNA in the eyes of the author. There is no one key required ingredient to make your application DNA-compliant. This figure does, however, suggest an arrangement that is typical of the DNA framework as touted by Microsoft.

> **Tip**
>
> If you are familiar with the three-tiered architecture model, you will notice its pattern in the following discussion. If you are not, you needn't worry because Chapter 2 covers it in depth.

FIGURE 1.1
The Windows DNA services.

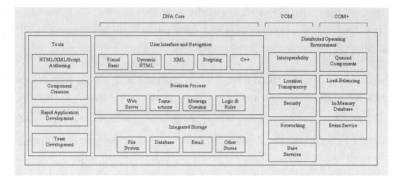

The Windows DNA Services: COM and COM+

In order to make DNA work, there must be support from the operating system kernel. An authority service must be present at all times to interpret and oversee communication protocols and component synergy. This is where COM/DCOM/COM+ (and the Service Control Manager, for that matter) come into the DNA picture as the Distributed Operating Environment (see Figure 1.1).

COM encompasses all the services shown in the first column on the far right side of Figure 1.1; COM+ encompasses the services in the second column. The COM+ library within the operating system provides the necessary glue, or plumbing services, between components that enables them to communicate and operate in a standard way. The services provided by the COM library are interoperability, location transparency, security, networking, and base services. Each is discussed in detail next. COM+ adds queued components, load balancing, in-memory database, and event service. The following two items compose the Distributed Operating Environment:

- Interoperability—For component technology to work, a consistent process of binary capability discovery must exist. Components should be able to query other components and, through a process of elimination, find whether requested behavior exists. COM provides access to this process via the `QueryInterface` mechanism of the `IUnknown` interface present in all components.

- Location Transparency—In a distributed environment like DNA, a component should not be aware of its physical location. Also, it should not have to hard-code the physical location of other components it wants to use. Of course, someone must know where components live. In COM this is the Windows Registry. The Registry enables DNA applications to execute as if they were in their own local environment even though they can really be spread out all over the Internet.

Security

Security is not to be taken lightly when working with DNA. Real exposure and threats exist when distributing a system over an intranet, or worse, the Internet.

Security can be divided into two main parts: client and server. For a client, there is the threat of executing downloaded binary images, components or otherwise, which expose the machine to viruses, Trojan horses, or blatant loss of data. These threats can be mitigated with the use of virus-detection software, certificate key technology, and a CA (Certificate Authority) to authenticate trusted sources. There is still no 100% guarantee of security because, even when certificates are authenticated, there is always a small chance of impersonation (a snooping entity claiming to be a trusted one, not to be confused with MTS Impersonation, which is discussed in later chapters).

For a typical enterprisewide DNA system, this is not normally a major concern because a physically isolated and firewalled intranet is used for the distributed environment, and any break-ins are likely to come from the inside (for which there is no known deterrent).

For a server, a security breach can have more profound consequences. A breach at the server level can create all kinds of problems including network-wide destruction of data and intellectual property theft. Windows NT Server provides government-approved, C2-level security at the kernel and file-system levels to help protect the server, but usually this is not enough. A middle network layer is required.

Between the client and server lie network security protocols like Secure Sockets Layer (SSL), TCP/IP firewalls, DCOM, or server-side, product-specific security (like MTS/MSMQ), depending on the communication medium.

DCOM security is discussed in length in Part III, "Component Management and Transactions" and TCP/IP firewalls are beyond the scope of this book, but their documentation is widely available.

MSMQ and MTS also have powerful security systems, including encryption, which are covered in subsequent parts of this book.

Despite all this security on the client and server, DNA applications are not immune to security breaches. No electronic system is infallible. Always have a contingency backup plan for your DNA system in case of electronic vandalism or theft. Nightly backups should always be performed, and spreading out tiers as physical machines will provide fault-tolerance. That is, one machine houses all presentation code, another machine serves application components, and a third machine houses all storage and Web servers.

> **Tip**
>
> For the utmost top-secret, confidential electronic information, the only way to keep it secure is to keep the machine physically isolated: behind locked doors and off a network. Even so, always keep in mind that there is no such thing as impenetrable security. Given enough time and resources, all forms of security can be broken, hacked, cracked, or otherwise rendered useless. Keep your data safe.
>
> Fortunately, COM+ comes with a robust security model. Developers can easily take advantage of it without a lot of extra code.

Networking

Networking is essential to a distributed system. In DNA, there are several high-level protocols you can use to network an application: COM+, DCOM, MSMQ, HTTP, and so on. All of them encapsulate the low-level layers of a network stack (like TCP/IP), which is very beneficial. The more encapsulation you can take advantage of, the more maintainable and reusable your DNA systems will be.

MSMQ, although not a network protocol, does enable applications to communicate with each other over a network. MSMQ can be configured to use many popular protocols like TCP/IP, but encapsulates all the protocol's communication details with simple send/receive–style API. MSMQ is covered in detail in later sections of the book.

Base Services

Other services required to make components work can be bundled in these categories—thread management, transactions, synchronization support, component registration, debugging, and so on.

We cannot take for granted the base COM services provided by the operating system. If all components had to carry code to understand the different threading models or participate in transaction contexts, the resulting component would be very bloated and slow. Furthermore, if components are hard-coded with base services like security, they would quickly become incompatible with other components in future security platforms.

The base services are essential for providing a backdrop in which components can be free to move about without concerns of networking or operating system implementation.

For example, the COM base services in a UNIX environment will certainly be implemented differently from those in NT or Windows 95. If a component is COM-compliant, it can interoperate across heterogeneous environments because the base services handle any compatibility issues. A component simply makes a call to a base service's API and lets the operating system do the rest.

The rest of this book focuses on these base services and how to take advantage of them.

Queued Components

Imagine that an application invokes a COM object on a remote server. If that server is unreachable for whatever reason, there's a problem with the communication (or lack thereof). Does the client keep trying until the remote server comes online? Or does the client abort its process entirely? These questions have plagued DCOM developers.

The answer to the problem lies in one of the new COM+ runtime services, known as queued components. This service allows a client object to make calls to a remote object, even if it's not currently reachable. The calls are recorded by a system utility, transmitted to the server through asynchronous protocols, and played back by another system utility into the server-side COM object when the server machine becomes available.

This takes the headache out of talking to remote objects because developers don't have to worry about their current state. If they're not reachable, the transaction will eventually be consummated.

Event Service

Suppose you have a system containing data that changes periodically, and refreshing the data on remote objects when the data changes is important if not essential. Without a special mechanism to signal data changes, you have to rely on a system of polling and retrieval when a change is reported.

COM+ adds something new named event service. It classifies programs in two ways: publishers and subscribers. A publisher provides information updates. A subscriber receives the information updates as notifications. The event service of COM+ provides an easy way for subscribers to sign up to receive these notifications from publishers, and for publishers to locate and make calls to their subscribers.

In-Memory Database

In-Memory Database (IMDB) offers a boost in performance to enterprise applications that primarily access read-only information from databases. What it does is cache the database information that's contained in back-end tables on middle-tier machines. Not having to access storage media and pull the data from memory is significantly faster.

Load Balancing

What happens when your enterprise application is too big for a single server? That's a problem that many DCOM developers don't have an answer for. That is, until COM+ added load balancing. The COM+ load-balancing service provides an automatic mechanism for distributing object creation requests among a number of servers in a pool, thereby spreading the load.

The Windows DNA Services: The DNA Core

In the center of Figure 1.1 are three tiers or layers of services. Each is bounded by well-defined interfaces that export public behavior only. They are User Interface and Navigation, Business Processes, and Integrated Storage. You examine what these tiers represent on a more generic level in Chapter 2, but here you learn them in the context of DNA.

User Interface and Navigation

Development tools like Visual Basic or Visual InterDev (VI) reside at the user-interface level because they are so popular for creating graphical interaction environments quickly and with controls (combo boxes, buttons, scrollbars, and so on). VB and VI are also becoming favorites among component developers because of their encapsulation of low-level COM details. VB, for example, makes it very easy to create COMcomponents with its ActiveX DLL Wizard, and Visual InterDev can turn scripts into COM-compliant scriptlets with a few mouse clicks.

Scripting technologies like ASP, VBScript, or ECMA JavaScript are popular because of their simplified syntax and user friendliness. They are a little slow and not as powerful as their compiled counterparts, but they can certainly add value to an application because they are easy to use and learn. Any time a language is interpreted (as with VBScript in ASPs) as opposed to being compiled into native code, there's a performance penalty.

C++ can also be used at this level, although not as quickly or easily as its RAD counterparts (VB, VI, VJ++, and so on). However, C++ gives the developer finer control over the graphical environment and hardware. VC++ also produces the smallest and most efficient binary images.

Business Processes

This is the heart, or *hot zone*, of DNA. Herein live the core server-side products that enable developers to focus on the solution and not the implementation details. Most of the plumbing required for managing transactions, for example, is provided by MTS. If queuing services are required, MSMQ exports a simple interface to make this happen with minimal development and configuration effort. Finally, to connect the application to the Internet, an HTTP server, like Microsoft's IIS, must exist. As you will see in a later section, IIS does a lot more than interpret HTTP.

The application must also be solving a problem, so the logic and rules to accomplish this are present in this tier. It is preferable that the rules be encapsulated in components using COM+, but this is not a requirement. COM+ components allow for reusability and inter-operability across platforms, but as long as the business rules can be activated and information passed back and forth between tiers, any programming technology can be used.

Tip

Server-side products like MTS and MSMQ can certainly be used within a local, standalone environment. The DNA services do have a clear design goal of scalability, particularly Web traffic, but this does not imply they can be used only within a distributed environment.

It is also important to note that MSMQ doesn't always belong in the middle tier. MSMQ can be used as a form of storage, in which case it would belong in the lowest tier: Integrated Storage. The hypothetical example presented in the next section illustrates this idea.

Integrated Storage

Not all storage must be tied to a database. Many forms of physical storage are acceptable and sometimes required. With DNA and its strong ties to the Internet, email or multimedia binary streams (like audio or video) are strong contenders for primary data sources or sinks. A file system can also be used as storage when relational data is not required. Log files, for example, are typically text files stored on the file system that are incrementally built as an application runs.

When data must be associated with other data, a relational database like SQL Server 7.0 can be used through Microsoft's Universal Data Access mechanisms. OLE DB and its superset, Active Data Objects, are perfect for DNA because of their component nature. Other methods of storage like collaboration streams can exist, too.

The Windows DNA Services: Tools

To use the services mentioned previously, tools must exist to aid in the integration of a DNA application. There is some overlap here with the tools mentioned in the DNA core section, but this layer is mostly oriented toward developing within the DNA core and the distributed environment.

HTML Authoring

HTML is the gateway between DNA and browser-agnostic applications everywhere. When the front end of an application needs to be accessed by a heterogeneous set of platforms, HTML is the only way to go. HTML is not just a language, but a ubiquitous platform in its own right. With HTML and server- or client-side scripting, rich applications can be created without hardware or platform assumptions by the developer. Developers need not be concerned about front-end configurations, operating systems, drivers, and so on. Plus, deployment becomes a nonissue. The application is fresh and new each time it is accessed.

> **Note**
>
> The HTML ideal and reality can be different, and in recent years, this is even more evident. Yes, HTML is intended to be cross-platform and allow developers the luxury of writing once for everyone. But with the advent of scripting and components, it can prove to be as disparate as writing native code applications in some cases.

Although many great tools exist for creating HTML, it is not surprising to note that one of the more popular tools for creating HTML content is Notepad. Notepad is a plain, bare-bones text editor that ships with the operating system. The reason for its popularity is simplicity. HTML is straightforward. There is no logic, no state, or control flow—just markup tags. Although WYSIWYG HTML editors are very convenient to use, particularly if graphics are involved, HTML is simple enough to be written in a quick and dirty way, usually with a trial-and-error design method (not recommended).

As mentioned earlier, HTML alone is not sufficient for rich, powerful applications with complex user interfaces. Server-side scripting technologies like Active Server Pages and client-side components like Java applets or COM ActiveX controls can be used to augment the plain functionality of HTML. Even if browsers are interpreting HTML in a different way, it is possible to use HTTP to let the client communicate with the server. That's a true step forward compared to TCP/IP sockets.

Component Creation

Components are orders of magnitude more sophisticated and powerful than HTML. The Visual Studio 6.0 Suite is the ideal development environment for building DNA components because of its compatibility with server-side products like IIS, MSMQ, SNA Server, and MTS. Either Visual Basic, Visual InterDev, Visual J++, or Visual C++ can be used to create components and, through the magic of COM+, they can all interoperate in harmony.

After a component is compiled and registered, it can be used by any tier in the DNA framework. The location transparency properties of COM allow the tiers to be completely distributed, without any programming effort by the component developer.

Rapid Application Development

Rapid Application Development (RAD) tools like Visual Basic were mentioned earlier in the Presentation and Navigation tier of the DNA core. This is not the only place where they can be used. RAD can certainly span the whole DNA spectrum and sometimes, when you are working with prototypes, it is the only choice.

RAD development is important to DNA and COM developers when trying to approach the most efficient DNA solution, whether it's a prototype or the real thing. Even with a thorough application design, DNA is very difficult to map. It is quite huge, and the combinations of tools and products that can be used at each level are complex and sometimes redundant. You need all the help you can get from tools like Visual Studio to quickly get something working and presented to users, identifying constraints and deficiencies in the process.

A good example of using RAD tools to quickly generate prototypes is the DTC (Design Time Control) library that ships with Visual InterDev 6.0. The data-bound HTML DTCs can reduce the time it takes to create database browser-based applications. With a few mouse clicks and property settings, a grid-control DTC, for example, can connect to a database, locate table information, and populate a grid with row and column data. This prototype can then be expanded with components, and quickly evolved to the finished product.

Team Development

DNA is distributed, and its development environment should be distributed as well. It is possible for one person to carry out all the responsibilities a DNA system entails, but it is more productive to separate the work by approaching it as a team project.

With traditional Windows applications, it was difficult to break down tasks across a team of developers because there was so much coupling involved. With DNA (and component-based software in general), it is much easier to delegate developers to loosely coupled tiers without integration being a major issue.

Content authors, for example, can work independently of data service component developers because they are so far apart in the DNA framework. There is a common goal and vision for the application, but the team can work independently and periodically checkpoint and validate the solution as a whole.

One of the most important tools to use at this level is Visual SourceSafe, which allows version control and a limited form of component management (binary files). VSS enables developers to lock files to prevent versioning problems that occur from multiple people working on the same files at once. VSS can also work as a database for application artifacts like design and specification documents, user documentation, demos, prototypes, and so on. With its capability to store the history (or evolution) of a file, VSS can be of tremendous help when projects are transitioned or passed on to other developers.

Another good tool for managing a component's life cycle is the Visual Component Manager, which ships with Visual Studio 6.0 Enterprise Edition. This tool does not provide versioning like VSS does, but exports a very user-friendly model for storing, packaging, and deploying components and any ancillary files like online help, examples, and so on. Figure 1.2 shows Component Manager in action.

FIGURE 1.2

The Visual Component Manager simplifies team development and component deployment.

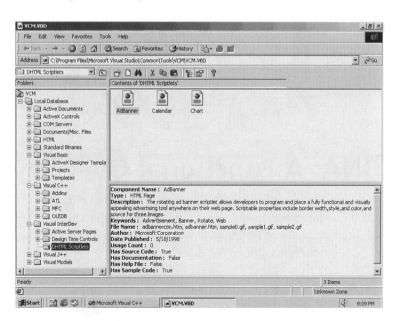

Evolving Your Applications

It is possible that your current applications are not yet ready to be taken to the level of a full-scale Web-enabled DNA application with all the tiers represented. A typical corporation will experiment first, manage the risks, and gradually evolve in phases.

Even Fortune 500 companies first take a static approach to the Web by publishing simple marketing content on their Web sites. With time and competition, their Web sites begin to incorporate interactive and dynamic elements: a search option here, a page counter there, maybe a form-based email contact page. As traffic on their Web site grows, equipment must be upgraded, security considered, and a new strategy planned.

Unfortunately, this is an expensive endeavor, and many companies are skeptical of the benefits of getting on the Internet. Skilled professionals in this area are not abundant (especially for dynamic Web content and component programming), and new Internet frameworks (like DNA) are emerging every day. A corporation faces definite risks in choosing tools to train, develop, build, and deploy a Web solution. All kinds of incompatibilities can arise when one particular technology is chosen over another (like VBScript over JavaScript) because browsers are not standard beyond HTML interpretation.

A wait-and-see approach doesn't work because the pressure to give customers what they want is real and constant. Eventually, with more and more people wanting more and more interaction with a Web site, a Web must evolve and begin incorporating the new technologies to accomplish this.

By taking on DNA in phases, it becomes more manageable and cost-effective to produce successful Web applications. Chapter 2 elaborates more on how to plan for Web convergence and, as much as possible, avoid rewrites.

DNA: A Functional Overview

Having discussed the general DNA framework and some of the Microsoft tools and products it encompasses, you can dive into more detail with a specific (but strictly hypothetical) example. In the following sections, you learn about the server-side products and tools shown in Figure 1.3.

The Browser

You begin the journey into a DNA application with a browser. This is depicted in Figure 1.3 as a computer connected to HTTP, the Internet protocol. In DNA, a browser really means Internet Explorer (IE). Microsoft has ported IE to many platforms such as

Macintosh, Windows, Solaris, and SunOS, with others in the works. IE is the ideal target browser because of its wide platform support, integration with COM (ActiveX), and relentless pursuit of world dominance in the browser wars.

FIGURE 1.3
A typical DNA application.

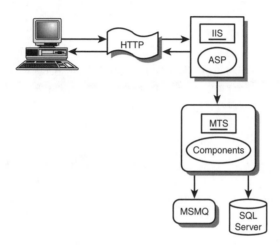

IIS

The next point of contact is Microsoft's Internet Information Server (IIS), a critical server-side product that makes DNA possible. One of its main goals is to serve HTML pages over the HTTP protocol efficiently and reliably. IIS is not the only HTTP server out there. Competitors like Apache and Netscape have long been in the server business and have produced commendable, inexpensive (or free) HTTP servers, but their main focus has been to serve static content as fast as possible. With IIS, however, you get much more than an optimized content server. You get session management, security, and ISAPI, to name a few features. To a COM developer, the most relevant of these is ISAPI and its family of component extensions, like ASP, that allows server-side scripting and dynamic content creation.

New Web Servers Are on the Horizon

Several new startup companies have recently introduced robust and dynamic Web servers. Most notably are Silver Stream and NetDynamics, which rival IIS in HTTP interpretation and claim to beat it in reliability and performance.

Session management is important to COM developers because it enables components to save state for a particular connection (client) on the server. The component itself is stateless, but information about the current executing environment can be persisted in the form of application (global) or session (local) IIS variables.

IIS can be integrated into components directly, or preferably through a scripting language like ASP.

ASP

ASP adds dynamics to HTML, a static markup language that by itself does not allow interaction with a user. In the past, HTML relied on external server-side Common Gateway Interface (CGI) programs or Perl scripts that would generate HTML based on some input. This gave the illusion of interaction, but at the cost of user-observed latency because of the many round trips required.

This was the situation *circa* 1995. Since then a whole slew of new technologies has changed the way developers write HTML-based applications. It is now possible to execute code based on user input on the client itself, without having to repeatedly query a server. This increases reliability and performance but adds coupling to the application.

Active Server Pages (ASP) encapsulate the complicated task of trying to create the illusion of a dynamic, user-driven application when only static, canned data exists. ASP enables a Web application to create individual environments controlled by the user. This is not a new concept. CGI has been around since HTML and has provided a limited form of dynamic Web content. If you've ever programmed with CGI, you are aware of its delicate and awkward user interface. ASP, although still having a few subtleties of its own (like VBScript syntax and difficulty with real-time debugging), takes CGI to the next level and creates an easy-to-program bridge between Web users and server COM components.

The addition of ASP has enabled an even finer control of Internet applications. With its capability to seamlessly instantiate COM components, Internet applications are virtually indistinguishable in functionality from their Win32 or similar GUI counterparts. Consider the following ASP script, which creates a COM object, locates an interface, calls a method, and stores a result in a variable, all with only two lines of code:

```
<%

set myobject = Server.CreateObject("Object.ImyInterface")
result= myobject.MyMethod(argument1, argument2)

%>
```

Tip

The configuration and administration of IIS is beyond the scope of COM programming and would probably merit a book of its own. Fortunately, the installation program included with IIS does a good job of setting up a default working environment. For a staging, development environment, where security and optimization are not critical, the default configuration of IIS has proven very effective. If you are deploying the system on a production server, it is highly recommended that you review the online IIS documentation on security and configuration.

MTS

Below IIS lives the Microsoft Transaction Server (MTS). In this example, a client will never see beyond ASP, so MTS is strictly playing a role behind the scenes. And MTS does more than its name implies. It certainly does a great job of automatically coordinating transactions within and across components and databases, but it also manages the caching and pooling of resources, producing scalability as a free-side effect.

MTS is normally used as a container for components in the DNA framework. The features of MTS are covered in detail in Part IV, "Asynchronous Component Programming," but for the purpose of this discussion, I treat MTS as a component manager or broker. Components do not need to be involved in transactions or require security to profit from the benefits of MTS. The components need not be confined to one MTS environment, either. They can be distributed across multiple machine boundaries.

Caution

Not all COM components will work with MTS. There are some constraints imposed on MTS-compatible components that are discussed in detail in Part IV.

A compliant COM+ component is different and will work with MTS without problems.

MSMQ and SQL Server

If your application must asynchronously communicate with another application or data store over a high-latency network, the Microsoft Message Queue (MSMQ) can be of tremendous help. MSMQ coordinates the complex synergy involved in the delivery, reception, and acknowledgment of synchronous or asynchronous messages. Because

MSMQ is COM-aware, components themselves can be messages and automatically managed. The developer need only provide the necessary implementation for the COM `IPersist` interfaces and let MSMQ take over in a reliable and fault-tolerant manner.

> **Tip**
>
> It can be debated whether MSMQ is a form of data store or a communication device. In this regard, it works as a storage medium like SQL Server. Our hypothetical DNA application will likely have asynchronous data requirements, which is where they fit in the picture.

For distributed applications that must communicate with each other remotely, or even within a local machine, MSMQ relieves the COM programmer from the burden of low-level communication details like WinSock, spawning threads, and concurrency control. MSMQ is covered in depth in Part IV.

> **Tip**
>
> The MSMQ, like its close cousin MTS, also manages resources along with components.

Visual Studio 6.0

So where does Visual Studio fit into DNA? Figure 1.3 shows you typical uses of the Visual Studio tools within a DNA application. Once again, the model depicted in Figure 1.3 is a typical example, but by no means the rule. VS6 provides a very rich set of tools, and Figure 1.4 only illustrates where three of them (a small but important subset) fit in.

Visual InterDev is the *de facto* industry standard for creating Web applications under IIS. It provides a set of tools (Design Time Controls), COM compatibility, team development support, and WYSYWIG editors, just to name a few features.

Visual Basic and Visual C++ are excellent tools for creating components, as well as Visual J++. Other COM development tools like Microfocus COBOL can do a good job of creating COM components (although at this writing, they don't support COM+).

These tools are discussed in detail next.

FIGURE 1.4
Visual Studio and DNA.

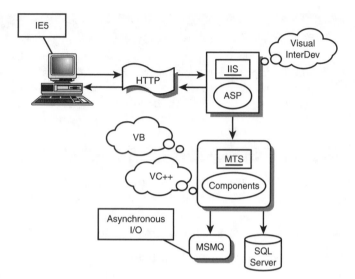

Visual InterDev

Visual InterDev 6.0 is Microsoft's newest development tool for Internet applications, particularly if ASP scripting is involved. Figure 1.4 illustrates its place in the DNA. Many good books have been written on Visual InterDev, and I won't attempt to introduce its many features or functions here. However, if you are already working with VI or plan to, here are some guidelines you can follow to make programming with COM and COM+ more productive.

Avoid Data-Bound Controls

The use of data-bound DTCs (Design Time Controls) was mentioned earlier in the chapter to highlight their prototyping qualities. However, it's important to note that in general, any introduction of coupling across logical programming boundaries, such as between the GUI and database, is a bad idea. (Design of multitiered architectures is covered in Chapter 2.) VI provides a set of SQL-ready DTC controls to quickly develop Web applications that access databases directly. There are some legitimate cases in which this sort of rapid development is required.

If you are creating a small intranet Web, for example, and must do it as quickly and reliably as possible, data-bound controls are a good option. If you choose to use the controls as opposed to delegating the logic to external components, you should be aware of risking a rewrite in the future if your application ever must be ported to another programming environment that doesn't support VI6 controls (like Win32).

> **Caution**
>
> Unless you are absolutely sure your application will never be evolved or upgraded, avoid using controls that directly bind your UI and a specific database. Binding physical data to a UI does not scale well and inhibits reusability, a key goal of DNA.

Balance Client/Server Scripting and Validation

There are many benefits to distributing a share of the server's work out to a client. If a client browser supports scripting, it should take advantage of it in a dynamic interactive environment to do simple, cosmetic validation. This can greatly reduce the number of round trips (and observed latency) otherwise required to process a form.

Another benefit to client scripting is the capability to render and manipulate UI controls on the client side. The server can send the client custom ActiveX components and controls to be contained within the browser or as standalone applications. Events can be fired and captured as if the browser were a Win32 application, and because it's all happening locally, there are no delays. This is a relief to Web surfers everywhere.

But balance is the key. It is not wise to send everything down to the client because that would make the client too independent, requiring long downloads all at once.

It is also not a good idea to put everything in the server because of the high-latency environment in which it's expected to run. If the user fills out an entire form, for example, but forgets one field, a whole round trip would be wasted because the server must reject. The rule of thumb is to put processing on the client to validate user data on a cosmetic level. (For example: Is data alphanumeric? Is data empty? Is data in date format?) Leave it to the server to do the more business-specific processing.

Visual Basic

VB is quickly becoming the *de facto* industry standard for quickly building COM components. VB encapsulates many of the gory COM and COM+ details (which I cover in this book) with its ActiveX controls and objects. This enables a developer to spend time solving the problem at hand and not worry too much about implementation issues. Although VB can get a component working in a short time, it depends on many other DLLs and can be very large. ATL (Active Template Library) might be a better long-term solution than VB components.

Unfortunately, VB does have some limitations. Although it can compile natively, it is still relying on an unpredictable garbage collector, which can slow down execution at random

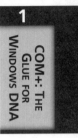

times. Its error-handling mechanism is very primitive, and it can produce spaghetti code. Furthermore, the flow control during an error is difficult to manage (the Resume and Resume Next clauses, for example).

Because it does not support implementation inheritance (only interface inheritance), some object-oriented purists will see it as inferior when an OO solution is called for.

Despite these restrictions, VB is an extremely powerful tool in the DNA framework and should definitely make up the majority of your components. Temper your needs for components that must be developed quickly with your needs for efficiency and speed. Your decision on how to proceed (VB or ATL) will depend on these factors.

Visual C++

With the ATL present in VC++, and COM support from MFC, COM and COM+ programming in C++ has become much easier. The ATL can generate very lightweight components with only the bare essentials. There is significantly more work to be done than with VB, but the components that result are as good or better than raw, hand-coded COM and COM+.

Within DNA, you will normally want to use VB for most of your business rule components and leave the ATL for only the mission critical, pedal-to-the-metal tasks. More debugging and testing are involved with the ATL, and creating large components (many methods and interfaces) is not recommended. The effort invested in developing large, complex components becomes counterproductive when trying to debug, make upgrades, or maintain the code.

Summary

In this chapter, you learned about DNA, the overriding and encompassing technology ideal behind distributed applications. It's an ideal that offers a framework under which enterprise applications can be effectively developed.

HTML provides the link between the multitude of platforms out there and the native applications. HTML does a good job in making it manageable for developers to create cross-platform code. With this said, there is a divergence with the advent of scripting and components.

COM+ enters the picture to resolve a number of development issues. It can solve many of the problems created by the statelessness of HTML. COM+ components add a performance advantage not known by HTML and scripting because it's compiled to native code. It makes it easy for developers to allow communication over disparate WAN links with location transparency.

Multitiered Component Architectures

Although COM and COM+ are groundbreaking new technologies that will surely change the way software is developed for the next decade, it is no silver bullet. COM and COM+ by themselves do not guarantee robust and reliable architectures, or even ones that work, for that matter. Good design principles are critical for any software system, regardless of the model or framework on which it is based. It is essential that sufficient time is spent analyzing the problem to be solved (the *what*), followed by more time spent designing a working solution (the *how*).

> **Tip**
>
> The analysis and requirement-gathering phases of software engineering, albeit critical, are not related to COM and COM+ programming, so they are not covered here. Design, however, does impact COM and COM+ components and merits a chapter of its own. Without a solid foundation created during the design phase of an application's development, it is unlikely the application will be successful over time. When it comes time to modify or augment the application, the lack of design will be evident and the likelihood of a rewrite is high.
>
> This chapter lays the groundwork on which all COM and COM+ programming should stand.

Chapter 1, "COM+: The Glue for Windows DNA," discussed Windows DNA as a road map. The task at hand is to correctly follow this map and build reliable, maintainable, and scalable applications with it. The design principles discussed here add value to all COM and COM+ solutions, but are essential for Windows DNA applications in particular.

An emphasis is placed on multitiered design for both its success in software design in general and its seamless adaptation to COM and COM+ solutions. I will cover traditional design methods first, three-tiered models, and finally multiple tiers in the sections that follow.

Ad-Hoc Design

Trial-and-error or nonexistent design techniques are likely to fail when you are developing software in general. Surprisingly, even when lack of design has been proven to cause late and over-budget projects that do not work or are never delivered, software developers continue to ignore this part of the development cycle. It seems as if there are never enough resources or days in the week for this seemingly empty and intangible phase.

With the component orientation inherent to COM, a flawed design is more pronounced as the application evolves. Although it is true that there are great benefits to component-based software, all advantages quickly disappear if components are assembled into monolithic, rigid structures. It is very difficult (and indeed, sometimes impossible) to scale or upgrade components without a rewrite unless they have been properly designed. It must also be taken into consideration that COM is not an easy subject to master and might even present false hopes as the solution to flawless software development. Add to that the training investment COM requires, and the pressure rises even more. A failed COM project will not be as forgivable as a traditional one. With all of its complexity, COM might seem shrouded in mystery to the uninitiated. Because we fear what we don't understand, it is very easy to blame COM technology in general when an ill-designed COM-based project fails.

Even when the technology is used correctly, components themselves don't solve all known software problems; in fact, they introduce a few of their own. If you've ever worked with DCOM, you can probably attest to this statement. (COM+ solves some of the complexities of DCOM, but more on this later.) COM takes time to learn. There is a considerable setup and configuration phase not normally associated with other programming paradigms or languages. Its benefits, however, surpass all these costs with intangible rewards like reusability, maintainability, and scalability.

> **Caution**
>
> Programming with COM+ in the Windows environment is very challenging. The challenge is not just understanding COM+ and its intricate API, but also mastering the ancillary system administration skills and domain knowledge that compound the development effort.

Fundamental Application Boundaries: Presentation, Logic, and Data Services

Designing software with components is slightly different from designing with other traditional methods. First, components are inherently independent, standalone entities. Components communicate with each other only through known public interfaces. A process of discovery reliably tests what a component can and cannot do.

If components are grouped into one monolithic, tightly coupled pile, they lose all their intrinsic benefits and add maintenance complexity. What is required is to view components as heterogeneous sets of tiers or layers, where each component has something in common with the other, but solves a different problem.

The idea of partitioning the work is not new. This highly successful model is known as the three-tiered model in the client/server community. You learn it here as a primary design guideline for all COM+ programming.

Loosely Coupled Versus Tightly Coupled Tiers

When I say a system is tightly coupled, I am referring to its interdependencies.

A coupled architecture will be rigid and inflexible, but easy to design and implement. Coupled architectures are synonymous to monoliths because they are regarded as single entities with little or no interchangeable objects or components—very much like huge blocks of granite.

Tightly coupled applications are difficult to maintain. When it is time to modify a monolithic system, the development team members might find they are painted into a corner. Making modifications to the system, however minor, is risky. A single change in a line of code in one function in one module can have a domino effect that causes another function in a separate module to break, causing the entire system to fail in strange and unpredictable ways.

Coupling can be divided into many forms. The most important are architectural, intra-procedural, inter-procedural, and inter-modular. They are listed here in order of greatest impact on the system:

- Architectural coupling ties the presentation (or GUI) code to the data and logic rules of the application or vice versa. When the presentation code of an application (the code in charge of communicating with a user via buttons, windows, events, and so on) knows about and assumes the existence of a vendor-specific database and uses that database's proprietary API, it becomes very difficult to change the application in the future when a new presentation technology (like the Web browser) or database emerges.

- Intra-procedural coupling tangles the control flow within a procedure or function. This form of coupling, the hardest of all coupling types to remove, is achieved by the frequent use of GOTO and GOSUB commands within a procedure, which quickly yields spaghetti code that is almost impossible to follow and maintain. This practice usually requires a rewrite of the procedure when a new developer must make a change.

- Inter-procedural coupling ties together functions or procedures within a module via global memory sharing. Global variables and constants form the two-edged sword of software development. They make programming very easy and quick, but in the face of change can create bug-inducing side effects that are very difficult and sometimes impossible to locate. Because the global variables are anonymous, they can be modified by anyone within the program, producing a chaotic, disorganized runtime. And it is more difficult to write thread-safe code.

- Inter-modular coupling creates dependencies across modules. Most monolithic applications will rely on a few commonly used modules or libraries. This can be a problem because a change in any of the library files will require a recompilation of the entire application. This is important when considering remote deployment of the application. Contrast this with COM+ that does not require its clients to recompile or be aware that any changes were made. As discussed in the last sections of this chapter, and in many other chapters to follow, COM+ interfaces should be eternal.

A loosely coupled architecture, on the other hand, is one composed of independent, interoperable components or objects. Changes to the architecture are isolated to one component at a time. The probability of a domino effect as previously described is almost zero. However, loosely coupled architectures incur a performance and development time trade-off. They take considerably more effort to design, there is significant communication overhead introduced by the components, and in general they are harder to implement.

Nonetheless, the benefits of loosely coupled systems far outweigh their cost, as you will see in the rest of this chapter.

Three-Tiered Design

One of the most successful models to emerge from the client/server world has been the three-tiered model. A tier, or layer, is a collection or set of independent homogenous objects (each solving a small problem) that together solve a larger but common problem.

Consider a typical PC application today. It most likely interacts with a user, processes some data, and perhaps persists its state somewhere—hence three tiers.

The three tiers are generally known as presentation, business logic, and data services. Figure 2.1 illustrates this idea and compares it to the monolithic approach, in which abstractions such as business logic and user interfaces are all bundled into one.

It is very likely that you will encounter this model under different names at different times (integrated storage instead of data services, or navigation in place of presentation, for example), but the concept is the same in any case. Within each tier live components that, in turn, contain public interfaces to the private functions or methods that do the actual work.

FIGURE 2.1

Monolithic versus three-tiered design.

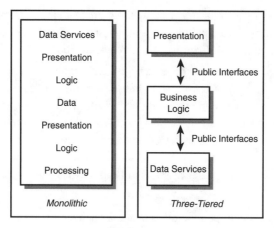

COM and COM+ are about having rigid implementation boundaries encapsulated by well-known public interfaces. Tiers are no different. The interfaces for a tier are more general and at a coarser level of granularity than for a component, but encapsulation is still the foundation.

A particular tier should know nothing whatsoever about its adjacent tiers other than their exposed public interfaces. From a procedural standpoint, this indifference seems like a restriction, but it's really a liberating mechanism.

Herein lies the strength of the model: Changes in one tier have minimal impact on the others. This rule puts the architecture in a comfortable position to be easily expanded and freely upgraded with time.

Communication across tiers exists only through public interfaces in a well-designed, three-tiered architecture. When tiers are loosely coupled, it is simple to swap out components (or entire tiers) to adapt to changing requirements without demanding a rewrite or system retest. For this reason, tiers should be completely unaware and carefree about the implementation of adjacent layers. A tier should see only the public interfaces of its immediate neighbors. In Figure 2.1, the arrows between the tiers represent the interfaces.

This highly effective and universal model has been around for years but is surprisingly uncommon outside the client/server world (one machine stores data, another reports it). With the advent of COM+ (interface-driven) and DNA, the three-tiered model is seeing tremendous use. COM+ makes it a cinch for developers to create components that communicate transparently across tier boundaries.

The following is a description of the main tiers in the three-tiered model as shown in Figure 2.1:

- Presentation—The presentation tier involves all interaction with the user. Specific GUI-only operations, like repainting a window, capturing mouse-up clicks, text input, and so on, live here. The model does not allow interaction with the user at any other tier. Doing so would couple the lower layers with this responsibility and render the model inflexible with time.

  Minimal validation of data can be done at this layer, but is better suited for the adjacent business tier below. The presentation tier does not know about any particular data store technology (if one exists) or where its data originates. This layer has a defined set of interfaces that enable it to communicate to the business layer, and that's the only capability it has.

- Business Logic—Next is the middle or business logic tier in which most of the processing is carried out. All business-specific rules are grouped into this tier. This is the part of the application that actually solves the problem. It is the middleware between the user and any physical data storage. Like its parent tier, the business tier should not know the specific details of its neighboring tiers, the data services tier below, and the tier above. It should only process data, not store it or present it.

- Data Services—Data services are in charge of any physical persistence required by the application. Specific data services mechanisms like low-level database access or SQL should go here. When the time comes to upgrade or change physical stores, nothing but this layer is affected and nothing else breaks or requires extensive retesting. Typical client/server three-tiered models involve a structured relational database storage of some type (such as Oracle or SQL Server), but this is not the case in modern three-tiered designs.

  An application does not require a database to benefit from a three-tiered model. Any kind of persistent storage can be placed here (file systems, email, multimedia streams, and so on), away from the presentation and logic layers to increase the potential for maintainability and evolution of the system in the future.

Keeping Tiers Balanced

Consider Figure 2.2, in which a well-balanced three-tiered architecture sits atop a delicate fulcrum. On the left rests all the presentation code; in the middle, the business logic; and on the right, any data services.

Although it is likely that the business logic middle tier will carry most of the weight in a system, it can be disastrous for future evolution if too much weight is placed on either extreme. Putting too much weight on either side will tilt the balanced objects and cause the application to collapse.

FIGURE 2.2

A well-balanced application.

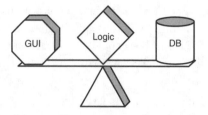

On the presentation side, this could mean adding data-aware or data-bound controls that talk directly to the data-access tier (see Figure 2.3).

FIGURE 2.3

Too much responsibility on the GUI.

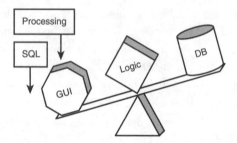

In turn, relying heavily on database-specific logic mechanisms like stored procedures or triggers on the data services tier will have the opposite effect, tipping the balance to the data services side (see Figure 2.4).

FIGURE 2.4

Too much responsibility on the server.

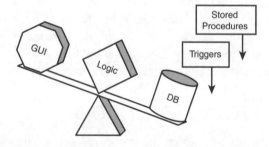

Now consider Figure 2.5, in which a solid three-tiered design rests on an immovable foundation of logic that eliminates the fulcrum and the chance of disturbing the balance. A square represents a rigid foundation, unshaken by future upgrades or modifications to any tier.

FIGURE 2.5
A solid, robust design.

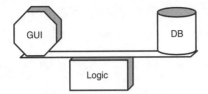

This rigid foundation is achieved by the clear separation of presentation and data logic from the business rules. As long as the problems that the application is trying to solve are oblivious to where the data comes from (if any), or how it is presented, it will remain scalable and robust with time.

The three-tiered architecture is not just for client/server environments. Virtually all applications can be divided into at least three tiers as described. (As an exception, however, consider device drivers and other low-level hardware manipulation programs in which the extra three-tiered design effort can be counterproductive.)

Whether you are building a small Win32-based application or a full-blown, Web-enabled e-commerce system, these principles are applied equally. No matter how complex the problem, software always deals with data in some form (or there would be no work to do) and can always be separated by behavior into distinctive layers.

Multitiered Design

As applications evolve and become more complex, it is sometimes necessary to break one particular tier into two or more. This results in multitiered, or n-tiered, architectures. Although the fundamental interaction with a user might be the same (present data, gather data, and store data), it is sometimes easier to break the three basic tiers into several pieces.

For large complex applications with dozens of developers, it is much easier to work with an n-tiered architecture than a three-tiered one because the work can be carried out separately in finer granularity. COM+ assists in n-tier development because developers can create components that transparently communicate across boundaries.

Consider Figure 2.6. This is an actual architecture diagram I used for a complex Web-based project. What once was the presentation tier in the three-tiered model has been broken into two independent tiers: Win32 and HTML.

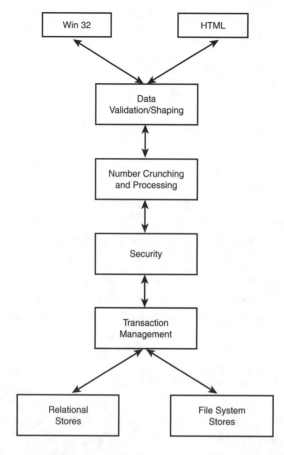

When examining Figure 2.6, you might be asking yourself, "Why not keep one tier, as before, and two components that handle HTML and Win32, respectively, adding interfaces and methods as required?" The answer is Win32 can be so complex that it would require a large set of homogenous Win32 components to coexist with another large set of homogenous HTML components. Win32 is inherently different from HTML processing (linear and event-driven instead of nonlinear and static).

As you might recall, a *tier* is defined as a collection of independent homogenous objects that work together to solve a common goal. By breaking down the tiers, and thus the number of components in each tier, you can greatly reduce the development and testing complexity of an application in a team environment. Independently developing and maintaining 5 components is much easier than doing so with 20.

The more components you have in a tier, the more the tier approaches a monolithic model (too much coupling), defeating the purpose of tiered architectures. In the case of

HTML and Win32 as presentation choices, separating them into two tiers is a sound logical choice.

> **Note**
>
> Do not confuse Figure 2.6 with a flow control diagram. It shows only the main problems of the application as abstracted in human terms. From this diagram, you cannot infer or assume communication interfaces or how data might flow throughout the application (uni- or bi-directional, concurrently, asynchronously, and so on).

> **Caution**
>
> There must certainly be a threshold set in the minimum number of components a tier should contain. If you were to make each component its own tier, you would be back where you started (all components, no homogeneous organization). When architecting an application, use tiers to your advantage but be frugal in their quantity.

Moving down from the top presentation tiers are four separate tiers that would normally be contained in the business tier. By breaking them apart according to general functional goals, it is much easier to understand what the application is doing: validating data, crunching data, securing data (encryption, authentication, and so on), and transacting data. Each of these actions could certainly be contained in a single tier, but doing so would crowd the tier and render it unmanageable—a contradiction of the model's main purpose.

Figure 2.7 shows a closer view on the Data Validation/Shaping tier. You can see it contains many different, but functionally similar, components. Each one solves a different problem within the validation domain of the application. Although validation can be considered a business-tier functionality, the validation components have little or no relation to crunching the data itself.

The next section talks about where your tiers should be physically placed in a deployment configuration.

FIGURE 2.7

Focusing on the Data Validation tier.

Data Validation/Shaping Tier

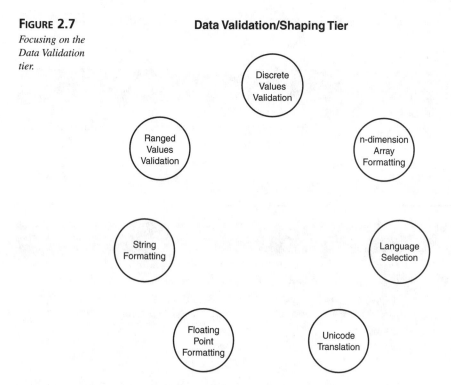

Local or Distributed?

Do not be fooled by the apparent distribution of the disconnected layers in a multitiered architecture. Programming with tiers does not imply a distributed relationship or even the presence of a database. It is a road map to follow and can be used for any application. Some applications do not even require a presentation layer. They might be services, for example, listening for non-interactive requests. Likewise, a data services tier can be absent if the application doesn't involve persistence (like the calculator usually found under the Accessories menu in Windows).

Good Design Techniques

Fortunately, sound design principles are very easy to apply to component-based software. You will not examine the more involved object-oriented approaches that exist, but instead will cover tried-and-true techniques for designing multitiered COM+ architectures. In order of importance, they are

1. Abstract the application into heterogeneous functional tiers.

2. Identify components to carry out finely grained behaviors.

3. Create interfaces or glue between the layers.

4. Implement the component interfaces and their methods.

From these techniques or principles, it is clear we are following an inductive approach. We start from the general and delve into the details.

Abstract the Application into Tiers

All useful software is created to solve one or more problems. All problems can always be divided or separated into subproblems. With components, it is important to split large and sophisticated problems into smaller, more manageable ones. By using this divide-and-conquer approach, we ensure that the problem as a whole will be solved and also create a robust and easily maintainable architecture. It is much easier to modify and upgrade a single component consisting of a subproblem than to try to tackle an entire monolithic problem, with the usual retesting and debugging.

Identify Components

This phase is a little more challenging and requires foresight (and hindsight). It's probably the most fun and creative phase of all because it brings together past experiences, current technology, and analytical problem solving.

Again, although not all applications can seamlessly fit the three-tiered model, they can always be logically separated into this abstraction at some level.

Start with presentation. Will the application interact with a user via a graphic interface or is it a service that fulfills requests blindly? Creating intuitive and user-friendly GUIs is not a trivial task. All too often, you see GUIs that are plagued with inconsistencies from screen to screen or are too busy. This only compounds the problems when you are working with browsers and their lack of rich control sets or state.

You won't learn GUI design here, but it is worth mentioning that it should not be taken lightly. Remember that although the presentation tier is just the tip of the iceberg, it is the one and only communication link between a user and what constitutes the application. The tiny presentation tier can be sitting on the shoulders of a huge sophisticated business tier, but if it's not exporting a user-friendly working environment, or is inconsistent, the user might unfairly dismiss the entire application.

After you have decided what visual or nonvisual technology to use (Win32, browser, console, and so on), separate the presentation into functional units. One component could handle menu options, another tabs, and yet another ToolTips. Or in a browser, a component can be delegated to track context menus that change from page to page, whereas others can be in charge of tracking combo and text boxes. The more you separate your presentation into standalone objects, the easier it will be to maintain and upgrade.

From experience, it is safe to say that the presentation tier undergoes the most changes. It is impossible to satisfy all users on how interaction should occur, but a common ground that will satisfy the majority of users can be found and a compromise reached.

The other two tiers should follow the same idea. The business tier is in charge of validating and processing. That's two components. A validation component can be in charge of filtering any data before it is passed on for processing. The processing component, in turn, does not have to worry about bad data because it has already been validated. This removes the burden of having to carry out both actions simultaneously, which can cause errors. COM+ assists here because it can participate in a transactional manner—exactly what is called for in this architecture.

If your application will require data access, the third (but by no means final) tier can be in charge of all data access. If your application communicates with a typical relational database, you can have two components: query and update. For example, each will have its own set of interfaces for carrying out vendor-specific SQL commands. Avoid using stored procedures whenever possible. They couple the underlying physical database with the rest of the application at the sometimes negligible reward of increased performance. If you offset stored procedures into components instead, the processing is generic and can be applied to any database technology in the future.

Stored Procedures Can Be Expensive

True story: Your consulting author once worked with a client who wanted to migrate his Sybase application to SQL Server. The PowerBuilder application in question was huge (about 400,000 lines of code) and had consumed dozens of man years. A hybrid-tiered architecture was used (2 1/2 tiers), but there was a tremendous amount of Sybase-specific stored procedures (which are not compatible with SQL Server). About 70% of the business rules were in stored procedures and triggers.

After a careful evaluation and thousands of dollars in consulting fees, the migration was deemed unfeasible. The $5 million application was abandoned and a new one written.

Moral of the story: Stored procedures can be very expensive.

Create Interfaces

Interfaces are at the heart of COM. They are powerful abstractions that enable you to separate advertised behavior from internal implementation. An interface should describe only what public services an object offers. The private state of an object should never be disclosed via public interfaces.

An interface in COM+ is the binding contract between a component and its clients. An interface at its core is a collection of semantically similar methods or functions accessed via a `vtable` pointer at runtime.

An interface itself does not have any functionality. It merely points to the implementation. Interfaces can be reused (polymorphically or with inheritance) across components and upgraded. New methods can be added, but old ones should always remain.

When designing interfaces, keep in mind that all the methods contained in an interface should have something in common. There is no limit to how many methods an interface supports, but a good rule of thumb is to keep the number below 10. This keeps the interface from becoming unmanageable and monolithic, defeating the purpose of COM.

Implement the Components

Finally, after you have created a conceptual model separated across tiers and interfaces, it is time to implement the behavior. Depending on the complexity of the application, this can be the quickest part of all. With the interfaces serving as a blueprint, and with the confidence of a sound design architecture, the requirements of the application can be implemented in code.

Design Constraints

When designing applications, be they multitiered or monolithic, a whole slew of requirements imposes constraints on the finished product. Sometimes the requirements are conflicting or require bargaining tradeoffs. Size versus speed, for example, has historically been a major tradeoff facing software architects. With memory prices constantly dropping, this particular tradeoff is not as relevant today as it was a decade ago. Many new tradeoffs have emerged to take its place. These are discussed next.

When working with modern-day multitiered architectures, there are many real and measurable forces acting on the overall shape of the architecture. The following are some of the most important:

- Leveraging existing technology and skills
- Time to market
- Platform deployment

Leveraging Existing Technology and Skills

It is unrealistic to assume that new projects will use all the latest high-tech tools, programming languages, and server-side products, setting aside all existing technology investments. In the real world, significant resources have been invested into software development: hardware, software, training, and sky-rocketing IS salaries all add up to a huge expense for any corporation.

Fortunately, programming with COM+ does not require a major IS overhaul. It is possible to develop successful COM+-based applications inexpensively and without having to throw in all the bells and whistles Microsoft has to offer. For example, expensive database products like SQL Server 7.0 might not be necessary if a corporation already owns another database. The same can be said for operating systems. Although it is ideal for everyone to be running Windows NT workstations, Windows 95 or Windows 98 works just fine with COM+.

Existing legacy code is not a problem either. SNA Server, Microsoft's bridge to the mainframe world, ships with the COM Transaction Integrator (COMTI). COMTI is a tool for creating COM components that transparently access mainframe resources. Chapter 19, "The COM Transaction Integrator," of this book covers COMTI in detail.

For interoperability with UNIX, several vendors (ChiliSoft, for example) have announced COM libraries for UNIX and VMS operating systems. At this writing it is unclear whether they will move to COM+.

Time to Market

Software projects are consistently late and over budget. There are many reasons for this, but implementation and integration issues always seem to emerge as primary culprits.

Although C++ is the ideal choice for COM, it is not always optimal. If the application requires real-time guarantees or is performance-critical, a medium-level language like C/C++ can be the only choice. However, the majority of applications built today are not time-critical and can benefit tremendously from a Rapid Application Development (RAD) boost. As discussed in Chapter 1, many excellent RAD tools exist; the most popular ones are Visual Basic, Visual InterDev, and Visual J++.

With their COM+ support, these tools are well suited for creating prototypes that will scale to the real thing over time. Even better, a combination of C++ and RAD can prove to be the best choice because the developer can quickly create a UI with RAD, but with the speed and efficiency of pedal-to-the-metal C++. All this, of course, is married through COM+ for reusability and maintainability

Platform Deployment

Even with the growing popularity of the PC, many companies are not yet ready to leave behind legacy systems. Their current systems might work correctly and not need fixing. Why invest so much money in new equipment and training when the current systems get the job done?

The concerns are legitimate. Software has always been a very expensive craft, and business wants to milk its investments as much as consumers will tolerate.

With the advent of the Internet and Web commerce, the software industry has witnessed an acceleration of new high-tech development with the latest tools and programming paradigms. It is not surprising that so many managers are overwhelmed by the choices and, in frustration, keep their existing obsolete systems. They think waiting another six months will bring down prices and increase performance.

Fortunately, one platform is virtually universal and seamlessly adapts to future hardware and software changes: the Web browser.

HTML interpreters have been written for all operating systems imaginable, even telephones. The reality of an Internet-ready toaster doesn't seem so comical anymore. HTML is here to stay for a while and makes perfect sense as a "platform." Consider HTML as your target platform.

Design Goals

In today's world of distributed computing and Internet applications, memory is cheap. It is reliability, not size, that matters. But reliability alone is not sufficient to justify an application to a modern user. There are several key intangibles that you must aim for as a developer. The following is a list of the most important ones:

- Maintainability
- Reliability
- Availability
- Scalability
- Portability
- Security
- Reusability
- Locality (distributed or local; ties closely with performance)

Maintainability

How effective is a software system if it cannot be upgraded or evolved over time? If there is one lesson we have learned from the Y2K problem, it is that computer programmers should be more judicious and critical of the assumptions they make about the future. Foresight and flexibility during design and implementation will be greatly rewarded. A narrow and specific solution usually must be rewritten several times as new features are requested and unexpected requirements arise.

Instead of attacking the problem in the particular, strive to solve the problem in general with additional rules for the specific problem at hand. All too often we come back to old code and wish we'd put a little extra effort into decoupling a large procedure or function. It's no fun to have to spend valuable time in a partial or complete rewrite.

With COM, this is easy to accomplish with interface inheritance. Create generic interfaces, and then implement specific behaviors to suit your problem. A great example of this technique can be seen in the `IPersist` family of interfaces, which are discussed in Chapter 4, "Persistent Storage."

Reliability

Probably the single most popular complaint about PCs is their instability. Whether it's the fault of the operating system or third-party software, it is the user who is left with a hung program and hours of work lost.

PC versus UNIX reliability flames wars of biblical proportions have raged on Usenet for years, with no end in sight. The issue of UNIX versus PC reliability is not to be dismissed quickly, and for time-critical or life-support systems it can be a matter of life and death. Consider medical equipment with embedded software, or the navigation software on airplanes. If the patient or passenger had the option of choosing which OS they would trust their lives on, what would be the most common answer? (I would most certainly pick UNIX.)

Having worked on both platforms for almost 18 years, I have experienced the cold but faithful glow of a UNIX command prompt along with the warm, but fragile charm of a colorful PC window.

But "COM," as Don Box once said, "is about love." COM embraces all strangers (IUnknowns), and does not discriminate across platforms (as long as they support COM).

So we won't discuss which operating system is more reliable, and frankly, as COM+ developers, we have little control of this part. We are normally faced with platform constraints and might not always have an option of which OS to work under.

We can, however, ensure that our code adheres to Microsoft guidelines for well-behaved components and can be ported not just to UNIX, but VMS or other systems that COM+ supports. These guidelines transcend your tried-and-true wisdom such as "Don't use global variables" or "Avoid GOTO statements." They have more real-world implications like concurrency, threading models, or interprocess communication.

Techniques for creating reliable components are covered in the rest of the book.

Availability

In the 2000s, consumers are educated and careful. Gone are the days when it was the status quo to accept "system down" signs at bank tellers' posts or busy signals for customer service lines. Today's consumer is Web-enabled and spoiled to near instant transactions. If a Web site doesn't load in a few seconds, a few impatient mouse clicks land the user in one that does.

Availability is expensive and difficult to achieve in a typical nondistributed PC environment. However, it is not necessary to create fault-tolerant rollover cluster systems to give the illusion of high availability. Windows DNA provides server-side products that offer users real-enough-time for the most demanding environments. Chapters 26 and 27 on loosely coupled events elaborate this point further.

Scalability

Historically, applications have been built to tackle current problems without foresight into evolving requirements that will place unforeseen demands on all or part of its components. A well-designed application can scale or absorb a changing environment, even under circumstances the developer didn't account for or imagine.

As COM+ programmers, we were fortunate to have MTS, the *scalability machine*. Now with COM+, we don't even worry about MTS. We put regular but well-behaved components in one end and watch them be transformed into scalable, robust objects on the other.

But if it were only that easy. MTS and COM+ do give us a lot of scalability for free, but that should not be used as an excuse to code resource-abusive components.

When working with resources, try to be as frugal as possible and never hold a resource longer than is necessary.

Portability

There are two levels of portability. One is at the implementation level, and the other is at the user or finished-product level. Before browsers and HTML, portable applications were written in languages like C or C++ and then compiled for each desired platform. This technique didn't always work because C does not provide a standard API for rich user interfaces. To exacerbate the problem, presentation code was written along with business logic, coupling the application and producing monoliths. Porting was a whole project in its own right and required significant resources to accomplish.

Today there are browsers and platform-neutral markup languages like HTML or the new XML. It is only necessary to write the application for one platform and rely on the presentation layer to produce compatible HTML for universal compatibility.

There is one disadvantage to browsers, however. They lack rich UI controls. Technologies like Java Applets, Dynamic HTML, and ActiveX can alleviate the problem but at the cost of introducing incompatibilities among browsers.

To be truly browser-agnostic, we must do what we can with standard HTML and its primitive forms capability. In practice, this is not the sacrifice third-party ActiveX and Java component vendors would want you to believe. If buttons and text boxes are not rich enough for your application, it is possible to use image maps and offer the illusion of a sophisticated GUI.

Once again, if you haven't done so already, consider using an HTML browser as your presentation tier.

Reusability

The most widely accepted definition of software utopia is that place where software can be built effortlessly by assembling ready-made standard components, much the way circuit boards or vehicles are manufactured today. Although we are still many decades from achieving such a grand goal, we can certainly build COM+ components today and plan to reuse them a few months from now.

The versioning properties of well-written COM+ objects guarantee that an existing interface today will continue to work (in some capacity) for the lifetime of the object. So even if new features are added to an otherwise old component, its past and present clients will not break. They just use what they need.

The COM+ specification speaks of immutable interfaces but, in reality, this turns out to be more of a suggestion. It is specified by COM+ that once a component interface is published, it should never be changed.

But it is possible to change the interface (or delete it altogether) and break the rule. This also breaks the binding contract between a COM+ object and its clients who expect to always find a specific interface. Blissfully ignorant clients of a misbehaving component will simply die after an illegal memory address rather than check to see if an interface query was successful.

COM+ does not "catch" these breaches of contract and does not warn the developer of COM+ Specification violations. That is entirely up to the developer.

Some of the tools in Visual Studio (like VB or VI) do give a warning message when deleting interfaces, but it's still up to the developer to exercise the contract.

Without this contract, the lifetime of a component is limited and its reusability compromised.

Avoid changing interfaces after they have been published and always exercise top-down discovery (via `QueryInterface`) when working with other components.

Locality

How large is the application? Does it need to be spread across machine boundaries to meet performance requirements or is one address space sufficient?

With COM's location transparency features, it is not necessary to foresee a distributed architecture at design time to be able to use one at installation time.

With the help of MTS, components can be distributed easily across machines without either client or server knowing the difference. Only the registry knows the true location of a component and whether any proxies are used. As far as a client is concerned, a server component is living in the same address space.

Design Tools

Many computer-aided software engineering (CASE) software tools exist to help the software architect articulate human ideas into coherent designs. One of the more popular tools for modeling architectures is Rational Rose, which is shipped with Visual Studio as Visual Modeler. Although an understanding of the unified modeling language (UML) is preferred, Visual Modeler has well-written, online documentation and tutorials to help guide UML newcomers.

Not surprisingly, the default template for building new projects in Visual Modeler is the three-tiered model (see Figure 2.8). Object-oriented fans will feel right at home with VM. Its rich feature set can overwhelm non-OO programmers, however.

FIGURE 2.8

*Visual Modeler
with a default
three-tiered tem-
plate.*

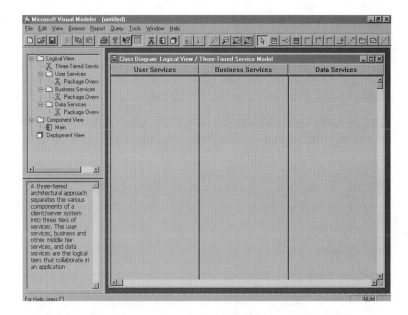

Fortunately, COM+ does not require OO skills because it is not object-oriented itself (at the binary level at least). COM, is, after all, about binary interoperability.

Beyond Object Orientation

In the last two decades, software engineering as we know it has been gradually phasing out of the procedural paradigm and into the object-oriented one. With COM/COM+, object-orientation can be taken to the next level: binary interoperability.

As a designer, this enables you to create objects that are compatible not only at a local source level, but at the application, runtime level. Being able to call on libraries or objects at runtime is not new, but doing so in an explorative way with language independence is new.

Summary

The cost of maintaining a software system is estimated to be many times its development cost. Computer code, regardless of the language, is still a mechanized and volatile expression of human thought. We all solve problems differently, and it is reflected in the code we write. But code rots with time. It becomes obscure and unreadable. This is an inevitable fact of the software life cycle.

With sound design principles, we can mitigate code rot and maximize code reuse.

Code reuse is good, but binary component reuse is even better. COM+ allows us to reuse objects without understanding their implementation. By strategically abstracting objects in our architecture tiers, we are in a much more comfortable position for reuse and scalability.

In essence, multitiered architectures are good. They blend perfectly with the COM+ methodology and embrace COM+'s encapsulation properties.

If you plan to program with COM or COM+, you should also design with tiers in mind.

Advanced COM Programming Techniques

PART

II

COM+
Architecture and
Administration

IN THIS CHAPTER

Up to now, we have talked about COM+ in relation to the traditional COM architecture. In this chapter, we will look at the new COM+ architecture. COM+ is intended to fully support the Windows DNA ideal. Of course, MTS got things started by enabling COM components to be used in multiuser and n-tiered enterprise applications. COM+ picks up where MTS left off. It marries MTS and COM. MTS and COM components that were developed before COM+ still work as they always have. But the layers that consisted of MTS and COM are now a single layer, encapsulated by COM+. COM+ is really more than the marriage of COM and MTS. It brings with it a runtime environment that explicitly supports the marriage. In addition to what MTS offers developers, COM+ adds useful items such as queued components (see Chapter 27).

Two features of note that were supposed to be delivered with COM+ are *In Memory Database (IMDB)* support and *Component Load Balancing (CLB)*. Neither feature made it in the final cut of the Windows 2000 COM+ runtime. IMDB turned out to create more problems than it solved, and it will probably never see the light of day. If you want to read the reasons Microsoft gives, go to `http://msdn.microsoft.com/library/techart/whatimdb.htm`. Component Load Balancing was in release candidate two but was removed from release candidate three and the final release of Windows 2000. It wasn't quite ready, but will appear in AppCenter Server sometime soon. You can read about Microsoft's plans for Component Load Balancing at `http://msdn.microsoft.com/library/techart/complusload.htm`.

The Evolution of COM+

COM is a direct outgrowth of OLE, or, more specifically, out of OLE 2. The central idea behind the technology is that applications are built around component objects. These components can and many times do have multiple interfaces. Developers who create COM objects must always be careful to leave old interfaces intact. In a sense, there is a contract between COM interfaces and applications. The implicit understanding is that interfaces, once they are introduced, will not change. New interfaces can be added, whereas the old interfaces are constant. The designers of COM, somewhere along the way, decided to separate the ideas of OLE and COM. Many technologies have arisen to augment COM, including ActiveX, automation, and many more sophisticated techniques. Components are treated as black boxes. In this case, the developer can only see the interface. Once defined, however, the interface itself for a component must be immutable. It is this strict definition of the interface that allows for effective component reuse.

You might be asking yourself, why do we need COM+? After all, COM provides the component architecture that developers have come to rely on. My first response would be that COM is fundamentally unchanged in COM+. As I said earlier, we would not want to change any previously published COM interfaces. In other words, we do not want to break any COM contracts. COM+ follows in the traditional COM footsteps. It adds services through new interfaces, and does not change existing interfaces and services.

COM works in the COM+ runtime because COM+ implements a system of interception and does transparently what is necessary for COM to work. There are, however, things that COM+ adds (such as loosely coupled events), and if component developers take advantage of these, they have more tools to work with.

You must also be aware that not all tools work to support COM+. At a minimum, you must have Visual C++ 6.0/6.01. The next release of Visual Studio will have complete COM+ development support for Visual C++, Visual Basic, and Visual J++.

It can be said that COM has been a faithful servant to developers thus far. It has enabled developers to more quickly create robust applications. But even with this said, times change and so must COM. The driving force behind the need for change is the widespread desire and use of enterprise applications. This has been accelerated by the tremendous growth of e-commerce on the Internet. Although traditional COM and MTS helped, COM+ becomes an integral tool for enterprise development. Managing increased and highly dynamic call loads, integrating browser-based clients, and tackling new highly distributed security models are only a few of the common issues on the plate of the n-tier programmer. COM+ shifts the focus of COM to better address these critical issues. New implementations of traditional services, more powerful object management, and new COM+–specific services provide support for advanced security, data access, and asynchronous communications, among other features.

What if you have applications built around COM objects? Will they still work? The answer is yes. Traditional COM and MTS applications function as they always have. COM+ simply adds to the framework so that developers can more easily develop large-scale applications.

3

COM+
ARCHITECTURE AND
ADMINISTRATION

MTS Shortcomings

COM+ solves a number of deficiencies in MTS. For starters, not all the MTS services are even implemented in the comprehensive way that we see them in COM+. MTS ostensibly supports object pooling with a set of documented methods. These methods, however, are not implemented in the MTS runtime. One can actually implement object pooling in MTS, but it requires writing a resource dispenser. In most cases, this is not required in COM+. Another drawback to MTS is the fact that MTS and COM overlap somewhat. This is because MTS is a layer on top of COM and duplicates some of the COM functionality. It is preferred that you call the MTS functions rather than their equivalent COM functions. This avoids potential problems at runtime. One example of a problem that can occur is during object construction and referencing when there might be a difference in whether the context is available. COM+, in combining COM and MTS, eliminates this problem.

Another extremely important omission from MTS is dynamic load balancing. MTS supports static load balancing, which allows network administrators to assign clients to different application server hosts. Static load balancing solves load balancing issues in small to medium-sized networks. It does not, however, provide the kind of solution necessary for high-performance networks in large-scale applications. Dynamic load balancing is an integral part of COM+.

Microsoft has maintained that MSMQ was a good solution to the need for load balancing. Yes, it solved the problem to an acceptable degree for most situations. But MSMQ is a loosely coupled architecture (more on this in Chapter 22), and many times only a tightly-coupled architecture will suffice. For this reason, Microsoft introduced Component Load Balancing. (As I said earlier, the CLB feature isn't quite ready at the writing of this book.)

OLE 2 was a complete rewrite of OLE 1. OLE 2 took all the component architecture experience provided by OLE 1 and rolled it into a completely modular and extensible framework based on a core object technology called COM. Because of this, OLE 1 developers faced significant changes in the application development cycle presented by OLE 2. Fortunately, the careful design of COM as the cornerstone of OLE 2 has proved worth the effort and remains at the heart of the Microsoft component-programming infrastructure. COM+ is more a synthesis of the meticulously designed COM component framework and the advanced application server environment introduced by MTS. MTS and standard COM components can be readily deployed in a COM+ environment, and developers having the available resources can add new COM+ functionality to existing COM and MTS components, making them even more powerful.

COM+ Architecture

This section examines some of the basic architectural principles behind COM+. You will take a look at the key object management strategies implemented by COM+ and examine guidelines and techniques for using new COM+ features.

COM+ introduces several new core architectural facets to the COM programming world. Most of these additions are carefully targeted at improving the performance and functionality of its MTS predecessor. Because of this, developers should seriously consider the MTS style of application development when specifying new projects. The MTS/COM+ model is a mandate from Microsoft. Sure, you can develop application components that don't use the MTS/COM+ specific services. The unfortunate side effect is that you will either have to develop sophisticated transaction services and scalability features yourself or do without. COM+ makes MTS and COM inseparable and entices you by adding even more performance advantages.

A good MTS component is a good COM+ component. If a developer has taken the time to reason through the issues related to enterprise applications when designing an MTS component, chances are that these will carry through to a COM+ component. There are several specific areas in which COM+ stands apart from MTS. COM+ improves the scalability features introduced by MTS through the implementation of object pooling and dynamic load balancing. (Dynamic load balancing is not here at this moment, but it will be very soon.) Well-written MTS components can immediately take advantage of these services. COM+ also simplifies the creation of constituent objects within an MTS activity. Because COM+ unifies MTS and COM, object construction need no longer be an MTS–specific behavior. COM+ introduces additional object construction hooks (such as parameterized object creation), presenting developers with extended performance facilities.

Creating COM+ Objects

COM+ creates all object instances of COM+ classes in much the same way as MTS would create an MTS-configured, server-based object. Standard COM objects operate in much the same way as they always have. The unification of COM and MTS in COM+ has cleared the way for several enhancements to the MTS interception mechanism. Most notable is the fact that context objects and interception functionality have been merged into the standard COM proxy/stub mechanism. This means that you can create a new object using CoCreateInstanceEx() without losing context. MTS developers must use the IObjectContext::CreateInstance() method in order to construct new objects within the current context. The CreateInstance() approach works in COM+ as well, however, providing complete compatibility with existing MTS components.

Context and interception are discussed in Chapter 15, "MTS."

Parameterized Object Construction

COM+ also introduces a parameterized object construction mechanism. The standard COM and MTS object-creation facilities do not supply a way to differentiate creation requests targeting the same class. A COM+ class can choose to support the IObjectConstructor interface that supports parameterized construction. The Component Services Manager (equivalent to the MTS Explorer) shown in Figure 3.1 can be used to configure a string parameter for object construction of any given COM+ class. The IObjectConstructor interface can be used by the new object to retrieve the construction string configured by the COM+ administrator. This would enable an administrator to define a message queue path to be used by objects associated with a set of clients, for example. Currently, COM+ 1.0 allows classes to be associated with only one application at a time. This restricts administrators to one construction string per class. This is shown in Chapter 5, "Monikers."

FIGURE 3.1

The Component Services Manager.

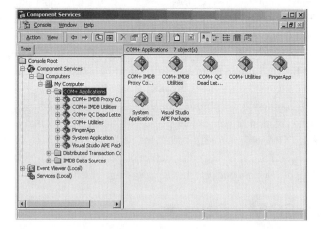

Monikers

Monikers are objects that are capable of reconstituting some other type of object through a simple string name (see Chapter 5). COM+ provides a *"new moniker"* that enables you to construct new objects from a simple string name, such as `"new:OrderEntry.Order.1"`. Of course, monikers are interface-based COM objects that anyone can create and are therefore much more flexible than strict API calls such as `CoCreateInstance()`. For example, using a moniker, the caller can pass initialization parameters to be used during object creation, something that can't be done with the standard COM object creation functions.

The Neutral-Threaded Apartment

COM+ introduces a new threading model known as the neutral-threaded apartment. This new apartment model is in direct response to the specific performance requirements of transaction-based application servers (such as MTS and COM+). The neutral apartment is also the preferred COM+ component threading model.

Recall that COM threading models are designed to control concurrency within COM components. An apartment is a collection of objects and the definition of which process threads can execute the methods of those objects. Calls across apartment boundaries usually cause expensive marshaling services to be invoked. In this way, COM can control the concurrency within an apartment. The preferred MTS threading model is the single-threaded apartment (STA). The STA model collects created objects into the apartment of the single thread creating them. Any calls to STA objects from outside the apartment must be marshaled by the calling thread and dispatched by the target STA thread. The advantage of this system is that you can build STA components quickly without worrying about the complexity of synchronization in a multithreaded application environment. The disadvantage is that COM serializes all method calls into the apartment, whether or not serialization is required. To further exacerbate the performance bottleneck, all external calls into the apartment must be marshaled. This can easily more than triple the method call overhead. COM threading is discussed in detail in Chapter 7.

So what's the solution? Current COM supports one multithreaded apartment (MTA) per process. The MTA can be equipped with a free-threaded marshaler (FTM) that allows any thread in the process (even those from STAs) to call directly into MTA object methods without marshaling. Sounds like just the ticket, right? Well, not really. The MTA basically eliminates the concurrency controls supplied by MTS/COM+ and reintroduces all the complexity and overhead involved with managing synchronization and threads in multithreaded applications, not to mention the contention introduced between application-specific and MTS/COM+–style thread management. In general, MTA components should not be implemented within MTS or COM+. A new threading solution is required to improve performance in COM+.

The neutral-threaded apartment is the solution. Neutral-threaded components are always created in the neutral apartment. The neutral apartment contains objects but no threads. Otherwise, the neutral apartment is similar to the MTA in that it enables many threads to execute concurrently on its objects. The advantage is that COM+ still takes care of the thread management and concurrency tasks, ensuring that no single object receives more than one method call at a time.

Object Pooling

COM+ is the first application server to actually implement the object-pooling system provided for in MTS. Components adhering to the basic pooling guidelines of MTS can be pooled in COM+. Administrators use the Component Services Manager to configure capable components for object pooling. Pooling enables objects to be created once and then reused over several sequential transactions for various clients. Object pooling eliminates the overhead of constructing and destroying objects on a per-transaction basis. Objects must carefully reinitialize any state they require through use of the `IObjectControl` interface and must report support for pooling through `IObjectControl` as well.

Objects that supported pooling in MTS might break under COM+ if they aren't well written. MTS never really pooled objects, but acted as if it did. Objects supporting pooling would receive all the appropriate IObjectControl calls, but MTS deleted the objects upon transaction completion instead of pooling them. This means that initialization bugs that don't appear when constructors and destructors are called at transaction boundaries will show up in COM+, where the objects are not really destroyed but pooled instead. It's also important to note that pooled objects cannot be single threaded or apartment threaded. Objects created in an STA live in the same STA for their entire lifetime, and must always be called on the thread associated with the STA. This would have a serious impact on the performance of your application. COM+ lets you set many of the object-pooling parameters administratively, as shown in Figure 3.2.

FIGURE 3.2

Setting object-pooling character-istics.

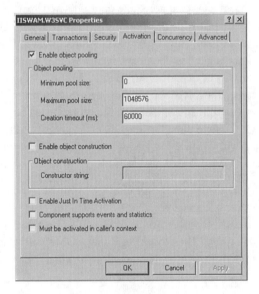

Object Pooling Administration

There is an administrative side of the pooling coin as well. Administrators who want to enable object pooling on a specific class must first ensure that the class is pool capable. Next, the Component Services Manager (the functional equivalent of the MTS Explorer) is used to enable pooling on the class in question. The Component Services Explorer also supplies minimum and maximum pool limits, as well as a client timeout setting used when no objects from the pool are available. The savvy administrator can carefully tune pool settings to improve overall server performance.

Dynamic Load Balancing

MTS enables administrators to configure client applications to use a specific server within a set of servers. This is called *static load balancing*. It is a load-balancing solution because it enables administrators to spread the burden of executing client requests across several servers. It's static because it doesn't adjust to the prevalent conditions. If you place 10 clients on each server, and all 10 members of the first set of clients need services at the same time while the 10 clients in the second set are all out to lunch, one server is going to be overloaded while another sits idle. Your options are staggered lunch shifts or dynamic load balancing. Microsoft's not quite powerful enough to mandate the lunch thing yet, so it has opted for the dynamic load-balancing solution in COM+.

Load balancing is a type of loose server clustering that allows a particular tier of an application to be spread across several systems. COM+ enables administrators to configure server applications to run on a specific cluster of servers. In a dynamic load-balancing scenario, server load information is reported by all the systems in the cluster, and client object creation requests are then forwarded to the most available system.

The COM+ machine that tracks server load information and redirects client requests is known as the *load-balancing router*. COM+ clients are configured to request services from the router and then use objects running on the most available system in the application group. As you can see, this is purely an administrative function, and no developer interaction is required. Any good COM+ component will operate well when deployed in a dynamic load-balancing scenario.

Dynamic load balancing has advantages beyond that of improved performance and better server utilization. The load-balancing router will not direct clients to failed servers in the server group. This provides the server platform with an element of fault tolerance. The router itself is the Achilles' heel in this case. Fortunately, the load-balancing router can be configured on a Windows 2000 fail-over cluster. This provides high-performance dynamic load balancing and eliminates the single point of failure posed by a load-balancing router operating on a standalone system.

COM+ Deployment Services

COM+ joins Windows 2000 in addressing one of the most critical concerns in a large enterprise, that of application deployment. The MTS Explorer and MTS packages greatly simplify distributed application configuration in the MTS world, and the Component Services Manager supports COM+ configuration in a similar manner. In order to take full advantage of the COM+ deployment services, a component should be fully self-describing. This means that components should supply a complete type library. Configured attributes and other component-centric information are stored in a component library that defines all the component's installation and registration requirements. Unfortunately no component library creation tools are available at the time of this writing. `DllRegisterServer()` is still required in order to support non–COM+ environments. In order to fully support dynamic configuration and deployment using the Microsoft Installer (MSI), COM+ components are prohibited from relying on registry data not established by the component itself and should clean up all configured states during uninstallation.

COM+ enables administrators to export client and server applications. COM+ server applications are much like MTS packages with the exception that they are called applications and are exported as application libraries with an .APL extension. Client-side exports create an MSI application. Client installers can be distributed through the Active Directory, which is discussed in the Chapter 16, "COM+ as a Component Manager."

Resource Management with COM+

One of the real tricks to developing highly scalable applications is effective resource management. COM+ supports many new mechanisms that enable developers to improve their resource allocation and retention tactics, such as object pooling and parameterized object construction. Enlisting resources in transactions is another important part of the MTS/COM+ application server behavior. COM+ supports the same architecture for DTC transactions—resource dispensers and resource managers—that MTS pioneered. Developing a COM+ resource manager or resource dispenser is no trivial endeavor and many times entails considerable overhead.

Compensating Resource Managers

In order to enable developers to support transactions in a lightweight context, COM+ introduces the *Compensating Resource Manager (CRM)*. CRMs are composed through two separate COM+ classes. The CRM Worker performs the business at hand, and the CRM Compensator unwinds the operations of the Worker in the case of a failed transaction. COM+ implements CRM-specific interfaces supporting transaction logging facilities that enable the developer-created CRM to recover in the case of system failure. Clients create CRM Worker objects to perform transactional tasks, and COM+ creates Compensator objects to monitor the Worker objects' transaction activity. By the way, MTS programmers pronounce CRM as "crumb." The next time you're with your COM+ buddies, make sure that you say "crumb" or they'll likely laugh you out of wherever you are.

Developing COM+ Applications

Developing COM+ applications is similar structurally to developing a high-quality MTS application. COM+ introduces several new facilities that enhance the services introduced by MTS, as well as features that extend the basic COM/DCOM system. In this section, you'll take a look at some design issues and several new COM+ features. You'll also look at some of the new base COM feature updates tagging along for the ride.

Designing COM+ Components

The most important thing to remember when considering COM+ as an application server platform is that the application server side of COM+ is simply an update to MTS. Although this is not an insignificant update, the fundamental MTS paradigm stands throughout. So one way you can begin the trek to COM+ is to build high-quality MTS in-process components. COM+ gains many practical benefits by merging the MTS service model with basic COM features.

The next step is to consider the environment in which your components will be operating. COM+ doesn't function on any platform other than Windows 2000 for now. This means that if you are designing components that need to run on NT 4, you should stick to the guidelines presented with MTS 2.0. Your components will still work just fine under COM+. If, on the other hand, you are planning to deploy on Windows 2000 exclusively, you can take advantage of several new and powerful enterprise features.

Queued Components

The Microsoft Message Queue Server (MSMQ) has opened up a whole new world of possibilities for COM developers. MSMQ enables applications to uncouple themselves from external services they might require. This, in turn, can greatly improve scalability, allowing all parts of an enterprise application to run as quickly as they can independently of each other. MSMQ also presents another significant advantage through disconnected queues. Parts of a larger application can be temporarily disconnected and then reattached, causing MSMQ to store queued messages until such time as they can be delivered.

So what does all this MSMQ stuff have to do with COM+? I'm glad you asked. MSMQ has a standard function-call interface at the native level, and although it integrates with COM applications and MTS applications nicely, MSMQ still represents a slight step out of the fully native COM world. COM applications are required to bundle call information into messages for transmission rather than just make an interface method call. COM+ changes this with queued components. The COM+ queued component system uses

3

MSMQ as a transport system. It enables clients to make COM calls to servers in an asynchronous way.

This means that a client application running on a disconnected laptop can still make as many calls as it likes to a nonexistent server using standard COM technology. The queued component recorder running on the client queues the COM method calls for later delivery. When the server network is once again available, the queued COM calls are delivered to the target queue. The queued component listener on the server network retrieves COM call messages from the queue and passes them to the queued component player. The player then makes the escrowed calls against the live COM server.

The main restriction to using any asynchronous technology is that the component cannot return data to the caller as you would see in a synchronous, blocked call. For example, if a component calls a queued component's `CreateOrder` method, the component cannot return a value (indicating success or failure) or any other value (such as an order confirmation number). Instead, the component must live by the rules of a distributed, asynchronous system and use a callback mechanism to return relevant data to the client. The mechanisms for doing this are discussed in more depth in Chapter 27.

Queued Transactions

The queued component system uses the underlying MSMQ transaction support to manage transactional interactions even when clients are disconnected. As a client makes calls to any component interfaces configured for queuing, the recorder gathers the calls into a single message. If the message cannot be committed, the transaction is aborted. Similar transactional behavior takes place on the server side. Should the message fail to be successfully dequeued, the transaction will abort, and MSMQ will remove the message to the appropriate dead-letter queue.

Administering Queued Components

As with any enterprise scale system, administrators play an enhanced role in the management of queued component applications. Administrators configure and deploy queued component applications using the Component Services Manager. COM+ applications and the necessary class interfaces are configured to use the queued component service with the COM Explorer. The COM Explorer will then export client applications with appropriate queue information. Note that queued component configuration is operative at the interface level. This means that a class can have some direct interfaces and some queued interfaces. Clients can also choose to use a component in normal mode or in queued mode. This enables components to operate in the normal tightly coupled fashion or in a queued fashion at the client's discretion. Queued components are created using a queue moniker such as `queue:/new:OrderEntry.Order.1`.

After it is created, a queued component operates just as any other COM object does. There are, however, a few limitations. As you might have already noticed, the queued component service provides a one-way communications channel. This means that interfaces configured for queuing must support only [in] parameters. There is no way for the server to respond to client calls in a disconnected scenario. Furthermore, if transactions have an affect on client-side resources, developers must build in a way to detect transactions that have failed on the server and rollback any necessary client operations. Two popular approaches to client-side recovery are queuing messages to the client and posting results in an appropriate database.

Loosely Coupled Events

One of the shortcomings of the COM technology set has traditionally been a lack of broadcast style services. Clients interested in notifications from COM servers have relied on custom solutions or perhaps COM connection points. Where COM is involved, both these types of solutions require the server to make a separate interface method call to each constituent client. This is far from optimal behavior and also presents an implementation dysfunction in designs that clearly call for the simplicity of broadcast semantics. As we have seen through queued components, COM+ is mending the tightly coupled, synchronous, bi-directional ways of traditional COM.

Using Loosely Coupled Events (LCE)

Loosely coupled events (LCE) introduce a publish and subscribe model for event distribution. Servers offering to fire events (make method calls) publish this information through the COM+ event service. Clients wanting to receive a particular published event subscribe to the event in question through the COM+ event service. When servers fire events, the COM+ event service broadcasts the event to all interested clients.

There are several important aspects of the loosely coupled event system. The LCE system provides a broadcast-style mechanism at the native COM level. Servers need not know which clients, if any, are listening. Events can be distributed across process boundaries and networks much more efficiently because only a single event message is transmitted from the server. This is in high contrast to the connection point architecture, which requires servers to call each client in turn. Presently, COM+ makes synchronous calls to all event clients before returning to the server. A server could, however, derive asynchronous behavior from the LCE system through queued components. The architecture also paves the way for the addition of more broadcast-oriented performance enhancements in the future. The LCE system also enables publishers to filter events, controlling which clients can receive which events. Subscribers can implement filters as well through the `ISubscriberControl` interface. This interface enables clients to discard or redirect particular events.

Take for instance an order entry system. During design it was decided that availability information could be sent once the order was received, but wasn't essential to the real-time order entry. This decision could be the result of a traffic estimate. The loosely coupled architecture (where no real-time availability information is available) can more effectively amortize the use of the applications servers over time. After an order is placed, the subscriber can be notified of any availability problems.

> **Note**
>
> LCE is yet another very powerful tool in the COM+ kit. Much like queued components, LCE services address a critical gap in previous COM implementations. queued components offer COM level one way of decoupled method invocation, and LCE provides a native COM broadcast mechanism. The features presented through the queued component and LCE services of COM+ solve problems that have caused many a developer to invent extensive custom software.

Accessing Data with COM+

Data access in COM+ is much the same as that presented in MTS. In particular, OLE DB and ADO are the access mechanisms of choice. OLE DB supplies a very powerful and extensible architecture supporting various types of underlying data stores, including any ODBC source. OLE DB is necessarily complex because of its flexibility and performance. ATL consumer and producer templates can ease the burden of OLE DB development in C++. By far, the most popular mechanism for programming OLE DB is, of course, ActiveX Data Objects (ADO). ADO provides a dual interface component implementation operating on top of OLE DB that can easily be used by compiled applications and scripts alike. Of course, if you're like many developers, you already have very large ODBC-based systems that are fully supported in this environment as well.

Read Optimized Data Access

IMDB is a smart in-memory database caching system optimized for read operations. IMDB allows static data to be loaded once and queried against many times. The performance advantages achievable with this type of in-memory data support are enormous. Queries satisfied locally through IMDB require neither network nor disk access. IMDB also supports write operations. It backlogs updates until they are committed. At that point, changes are submitted to the underlying database. Obviously, the real performance advantages lie in the arena of caching static-read weighted data.

Applications access the IMDB in much the same way as they would any other modern database. IMDB is an OLE DB provider, which ensures built-in support for most programming languages and scripting environments through ADO.

The Transactional Shared Property Manager

The MTS Shared Property Manager (SPM) is a valuable asset to JIT-activated and early released components, providing a stable shared data store within a particular server process. COM+ implements the Shared Property Manager interfaces on top of IMDB. This new construct is referred to as the Transactional Shared Property Manager. Make sure that if you're out with your COM+ buddies, you pronounce SPM as "spam."

COM+ Security

COM+ presents the same basic application server security features introduced by MTS. COM+ applications can use standard COM security, as well as declarative and procedural role-based security. COM+ has extended role-based security to the interface method, enabling administrators to control access at the most fundamental level (recall that MTS supports role membership only to the interface level). Unlike MTS, COM+ also supports role-based security in library packages. Enhanced security information is provided in COM+ through the ISecurityCallContext interface. The ISecurityCallContext interface supercedes the MTS ISecurityProperty interface and provides detailed information about all callers in the chain back to the base client. COM+ security is covered in more detail in Chapter 18.

Base COM Features

MTS and COM/DCOM represent distinct paths of development supported by distinct development units at Microsoft. Such is the case with COM+ (the MTS successor) and the core COM services in Windows 2000. In this section, you'll look at some of the new base COM services that are packaged along with COM+ in Windows 2000.

Structured Storage

Structured storage is a powerful compound file management service, supporting a file system within a file. The great thing about structured storage is that it is a standard mechanism supported directly by Windows and many application products. Windows 2000 promises to integrate structured storage into even more file system and shell features. Link tracking is a new feature enabling Windows 2000 to update OLE links within a structured storage file when the target object is moved. All the Win32 MoveFile() routines coordinate with the link tracking service, including the new MoveFileWithProgress() routine. The link tracking feature only functions on NTFS volumes, but presents a long-awaited solution to a common problem.

The structured storage system also introduces new routines for creating and opening compound files. These are as follows:

- `StgCreateStorageEx()`
- `StgOpenStorageEx()`

The `StgCreateStorageEx()` routine supersedes the `StgCreateDocfile()` routine and should be used by all new Windows 2000 applications. Enhancements to the structured storage system will be exposed through the two new Ex routines.

Windows 2000 includes an upgraded version of NTFS (NTFS v5) that enables many of the new disk-based services. Compound documents residing on NTFS v5 volumes can take advantage of the STGFMT_NATIVE storage format. NTFS Native Structured Storage (NSS) uses the native property-based storage features of NTFS to improve compound document efficiency.

Windows 2000 structured storage also supports the new `IDirectWriterLock` interface, which enables a writer to obtain exclusive access to a root storage object opened in direct mode. Several readers can then concurrently access the storage.

Canceling Outstanding COM Calls

Synchronous COM calls can block for extended periods of time while waiting for failed server requests to timeout. On the other hand, the very nature of asynchronous calls can introduce the need for some applications to cancel outstanding calls that have not completed before an outdating event takes place. COM supplies several call control interfaces that can be used to manage asynchronous method calls. COM+ creates and manages Cancel objects for all calls that use standard marshaling by calling `CoSetCancelObject()` before and after each method call. COM Cancel objects support the `ICancelMethodCalls` interface. The `ICancelMethodCalls` interface of a particular Cancel object can be obtained by calling the `CoGetCancelObject()` component library routine with the `IID_ICancelMethodCalls` interface ID. The `CoGetCancelObject()` prototype is displayed as follows:

```
HRESULT CoGetCancelObject(
...............DWORD dwThreadId,....//Thread with pending call
...............REFIID riid,........ //ID of requested interface
...............void ** ppUnk ....); //Pointer to the requested interface
```

The `ICancelMethodCalls` supports the methods in Table 3.1.

TABLE 3.1 `ICancelMethodCalls` Methods

`ICancelMethodCalls` *Method*	*What It Does*
`Cancel()`	Requests that the method be canceled.
`TestCancel()`	Checks to see whether the call has been canceled.
`SetCancelTimeout()`	Sets an automatic cancel timeout for the call.

The process of getting the Cancel object interface and invoking the `Cancel()` method has a wrapper equivalent in the `CoCancelCall()` routine. `CoTestCancel()` provides a similar shortcut for the call to the `TestCancel()` method. Together these features make it easy to take call-level control of pending methods.

Summary

COM+ is the next logical step in COM evolution. It isn't a radical departure from COM, keeping the best of the COM architecture and adding enhancements.

One of the greatest advances is the capability to load balance and pool, unlike MTS that didn't actually implement these features.

Many of the COM+ additions are improvements for the performance and functionality of its MTS predecessor. The MTS/COM+ model is a mandate from Microsoft, and you should be sure that you're following its lead. COM+ makes MTS and COM inseparable and entices you by adding even more performance advantages.

The rest of the book shows you how to use COM+ to develop component applications and maximize its effectiveness.

Persistent Storage

CHAPTER 4

One of the challenges that developers face is maintaining the state of a COM object. At runtime, when a COM object loads, it might be desirable for it to remember and revert to a previous state. In this case, the object would be loading persistent storage data so that it can resume operation in a previous state. When a COM object is destroyed, it might also find it necessary to save its state so that the current application, or another application, can assume a state identical to the state it was in when destroyed. In this case, the object would be saving persistent data.

A good example of a use for persistent storage is Visual Basic's treatment of ActiveX controls. In the ActiveX control property sheet, you can see that Visual Basic keeps the same property values from session to session. In other words, if you set the properties of the control to some desirable values while running Visual Basic, when you rerun Visual Basic, that control retains the property settings from the last session.

This chapter shows you how to load and save persistent data to and from objects. Our discussion will focus on the `IPersistStreamInit` and the `IStream` interfaces. However, the techniques shown in this chapter are not the only ones you can use for persistent data storage.

Two sample controls and two sample programs that use the controls will illustrate the techniques. The first control was kept simple so that you could easily see and understand the material. The client application that loads the first sample control is also simple. It shows you how to use persistent storage techniques without relying on ClassWizard-generated classes.

The second sample program does more than the first in that it responds to user mouse clicks. However, I resorted to using ClassWizard to help make things easy. Therefore, the second sample program did not take me any more time to create than the first sample program.

The `IPersist` Interfaces

Several standard persistence interfaces allow a client application to obtain and save the state of an object. An object declares its capability to serialize state by implementing one or more of these interfaces. Persistence interfaces also enable a client to clone an object by loading its serialized data back into an object. I have already mentioned Visual Basic's use of property persistence. Microsoft Message Queue (MSMQ) uses the persistence interfaces to save an object's state for transmission in a message. Table 4.1 shows the six standard persistence interfaces.

TABLE 4.1 The Standard Persistence Interfaces

Interface	Description
IStorage	The IStorage interface supports the creation and management of structured storage objects
IStream	The IStream interface supports reading and writing data to stream objects
IPersist	The IPersist interface defines the single method GetClassID, which is designed to supply the CLSID of an object that can be stored persistently in the system
IPersistStorage	The IPersistStorage interface defines methods that enable a container application to pass a storage object to one of its contained objects and to load and save the storage object
IPersistStream	The IPersistStream interface provides methods for saving and loading objects that use a simple serial stream for their storage needs
IPersistFile	The IPersistFile interface provides methods that permit an object to be loaded from or saved to a disk file, rather than a storage object or stream

All the persistence interfaces are derived from the IPersist interface. This interface simply allows a client to obtain the class identifier (CLSID) of the object. Typically, a client application stores the class identifier of an object together with the object's state. In this way, the client application knows which object to activate when it reinstantiates the class. For stateless objects, the IPersist interface is sufficient because the client application needs to know only which class to activate. Most objects, however, need to store data in addition to their CLSID. Those objects can choose among several types of persistence interfaces that derive from the base IPersist interface.

IPersistStorage

The IPersistStorage interface provides methods that allow a container application to pass a storage object to one of its contained objects, and to load and save the storage object. The IPersistStorage interface is normally used for a compound object. One common application of this interface is for clipboard or drag-and-drop operations. The container uses the interface to initialize the object and put it in the loaded or running state. The following is the interface declaration:

```
interface IPersistStorage : IPersist
{
    HRESULT IsDirty
    (
        void
    );

    HRESULT InitNew
    (
```

4

PERSISTENT
STORAGE

```
        [in, unique] IStorage *pStg
    );

    HRESULT Load
    (
        [in, unique] IStorage *pStg
    );

    HRESULT Save
    (
        [in, unique] IStorage *pStgSave,
        [in] BOOL fSameAsLoad
    );

    HRESULT SaveCompleted
    (
        [in, unique] IStorage *pStgNew
    );

    HRESULT HandsOffStorage
    (
        void
    );
};
```

IPersistFile

The IPersistFile interface provides methods that allow objects to be loaded from or saved to a disk file. The examples in this chapter load and save using a stream object. The IPersistFile interface contrasts what we do in the examples in this way: You would implement the IPersistFile interface when you want to read or write information from a separate file. The interface declaration follows:

```
interface IPersistFile : IPersist
{
    HRESULT IsDirty
    (
        void
    );

    HRESULT Load
    (
        [in] LPCOLESTR pszFileName,
        [in] DWORD dwMode
    );

    HRESULT Save
    (
        [in, unique] LPCOLESTR pszFileName,
```

```
        [in] BOOL fRemember
    );

    HRESULT SaveCompleted
    (
        [in, unique] LPCOLESTR pszFileName
    );

    HRESULT GetCurFile
    (
        [out] LPOLESTR *ppszFileName
    );
};
```

IPersistStreamInit

The IPersistStreamInit interface is actually designed to be a replacement for the
IPersistStream interface. It adds a single method called InitNew(). The IsDirty(),
Load(), Save(), and GetSizeMax() are derived from IPersistStream. All the
IPersistStreamInit methods can be seen in Table 4.2. You can see the interface decla-
ration below:

```
interface IPersistStreamInit : IPersist
{
    HRESULT IsDirty
    (
        void
    );

    HRESULT Load
    (
        [in, unique] IStream *pStm
    );

    HRESULT Save
    (
        [in, unique] IStream *pStm,
        [in] BOOL fClearDirty
    );

    HRESULT GetSizeMax
    (
        [out] ULARGE_INTEGER *pcbSize
    );

    HRESULT InitNew
    (
        void
    );
};
```

TABLE 4.2 The `IPersistStreamInit` Interface

Method	Description
QueryInterface	Inherited from `IUnknown`
AddRef	Inherited from `IUnknown`
Release	Inherited from `IUnknown`
GetClassID	Inherited from `IPersist`
IsDirty	Checks the object for changes since it was last saved
Load	Initializes an object from the stream where it was previously saved
Save	Saves an object into the specified stream and indicates whether the object should reset its `dirty` flag
GetSizeMax	Returns the size in bytes of the stream needed to save the object
InitNew	Initializes the object to a default state

The `IStream` Interface

The `IStream` interface supports reading and writing data to stream objects. Stream objects contain the data in a structured storage object. Simple data can be written directly to a stream, but most frequently, streams are elements nested within a storage object. They are similar to standard files.

The `IStream` interface defines methods similar to the MS-DOS file functions. For example, each stream object has its own access rights and a seek pointer. The main difference between a stream object and a DOS file is that streams are not opened using a file handle, but through an `IStream` interface pointer.

The methods in this interface present your object's data as a contiguous sequence of bytes that you can read or write. There are also methods for committing and reverting changes on streams open in transacted mode and methods for restricting access to a range of bytes in the stream.

Streams can remain open for long periods of time without consuming file system resources. The `IStream::Release` method is similar to a close function on a file. Once it is released, the stream object is no longer valid and cannot be used.

Table 4.2 shows the `IStream` methods and gives a short description of each.

TABLE 4.3   The IStream Interface

Method	Description
QueryInterface	Inherited from IUnknown.
AddRef	Inherited from IUnknown.
Release	Inherited from IUnknown.
Read	Inherited from ISequentialStream. Reads a specified number of bytes from the stream object into memory starting at the current seek pointer.
Write	Inherited from ISequentialStream. Writes a specified number of bytes into the stream object starting at the current seek pointer.
Clone	Creates a new stream object that references the same bytes as the original stream but provides a separate seek pointer to those bytes.
Commit	Ensures that any changes made to a stream object open in transacted mode are reflected in the parent storage object.
CopyTo	Copies a specified number of bytes from the current seek pointer in the stream to the current seek pointer in another stream.
LockRegion	Restricts access to a specified range of bytes in the stream. Supporting this functionality is optional because some file systems do not provide it.
Revert	Discards all changes that have been made to a transacted stream since the last IStream::Commit call.
Seek	Changes the seek pointer to a new location relative to the beginning of the stream, the end of the stream, or the current seek pointer.
SetSize	Changes the size of the stream object.
Stat	Retrieves the STATSTG structure for this stream.
UnlockRegion	Removes the access restriction on a range of bytes previously restricted with IStream::LockRegion.

4

PERSISTENT STORAGE

The next sections show examples of the methods of the IStream interface that I use in the examples.

IStream::Write()

The code in Listing 4.1 shows how to use IStream::Write() to write to an IStream object.

LISTING 4.1   Write to an `IStream` Object

```
#include <windows.h>

int main()
{
    IStorage *pStg = NULL;
    IStream *pStream = NULL;
    LONG l = ::StgOpenStorage( L"C:\\MyStorageFile", NULL,
        STGM_READWRITE|STGM_DIRECT|STGM_SHARE_EXCLUSIVE,
        NULL, 0, &pStg );

    if( FAILED( l ) )
    {
        cout << "StgOpenStorage() failed.\n";
        exit( 0 );
    }
    HRESULT hRes = pStg->OpenStream( L"MyStream", NULL,
        STGM_READWRITE|STGM_DIRECT|STGM_SHARE_EXCLUSIVE,
        0, &pStream );
    if( FAILED( hRes ) )
    {
        pStg->Release();
        cout << "OpenStream() failed.\n";
        exit( 0 );
    }
    ULONG cb;
    hRes = stream->Write( L"Hello", 12, &cb );
    if( FAILED( hRes ) )
        cout << "Write() failed\n";
    pStream->Release();
    pStg->Release();
    return 0;
}
```

`IStream::Read()`

The code in Listing 4.2 shows how to use `IStream::Read()` to read from an `IStream` object.

LISTING 4.2   Read from an `IStream` Object

```
#include <windows.h>
#include <iostream>

int main()
{
    IStorage *pStg = NULL;
    IStream *pStream = NULL;
```

LISTING 4.2   Continued

```
    LONG l = ::StgOpenStorage( L"C:\\MyStorageFile", NULL,
        STGM_READWRITE|STGM_DIRECT|STGM_SHARE_EXCLUSIVE,
        NULL, 0, &pStg );

    if( FAILED( l ) )
    {
        cout << "StgOpenStorage() failed.\n";
        exit( 0 );
    }

    HRESULT hRes = pStg->OpenStream( L"MyStream", NULL,
        STGM_READWRITE|STGM_DIRECT|STGM_SHARE_EXCLUSIVE,
        0, &pStream );

    if( FAILED( hRes ) )
    {
        pStg->Release();
        cout << "OpenStream() failed.\n";
        exit( 0 );
    }

    unsigned short olestr[256];
    char s[256];
    ULONG cb;
    hRes = pStream->Read( olestr, 255, &cb );
    if( FAILED( hRes ) )
        cout << "Read() failed.\n";
    wcstombs( s, olestr, 255 );
    std::cout << s << std::endl;
    pStream->Release();
    pStg->Release();
    return 0;
}
```

`IStream::Seek()`

The code in Listing 4.3 shows how to use `IStream::Seek()` to move the cursor in an `IStream` object.

LISTING 4.3   Move the Cursor in an `IStream` Object

```
#include <windows.h>
#include <iostream>

int main()
{
    IStorage *pStg = NULL;
```

4

PERSISTENT STORAGE

LISTING 4.3   Continued

```
IStream *pStream = NULL;
LONG l = ::StgOpenStorage( L"C:\\MyStorageFile", NULL,
    STGM_READWRITE|STGM_DIRECT|STGM_SHARE_EXCLUSIVE,
    NULL, 0, &pStg );

if( FAILED( l ) )
{
    cout << "StgOpenStorage() failed.\n";
    exit( 0 );
}

HRESULT hRes = pStg->OpenStream( L"MyStream", NULL,
    STGM_READWRITE|STGM_DIRECT|STGM_SHARE_EXCLUSIVE,
    0, &pStream );

if( FAILED( hRes ) )
{
    pStg->Release();
    cout << "OpenStream() failed.\n";
    exit( 0 );
}

unsigned short olestr[256];
char s[256];
ULONG cb;
LARGE_INTEGER li;
LISet32(li, 2);
hRes = pStream->Seek( li, STREAM_SEEK_SET, NULL );

if( FAILED( hRes ) )
    cout << "Seek() failed.\n";

hRes = pStream->Read( olestr, 255, &cb );

if( FAILED( hRes ) )
    cout << "Read() failed.\n";

wcstombs( s, olestr, 255 );
std::cout << s << std::endl;
pStream->Release();
pStg->Release();
return 0;
}
```

Creating an ATL Object That Implements `IPersistStreamInit`

I have read a number of books where the author spent an entire chapter explain something. And I dutifully followed the topic for the entire chapter. In most cases, I felt that I understood the material. But when it came time to actually put it into practice, I did not know how to proceed. For that reason, I will run the risk of showing you something that you already know. I am going to give you a step-by-step set of instructions to create an ATL project that implements persistent storage. With Visual C++ running, create a new ATL project. For simplicity, use the default settings.

From the Insert menu, select New ATL Object. Then, insert a full control into the ATL project. If you want persistent storage, the reason to use a full control is that a full control inherits from the `IPersistStreamInit` interface. This simplifies your first foray into the persistent data storage arena. IPersistStreamInit actually implements nothing because it's an interface. In order to have the default ATL implementation for this interface, you must use `IPersistStreamInitImpl`.

IPersistStreamInit already implements the `GetClassID()`, `Load()`, `Save()`, `InitNew()`, `IsDirty()`, and `GetSizeMax()` methods. But there's a good chance that you want to override those methods in your control. The methods you want to override must be added to the class definition for the full control you inserted as follows:

```
// IPersistStream
HRESULT __stdcall IsDirty( void );
HRESULT __stdcall Load( IStream * );
HRESULT __stdcall Save( IStream *, BOOL );
HRESULT __stdcall GetSizeMax( ULARGE_INTEGER * );

// IPersistStreamInit
HRESULT __stdcall InitNew( void );

// IPersist
HRESULT __stdcall GetClassID( CLSID* pClassID );
```

Next, you must actually implement the methods. Open the .cpp file for the full control you added, and add the following (empty) methods:

```
HRESULT CPersistClass1::InitNew( void )
{
    return S_OK;
}

HRESULT CPersistClass1::GetClassID( CLSID* pClassID )
{
```

```
        return S_OK;
}

HRESULT CPersistClass1::IsDirty( void )
{
        return S_OK;
}

HRESULT CPersistClass1::Load( IStream *pStm )
{
        return S_OK;
}

HRESULT CPersistClass1::Save( IStream *pStm, BOOL bClearDirty )
{
        return S_OK;
}

HRESULT CPersistClass1::GetSizeMax( ULARGE_INTEGER *pcbSize )
{
        return S_OK;
}
```

One thing to note is that you don't really have to implement IsDirty() and GetClassID() because IPersistStreamInitImpl already does this. They are shown above for completeness. After the empty methods exist, you can do with them as you want. Most of the time, the Save() and Load() methods are most important.

Listing 4.4 shows highlights the .h file for the first example control. (It's in the Chapter03 directory under the AtlPersistControl1 subdirectory.) The control class is named PersistClass1. If you look at the listing, you'll notice that in addition to the method prototypes, I added a data structure. This data structure is an example of data that you might want to implement as persistent. (I actually use this data structure in the second example.) Its purpose is to hold a text string that is displayed with the control window draws. You can see it's initialized in the constructor, as well as the InitNew() method (shown in Listing 4.5).

LISTING 4.4   PersistClass1.h (Partial)—IPersistStorageInit Member Methods Overridden

```
public:
    CPersistClass1()
    {
        // Clear the data structure.
        memset( &m_TextData, 0, sizeof( TEXTDATA ) );
        // Initialize with the clock tick count.
        wsprintf( m_TextData.szText, "GetTickCount()=%d",
            GetTickCount() );
```

LISTING 4.4   Continued

```
        // Set the color.
        m_TextData.Color = RGB( 255, 255, 0 );

    }

    typedef struct{
        char szText[400];
        COLORREF Color;
    } TEXTDATA;

    TEXTDATA m_TextData;

    // IPersistStream
    HRESULT __stdcall IsDirty( void );
    HRESULT __stdcall Load( IStream * );
    HRESULT __stdcall Save( IStream *, BOOL );
    HRESULT __stdcall GetSizeMax( ULARGE_INTEGER * );

    // IPersistStreamInit
    HRESULT __stdcall InitNew( void );

    // IPersist
    HRESULT __stdcall GetClassID( CLSID* pClassID );
```

The source code for the implemented methods can be seen in Listing 4.5. As mentioned
previously, the `InitNew()` method performs the same initialization as the constructor.
The `Load()` and `Save()` methods use an `IStream` object to read and write the data that
will persist (the `m_TextData` structure).

LISTING 4.5   PersistClass1.cpp—`IPersistStorageInit` Member Method Override
Implementations

```
HRESULT CPersistClass1::InitNew( void )
{

    // Clear the data structure.
    memset( &m_TextData, 0, sizeof( TEXTDATA ) );
    // Initialize with the clock tick count.
    wsprintf( m_TextData.szText, "GetTickCount()=%d",
        GetTickCount() );
    // Set the color.
    m_TextData.Color = RGB( 255, 255, 0 );
    return S_OK;
}

HRESULT CPersistClass1::GetClassID( CLSID* pClassID )
{
```

LISTING 4.5   Continued

```
    // Return the CLSID
    *pClassID = CLSID_PersistClass1;

    return S_OK;
}

HRESULT CPersistClass1::IsDirty( void )
{

    return S_OK;

}

HRESULT CPersistClass1::Load( IStream *pStm )
{
    ULONG lRead = 0;

    // Read the data.
    pStm->Read( &m_TextData, sizeof( TEXTDATA ), &lRead );

    return S_OK;

}

HRESULT CPersistClass1::Save( IStream *pStm, BOOL bClearDirty )
{
    ULONG lWritten = 0;

    // Write the data.
    HRESULT hr = pStm->Write( &m_TextData, sizeof( TEXTDATA ), &lWritten );

    return S_OK;

}

HRESULT CPersistClass1::GetSizeMax( ULARGE_INTEGER *pcbSize )
{

    // Return the size of the data.
    (*pcbSize).QuadPart = sizeof( TEXTDATA );

    return S_OK;
}
```

Creating Simple ATL Controls

What if you don't want a full control? What if all you want is a simple control that's lean and mean? You know: the kind of control for which ATL is famous. Relax, you can still have your cake and eat it, too. If you create an ATL object, you can insert a simple object. Then you simply make some changes to your class definition.

Specifically, you must do two things: derive from `IPersistStream` and `IPersistStreamInit`, and add a variable and method.

To derive from `IPersistStream` and `IPersistStreamInit`, add the following:

```
public IPersistStreamInitImpl<CMyClass>,
public IPersistStorageImpl<CMyClass>
```

The variable and method you must add are as follows:

```
BOOL m_bRequiresSave;

static ATL_PROPMAP_ENTRY *GetPropertyMap()
{
    return( NULL );
}
```

By the way, this won't work if you need the `GetProperyMap()` method to return a valid value. If that is the case, you want a full control anyway; so much for lean and mean.

The `include` file for a class named `CMyClass` follows so that you can see exactly what it should look like:

```
class ATL_NO_VTABLE CMyClass :
    public CComObjectRootEx<CComSingleThreadModel>,
    public CComCoClass<CMyClass, &CLSID_MyClass>,
    public IDispatchImpl<IMyClass, &IID_IMyClass, &LIBID_TEST132Lib>,
    public IPersistStreamInitImpl<CMyClass>,
    public IPersistStorageImpl<CMyClass>

{
public:
    CMyClass()
    {
    }

    BOOL m_bRequiresSave;

    static ATL_PROPMAP_ENTRY *GetPropertyMap()
    {
        return( NULL );
    }

DECLARE_REGISTRY_RESOURCEID(IDR_MYCLASS)

DECLARE_PROTECT_FINAL_CONSTRUCT()

BEGIN_COM_MAP(CMyClass)
```

```
    COM_INTERFACE_ENTRY(IMyClass)
    COM_INTERFACE_ENTRY(IDispatch)
END_COM_MAP()

// IMyClass
public:
};
```

Using an Object with Persistence

The next thing to do is create a client application that uses the `PersistClass1` control. The example on the CD is named PersistClient1. (It's in the Chapter03 directory under the PersistClient1 subdirectory.)

The PersistClient1 application is a simple MFC single-document program. The only code that was added can be found in the view class's constructor and destructor. A few member variables were added to the .h file, and they can be seen in Listing 4.6.

LISTING 4.6 PersistClient1View.h—Member Variables Used for Persistent Storage

```
BOOL m_bCoInitialized;
IUnknown *m_pUnknown;
IPersistStreamInit *m_pPersistStreamInit;
IStream *m_pStream;
```

At runtime, the program goes through a predictable set of steps to initialize and load the control. These steps can be seen in Listing 4.7 as calls to the `CoInitialize()`, `CoCreateInstance()`, and `QueryInterface()` methods are made.

The first code to make note of is the call to `CreateStreamOnHGlobal()`. This creates an `IStream` object that uses memory to which it reads and writes. This `IStream` object can then be used with the control's `Load()` and `Save()` methods.

Before doing the save, the `InitNew()` method is called so that the control is set to its default properties.

The code in the destructor simply cleans up everything. The `IStream`, `IPersistStreamInit`, and `IUnknown` objects are all released. `CoUninitialize()` is called for the final clean up. The `CLSID` below can be found in the .rgs file.

LISTING 4.7 PersistClient1View.cpp—Constructor and Destructor Implementing In-Memory Persistent Storage

```
const CLSID CLSID_PersistClass1 =
    {0x33733D5B, 0xd350, 0x11d3, { 0x8d, 0x44,
```

LISTING 4.7   Continued

```cpp
    ➥ 0x0, 0x10, 0x5a, 0xa7, 0x21, 0xbe }};
CPersistClient1View::CPersistClient1View()
{
    HRESULT hRes;

    m_bCoInitialized = TRUE;
    m_pUnknown = NULL;
    m_pPersistStreamInit = NULL;
    m_pStream = NULL;

    // Initialize.
    hRes = CoInitialize( NULL );

    // Return if initialization failed.
    if( FAILED( hRes ) ){
        m_bCoInitialized = FALSE;
        return;
        }

    // Create the object.
    hRes = CoCreateInstance( CLSID_PersistClass1, NULL,
        CLSCTX_INPROC_SERVER, IID_IUnknown, (void **) &m_pUnknown );

    // Return if object creation failed.
    if( FAILED( hRes ) ){
        m_pUnknown = NULL;
        return;
        }

    // Attempt to get the IPersistStreamInit interface object.
    hRes = m_pUnknown->QueryInterface( IID_IPersistStreamInit,
        (void **) &m_pPersistStreamInit );

    // If we didn't get the IPersistStreamInit interface
    // object, return.
    if( FAILED( hRes ) ){
        m_pPersistStreamInit = NULL;
        return;
        }

    // Create a memory-based stream.
    hRes = CreateStreamOnHGlobal( NULL, TRUE, &m_pStream );

    // If the creation of the memory-based stream failed, return.
    if( FAILED( hRes ) ){
        m_pStream = NULL;
        return;
        }
```

LISTING 4.7   Continued

```
// Initialize the object to its default state.
    hRes = m_pPersistStreamInit->InitNew();

    // Return if the InitNew() method failed.
    if( FAILED( hRes ) )
        return;

    // Save the object to the stream.
    hRes = m_pPersistStreamInit->Save( m_pStream, TRUE );

}

CPersistClient1View::~CPersistClient1View()
{

    // Release the IStream object.
    if( m_pStream != NULL )
        m_pStream->Release();

    // Release the IPersistStreamInit object.
    if( m_pPersistStreamInit != NULL )
        m_pPersistStreamInit->Release();

    // Release the object.
    if( m_pUnknown != NULL )
        m_pUnknown->Release();

    // Uninitialize.
    if( m_bCoInitialized )
        CoUninitialize();

}
```

Simplify Persistent Object Creation

Visual C++ does some of the work for you when you create a control. Instead of manually adding methods to the class, you can add methods from the ClassView window. This
not only adds the prototype to the .h file, but it gives you an empty method into which
you can place your code.

Follow the same steps you followed to create an ATL project with a full control. From
the ClassView window, add the Load(), Save(), InitNew(), and IsDirty() methods.
(You can add GetClsID() and GetSizeMax() if you want, but for the second example I
didn't anticipate using them.)

The rest is easy. Just add your code to Load() and Save(), and the control will persist the desired data.

The second sample object is named AtlPersistControl2. (It's in the Chapter03 directory under the AtlPersistControl2 subdirectory.) The full control class that was added is named PersistClass2. If you take a look at Listing 4.8, you'll see the salient portions of the PersistClass2.h file. The constructor does not perform the same initialization that I pointed out in the first example. This time around, we'll actually use the data. You can also see the methods that were added. Finally, note the OnDraw() method. It uses the m_TextData structure to draw to the window.

LISTING 4.8   PersistClass2.h (Partial)—Data Structure Initialization, Added Method Overrides, and Altered OnDraw() Method

```
public:
    CPersistClass2()
    {
        // Clear the data structure.
        memset( &m_TextData, 0, sizeof( TEXTDATA ) );
        // Initialize with the clock tick count.
        wsprintf( m_TextData.szText, "GetTickCount()=%d",
            GetTickCount() );
        // Set the color.
        m_TextData.Color = RGB( 255, 255, 0 );
    }

    typedef struct{
        char szText[400];
        COLORREF Color;
    } TEXTDATA;

    TEXTDATA m_TextData;

    // Other stuff here…

// IPersistClass2
public:
    STDMETHOD(InitNew)(void);
    STDMETHOD(Save)(IStream *pStm, BOOL bClearDirty);
    STDMETHOD(Load)(IStream *pStm);
    STDMETHOD(IsDirty)(void);

    HRESULT OnDraw(ATL_DRAWINFO& di)
    {
        RECT& rc = *(RECT*)di.prcBounds;
        Rectangle(di.hdcDraw, rc.left, rc.top, rc.right, rc.bottom);

        SetTextAlign(di.hdcDraw, TA_CENTER|TA_BASELINE);
```

LISTING 4.8   Continued

```
        LPCTSTR pszText = _T("ATL 3.0 : PersistClass2");
        TextOut(di.hdcDraw,
            (rc.left + rc.right) / 2,
            (rc.top + rc.bottom) / 2,
            m_TextData.szText,
            lstrlen(m_TextData.szText));

        return S_OK;
    }
```

The only thing added to the implementation of the methods is in the InitNew() and Load() methods as can be seen in Listing 4.9. When the control is reinitialized or reloaded, the data in the m_TextData structure changes. It's important, then, to redraw the window. After doing a simple check to make sure the control window is valid, I called InvalidateRect() and UpdateWindow(). Users then see the new string data drawn in the window.

LISTING 4.9   AtlPersistControl2.cpp—Implementation of the Methods Used in the ATL Class for Persistent Storage

```
STDMETHODIMP CPersistClass2::IsDirty()
{

    return S_OK;

}

STDMETHODIMP CPersistClass2::Load(IStream *pStm)
{
    ULONG lRead = 0;

    // Read the data.
    pStm->Read( &m_TextData, sizeof( TEXTDATA ), &lRead );

    // If the window is valid, cause a redraw.
    if( ::IsWindow( m_hWnd ) ){
        InvalidateRect( NULL, TRUE );
        UpdateWindow();
        }

    return S_OK;

}

STDMETHODIMP CPersistClass2::Save(IStream *pStm, BOOL bClearDirty)
{
```

LISTING 4.9   Continued

```
    ULONG lWritten = 0;

    // Write the data.
    HRESULT hr = pStm->Write( &m_TextData, sizeof( TEXTDATA ), &lWritten );

    return S_OK;

}

STDMETHODIMP CPersistClass2::InitNew()
{

    // Initialize the data.
    memset( &m_TextData, 0, sizeof( TEXTDATA ) );
    wsprintf( m_TextData.szText, "GetTickCount()=%d",
        GetTickCount() );
    m_TextData.Color = RGB( 255, 255, 0 );

    // If the window is valid, cause a redraw.
    if( ::IsWindow( m_hWnd ) ){
        InvalidateRect( NULL, TRUE );
        UpdateWindow();
        }

    return S_OK;
}
```

Simplify Persistent Object Use

I've always thought that adding the code to load and unload a COM object was harder than it had to be. Don't get me wrong; I don't mind writing code. But why write extra code I don't need to?

This actually reminds me of a funny story. I was at an Insider's Summit at Microsoft, and I was having lunch at the table with the Microsoft ADO developers. The project manager looked at me and asked, "What is it about you C++ programmers? What do you have against RAD tools?" (RAD means Rapid Application Development.) Of course, the project manager's implication was that C++ programmers love to write line after line of code for the sheer enjoyment of writing code. Well, after composing myself and remembering that I was an invited guest of Microsoft, I made some sort of polite reply.

The point is this: There are times when we do write more code than we have to. Many times we're afraid of giving away some control of the development to RAD tools, or of adding extra bloat to our applications. Fear not. Visual C++ can wrap an ActiveX control in a class with a minimal amount of extra code, and your job becomes much easier.

4

PERSISTENT STORAGE

You veterans can skip this paragraph. I don't want you to be insulted. For non-veterans, here's how to create a wrapper class for an ActiveX control: Select Add To Project from the Project menu. A dialog box appears, and one of the choices is Components and Controls; select that choice. Then you must select Registered ActiveX Controls. A list of available ActiveX controls will be developed. All you do to create a wrapper class for a control is double-click the control you want in the list, and answer OK when it asks whether you want to insert the control. You can name the class or simply use the suggested name. (I usually choose the suggested name.) Now the control is wrapped in a class and you don't have to worry about `CoInitialize()` or `CoCreateInstance()`. Easy, isn't it?

The preceding steps are what I did to create a class for the `AtlPersistControl2` object and add it to the PersistClient2 program. (It's in the Chapter03 directory under the PersistClient2 subdirectory.) The name of the class is `CPersistClass2`, and the variable name I added to the view class's .h file is `m_Persist`. I also declared an `IStream` object. You can see the two variables I added in Listing 4.10.

LISTING 4.10   PersistClient2View.h—Member Variables Used for Persistent Storage

```
CPersistClass2 m_Persist;
IStream *m_pStream;
```

With ClassWizard, I added three functions to the `CPersistClient2View` class: `OnInitialUpdate()`, `OnLButtonDown()`, and `OnRButtonDown()`. In the `OnInitialUpdate()` function, I called the control's `Create()` function so that it would create its window and attach to the view window. I also created the `IStream` object that is used in the control's `Load()` and `Save()` functions. As a matter of fact, the last thing that happens in the `OnInitialUpdate()` function is that the control's data is saved to the `IStream` object.

The `OnLButtonDown()` function simply causes the control's `InitNew()` method to be called. Because this method causes the control's text string to be updated with the clock ticks, the number displayed in the control's window will change. (Remember not to left-click on the control, but on the view window.)

The `OnRButtonDown()` function causes the saved data to be reloaded into the control. This causes the control to display the number it displayed when it first became visible. The `Load()` method takes the `IStream` object and gets the data. An important point is that we must seek back to the beginning of the data stream before calling the `Load()` method. Because the data was saved at the beginning, that's where we must read. If we try to read without seeking back to the beginning, nothing will be loaded back into the control because the stream pointer is past the data high mark. It's like trying to read the 101st byte from a text file that's only 100 bytes; it just won't work.

Remember, too, that the Load() method in the control causes a redraw. This is important because just restoring the data doesn't cause the control window to redraw. The three functions that were added to the CPersistClient2View class can be seen in Listing 4.11.

LISTING 4.11   PersistClient2View.cpp—Use of Persistent Storage in the Program

```cpp
void CPersistClient2View::OnInitialUpdate()
{
    CView::OnInitialUpdate();

    // Create the control.
    RECT Rect;
    Rect.left = Rect.top = 0;
    Rect.right = 250;
    Rect.bottom = 100;
    m_Persist.Create( "Persist", WS_VISIBLE, Rect, this, 0x11111 );

    // Create a memory-based stream.
    HRESULT hRes = CreateStreamOnHGlobal( NULL, TRUE, &m_pStream );

    // If the creation of the memory-based stream failed, return.
    if( FAILED( hRes ) ){
        m_pStream = NULL;
        return;
        }

    // Save the object to the stream.
    m_Persist.Save( m_pStream, TRUE );

}

void CPersistClient2View::OnLButtonDown(UINT nFlags, CPoint point)
{

    // Reinitialize the control.
    m_Persist.InitNew();

    CView::OnLButtonDown(nFlags, point);
}

void CPersistClient2View::OnRButtonDown(UINT nFlags, CPoint point)
{

    // Load the object from the stream.
    if( m_pStream != NULL ){
        // We need a LARGE_INTEGER and a ULARGE_INTEGER.
        LARGE_INTEGER GoTo;
        ULARGE_INTEGER NewPos;
        GoTo.QuadPart = 0;
```

LISTING 4.11   Continued

```
        // Seek to the beginning.
        m_pStream->Seek( GoTo, STREAM_SEEK_SET, &NewPos );
        // Call the Load() method.
        m_Persist.Load( m_pStream );
        }

    CView::OnRButtonDown(nFlags, point);

}
```

When you run the PersistClient2 programyou'll see the control window, as shown in Figure 4.1, with text saying something like `GetTickCount()=432984395`. Left-click the mouse in the view window (but not in the control window), and you'll see the number change. When you right-click in the view window, the number will be restored to its original number.

FIGURE 4.1

The PersistClient2 program.

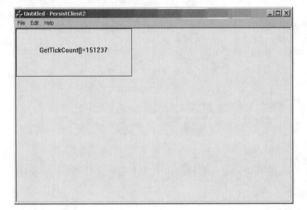

Summary

Persistent data is important for almost every COM object. Persistent data is not hard to implement with the many interfaces that are available. You've learned about the standard interfaces and where they are used. Two examples showed you exactly how to put the persistent interfaces to work in your programs.

The best way to learn is to expand the two examples in this chapter. I'd suggest expanding the amount of data that remains persistent, and using it in a variety of ways.

Monikers

IN THIS CHAPTER

COM+ Objects and Monikers

Monikers are objects that offer services to other COM+ objects; they give you the ability to identify COM+ objects by name. The services that moniker objects provide are all related to providing pointers to the objects that the moniker identifies. The entire process of identification and the subsequent pointer access is known as *binding*.

Monikers are objects that implement the IMoniker interface, and are generally implemented in DLLs as COM+ objects. There are two ways of viewing the use of monikers: as a moniker client, a component that uses a moniker to get a pointer to another object; and as a moniker provider, a component that supplies monikers identifying its objects to moniker clients.

COM+ uses monikers to connect to and activate objects, whether they are in the same machine or across a network. A very important use is for network connections. They are also used to identify, connect to, and run Compound Document link objects. In this case, the link source acts as the moniker provider, and the container holding the link object acts as the moniker client.

Think for a moment about a standard, mundane filename. That filename refers to a collection of data that happens to be stored somewhere on disk. We can call the file's contents an object—the contents are information, and there's probably some code lying around that knows how to provide some functionality for that information. An object such as this would allow clients to manipulate its contents through interface pointers.

Now, the filename itself is not the object but is merely a reference to where the object exists in a passive state. The intelligence about how to use that name is concerned with bringing the object—the file—from its passive state to its running state. But a filename by itself is unintelligent; all the knowledge about how to run the object and how to manage that filename persistently must be coded into the client that intends to use the file object. Usually this isn't much of a problem because applications have been working with file objects for a long time.

In a component software environment, however, more types of objects exist than those whose data exists in a file. There are objects that passively reside in databases, in email messages, and in specific locations inside other files as well. Other objects represent some running process and don't have a passive state at all. Nevertheless, clients need to maintain symbolic links—that is, clients need persistent names that they can bind in order to run objects and retrieve interface pointers for them. Clients also need names to describe specific parts of a file (or parts of parts of files), database queries, remote computations, administrative operations, and so on. Literally any data set and any process or function in a computing environment can be given a name, and a naming and binding architecture allows clients to exploit those resources in efficient and powerful ways.

Nonsensical names can be a problem for this very reason. In fact, they are contrary to the ideals of component software. Adding a new naming tool requires revisions to all the clients that want to make use of that new type of name. In other words, each client has to contain specific code in order to work with any particular type of name for particular resources. If they don't know how to use the name, the resource is unavailable to them. This is completely impractical in a component software system, in which we have the ability to change, modify, update, and redeploy software components independently of any other component and in which QueryInterface() allows us to add new interfaces and new features without losing compatibility with existing clients.

Using Monikers

Suppose that you have product X sales information for fourth quarter 1999 of the UNITEDSTATES division of the Central Region. This information might be stored on the \\salesinfo server, in a specific table and a specific range of cells. An application needs to perform some typical operations on this data: "How do sales of product X compare to sales of product Y this quarter?" "How do sales of product X compare between Q1 this year and Q1 last year?" "Add this figure with 10% of this figure, and update the table for next year's sales quota that resides on www.sourcedna.com/sales/infox/budget.xyz."

Listing 5.1 illustrates how this last example could be encapsulated using monikers and a COM+ object that implements the necessary business logic.

LISTING 5.1 Encapsulating with a Moniker

```
HRESULT hRes = S_OK;
IBindCtx *pBC = NULL;
hRes = CreateBindCtx( NULL, &pBC );

if( SUCCEEDED( hRes ) ){
    DWORD dwValue;
    IMoniker *pMoniker = NULL;

    // Create the moniker object.
    HRes = MkParseDisplayName( pBC,
    ➥ L"file:\\\\\salesinfo\\sales\\infox\\salesQ499.xyz!Summary",
        &dwValue, &pMoniker );

    if( SUCCEEDED( hRes ) ){

        // Connect to the actual business object, create and
        // initialize it if necessary.
        HRes = pMoniker->BindToObject( pBC, NULL, IID_ISalesInfo, &pSales );

        if( SUCCEEDED( hRes ) ){
```

5

MONIKERS

LISTING 5.1 Continued

```
        // Perform the operation.
        pSales->Add( 1.1,
        ➥"http://www.sourcedna.com/sales/infox/budget.xyz" );
        pSales->Release();
        }

    pMoniker->Release();
    }

  pBC->Release();

}
```

This code first creates an `IBindCtx` object with a call to `CreateBindCtx()`. The `IBindCtx` interface provides access to a bind context, which is an object that stores information about a particular moniker binding operation. The `IMoniker` object is created with a call to `MkParseDisplayName()`.

If both of these calls succeed, the actual business object is created with a call to `BindToObject()`. The object is used when the `Add()` function is called.

Everything is finally cleaned up with `Release()` calls.

IMoniker::BindToObject()

The `IMoniker::BindToObject()` method creates an instance of the implementation COM object associated with the moniker. Listing 5.2 is an example of using the `IMoniker::BindToObject()` method.

LISTING 5.2 Using `IMoniker::BindToObject()`

```
#include <windows.h>

IUnknown * CreateAndBind(WCHAR * szDisplayName)
{
  IBindCtx *pbindctx;
  IMoniker *pmoniker;
  ULONG ul;
  IUnknown *punknown;

  HRESULT hresult = ::CreateBindCtx(0, &pbindctx);
  hresult = ::MkParseDisplayName(pbindctx, szDisplayName,
                                   &ul, &pmoniker);
  hresult = pmoniker->BindToObject(pbindctx, NULL,
                         IID_IUnknown, (void**)&punknown);
  pbindctx->Release();
```

LISTING 5.2 Continued

```
  pmoniker->Release();
  return punknown;
}

int main()
{
  ::CoInitialize(NULL);
  IUnknown * pu = CreateAndBind(L"e:\\old.doc");
  pu->Release();
  ::CoUninitialize();

  return 0;
}
```

IMoniker::BindToStorage()

The IMoniker::BindToStorage() method retrieves an instance to the storage interface
(usually IStorage or IStream interfaces) for the moniker. This does not load an instance
of the implementation COM object.

IMoniker::ComposeWith()

The IMoniker::ComposeWith() method creates a new composite moniker from this
moniker and another moniker. This moniker is considered to be the left moniker in the
composite.

For a description of composite monikers, see the "Composite Monikers" section later in
this chapter.

IMoniker::Enum()

The IMoniker::Enum() method retrieves an instance of the IEnumMoniker object for the
composite moniker. The IEnumMoniker object can be used to enumerate the component
monikers of the composite.

IMoniker::IsEqual() and IMoniker::Reduce()

The IMoniker::IsEqual() method determines whether two monikers are equal. Call the
IMoniker::Reduce() method before calling the IMoniker::IsEqual() method to reduce
the moniker to its most specific form.

IMoniker::Hash()

The IMoniker::Hash() method returns a DWORD. The DWORD can be used by other components to bucket sort monikers.

IMoniker::GetTimeOfLastChange()

The IMoniker::GetTimeOfLastChange() method can be used to determine the last time the moniker was changed. This is useful if you are caching data from the moniker.

IMoniker::CommonPrefixWith() and IMoniker::RelativePathTo()

The IMoniker::CommonPrefixWith() method creates a new moniker that determines the commonality with this moniker and another moniker. As an example, the file monikers c:\mydir\subdir\myfile.doc and c:\mydir\otherdir\myfile.doc would have a common prefix of c:\mydir.

The IMoniker::RelativePathTo() method creates a new relative moniker that determines the relative path from this moniker to another moniker. Using the previous sample file monikers, the resulting relative moniker would have the display name ..\otherdir\myfile.doc.

IMoniker::GetDisplayName()

The IMoniker::GetDisplayName() method retrieves the display name of the moniker. For file monikers, this function would return the same filename you used to create the moniker.

IMoniker::IsSystemMoniker()

The IMoniker::IsSystemMoniker() method returns the moniker type. Listing 5.3 shows an example of using the IMoniker::IsSystemMoniker() method. This listing dumps the number two to cout, which is the type of file moniker.

LISTING 5.3 Using IMoniker::IsSystemMoniker()

```
#include <windows.h>
#include <iostream>

int main()
{
  IBindCtx *pbindctx;
  IMoniker *pmoniker;
  ULONG ul;
  HRESULT hresult = ::CreateBindCtx(0, &pbindctx);
  hresult = ::MkParseDisplayName(pbindctx, L"e:\\old.doc", &ul,
  ➡&pmoniker);
  DWORD dw;
  pmoniker->IsSystemMoniker(&dw);
  std::cout << dw << std::endl;
  pbindctx->Release();
```

Listing 5.3   Continued

```
  pmoniker->Release();

  return 0;
}
```

Exploring Moniker Types

The component that provides a moniker makes the moniker accessible to other objects. It is important to understand the differences between the various system-supplied moniker classes to know which are appropriate for a given object. COM also provides functions for creating monikers using the COM-supplied moniker classes. In this section I'll cover file monikers, the Running Object Table, item monikers, class monikers, and pointer monikers.

File Monikers

The simplest moniker types are file monikers. They can be used to identify any object that's stored in a file of its own. File monikers act as wrappers for the pathname the native file system assigns to the file. Calling `IMoniker::BindToObject()` for this moniker would cause this object to be activated and then would return an interface pointer to the object. The source of the object named by the moniker must provide an implementation of the `IPersistFile` interface to support binding a file moniker. (See Chapter 4, "Persistent Storage," for more details. You can also find the interface declaration later in this chapter.) File monikers can represent either a complete or a relative path.

For example, the file moniker for a spreadsheet object stored as the file C:\FINANCIAL\ PROJECTIONS.XLS would contain information equivalent to that pathname. The moniker would not necessarily consist of the same string, however. The string is just its display name, a representation of the moniker's contents that is meaningful to an end user. The display name, which is available through the `IMoniker::GetDisplayName()` method, is used only when displaying a moniker to an end user. This method gets the display name for any of the moniker classes. Internally, the moniker might store the same information in a format that's more efficient for performing moniker operations, but isn't meaningful to users. Then, when this same object is bound through a call to the `BindToObject()` method, the object would be activated, probably by loading the file into the spreadsheet.

COM+ offers moniker providers and the helper API `CreateFileMoniker()`, which creates a file moniker object and returns its pointer to the provider.

COM+ supports three activation primitives: binding to class objects, binding to new class instances, and binding to persistent objects stored in files. This can be seen in the COM+ API function `CoGetInstanceFromFile()`, as shown in Listing 5.4.

LISTING 5.4   The `CoGetInstanceFromFile` Declaration

```
HRESULT CoGetInstanceFromFile(
    [in, unique] COSERVERINFO *pcsi, // host/security info
    [in, unique] CLSID      *pClsid,  // explicit CLSID (opt)
    [in, unique] IUnknown *punkOuter,// for aggregation
    [in] DWORD dwClsCtx,   // locality?
    [in] DWORD grfMode,    // file open mode
    [in] OLECHAR *pwszName,   // file name of object
    [in] DWORD cmqi,    // how many interfaces?
   [out, size_is(cmqi)] MULTI_QI *prgmq // where to put itfs
);
```

The `CoGetInstanceFromFile()` routine takes a filename as input. This filename refers to the persistent state of an object. Using the `CoGetInstanceFromFile()` method guarantees that the object is running. Then, it returns one or more interface pointers to the activated (or reactivated) object. To carry this out, `CoGetInstanceFromFile()` first needs to determine the `CLSID` of the object. The `CLSID` is needed for two reasons. First, if the object is not running, COM+ will need this `CLSID` to create a new instance to be initialized from the persistent image. Second, if the caller doesn't specify an explicit hostname to forward the activation call to, COM+ will use the `CLSID` to determine on which machine to activate the object.

If the `CLSID` is not passed explicitly by the caller, the `CoGetInstanceFromFile()` function derives the `CLSID` from the file itself by calling the COM+ API function `GetClassFile()`:

```
HRESULT GetClassFile([in, string] OLECHAR *pwszFileName,
                     [out] CLSID *pclsid);
```

`GetClassFile()` uses header information in the file as well as registry information to determine what type of object is contained in the file.

Once the class and host machine are determined, COM+ examines the Running Object Table (ROT) on the target host machine to determine whether the object has already been activated. The ROT is a facility of the SCM that maps arbitrary monikers onto running instances on the local host machine. Persistent objects are expected to register themselves at load time in the local ROT. To represent the persistent object's filename as a moniker, COM+ provides a standard moniker type called the File Moniker that wraps a filename behind the `IMoniker` interface. File monikers can be created either by passing the filename to `MkParseDisplayName()` or by calling the explicit API function

```
CreateFileMoniker():
```

```
HRESULT CreateFileMoniker(
        [in, string] const OLECHAR *pszFileName,
        [out] IMoniker **ppmk);
```

If the persistent object has already registered its File Moniker in the ROT, `CoGetInstanceFromFile()` simply returns a pointer to the already running object. If the object is not found in the ROT, COM+ creates a new instance of the file's class and initializes it from the persistent image via the instance's `IPersistFile::Load()` method, as seen in Listing 5.5.

LISTING 5.5   The `IPersistFile` Interface Declaration

```
[ object, uuid(0000010b-0000-0000-C000-000000000046) ]
interface IPersistFile : IPersist {
// called by CoGetInstanceFromFile to initialize object
  HRESULT Load(
        [in, string] const OLECHAR * pszFileName,
        [in] DWORD grfMode
  );
// remaining methods deleted for clarity
}
```

It's the responsibility of the object implementation to load any persistent state from the file as well as to register itself with the local ROT to ensure that only one instance per file is running at a time. This can be seen in Listing 5.6.

LISTING 5.6   Loading the Persistent State

```
STDMETHODIMP Example::Load(const OLECHAR *pszFileName,
                           DWORD grfMode) {
// read in persisted object state
  HRESULT hr = this->MyReadStateFromFile(pszFile, grfMode);
  if (FAILED(hr)) return hr;
// get pointer to ROT from SCM
  IRunningObjectTable *prot = 0;
  hr = GetRunningObjectTable(0, &prot);
  if (SUCCEEDED(hr)) {
// create a file moniker to register in ROT
    IMoniker *pmk = 0;
    hr = CreateFileMoniker(pszFileName, &pmk);
    if (SUCCEEDED(hr)) {
// register self in ROT
      hr = prot->Register(0, this, pmk, &m_dwReg);
      pmk->Release();
    }
    prot->Release();
  }
  return hr;
}
```

The newly created instance's IPersistFile::Load() method will be called by the SCM during the execution of CoGetInstanceFromFile(). The previous example uses the COM+ API function GetRunningObjectTable() to get an IRunningObjectTable interface pointer into the SCM. It then uses this interface to register its moniker in the ROT so that subsequent calls to CoGetInstanceFromFile() using the same filename won't fail when creating new objects, but will return references to this object.

The file moniker exists for two reasons. One reason is to allow objects to register themselves in the ROT so that CoGetInstanceFromFile() can find them. The second reason is to hide the use of CoGetInstanceFromFile() from the client behind the IMoniker interface. The file moniker's implementation of BindToObject() simply calls CoGetInstanceFromFile(), as seen in Listing 5.7.

LISTING 5.7   The Implementation of BindToObject()

```
// pseudo-code from OLE32.DLL
STDMETHODIMP FileMoniker::BindToObject(IBindCtx *pbc,
                IMoniker *pmkToLeft,
                REFIID riid, void **ppv) {
// assume failure
  *ppv = 0;
  HRESULT hr = E_FAIL;
  if (pmkToLeft == 0) { // no moniker to left
    MULTI_QI mqi = { &riid, 0, 0 };
    COSERVERINFO *pcsi;
    DWORD grfMode;
    DWORD dwClsCtx;
// these three parameters are attributes of the BindCtx
    this->MyGetFromBindCtx(pbc, &pcsi, &grfMode, &dwClsCtx);
    hr = CoGetInstanceFromFile(pcsi, 0, 0, dwClsCtx,
                               grfMode, this->m_pszFileName,
                               1, &mqi);
    if (SUCCEEDED(hr))
      *ppv = mqi.pItf;
  }
  else { // there's a moniker to the left
    // ask object to left for IClassActivator
    // or IClassFactory
  }
  return hr;
}
```

Given the behavior of the file moniker, the function in Listing 5.8 that calls CoGetInstanceFromFile():

LISTING 5.8   The CoGetInstanceFromFile() Function

```
HRESULT GetInfo(IInf * &rpInf) {
  OLECHAR *pwszObject =
              OLESTR("\\\\server\\public\\information.expl");
  MULTI_QI mqi = { &IID_IInf, 0, 0 };
  HRESULT hr = CoGetInstanceFromFile(0, 0, 0, CLSCTX_SERVER,
                    STGM_READWRITE, pwszObject, 1, &mqi);
  if (SUCCEEDED(hr))
    rpInf = mqi.pItf;
  else
    rpInf = 0;
  return hr;
}
```

could be simplified by calling CoGetObject instead:

```
HRESULT GetCornelius(IInf * &rpInf) {
  OLECHAR *pwszObject =
              OLESTR("\\\\server\\public\\ information.expl ");
  return CoGetObject(pwszObject,0,IID_IInf, (void**)&rpInf);
}
```

As in the case when the class moniker was used previously, the level of indirection afforded by CoGetObject() allows the client to specify arbitrarily complex activation policies without changing one line of code.

An alternative version of this API function, CoGetInstanceFromIStorage(), accepts a pointer to a hierarchical storage medium instead of a filename.

In addition to the normal rerouting of CLSIDs to host machines that is used by CoGetClassObject()/CoCreateInstanceEx(), CoGetInstanceFromFile() can use the UNC hostname of the file to reroute the activation request to the host machine in which the file resides.

Technically, the ROT is not a machine-wide table but rather a Winstation-wide table, which means that by default, not all logon sessions will have access to the object. To ensure that the object is visible to all possible clients, the object should specify the ROTFLAGS_ALLOWANYCLIENT flag when calling IRunningObjectTable::Register().

Running Object Table

The *Running Object Table (ROT)* is a globally accessible table on each computer that keeps track of all COM+ objects in the running state that can be identified by a moniker. Moniker providers register an object in the table, which increments the object's reference count. Before the object can be destroyed, its moniker must be released from the table

The `IROTData` interface; is implemented by monikers to enable the ROT to compare monikers against each other. The ROT uses the `IROTData` interface to test whether two monikers are equal. The ROT must do this when, for example, it checks whether a specified moniker is registered as running.

You must implement `IROTData` if you are writing your own moniker class (that is, writing your own implementation of the `IMoniker` interface), and if your monikers are meant to be registered in the ROT.

You typically do not need to use this interface. It is used by the system's implementation of the ROT.

Item Monikers

Another implemented moniker class is the item moniker, which can be used to identify an object contained in another object. One type of contained object is an OLE object embedded in a compound document. A compound document could identify the embedded objects it contains by assigning each one an arbitrary name, such as "myobj1," "myobj2," and so forth. Another type of contained object is a user selection in a document, such as a range of cells in a spreadsheet or a range of characters in a text document. An object that consists of a selection is called a *pseudo-object* because it isn't treated as a distinct object until a user marks the selection. A spreadsheet might identify a cell range using a name such as "2C:8H," whereas a word-processing document might identify a range of characters using the name of a bookmark.

An item moniker is useful primarily when concatenated—or "composed"—with another moniker, one that identifies the container. An item moniker is usually created, and then composed onto a file moniker to create the equivalent of a complete path to the object. You can compose the file moniker "C:\stuff\games.doc" (which identifies the container object) with the item moniker "embedobj1" (which identifies an object within the container) to form the moniker "C:\stuff\games.doc\myobj1," which uniquely identifies a particular object within a particular file. You can also concatenate additional item monikers to identify deeply nested objects. For example, if "myobj1" is the name of a spreadsheet object, to identify a certain range of cells in that spreadsheet object, you could append another item moniker to create a moniker that would be the equivalent of "C:\stuff\games.doc\myobj1\."

Item Monikers and File Monikers

When combined with a file moniker, an item moniker forms a complete path. Item monikers thus extend the notion of pathnames beyond the file system, defining pathnames to identify individual objects, not just files.

There is a significant difference between an item moniker and a file moniker. The path contained in a file moniker is meaningful to anyone who understands the file system, whereas the partial path contained in an item moniker is meaningful only to a particular container. Everyone knows what "c:\stuff\games.doc" refers to, but only one particular container object knows what "1A:7F" refers to. One container cannot interpret an item moniker created by another application; the only container that knows which object is referred to by an item moniker is the container that assigned the item moniker to the object in the first place. For this reason, the source of the object named by the combination of a file and item moniker must not only implement `IPersistFile` to facilitate binding the file moniker, but also `IOleItemContainer` to facilitate resolving the name of the item moniker into the appropriate object, in the context of a file.

The advantage of monikers is that someone using a moniker to locate an object doesn't need to understand the name contained within the item moniker, as long as the item moniker is part of a composite. Generally, it would not make sense for an item moniker to exist on its own. Instead, you would compose an item moniker onto a file moniker. You would then call `IMoniker::BindToObject()` on the composite, which binds the individual monikers within it, interpreting the names.

Creating an Item Moniker

To create an item moniker object and return its pointer to the moniker provider, OLE provides the helper API `CreateItemMoniker()`.

Composite Monikers

One of the most useful features of monikers is that you can concatenate or compose monikers together. A composite moniker is a moniker that is a composition of other monikers, and can determine the relation between the parts. This lets you assemble the complete path to an object given two or more monikers that are the equivalent of partial paths. You can compose monikers of the same class (like two file monikers) or of different classes (like a file moniker and an item moniker). If you were to write your own moniker class, you could also compose your monikers with file or item monikers. The basic advantage of a composite is that it gives you one piece of code to implement every possible moniker that is a combination of simpler monikers. That reduces tremendously the need for specific custom moniker classes.

Because monikers of different classes can be composed with one another, monikers provide the ability to join multiple namespaces. The file system defines a common namespace for objects stored as files because all applications understand a file-system pathname. Similarly, a container object also defines a private namespace for the objects that it contains because no container understands the names generated by another container. Monikers allow these namespaces to be joined because file monikers and item

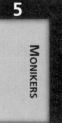

5

MONIKERS

monikers can be composed. A moniker client can search the namespace for all objects using a single mechanism. The client simply calls `IMoniker::BindToObject()` on the moniker, and the moniker code handles the rest. A call to `IMoniker::GetDisplayName()` on a composite creates a name using the concatenation of all the individual monikers' display names.

Furthermore, because you can write your own moniker class, moniker composition allows you to add customized extensions to the namespace for objects.

Sometimes two monikers of specific classes can be combined in a special way. For example, a file moniker representing an incomplete path and another file moniker representing a relative path can be combined to form a single file moniker representing the complete path. For example, the file moniker c:\stuff\music could be composed with the relative file moniker ..\backup\myfile.doc to equal c:\stuff\backup\myfile.doc. This is an example of *non-generic* composition.

Generic composition, on the other hand, permits the connection of any two monikers, no matter what their classes. For example, you could compose an item moniker onto a file moniker, though not, of course, the other way around.

Because a non-generic composition depends on the class of the monikers involved, its details are defined by the implementation of a particular moniker class. You can define new types of non-generic compositions if you write a new moniker class. By contrast, generic compositions are defined by OLE. Monikers created as a result of generic composition are called generic composite monikers.

These three types—file monikers, item monikers, and generic composite monikers—all work together, and they are the most commonly used classes of monikers.

Moniker clients should call `IMoniker::ComposeWith()` to create a composite on one moniker with another. The moniker it's called on internally decides whether it can do a generic or non-generic composition. If the moniker implementation determines that a generic composition is usable, OLE provides the `CreateGenericComposite()` API function to facilitate this.

Class Monikers

Although classes are typically identified directly with `CLSID`s to APIs such as `CoCreateInstance()` or `CoGetClassObject()`, they can also now be identified with a moniker called a class moniker. Class monikers bind to the class object of the class for which they are created.

The ability to identify classes with a moniker supports useful operations that are otherwise unwieldy. For example, file monikers traditionally only supported rich binding to the class associated with the class of file they referred to—a moniker to an Excel file would bind to an instance of an Excel object, and a moniker to a GIF image would bind to an instance of the currently registered GIF handler. Class moniker allows you to indicate the class you want to use to manipulate a file through composition with a file moniker. A class moniker for a 3D charting class composed with a moniker to an Excel file yields a moniker that binds to an instance of the 3D charting object and initializes the object with the contents of the Excel file.

Class monikers are therefore most useful in composition with other types of monikers, such as file monikers or item monikers.

Class monikers might also be composed to the right of monikers supporting binding to the `IClassActivator` interface. When composed in this manner, `IClassActivator` simply gives access to the class object and instances of the class through `IClassActivator::GetClassObject`. Class monikers can be identified through `IMoniker::IsSystemMoniker`, which returns `MKSYS_CLASSMONIKER` in pdwMkSys.

Pointer Monikers

A pointer moniker identifies an object that can exist only in the active or running state. This differs from other classes of monikers, which identify objects that can exist either in the passive or active state.

Suppose that, for example, an application has an object that has no persistent representation. Normally, if a client of your application needs access to that object, you could simply pass the client a pointer to the object. However, suppose that your client is expecting a moniker. The object cannot be identified with a file moniker because it isn't stored in a file, nor with an item moniker because it isn't contained in another object.

Instead, your application can create a pointer moniker, which is a moniker that simply contains a pointer internally, and pass that to the client. The client can treat this moniker like any other. However, when the client calls `IMoniker::BindToObject()` on the pointer moniker, the moniker code doesn't check the Running Object Table (ROT) or load anything from storage. Instead, the moniker code simply calls `IUnknown::QueryInterface()` on the pointer stored inside the moniker.

Pointer monikers allow objects that exist only in the active or running state to participate in moniker operations and be used by moniker clients. One important difference between pointer monikers and other classes of monikers is that pointer monikers cannot be saved to persistent storage. If you do, calling the `IMoniker::Save()` method returns an error. This means that pointer monikers are useful only in specialized situations. You can use the `CreatePointerMoniker()` API function if you need to use a pointer moniker.

Summary

Monikers provide a way to access a COM object with a name. This can be a real benefit to developers. Monikers also give COM objects a way to initialize with an initialization string, simplifying code and instantiations.

In this chapter you learned about the different moniker types and how to use them. You also learned about the all-important topic of the Running Object Table.

How many times have you implemented map containers that identify distinct object instances of the same class by name? I know I've done it at least a hundred times. Monikers and the Running Object Table are COM's implementation of the map container for COM objects. I've already run across a few instances where the Running Object Table looked very tempting. Unfortunately, due to the complexity of programming using monikers and the Running Object Table, you may have yet to implement anything beyond the trivial. I'm hoping that this chapter provided you with the fuel you need to use monikers in your applications.

Connectable Objects

CHAPTER

6

This chapter shows you how to create and use events in Visual C++ and Visual Basic. COM+ does not inherently support the event model or callback functions. In many object models, classes can have three types of members: properties, methods, and events. Visual Basic and Delphi are object-oriented tools that provide these types of models.

COM+ provides direct support for COM+ classes having both properties and methods, but no COM+ structure is the equivalent of an event. This makes implementing COM+ events very difficult.

The model suggested by ActiveX is to provide a connection point where a client can register an event sink. You can think of the event sink as a *callback class*, that is, a class whose methods are invoked to provide for event notification. The event server (or source) is the server that will provide notification (events) to zero or more event sink objects. This implementation is shown in Figure 6.1.

FIGURE 6.1

The connectable object model.

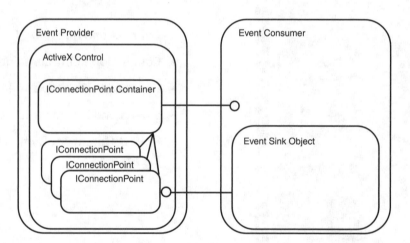

The event source defines an event sink interface and implements one or more connection point classes and a connection point container class. The client implements the event sink interface defined by the event source and registers the event sink object with a connection point object. When the event is triggered, the connection point object calls methods in the event sink object. This is not the easiest process to understand or implement.

Connection Points

The connection point class is an implementation of the `IConnectionPoint` interface. Listing 6.1 shows the definition of the `IConnectionPoint` interface.

LISTING 6.1 Definition of the `IConnectionPoint` Interface

```
interface IConnectionPoint : IUnknown
{
  HRESULT GetConnectionInterface([out] IID * piid);
  HRESULT GetConnectionPointContainer(
    [out] IConnectionPointContainer ** ppCPC)
  HRESULT Advise([in] IUnknown * pUnkSink,
    [out] DWORD * pdwCookie);
  HRESULT Unadvise([in] DWORD dwCookie);
  HRESULT EnumConnections(
    [out] IEnumConnections ** ppEnum);
}
```

The `IConnectionPoint::GetConnectionInterface()` method returns the interface identifier (IID) of the event sink interface. The `IConnectionPoint::GetConnectionPointContainer()` method returns the connection container object. When the client wants event notification, it creates the event sink object defined by the server and calls the `IConnectionPoint::Advise()` method with an `IUnknown` pointer to the event sink object.

This architecture enables one connection sink to be serviced by multiple connection points and multiple connection sinks to be serviced by one connection point. In order to enumerate all the event sinks serviced by a connection point, the client can call the `IConnectionPoint::EnumConnections()` method. The returned `IEnumConnections` object can be used to enumerate all the event sinks that require notification. Listing 6.2 shows the definition of the `IEnumConnections` interface.

LISTING 6.2 Definition of the `IEnumConnections` Interface

```
interface IEnumConnections : IUnknown
{
  HRESULT Next([in] ULONG cConnections,
    [out] CONNECTDATA * rgcd,
    [out] ULONG * lpcFetched);
  HRESULT Skip([in] ULONG celt);
  HRESULT Reset();
  HRESULT Clone([out] IEnumConnections * ppenum);
}
```

The call to the `IEnumConnections::Next()` method returns a `CONNECTDATA` structure. Listing 6.3 shows the definition of the `CONNECTDATA` structure.

LISTING 6.3   Definition of the CONNECTDATA Structure

```
typedef struct tagCONNECTDATA
{
  IUnknown * pUnk;
  DWORD dwCookie;
} CONNECTDATA;
```

The cookie in the CONNECTDATA structure is the value that was returned in the call to the IConnectionPoint::Advise() method. The IUnknown interface pointer can be used by the connection point to query the event sink interface and call methods on the event sink object. (This method call on the event sink is the actual event being triggered in the client.)

Connection Point Container

The server can implement an IConnectionPointContainer class to dispense connection point objects. Listing 6.4 shows the definition of the IConnectionPointContainer interface.

LISTING 6.4   Definition of the IConnectionPointContainer Interface

```
interface IConnectionPointContainer : IUnknown
{
  HRESULT EnumConnectionPoints(
    [out] IEnumConnectionPoints ** ppEnum);
  HRESULT FindConnectionPoint([in] REFIID riid,
    [out] IConnectionPoint ** ppCP);
}
```

The IConnectionPointContainer::FindConnectionPoint() method returns the IConnectionPoint object that services a particular interface identifier.

The IEnumConnectionPoints object is a standard enumeration class. Listing 6.5 shows the definition of the IEnumConnectionPoints interface.

LISTING 6.5   Definition of the IEnumConnectionPoints Interface

```
interface IEnumConnectionPoints : IUnknown
{
HRESULT Next([in] ULONG cConnections,
    [out] IConnectionPoint ** rgcd,
    [out] ULONG * pcFetched);
  HRESULT Skip([in] ULONG celt);
  HRESULT Reset();
  HRESULT Clone([out] IEnumConnectionPoints * ppenum);
}
```

Connection Point Example

In order to demonstrate how connection points are used, I will use ATL's
`IConnectionPointContainerImpl` class. This implementation provides most of the functionality that is necessary to work with connection points from the server-side point of
view.

The demonstration consists of three components: an event server (source) that will trigger events, an event sink that will capture events, and a control program. The event sink
and control program will reside in the client process, and the event source will reside in
the server process. This best simulates the event sink–event source model that is typical
in most programs. This example is available on the CD-ROM in the Chapter06 directory
in the ComEvents subdirectory.

We begin by examining the IDL for the event source (see Listing 6.6).

LISTING 6.6   The IDL for the Event Source

```
// EventServer.idl : IDL source for EventServer.dll
//

// This file will be processed by the MIDL tool to
// produce the type library (EventServer.tlb) and marshaling
// code.

import "oaidl.idl";
import "ocidl.idl";

  [

    uuid(1579753F-41A7-11D2-BEA1-00C04F8B72E7),
    dual,
    helpstring("IMyEventTrigger Interface"),
    pointer_default(unique)
  ]
  interface IMyEventTrigger : IDispatch
  {
    [helpstring("method Fire")] HRESULT Fire();
  };

  [
    object,
    uuid(15797541-41A7-11D2-BEA1-00C04F8B72E7),
    dual,
    helpstring("IMyEventSink Interface"),
    pointer_default(unique)
  ]
```

LISTING 6.6   Continued

```
interface IMyEventSink : IDispatch
{
  [helpstring("method Hello")] HRESULT Hello();
};

[
  uuid(15797532-41A7-11D2-BEA1-00C04F8B72E7),
  version(1.0),
  helpstring("EventServer 1.0 Type Library")
]
library EVENTSERVERLib
{
  importlib("stdole32.tlb");
  importlib("stdole2.tlb");

  [
    uuid(15797540-41A7-11D2-BEA1-00C04F8B72E7),
    helpstring("MyEventTrigger Class")
  ]
  coclass MyEventTrigger
  {
    [default] interface IMyEventTrigger;
    [default, source] interface IMyEventSink;
  };
};
```

I've created two interfaces, one to trigger events and one to capture events (an event sink). Each interface has one method that defines the trigger method and sink method. When the trigger method in the event source is called, the sink methods in the event sinks will be called.

In the coclass definition, I included the interface attributes [default, source] for the event interface. That means this interface is the default interface for events. It is important to add the [source] attribute to mark interfaces as being event sink interfaces, rather than interfaces exposed by the class. Languages such as Delphi and Visual Basic use the [source] attribute to differentiate events from methods and properties.

Next, look at the trigger's class declaration in Listing 6.7.

LISTING 6.7   The Class Declaration of the Trigger

```
// MyEventTrigger.h : Declaration of the CMyEventTrigger

#ifndef __MYEVENTTRIGGER_H_
#define __MYEVENTTRIGGER_H_
```

LISTING 6.7 Continued

```c
#include "resource.h"        // main symbols

//////////////////////////////////////////////////////////////////////
// CMyEventTrigger
class ATL_NO_VTABLE CMyEventTrigger :
  public CComObjectRootEx<CComSingleThreadModel>,
  public CComCoClass<CMyEventTrigger, &CLSID_MyEventTrigger>,
  public IConnectionPointContainerImpl<CMyEventTrigger>,
  public IDispatchImpl<IMyEventTrigger, &IID_IMyEventTrigger,
                       &LIBID_EVENTSERVERLib>,
  public IConnectionPointImpl<CMyEventTrigger,
                             &IID_IMyEventSink>
{
public:
  CMyEventTrigger()
  {
  }

DECLARE_REGISTRY_RESOURCEID(IDR_MYEVENTTRIGGER)

BEGIN_COM_MAP(CMyEventTrigger)
  COM_INTERFACE_ENTRY(IMyEventTrigger)
  COM_INTERFACE_ENTRY(IDispatch)
  COM_INTERFACE_ENTRY_IMPL(IConnectionPointContainer)
END_COM_MAP()

BEGIN_CONNECTION_POINT_MAP(CMyEventTrigger)
  CONNECTION_POINT_ENTRY(IID_IMyEventSink)
END_CONNECTION_POINT_MAP()


// IMyEventTrigger
public:
  STDMETHOD(Fire)();
};

#endif //__MYEVENTTRIGGER_H_
```

In the class declaration, note that I've implemented the IMyEventTrigger interface. This interface will be called later in order to trigger the event. I've inherited from both the IConnectionPointImpl and IConnectionPointContainerImpl in order to use all the default template code implemented in ATL. The entry CONNECTION_POINT_ENTRY() tells the IConnectionPointContainerImpl which event sink interfaces are handled by the connection point.

The trigger's class definition is very simple because only one method is implemented (see Listing 6.8).

LISTING 6.8 The Class Definition of the Trigger

```
// MyEventTrigger.cpp : Implementation of CMyEventTrigger
#include "stdafx.h"
#include "EventServer.h"
#include "MyEventTrigger.h"

/////////////////////////////////////////////////////////////////////
// CMyEventTrigger


STDMETHODIMP CMyEventTrigger::Fire()
{
  // TODO: Add your implementation code here
  IUnknown ** ppunknown = m_vec.begin();
  if (*ppunknown != NULL)
  {
    IMyEventSink * pmyeventsink = (IMyEventSink *)*ppunknown;
    pmyeventsink->Hello();
  }

  return S_OK;
}
```

The IUnknown pointers contained in the connection point are saved in a
CComDynamicUnkArray container member variable named m_vec. You can navigate this
entire array by using code similar to Listing 6.9.

LISTING 6.9 Navigating the CComDynamicUnkArray Container Class

```
IUnknown** ppunknown = m_vec.begin();
while (ppunknown < m_vec.end())
{
  if (*ppunknown != NULL)
  {
    IMyEventSink * pmyeventsink = (IMyEventSink *)*ppunknown;
    (*pmyeventsink)->Hello();
  }
  ppunknown++;
}
```

That's the entire event server. There's not that much code because the
IConnectionPointContainerImpl and IConnectionPointImpl templates are doing
everything for you.

The Event Sink

The event sink object is an in-process server. This server has no new interfaces and one
COM+ class (see Listing 6.10).

LISTING 6.10 The Event Sink Object IDL

```
// EventClient.idl : IDL source for EventClient.dll
//

// This file will be processed by the MIDL tool to
// produce the type library (EventClient.tlb) and marshaling
// code.

import "oaidl.idl";
import "ocidl.idl";



[
  uuid(7BBCFB61-41AB-11D2-BEA1-00C04F8B72E7),
  version(1.0),
  helpstring("EventClient 1.0 Type Library")
]
library EVENTCLIENTLib
{
  importlib("stdole32.tlb");
  importlib("stdole2.tlb");
  importlib("..\\EventServer\\EventServer.tlb");


  [
    uuid(7BBCFB6F-41AB-11D2-BEA1-00C04F8B72E7),
    helpstring("MyEventSink Class")
  ]
  coclass MyEventSink
  {
    [default] interface IMyEventSink;
  };

};
```

The important thing to note in the IDL is that I am importing the type library of the event source and implementing the `IMyEventSink` interface in the event sink class.

The class declaration (see Listing 6.11) and class definition (see Listing 6.12) of the event sink object are straightforward.

LISTING 6.11 The Event Sink Object Class Declaration

```
// MyEventSink.h: Definition of the MyEventSink class
//
//////////////////////////////////////////////////////////////
```

Listing 6.11 Continued

```
#if !defined(AFX_MYEVENTSINK_H_INCLUDED_)
#define AFX_MYEVENTSINK_H_INCLUDED_

#if _MSC_VER >= 1000
#pragma once
#endif // _MSC_VER >= 1000

#include "resource.h"       // main symbols

#include "..\\EventServer\\EventServer.h"

/////////////////////////////////////////////////////////////
// MyEventSink

class MyEventSink :
  public CComObjectRoot,
  public CComCoClass<MyEventSink,&CLSID_MyEventSink>,
  public IDispatchImpl<IMyEventSink, &IID_IMyEventSink,
                       &LIBID_EVENTSERVERLib>
{
public:
  MyEventSink() {}
BEGIN_COM_MAP(MyEventSink)
  COM_INTERFACE_ENTRY(IDispatch)
  COM_INTERFACE_ENTRY(IMyEventSink)
END_COM_MAP()
//DECLARE_NOT_AGGREGATABLE(MyEventSink)
// Remove the comment from the line above if you don't want
// your object to support aggregation.

DECLARE_REGISTRY_RESOURCEID(IDR_MyEventSink)

// IMyEventSink
public:
  STDMETHOD(Hello)();

};

#endif // !defined(AFX_MYEVENTSINK_H_INCLUDED_)
```

Listing 6.12 The Event Sink Object Class Definition

```
// MyEventSink.cpp : Implementation of CEventClientApp and
// DLL registration.

#include "stdafx.h"
#include "EventClient.h"
#include "MyEventSink.h"
```

LISTING 6.12   Continued

```
#include <iostream>

#include "..\\EventServer\\EventServer_i.c"

//////////////////////////////////////////////////////////
//

STDMETHODIMP MyEventSink::Hello()
{
  // TODO: Add your implementation code here
  std::cout << "The event was fired.  Hurray!" << std::endl;

  return S_OK;
}
```

Both the definition and declaration are standard implementations of a dual interface.
They inherit from the `IDispatchImpl` ATL class template and implement all the methods
of the interface (`IMyEventSink`). In this case, one method sends a message to the standard output when the event is fired. About the only code out of the ordinary in this declaration and definition is that the event server's header file (`EventServer.h`) comes before
the class declaration, and the event server's type library source file (`EventServer_i.c`)
comes before the class definition. These files contain the C++ definition of the event sink
interface (in the header file) and the GUIDs of the event sink interface (in the source
file).

The control program is where all the action is (see Listing 6.13).

LISTING 6.13   Event Control Program

```
#include <windows.h>
#include <iostream>
#include <atlbase.h>
#include "EventServer\\EventServer.h"

#include "EventServer\\EventServer_i.c"

char s[1024];

HRESULT GetUnknown(WCHAR * strProgID, IUnknown ** ppunknown)
{
  CLSID clsid;
  HRESULT hresult = ::CLSIDFromProgID(strProgID, &clsid);
  if (FAILED(hresult))
  {
    // CLSIDFromProgID failed
    std::cout << "CLSIDFromProgID failed = "
```

LISTING 6.13   Continued

```
                    << _ltoa(hresult, s, 16) << std::endl;
    ATLASSERT(FALSE);
    return hresult;
  }

  hresult = ::CoCreateInstance(clsid, NULL, CLSCTX_SERVER,
                            IID_IUnknown, (void **)ppunknown);
  if (FAILED(hresult))
  {
    // CoCreateInstance failed
    std::cout << "CoCreateInstance failed = "
              << _ltoa(hresult, s, 16) << std::endl;
    ATLASSERT(FALSE);
    return hresult;
  }

  return S_OK;
};

HRESULT GetInterface(IUnknown * punknown, REFIID riid,
                     IUnknown ** ppunknown)
{
  HRESULT hresult = punknown->QueryInterface(riid,
                                         (void **)ppunknown);
  if (FAILED(hresult))
  {
    // QueryInterface failed
    std::cout << "QueryInterface failed = "
              << _ltoa(hresult, s, 16) << std::endl;
    ATLASSERT(FALSE);
    return hresult;
  }

  return S_OK;
};

int main()
{
  //======================================
  // Start the test app
  //======================================
  ::CoInitialize(NULL);
  std::cout << "Start" << std::endl;

  //======================================
  // initialize all my interfaces
  //======================================
  IUnknown * punknownserver = 0;
  IUnknown * punknownclient = 0;
```

LISTING 6.13   Continued

```cpp
IMyEventSink * pmyeventsink = 0;
IConnectionPointContainer * pmyconnectionpointcontainer = 0;
IConnectionPoint * pmyconnectionpoint = 0;
IMyEventTrigger * pmyeventtrigger = 0;

//=====================================
// Get my server IUnknown
//=====================================
HRESULT hresult =
  GetUnknown(L"MyEventTrigger.MyEventTrigger.1",
             &punknownserver);
if (FAILED(hresult))
{
  // GetUnknown failed
  std::cout << "GetUnknown failed = "
            << _ltoa(hresult, s, 16) << std::endl;
  ATLASSERT(FALSE);
  return hresult;
}


//=====================================
// Get my client IUnknown
//=====================================
hresult = GetUnknown(L"EventClient.MyEventSink.1",
                     &punknownclient);
if (FAILED(hresult))
{
  // GetUnknown failed
  std::cout << "GetUnknown failed = "
            << _ltoa(hresult, s, 16) << std::endl;
  ATLASSERT(FALSE);
  return hresult;
}


//=====================================
// Get my server interface
//=====================================
hresult = GetInterface(punknownserver,
                IID_IConnectionPointContainer,
                (IUnknown **)&pmyconnectionpointcontainer);
if (FAILED(hresult))
{
  // GetInterface failed
  std::cout << "GetInterface failed = "
            << _ltoa(hresult, s, 16) << std::endl;
  ATLASSERT(FALSE);
  return hresult;
}
```

LISTING 6.13   Continued

```
//======================================
// Get the container
//======================================
hresult = pmyconnectionpointcontainer->FindConnectionPoint(
                    IID_IMyEventSink, &pmyconnectionpoint);
if (FAILED(hresult))
{
  // FindConnectionPoint failed
  std::cout << "FindConnectionPoint failed = "
            << _ltoa(hresult, s, 16) << std::endl;
  ATLASSERT(FALSE);
  return hresult;
}


//======================================
// Add the advise notification
//======================================
DWORD dwcookie = 0;
hresult = pmyconnectionpoint->Advise(punknownclient,
                                     &dwcookie);
if (FAILED(hresult))
{
  // Advise failed
  std::cout << "Advise failed = "
            << _ltoa(hresult, s, 16) << std::endl;
  ATLASSERT(FALSE);
  return hresult;
}


//======================================
// Get my server interface
//======================================
hresult = GetInterface(punknownserver, IID_IMyEventTrigger,
                       (IUnknown **)&pmyeventtrigger);
if (FAILED(hresult))
{
  // GetInterface failed
  std::cout << "GetInterface failed = "
            << _ltoa(hresult, s, 16) << std::endl;
  ATLASSERT(FALSE);
  return hresult;
}


//======================================
// Fire the event
//======================================
hresult = pmyeventtrigger->Fire();
if (FAILED(hresult))
{
```

Events and Visual Basic

I fired the event in the previous example using the vtable. Visual Basic generates automation code only for its event sinks and does not generate any vtable code to capture event notifications. That means I must call the `IDispatch::Invoke` method in order to fire the event in a Visual Basic client.

Black Hole of Events

This is one of the big black holes in Microsoft's object-oriented architecture. How is the programmer supposed to know which interface to fire the event with, the dispatch or the vtable interface? It is simply not possible without imposing limits on the model.

You could impose a rule on COM servers that they must call both the vtable and dispatch interface, but this would result in additional client code to ensure that an event was not received twice.

The only rule that works is to limit everyone to using the dispatch interface when invoking event sink methods. This removes any advantage of using the vtable and increases the learning curve by requiring developers to understand automation in order to use events.

Listing 6.14 shows the necessary code to call the `IDispatch::Invoke` method in order to invoke events using the dispatch interface.

LISTING 6.14   Call Event Handler Through `IDispatch` Interface

```
VARIANTARG* pvars = new VARIANTARG[1];
for (int i = 0; i < 1; i++)
{
  VariantInit(&pvars[i]);
}
IUnknown** pp = m_vec.begin();
while (pp < m_vec.end())
{
  if (*pp != NULL)
  {
    pvars[0].vt = VT_I4;
    pvars[0].lVal= lFlags;
    DISPPARAMS disp = { pvars, NULL, 1, 0 };
    IDispatch* pDispatch = reinterpret_cast<IDispatch*>(*pp);
    pDispatch->Invoke(0x1, IID_NULL, LOCALE_USER_DEFAULT,
                  DISPATCH_METHOD, &disp, NULL, NULL, NULL);
  }
```

LISTING 6.14   Continued

```
    pp++;
}
delete[] pvars;
```

Rewriting the Event Source

A few things must be rewritten in the event source in order to comply with this event model. The IMyEventSink interface must be rewritten as a dispatch interface. Listing 6.15 shows the content of the new IDL file.

LISTING 6.15   IDL for New Event Source

```
// vbsink.idl : IDL source for vbsink.dll
//

// This file will be processed by the MIDL tool to
// produce the type library (vbsink.tlb) and marshaling
// code.

import "oaidl.idl";
import "ocidl.idl";

    [
      object,
      uuid(18C9E28D-8D36-11D2-9C2B-DC6F06C10000),
      dual,
      helpstring("IMyEventSource Interface"),
      pointer_default(unique)
    ]
    interface IMyEventSource : IDispatch
    {
      [id(1), helpstring("method FireEvent")]
        HRESULT FireEvent(long lSeconds);
    };
[
  uuid(18C9E280-8D36-11D2-9C2B-DC6F06C10000),
  version(1.0),
  helpstring("vbsink 1.0 Type Library")
]
library VBSINKLib
{
  importlib("stdole32.tlb");
  importlib("stdole2.tlb");

    [
      uuid(A0281EE1-8D36-11d2-9C2B-DC6F06C10000),
```

LISTING 6.15 Continued

```
  nonextensible,
  helpstring("DIMyEventSink Dispatch Interface")
]
dispinterface DIMyEventSink
{
  properties:
  methods:
    [id(1)] void Timeout();
};

[
  uuid(18C9E28E-8D36-11D2-9C2B-DC6F06C10000),
  helpstring("MyEventSource Class")
]
coclass MyEventSource
{
  [default] interface IMyEventSource;
  [default, source] dispinterface DIMyEventSink;
};
};
```

Another change added was to delay the event trigger by a selected number of seconds to make the event notification process more obvious. In order to introduce the delay, I must create a second thread so that the first thread does not block the client application. Listing 6.16 shows the implementation of the new event source class.

LISTING 6.16 Firing the Delayed Event in a Separate Thread

```
// MyEventSource.cpp : Implementation of CMyEventSource
#include "stdafx.h"
#include "vbsink.h"
#include "MyEventSource.h"


//////////////////////////////////////////////////////////////
// CMyEventSource


STDMETHODIMP CMyEventSource::FireEvent(long lSeconds)
{
  m_lSeconds = lSeconds;

  DWORD dw;
  if (::CreateThread(NULL, 0,
    (LPTHREAD_START_ROUTINE)&CMyEventSource::ThreadStart,
    this, 0, &dw))
  {
    return S_FALSE;
  }

  return S_OK;
```

LISTING 6.16   Continued

```
}

DWORD WINAPI CMyEventSource::ThreadStart(void * pCookie)
{
  CMyEventSource * object = (CMyEventSource *)pCookie;
  Sleep(1000*object->m_lSeconds);
  object->Fire_Timeout();
  return 0;
}
```

This type of thread, as explained in Chapter 7, "COM+ Threading," is known as a *worker thread*. It enables the main thread to continue normal processing while the task is performed in the background. In this case, the background task is the `CMyEventSource::ThreadStart` static method that simply waits for the selected amount of seconds before firing the timeout event.

I could have written the code to call the event sink handling routine by writing the `CMyEventSource::FireEvent()` to read like Listing 6.14. But Visual C++ provides an alternative, safer, and easier method for deriving this code. Using this method, I was able to reduce the event notification code to one line, that is, `CMyEventSource->Fire_Timeout()`. The code behind `CMyEventSource::Fire_Timeout()` was generated by Visual C++ 6.0's ATL Proxy Generator.

The ATL Proxy Generator

The ATL proxy generator has a function that generates the source code necessary to broadcast an event notification to all connected event sinks. This makes coding much easier because event notification in the event source requires only one line of code rather than the 20 or so used in Listing 6.14.

> **Note**
>
> The ATL Proxy Generator is no longer available in Visual C++ 6.0. It has been integrated into the DevStudio's ClassView pane. Save your IDL and compile it, so that you generate a type library. You can compile your IDL by right-clicking the IDL file in DevStudio's FileView pane and selecting the Compile option in the pop-up menu.
>
> After the type library is compiled, right-click your event source class in the ClassView pane and select Implement Connection Point in the pop-up menu. From the Implement Connection Point dialog that appears, you can select your event interface and click OK.
>
> The IDE will generate a header file similar to Listing 6.17, and it will automatically generate the code to inherit from the newly generated proxy class.

In order to generate the event source proxy code, save your IDL file and compile it into the necessary type library. In this case, the type library file is vbsink.tlb. Now, from the IDE, select Project, Add To Project, Component and Controls. Select the Developer Studio Components folder, followed by the ATL Proxy Generator item. Select Insert and click OK in the confirmation pop-up box. The ATL Proxy Generator dialog box appears and should look like Figure 6.2.

FIGURE 6.2

The ATL Proxy Generator.

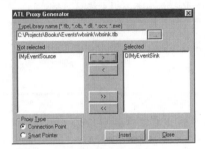

From the dialog box, add the type library filename with full path in the TypeLibrary Name edit control. You can use the ellipsis notation button to browse for your type library. Highlight the event sink dispatch interface and click -> to move the interface from the Not Selected to the Selected pane. Select Connection Point in the Proxy Type box, and click the Insert button. The code generator will ask for a filename. You can simply accept the filename provided by the code generator by clicking the Save button.

Listing 6.17 shows the code generated from your type library.

LISTING 6.17   IConnectionPoint Handler

```
/////////////////////////////////////////////////////////////////
// CProxyDIMyEventSink
template <class T>
class CProxyDIMyEventSink :
  public IConnectionPointImpl<T, &DIID_DIMyEventSink,
                             CComDynamicUnkArray>
{
public:
//methods:
//DIMyEventSink : IDispatch
public:
  void Fire_Timeout()
  {
    T* pT = (T*)this;
    pT->Lock();
    IUnknown** pp = m_vec.begin();
    while (pp < m_vec.end())
```

LISTING 6.17 Continued

```
     {
       if (*pp != NULL)
       {
         DISPPARAMS disp = { NULL, NULL, 0, 0 };
         IDispatch* pDispatch =
                           reinterpret_cast<IDispatch*>(*pp);
         pDispatch->Invoke(0x1, IID_NULL, LOCALE_USER_DEFAULT,
                   DISPATCH_METHOD, &disp, NULL, NULL, NULL);
       }
       pp++;
     }
     pT->Unlock();
   }
};
```

In order to implement this connection point template class, simply derive the event source class from this template and add the dispatch interface ID to the connection point map. Listing 6.18 shows the new event source class declaration.

LISTING 6.18 The Event Source Class

```
// MyEventSource.h : Declaration of the CMyEventSource

#ifndef __MYEVENTSOURCE_H_
#define __MYEVENTSOURCE_H_

#include "resource.h"       // main symbols
#include "cpvbsink.h"

/////////////////////////////////////////////////////////////
// CMyEventSource
class ATL_NO_VTABLE CMyEventSource :
  public CComObjectRootEx<CComMultiThreadModel>,
  public CComCoClass<CMyEventSource, &CLSID_MyEventSource>,
  public IConnectionPointContainerImpl<CMyEventSource>,
  public IDispatchImpl<IMyEventSource, &IID_IMyEventSource,
                       &LIBID_VBSINKLib>,
  public CProxyDIMyEventSink<CMyEventSource>
{
public:
  CMyEventSource()
  {
  }

DECLARE_REGISTRY_RESOURCEID(IDR_MYEVENTSOURCE)

BEGIN_COM_MAP(CMyEventSource)
```

LISTING 6.18   Continued

```
  COM_INTERFACE_ENTRY(IMyEventSource)
  COM_INTERFACE_ENTRY(IDispatch)
  COM_INTERFACE_ENTRY_IMPL(IConnectionPointContainer)
END_COM_MAP()

BEGIN_CONNECTION_POINT_MAP(CMyEventSource)
  CONNECTION_POINT_ENTRY(DIID_DIMyEventSink)
END_CONNECTION_POINT_MAP()


// IMyEventSource
public:
  STDMETHOD(FireEvent)(long lSeconds);
private:
  long m_lSeconds;
  static DWORD WINAPI ThreadStart(void * pCookie);
};

#endif //__MYEVENTSOURCE_H_
```

I didn't rewrite the control program or the event sink client. Instead, I'll write the client in Visual Basic, as a proof of the concept that this type of event handling is compatible with Visual Basic.

Writing the Visual Basic Client

Writing the VB client is quite easy. Create a simple Visual Basic executable with one form and one class file. Go to Projects, References and enable the reference to the type library that contains the COM object you are using. Add the code in Listing 6.19 to your form source code.

LISTING 6.19   Initiate the Event

```
Option Explicit
Dim vbsinkcls As Class1

Private Sub Command1_Click()

    Set vbsinkcls = New Class1
    DoEvents
    vbsinkcls.Go

End Sub
```

Note that Class1 is the name of your one class file. If you changed the name of your one class file, you also must change the code in the form source code.

Finally, you must create the COM object, call the `FireEvent` method, and respond to the `Timeout` event notification. Listing 6.20 shows the code in the class file that performs these activities.

LISTING 6.20   Class to Call Event Trigger and Handle Event Notification

```
Option Explicit
Dim WithEvents vbsink As VBSINKLib.MyEventSource
Attribute vbsink.VB_VarHelpID = -1

Private Sub Class_Initialize()

    Set vbsink = New VBSINKLib.MyEventSource

End Sub

Private Sub Class_Terminate()

    Set vbsink = Nothing

End Sub

Private Sub vbsink_Timeout()

    MsgBox "Timeout"

End Sub

Sub Go()

    vbsink.FireEvent 10

End Sub
```

The type of the `vbsink` object must be the type library name defined in your IDL file and the class name of your `coclass`, also defined in your IDL file. The COM class is created in the `Class_Initialize()` subroutine and destroyed in the `Class_Terminate()` subroutine. The `Go()` subroutine calls the `FireEvent` method of the COM object with a parameter indicating a 10-second delay before the timeout event is sent.

The most important part of this class file is the `vbsink_Timeout()` subroutine that receives the event notification. When Visual Basic receives the event notification, it looks for a subroutine name that matches the object name, followed by an underscore, followed by the notification method's name.

Run the VB executable and click the Trigger button. Ten seconds later, the event notification will be sent and a message box with the caption Timeout will be displayed. That's it.

Both the VB and ATL projects for this last experiment are available on the CD-ROM in the Chapter06 directory, in a subdirectory named vbsink.

How Different Tools Implement Events

The next two sections are experiments that I believe are most useful in understanding how COM events work. These experiments show how different compilers generate their own event interfaces.

Events and Visual Basic

If you create a VB ActiveX control and compile the project into an OCX, you can use OLEView to read the OCX's type library. Start OLEView and select File, View TypeLib from the menu bar. Select your newly created OCX and click the Open button. The right pane of the ITypeLib viewer displays the content of the type library in IDL format. Listing 6.21 is the default IDL generated for a Visual Basic ActiveX control.

LISTING 6.21   IDL of Visual Basic ActiveX Control

```
// Generated .IDL file (by the OLE/COM Object Viewer)
//
// typelib filename: Project1.ocx
// Forward declare all types defined in this typelib
interface _UserControl1;
dispinterface __UserControl1;

[
  uuid(700BD9B9-8D5F-11D2-9C2B-DC6F06C10000),
  version(1.0),
  helpstring("Project1")
]
library Project1
{
    // TLib : OLE Automation :
    // {00020430-0000-0000-C000-000000000046}
    importlib("STDOLE2.TLB");

    [
      odl,
      uuid(700BD9B6-8D5F-11D2-9C2B-DC6F06C10000),
      version(1.0),
      hidden,
      dual,
      nonextensible,
```

LISTING 6.21   Continued

```
    oleautomation
    ]
    interface _UserControl1 : IDispatch {
    };

    [
        uuid(700BD9B7-8D5F-11D2-9C2B-DC6F06C10000),
        version(1.0),
        noncreatable,
        control
    ]
    coclass UserControl1 {
        [default] interface _UserControl1;
        [default, source] dispinterface __UserControl1;
    };

    [
        uuid(700BD9B8-8D5F-11D2-9C2B-DC6F06C10000),
        version(1.0),
        hidden,
        nonextensible
    ]
    dispinterface __UserControl1 {
        properties:
        methods:
    };
};
```

Note that the control implements two interfaces, one dual interface and one dispatch interface. The dual interface contains the properties and methods of the ActiveX object. The dual interface has the name of the control with a prefixed underscore.

The dispatch interface contains the events of the ActiveX object and has the name of the control with two prefixed underscores. This is a confusing convention because it is sometimes difficult to tell the difference between one and two leading underscores, but the convention works in that it now is easy to differentiate which interfaces belong to which controls.

If you compare the IDL in Listing 6.22 to the IDL in Listing 6.15, you will note that they are very similar. This is the similarity we were trying to achieve so that Visual Basic modules can take advantage of our events.

Events and C++Builder

Another interesting experiment is to view the content of an ActiveForm built using Inprise's C++Builder or Delphi. Listing 6.22 shows the default IDL generated when creating an ActiveForm with C++Builder.

LISTING 6.22   IDL of C++Builder ActiveForm

```
// Generated .IDL file (by the OLE/COM Object Viewer)
//
// typelib filename: <could not determine filename>
// Forward declare all types defined in this typelib
interface IActiveFormX;
dispinterface IActiveFormXEvents;

[
  uuid(18C9B680-8CA9-11D2-9C2B-DC6F06C10000),
  version(1.0),
  helpstring("ActiveFormProj1 Library")
]
library ActiveFormProj1
{
    // TLib : OLE Automation :
    // {00020430-0000-0000-C000-000000000046}
    importlib("STDOLE2.TLB");

    [
      odl,
      uuid(18C9B681-8CA9-11D2-9C2B-DC6F06C10000),
      version(1.0),
      helpstring("Dispatch interface for ActiveForm Control"),
      dual,
      oleautomation
    ]
    interface IActiveFormX : IDispatch {
        [id(0x00000001), propget]
        HRESULT _stdcall Visible(
          [out, retval] VARIANT_BOOL* Value);
        [id(0x00000001), propput]
        HRESULT _stdcall Visible([in] VARIANT_BOOL Value);
        [id(0x00000002), propget]
        HRESULT _stdcall AutoScroll(
          [out, retval] VARIANT_BOOL* Value);
        [id(0x00000002), propput]
        HRESULT _stdcall AutoScroll([in] VARIANT_BOOL Value);
        [id(0x00000003), propget]
        HRESULT _stdcall AxBorderStyle(
          [out, retval] TxActiveFormBorderStyle* Value);
        [id(0x00000003), propput]
        HRESULT _stdcall AxBorderStyle(
          [in] TxActiveFormBorderStyle Value);
        [id(0xfffffdfa), propget]
        HRESULT _stdcall Caption([out, retval] BSTR* Value);
        [id(0xfffffdfa), propput]
        HRESULT _stdcall Caption([in] BSTR Value);
        [id(0xfffffe0b), propget]
        HRESULT _stdcall Color([out, retval] OLE_COLOR* Value);
```

LISTING 6.22   Continued

```
[id(0xfffffe0b), propput]
HRESULT _stdcall Color([in] OLE_COLOR Value);
[id(0xfffffe00), propget]
HRESULT _stdcall Font(
  [out, retval] IFontDisp** Value);
[id(0xfffffe00), propput]
HRESULT _stdcall Font([in] IFontDisp* Value);
[id(0xfffffe00), propputref]
HRESULT _stdcall Font([in] IFontDisp* Value);
[id(0x00000004), propget]
HRESULT _stdcall KeyPreview(
  [out, retval] VARIANT_BOOL* Value);
[id(0x00000004), propput]
HRESULT _stdcall KeyPreview([in] VARIANT_BOOL Value);
[id(0x00000005), propget]
HRESULT _stdcall PixelsPerInch(
  [out, retval] long* Value);
[id(0x00000005), propput]
HRESULT _stdcall PixelsPerInch([in] long Value);
[id(0x00000006), propget]
HRESULT _stdcall PrintScale(
  [out, retval] TxPrintScale* Value);
[id(0x00000006), propput]
HRESULT _stdcall PrintScale([in] TxPrintScale Value);
[id(0x00000007), propget]
HRESULT _stdcall Scaled(
  [out, retval] VARIANT_BOOL* Value);
[id(0x00000007), propput]
HRESULT _stdcall Scaled([in] VARIANT_BOOL Value);
[id(0x00000008), propget]
HRESULT _stdcall Active(
  [out, retval] VARIANT_BOOL* Value);
[id(0x00000009), propget]
HRESULT _stdcall DropTarget(
  [out, retval] VARIANT_BOOL* Value);
[id(0x00000009), propput]
HRESULT _stdcall DropTarget([in] VARIANT_BOOL Value);
[id(0x0000000a), propget]
HRESULT _stdcall HelpFile([out, retval] BSTR* Value);
[id(0x0000000a), propput]
HRESULT _stdcall HelpFile([in] BSTR Value);
[id(0x0000000b), propget]
HRESULT _stdcall WindowState(
  [out, retval] TxWindowState* Value);
[id(0x0000000b), propput]
HRESULT _stdcall WindowState(
  [in] TxWindowState Value);
[id(0xfffffdfe), propget]
HRESULT _stdcall Enabled(
```

LISTING 6.22   Continued

```
        [out, retval] VARIANT_BOOL* Value);
    [id(0xfffffdfe), propput]
    HRESULT _stdcall Enabled([in] VARIANT_BOOL Value);
    [id(0x0000000c), propget]
    HRESULT _stdcall Cursor([out, retval] short* Value);
    [id(0x0000000c), propput]
    HRESULT _stdcall Cursor([in] short Value);
};
[
  uuid(18C9B683-8CA9-11D2-9C2B-DC6F06C10000),
  version(1.0),
  helpstring("Events interface for ActiveFormX Control")
]
dispinterface IActiveFormXEvents {
    properties:
    methods:
        [id(0x00000001)]
        void OnActivate();
        [id(0x00000002)]
        void OnClick();
        [id(0x00000003)]
        void OnCreate();
        [id(0x00000004)]
        void OnDblClick();
        [id(0x00000005)]
        void OnDestroy();
        [id(0x00000006)]
        void OnDeactivate();
        [id(0x0000000f)]
        void OnPaint();
};

[
  uuid(18C9B685-8CA9-11D2-9C2B-DC6F06C10000),
  version(1.0),
  helpstring("ActiveFormX Control"),
  control
]
coclass ActiveFormX {
    [default] interface IActiveFormX;
    [default, source] dispinterface IActiveFormXEvents;
};

typedef [uuid(18C9B687-8CA9-11D2-9C2B-DC6F06C10000),
         version(1.0)]
enum {
    afbNone = 0,
    afbSingle = 1,
    afbSunken = 2,
```

LISTING 6.22   Continued

```
        afbRaised = 3
} TxActiveFormBorderStyle;

typedef [uuid(18C9B688-8CA9-11D2-9C2B-DC6F06C10000),
         version(1.0)]
enum {
    poNone = 0,
    poProportional = 1,
    poPrintToFit = 2
} TxPrintScale;

typedef [uuid(18C9B689-8CA9-11D2-9C2B-DC6F06C10000),
         version(1.0)]
enum {
    mbLeft = 0,
    mbRight = 1,
    mbMiddle = 2
} TxMouseButton;

typedef [uuid(18C9B68A-8CA9-11D2-9C2B-DC6F06C10000),
         version(1.0)]
enum {
    wsNormal = 0,
    wsMinimized = 1,
    wsMaximized = 2
} TxWindowState;
};
```

If you simply skip over the default properties and events that were generated by
C++Builder, you'll note again that this IDL file is almost identical to Visual Basic's IDL
in Listing 6.22 and the IDL in Listing 6.15. I prefer C++Builder's convention of naming
its event dispatch interface with an `Events` suffix rather than Visual Basic's leading
underscores.

Summary

I recognize that most developers have a fear of COM connection points and events. But
my own experience is that the fear is often squashed by simply taking the time to create
on your own a couple of COM controls that implement different types of events. If
you're not already comfortable with events, I suggest you take the time to create your
own ATL COM project that implements events. And don't stop at creating a COM
server; you must also create a client that implements the events in your COM server.

COM+ Threading

CHAPTER

7

Understanding threading in the COM+ universe is a large undertaking. With a half-dozen or so different thread types, a multitude of thread-synchronization issues, and different threading models, you could read a bible on threading and still grasp only the basics of the issues that need to be understood.

The threading subject is so vast primarily because of the legacy that threading has created as it evolved on the PC.

The Evolution of PC Threading

Originally, PCs were not capable of threading or even multitasking. You can think of multitasking as the capability of a computer system to run more than one task or program at a time. Eventually, as the PC moved to 32-bit operating systems, programmers began to refer to individual tasks or programs as processes. This language translated well from the UNIX world, where processes have existed for decades.

Windows 95 and Windows NT were the platforms that launched the success of multitasking on PCs. 16-bit Windows also provided for multitasking, but the operating system lacked many features that a multitasking system such as UNIX provided to high-end machines. The most important of these features included preemptive task switching and isolating task failures.

Without preemptive task switching, a task had to explicitly call functions that yielded control to the operating system. A task could either maliciously or accidentally refuse to yield control to the operating system and lock all other running tasks.

Isolating task failures was another important feature of 32-bit Windows multitasking. Previously, versions of Windows would easily become unstable when failure occurred in any running tasks. Frustration and rebooting the PC typically followed failures in 16-bit Windows. Failures in 32-bit Windows are also followed by frustration, but recovery is generally possible without having to reboot the PC.

With the advent of 32-bit Windows, we were also introduced to the concept of having multiple threads of execution in one process. Not only were we able to have multiple processes running simultaneously, but we could also have multiple running threads in each process.

A lot of changes took place over those few years. Meanwhile, a young version of OLE was also being ported to 32-bit Windows. Around this time, Microsoft's object computing strategy became known as COM. With the implementation of COM came the idea of an apartment thread. Because this book is about COM+, and this chapter is about threading, the discussion is concerned primarily with apartment threads.

The first paragraph of this chapter identified three areas that are important to understand in order to thread with the best of them. These areas are thread types, COM+ threading models, and thread synchronization. You will learn each in turn.

> **Note**
>
> I must warn you that this chapter was written with the assumption that you are familiar with Win32 threading basics. If you don't know the `CreateThread()` function, I suggest you familiarize yourself with it quickly because I'll be using it in almost every code listing.
>
> I did not include any header files in the code listings. I did, however, include all the code in this chapter on the CD-ROM that accompanies this book in the Chapter07 directory. The code on the CD-ROM includes the appropriate header files.

COM+ Thread Types

The thread type indicates the amount of support that the thread is providing. Here, *support* means the quantity of features implemented by the thread. The difference in quantity of features is important only to the programmer. The user does not really care, nor should he care, what thread types are used in his application. The operating system is also completely unaware of the different types of threads.

You'll learn about thread pools and the following thread types in this chapter:

- Worker threads
- Message queue threads
- Window threads
- Apartment threads

> **Note**
>
> Each of the thread types that I discuss will contain the features of the previous thread type and one or more additional features. The message queue thread type is similar to the worker thread type and additionally contains a message queue. The window thread type is similar to the message queue type and additionally contains a GUI window. The apartment thread type is similar to the window thread type and additionally initializes the COM library.

Worker Threads

The most basic thread type is the worker thread. The worker thread is commonly used to simulate background processing. You can easily provide background-processing capabilities to your program by initiating sequences of code in a separate thread. Listing 7.1 shows how to use a worker thread to initiate background processing.

LISTING 7.1   An Example of a Worker Thread

```
class WorkerThread
{
public:
  int DoWork();
  static DWORD WINAPI ThreadProc(void * p);
  WorkerThread();
  virtual ~WorkerThread();
};

WorkerThread::WorkerThread () {}

WorkerThread::~WorkerThread () {}

DWORD WINAPI Worker::ThreadProc(void *p)
{
  ///////////////////////////////////
  // TODO
  // Add background processing code here
  //
  std::cout << "Hello World!" << std::endl;
  Sleep(1000);
  std::cout << "Goodbye World!" << std::endl;
  return 0;
}

int WorkerThread::DoWork()
{
  DWORD dw;
  HANDLE thread = ::CreateThread(NULL, 0, ThreadProc, NULL, 0, &dw);
  ::CloseHandle(thread);
  return 0;
}
```

Note that the DoWork() method returns to the caller before the real work has finished. This is one of the difficulties with creating PauseWork() and StopWork() methods; the thread is busily working and a simple method that stops the action must somehow signal the executing thread. The thread must be looking for the signal as well.

Message Queue Threads

The next step forward in thread functionality is the message queue thread. The advantage of the message queue thread is that you can post Windows messages to the thread. Listing 7.2 shows an example of starting and posting messages to a message queue thread.

LISTING 7.2   An Example of a Message Queue Thread

```
class MessageQueue
{
public:
  static DWORD WINAPI ThreadProc(void *p);
  int DoWork();
  MessageQueue();
  virtual ~MessageQueue();

private:
  DWORD m_idThread;
};

#define MYMESSAGE (WM_USER+1000)

MessageQueue::MessageQueue()
{
  HANDLE thread = ::CreateThread(NULL, 0, ThreadProc, NULL, 0,
                                 &m_idThread);
  ::CloseHandle(thread);
}

MessageQueue::~MessageQueue()
{
  ::PostThreadMessage(m_idThread, WM_QUIT, 0, 0);
}

DWORD WINAPI MessageQueue::ThreadProc(void *p)
{
  MSG msg;
  while (::GetMessage(&msg, NULL, 0, 0))
  {
    switch (msg.message)
    {
      case MYMESSAGE:
      ////////////////////////////////////
      // TODO
      // Add background processing code here
      //
      std::cout << "Hello World!" << std::endl;
      Sleep(1000);
```

7

COM+
THREADING

LISTING 7.2 Continued

```
        std::cout << "Goodbye World!" << std::endl;
      default:
      break;
    };
  };
  return 0;
}

int MessageQueue::DoWork()
{
  ::PostThreadMessage(m_idThread, MYMESSAGE, 0, 0);
  return 0;
}
```

Messages are posted to a message queue thread by calling the PostThreadMessage()
function. You captured the thread ID when you created the thread and are able to post
messages to the thread using this identifier.

The message queue thread retrieves messages from its message queue with the
GetMessage() function. It is highly likely that you've used the GetMessage() function to
retrieve Windows messages for a GUI object. In this case, you've specified a window
handle of NULL. Had you specified a non-NULL window handle, Windows would
return only messages destined for the specified window.

DoWork() calls are synchronized automatically by GetMessage(). If you call DoWork()
three times, the caller does not wait on any DoWork() call. But because the real job is
done upon reception of MYMESSAGE, the next order can be known only when the first
job is finished, the switch exited and the GetMessage() API called. If you choose to
make it invisible, remove the WM_PAINT handler from the window procedure and
TranslateMessage().

Window Threads

The window thread type has a window in addition to a message queue. The window
thread type also uses the GetMessage() function to retrieve message from its message
queue; but to retrieve the message, the thread specifies a window's handle rather than a
thread ID to retrieve its messages. Listing 7.3 shows an example of a window thread.
Note that the window is visible but in many cases you might want it to be invisible
because someone can close it and make the class useless.

LISTING 7.3   An Example of a Window Thread

```cpp
class Window
{
public:
  static LRESULT CALLBACK WndProc(HWND hwnd, UINT idMessage,
                                  WPARAM wParam, LPARAM lParam);
  static DWORD WINAPI ThreadProc(void * p);
  int DoWork();
  Window();
  virtual ~Window();

private:
  DWORD m_idThread;
  HWND m_hwnd;
};
#define MYMESSAGE (WM_USER+1000)

Window::Window()
{
  HANDLE thread = ::CreateThread(NULL, 0, ThreadProc, &m_hwnd, 0,
                                 &m_idThread);
  ::CloseHandle(thread);
}

Window::~Window()
{
  ::PostMessage(m_hwnd, WM_QUIT, 0, 0);
}

LRESULT CALLBACK Window::WndProc(HWND hwnd, UINT idMessage,
                                 WPARAM wParam, LPARAM lParam)
{
  HDC hDC;
  PAINTSTRUCT ps;
  RECT rect;
  switch (idMessage)
  {
    case WM_PAINT:
      hDC = BeginPaint (hwnd, &ps);
      GetClientRect (hwnd, &rect);
      DrawText (hDC, "Hello Thread", -1, &rect,
          DT_SINGLELINE | DT_CENTER | DT_VCENTER);
      EndPaint (hwnd, &ps);
      break;
    case WM_DESTROY:
      PostQuitMessage(0);
      break;
    case MYMESSAGE:
        /////////////////////////////////////
        // TODO
```

7

COM+
THREADING

LISTING 7.3   Continued

```cpp
          // Add background processing code here
          //
          std::cout << "Hello World!" << std::endl;
          Sleep(1000);
          std::cout << "Goodbye World!" << std::endl;
      break;
    default:
      return DefWindowProc (hwnd, idMessage, wParam, lParam);
  }
  return (0L);
}

DWORD WINAPI Window::ThreadProc(void *p)
{
  WNDCLASSEX wndclass;
  static char  szWndClassName[] = "Threading Example";

  wndclass.cbSize = sizeof (wndclass);
  wndclass.style=CS_HREDRAW | CS_VREDRAW;
  wndclass.lpfnWndProc = WndProc;
  wndclass.cbClsExtra = 0;
  wndclass.cbWndExtra = 0;
  wndclass.hInstance = ::GetModuleHandle(NULL);
  wndclass.hIcon = ::LoadIcon(NULL,IDI_APPLICATION);
  wndclass.hCursor = ::LoadCursor(NULL, IDC_ARROW);
  wndclass.hbrBackground = (HBRUSH) ::GetStockObject(WHITE_BRUSH);
  wndclass.lpszMenuName = NULL;
  wndclass.lpszClassName = szWndClassName;
  wndclass.hIconSm = ::LoadIcon(NULL,IDI_APPLICATION);

  RegisterClassEx (&wndclass);

  HWND hwnd;
  MSG msg;

  hwnd = CreateWindow (
    szWndClassName,
    "The Hello Program",
    WS_OVERLAPPEDWINDOW,
    CW_USEDEFAULT,
    CW_USEDEFAULT,
    CW_USEDEFAULT,
    CW_USEDEFAULT,
    NULL,
    NULL,
    GetModuleHandle(NULL),
    NULL);

  *(HWND *)p = hwnd;
```

LISTING 7.3 Continued

```
  ShowWindow(hwnd, SW_SHOWNORMAL);
  UpdateWindow(hwnd);

  while (GetMessage(&msg,hwnd,0,0))
  {
    TranslateMessage(&msg);
    DispatchMessage(&msg);
  }
  return msg.wParam;
}

int Window::DoWork()
{
  ::PostMessage(m_hwnd, MYMESSAGE, 0, 0);
  return 0;
}
```

You can see how the example differs from the previous message queue thread in that the thread creates a window and retrieves messages for that window.

Apartment Threads

The last basic thread type is the apartment thread. Any thread used to execute calls to component objects is configured as "apartment threaded." Each object "lives in an apartment" (thread) for the life of the object. All calls to that object execute on the apartment thread.

Listing 7.4 shows an example of a minimal apartment thread.

LISTING 7.4 A Minimal Apartment Thread

```
class Apartment
{
public:
  static DWORD WINAPI ThreadProc(void * p);
  int DoWork();
  Apartment();
  virtual ~Apartment();

};

Apartment::Apartment() {}

Apartment::~Apartment() {}

DWORD WINAPI Apartment::ThreadProc(void *p)
```

LISTING 7.4 Continued

```
{
  ::CoInitialize(NULL);
  ///////////////////////////////////////
  // TODO
  // Add background processing code here
  //
  std::cout << "Hello World!" << std::endl;
  Sleep(1000);
  std::cout << "Goodbye World!" << std::endl;

  ::CoUninitialize();
  return 0;
}

int Apartment::DoWork()
{
  DWORD dw;
  HANDLE thread = ::CreateThread(NULL, 0, ThreadProc, NULL, 0, &dw);
  ::CloseHandle(thread);
  return 0;
}
```

Note that this thread type does not appear to have a message loop or a window. The call to the `CoInitialize()` function automatically creates its own message queue where the COM+ subsystem can place calls to objects and receive COM+ calls from clients that exist in other threads. This queue is created the first time it is needed.

Originally, each thread had to have its own apartment in order to communicate with the COM/COM+ subsystem. These apartments were called single-threaded apartments (STAs). When COM introduced the multithreaded apartment (MTA), the apartment thread became a misnomer; that is, apartments were no longer actually tied to one thread.

If you call the `CoInitializeEx(NULL, COINIT_MULTITHREADED)` function, your thread will start a multithreaded apartment. All threads created in the same process automatically have access to this multithreaded apartment. Each thread can still initialize its own single-threaded apartment by calling the `CoInitialize(NULL)` function, but the thread can exist in only one apartment (either one STA or one MTA).

In a process, a thread must enter an apartment before being able to use a COM object (through a call to `CoInitialize(Ex)()`). `CO_INIT_MULTITHREADED` lets a thread enter the one and only multithreaded apartment and `CoInitialize()` lets the thread enter a single-threaded apartment.

The advantages and disadvantages of your choice of single-threaded or multithreaded apartment are discussed in detail later in this chapter in the section, "COM+ Threading Models."

Thread Pools

Thread pools are not a thread type, but rather an implementation option. In other words, COM is using a thread pool to implement how COM calls to single- and multithreaded apartments. Any of the previous four thread types could be extended to provide for a thread pool. Listing 7.5 shows an example of a thread pool using message queue threads.

LISTING 7.5   Worker Thread Pool

```
class Pool
{
public:
  static DWORD WINAPI ThreadProc(void * p);
  int DoWork();
  Pool();
  virtual ~Pool();

private:
  std::queue<DWORD> m_qidThread;

};

#define MYMESSAGE (WM_USER+1000)
#define NUMTHREADS 10

Pool::Pool()
{
  for (int i=0;i<10;i++)
  {
    DWORD dw;
    HANDLE thread = ::CreateThread(NULL, 0, ThreadProc, NULL, 0, &dw);
    ::CloseHandle(thread);
    m_qidThread.push(dw);
  }
}

Pool::~Pool()
{
  while (!m_qidThread.empty())
  {
    ::PostThreadMessage(m_qidThread.front(), WM_QUIT, 0, 0);
    m_qidThread.pop();
  }
}

DWORD WINAPI Pool::ThreadProc(void *p)
{
  MSG msg;
  while (::GetMessage(&msg, NULL, 0, 0))
```

Listing 7.5 Continued

```
    {
      switch (msg.message)
      {
        case MYMESSAGE:
          /////////////////////////////////////////
          // TODO
          // Add background processing code here
          //
          std::cout << "Hello World!" << std::endl;
          std::cout << "From Thread Number: " << ::GetCurrentThreadId()
                    << std::endl;
        default:
        break;
      };
    };
    return 0;
}

int Pool::DoWork()
{
    DWORD dw = m_qidThread.front();
    ::PostThreadMessage(dw, MYMESSAGE, 0, 0);
    m_qidThread.pop();
    m_qidThread.push(dw);
    return 0;
}
```

An important implementation of thread pool is apartment thread pooling. In the apartment-threading model, COM+ allocates several apartment threads where COM+ objects can be created. This type of model can provide for a multithreaded server where each individual object is single-threaded and, therefore, does not need to consider concurrency issues. You learn this threading model in more detail in the next section.

COM+ Threading Models

The following are the four most common types of COM+ threading models:

- Single-threaded
- Apartment-threaded
- Neutral-threaded
- Free-threaded

The Single-Threaded Server

Most COM+ servers to date have been developed using the single-threaded server threading model. In this model, all method calls to all objects are done by the same thread. The single thread has one apartment where out-of-process calls to the COM+ server are serialized. Each out-of-process COM+ call is placed on the apartment's message queue. Calls on the message queue are processed one at a time by the apartment thread. This threading model completely eliminates any concurrency problems involving either per-object data or shared data.

The apartments in this model are commonly referred to as STAs (single-threaded apartments). The meaning is quite clear: Methods of objects in a single-threaded apartment are only called by the same thread and one at a time.

The single-threaded server has a major bottleneck in the apartment's message queue. Because all calls are serialized through the message queue and only one thread retrieves calls from the message queue, it is not hard to imagine how performance is limited. In addition, the indirection provided by the message queue requires several milliseconds of processing time per COM+ method call to place and retrieve messages on the queue.

In order to relate the discussion to a more concrete understanding, we're going to take some time to work through a simple example. It will use ATL to demonstrate a simple single-threaded example. Creating an ATL server that uses the single-threaded model is simple. Create the ATL executable application using the ATL AppWizard. From the menu bar, select Insert, New ATL Object. Select Simple Object in the ATL Object Wizard and click the Next button. From the Attribute property page of the ATL Object Wizard Properties Form, select Single as the Threading Model (see Figure 7.1). On the Names property page of the ATL Object Wizard Properties Form, type whatever Short Name you want for your object and click OK. That's it.

FIGURE 7.1

Selecting the threading model.

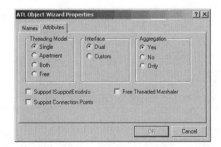

There are several ways to eliminate this bottleneck. You can create additional apartment threads so that individual objects can run simultaneously (apartment-threaded model) or you can allow multiple threads to exist in an apartment (free-threaded model).

The Apartment-Threaded Server

The second type of COM+ server that is used by experienced COM+ programmers is the apartment-threaded server. This server type differs from the single-threaded server in that the COM+ server has one or more apartment threads (STAs).

Each object exists in only one apartment thread (STA), and incoming calls are still serialized on the apartment thread's message queue. That means no concurrency issues exist for per-object data. Because objects running in separate apartment threads can share global data and run concurrently, a concurrency problem now exists for global data.

Once again, to relate the discussion to a concrete example, we'll take some time out to use ATL and work through an example. Creating an ATL server that uses the apartment-threaded model is slightly more difficult than creating a single-threaded server. Follow the same steps as for creating a single-threaded server, except select Apartment as the Threading Model on the Attributes property page of the ATL Object Wizard Properties form (refer to Figure 7.1). Three additional changes are required. You must modify your CExeModule class to inherit from the CComAutoThreadModule template class (see Listing 7.6).

LISTING 7.6 Inherit from CComAutoThreadModule Template Class

```
class CExeModule
  : public CComAutoThreadModule<CComSimpleThreadAllocator>
{
public:
  LONG Unlock();
  DWORD dwThreadID;
  HANDLE hEventShutdown;
  void MonitorShutdown();
  bool StartMonitor();
  bool bActivity;
};
```

You must modify your CExeModule::Unlock() method to call the CComAutoThreadModule::Unlock() method (see Listing 7.7).

LISTING 7.7 Call CComAutoThreadModule::Unlock Method

```
LONG CExeModule::Unlock()
{
    LONG l = CComAutoThreadModule<CComSimpleThreadAllocator>::Unlock();
    if (l == 0)
    {
        bActivity = true;
```

Listing 7.7 Continued

```
        SetEvent(hEventShutdown);
        // tell monitor that we transitioned to zero
    }

    return 1;
}
```

You must add the DECLARE_CLASSFACTORY_AUTO_THREAD() macro to your COM+ class definitions (see Listing 7.8).

Listing 7.8 Implement AUTO_THREAD() Class Factory

```
class ATL_NO_VTABLE CATObject :
  public CComObjectRootEx<CComSingleThreadModel>,
  public CComCoClass<CATObject, &CLSID_ATObject>,
  public IDispatchImpl<IATObject, &IID_IATObject,
                       &LIBID_APARTMENTTHREADEDLib>
{
public:
  CATObject()
  {
  }

DECLARE_REGISTRY_RESOURCEID(IDR_ATOBJECT)

DECLARE_PROTECT_FINAL_CONSTRUCT()

DECLARE_CLASSFACTORY_AUTO_THREAD()

BEGIN_COM_MAP(CATObject)
  COM_INTERFACE_ENTRY(IATObject)
  COM_INTERFACE_ENTRY(IDispatch)
END_COM_MAP()

// IATObject
public:
  STDMETHOD(get_Thread)(/*[out, retval]*/ long *pVal);
};
```

The apartment-threaded server exists so that legacy thread-unsafe COM+ objects can continue to exist without causing concurrency issues in these objects that are assumed to be incapable of maintaining integrity in a multithreaded environment. If you are willing to take the time to make your COM+ object thread-safe, I suggest you create your COM+ servers using the free-threaded threading model.

7

COM+
THREADING

The Neutral-Threaded Server

COM+ includes a new threading model called the neutral threading. The neutral model supports execution of objects on any thread type. The benefit of neutral apartment threading is that it does not require the developer of objects running in a neutral apartment to make the object thread safe.

Although apartments determine which threads are dispatched to the object, setting the synchronization attribute controls when these calls are dispatched. An activity groups one or more contexts with the same concurrency requirements. Activities span more than a single context and object, but although each context in a process belongs to just one activity, some contexts do not belong to any activity. If the context does not belong to an activity, any thread in the apartment can enter the context at any time. If the apartment is a single-threaded apartment, only one thread can enter. In the case of a neutral apartment or multithreaded apartment, there can be concurrent access to the context.

The Free-Threaded Server

The free-threaded model does not use an apartment message queue to serialize incoming COM+ calls. This type of server enables incoming COM+ calls to call the methods directly on the incoming RPC thread. That means your COM+ objects can span one or more threads, thus introducing concurrency issues for both per-object data and global data.

Creating a free-threaded COM+ server is almost as easy as creating a single-threaded COM+ server. Follow the same steps as for creating a single-threaded server, except select Free under the heading Threading Model on the Attributes property page of the ATL Object Wizard Properties Form (refer to Figure 7.1). The only other change is in your precompiled header file. You must undefine the _ATL_APARTMENT_THREADED constant and define the _ATL_FREE_THREADED constant (see Listing 7.9).

LISTING 7.9 Defining _ATL_FREE_THREADED

```
// stdafx.h : include file for standard system include files,
//      or project specific include files that are used frequently,
//      but are changed infrequently

#if !defined(AFX_STDAFX_H)
#define AFX_STDAFX_H

#if _MSC_VER > 1000
#pragma once
#endif // _MSC_VER > 1000
```

LISTING 7.9 Continued

```
#define STRICT
#ifndef _WIN32_WINNT
#define _WIN32_WINNT 0x0400
#endif
//#define _ATL_APARTMENT_THREADED
#define _ATL_FREE_THREADED

#include <atlbase.h>
//You may derive a class from CComModule and use it if you want to
//override something, but do not change the name of _Module
class CExeModule : public CComModule
{
public:
  LONG Unlock();
  DWORD dwThreadID;
  HANDLE hEventShutdown;
  void MonitorShutdown();
  bool StartMonitor();
  bool bActivity;
};
extern CExeModule _Module;
#include <atlcom.h>

//{{AFX_INSERT_LOCATION}}
// Microsoft Visual C++ will insert additional declarations immediately
// before the previous line.

#endif // !defined(AFX_STDAFX_H)
```

A free-threaded COM+ server does not suffer from the bottlenecks of the two previous models. If you are interested in performance and are willing to take the additional time to make your object thread-safe, the free-threaded COM+ server is your preferred alternative.

Three COM+ local servers are included on the CD-ROM in the Chapter07 directory. A single-threaded server is included in the Singlethreaded project. An apartment-threaded server is in the Apartmentthreaded project. A free-threaded server is in the Freethreaded project. Each has one object that has one read-only property that returns the thread ID of the executing server thread. Another project called Controller, also on the CD-ROM, creates and calls the method of each type of server (see Listing 7.10).

LISTING 7.10 Calling Various Threaded Servers

```
CRITICAL_SECTION cs;

DWORD WINAPI ThreadProc(void *p)
{
  Automation * object = (Automation *) p;
```

LISTING 7.10   Continued

```cpp
  long l = object->Get(L"Thread").lVal;
  ::EnterCriticalSection(&cs);
  std::cout << "Thread ID = " << l << "\t";
  ::LeaveCriticalSection(&cs);
  return 0;
}

int main(int argc, char* argv[])
{
  ::CoInitializeEx(NULL, COINIT_MULTITHREADED);
  {
    std::vector<Automation> v;
    int i=0;
    for (i=0;i<10;i++)
    {
      Automation object;
      object.CreateObject(L"Singlethreaded.STObject");
      v.push_back(object);
    }
    for (i=0;i<10;i++)
    {
      Automation object;
      object.CreateObject(L"Apartmentthreaded.ATObject");
      v.push_back(object);
    }
    for (i=0;i<10;i++)
    {
      Automation object;
      object.CreateObject(L"Freethreaded.FTObject");
      v.push_back(object);
    }

    ::InitializeCriticalSection(&cs);
    std::vector<Automation>::iterator j = v.begin();
    for (;j!=v.end();j++)
    {
      DWORD dw;
      HANDLE thread = ::CreateThread(NULL, 0, ThreadProc,
                             (void *)(Automation *)j, 0, &dw);
      ::CloseHandle(thread);
    }

    j = v.begin();
    for (;j!=v.end();j++)
    {
      DWORD dw;
      HANDLE thread = ::CreateThread(NULL, 0, ThreadProc,
                             (void *)(Automation *)j, 0, &dw);
      ::CloseHandle(thread);
```

LISTING 7.10 Continued

```
        }
        Sleep(10000);
        ::DeleteCriticalSection(&cs);
    }
    ::CoUninitialize();
    return 0;
}
```

If you run the Controller application, you'll note that you are returned about 20 or so thread IDs. All the objects in the single-threaded server are returning the same thread ID. Each individual object in the apartment-threaded server always returns the same thread ID; but distinct objects usually, although not always, have distinct thread IDs. The objects in the free-threaded server return random thread IDs.

> **Note**
>
> I had to add a sleep call in the free-threaded server method call because the method returned so quickly that the same thread was always used to process the call.

An interesting experiment is to comment out two or three for loops that create automation objects. By doing this, you can get a feel for what thread IDs are being returned from each server type.

Free-threaded objects do not exist in a single-threaded apartment. They exist in the multi-threaded apartment (MTA) of the process. In an MTA, one or more threads share a common apartment, but there may only be one MTA in any process. In addition, a process that has an MTA can also have one or more STAs. This enables the programmer to create new thread-safe COM classes in an MTA and use existing thread-unsafe COM classes in separate STAs.

Because free-threaded objects exist in MTAs, each call to an object can be processed using a different thread. That also means two or more threads can process calls on the same object concurrently. Because of this, objects that exist in an MTA usually have concurrency issues that must be resolved. The next section on thread synchronization describes the programming aids that can help you resolve these concurrency issues.

Thread Synchronization

From the server point of view, after you have decided on a threading model, you must consider concurrency issues. Actually, if you select the single-threaded threading model, you don't have to consider any concurrency issues. If you select the apartment-threading model, you must consider concurrency issues only for global data. If you select the free-threading model, you must consider concurrency for both per-object data and global data.

But what is per-object data and what is global data? Per-object data is data that is local only to the current object. The most common type of per-object data is nonstatic C++ class members. All function local data that is allocated on the stack or the heap is also per-object data. All data that is not per-object data is global data. But this definition is not quite complete without some exceptions.

For instance, it is possible to make nonstatic C++ class member data directly available to external threads without using COM+. This type of data, although it's per-object data, must be treated as global data because several STAs might have access to the data.

Thread Local Storage

Thread local storage (TLS) is a special storage type that limits access to one current thread. If only one thread has access to the thread local storage, it is not possible for concurrency issues to arise. With TLS, it is possible to associate some amount of memory per thread. Therefore, each thread has its own storage that can only be accessed by that thread. This might or might not alleviate concurrency issues with any one implementation of thread local storage. Whether concurrency issues exist with one implementation of thread local storage is sometimes difficult to determine. It is sometimes best to assume that all thread local storage is global data and eliminate all possible concurrency problems. This might lead to a bottleneck in your application. If a bottleneck does occur, I suggest you remove the concurrency problem by redesigning the application.

One problem that might arise is the assumption that free-threaded objects always have the same thread context. This is an obviously incorrect assumption.

Eliminating Concurrency Problems

The Windows API has a large number of functions that can be used to eliminate concurrency problems. The most basic of these structures is the critical section. Other concurrency structures exist, including mutexes, semaphores, and events.

Critical Sections

This is the minimal implementation of concurrency controls. Listing 7.11 shows an example of using a critical section object.

LISTING 7.11 Using Critical Sections

```
class Pool
{
public:
  static DWORD WINAPI ThreadProc(void * p);
  int DoWork();
  Pool();
  virtual ~Pool();

private:
  static CRITICAL_SECTION sm_csToProtectCout;
  std::queue<DWORD> m_qidThread;

};

#define MYMESSAGE (WM_USER+1000)
#define NUMTHREADS 10

CRITICAL_SECTION Pool::sm_csToProtectCout;

Pool::Pool()
{
  ::InitializeCriticalSection(&sm_csToProtectCout);
  for (int i=0;i<10;i++)
  {
    DWORD dw;
    HANDLE thread = ::CreateThread(NULL, 0, ThreadProc, NULL, 0, &dw);
    ::CloseHandle(thread);
    m_qidThread.push(dw);
  }
}

Pool::~Pool()
{
  while (!m_qidThread.empty())
  {
    ::PostThreadMessage(m_qidThread.front(), WM_QUIT, 0, 0);
    m_qidThread.pop();
  }
  ::DeleteCriticalSection(&sm_csToProtectCout);
}

DWORD WINAPI Pool::ThreadProc(void *p)
{
  MSG msg;
  while (::GetMessage(&msg, NULL, 0, 0))
```

LISTING 7.11   Continued

```
    {
      switch (msg.message)
      {
        case MYMESSAGE:
        ///////////////////////////////////////
        // TODO
        // Add background processing code here
        //
          ::EnterCriticalSection(&sm_csToProtectCout);
          std::cout << "Hello World! from Thread Number: "
                    << ::GetCurrentThreadId() << std::endl;
          ::LeaveCriticalSection(&sm_csToProtectCout);
        default:
        break;
      };
    };
    return 0;
}

int Pool::DoWork()
{
  DWORD dw = m_qidThread.front();
  ::PostThreadMessage(dw, MYMESSAGE, 0, 0);
  m_qidThread.pop();
  m_qidThread.push(dw);
  return 0;
}
```

The code in Listing 7.11 is similar to the thread pooling shown earlier in Listing 7.6. In order to safeguard against multiple threads writing to cout at the same time, enclose the cout routines in a critical section to remove any concurrency problems.

There is another concurrency issue that I haven't mentioned. Take for example, the following:

```
void Function( void )
{
  Pool p;
  p.DoWork();
  p.DoWork();
  p.DoWork();
}
```

It is possible that if DoWork() takes a long time to run, p might be destroyed before the last DoWork() ends but after the critical session has been deleted. Starting and ending multithreaded code is always hard to perfectly implement.

If you run the code in Listing 7.12 without the critical section in place, you will produce some horrific output in the standard out (see Listing 7.13). This is because the individual threads are being swapped out in the middle of the cout command. The next thread then begins writing its output before the previous thread completes. This continues until you have a very psychedelic output.

LISTING 7.12   Thread-Safety Checking

```
int main(int argc, char* argv[])
{
  Pool thread;
  Sleep(1000);
  for (int i=0;i<20;i++)
  {
    thread.DoWork();
  }
  Sleep(2000);
  return 0;
}
```

7

COM+ THREADING

LISTING 7.13   Unsynchronized Output

```
HelloH HHeHWHeeHleHoelHlelHlerllellelllolololollold o l ol o!W WoW oW  oWo oW oWfr
orWroWrorlrlolrolrodldrdlrdlm!d!l!dl!d  ! d !d !Tf f!f !f hrfr rf rfroroforforem
omrmormoa m o mo mdT TmT mT  hTh hT hTNrhrTrhTrhuereherhermaearaeraebdadedaedae
d a da drN NdN dN :uNu uN uN mumNmuNmu4bmbubmubm7ebemebmeb2rerbrebre:r:e:re:r :
r :r :3 5:3 :5 252 13 039022655672585382t
Hello World! from Thread Number: 472
Hello World! from Thread Number:
Hello World! from Thread Number: 522
Hello World! from Thread Number:
Hello World! from Thread Number: 506
Hello World! from Thread Number: 502
Hello World! from Thread Number: 358
Hello World! from Thread Number: 373
Hello World! from Thread Number: 258
Hello World! from Thread Number: 552
329

316
```

If you run the same Listing 7.12 with the critical section in place, the output is more readable (see Listing 7.14).

LISTING 7.14   Synchronized Output

```
Hello World! from Thread Number: 492
Hello World! from Thread Number: 353
Hello World! from Thread Number: 465
Hello World! from Thread Number: 518
Hello World! from Thread Number: 450
Hello World! from Thread Number: 510
Hello World! from Thread Number: 435
Hello World! from Thread Number: 416
Hello World! from Thread Number: 69
Hello World! from Thread Number: 452
Hello World! from Thread Number: 492
Hello World! from Thread Number: 353
Hello World! from Thread Number: 465
Hello World! from Thread Number: 518
Hello World! from Thread Number: 450
Hello World! from Thread Number: 510
Hello World! from Thread Number: 435
Hello World! from Thread Number: 416
Hello World! from Thread Number: 69
Hello World! from Thread Number: 452
```

The critical section object exists as a process or thread local object and, therefore, will limit access to only a resource that has the same context as the critical section object. If the critical section object is instantiated as a nonstatic member of a non-singleton class, it cannot be used to limit access to a global object. If the critical section is a global object, it can be used to limit access to a nonstatic member of non-singleton class, but the critical section is too limiting because it will guard against current access to every instance of the data member.

> **Note**
>
> What do I mean by "the critical section is too limiting"? It is quite convenient to create one critical section and resolve more than one concurrency problem with just this one critical section. But this might create a bottleneck in the critical section. It is sometimes preferred to create multiple critical sections, one for each concurrency problem, rather than sharing one critical section between multiple concurrent access to a global resource problem.

If you inherit from the CComCriticalSection or CComAutoCriticalSection class, ATL automatically implements a critical section object in your class. All your ATL objects implement a CComAutoCriticalSection object using association. Your ATL objects have methods called Lock() and Unlock() that are redirected to a member object derived from the CComAutoCriticalSection class. Listing 7.15 shows the definition of the CComObjectRootEx class from which all ATL objects derive.

LISTING 7.15 Definition of `CComObjectRootEx`

```
template <class ThreadModel>
class CComObjectRootEx : public CComObjectRootBase
{
public:
  typedef ThreadModel _ThreadModel;
  typedef _ThreadModel::AutoCriticalSection _CritSec;
  typedef CComObjectLockT<_ThreadModel> ObjectLock;

  ULONG InternalAddRef()
  {
    ATLASSERT(m_dwRef != -1L);
    return _ThreadModel::Increment(&m_dwRef);
  }
  ULONG InternalRelease()
  {
    ATLASSERT(m_dwRef > 0);
    return _ThreadModel::Decrement(&m_dwRef);
  }

  void Lock() {m_critsec.Lock();}
  void Unlock() {m_critsec.Unlock();}
private:
  _CritSec m_critsec;
};
```

The `_CritSec` typedef is defined as `_ThreadModel::AutoCriticalSection`. Depending on the type definition of `_ThreadModel`, this is defined as `CComAutoCriticalSection` or `CComFakeCriticalSection`. If your object is free-threaded, it implements `CComAutoCriticalSection`; otherwise, it implements `CComFakeCriticalSection`.

Swiss Army Knife

All these typedefs are quite confusing because Microsoft attempted to create an all-purpose critical section that does nothing when the threading model does not require it. This type of all-purpose design typically leads to confusing code. And it did.

One of Microsoft's design considerations was to enable the programmer to write his class without concern for the threading model being used. For the sake of a few programmers who will someday take advantage of this feature, Microsoft has created multiple levels of typedefs to confuse the rest of us.

This type of overdesign is sometimes called the Swiss Army Knife design pattern. Another example of Microsoft using the Swiss Army Knife design pattern is MFC's `CString` class. I think the `CString` class has a method that translates the string into 40 different languages. I could be wrong.

So, you can already have critical sections defined for your objects. These can be used to implement concurrency control for per-object data. Unfortunately, this critical section— applied without any thought—might cause another bottleneck as each thread waits its turn to acquire the critical section. If this situation arises, you can create additional critical sections to reduce the bottleneck.

Mutexes

The mutex kernel object enables you to create and manage access to a resource that cannot be guarded by critical sections. Resources that span process boundaries cannot be guarded by a critical section, but can be guarded by a mutex. Listing 7.16 shows an example of using the mutex object. Note that mutexes are shared by name among different processes, but this is not the case for critical sections.

LISTING 7.16   Using Mutexes

```
class Pool
{
public:
  static DWORD WINAPI ThreadProc(void * p);
  int DoWork();
  Pool();
  virtual ~Pool();

private:
  static HANDLE sm_mutex;
  std::queue<DWORD> m_qidThread;

};

#define MYMESSAGE (WM_USER+1000)
#define NUMTHREADS 10

HANDLE Pool::sm_mutex;

Pool::Pool()
{
  sm_mutex = ::CreateMutex(NULL, FALSE, "MYMUTEX");
  for (int i=0;i<10;i++)
  {
    DWORD dw;
    HANDLE thread = ::CreateThread(NULL, 0, ThreadProc, NULL, 0, &dw);
    ::CloseHandle(thread);
    m_qidThread.push(dw);
  }
}

Pool::~Pool()
```

LISTING 7.16   Continued

```cpp
{
  while (!m_qidThread.empty())
  {
    ::PostThreadMessage(m_qidThread.front(), WM_QUIT, 0, 0);
    m_qidThread.pop();
  }
  ::WaitForSingleObject(m_qidThread.front(), 5000 );
  ::CloseHandle(sm_mutex);
}

DWORD WINAPI Pool::ThreadProc(void *p)
{
  MSG msg;
  while (::GetMessage(&msg, NULL, 0, 0))
  {
    switch (msg.message)
    {
      case MYMESSAGE:
        /////////////////////////////////////
        // TODO
        // Add background processing code here
        //
        ::WaitForSingleObject(sm_mutex, INFINITE);
        std::cout << "Hello World! from Thread Number: "
                  << ::GetCurrentThreadId() << std::endl;
        ::ReleaseMutex(sm_mutex);
      default:
      break;
    };
  };
  return 0;
}

int Pool::DoWork()
{
  DWORD dw = m_qidThread.front();
  ::PostThreadMessage(dw, MYMESSAGE, 0, 0);
  m_qidThread.pop();
  m_qidThread.push(dw);
  return 0;
}
```

Remember that critical sections are process local objects and, therefore, cannot limit access to a resource that spans more than one process.

With the mutexes in Listing 7.16, you could have one or more processes running one instance each of the Pool class, and they would share the same named mutex called MYMUTEX. With the critical section example in Listing 7.11, each process has its own distinct critical section.

7

COM+
THREADING

Semaphores and Events

Semaphores and events are more complex kernel objects that limit access to resources. Semaphores are actually a more generalized implementation that enables the programmer to specify how many threads can have simultaneous access to a resource. A semaphore has a counter that moves between zero and a maximum amount specified by the programmer. The semaphore is nonsignaled when the count reaches zero and signaled when the count is non-zero.

The event object is also a two-state object like the mutex; that is, it is either signaled or nonsignaled. But the event and semaphore objects can be moved from nonsignaled to signaled by any thread. The mutex object can be moved from nonsignaled to signaled only by the thread that originally moved the mutex's state from signaled to nonsignaled. Your choice of which synchronization object works best for you depends primarily on your concurrency problems. Some concurrency problems lend themselves well to critical sections, others to mutexes, semaphores, or events.

Summary

In this chapter, you learned how COM+ fits into the various Windows threading paradigms. You should understand which thread types, threading models, and synchronization objects are available to you, the programmer, and which one is best for your project. The next time you write a COM+ server or implement concurrency control, you'll have some added knowledge to justify your design.

We spent a good deal of time discussing concurrency issues, which should help you prevent and resolve the problems in your programming. These issues can be the most difficult to deal with in multithreaded applications.

COM and the Registry

CHAPTER 8

This chapter talks about the registry as it relates to COM+. If you've ever wondered how applications know how to find COM+ objects when they're instantiated, you'll find this chapter enlightening. As you will see, the registry is the repository for information about COM+ servers. This information is used to locate and know about COM+ servers that are used by applications.

Registry API

Reading and writing to the registry tends to be a lot more difficult than it should be. An example is the RegCreateKeyEx() API, which clearly has too many parameters. With one function, you can create and open registry keys and set security permissions for registry keys. This can all be done in one call. This is nice if your performance is evaluated by how much you can accomplish with the least amount of code.

In Listing 8.1, I've coded a small C++ class, CRegistry, that removes most of the complexity from the registry APIs. This class has three functions that perform the three basic operations needed: setting values in the registry, retrieving values from the registry, and deleting registry keys. The class constructor automatically opens the specified key and creates the key if it does not already exist.

LISTING 8.1   Easy-to-Use Registry Class

```
class CRegistry
{

public:
    CRegistry();
    CRegistry( HKEY, const char * );
    ~CRegistry();

    BOOL Open( HKEY, const char * );
    BOOL Close( void );

    BOOL ReadDWORD( const char *, DWORD *, DWORD *pdwLastError = NULL );
    BOOL ReadString( const char *, LPVOID, int, DWORD *pdwLastError = NULL );

    BOOL WriteDWORD( const char *, DWORD, DWORD *pdwLastError = NULL );
    BOOL WriteString( const char *, LPVOID, DWORD *pdwLastError = NULL );
    BOOL Write( const char *, LPVOID, DWORD, int );

    void BuildList( const char *, CStringArray& );
    void StoreList( const char *, CStringArray& );

protected:
    HKEY m_hKey;
```

LISTING 8.1 Continued

```
    DWORD m_dwLastError;

    BOOL Read( const char *, LPVOID );

    DWORD m_dwSize;

};
CRegistry::CRegistry()
{

    // Member variable m_hKey set to NULL so
    // we know we don't have to close it when Close()
    // is called from the destructor.
    m_hKey = NULL;

}

CRegistry::CRegistry( HKEY hKey, const char *lpszSubKey )
{

    // Member variable m_hKey set to NULL so
    // we know we don't have to close it when Close()
    // is called from the destructor.
    m_hKey = NULL;

    // This constructor opens the registry key.
    Open( hKey, lpszSubKey );

}

CRegistry::~CRegistry()
{

    // Call the close function from the destructor
    // to make sure the registry key is close (if it
    // was opened).
    Close();

}

BOOL CRegistry::Open( HKEY hKey, const char *lpszSubKey )
{

    // First try to close the registry. (It may not be
    // opened, but we want to be sure.)
    Close();

    // Reset our error variable.
    m_dwLastError = 0;
```

8

COM AND THE
REGISTRY

LISTING 8.1   Continued

```
    // Open the registry key. We use KEY_ALL_ACCESS to avoid
    // any problems.
    if( ::RegOpenKeyEx( hKey, lpszSubKey, 0,
        ➡ KEY_ALL_ACCESS, &m_hKey ) != ERROR_SUCCESS ){

        // Get the error and return.
        m_dwLastError = GetLastError();
        return( FALSE );


        }

    // Return success.
    return( TRUE );

}

BOOL CRegistry::Close( void )
{
    BOOL bRet = TRUE;

    // If m_hKey is NULL then the registry key
    // isn't opened. If this is the case, return
    // indicating that Close() wasn't successful.
    if( m_hKey == NULL )
        return( FALSE );

    // Close the registry key.
    bRet = ( ::RegCloseKey( m_hKey ) == ERROR_SUCCESS );

    // Get the error (if any).
    m_dwLastError = GetLastError();

    // Set the key handle to NULL so we don't accidentally
    // close it again.
    m_hKey = NULL;

    // Return success or failure
    return( bRet );

}

BOOL CRegistry::Read( const char *lpszValueName, LPVOID lpReturnBuffer )
{

    // Generic read function.

    // If the key is not opened, return with failure.
    if( m_hKey == NULL )
        return( FALSE );
```

LISTING 8.1 Continued

```
    // Set the local variable to our size.
    DWORD dwSize = m_dwSize;

    // Clear the return buffer.
    memset( lpReturnBuffer, 0, dwSize );

    // Read the registry value.
    BOOL bRet = ( ::RegQueryValueEx( m_hKey, lpszValueName, NULL, NULL,
      (unsigned char *) lpReturnBuffer, &dwSize ) == ERROR_SUCCESS );

    // Get the error (if any).
    m_dwLastError = GetLastError();

    // Return success or failure
    return( bRet );

}

BOOL CRegistry::ReadDWORD( const char *lpszValueName, DWORD *pdwData,
  ➥DWORD *pdwLastError )
{

    // If the key is not opened, return with failure.
    if( m_hKey == NULL )
        return( FALSE );

    // Set the m_dwSize value so that we can call the
    // generic Read function.
    m_dwSize = sizeof( DWORD );

    // Call the read function.
    BOOL bRet = Read( lpszValueName, pdwData );

    // If caller wants the error code, store the value.
    if( pdwLastError != NULL )
        *pdwLastError = m_dwLastError;

    // Return success or failure
    return( bRet );

}

BOOL CRegistry::ReadString( const char *lpszValueName, LPVOID lpReturnBuffer,
  ➥int nSize, DWORD *pdwLastError )
{

    // If the key is not opened, return with failure.
    if( m_hKey == NULL )
        return( FALSE );
```

8

COM AND THE
REGISTRY

LISTING 8.1 Continued

```
// Set the m_dwSize value so that we can call the
    // generic Read function.
    m_dwSize = nSize;

    // Call the read function.
    BOOL bRet = Read( lpszValueName, lpReturnBuffer );

    // If caller wants the error code, store the value.
    if( pdwLastError != NULL )
        *pdwLastError = m_dwLastError;

    // Return success or failure
    return( bRet );

}

BOOL CRegistry::WriteDWORD( const char *lpszValueName, DWORD dwData,
    DWORD *pdwLastError )
{

    // If the key is not opened, return with failure.
    if( m_hKey == NULL )
        return( FALSE );

    // Call the write function.
    BOOL bRet = Write( lpszValueName, &dwData, REG_DWORD, sizeof( DWORD ) );

    // If caller wants the error code, store the value.
    if( pdwLastError != NULL )
        *pdwLastError = m_dwLastError;

    // Return success or failure
    return( bRet );

}

BOOL CRegistry::WriteString( const char *lpszValueName, LPVOID lpData,
    ➡DWORD *pdwLastError )
{

    // If the key is not opened, return with failure.
    if( m_hKey == NULL )
        return( FALSE );

    // Call the write function.
    BOOL bRet = Write( lpszValueName, lpData, REG_SZ,
        (DWORD) strlen( (const char *) lpData ) + 1 );

    // If caller wants the error code, store the value.
```

LISTING 8.1 Continued

```
    if( pdwLastError != NULL )
        *pdwLastError = m_dwLastError;

    // Return success or failure
    return( bRet );

}

BOOL CRegistry::Write( const char *lpszValueName, LPVOID lpData, DWORD dwType,
    ➥int nSize )
{

    // Generic write function.

    // If the key is not opened, return with failure.
    if( m_hKey == NULL )
        return( FALSE );


    // Call the RegSetValueEx() function.
    BOOL bRet = ( ::RegSetValueEx( m_hKey, lpszValueName, 0, dwType,
        (unsigned char *) lpData, nSize ) == ERROR_SUCCESS );
    // Get the error (if any).
    m_dwLastError = GetLastError();

    // Return success or failure
    return( bRet );

}

void CRegistry::BuildList( const char *lpszValueName, CStringArray& List )
{
    CString strTemp;
    char szTemp[1000];

    // This function builds a char ** list of values in a
    // single registry value.

    // For instance: This;That;TheOther
    // creates a list of three char buffers
    // containing This, That, and TheOther

    // Clear our local temp buffer
    memset( szTemp, 0, sizeof( szTemp ) );

    // Read the Registry value.
    if( !ReadString( lpszValueName, szTemp, sizeof( szTemp ) ) )
        return;
```

8

COM AND THE
REGISTRY

LISTING 8.1   Continued

```
// Clear the list.
   List.RemoveAll();

   // Store in a CString for easier manipulation.
   strTemp = szTemp;

   // Look for ';' -- that's the delimiter.
   int nIndex = strTemp.Find( ";" );

   while( nIndex != -1 ){

       // Get the partial string.
       CString strNew = strTemp.Left( nIndex );

       // Kill the ';' character.
       strTemp = strTemp.Right( strTemp.GetLength() - nIndex - 1 );

       // If the string has any length, add it.
       if( strNew.GetLength() > 0 )
           List.Add( strNew );

       // Look for the next string.
       nIndex = strTemp.Find( ";" );
       }

   // If we have text that didn't end with ';',
   // it'll need to be added also.
   if( strTemp.GetLength() > 0 )
       List.Add( strTemp );

}

void CRegistry::StoreList( const char *lpszValueName, CStringArray& List )
{
   CString strTemp;

   // Given a char ** list, store these values into
   // a single registry item separated by ';'

   // Loop through for each string.
   for( int i=0; i<List.GetSize(); i++ ){

       // If there's already data in strTemp,
       // add the ';' delimiter.
       if( strTemp.GetLength() > 0 )
           strTemp += ";";

       // Now add the string data.
       strTemp += List.GetAt( i );
```

LISTING 8.1   Continued

```
    }

    // If we didn't actually get any data, just return.
    if( strTemp.GetLength() == 0 )
        return;

    // Write the string to the registry.
    WriteString( lpszValueName, strTemp.GetBuffer( 0 ) );

}
```

Regedit and Regedt32

Microsoft has provided two different editors to view and manipulate the Windows system registry: Regedit and Regedt32.

Regedit provides the basic functionality necessary to view and make some alterations to the system registry. The user interface is fashioned in the classic explorer-style view (splitter windows with tree view on the left and list view on the right) as shown in Figure 8.1.

FIGURE 8.1

The Regedit user interface.

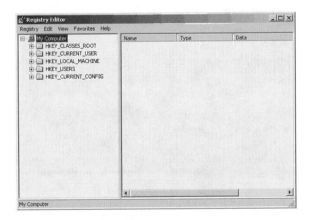

Regedt32 does nearly everything that Regedit does and more. The user interface is fashioned in the classic MDI style, as shown in Figure 8.2. Each key can be opened as a separate MDI child window. You should be aware, though, that Regedt32 is not available on Windows 9x platforms.

FIGURE 8.2

The Regedt32 *user interface.*

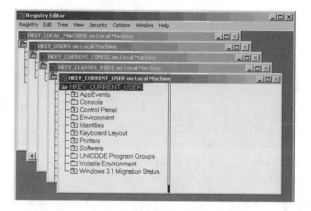

Each registry key has permissions that allow and deny read-and-write access to different users and user groups. The Regedt32 editor provides the capability to view and modify these registry permissions, as shown in Figure 8.3.

FIGURE 8.3

The Regedt32
Permissions dialog box.

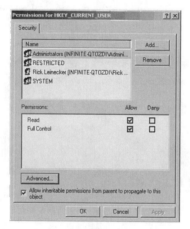

I use a mixture of the two editors. Regedit has a few bugs that are not in Regedt32, but Regedit is much easier to type from the command line, and for this reason it's my preferred registry editor.

Importing and Exporting Registration Files

The Regedit registry editor has functions that import and export registration files. These files typically have an .RGS extension. Coding wizards often generate the registration files in order to facilitate registering COM objects.

Registration files are well suited for copying registry settings from one computer to another computer. If you have all the registry settings correct on one computer, it is possible to export the settings to a registration file and import the registration file to another computer.

`Regedt32` also has functions to import and export registry keys, but it saves them in an unreadable format, whereas `Regedit` saves the key as a readable text file.

COM Registry Structure

COM uses the `HKEY_CLASSES_ROOT` hive in the system registry to maintain object initialization parameters. Six categories of information are included in this key:

- File extensions
- `ProgIDs`
- `AppIDs`
- `CLSIDs`
- Interfaces
- `TypeLibs`

COM also uses the `HKEY_LOCAL_MACHINE\SOFTWARE\Microsoft\Ole` key to maintain security information. You learn both of these hives in the following sections.

File Extensions

File extensions are subkeys of the `HKEY_CLASSES_ROOT` key. The file extension key has the following structure, as shown in Figure 8.4:

```
HKEY_CLASSES_ROOT
    { .extension } = { prog-id }
```

FIGURE 8.4

The file extension key.

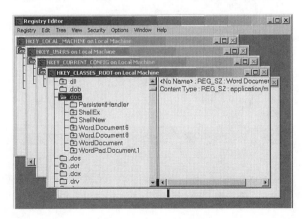

This value indicates where COM should look to find the `ProgID` for the COM object type. After the `ProgID` is located, COM can determine the object `CLSID`. With the `CLSID`, COM can start an instance of the object and bind the file to the object.

For some system registry keys, I will give a short function that can be used to configure the key. Listing 8.2 can be used to configure the file extension keys.

LISTING 8.2 Configuring the File Extension Registry Key

```
int BuildFileExtensionKey(LPSTR szExtension,
                          LPSTR szProgId)
{
    CRegistry key(HKEY_CLASSES_ROOT, szExtension);
    key.SetValue(NULL, szProgId);
    return 0;
}
```

ProgIDs

`ProgIDs` are also subkeys of the `HKEY_CLASSES_ROOT` key. Because both file extensions and `ProgIDs` are subkeys of the same root key, it makes for quite a messy key. The `ProgID` key (see Figure 8.5) has the following structure:

```
HKEY_CLASSES_ROOT
    { ModuleName.ObjectName } = Description
        CLSID = { class-id-as-guid }
        CurVer = { version-dependent-prog-id }
    { ModuleName.ObjectName.VersionNumber } = Description
        CLSID = { class-id-as-guid }
```

FIGURE 8.5

The ProgID key structure.

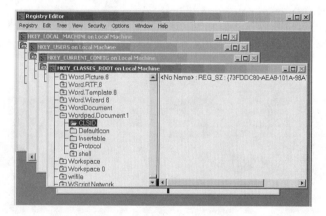

Listing 8.3 can be used to configure the `ProgID` system registry key. This listing uses two new APIs called `StringFromCLSID()` and `WideCharToMultiByte()`. `StringFromCLSID()` takes a

GUID structure and converts it into a human-readable string. WideCharToMultiByte() converts double-byte character strings into the familiar single-byte character strings (as long as you're not coding for unicode platforms).

LISTING 8.3 Configuring the ProgID Registry Key

```
int BuildProgIDKey(LPSTR szProgID, LPSTR szDescription,
                CLSID clsid, LPSTR szProgIDVersionIndependent)
{
    // version dependent description
    CRegistry key(HKEY_CLASSES_ROOT, szProgID);
    key.SetValue(NULL, szDescription);

    // version dependent CLSID key
    LPSTR strCLSID = "CLSID";
    LPSTR str = new char[::lstrlen(szProgID)
                        +::lstrlen(strCLSID)+2];
    ::lstrcpy(str, szProgID);
    ::lstrcat(str, "\\");
    ::lstrcat(str, strCLSID);
    CRegistry key2(HKEY_CLASSES_ROOT, str);
    delete[] str;

    // version dependent CLSID value
    LPOLESTR olestr = NULL;
    str = NULL;
    ::StringFromCLSID(clsid, &olestr);
    int i = ::WideCharToMultiByte(CP_ACP, 0, olestr, -1, str,
                                  0, NULL, NULL);
    str = new char[i+1];
    ::WideCharToMultiByte(CP_ACP, 0, olestr, -1, str,
                          i, NULL, NULL);
    key2.SetValue(NULL, str);
    delete[] str;

    // version independent description
    CRegistry key3(HKEY_CLASSES_ROOT,
                   szProgIDVersionIndependent);
    key3.SetValue(NULL, szDescription);

    // version independent CLSID key
    str = new char[::lstrlen(szProgIDVersionIndependent)
                   +::lstrlen(strCLSID)+2];
    ::lstrcpy(str, szProgIDVersionIndependent);
    ::lstrcat(str, "\\");
    ::lstrcat(str, strCLSID);
    CRegistry key4(HKEY_CLASSES_ROOT, str);
    delete[] str;
```

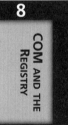

8

COM AND THE
REGISTRY

LISTING 8.3   Continued

```
// version independent CLSID value
str = NULL;
i = ::WideCharToMultiByte(CP_ACP, 0, olestr, -1, str,
                          0, NULL, NULL);
str = new char[i+1];
::WideCharToMultiByte(CP_ACP, 0, olestr, -1, str,
                      i, NULL, NULL);
key4.SetValue(NULL, str);
delete[] str;

// current version
LPSTR strCurVer = "CurVer";
str = new char[::lstrlen(szProgIDVersionIndependent)
            +::lstrlen(strCurVer)+2];
::lstrcpy(str, szProgIDVersionIndependent);
::lstrcat(str, "\\");
::lstrcat(str, strCurVer);
CRegistry key5(HKEY_CLASSES_ROOT, str);
delete[] str;
key5.SetValue(NULL, szProgID);

return 0;
}
```

ProgID and CLSID

Each `ProgID` has a subkey denoting its `CLSID`. This subkey has one value, a GUID representing the `CLSID` for the `ProgID`. The GUIDs generated by COM are too complex for programmers to work with. Therefore, to make working with COM easier, COM provides `ProgID`s as a simpler mechanism for identifying objects. The `CLSID` value is the translation of the simpler `ProgID` to the complex GUID. COM provides two APIs that translate between `ProgID`s and CLSIDs:

```
WINOLEAPI ProgIDFromCLSID (REFCLSID clsid, LPOLESTR FAR* lpszProgID);

WINOLEAPI CLSIDFromProgID (LPCOLESTR lpszProgID, LPCLSID lpclsid);
```

Version-Dependent `ProgID`s

`ProgID`s have the following syntax:

ModuleName.ObjectName.VersionNumber

All objects in the same module would have the same *ModuleName*, but the *ObjectName* would uniquely identify each object in the module. The *VersionNumber* is an integer (starting at 1) identifying the version of the object. For example, the first implementation of your object would have the `ProgID` MyModuleName.MyObjectName.1. The second implementation would have the `ProgID` MyModuleName.MyObjectName.2. This convention enables you to have multiple versions of your COM class installed on the same machine. Each version will be tagged with an incrementing integer suffix.

Version-Independent `ProgIDs`

It is convenient to also have a version-independent `ProgID`. The version-independent `ProgID` has the following syntax:

```
MyModuleName.MyObjectName
```

This `ProgID` makes it possible for client programmers to use objects without having to check which version of the object is installed on the system.

AppIDs

`AppIDs` are subkeys of the key `HKEY_CLASSES_ROOT\AppID`.

The `AppID` key (see Figure 8.6) has the following structure:

```
HKEY_CLASSES_ROOT
APPID
{ app-id-as-guid }
    RemoteServerName = { DNS or UNC of server } // client machine only
    DLLSurrogate = { path\surrogate.exe or NULL for DllHost.exe }
    // server machine only
    LaunchPermission = REG_BINARY { self-relative security descriptor }
    AccessPermission = REG_BINARY { self-relative security descriptor }
    ActivateAtStorage = { Y or N }
    LocalService =
        ServiceParameters =
        RunAs = { none | "Interactive User" | user account }
            AuthenticationLevel =
```

FIGURE 8.6

The AppID *key structure.*

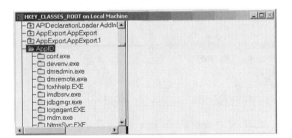

The `AppID` provides information on how to launch the COM server. COM servers can be configured to run remotely, with security, permissions, and as services.

Remote In-Process Servers

In order to launch in-process servers on remote machines, you must use a surrogate. The value data specified in the DLLSurrogate value name is the executable that will serve as the surrogate. If you leave this value empty, DCOM will use the default surrogate (DLLHost.exe). To set up an in-process server to run remotely, you must specify the DLLSurrogate value name on the server (remote) machine and the RemoteServerName value on the client (local) machine.

Remote Out-of-Process Server

If the object has a RemoteServerName value name in the CLSID key, the object can be launched and accessed as a remote out-of-process server. The value is the location of the server where the server will be launched.

Permissions and Security

COM enables you to set permissions for launching (LaunchPermission) and accessing (AccessPermission) objects on the local computer. These permissions are saved in the registry as self-relative security descriptors.

Listing 8.4 shows how you can save a security descriptor in the registry. The same technique would apply to saving the security descriptor to a file or transmitting the security descriptor to another process.

LISTING 8.4 Saving a Security Descriptor in the Registry

```
//-------------------------
// RegSaveSecurityDescriptor
//-------------------------
int RegSaveSecurityDescriptor(PSECURITY_DESCRIPTOR pSD,
                              HKEY hkey, LPSTR szValueName)
{
    // convert the security descriptor to
    // self-relative security description
    PSECURITY_DESCRIPTOR pSRSD = NULL;
    DWORD cbSD = 0;
    if (!::MakeSelfRelativeSD(pSD, pSRSD, &cbSD))
    {
        DWORD dw = ::GetLastError();
        if( dw != ERROR_INSUFFICIENT_BUFFER )
        {
            std::cout << "Error ::MakeSelfRelativeSD "
                    << dw << endl;
            return 0;
        }
    }
```

LISTING 8.4   Continued

```
pSRSD = (PSECURITY_DESCRIPTOR) ::LocalAlloc(LPTR, cbSD);
if (!::MakeSelfRelativeSD(pSD, pSRSD, &cbSD))
{
    std::cout << "Error ::MakeSelfRelativeSD "
              << ::GetLastError() << endl;
    return 0;
}

// save the self-relative security description
// in the registry
if (::RegSetValueEx(hkey, szValueName, 0, REG_BINARY,
                    (BYTE *)pSRSD, cbSD)!=ERROR_SUCCESS)
{
    std::cout << "Error ::RegSetValueEx "
              << ::GetLastError() << endl;
    g::LocalFree((HLOCAL) pSRSD);
    return 0;
}

if(pSRSD != NULL)
{
    ::LocalFree((HLOCAL) pSRSD);
}

return 0;
}
```

In order to save the security descriptor, you must call `MakeSelfRelativeSD()` to convert the absolute security descriptor into a self-relative security descriptor. Self-relative security descriptors are flat structures that are completely self contained. Absolute security descriptors contain references to objects outside the structure.

Authentication

Windows 2000 has an additional value in this key. It enables you to change the default authentication level.

Remote Activation

Normally when you call `IMoniker::BindToObject()`, the object is created and loaded locally. When the `ActivateAtStorage` value is missing or set to `N`, the object will be created and loaded locally. If the `ActivateAtStorage` value is set to `Y`, however, COM will attempt to load the object on the machine on which it resides. So, if you create a file `IMoniker::BindToObject()`, the object will be created on the remote machine (see Figure 8.7).

FIGURE 8.7
The
`ActivateAtStorage`
setting.

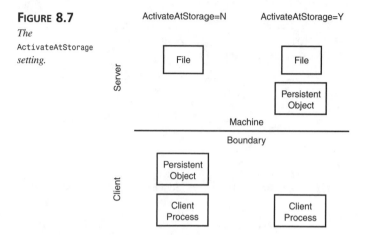

Objects as Services

If a COM object wants to install itself as an NT service, it must set the `LocalService` registry entry with the service name. In addition, it is possible to pass parameters to the service when it is launched. By setting the value of the `ServiceParameters` registry entry, the value will be passed as a parameter to the service.

Identity

Using the `RunAs` value, it is possible to launch an object's module into a process with the security context of another user. In addition to the launching user, you can also give the process the security context of the interactive user or the security context of a specific user.

CLSIDs

CLSIDs are subkeys of the key `HKEY_CLASSES_ROOT\CLSID`. The `CLSID` key (see Figure 8.8) has the following structure:

```
HKEY_CLASSES_ROOT
    CLSID
    { class-id-as-guid } = Description
            AppID = { app-id-as-guid }
            ProgID = { ModuleName.ObjectName.VersionNumber }
            VersionIndependentProgID = { ModuleName.ObjectName }
            InprocServer32 = { mypath\mymodule.dll }
                ThreadingModel = { [no value] | Apartment | Free | Both }
            InprocHandler32 = { mypath\myhandler.dll }
            LocalServer32 = { mypath\mymodule.exe }
            DefaultIcon = { mypath\mymodule, resource id }
            TypeLib = { type-library-id-as-guid }
    }
```

FIGURE 8.8

The CLSID key structure.

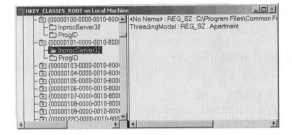

Listing 8.5 can be used to configure the CLSID system registry key.

LISTING 8.5   Configuring the CLSID Registry Key

```
int BuildCLSIDKey(CLSID clsid, LPSTR szDescription,
          LPSTR szProgID, LPSTR szProgIDVersionIndependent)
{
    // build the CLSID
    LPOLESTR olestr = NULL;
    LPSTR str = NULL;
    ::StringFromCLSID(clsid, &olestr);
    int i = ::WideCharToMultiByte(CP_ACP, 0, olestr, -1, str,
                                  0, NULL, NULL);
    str = new char[i+1];
    ::WideCharToMultiByte(CP_ACP, 0, olestr, -1, str,
                          i, NULL, NULL);

    // build the subkey
    LPSTR str2 = NULL;
    LPSTR strCLSID = "CLSID";
    str2 = new char[::lstrlen(strCLSID)+::lstrlen(str)+2];
    ::lstrcpy(str2, strCLSID);
    ::lstrcat(str2, "\\");
    ::lstrcat(str2, str);

    // set description
    CRegistry key(HKEY_CLASSES_ROOT, str2);
    key.SetValue(NULL, szDescription);
    delete[] str2;

    // build CLSID\{CLSID}\ProgID string
    LPSTR strProgID = "ProgID";
    str2 = new char[::lstrlen(strCLSID)+::lstrlen(str)
                   +::lstrlen(strProgID)+3];
    ::lstrcpy(str2, strCLSID);
    ::lstrcat(str2, "\\");
    ::lstrcat(str2, str);
    ::lstrcat(str2, "\\");
    ::lstrcat(str2, strProgID);
```

LISTING 8.5 Continued

```
// set progid
CRegistry key2(HKEY_CLASSES_ROOT, str2);
key2.SetValue(NULL, szProgID);
delete[] str2;

// build CLSID\{CLSID}\VersionIndependentProgID string
LPSTR strProgIDV = "VersionIndependentProgID";
str2 = new char[::lstrlen(strCLSID)+::lstrlen(str)
                +::lstrlen(strProgIDV)+3];
::lstrcpy(str2, strCLSID);
::lstrcat(str2, "\\");
::lstrcat(str2, str);
::lstrcat(str2, "\\");
::lstrcat(str2, strProgIDV);

// set version independent progid
CRegistry key3(HKEY_CLASSES_ROOT, str2);
key3.SetValue(NULL, szProgIDVersionIndependent);
delete[] str2;

delete[] str;

return 0;
}
```

The CLSID key provides information as to how to launch the COM class. The most important information in this key is the location values; that is, the location of the module that implements the COM class.

Location

If the object has an InprocServer32 value name in the CLSID key, the object can be launched and accessed as an in-process server. The value is the location of the DLL (dynamic link library). It is the role of COM+ to take the threading model into account to provide location transparency. I'll talk more about this later. You could imagine an in-process server that is not thread safe being accessed by a free-threaded, multithreaded client. To advise COM+ of the threading model, simply set the ThreadingModel value in the InprocServer32 registry key.

If the object has an InprocHandler32 value name in the CLSID key, the object uses the custom object handler (custom IMarshall interface). The value is the file location of the custom handler module. To use standard marshaling, set this value to OLE32.DLL.

If the object has a LocalServer32 value name in the CLSID key, the object can be launched and accessed as a local out-of-process server. The value is the location of the exe (executable module).

The in-process handlers are used to register custom marshaling. The custom marshaling handler (the DLL) is loaded in-process in both the client and server processes and is responsible for marshaling between the client process and the server process.

CLSID Type Library

The `TypeLib` setting is the `CLSID` of the type library. The `CLSID` in turn can be found in the `HKEY_CLASSES_ROOT\TypeLib` key.

Interfaces

Interfaces are subkeys of the key `HKEY_CLASSES_ROOT\Interface`. The Interface key (see Figure 8.9) has the following structure:

```
HKEY_CLASSES_ROOT
    Interface
        { interface-as-guid } = Description
            ProxyStubClsid32 = { class-id-as-guid }
            TypeLib = { type-library-id-as-guid }
```

FIGURE 8.9

The Interface *key structure.*

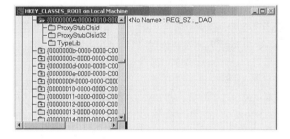

The `DLLRegisterServer` and `DLLUnregisterServer` functions in your marshaler should be coded to add and remove this registry key and its values. One `Interface` subkey will be added for each interface that can be marshaled.

The interface subkeys are quite small. For standard or custom marshaling, we are interested in the `CLSID` of proxy-stub that implements the marshaling for this interface. For type library marshaling, we are interested in the `CLSID` of the type library.

Proxy-Stub

The `ProxyStubClsid32` is the `CLSID` for the proxy-stub pair that will perform marshaling of the interface. The default proxy-stub class ID—that is, the one for `IDispatch`—is `{00020420-0000-0000-C000-000000000046}`.

8

COM AND THE
REGISTRY

Type Library

The `TypeLib` is the `CLSID` for the type library that is registered in the `TypeLib` key.

TypeLibs

`TypeLibs` are subkeys of the key `HKEY_CLASSES_ROOT\TypeLib`. The type library key (see Figure 8.10) has the following structure:

```
HKEY_CLASSES_ROOT
    TypeLib
        { type-library-id-as-guid } = Description
            { major.minor } = Description
                { locale-id }
                    { platform } = { module }
                FLAGS = 0
                HELPDIR = { helppath }
```

FIGURE 8.10

The `TypeLib` *key structure.*

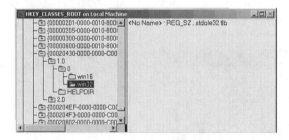

The `locale-id` is a one- to four-digit hex string denoting the locale ID. A value of zero denotes the `LANG_SYSTEM_DEFAULT(0)` setting (this is used for internationalization). The `platform` is a string that can be `win16`, `win32`, `mac`, or `other`. The `module` can be a TLB (type library), a DLL, or an EXE.

RegisterTypeLib

The function `RegisterTypeLib()` will automatically create the `TypeLib` key. To invoke the function, you must first acquire a pointer to the `ITypeLib` object for the type library. Listing 8.6 shows how to use the `RegisterTypeLib()` function.

LISTING 8.6   Using `RegisterTypeLib()`

```
int MyRegisterTypeLib(LPOLESTR lpszModule,
                      LPOLESTR lpszHelpDir)
{
    ITypeLib* pTypeLib;
    HRESULT hr = ::LoadTypeLib(lpszModule, &pTypeLib);
```

LISTING 8.6 Continued

```
    if (SUCCEEDED(hr))
    {
        ::RegisterTypeLib(pTypeLib, lpszModule, lpszHelpDir);
    }
    if (pTypeLib != NULL)
    {
        pTypeLib->Release();
    }
    return 0;
}
```

Flags

The following flags are available in the TypeLib structure:

- 1—Restricted. You cannot view or use the type library.
- 2—Control. Contains description of controls.
- 4—Hidden. Users cannot view this type library, but it can be used by controls.

Help Directory

Type libraries can provide context-sensitive help. The HELPDIR = value is the path to the files providing the help. If you exclude this key, you must provide the path to the help files at build time.

HKEY_LOCAL_MACHINE\SOFTWARE\ Microsoft\Ole

This key contains all the default security information that COM requires. The Ole key (see Figure 8.11) has the following structure:

```
HKEY_LOCAL_MACHINE
    SOFTWARE
        Microsoft
        Ole
                EnableDCOM = { Y or N }
            DefaultAccessPermission = REG_BINARY
                                { self-relative security descriptor }
            DefaultLaunchPermission = REG_BINARY
                                { self-relative security descriptor }
            LegacyAuthentication =
            LegacyImpersonation =
LegacySecureReferences = { Y or N }
```

FIGURE 8.11

The
Microsoft\Ole *key*
structure.

The next few sections describe the various settings in the OLE registry subkey.

Enabling and Disabling DCOM

The EnableDCOM value enables you to enable and disable remote objects. Setting this
value to N disables remote objects but does not disable DCOM security.

Default Permissions

The DefaultLaunchPermission and DefaultAccessPermission values are used when a
COM server does not provide values in its AppID key for the LaunchPermission and
AccessPermission. If the AppID's LaunchPermission is missing, the
DefaultLaunchPermission is used. If the AppID's AccessPermission is missing, the
DefaultAccessPermission is used.

Managing the permissions for hundreds of COM servers on your machine on an individual basis is not really possible. Therefore, I have taken the approach to use the default
permissions rather than configure COM servers individually. If a COM server proves that
it needs additional or less security, then and only then do I add custom permissions.

Legacy Security

COM+ provides values to set default security settings that apply to components that do
not implement specific security in these areas. The following authentication levels are
available:

- RPC_C_AUTHN_LEVEL_DEFAULT—Uses the authentication service's default authenti-
  cation level.
- RPC_C_AUTHN_LEVEL_NONE—No authentication.
- RPC_C_AUTHN_LEVEL_CONNECT—Authenticates only at connection.
- RPC_C_AUTHN_LEVEL_CALL—Authenticates every call.
- RPC_C_AUTHN_LEVEL_PKT—Authenticates every packet.

- RPC_C_AUTHN_LEVEL_PKT_INTEGRITY—Same as RPC_C_AUTHN_LEVEL_PKT and verifies that the data was not modified during transit.

- RPC_C_AUTHN_LEVEL_PKT_PRIVACY—Same as RPC_C_AUTHN_LEVEL_PKT_INTEGRITY and encrypts the packet.

COM+ provides the capability for servers to take on the security context of other users by impersonating those users. The LegacyImpersonation value enables you to limit the kinds of impersonation that servers can use. The following impersonation levels are available:

- Anonymous—No impersonation is allowed.
- Identify—No impersonation is allowed, except for checking client permissions.
- Impersonate—Impersonation is allowed, except when calling other objects.
- Delegate—Impersonation is allowed, even when calling other objects.

If LegacySecureReferences has the value Y, calls to AddRef() and Release() by objects that do not call CoInitializeSecurity() are secured. That means COM+ will apply security on those calls. COM+ is slower when LegacySecureReferences is set to Y.

Registering a COM+ Server

That's a lot of registry subkeys and values that I've tried to explain in this chapter. I'll let you finish watching *The Simpsons* before I tell you the bad news that it is your COM+ server's responsibility to register a lot of these settings. The next few sections describe where your registration code should be located.

Regsvr32

The DllUnregisterServer and DllRegister functions are exported from the DLL.

The Regsvr32 application performs the following three tasks to register or unregister an in-process server:

- Calls LoadLibrary to load the module
- Calls GetProcAddress to retrieve a function pointer for DllRegister or DllUnregister
- Calls the DllRegister or DllUnregister function
- Calls FreeLibrary

DLLRegisterServer and DLLUnregisterServer

In-process servers use the DLLRegisterServer and DLLUnregisterServer to perform self-registration. You can register a self-registering DLL by running the DLLRegisterServer function. This is done automatically in a module named module.dll by executing the command line `REGSVR32 module.dll`. To unregister, remove the system registry entries by running the `DLLUnregisterServer` function. This is done automatically in a module named module.dll by executing the comment line `REGSVR32 /U module.dll`.

Self-registering DLLs should include the string `"OLESelfRegister"` in its `VERSIONINFO` resource. Listing 8.7 shows where the `OLESelfRegister` string occurs in the `VERSIONINFO` resource.

LISTING 8.7 `OLESelfRegister` String in `VERSIONINFO` Resource

```
VS_VERSION_INFO VERSIONINFO
    ...
BEGIN
    BLOCK "StringFileInfo"
    BEGIN
        BLOCK "040904E4" // Lang=US English, CharSet=Windows Multilingual
        BEGIN
            ...
            VALUE "OLESelfRegister", "\0"
        END
        ...
    END
    ...
END
```

Your `DLLRegisterServer` and `DLLUnregisterServer` functions must be exported from your DLL, and they must not contain C++ name mangling. If the exported functions have C++ name mangling, clients such as `REGSVR32` will fail when calling the functions. The stubs for implementing `DLLRegisterServer` and `DLLUnregisterServer` are shown in Listing 8.8.

LISTING 8.8 Stubs for Implementing `DLLRegisterServer`

```
//------------------
// DllRegisterServer
//------------------
STDAPI DllRegisterServer()
{
    // use RegCreateKey() and RegSetValue() to add keys
    ...
    return NOERROR;
}

//--------------------
// DllUnregisterServer
```

LISTING 8.8   Continued

```
//------------------
STDAPI DllUnregisterServer()
{
// use RegDeleteKey() to remove keys

    ...
    return NOERROR;
}
```

Most frameworks like ATL and MFC automatically generate the necessary code for the
DLLRegisterServer() and DLLUnregisterServer() functions.

Self-Registering Out-of-Process Servers

Out-of-process servers should register and unregister themselves from the command line.
That is, they should check for the command-line parameters /RegServer and
/UnRegServer. Listing 8.9 shows how to implement your WinMain() function in order to
process the registration parameters.

LISTING 8.9   Checking the Command-Line Parameters for Self Registration

```
//------------
// MatchOption
//------------
BOOL MatchOption(LPTSTR lpsz, LPTSTR lpszOption)
{
    if (lpsz[0] == '-' || lpsz[0] == '/')
    {
        lpsz++;
    }
    if (lstrcmpi(lpsz, lpszOption) == 0)
    {
        return TRUE;
    }
    return FALSE;
}

//--------
// WinMain
//--------
int WINAPI WinMain(HINSTANCE hInstance,
                   HINSTANCE hPrevInstance,
                   LPSTR lpCmdLine, int nCmdShow)
{
    LPTSTR szCmdLine = lpCmdLine;
    TCHAR szTokens[] = _TEXT(" -/");
    LPTSTR szNextToken = _tcstok(szCmdLine, szTokens);
```

LISTING 8.9 Continued

```
    while (NULL != szNextToken)
    {
        if (MatchOption(szNextToken, TEXT("UnregServer"))
        {
            // Unregister the server
            // use RegDeleteKey()
            ...
            return FALSE;
        }
        else if (MatchOption(szNextToken, _TEXT("RegServer")))
        {
            // Register the server
            // use RegCreateKey() and RegSetValue()
            ...
            return FALSE;
        }
        else if (MatchOption(szNextToken, _TEXT("Embedding")))
        {
            break;
        }
        //Find the next token
        szNextToken = _tcstok(NULL, szTokens) ;
    }
    // Initialize the COM Library.
    HRESULT hr = CoInitialize(NULL);
    if (FAILED(hr))
        return FALSE;
    ...
    // Uninitialize the COM Library.
    CoUninitialize();
    return (msg.wParam);
}
```

Frameworks

Visual Basic and Visual C++ (MFC and ATL) provide built-in facilities that automatically register both in-process and out-of-process servers.

If you look at the MFC source code, you'll notice two functions called
`AfxOleRegisterServerClass()` and `AfxOleUnregisterServerClass()` that provide
some of the necessary functionality of registering and unregistering your COM servers.
In ATL, you have two similar functions called `AtlModuleRegisterServer()` and
`AtlModuleUnregisterServer()`.

MFC has two functions to register type libraries, `AfxOleRegisterTypeLib()` and
`AfxOleUnregisterTypeLib()`. ATL has a function, `AtlModuleRegisterTypeLib()`, that
also helps in registering type libraries.

ATL also provides several mechanisms for embedding your .REG files as a resource in your module (DLL or EXE) and a function to invoke this functionality: `AtlModuleUpdateRegistryFromResourceD()`.

Summary

This section tackled the often-difficult subject of the registry. Acting as a repository for the COM+ server information, it is an important topic to understand if you want to develop component applications.

A special class was presented that gives you an easy way to access the registry without having to rely on some of the more limiting API calls. This class was shown along with its use.

You also saw how to use `Regedit` and `RegEdt32` in your quest to learn, understand, and edit the registry.

8

COM AND THE
REGISTRY

COM+ Optimization, Inheritance, and Aggregation

CHAPTER 9

COM+ is not 2,000 times slower than equivalent C++ as some would suggest. Six times slower (or about 20 microseconds per object constructor call) might be more accurate. Later in the chapter, I'll clarify how I calculated this speed difference.

> **Note**
>
> When I talk about differences in speed, I am referring to numbers that were compiled with one computer. Other computers will produce slightly different results. I have a Windows 2000 installation that suggests that COM+ is 11 times slower than equivalent C++.
>
> I occasionally talk about equivalent C++. C++ is not a language that lends itself to calling out-of-process object methods. So when I use the term *equivalent C++*, I mean equivalent in-process C++. Obviously, it is not fair to compare in-process C++ to out-of-process DCOM. However, I'm using the equivalent C++ as the baseline when comparing the speeds of different types of DCOM invocations.

Speed of DCOM

So, why is DCOM six times or 20 microseconds slower? You can attribute the slower speed to COM+'s support for security, remoting, location transparency, class factories, and multiple interfaces. When you invoke a COM+ object, COM+ searches the registry to determine whether you have access to the object, whether the object needs to be constructed on a remote computer, and whether the object needs to be constructed in-process or out-of-process. COM+ also spends valuable microseconds retrieving the class factory that creates the COM+ class and the interfaces required by the client.

This time is not wasted, however. Class factories, multiple interfaces, security, remoting, and location transparency are all valuable features provided by DCOM. C++ does not inherently provide any of these features. So, when you decide whether DCOM is worth the 20 microseconds, weigh the 20 microseconds against the aforementioned features.

The 20-microsecond delay occurs when the object is constructed (and destroyed), not when methods are invoked on the object. This might be important in determining whether you are willing to incur the overhead of COM+. That is, if you have a lot of object construction, the overhead might be apparent. If you have very little object construction, the overhead is negligible.

At this point, some of you are saying, "You haven't seen my COM+ application crawl." I believe you. I've seen some implementations that move like turtles. That's why I'm going to show you what is happening under the hood to make your applications move so slowly.

Object Location

Several questions are important when designing your DCOM objects. The key question is, "What is the minimal location relationship that can exist between an object's server and client?" Does the object server have to be remote or local to the client process (that is, in-process or out-of-process)? Does the object server have to be remote or local to the client machine? Remember that in-process servers are about six times slower than equivalent C++. DCOM out-of-process servers are 2,000 times slower than equivalent C++.

Two thousand times slower might be a problem. Your goal should be to make COM+ object servers as local to the client as possible.

A year ago, a friend of mine wrote a good example of poor design that placed COM+ objects out-of-process. It was a database connection pool manager. In this application, the connection manager object had to be out-of-process in order to provide a single point of access to the database connections. Unfortunately, this meant that the individual database connections were also out-of-process. In turn, every call to the out-of-process server incurred the 2,000-times-slower penalty. In the end, the application could process (at most) three transactions at a time and slightly more per second. Because it could use only three database connections at a time, there was no need to pool database connections.

This type of bad architecture is why some people think COM+ is slow. I don't blame them; bad architecture is the norm because most COM+ programmers couldn't tell you the difference between an in-process and out-of-process server.

Out-of-process servers are slow. But remote servers are even slower. I can't tell you just how slow because it depends primarily on the network distance between the two computers. Whenever possible, reduce the number of cycles between computers. Cycles are important.

Network Cycles

The same project that produced the previous connection manager example also had another classic failure in design. The business engine was designed to run remotely from its client, and calls to business objects were on a property-by-property basis. The client executable began by loading a small percentage of the business model, or about 1,000,000 atomic items. Each property was retrieved in a separate PROPERTY GET invocation.

Imagine how long it took to send 1,000,000 packets back and forth between two computers. One packet sent from the client and a second packet returned from the server is referred to as one cycle. The previous example has 1,000,000 cycles. The client has never once successfully loaded using this design. The proper design should retrieve as many items as possible at one time.

On another occasion, I had a much faster business engine that retrieved entire objects (database records) all at once. The client executable again tried to load a small percentage of the business model, about 1,000,000 atomic items or 100,000 rows. Forty-five minutes later, the client was loaded. By packaging (marshaling) the business model in rows rather than atoms, I was able to reduce the startup time from infinity to 45 minutes. But 45 minutes is still not acceptable.

I then decided to transfer more than one record at a time. After I found the optimum number of records to send at one time, I was able to load the client in less than one minute. Imagine that. A good general rule is to learn the optimal approach and build code based on your experiments.

Mixed Threading Models

Another way to slow down COM+ is by mixing threading models. Older single-threaded COM+ classes didn't have to be thread-safe because all COM+ method calls were serialized through a Windows message queue. Because these legacy COM+ classes have no requirement to be thread-safe, COM+ must continue serializing calls to these legacy COM+ classes. This is not a problem for out-of-process servers because the COM+ objects exist in their own single-threaded apartments, and COM+ method calls are serialized appropriately.

A problem does arise when the COM+ class is part of an in-process server. Because in-process COM+ objects exist in the apartment of the thread that created the object, the COM+ object might be created in a single-threaded or in a multithreaded apartment. The choice of threading model is determined by the calling client, not the server designer. If the COM+ object is created in a multithreaded apartment and is not thread-safe, there is a problem.

COM+ resolves this problem by creating another apartment where the in-process COM+ object is created when the threading model of the client does not match the threading model of the server.

In Chapter 8, "COM and the Registry," you learned the registry key that enables you to specify the threading model of an in-process server. COM+ determines the threading model of the in-process server using this registry value. If the threading model of the in-process COM+ server does not match that of the client, COM+ creates the object in a new apartment, thus forcing COM+ method calls to be marshaled between the apartments. This causes another performance problem when COM+ method calls are serialized on a message queue.

I included a project on the CD-ROM called Dcomvscpp; it's in a subdirectory in the Chapter09 directory. I use this project to demonstrate the speed of DCOM relative to equivalent C++. The heart of this project is the controller executable that constructs, calls, and deletes objects of various types and reports on the milliseconds that it takes to construct, call, and delete these objects. Listing 9.1 shows all the code in this executable.

LISTING 9.1   Controller Source Code

```
// controller.cpp : Defines the entry point for the console application.
//

#include "stdafx.h"
#include "../cpp/cpp.h"
#include "../dcom/dcom.h"
#include "../dcom/dcom_i.c"
#include "../dcomserver/dcomserver.h"
#include "../dcomserver/dcomserver_i.c"

CRITICAL_SECTION cs;

DWORD WINAPI CppThread(void * p)
{
  DWORD dw = ::GetTickCount();
  for (int j=0;j<(int)((DWORD *)p)[0];j++)
  {
    CCpp * i = new CCpp();
    i->Hello();
    delete i;
  }
  dw = ::GetTickCount() - dw;
  ::EnterCriticalSection(&cs);
  std::cout << "\nCppThread ticks " << dw << std::endl;
  ::LeaveCriticalSection(&cs);
  return 0;
};

static IClassFactory * pclassfactory = NULL;
HRESULT GetUnknown(CLSID clsid, REFIID riid, IUnknown ** ppUnknown)
{
  if (pclassfactory==NULL)
  {
    ::CoGetClassObject(clsid, CLSCTX_ALL, NULL, IID_IClassFactory,
                       (void **)&pclassfactory);
    if( pclassfactory == NULL )
        return( -1 );
  }
  pclassfactory->CreateInstance(NULL, riid, (void **)ppUnknown);

  return S_OK;
};
```

LISTING 9.1   Continued

```
DWORD WINAPI DComThreadServer(void * p)
{
  ::CoInitialize(NULL);
  DWORD dw = ::GetTickCount();
  for (int j=0;j<(*((DWORD *)p));j++)
  {
    ITestServer * i;
    GetUnknown(CLSID_TestServer, IID_ITestServer, (IUnknown **)&i);
    i->Hello();
    i->Release();
  }
  pclassfactory->Release();
  pclassfactory=NULL;
  dw = ::GetTickCount() - dw;
  ::EnterCriticalSection(&cs);
  std::cout << "\nDComThread server ticks " << dw << std::endl;
  ::LeaveCriticalSection(&cs);
  ::CoUninitialize();
  return 0;
};

DWORD WINAPI DComThread(void * p)
{
  ::CoInitialize(NULL);
  DWORD dw = ::GetTickCount();
  for (int j=0;j<(*((DWORD *)p));j++)
  {
    ITestObject * i;
    GetUnknown(CLSID_TestObject, IID_ITestObject, (IUnknown **)&i);
    i->Hello();
    i->Release();
  }
  pclassfactory->Release();
  pclassfactory=NULL;
  dw = ::GetTickCount() - dw;
  ::EnterCriticalSection(&cs);
  std::cout << "\nDComThread ticks " << dw << std::endl;
  ::LeaveCriticalSection(&cs);
  ::CoUninitialize();
  return 0;
};

DWORD WINAPI DComThreadServer2(void * p)
{
  ::CoInitialize(NULL);
  DWORD dw = ::GetTickCount();
  for (int j=0;j<(*((DWORD *)p));j++)
  {
    ITestServer * i;
```

LISTING 9.1 Continued

```
    GetUnknown(CLSID_TestServer, IID_ITestServer, (IUnknown **)&i);
    i->Hello();
    i->Release();
  }
  pclassfactory->Release();
  pclassfactory=NULL;
  dw = ::GetTickCount() - dw;
  ::EnterCriticalSection(&cs);
  std::cout << "\nOld DComThread server ticks " << dw << std::endl;
  ::LeaveCriticalSection(&cs);
  ::CoUninitialize();
  return 0;
};

DWORD WINAPI DComThread2(void * p)
{
  ::CoInitialize(NULL);
  DWORD dw = ::GetTickCount();
  for (int j=0;j<(*((DWORD *)p));j++)
  {
    ITestObject * i;
    GetUnknown(CLSID_TestObject, IID_ITestObject, (IUnknown **)&i);
    i->Hello();
    i->Release();
  }
  pclassfactory->Release();
  pclassfactory=NULL;
  dw = ::GetTickCount() - dw;
  ::EnterCriticalSection(&cs);
  std::cout << "\nOld DComThread ticks " << dw << std::endl;
  ::LeaveCriticalSection(&cs);
  ::CoUninitialize();
  return 0;
};

int main(int argc, char* argv[])
{

  ::InitializeCriticalSection(&cs);
  DWORD dw=0;
  DWORD times=10000;
  HANDLE handle;

  handle = ::CreateThread(NULL, 0, DComThread2, &times, 0, &dw);
  ::WaitForSingleObject(handle, INFINITE);
  ::CloseHandle(handle);

  handle = ::CreateThread(NULL, 0, DComThreadServer2, &times, 0, &dw);
  ::WaitForSingleObject(handle, INFINITE);
```

LISTING 9.1 Continued

```
  ::CloseHandle(handle);

  handle = ::CreateThread(NULL, 0, DComThread, &times, 0, &dw);
  ::WaitForSingleObject(handle, INFINITE);
  ::CloseHandle(handle);

  handle = ::CreateThread(NULL, 0, DComThreadServer, &times, 0, &dw);
  ::WaitForSingleObject(handle, INFINITE);
  ::CloseHandle(handle);

  handle = ::CreateThread(NULL, 0, CppThread, &times, 0, &dw);
  ::WaitForSingleObject(handle, INFINITE);
  ::CloseHandle(handle);

  ::DeleteCriticalSection(&cs);


  return 0;
}
```

The controller simply creates five different threads to test the five different types of objects. The five objects are native C++ objects (CppThread), in-process one-threading model (DComThread), out-of-process one-threading model (DComThreadServer), in-process mixed-threading model (DComThread2), and out-of-process mixed-threading model (DComThreadServer2).

The executable demonstrates how in-process COM+ servers that use a threading model different than the client's threading model are nearly as slow as out-of-process COM+ servers, as shown in both Table 9.1 and Figure 9.1. This is because COM+ is marshaling calls between the apartments.

TABLE 9.1 Comparison of Clock Ticks for 350MHz Pentium

Thread	Ticks
Old DComThread	73556
Old DComThread server	78984
DComThread	200
DComThread server	76320
CppThread	10

FIGURE 9.1

The results of running the controller program.

The lesson here is that in order to run at reasonable speeds, your in-process COM+ servers must have the same threading model as the calling client. Unfortunately, it is not always possible to have the same threading model as all calling clients. Or is it? COM+ has conveniently provided the capability to specify an in-process COM+ server as being both single-threaded and multithreaded. In order for your in-process COM+ server to be capable of both single-threaded and multithreaded use, you must ensure that the COM+ classes in this server are thread-safe.

So, to maximize the speed of your in-process COM+ server, you must specify in the registry that it is capable of being both single-threaded and multithreaded, and it must also be thread-safe.

I've explained some optimizations that, when applied correctly, can greatly increase the speed of your application. But hundreds of other optimizations are out there. The best way to help you optimize is to describe what is going on underneath the hood and hope that you can use this information to find optimizations for your own applications.

I'll begin by explaining how the D (distributed) works in DCOM. How does COM+ provide for remote activation, reference counting, pinging, marshaling, and all that jazz?

Remote Activation

The Service Control Manager (SCM) is responsible for launching local and remote COM+ servers. The SCM launches remote COM+ servers using the IRemoteActivation interface. Listing 9.2 shows the definition for the IRemoteActivation interface.

LISTING 9.2 Interface Definition of IRemoteActivation

```
interface IRemoteActivation
{
    HRESULT RemoteActivation(
      [in] handle_t                      hRpc,
      [in] ORPCTHIS                      *ORPCthis,
```

LISTING 9.2   Continued

```
            [out] ORPCTHAT                          *ORPCthat,
            [in] GUID                               *Clsid,
            [in, string, unique] WCHAR              *pwszObjectName,
            [in, unique] MInterfacePointer          *pObjectStorage,
            [in] DWORD                               ClientImpLevel,
            [in] DWORD                               Mode,
            [in] DWORD                               Interfaces,
            [in,unique,size_is(Interfaces)] IID     *pIIDs,
            [in] unsigned short                      cRequestedProtseqs,
            [in, size_is(cRequestedProtseqs)]
                unsigned short                       RequestedProtseqs[],
            [out] OXID                              *pOxid,
            [out] DUALSTRINGARRAY                   **ppdsaOxidBindings,
            [out] IPID                              *pipidRemUnknown,
            [out] DWORD                             *pAuthnHint,
            [out] COMVERSION                        *pServerVersion,
            [out] HRESULT                           *phr,
            [out,size_is(Interfaces)] MInterfacePointer **ppInterfaceData,
            [out,size_is(Interfaces)] HRESULT       *pResults
            );
}
```

The SCM on the client machine calls the SCM on the server machine by using this RemoteActivate() RPC function. The server SCM reads the Clsid parameter and creates a local COM object with the CLSID. The local COM object is queried for all the interfaces matching in the pIIDs array parameter. The server SCM returns an array of marshaled interfaces (ppInterfaceData).

The RemoteActivate() RPC function also returns an interface pointer identifier (IPID). IPIDs are similar to interface pointers, except that they also identify the server where the object behind this interface is active. The returned pipidRemUnknown parameter is the IPID of the IRemUnknown interface of the object. The IRemUnknown interface is described later in this chapter.

The MInterfacePointer structure contains the marshaled interface pointers that are returned to the client machine. The SCM on the client machine can now refer to the remote object by using the returned data structures.

Remote Reference Counting

How many times does an application call the IUnknown::AddRef() and IUnknown::Release() methods? How many ants live in North America? Because COM+ uses the IUnknown::AddRef() and IUnknown::Release() methods to perform reference counting, it would be a drain on performance if you waited one network cycle every time somebody called the reference counting functions. To remove this potential flaw, DCOM implements the `IRemUnknown` interface. Listing 9.3 shows the IDL (interface definition language) for the `IRemUnknown` interface.

LISTING 9.3   Interface Definition of `IRemUnknown`

```
interface IRemUnknown : IUnknown
{
  HRESULT RemQueryInterface(
    [in] REFIPID ripid,
    [in] unsigned long cRefs,
    [in] unsigned short cIids,
    [in, size_is(cIids)] IID * iids,
    [out, size_is(cIids) REMQIRESULT ** ppQIResults);
  HRESULT RemAddRef(
    [in] unsigned short cInterfaceRefs,
    [in, size_is(cInterfaceRefs)] REMINTERFACEREF InterfaceRefs[],
    [out, size_is(cInterfaceRefs)] HRESULT * pResults);
  HRESULT RemRelease(
    [in] unsigned short cInterfaceRefs,
    [in, size_is(cInterfaceRefs)] REMINTERFACEREF InterfaceRefs[]);
}
```

The client calls the `IRemUnknown::RemAddRef()` and `IRemUnknown::RemRelease()` methods once to increase and decrease the OID's (object identifier's) reference counts by any amount. This reduces the network cycles from one cycle per call to `IUnknown::AddRef()` or `IUnknown::Release()` to one cycle for multiple calls to `IUnknown::AddRef()` and `IUnknown::Release()`. Calls to `IUnknown::AddRef()` and `IUnknown::Release()` do not translate directly into calls to the `IRemUnknown::RemAddRef()` and `IRemUnknown::RemRelease()` methods. The standard proxy implementation does not issue a call to `IRemUnknown::RemRelease()` until all local references to all the objects IPIDs have been released.

Whenever you use remote objects, remember that calls to the `IUnknown::AddRef()` and `IUnknown::Release()` methods are somewhat optimized.

That's all great, but what happens when a caller object terminates abnormally without calling `IRemUnknown::RemRelease()`?

Pinging the Client

Eventually, the COM+ server object will be released. The COM+ attempts to ping the client, and after a determined number of failed attempts, all references to the COM+ server object are released. This could prove very inefficient if the pinging occurs for each remote object. Pings are combined to generate ping sets. The ping sets attempt to resolve pings for each remote machine, rather than for each object.

You might also be wondering about how COM+ implements remote in-process servers. Remote in-process servers are implemented using surrogate processes.

Surrogate Processes

Surrogate processes were introduced to Windows NT 4.0 in the Service Pack version 2.0. The original release of DCOM enabled only remote access to out-of-process servers and did not include any support for remote in-process servers. Having remote in-process servers is quite a contradiction because it is not possible to have in-process objects that span processors. In order to use in-process servers remotely, COM introduced the concept of the surrogate process. The surrogate process is started on the remote machine, and the in-process object is loaded into the surrogate's process space (see Figure 9.2).

FIGURE 9.2

Surrogate model.

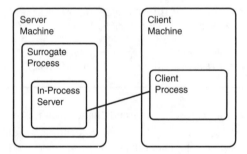

Some interesting advantages become available to surrogate processes. The process can have a process and security context that are different from the caller process. Damage caused by bad and malicious programming that occurs in the in-process server is limited to the process space of the surrogate and can be prevented by limiting the security context of the surrogate. Neither the damage in the process space of the surrogate nor the limiting security context of the surrogate affects the caller process.

The biggest disadvantages are speed (because out-of-process calls are slower than in-process calls) and the inability to share process memory space. Although in-process servers can be programmed to share process memory space with their caller, this is not possible when a surrogate is involved. Sharing of process memory space can be simulated by having the surrogate take special actions to retrieve and update process memory space in the caller, but this taxes the performance of the surrogate.

Listing 9.4 shows an example of calling an in-process server, but loading it in a local surrogate process. Additional code is available on the CD-ROM as Surrogate; it's a subdirectory in the Chapter09 directory.

LISTING 9.4   Calling a Surrogate DLL

```cpp
#include <windows.h>
#include <iostream>
#include <atlbase.h>
#include "inprocess\\inprocess.h"
#include "inprocess\\inprocess_i.c"

char s[1024];

HRESULT GetUnknown(WCHAR * strProgID, IUnknown ** ppUnknown)
{
  CLSID clsid;
  HRESULT hRes = ::CLSIDFromProgID(strProgID, &clsid);
  if (FAILED(hRes))
  {
    // CLSIDFromProgID failed
    std::cout << "CLSIDFromProgID failed = " << _ltoa(hRes, s, 16)
              << std::endl;
    ATLASSERT(FALSE);
    return hRes;
  }

  IClassFactory * pCF;
  hRes = ::CoGetClassObject(clsid, CLSCTX_LOCAL_SERVER, NULL,
                            IID_IClassFactory, (void **)&pCF);

  if (FAILED(hRes))
  {
    *ppUnknown = 0;
    std::cout << "CoGetClassObject failed = " << _ltoa(hRes, s, 16)
              << std::endl;
    ATLASSERT(FALSE);
    return hRes;
  }

  hRes = pCF->CreateInstance(NULL, IID_IUnknown, (void **)ppUnknown);
  pCF->Release();

  if (FAILED(hRes))
  {
    *ppUnknown = 0;
    std::cout << "CreateInstance failed = " << _ltoa(hRes, s, 16)
              << std::endl;
    ATLASSERT(FALSE);
    return hRes;
  }

  return S_OK;
};
```

9

OPTIMIZATION,
INHERITANCE, AND
AGGREGATION

LISTING 9.4   Continued

```cpp
HRESULT GetInterface(IUnknown * pUnknown, REFIID riid,
                     IUnknown ** ppUnknown)
{
  HRESULT hRes = pUnknown->QueryInterface(riid, (void **)ppUnknown);
  if (FAILED(hRes))
  {
    // QueryInterface failed
    std::cout << "QueryInterface failed = " << _ltoa(hRes, s, 16)
              << std::endl;
    ATLASSERT(FALSE);
    return hRes;
  }

  return S_OK;
};
int main()
{
  CoInitialize(NULL);
  std::cout << "Start" << std::endl;

  IUnknown * pUnknown;
  HRESULT hRes = GetUnknown(L"Inprocess.MyInterface.1", &pUnknown);
  if (FAILED(hRes))
  {
    CoUninitialize();
    // GetUnknown failed
    return hRes;
  }

  IMyInterface * p;
  hRes = GetInterface(pUnknown, IID_IMyInterface, (IUnknown **)&p);
  if (FAILED(hRes))
  {

    pUnknown->Release();
    CoUninitialize();

    // GetUnknown failed
    return hRes;
  }

  long l=0;
  p->get_processid(&l);
  std::cout << "Object Process = " << l << std::endl;
  p->get_threadid(&l);
  std::cout << "Object Thread = " << l << std::endl;

  std::cout << "Process = " << ::GetCurrentProcessId() << std::endl;
  std::cout << "Thread = " << ::GetCurrentThreadId() << std::endl;
```

LISTING 9.4 Continued

```
std::cout << "End" << std::endl;
p->Release();
pUnknown->Release();
CoUninitialize();

return 0;
}
```

It's important to note that I used `CLSCTX_LOCAL_SERVER` for the class context parameter in the call to the `CoGetClassObject()` function. Had I specified `CLSCTX_SERVER` or `CLSCTX_INPROC_SERVER` as the class context, the in-process server would not have used the surrogate process. I manually created the registry settings in Listing 9.5 over and above the settings that were written in the registry from my `DllRegisterServer()` function.

When using surrogates, you can use the standard surrogate or you can create a custom surrogate. To configure an in-process server to use a surrogate, set the `RemoteServerName` value in the `AppID` registry key on the client machine to the address or name of the remote server. To use the standard surrogate, set the `DllSurrogate` value in the `AppID` registry key on the server machine's registry to empty. To use a custom surrogate, set this same registry value to the path of your custom surrogate module. Listing 9.5 shows the registry settings necessary to make an in-process server use a surrogate.

LISTING 9.5 Registry Settings for Surrogate Activation

```
[HKEY_CLASSES_ROOT \ AppID \ {E7523002-4382-11D2-BEA2-00C04F8B72E7}]
  = s 'inprocess'
[HKEY_CLASSES_ROOT \ AppID \ {E7523002-4382-11D2-BEA2-00C04F8B72E7}]
  DllSurrogate = s ''
[HKEY_CLASSES_ROOT \ CLSID \ {E7523002-4382-11D2-BEA2-00C04F8B72E7}]
  AppID = {E7523002-4382-11D2-BEA2-00C04F8B72E7}
```

Custom Surrogate

The default surrogate (DllHost.exe) is adequate for most object implementations. The default surrogate is not adequate when your in-process server requires access to global memory that is normally available only in the client process. When writing a custom surrogate, the surrogate implements the `ISurrogate` interface. Listing 9.6 shows the definition of the `ISurrogate` interface.

LISTING 9.6   Interface Definition of `ISurrogate`

```
interface ISurrogate : IUnknown
{
  HRESULT LoadDllServer([in] REFCLSID clsid);
  HRESULT FreeSurrogate();
}
```

The surrogate must register itself by calling the `CoRegisterSurrogate()` function.
COM+ will call the `ISurrogate::LoadDllServer()` method to load a server and the
`ISurrogate::FreeSurrogate()` method to release the surrogate.

IClassFactory

Class factories used to be the talk of COM+. The most important interface in COM+ was
the class factory. Over time, the class factory has lost its popularity because everything
that needed to be said about class factories has already been said. Most COM+ frameworks implement a class's `IClassFactory` class with boilerplate code hidden behind layers of macros.

The `IClassFactory` interface still remains central to everything that is COM+.
When you create COM+ objects, as with calls to the `CoCreateInstance()`
or `CoCreateInstanceEx()` functions, you are in essence calling the
`IClassFactory::CreateInstance()` method.

You might also have noticed that COM+ DLLs export a function called
`DllGetClassObject()`. COM+ calls this function in order to retrieve the class factories
from your in-process server. Figure 9.3 depicts how COM uses the
`DllGetClassObject()` exported function and the `IClassFactory` classes to create a new
COM object. Note how a call to the `CoCreateInstance()` function creates or retrieves an
instance of the class factory. The class factory in turn creates the object.

Listing 9.7 is a simplified version showing how the `CoCreateInstance()` function uses
the `IClassFactory` object.

LISTING 9.7   Code Behind the `CoCreateInstance()` Function

```
HRESULT CoCreateInstance(REFCLSID clsid, IUnknown * pUnkOuter,
  DWORD grfContext, REFIID iid, void * ppvObj)
{
  IClassFactory * pCF;
  HRESULT         hr = ::CoGetClassObject(clsid, grfContext,
                    NULL, IID_IClassFactory, (void **)&pCF);

  if (FAILED(hr))
  {
    return hr;
```

LISTING 9.7   Continued

```
}

hr=pCF->CreateInstance(pUnkOuter, iid, (void **)ppv);
pCF->Release();

if (FAILED(hr))
{
  *ppv = 0;
}

return hr;
}
```

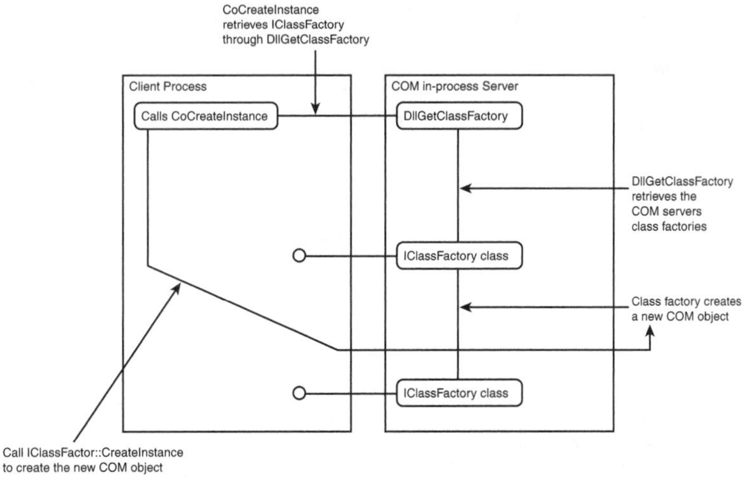

FIGURE 9.3
*Class factory
creating the
COM object.*

The CoCreateInstanceEx() function has a similar implementation (see Listing 9.8). The
CoCreateInstanceEx() function uses an array of MULTI_QI structures in order to retrieve
more than one interface to the object. The code in Listing 9.8 is pseudo-code as there are
some optimizations that are implemented. CoCreateInstanceEx() can also be used to
choose on which server the object gets instantiated.

LISTING 9.8   Code Behind the CoCreateInstanceEx() Function

```
struct tagMULTI_QI
{
  REFIID riid;
  void * pvObj;
  HRESULT hr;
} MULTI_QI;
```

LISTING 9.8   Continued

```
HRESULT CoCreateInstanceEx(REFCLSID clsid,
  IUnknown * pUnkOuter, DWORD grfContext,
  COMSERVERINFO * pServerInfo, DWORD dwCount,
  MULTI_QI * rgMultiQI)
{
  IClassFactory * pCF;
  HRESULT hr = ::CoGetClassObject(clsid, grfContext,
                  pServerInfo, IID_IClassFactory, (void *)pCF);

  if (FAILED(hr))
  {
    return hr;
  }

  hr=pCF->CreateInstance(pUnkOuter, iid, (void *)ppv);
  pCF->Release();
  for (DWORD i=0; i<dwCount; i++)
  {
    rgMultiQI[I].hr = punk->QueryInterface(rgMultiQI[i].riid,
                                           &rgMultiQI[i].pvObj);
  }

  if (FAILED(hr))
  {
    *ppv = 0;
  }

  return hr;
}
```

With the class factory object, you can perform something that most believe is not possible in COM: implementation inheritance.

Inheritance

COM+ enables you to use both interface and implementation inheritance. Using interface inheritance, one interface can inherit methods from another interface. An example of interface inheritance is the IDispatch interface, which inherits the QueryInterface(), AddRef(), and Release() methods from the IUnknown interface.

COM+ also enables you to use implementation inheritances. This type of inheritance enables one COM+ class to inherit an implementation from another COM+ class. Implementation inheritance is not fully implemented in COM+. That is, COM+ classes that inherit an implementation from another COM+ class do not have access to the implementation data of the inherited class. Because of this shortcoming, it is sometimes said that COM does not support implementation inheritance.

Two types of implementation inheritance are provided for in COM+: containment and aggregation. Containment inheritance is implemented by having a COM+ class reimplement the methods of the inherited class. These implementations would simply redirect calls to the contained COM+ class.

Aggregation

Aggregation inheritance enables clients to call inherited methods directly. One disadvantage of this method is that the aggregated object's IUnknown methods must be integrated with the aggregator's IUnknown methods. Another disadvantage is that only in-process servers can implement aggregation inheritance.

Aggregation inheritance is accomplished using the IClassFactory interface. Each COM+ class, whether it can be aggregated or not, must implement a class factory object that implements the IClassFactory interface. The class factory object is responsible for creating the COM+ class. Listing 9.9 shows the definition of the IClassFactory interface.

LISTING 9.9   Definition of the IClassFactory Interface

```
interface IClassFactory : IUnknown
{
  HRESULT CreateInstance(IUnknown * punk,
    REFIID iid, void * * ppvobj);
  HRESULT LockServer(BOOL fLock);
}
```

All COM+ objects are created by calling this IClassFactory::CreateInstance() method. If the first parameter of the call to the IClassFactory::CreateInstance() method is NULL, the object being created will not be aggregated. If this same parameter is a pointer to an IUnknown, the object being created will be aggregated and delegate all calls to IUnknown methods to the alternate IUnknown interface.

Aggregation is a very powerful feature of COM+ that is rarely used. ATL enables you to take advantage of aggregation without having to write too much code. In aggregation inheritance, we say that an aggregator inherits the implementation of an aggregate. You'll need to know this to understand the next ATL code listings.

ATL classes can serve as aggregates as long as they do not define the DECLARE_NOT_AGGREGATABLE macro. This makes coding aggregates easy because it requires no additional code in the aggregate. Listing 9.10 shows the class that I will be using as the aggregate. Again, no additional coding is needed to support aggregation in the aggregate.

9

OPTIMIZATION,
INHERITANCE, AND
AGGREGATION

LISTING 9.10 Declaration of Aggregate Class

```
// MyAggregate.h : Declaration of the CMyAggregate

#ifndef __MYAGGREGATE_H_
#define __MYAGGREGATE_H_

#include "resource.h"        // main symbols

/////////////////////////////////////////////////////////////////////////////
// CMyAggregate
class ATL_NO_VTABLE CMyAggregate :
  public CComObjectRootEx<CComSingleThreadModel>,
  public CComCoClass<CMyAggregate, &CLSID_MyAggregate>,
  public IDispatchImpl<IMyAggregate, &IID_IMyAggregate,
                    &LIBID_AGGREGATELib>
{
public:
  CMyAggregate()
  {
  }

DECLARE_REGISTRY_RESOURCEID(IDR_MYAGGREGATE)

BEGIN_COM_MAP(CMyAggregate)
  COM_INTERFACE_ENTRY(IMyAggregate)
  COM_INTERFACE_ENTRY(IDispatch)
END_COM_MAP()

// IMyAggregate
public:
  STDMETHOD(Hello)();
};

#endif //__MYAGGREGATE_H_
```

The ATL aggregator is slightly more complex. As with the aggregate earlier, I generated a standard ATL class using the ATL object wizard and added one method called Hello. Listing 9.11 shows an aggregator class declaration.

LISTING 9.11 Declaration of Aggregator Class

```
// MyAggregator.h : Declaration of the CMyAggregator

#ifndef __MYAGGREGATOR_H_
#define __MYAGGREGATOR_H_

#include "resource.h"        // main symbols
#include "..\\aggregate\\aggregate.h"
```

LISTING 9.11   Continued

```
////////////////////////////////////////////////////////////////////
// CMyAggregator
class ATL_NO_VTABLE CMyAggregator :
  public CComObjectRootEx<CComSingleThreadModel>,
  public CComCoClass<CMyAggregator, &CLSID_MyAggregator>,
  public IDispatchImpl<IMyAggregator, &IID_IMyAggregator,
                      &LIBID_AGGREGATORLib>
{
public:
  CMyAggregator()
  {
  }
  void FinalRelease()
  {
    m_pAggregateUnknown.Release();
  };

DECLARE_REGISTRY_RESOURCEID(IDR_MYAGGREGATOR)

BEGIN_COM_MAP(CMyAggregator)
  COM_INTERFACE_ENTRY(IMyAggregator)
  COM_INTERFACE_ENTRY(IDispatch)
  COM_INTERFACE_ENTRY_AUTOAGGREGATE_BLIND(m_pAggregateUnknown.p,
                                          CLSID_MyAggregate)
END_COM_MAP()

CComPtr<IUnknown> m_pAggregateUnknown;

DECLARE_GET_CONTROLLING_UNKNOWN()

// IMyAggregator
public:
  STDMETHOD(MyHello)();
};

#endif //__MYAGGREGATOR_H_
```

Six changes were required. I included the aggregate.h header file at the beginning of my aggregator class's header file. I had to implement the CComObjectRootEx::FinalRelease() method to release the IUnknown of the aggregate. I added the COM_INTERFACE_ENTRY_AUTOAGGREGATE_BLIND macro that automatically creates the aggregate object and interface pointers. I added a member variable for the aggregate IUnknown interface pointer. I added the DECLARE_GET_CONTROLLING_UNKNOWN macro to my aggregator's declaration. Finally, I included the aggregate_i.c source file to my aggregator implementation file (see Listing 9.12).

LISTING 9.12 Definition of Aggregator Class

```cpp
// MyAggregator.cpp : Implementation of CMyAggregator
#include "stdafx.h"
#include "aggregator.h"
#include "MyAggregator.h"
#include <iostream>

#include "..\\aggregate\\aggregate_i.c"

//////////////////////////////////////////////////////////////////////
// CMyAggregator


STDMETHODIMP CMyAggregator::Hello()
{
  // TODO: Add your implementation code here
  std::cout << "This is the aggregator being called" << std::endl;

  return S_OK;
}
```

That's all. Now my aggregator class has inherited the implementation of my aggregate class. Listing 9.13 shows how to call aggregate methods of an aggregator class. This listing is no different than having one class with two interfaces.

LISTING 9.13 Aggregation in Action

```cpp
#include <windows.h>
#include <iostream>
#include "aggregator\\aggregator.h"
#include "aggregator\\aggregator_i.c"
#include "aggregate\\aggregate.h"
#include "aggregate\\aggregate_i.c"

char s[1024];

HRESULT GetUnknown(WCHAR * strProgID, IUnknown ** ppUnknown)
{
  CLSID clsid;
  HRESULT hRes = ::CLSIDFromProgID(strProgID, &clsid);
  if (FAILED(hRes))
  {
    // CLSIDFromProgID failed
    std::cout << "CLSIDFromProgID failed = " << _ltoa(hRes, s, 16)
            << std::endl;
    ATLASSERT(FALSE);
    return hRes;
  }
```

LISTING 9.13   Continued

```cpp
    hRes = ::CoCreateInstance(clsid, NULL, CLSCTX_SERVER,
                              IID_IUnknown, (void **)ppUnknown);
    if (FAILED(hRes))
    {
      // CoCreateInstance failed
      std::cout << "CoCreateInstance failed = " << _ltoa(hRes, s, 16)
               << std::endl;
      ATLASSERT(FALSE);
      return hRes;
    }

    return S_OK;
};

HRESULT GetInterface(IUnknown * pUnknown, REFIID riid,
                     IUnknown ** ppUnknown)
{
  HRESULT hRes = pUnknown->QueryInterface(riid, (void **)ppUnknown);
  if (FAILED(hRes))
  {
    // QueryInterface failed
    std::cout << "QueryInterface failed = " << _ltoa(hRes, s, 16)
             << std::endl;
    ATLASSERT(FALSE);
    return hRes;
  }

  return S_OK;
};

int main()
{
  CoInitialize(NULL);
  std::cout << "Start" << std::endl;

  IUnknown * pUnknown;
  HRESULT hRes = GetUnknown(L"MyAggregator.MyAggregator.1",
                           &pUnknown);
  if (FAILED(hRes))
  {

    CoUninitialize();

    // GetUnknown failed
    return hRes;
  }
```

LISTING 9.13 Continued

```
IMyAggregator * p_tor;
  hRes = GetInterface(pUnknown, IID_IMyAggregator,
                            (IUnknown **)&p_tor);
  if (FAILED(hRes))
  {
    pUnknown->Release();
    CoUninitialize();
    // GetInterface failed
    return hRes;
  }
  p_tor->Hello();

  IMyAggregate * p_te;
  hRes = GetInterface(pUnknown, IID_IMyAggregate, (IUnknown **)&p_te);
  if (FAILED(hRes))
  {
    // GetInterface failed
    return hRes;
  }
  p_te->Hello();

  std::cout << "End" << std::endl;
  p->Release();
  pUnknown->Release();
  CoUninitialize();
  return 0;
}
```

When you run the aggregation executable, the control program initially creates the object and acquires a pointer to its IMyAggregator interface. This interface is not aggregated, and there is nothing special when the call to the Hello() method is invoked. Next, it acquires a pointer to its IMyAggregate object. This interface was acquired just as any nonaggregate interface would have been acquired. Reading the control program, it looks as though nothing special took place, but COM actually acquired that interface pointer from the aggregated object.

When the Hello() method is invoked, it is invoked in the inherited class; thus, you have accomplished implementation inheritance through aggregation. Additional code is available on the CD-ROM as Aggregation, a subdirectory in the Chapter09 directory.

Summary

You can program in COM without knowing anything in this chapter. I've introduced nothing that is radically important. But this chapter introduces many tricks that you should store upstairs until that rainy day comes when you realize that your COM application is too slow or that you would really like to inherit the implementation of a COM object.

Run your COM+ applications through the same kind of benchmark testing discussed early in the chapter. You might be surprised at how much room there is for improvement. Remember that remote activation can surprise you, and many times experimentation reveals a story you couldn't predict.

Surrogate processes are another big can of worms. Learn about the surrogate processes and see if you can improve the performance of your remote activations.

You should also experiment in your applications to see how object creation is expensive compared to method call. It is easy to change your source code to measure the creation and then call the method 100,000 times.

Using NT Services

CHAPTER

10

Services are powerful features that are now beginning to see favor with developers. One reason services are not widely used is the limited amount of literature available describing how to create services. Another reason is the level of expertise required to start and communicate programmatically with services.

Suppose that you want your Windows 2000 machine to start a process whenever it starts. A service might be just the thing, especially if the process does not require a user interface. For instance, what if you need a process that checks the time of day and, at certain intervals, performs a database update function. You can create a service that does this automatically.

The limited amount of literature available describing how to create services is not due to the difficulty of programming these services. Creating a service, as you'll learn in the first sections of this chapter, is quite easy. Communicating with services is where the problem lies. But why is this the case? In order to explain this difficulty, it is best I start by describing what a service is and why you would want one in the first place.

> **Note**
>
> What I talk about in this chapter does not apply to Windows 9x platforms.

When a user signs on to a workstation (a machine context), he is immediately assigned a desktop (the user interface), and the desktop is activated. When the user starts a new process or thread, that process or thread is attached to the desktop. This is why you see all the GUI windows in your active desktop.

It is possible to create additional desktops and assign threads to those desktops. You can create windows in each of the threads, but only those windows in threads assigned to the active desktop are visible. If you switch desktops, a different set of windows becomes visible; these are the windows in threads assigned to the new active desktop. Listing 10.1 shows the code that would produce the events described in this paragraph. (MSDN provides a complete sample with source code called Switcher.)

LISTING 10.1 Switching Desktops

```
#include <windows.h>

HDESK hDesktopOrig = NULL;
HDESK hDesktop = NULL;
DWORD WINAPI ThreadProc(void * p)
{
```

LISTING 10.1   Continued

```
  ::MessageBox(NULL, "This is on the desktop", "Hey", MB_OK);
  return 0;
}
DWORD WINAPI AlternateDesktopThreadProc(void * p)
{
  ::SetThreadDesktop(hDesktop);
  ::MessageBox(NULL, "This is on an alternate desktop", "Hey", MB_OK);
  ::MessageBox(NULL, "To switch desktops", "Click OK", MB_OK);
  ::SwitchDesktop(hDesktopOrig);
  return 0;
}
int main()
{
  hDesktopOrig = ::GetThreadDesktop(::GetCurrentThreadId());
  DWORD dw;
  HANDLE hThread = ::CreateThread(NULL, 0, ThreadProc, NULL, NULL, &dw);
  hDesktop = ::CreateDesktop("MyDesktop", NULL, NULL, 0,
    DESKTOP_CREATEMENU | DESKTOP_CREATEWINDOW | DESKTOP_SWITCHDESKTOP, NULL);
  HANDLE hAltThread = ::CreateThread(NULL, 0, AlternateDesktopThreadProc,
                                     NULL, NULL, &dw);
  ::MessageBox(NULL, "To switch desktops", "Click OK", MB_OK);
  ::SwitchDesktop(hDesktop);
  ::MessageBox(NULL, "To shutdown this app", "Click OK", MB_OK);
  ::CloseHandle(hAltThread);
  ::CloseHandle(hThread);
  ::CloseDesktop (hDesktop);
  return 0;
}
```

The preceding code uses the Win32 API to do its magic. The functions that set the desktop are `SetThreadDesktop()` and `SwitchDesktop()`. A desktop is created with `CreateDesktop()`, and normal thread functions such as `CreateThread()` and `CloseHandle()` are used for the threads.

In the Win32 API, a *service* is an executable object about which information is installed in a registry database maintained by the service control manager. Included in this database is information that determines whether each installed service starts on demand or automatically when the system starts. The database can also contain logon and security information for a service, allowing it to run even when no user is logged on. System administrators can customize the security requirements for a particular service. Implementing a server application as a service provides a number of benefits that derive from the architecture of services.

A server application running as a service can do so using a unique service account for remote administration and control. For example, if a database application and a host

10

USING NT SERVICES

connectivity application are both running on the same server system, these applications can run as services under separate service accounts. This helps ensure that only designated host connectivity administrators can administer the host connectivity server application, and that only database administrators can administer database server applications. An additional benefit of this configuration is that it makes it possible for an administrator to control a group of services that work under a common user account.

Running as a service helps a server application impersonate a client while accessing objects on behalf of the client. This capability ensures that the server application can act on behalf of a client without requiring the server application to run with an inappropriately high privilege level. It also ensures that the server application cannot perform actions that would be denied the client directly.

Services can be configured to start automatically, either when the machine itself starts, or when the service is started by a dependent service that starts automatically. In either case, the service starts without human intervention; that is, without a user being required to log on and explicitly start the service. By starting automatically, a server application implemented as a service is guaranteed to be available whenever needed so long as the machine is running. Moreover, related services can be started easily and, where appropriate, automatically.

Finally, implementing a server application as a service allows the application to be installed and controlled using standard user and Win32 programming interfaces. Such a service can be started and stopped both locally and remotely, providing network administrators with an easy and consistent way to control the service across the network by using the control panel's Services applet or the services MMC.

If a server application is implemented as a collection of services, the application should use remote procedure calls (or similar remote mechanisms) between services to allow each service to run on separate computers. This distributed function provides users with the benefits of greater capacity and scalability.

Back to the original discussion. Why is it hard to communicate with a service? Because services have inactive desktops, they usually do not interact with users. The only other method of communicating with a process is using IPC (Inter-Process Communication). Creating an IPC protocol tends to be more difficult than creating a GUI front end, and that is why services have been more difficult to communicate with than most processes. But this is no longer true because ATL has introduced new classes that make communicating with services as easy as using COM objects. Later in this chapter, you learn both how easy it is to create a DCOM service with ATL and how easy it is to access ATL-DCOM services.

Service Anatomy

Services are started and stopped by the service control manager (SCM). In order for a module to start and stop like a service, it must register itself with this SCM.

main() and WinMain()

Services are also executable modules. Typically, service modules are constructed so that they can be launched both as a service and as an interactive process. *Interactive process* means a process that exists in the context of a desktop. Because services are also executable modules, they must have a main() or WinMain() entry point, just like all other executable modules. The purpose of the executable entry point is to initialize the service. Listing 10.2 shows how to initialize a service; that is, how to register the service's ServiceMain() routine (or routines) with the SCM.

LISTING 10.2   Service's main() Entry Point

```
void WINAPI ServiceMain(DWORD argc, LPTSTR * argv);
int WINAPI main(int argc, char * arg[])
{
  if ((argc==2) && (::strcmp(arg[1]+1, "Service")==0))
  {
    InstallAService(_T("MyBigService"));
    return 0;
  }
  SERVICE_TABLE_ENTRY servicetableentry[] =
  {
    { _T("MyBigService"), ServiceMain },
    { NULL, NULL }
  };
  ::StartServiceCtrlDispatcher(servicetableentry);
  return 0;
}
```

The StartServiceCtrlDispatcher() function registers the ServiceMain() routine with the SCM. The SCM then calls this ServiceMain() function to start the service. Listing 10.3 shows the definition of the SERVICE_TABLE_ENTRY structure.

LISTING 10.3   SERVICE_TABLE_ENTRY

```
typedef struct _SERVICE_TABLE_ENTRY
{
  LPTSTR lpServiceName;
  LPSERVICE_MAIN_FUNCTION lpServiceProc;
} SERVICE_TABLE_ENTRY, *LPSERVICE_TABLE_ENTRY;
```

10

USING NT SERVICES

This structure is the input parameter to the StartServiceCtrlDispatcher() function. You can also start more than one service in the main() entry function by specifying more than one SERVICE_TABLE_ENTRY structure in the call to the StartServiceCtrlDispatcher() function. Listing 10.4 shows an example of starting more than one service in a main() entry function.

LISTING 10.4   Service's main() Entry Point

```
void WINAPI ServiceMain1(DWORD argc, LPTSTR * argv);
void WINAPI ServiceMain2(DWORD argc, LPTSTR * argv);
int WINAPI main()
{
  SERVICE_TABLE_ENTRY servicetableentry[] =
  {
    { _T("My First Service"), ServiceMain1 },
    { _T("My Second Service"), ServiceMain2 },
    { NULL, NULL }
  };
  ::StartServiceCtrlDispatcher(servicetableentry);
  return 0;
}
```

Assuming your call to the StartServiceCtrlDispatcher() is successful, the SCM should call your ServiceMain() service initialization function. StartServiceCtrlDispatcher() can fail for two reasons: the specified dispatch table contains entries that are not in the proper format, and the process has already called StartServiceCtrlDispatcher(). (Each process can call StartServiceCtrlDispatcher() only one time.)

ServiceMain()

The SCM calls this function on a new thread after receiving a call from the StartServiceCtrlDispatcher() function. Listing 10.5 shows how the ServiceMain() function might be implemented.

LISTING 10.5   ServiceMain() Implementation

```
SERVICE_STATUS servicestatus;
SERVICE_STATUS_HANDLE servicestatushandle;
void WINAPI ServiceCtrlHandler(DWORD dwControl);
void WINAPI ServiceMain(DWORD argc, LPTSTR * argv)
{
  servicestatus.dwServiceType = SERVICE_WIN32;
  servicestatus.dwCurrentState = SERVICE_START_PENDING;
  servicestatus.dwControlsAccepted = SERVICE_ACCEPT_STOP;
```

LISTING 10.5 Continued

```
  servicestatus.dwWin32ExitCode = 0;
  servicestatus.dwServiceSpecificExitCode = 0;
  servicestatus.dwCheckPoint = 0;
  servicestatus.dwWaitHint = 0;

  servicestatushandle =
    ::RegisterServiceCtrlHandler(_T("MyBigService"), ServiceCtrlHandler);
  if (servicestatushandle == (SERVICE_STATUS_HANDLE)0)
  {
    // If RegisterServiceCtrlHandler fails, the
    // handle does not have to be closed.
    return;
  }

  BOOL bInitialized = false;
  // Initialize the service
  // ...
  // In this section, if initialization
  // is successful then bInitialized = true;

  servicestatus.dwCheckPoint = 0;
  servicestatus.dwWaitHint = 0;
  if (!bInitialized)
  {
    servicestatus.dwCurrentState = SERVICE_STOPPED;
    servicestatus.dwWin32ExitCode = ERROR_SERVICE_SPECIFIC_ERROR;
    servicestatus.dwServiceSpecificExitCode = 1;
  }
  else
  {
    servicestatus.dwCurrentState = SERVICE_RUNNING;
  }
  ::SetServiceStatus(servicestatushandle,  &servicestatus);
  return;
}
```

The first thing the service should do in its `ServiceMain()` function is initialize the service status structure and register the `ServiceCtrlHandler()` function by calling the `RegisterServiceCtrlHandler()` function.

After the service control handler is registered, the service should go about initializing the service-dependent global structures. The service should occasionally call `SetServiceStatus()` to notify the SCM whether the service's initialization is proceeding correctly, whether the initialization is complete, or whether it has failed. The `SetServiceStatus()` function has two parameters: the `SERVICE_STATUS` structure and the `SERVICE_STATUS_HANDLE` handle. The `SERVICE_STATUS_HANDLE` handle is the handle that was returned from the `RegisterServiceCtrlHandler()` function. Listing 10.6 shows the definition of the `SERVICE_STATUS` structure.

When a service receives a control request, the service's Handler function must call `SetServiceStatus()`, even if the service's status did not change. A service can also use this function at any time and by any of its threads to notify the service control manager of status changes. Examples of such unsolicited status updates include checkpoint updates that occur when the service is in transition from one state to another (that is, `SERVICE_START_PENDING`) and fatal error updates that occur when the service must stop because of a recoverable error. A service can call this function only after it has called `RegisterServiceCtrlHandler()` to get a service status handle.

LISTING 10.6 Definition of `SERVICE_STATUS` Structure

```
typedef struct _SERVICE_STATUS
{
  DWORD dwServiceType;
  DWORD dwCurrentState;
  DWORD dwControlsAccepted;
  DWORD dwWin32ExitCode;
  DWORD dwServiceSpecificExitCode;
  DWORD dwCheckPoint;
  DWORD dwWaitHint;
} SERVICE_STATUS, *LPSERVICE_STATUS;
```

The `SERVICE_STATUS::dwServiceType` member can have the following values:

- `SERVICE_WIN32_OWN_PROCESS`—There is one service in this process.
- `SERVICE_WIN32_SHARE_PROCESS`—There are more than one services in this process.
- `SERVICE_KERNEL_DRIVER`—The process is a device driver.
- `SERVICE_FILE_SYSTEM_DRIVER`—The process is a file system driver.
- `SERVICE_INTERACTIVE_PROCESS`—The process will interact with the desktop (should the process become active).

The `SERVICE_STATUS::dwCurrentState` member can have the following values:

- `SERVICE_STOPPED`—The service is not running.
- `SERVICE_START_PENDING`—The service is being initialized.
- `SERVICE_STOP_PENDING`—The service is being terminated.
- `SERVICE_RUNNING`—The service is running normally.
- `SERVICE_CONTINUE_PENDING`—The service is paused and is being unpaused.
- `SERVICE_PAUSE_PENDING`—The service is being paused.
- `SERVICE_PAUSED`—The service is paused.

The SERVICE_STATUS::dwControlsAccepted member can have the following values:

- SERVICE_ACCEPT_STOP—The service can be stopped.
- SERVICE_ACCEPT_PAUSE_CONTINUE—The service can be paused and unpaused.
- SERVICE_ACCEPT_SHUTDOWN—The service can be shut down.
- SERVICE_USER_DEFINED_CONTROL—The service accepts user-defined control messages.

SERVICE_STATUS::dwWin32ExitCode and SERVICE_STATUS::dwServiceSpecificCode members can be used to report errors to the SCM. A service can pass a Win32 error code by setting the SERVICE_STATUS::dwWin32ExitCode member. Or, a service can pass a proprietary error code by setting SERVICE_STATUS::dwWin32ExitCode to ERROR_SERVICE_SPECIFIC_ERROR and setting SERVICE_STATUS::dwServiceSpecificCode to the error code.

The SERVICE_STATUS::dwCheckPoint and SERVICE_STATUS::dwWaitHint members indicate to the SCM the progression of the services initialization or shutdown. SERVICE_STATUS::dwCheckPoint should be incremented with each call to the SetServiceStatus() function to indicate progress in the initialization or shutdown. The SERVICE_STATUS::dwWaitHint member should indicate the maximum amount of time in milliseconds that should elapse between the current call to the SetServiceStatus() function and the next call to the same function. If the time elapses before the next call to the SetServiceStatus() function, the SCM assumes that your service is not operating properly and suspends it.

When your service is properly initialized and registered by calling the RegisterServiceCtrlHandler() function, the SCM begins sending messages to your ServiceCtrlHandle() callback function.

ServiceCtrlHandle()

The ServiceCtrlHandle() function can receive five standard messages. You can also add additional control messages in the range 128–256. The five standard messages are as follows:

- SERVICE_CONTROL_PAUSE—The SCM is requesting that the service pause itself.
- SERVICE_CONTROL_CONTINUE—The SCM is requesting that the service unpause itself.
- SERVICE_CONTROL_STOP—The SCM is requesting that the service shut itself down.
- SERVICE_CONTROL_SHUTDOWN—The system is being shut down.
- SERVICE_CONTROL_INTERROGATE—The SCM is requesting the status of the service.

10

USING NT SERVICES

Listing 10.7 shows what your ServiceCtrlHandler() might look like.

LISTING 10.7   Sample ServiceCtrlHandler()

```
SERVICE_STATUS servicestatus;
SERVICE_STATUS_HANDLE servicestatushandle;
void WINAPI ServiceCtrlHandler(DWORD dwControl)
{
  switch (dwControl)
  {
    case SERVICE_CONTROL_PAUSE:
      servicestatus.dwCurrentState = SERVICE_PAUSE_PENDING;
      ::SetServiceStatus(servicestatushandle, &servicestatus);
      // TODO: add code to pause the service
      // not called in this service
      // ...
      servicestatus.dwCurrentState = SERVICE_PAUSED;
    break;

    case SERVICE_CONTROL_CONTINUE:
      servicestatus.dwCurrentState = SERVICE_CONTINUE_PENDING;
      ::SetServiceStatus(servicestatushandle, &servicestatus);
      // TODO: add code to unpause the service
      // not called in this service
      // ...
      servicestatus.dwCurrentState = SERVICE_RUNNING;
    break;

    case SERVICE_CONTROL_STOP:
      servicestatus.dwCurrentState = SERVICE_STOP_PENDING;
      ::SetServiceStatus(servicestatushandle, &servicestatus);
      // TODO: add code to stop the service
      // ...
      servicestatus.dwCurrentState = SERVICE_STOPPED;
    break;

    case SERVICE_CONTROL_SHUTDOWN:
      // TODO: add code for system shutdown
      // ...
    break;

    case SERVICE_CONTROL_INTERROGATE:
      // TODO: add code to set the service status
      // ...
      servicestatus.dwCurrentState = SERVICE_RUNNING;
    break;
  }
  ::SetServiceStatus(servicestatushandle,  &servicestatus);
}
```

> **Note**
>
> In some cases, I immediately set the status to pending. This should be done within 30 seconds of the entry into this function, or the SCM will assume your service is not operating properly and suspend the thread.

A service must at least respond to the SERVICE_CONTROL_INTERROGATE message. A service must also respond to those messages that are enumerated in the SERVICE_STATUS::dwControlsAccepted message when you call the RegisterServiceCtrlHandle() function.

A main() entry point function, a ServiceMain() initialization function, and a ServiceCtrlHandler() message processing function—that's all the code necessary to get a minimal service running. You might also be interested in programmatically starting, stopping, pausing, and unpausing a service. This is accomplished with the OpenSCManager() function and related API.

Source code for a sample NT service is available on the CD-ROM that accompanies this book in the ntservice subdirectory, which can be found in the chapter10 directory. You can install the service by running the executable with the command line /Service. After registering the service you can start, stop, pause, and unpause the service, but the service does nothing other than act as a service.

The only component missing from this service is an IPC protocol to talk to the service so that it can perform whatever operations it was designed to perform. This has always been a very difficult venture because IPC protocols are difficult to both develop and use. ATL provides the capability to develop COM classes with little effort.

ATL and Services

The ATL COM AppWizard provides a very easy method for generating all the code necessary to create a service that exposes COM objects. Simply start the wizard by selecting File, New from the Developer Studio menu bar. Select the Projects tab, and from the list view, select ATL COM AppWizard (see Figure 10.1).

Type the appropriate project name and the path in which you want your new project code to be generated. Click OK and the ATL COM AppWizard appears (see Figure 10.2).

FIGURE **10.1**
*Start the ATL
COM AppWizard.*

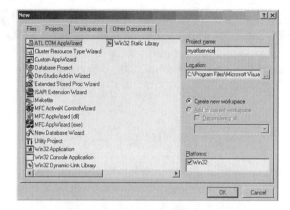

FIGURE **10.2**
*The ATL COM
AppWizard.*

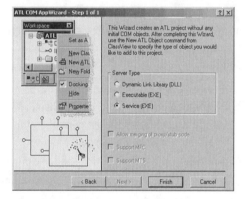

The wizard conveniently enables you to select Service as a server type. After selecting Service, click on the Finish button, and then click OK; Developer Studio will generate all the code necessary for your service. That's it. This short process generates code similar to all the code you learned about in the previous sections in this chapter.

The ATL COM AppWizard generates about a dozen files. Most of the files are typical boilerplate code necessary to build an ATL project; that is, precompiled header, resource scripts, and more. One of the generated files contains the code that implements your service. Listing 10.8 shows an example of the implementation generated by the ATL COM AppWizard.

LISTING 10.8   ATL Service Boilerplate

```
// myatlservice.cpp : Implementation of WinMain


// Note: Proxy/Stub Information
//       To build a separate proxy/stub DLL,
```

LISTING 10.8   Continued

```
//      run nmake -f myatlserviceps.mk in the project directory.

#include "stdafx.h"
#include "resource.h"
#include <initguid.h>
#include "myatlservice.h"

#include "myatlservice_i.c"


#include <stdio.h>

CServiceModule _Module;

BEGIN_OBJECT_MAP(ObjectMap)
END_OBJECT_MAP()


LPCTSTR FindOneOf(LPCTSTR p1, LPCTSTR p2)
{
    while (p1 != NULL && *p1 != NULL)
    {
        LPCTSTR p = p2;
        while (p != NULL && *p != NULL)
        {
            if (*p1 == *p)
                return CharNext(p1);
            p = CharNext(p);
        }
        p1 = CharNext(p1);
    }
    return NULL;
}

// Although some of these functions are big they are declared inline
// since they are only used once

inline HRESULT CServiceModule::RegisterServer(BOOL bRegTypeLib,
                                              BOOL bService)
{
    HRESULT hr = CoInitialize(NULL);
    if (FAILED(hr))
        return hr;

    // Remove any previous service since it may point to
    // the incorrect file
    Uninstall();

    // Add service entries
```

LISTING 10.8   Continued

```
    UpdateRegistryFromResource(IDR_Myatlservice, TRUE);

    // Adjust the AppID for Local Server or Service
    CRegKey keyAppID;
    LONG lRes = keyAppID.Open(HKEY_CLASSES_ROOT, _T("AppID"), KEY_WRITE);
    if (lRes != ERROR_SUCCESS)
        return lRes;

    CRegKey key;
    lRes =
      key.Open(keyAppID, _T("{B51F6322-99A5-11D2-BEC8-00C04F8B72E7}"),
               KEY_WRITE);
    if (lRes != ERROR_SUCCESS)
        return lRes;
    key.DeleteValue(_T("LocalService"));

    if (bService)
    {
        key.SetValue(_T("myatlservice"), _T("LocalService"));
        key.SetValue(_T("-Service"), _T("ServiceParameters"));
        // Create service
        Install();
    }

    // Add object entries
    hr = CComModule::RegisterServer(bRegTypeLib);

    CoUninitialize();
    return hr;
}

inline HRESULT CServiceModule::UnregisterServer()
{
    HRESULT hr = CoInitialize(NULL);
    if (FAILED(hr))
        return hr;

    // Remove service entries
    UpdateRegistryFromResource(IDR_Myatlservice, FALSE);
    // Remove service
    Uninstall();
    // Remove object entries
    CComModule::UnregisterServer(TRUE);
    CoUninitialize();
    return S_OK;
}

inline void CServiceModule::Init(_ATL_OBJMAP_ENTRY* p, HINSTANCE h,
                                 UINT nServiceNameID, const GUID* plibid)
```

LISTING 10.8   Continued

```
{
    CComModule::Init(p, h, plibid);

    m_bService = TRUE;

    LoadString(h, nServiceNameID, m_szServiceName,
               sizeof(m_szServiceName) / sizeof(TCHAR));

    // set up the initial service status
    m_hServiceStatus = NULL;
    m_status.dwServiceType = SERVICE_WIN32_OWN_PROCESS;
    m_status.dwCurrentState = SERVICE_STOPPED;
    m_status.dwControlsAccepted = SERVICE_ACCEPT_STOP;
    m_status.dwWin32ExitCode = 0;
    m_status.dwServiceSpecificExitCode = 0;
    m_status.dwCheckPoint = 0;
    m_status.dwWaitHint = 0;
}

LONG CServiceModule::Unlock()
{
    LONG l = CComModule::Unlock();
    if (l == 0 && !m_bService)
        PostThreadMessage(dwThreadID,  WM_QUIT, 0, 0);
    return l;
}

BOOL CServiceModule::IsInstalled()
{
    BOOL bResult = FALSE;

    SC_HANDLE hSCM = ::OpenSCManager(NULL, NULL, SC_MANAGER_ALL_ACCESS);

    if (hSCM != NULL)
    {
        SC_HANDLE hService = ::OpenService(hSCM, m_szServiceName,
                                           SERVICE_QUERY_CONFIG);
        if (hService != NULL)
        {
            bResult = TRUE;
            ::CloseServiceHandle(hService);
        }
        ::CloseServiceHandle(hSCM);
    }
    return bResult;
}

inline BOOL CServiceModule::Install()
{
```

10

USING NT
SERVICES

LISTING 10.8 Continued

```
    if (IsInstalled())
        return TRUE;

    SC_HANDLE hSCM = ::OpenSCManager(NULL, NULL,  SC_MANAGER_ALL_ACCESS);
    if (hSCM == NULL)
    {
        MessageBox(NULL, _T("Couldn't open service manager"),
                   m_szServiceName, MB_OK);
        return FALSE;
    }

    // Get the executable file path
    TCHAR szFilePath[_MAX_PATH];
    ::GetModuleFileName(NULL, szFilePath, _MAX_PATH);

    SC_HANDLE hService = ::CreateService(
        hSCM, m_szServiceName, m_szServiceName,
        SERVICE_ALL_ACCESS, SERVICE_WIN32_OWN_PROCESS,
        SERVICE_DEMAND_START, SERVICE_ERROR_NORMAL,
        szFilePath, NULL, NULL, _T("RPCSS\0"), NULL, NULL);

    if (hService == NULL)
    {
        ::CloseServiceHandle(hSCM);
        MessageBox(NULL, _T("Couldn't create service"), m_szServiceName,
                   MB_OK);
        return FALSE;
    }

    ::CloseServiceHandle(hService);
    ::CloseServiceHandle(hSCM);
    return TRUE;
}

inline BOOL CServiceModule::Uninstall()
{
    if (!IsInstalled())
        return TRUE;

    SC_HANDLE hSCM = ::OpenSCManager(NULL, NULL, SC_MANAGER_ALL_ACCESS);

    if (hSCM == NULL)
    {
        MessageBox(NULL, _T("Couldn't open service manager"),
                   m_szServiceName, MB_OK);
        return FALSE;
    }

    SC_HANDLE hService = ::OpenService(hSCM, m_szServiceName,
```

LISTING 10.8   Continued

```
                                    SERVICE_STOP | DELETE);

    if (hService == NULL)
    {
        ::CloseServiceHandle(hSCM);
        MessageBox(NULL, _T("Couldn't open service"), m_szServiceName,
                    MB_OK);
        return FALSE;
    }
    SERVICE_STATUS status;
    ::ControlService(hService, SERVICE_CONTROL_STOP, &status);

    BOOL bDelete = ::DeleteService(hService);
    ::CloseServiceHandle(hService);
    ::CloseServiceHandle(hSCM);

    if (bDelete)
        return TRUE;

    MessageBox(NULL, _T("Service could not be deleted"), m_szServiceName,
                MB_OK);
    return FALSE;
}

//////////////////////////////////////////////////////////////////////
// Logging functions
void CServiceModule::LogEvent(LPCTSTR pFormat, ...)
{
    TCHAR    chMsg[256];
    HANDLE   hEventSource;
    LPTSTR   lpszStrings[1];
    va_list  pArg;

    va_start(pArg, pFormat);
    _vstprintf(chMsg, pFormat, pArg);
    va_end(pArg);

    lpszStrings[0] = chMsg;

    if (m_bService)
    {
        /* Get a handle to use with ReportEvent(). */
        hEventSource = RegisterEventSource(NULL, m_szServiceName);
        if (hEventSource != NULL)
        {
            /* Write to event log. */
            ReportEvent(hEventSource, EVENTLOG_INFORMATION_TYPE, 0, 0,
                        NULL, 1, 0, (LPCTSTR*) &lpszStrings[0], NULL);
            DeregisterEventSource(hEventSource);
```

LISTING 10.8   Continued

```
        }
    }
    else
    {
        // As we are not running as a service, just write the error to
        // the console.
        _putts(chMsg);
    }
}

//////////////////////////////////////////////////////////////////////
// Service startup and registration
inline void CServiceModule::Start()
{
    SERVICE_TABLE_ENTRY st[] =
    {
        { m_szServiceName, _ServiceMain },
        { NULL, NULL }
    };
    if (m_bService && !::StartServiceCtrlDispatcher(st))
    {
        m_bService = FALSE;
    }
    if (m_bService == FALSE)
        Run();
}

inline void CServiceModule::ServiceMain(DWORD, LPTSTR*)
{
    // Register the control request handler
    m_status.dwCurrentState = SERVICE_START_PENDING;
    m_hServiceStatus = RegisterServiceCtrlHandler(m_szServiceName,
                                                  _Handler);
    if (m_hServiceStatus == NULL)
    {
        LogEvent(_T("Handler not installed"));
        return;
    }
    SetServiceStatus(SERVICE_START_PENDING);

    m_status.dwWin32ExitCode = S_OK;
    m_status.dwCheckPoint = 0;
    m_status.dwWaitHint = 0;

    // When the Run function returns, the service has stopped.
    Run();

    SetServiceStatus(SERVICE_STOPPED);
    LogEvent(_T("Service stopped"));
```

LISTING 10.8 Continued

```
}

inline void CServiceModule::Handler(DWORD dwOpcode)
{
    switch (dwOpcode)
    {
    case SERVICE_CONTROL_STOP:
        SetServiceStatus(SERVICE_STOP_PENDING);
        PostThreadMessage(dwThreadID, WM_QUIT, 0, 0);
        break;
    case SERVICE_CONTROL_PAUSE:
        break;
    case SERVICE_CONTROL_CONTINUE:
        break;
    case SERVICE_CONTROL_INTERROGATE:
        break;
    case SERVICE_CONTROL_SHUTDOWN:
        break;
    default:
        LogEvent(_T("Bad service request"));
    }
}

void WINAPI CServiceModule::_ServiceMain(DWORD dwArgc, LPTSTR* lpszArgv)
{
    _Module.ServiceMain(dwArgc, lpszArgv);
}
void WINAPI CServiceModule::_Handler(DWORD dwOpcode)
{
    _Module.Handler(dwOpcode);
}

void CServiceModule::SetServiceStatus(DWORD dwState)
{
    m_status.dwCurrentState = dwState;
    ::SetServiceStatus(m_hServiceStatus, &m_status);
}

void CServiceModule::Run()
{
    _Module.dwThreadID = GetCurrentThreadId();

    HRESULT hr = CoInitialize(NULL);
// If you are running on NT 4.0 or higher you can use the following call
// instead to make the EXE free threaded.
// This means that calls come in on a random RPC thread
// HRESULT hr = CoInitializeEx(NULL, COINIT_MULTITHREADED);

    _ASSERTE(SUCCEEDED(hr));
```

LISTING 10.8 Continued

```
        // This provides a NULL DACL which will allow access to everyone.
        CSecurityDescriptor sd;
        sd.InitializeFromThreadToken();
        hr = CoInitializeSecurity(sd, -1, NULL, NULL,
            RPC_C_AUTHN_LEVEL_PKT, RPC_C_IMP_LEVEL_IMPERSONATE, NULL,
            EOAC_NONE, NULL);
        _ASSERTE(SUCCEEDED(hr));

        hr = _Module.RegisterClassObjects(CLSCTX_LOCAL_SERVER |
                                          CLSCTX_REMOTE_SERVER,
                                          REGCLS_MULTIPLEUSE);
        _ASSERTE(SUCCEEDED(hr));

        LogEvent(_T("Service started"));
        if (m_bService)
            SetServiceStatus(SERVICE_RUNNING);

        MSG msg;
        while (GetMessage(&msg,  0, 0, 0))
            DispatchMessage(&msg);

        _Module.RevokeClassObjects();

        CoUninitialize();
}


/////////////////////////////////////////////////////////////////////////
//
extern "C" int WINAPI _tWinMain(HINSTANCE hInstance,
    HINSTANCE /*hPrevInstance*/, LPTSTR lpCmdLine, int /*nShowCmd*/)
{
    lpCmdLine = GetCommandLine(); //this line necessary for _ATL_MIN_CRT
    _Module.Init(ObjectMap, hInstance,  IDS_SERVICENAME,
                &LIBID_MYATLSERVICELib);
    _Module.m_bService = TRUE;

    TCHAR szTokens[] = _T("-/");

    LPCTSTR lpszToken = FindOneOf(lpCmdLine, szTokens);
    while (lpszToken != NULL)
    {
        if (lstrcmpi(lpszToken, _T("UnregServer"))==0)
            return _Module.UnregisterServer();

        // Register as Local Server
        if (lstrcmpi(lpszToken, _T("RegServer"))==0)
            return _Module.RegisterServer(TRUE, FALSE);

        // Register as Service
```

LISTING 10.8 Continued

```
        if (lstrcmpi(lpszToken, _T("Service"))==0)
            return _Module.RegisterServer(TRUE, TRUE);

        lpszToken = FindOneOf(lpszToken, szTokens);
    }

    // Are we Service or Local Server
    CRegKey keyAppID;
    LONG lRes = keyAppID.Open(HKEY_CLASSES_ROOT, _T("AppID"), KEY_READ);
    if (lRes != ERROR_SUCCESS)
        return lRes;

    CRegKey key;
    lRes =
      key.Open(keyAppID, _T("{B51F6322-99A5-11D2-BEC8-00C04F8B72E7}"),
            KEY_READ);
    if (lRes != ERROR_SUCCESS)
        return lRes;

    TCHAR szValue[_MAX_PATH];
    DWORD dwLen = _MAX_PATH;
    lRes = key.QueryValue(szValue, _T("LocalService"), &dwLen);

    _Module.m_bService = FALSE;
    if (lRes == ERROR_SUCCESS)
        _Module.m_bService = TRUE;

    _Module.Start();

    // When we get here, the service has been stopped
    return _Module.m_status.dwWin32ExitCode;
}
```

If you look at the member functions of the CServiceModule class, you'll note that they are similar to the code presented earlier in this chapter. As an example, the method CServiceModule::Init() initializes the SERVICE_STATUS array as I did at the beginning of the ServiceMain() function. The CServiceModule::Start() method calls the StartServiceCtrlDispatcher() function as I did in the main() function. The CServiceModule::ServiceMain() method, like the ServiceMain() function, registers the control dispatcher with the SCM by calling the RegisterServiceCtrlHandler() function.

Overall, you get the feeling that you are coding a service. But because the ATL COM Wizard is attempting to implement too many features, you tend to lose the ability to read the code. This is a common design flaw, known as the Blob or Swiss-Army Knife design pattern. That is, the designer tries to incorporate too much functionality into one class. The class does everything, and, therefore, lacks clarity. But trust me, the code works.

In addition to the code necessary to start and stop your service, the module class also implements, free-of-charge, event logging and ATL class registration. Later in this chapter, the "Using the Event Log" section discusses event logging in more detail.

So now you ask, how does ATL make it easier for me to communicate with services? To date, you've seen only the boilerplate code necessary to create a service. The next section describes how to use DCOM to communicate with a service.

DCOM IPC

Go back to the ATL service project workspace. Now that you have a basic ATL service project, you can add ATL classes with the ATL Object Wizard. As usual, you can create an ATL class by selecting Insert, New ATL Object from the menu bar. From the ATL Object Wizard pop-up dialog box, select Objects in the Category list box, Simple Object in the Objects list box, and click the Next button. In the ATL Object Wizard Properties pop-up dialog, type a short name for your object. I usually start by adding a singleton object to my services as a common entry point.

A *singleton* class is a COM class whose class factory creates only one instance of its class. This one instance is returned from all calls to the `IClassFactory::CreateInstance()`. That means all clients will share one instance of this object. Assuming this object is free-threaded and thread-safe, it can be used as a common entry point into your service. In order to make your ATL class a singleton, add the `DECLARE_CLASSFACTORY_SINGLETON` macro to your class declaration (see Listing 10.9).

LISTING 10.9 Singleton ATL Class

```
// singleton.h : Declaration of the Csingleton

#ifndef __SINGLETON_H_
#define __SINGLETON_H_

#include "resource.h"        // main symbols

/////////////////////////////////////////////////////////////////////////////
// Csingleton
class ATL_NO_VTABLE Csingleton :
  public CComObjectRootEx<CComMultiThreadModel>,
  public CComCoClass<Csingleton, &CLSID_singleton>,
  public IDispatchImpl<Isingleton, &IID_Isingleton,
                       &LIBID_MYATLSERVICELib>
{
public:
  Csingleton()
```

LISTING 10.9   Continued

```
  {
  }

DECLARE_CLASSFACTORY_SINGLETON(Csingleton)

DECLARE_REGISTRY_RESOURCEID(IDR_SINGLETON)

DECLARE_PROTECT_FINAL_CONSTRUCT()

BEGIN_COM_MAP(Csingleton)
  COM_INTERFACE_ENTRY(Isingleton)
  COM_INTERFACE_ENTRY(IDispatch)
END_COM_MAP()

// Isingleton
public:
};

#endif //__SINGLETON_H_
```

I included a project on the CD-ROM called myatlservice. It can be found in the myatlser-vice subdirectory in the chapter10 directory. This service has one ATL singleton class. I have encountered problems with the ATL wizards; they sometimes forget to include header files where necessary. The included workspace also contains an automation client that creates the ATL class. Listing 10.10 shows the code of this automation client.

LISTING 10.10   ATL Service Client

```
// controller.cpp : Defines the entry point for the console application.
//

#include "stdafx.h"
#include "automation.h"

int main(int argc, char* argv[])
{
  ::CoInitialize(NULL);
  {
    Automation object;
    object.CreateObject(L"Myatlservice.singleton.1");
  }
  ::CoUninitialize();
  return 0;
}
```

The client is quite simple. It creates the object as an automation object and quits. The Automation class included with the project on the CD-ROM is a simple automation wrapper that attempts to simulate Visual Basic automation syntax in C++.

In order to launch the module as a service, you must first register the service with the SCM. You can do this by simply running the Myatlservice.exe executable with the `-service` command-line parameter.

After registering the service with the SCM, step through the client code again, and the ATL module will launch as a service. You might be wondering how to tell whether a module is launched as a service or an executable. The next sections describe a few tools—including the Administrative Tools Services applet—that will help you determine the running state of a service.

Utilities for Working with Services

Four tools are invaluable when you are programming and working with services. These are the Administrative Tools Services applet, the Diagnostic utility, the Service Controller, and the Event Viewer.

Administrative Tools Services Applet

The Services applet enables you to start, stop, pause, unpause, and configure all the installed services on the machine. You can start the Services applet from the Windows 2000 Administrative Tools. Figure 10.3 shows the main dialog of the Services applet.

FIGURE 10.3

The Administrative Tools Services applet.

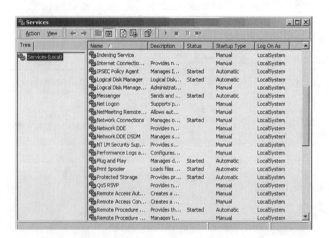

Starting, stopping, pausing, and unpausing services is quite easy and warrants little explanation. If you select a service and click the Configure button, the service configuration dialog box, shown in Figure 10.4, appears.

FIGURE 10.4

Configuring a service.

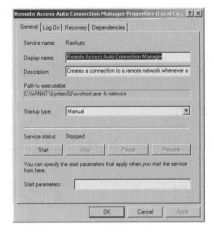

By selecting Automatic from the Startup Type group box, you can set up a service to launch automatically when the machine boots. Services typically run under the context of the system account, but from the service configuration dialog, you can configure a service to run in the context of any user.

Diagnostic Utility

Another great utility is the Diagnostic utility (WinMsd.exe). The utility can be found in the system32 directory. It lists all the services running or stopped on a machine. Figure 10.5 shows the Services tab of the Diagnostic utility.

With WinMsd, it is possible to know the state of the services. You can get the same list for any computer on the domain. That's why it is useful for administrators.

FIGURE 10.5

Diagnostic utility.

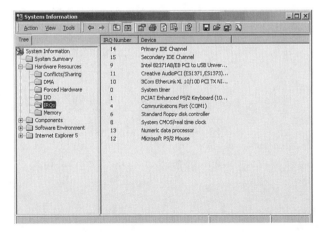

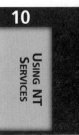

WinMsd is a tool of convenience because it is installed on most workstations. You can access the utility by selecting Run from the Start Menu, typing `winmsd`, and pressing Enter. This easy access is WinMsd's primary advantage over other tools such as the service controller.

Service Controller

The Service Controller utility, Sc.exe, provides all the functionality available in the two previous utilities, but it also enables you to start, stop, pause, unpause, and configure services on remote computers.

Unfortunately, the Service Controller utility is not pre-installed. You have to copy the executable from the bin directory of the installation CD-ROM to every computer that requires it. But the advantages of the Service Controller make it worth copying, at least on your personal workstation.

Event Viewer

The Event Viewer is located in the Program/Administrative Tools folder of the Start menu and in your System32 directory. Figure 10.6 shows the main window of the Event Viewer.

FIGURE 10.6

The Event Viewer.

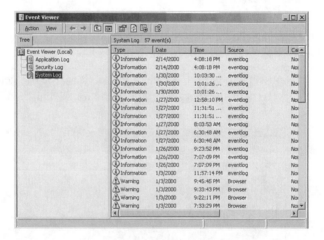

When you start using the Event Log, you will quickly learn how valuable this tool is. Later in the chapter, I describe how to send events to the event log.

OpenSCManager()

The OpenSCManager() function can be used to retrieve a handle to the SCM. After you've retrieved a handle to the SCM, you can begin communicating with services through the internal API.

> **Note**
>
> You should only start, stop, pause, and unpause a service using the SCM APIs. If you want to send other requests to a service, the service should provide an IPC protocol that supports client requests. This is a guideline, not a rule.

Service Handles

The first thing you must do is call the OpenService() function to acquire a handle to a specific service. After you've acquired a handle to a specific service, you can start the service by calling the StartService() function. You can close the service handle with the CloseServiceHandle() function. Listing 10.11 shows an example of starting a service using the StartService() function.

LISTING 10.11   StartService() Example

```
void StartAService(const char * szServiceName)
{
  SC_HANDLE handle = ::OpenSCManager(NULL, NULL, SC_MANAGER_ALL_ACCESS);
  SC_HANDLE hService = ::OpenService(handle, szServiceName,
                                    SERVICE_ALL_ACCESS);
  ::StartService(hService, 0, NULL);
  ::CloseServiceHandle(hService);
  ::CloseServiceHandle(handle);
}
```

The API prototypes just used are as follows:

```
SC_HANDLE OpenSCManager(
  LPCTSTR lpMachineName, // pointer to machine name string
  LPCTSTR lpDatabaseName, // pointer to database name string
  DWORD dwDesiredAccess // type of access
);

SC_HANDLE OpenService(
  SC_HANDLE hSCManager, // handle to service control manager database
```

10

USING NT SERVICES

```
  LPCTSTR lpServiceName, // pointer to name of service to start
  DWORD dwDesiredAccess // type of access to service
);

BOOL StartService(
  SC_HANDLE hService, // handle of service
  DWORD dwNumServiceArgs, // number of arguments
  LPCTSTR *lpServiceArgVectors // array of argument strings
);
```

Manipulating Services

After you have a handle to the service and the service is started, you can call the
ControlService() and the QueryServiceStatus() functions to pause, unpause, stop,
and query the status of the service. Listing 10.12 shows an example of using both of
these functions to stop a service.

LISTING 10.12   Stop a Service Example

```
void StopAService(const char * szServiceName)
{
  SC_HANDLE handle = ::OpenSCManager(NULL, NULL, SC_MANAGER_ALL_ACCESS);
  SC_HANDLE hService = ::OpenService(handle, szServiceName,
                                     SERVICE_ALL_ACCESS);
  SERVICE_STATUS servicestatus;
  ::QueryServiceStatus(hService, &servicestatus);
  if (servicestatus.dwCurrentState == SERVICE_RUNNING)
  {
    if( !::ControlService(hService, SERVICE_CONTROL_STOP, &servicestatus) )
    {
        // Handle situation where service did not stop.
    }
  }
  ::CloseServiceHandle(hService);
  ::CloseServiceHandle (handle);
}
```

You can also use the ControlService() function to send the proprietary messages discussed earlier in this chapter to the ServiceCtrlHandlers() function.

Installing Services via the Registry

In order to install a service on a machine, you must add a few values under the
HKEY_LOCAL_MACHINE\System\CurrentControlSet\Services key in the registry.

Although you can install the service by directly manipulating the registry, you might want to use the `CreateService()` function. Listing 10.13 shows an example of calling the `CreateService()` function in order to install a service.

LISTING 10.13   Example Using `CreateService()`

```
void InstallAService(const char * szServiceName)
{
  SC_HANDLE handle = ::OpenSCManager(NULL, NULL, SC_MANAGER_ALL_ACCESS);
  char szFilename[256];
  ::GetModuleFileName(NULL, szFilename, 255);
  SC_HANDLE hService = ::CreateService(handle, szServiceName,
    szServiceName, SERVICE_ALL_ACCESS, SERVICE_WIN32_OWN_PROCESS,
    SERVICE_DEMAND_START, SERVICE_ERROR_IGNORE, szFilename, NULL,
    NULL, NULL, NULL, NULL);
  ::CloseServiceHandle(hService);
  ::CloseServiceHandle (handle);
}
```

The `CreateService()` function installs your service by adding entries to the Windows system registry. Figure 10.7 shows an example of the entries added by the `CreateService()` function.

FIGURE 10.7

The registry and `CreateService()`.

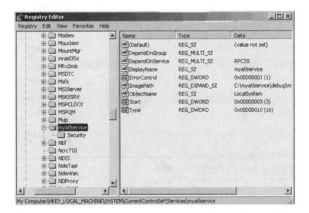

After you have installed the service, you can modify the configuration of your service by calling the `ChangeServiceConfig()` function. To uninstall the service, call the `DeleteService()` function. Note that delete service does not actually uninstall the service, it only marks the service for deletion. After all handles to the service are closed, the service is removed.

Using the Event Log

A subject related to services is the Event Log. Quite often, while debugging a service, you'll run into the problem of providing runtime feedback. Services should not provide direct feedback in the form of a message box or any other GUI component. Instead, they should log feedback in the Event Log. The next sections describe how to write events to the Event Log and how to read from the Event Log.

The information provided in the log is comprehensive enough that you usually get enough information to figure things out. In the log you'll get the event type, date, time, source, and category. You'll also know if the event was generated by an application, the system, or a service.

> **Note**
>
> There are actually at least three, if not more, event logs on any workstation or server. The three primary event logs are the Application, System, and Security event logs. In this chapter, I always refer to the Application event log.

Message Compiler (MC)

The first tool to familiarize yourself with in order to implement event logging is the message compiler. The message compiler uses as input a message script (.mc) file and outputs three files, a binary (.bin), a resource script (.rc), and a header file (.h). To run the message compiler, go to the command shell and type **mc -c *myatlservicemc***, where *myatlservicemc* is the name of the message script file you created. Listing 10.14 shows a sample message script file that creates three message resource strings.

LISTING 10.14 Sample Message Script File

```
MessageID=10
SymbolicName=MRS_HELLO
Language=English
My service has started
.
MessageID=
SymbolicName=MRS_ERROR
Language=English
Error: %1
.
MessageID=
SymbolicName=MRS_GOODBYE
Language=English
My service has stopped
.
```

After compiling this message script file, you will have generated the three necessary files. The resource script file should be compiled and linked into your service's module file. The resource script file will include the binary file, so it must be in the path when you compile the resource script. The header file can be included in your program code in order to use the symbolic names of your message resource strings. This is the resource script generated by MC:

```
LANGUAGE 0x9,0x1
1 11 MSG00001.bin
```

Listing 10.15 shows the resource script and header files that will be created by the message compiler.

LISTING 10.15 Header File Generated by MC

```
//
// Values are 32 bit values laid out as follows:
//
//  3 3 2 2 2 2 2 2 2 2 2 2 1 1 1 1 1 1 1 1 1 1
//  1 0 9 8 7 6 5 4 3 2 1 0 9 8 7 6 5 4 3 2 1 0 9 8 7 6 5 4 3 2 1 0
//  +---+-+-+---------------------+-----------------------------+
//  |Sev|C|R|     Facility        |            Code             |
//  +---+-+-+---------------------+-----------------------------+
//
// where
//
//      Sev - is the severity code
//
//          00 - Success
//          01 - Informational
//          10 - Warning
//          11 - Error
//
//      C - is the Customer code flag
//
//      R - is a reserved bit
//
//      Facility - is the facility code
//
//      Code - is the facility's status code
//
//
// Define the facility codes
//


//
// Define the severity codes
//
```

LISTING 10.15   Continued

```
//
// MessageId: MRS_HELLO
//
// MessageText:
//
//  %s
//
#define MRS_HELLO                       0x2000000AL

//
// MessageId: MRS_ERROR
//
// MessageText:
//
//  Error: %s
//
#define MRS_ERROR                       0x2000000BL
```

Finally, you must register the message strings by running the code in Listing 10.16. I've included additional source code, called EventLog, on the CD-ROM. It can be found in the EventLog subdirectory in the chapter10 directory. EventLog includes the entire event logging source code in this chapter. This sample extends your previous service by adding complete event logging capability.

LISTING 10.16   Register Event Server

```
USES_CONVERSION;
HKEY hkey;
::RegCreateKey(HKEY_LOCAL_MACHINE, "SYSTEM\\CurrentControlSet\\"
  "Services\\EventLog\\Application\\myatlservice", &hkey);
char sz[MAX_PATH];
::GetModuleFileName(NULL, sz, MAX_PATH);
::RegSetValueEx(hkey, "EventMessageFile", 0, REG_EXPAND_SZ, (LPBYTE) sz,
  ::strlen(sz)+ 1);
DWORD dwData = EVENTLOG_ERROR_TYPE | EVENTLOG_WARNING_TYPE |
              EVENTLOG_INFORMATION_TYPE;
::RegSetValueEx(hkey, "TypesSupported", 0, REG_DWORD,  (LPBYTE) &dwData,
  sizeof(DWORD));
::RegCloseKey (hkey);
```

RegisterEventSource(), DeregisterEventSource(), and Report Event()

Writing to the event log also quite easy. In order to open and close a handle that can be used to write to the registry, call the RegisterEventSource() and

`DeregisterEventSource()` functions. To write an entry to the event log, call the `ReportEvent()` function. Listing 10.17 is a generic routine that can be used to write entries to the event log.

LISTING 10.17   Writing to the Event Log

```
void WriteEventLogEntry(int idMessageString, const char * * pszString)
{
  HANDLE hEventSource = ::RegisterEventSource(NULL, szServiceName));
  if (hEventSource != NULL)
  {
    ::ReportEvent(hEventSource, EVENTLOG_INFORMATION_TYPE,
      0, idMessageString, NULL, 1, 0, szString, NULL);
    ::DeregisterEventSource(hEventSource);
  }
};
```

You will find that this function only writes information-type messages to the event log. This is because I hard coded the `EVENTLOG_INFORMATION_TYPE` parameter. Actually, five such constants are available:

> `EVENTLOG_ERROR_TYPE`
>
> `EVENTLOG_WARNING_TYPE`
>
> `EVENTLOG_INFORMATION_TYPE`
>
> `EVENTLOG_AUDIT_SUCCESS`
>
> `EVENTLOG_AUDIT_FAILURE`

After all your events are writing to the event log, you can use the Event Viewer. Another option for viewing the event log is to create your own event log viewer. The next section describes how to create such a viewer.

Event Log Viewer

Reading from the event log is even easier than writing to it. You open and close a handle to the event log by using the `OpenEventLog()` and `CloseEventLog()`functions. To read individual event log entries, call the `ReadEventLog()`function. But the individual event log entries contain only the strings that you passed to the `ReportEvent()`function. The individual event log entries do not contain the message strings. It is the viewer's responsibility to format the message. Listing 10.18 shows the source code for an event viewer that dumps the event log to the standard output.

10

USING NT SERVICES

LISTING 10.18   Dump Event Log

```cpp
// viewer.cpp : Defines the entry point for the console application.
//

#include "stdafx.h"

#include "windows.h"
#include "iostream.h"

int main()
{
    HANDLE handle = ::OpenEventLog(NULL, "Application");
    if (handle == NULL)
    {
        return 0;
    }

    DWORD dwRec=0;
    static const int c = 65536;
    DWORD dwRead, dwNext;
    BYTE by[c];
    while (1)
    {
        if (!::ReadEventLog(handle, EVENTLOG_BACKWARDS_READ +
                            EVENTLOG_SEQUENTIAL_READ,
                            1, by, c, &dwRead, &dwNext))
        {
            break;
        }
        DWORD dw=0;
        while (dwRead>dw)
        {
            EVENTLOGRECORD * p;
            p = (EVENTLOGRECORD *)(by+dw);
            char * sz = (char *)by+dw+56;
            cout << "Record: " << ++dwRec << '\n';
            TCHAR * tchar = (TCHAR *)(by+dw+p->StringOffset);
            cout << tchar << '\n';
            dw += p->Length;
        }
    }

    ::CloseEventLog(handle);
    return 0;
};
```

Remember that the reason you are using the event log is to provide runtime feedback to
programmers and operators. You are not able to provide feedback using message boxes
or other GUI elements because services do not have a desktop. You might be tempted to

send a lot of feedback to the event log in order to make debugging easier. This is not advisable. Only important information should be logged in the event log. The next few sections show you a few tricks you can use to debug services.

Debugging Your Services

There are several reasons why services are more difficult to debug than other processes. The first reason is that services do not have a desktop like other processes. Another reason is that services usually run using a special user account called the system account.

The System Account

The system account has special privileges that grant the account access to the file system and many other security resources. But the system account is quite limited and does not have access to any network resources. It is a null session account, and null session accounts do not have access to network resources, even if everyone was granted access to a network resource.

Finally, you cannot log on to a machine by using the system account. This makes it very difficult to debug bugs that are related to the fact that the service is running under an account with a set of access rights different from the rights of an interactive user.

Task Manager: Debug

You can debug a process, even a process running under the system account, by starting the debugging from Task Manager. From the Task Manager's Processes tab, you can right-click on a process to get its context menu. From the context menu, select Debug, which launches your registered debugger and attaches the current running process. You can also start Developer Studio with the switch /P followed by the process ID of the running service that you want to debug.

Start the Debugger with the AT Command

Another option for debugging is to acquire a command shell that runs in the security context of the system account. From the Start menu, select Run. Type the command **at 9:05 /interactive cmd.exe**, where 9:05 is one minute into the future—that is, if the current time were 10:06, you would type **at 10:07 /interactive cmd.exe**. When the clock reaches 10:07, the scheduler will launch a command shell. Because the scheduler runs with the security context of the system account, so will the command shell. From this command shell, you can start Developer Studio or any other process, and that process will also run in the security context of the system account.

Summary

In this chapter, you learned a lot about services: how to write them, use them, and debug them. Now that you've learned the basics of creating services and it's fresh in your mind, you should experiment and create some of your own design.

The registry is another thing you learned. Because most of the information about services is stored in the registry, and because services load most of their settings from the registry, this topic has a great bearing on services. The understanding of the registry with regard to services can sometime make or break you.

The Event Log and debugging round out the chapter. Surely the difficulties in debugging services can't be underestimated, but I talked about working through these difficulties, including using the Event Log.

Marshaling

Understanding Marshaling

The definition of marshaling is sometimes not very well understood, even by those who have successfully mastered the concept. The word marshaling was previously used to describe the process of gathering and organizing an army before battle. Marshaling in computer terms is the process of gathering and organizing data into a data packet that can be transferred to another process or thread. Unmarshaling, then, is the process of unpackaging the data packet and saving the data in local storage.

The client process starts by formulating a request for a server COM+ object. The request is marshaled into transmittable data packets and passed to the server object. The server object unmarshals the data packets and processes the request. The response is then marshaled and passed back to the calling client. The client unmarshals the data and interprets the response.

The client marshals and unmarshals data using a proxy object, which provides the same interfaces as the COM+ server. Instead of implementing the methods of the COM+ server, the proxy simply packages method parameters, sends them to the actual COM+ server, and unpackages the results returned from the COM+ server method.

The server usually has a stub thread that receives the incoming requests from the proxy and unmarshals the data to perform the actual call on the COM+ object (see Figure 11.1).

FIGURE 11.1
Proxy-stub marshaling.

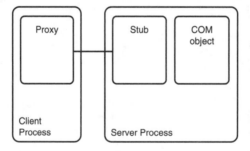

There are three types of marshaling: type library marshaling, standard marshaling, and custom marshaling. Although you need only one of the three techniques to marshal your interfaces, the following sections explain each type of marshaling so that you can choose the marshaling technique that best fits your needs.

Type Library Marshaling

Type library marshaling takes advantage of the fact that every installation already has an automation marshaler installed. As long as you are willing to limit yourself to data types

supported by the automation marshaler, you can use type library marshaling. That is, instead of installing proxy-stub modules on the client and server, you can use the proxy-stub pair used by automation. In place of installing the proxy-stub pairs, you now must install only the type library on the client and server machines. I almost always use type library marshaling because of its simplicity.

In order to use type library marshaling, you must indicate in the registry that you are using the automation marshaler and where to find your type library. Listing 11.1 shows the registration file for a COM+ interface that uses type library marshaling.

LISTING 11.1   Sample Registration File for Type Library Marshaling

```
[HKEY_CLASSES_ROOT \ Interface \ {my- interfaces-iid }]
@="IMyInterface"

[HKEY_CLASSES_ROOT \ Interface \ {my- interfaces-iid } \
  ProxyStubClsid32]
@="{00020424-0000-0000-C000-000000000046}"

[HKEY_CLASSES_ROOT \ Interface \ {my- interfaces-iid } \
  TypeLib]
@="{my-typelibs-guid}"
"Version"="1.0"

[HKEY_CLASSES_ROOT \ TypeLib \ {my-typelibs-guid} \ 1.0]
@="My Type Library"

[HKEY_CLASSES_ROOT \ TypeLib \ {my-typelibs-guid} \ 1.0 \
  Win32]
@="c:\\mypath\\mymodule.tlb"

[HKEY_CLASSES_ROOT \ TypeLib \ {my-typelibs-guid} \ 1.0 \
  Flags]
@="0"

[HKEY_CLASSES_ROOT \ TypeLib \ {my-typelibs-guid} \ 1.0 \
  HelpDir]
@=""
```

The previous registration file registers the IMyInterface interface in the registry. The related typelib, "My Type Library", is also registered. You should note that the .tlb file is registered as well.

Standard Marshaling

Standard marshaling is accomplished using the Microsoft interface definition language (MIDL) compiler. Assuming that you have an interface called IMyInterface and you

saved this interface in the file myinterface.idl, you can use the MIDL compiler to generate the proxy-stub code for the interface. The output of the MIDL compiler is made up of
the following five files:

- myinterface.h—A header file with the interface definition
- myinterface_i.c—A source file with the IID constant definitions
- myinterface_p.c—A source file with the proxy-stub code
- dlldata.c—A source file with the proxy-stub DLL entry points
- myinterface.tlb—The automation-capable type library to be used in type library
  marshaling

Listing 11.2 is a simple interface definition language (IDL) file used as input to generate
files with the MIDL compiler.

LISTING 11.2   Sample IDL File

```
// MyMidlExperiment.idl : IDL source for MyMidlExperiment.dll
//

// This file will be processed by the MIDL tool to
// produce the type library (MyMidlExperiment.tlb) and
// marshaling code.

import "oaidl.idl";
import "ocidl.idl";

  [

    uuid(CE00560E-40F0-11D2-BEA0-00C04F8B72E7),

    helpstring("IMyInterface Interface"),
    pointer_default(unique)
  ]
  interface IMyInterface : IUnknown
  {
    [helpstring("method Hello")] HRESULT Hello();
  };
[
  uuid(CE005601-40F0-11D2-BEA0-00C04F8B72E7),
  version(1.0),
  helpstring("MyMidlExperiment 1.0 Type Library")
]
library MYMIDLEXPERIMENTLib
{
  importlib("stdole32.tlb");
  importlib("stdole2.tlb");
```

LISTING 11.2   Continued

```
  [
    uuid(CE00560F-40F0-11D2-BEA0-00C04F8B72E7),
    helpstring("MyInterface Class")
  ]
  coclass MyInterface
  {
    [default] interface IMyInterface;
  };
};
```

If you execute the MIDL compiler with this IDL file, the output would be the type library and the four files in Listings 11.3, 11.4, 11.5, and 11.6, shown in the following sections.

Define the DLL Entry Points

Listing 11.3 is the dlldata.c source file. This source file defines all the DLL entry points for your proxy stub. The macro DLLDATA_ROUTINES creates the export routines required by the proxy stub. These can include DllGetClassObject(), DllCanUnloadNow(), GetProxyDllInfo(), DllRegisterServer(), and DllUnregisterServer().

The .cpp file lacks the familiar COM in-process server functions DllGetClassObject() and DllCanUnloadNow(). Explicit definitions of these functions are not needed because compiling .c generates default implementations for you. Those implementations, however, must still be exported from this DLL. Standard marshaling DLLs require the DllGetClassObject(), DllCanUnloadNow(), and exports. You need only export these three functions; you don't need to implement them within a standard marshaling DLL. Of course, you must also export the DllRegisterServer() and DllUnregisterServer() functions if you have defined them in the DLL.

LISTING 11.3   Output from MIDL Compiler (dlldata.c)

```
/***********************************************************
DllData file -- generated by MIDL compiler

        DO NOT ALTER THIS FILE

This file is regenerated by MIDL on every IDL file compile.

To completely reconstruct this file, delete it and rerun MIDL
on all the IDL files in this DLL, specifying this file for the
/dlldata command line option

***********************************************************/
```

LISTING 11.3 Continued

```
#include <rpcproxy.h>

#ifdef __cplusplus
extern "C"    {
#endif

EXTERN_PROXY_FILE( MyMidlExperiment )


PROXYFILE_LIST_START
/* Start of list */
  REFERENCE_PROXY_FILE( MyMidlExperiment ),
/* End of list */
PROXYFILE_LIST_END


DLLDATA_ROUTINES( aProxyFileList, GET_DLL_CLSID )

#ifdef __cplusplus
}   /*extern "C" */
#endif

/* end of generated dlldata file */
```

The Class Definition

Listing 11.4 is the mymidlexperiment.h header file. This header file contains the class definition. If you are going to refer directly to an `IMyInterface` object, you should include this file.

LISTING 11.4 Output from MIDL Compiler (mymidlexperiment.h)

```
/* this ALWAYS GENERATED file contains the definitions for the
interfaces */


/* File created by MIDL compiler version 3.03.0110 */
/* at Mon Aug 31 09:51:22 1998
 */
/* Compiler settings for MyMidlExperiment.idl:
    Oicf (OptLev=i2), W1, Zp8, env=Win32, ms_ext, c_ext
    error checks: none
*/
//@@MIDL_FILE_HEADING(  )


/* verify that the <rpcndr.h> version is high enough to
```

LISTING 11.4 Continued

```
compile this file*/
#ifndef __REQUIRED_RPCNDR_H_VERSION__
#define __REQUIRED_RPCNDR_H_VERSION__ 440
#endif

#include "rpc.h"
#include "rpcndr.h"

#ifndef __RPCNDR_H_VERSION__
#error this stub requires an updated version of <rpcndr.h>
#endif // __RPCNDR_H_VERSION__

#ifndef COM_NO_WINDOWS_H
#include "windows.h"
#include "ole2.h"
#endif /*COM_NO_WINDOWS_H*/

#ifndef __MyMidlExperiment_h__
#define __MyMidlExperiment_h__

#ifdef __cplusplus
extern "C"{
#endif

/* Forward Declarations */

#ifndef __IMyInterface_FWD_DEFINED__
#define __IMyInterface_FWD_DEFINED__
typedef interface IMyInterface IMyInterface;
#endif   /* __IMyInterface_FWD_DEFINED__ */


#ifndef __MyInterface_FWD_DEFINED__
#define __MyInterface_FWD_DEFINED__

#ifdef __cplusplus
typedef class MyInterface MyInterface;
#else
typedef struct MyInterface MyInterface;
#endif /* __cplusplus */

#endif   /* __MyInterface_FWD_DEFINED__ */


/* header files for imported files */
#include "oaidl.h"
#include "ocidl.h"

void __RPC_FAR * __RPC_USER MIDL_user_allocate(size_t);
```

LISTING 11.4   Continued

```
void __RPC_USER MIDL_user_free( void __RPC_FAR * );

#ifndef __IMyInterface_INTERFACE_DEFINED__
#define __IMyInterface_INTERFACE_DEFINED__

/*****************************************
 * Generated header for interface: IMyInterface
 * at Mon Aug 31 09:51:22 1998
 * using MIDL 3.03.0110
 *****************************************/
/* [object][unique][helpstring][uuid] */


EXTERN_C const IID IID_IMyInterface;

#if defined(__cplusplus) && !defined(CINTERFACE)

    MIDL_INTERFACE("CE00560E-40F0-11D2-BEA0-00C04F8B72E7")
    IMyInterface : public IUnknown
    {
    public:
        virtual /* [helpstring] */ HRESULT STDMETHODCALLTYPE
                                  Hello(void) = 0;

    };

#else   /* C style interface */

    typedef struct IMyInterfaceVtbl
    {
        BEGIN_INTERFACE

        HRESULT (STDMETHODCALLTYPE __RPC_FAR *QueryInterface)(
            IMyInterface __RPC_FAR * This,
            /*[in]*/ REFIID riid,
            /*[iid_is][out]*/ void __RPC_FAR *__RPC_FAR *
                        ppvObject);

        ULONG ( STDMETHODCALLTYPE __RPC_FAR *AddRef )(
            IMyInterface __RPC_FAR * This);

        ULONG ( STDMETHODCALLTYPE __RPC_FAR *Release )(
            IMyInterface __RPC_FAR * This);

        /* [helpstring] */ HRESULT ( STDMETHODCALLTYPE
                        __RPC_FAR *Hello )(
            IMyInterface __RPC_FAR * This);
```

11

LISTING 11.4   Continued

```
        END_INTERFACE
    } IMyInterfaceVtbl;

    interface IMyInterface
    {
        CONST_VTBL struct IMyInterfaceVtbl __RPC_FAR *lpVtbl;
    };



#ifdef COBJMACROS


#define IMyInterface_QueryInterface(This,riid,ppvObject)  \
    (This)->lpVtbl -> QueryInterface(This,riid,ppvObject)

#define IMyInterface_AddRef(This)  \
    (This)->lpVtbl -> AddRef(This)

#define IMyInterface_Release(This)  \
    (This)->lpVtbl -> Release(This)


#define IMyInterface_Hello(This)  \
    (This)->lpVtbl -> Hello(This)

#endif /* COBJMACROS */


#endif   /* C style interface */



/* [helpstring] */ HRESULT STDMETHODCALLTYPE
    IMyInterface_Hello_Proxy( IMyInterface __RPC_FAR * This);


void __RPC_STUB IMyInterface_Hello_Stub(
    IRpcStubBuffer *This,
    IRpcChannelBuffer *_pRpcChannelBuffer,
    PRPC_MESSAGE _pRpcMessage,
    DWORD *_pdwStubPhase);



#endif   /* __IMyInterface_INTERFACE_DEFINED__ */
```

LISTING 11.4 Continued

```
#ifndef __MYMIDLEXPERIMENTLib_LIBRARY_DEFINED__
#define __MYMIDLEXPERIMENTLib_LIBRARY_DEFINED__

/******************************************
 * Generated header for library: MYMIDLEXPERIMENTLib
 * at Mon Aug 31 09:51:22 1998
 * using MIDL 3.03.0110
 ******************************************/
/* [helpstring][version][uuid] */



EXTERN_C const IID LIBID_MYMIDLEXPERIMENTLib;

EXTERN_C const CLSID CLSID_MyInterface;

#ifdef __cplusplus

class DECLSPEC_UUID("CE00560F-40F0-11D2-BEA0-00C04F8B72E7")
MyInterface;
#endif
#endif /* __MYMIDLEXPERIMENTLib_LIBRARY_DEFINED__ */

/* Additional Prototypes for ALL interfaces */

/* end of Additional Prototypes */

#ifdef __cplusplus
}
#endif

#endif
```

You should note that the proxy and stub code is merged into one DLL. That's why the filename ends with ps (which stands for ProxyStub).

IRpcProxyBuffer interface is the interface by which the client-side infrastructure (for example, the proxy manager) talks to the interface proxy instances that it manages. When created, proxies are aggregated into some larger objects, as per the normal creation process (where pUnkOuter in IPSFactoryBuffer::CreateProxy() is nonNULL). The controlling unknown then calls QueryInterface() to the interface (from the interface proxy) it wants to expose.

On the server side, each interface stub implements IRpcStubBuffer, an internal interface. The server code acting as a stub manager calls IRpcStubBuffer::Connect and passes the interface stub the IUnknown pointer of its object.

Proxy and stub communicate by means of an RPC (remote procedure call) channel, which utilizes the system's RPC infrastructure for interprocess communication. The RPC channel implements a single interface `IRpcChannelBuffer`, an internal interface to which both interface proxies and stubs hold a pointer. The proxy and stub call the interface to obtain a marshaling packet, send the data to their counterpart, and destroy the packet when they are done. The interface stub also holds a pointer to the original object.

Defining the `IID`, `TypeLib` GUID, and `CLSID`

Listing 11.5 is the mymidlexperiment_i.c source file. This source file contains the definitions of the interface (`IID`), type library (`TypeLib` GUID) and class identifiers (`CLSID`).

LISTING 11.5 Output from MIDL Compiler (mymidlexperiment_i.c)

```
/* this file contains the actual definitions of */
/* the IIDs and CLSIDs */

/* link this file in with the server and any clients */


/* File created by MIDL compiler version 3.03.0110 */
/* at Mon Aug 31 09:51:22 1998
 */
/* Compiler settings for MyMidlExperiment.idl:
    Oicf (OptLev=i2), W1, Zp8, env=Win32, ms_ext, c_ext
    error checks: none
*/
//@@MIDL_FILE_HEADING(  )
#ifdef __cplusplus
extern "C"{
#endif


#ifndef __IID_DEFINED__
#define __IID_DEFINED__

typedef struct _IID
{
    unsigned long  x;
    unsigned short s1;
    unsigned short s2;
    unsigned char  c[8];(
} IID;

#endif // __IID_DEFINED__

#ifndef CLSID_DEFINED
#define CLSID_DEFINED
```

LISTING 11.5   Continued

```
typedef IID CLSID;
#endif // CLSID_DEFINED

const IID IID_IMyInterface = {0xCE00560E,0x40F0,0x11D2,
  {0xBE,0xA0,0x00,0xC0,0x4F,0x8B,0x72,0xE7}};


const IID LIBID_MYMIDLEXPERIMENTLib =
  {0xCE005601,0x40F0,0x11D2,
    {0xBE,0xA0,0x00,0xC0,0x4F,0x8B,0x72,0xE7}};


const CLSID CLSID_MyInterface =
  {0xCE00560F,0x40F0,0x11D2,
    {0xBE,0xA0,0x00,0xC0,0x4F,0x8B,0x72,0xE7}};


#ifdef __cplusplus
}
#endif
```

The Proxy and Stub Definitions

Listing 11.6 is the mymidlexperiment_p.c source file. This source file contains the actual proxy and stub definitions and code.

LISTING 11.6   Output from MIDL Compiler (mymidlexperiment_p.c)

```
/* this ALWAYS GENERATED file contains the proxy stub code */


/* File created by MIDL compiler version 3.03.0110 */
/* at Mon Aug 31 09:51:22 1998
 */
/* Compiler settings for MyMidlExperiment.idl:
    Oicf (OptLev=i2), W1, Zp8, env=Win32, ms_ext, c_ext
    error checks: none
*/
//@@MIDL_FILE_HEADING(  )

#define USE_STUBLESS_PROXY


/* verify that the <rpcproxy.h> version is high enough to
   compile this file*/
#ifndef __REDQ_RPCPROXY_H_VERSION__
#define __REQUIRED_RPCPROXY_H_VERSION__ 440
#endif
```

LISTING 11.6   Continued

```c
#include "rpcproxy.h"
#ifndef __RPCPROXY_H_VERSION__
#error this stub requires an updated version of <rpcproxy.h>
#endif // __RPCPROXY_H_VERSION__


#include "MyMidlExperiment.h"

#define TYPE_FORMAT_STRING_SIZE    1
#define PROC_FORMAT_STRING_SIZE    19

typedef struct _MIDL_TYPE_FORMAT_STRING
    {
    short          Pad;
    unsigned char  Format[ TYPE_FORMAT_STRING_SIZE ];
    } MIDL_TYPE_FORMAT_STRING;

typedef struct _MIDL_PROC_FORMAT_STRING
    {
    short          Pad;
    unsigned char  Format[ PROC_FORMAT_STRING_SIZE ];
    } MIDL_PROC_FORMAT_STRING;


extern const MIDL_TYPE_FORMAT_STRING __MIDL_TypeFormatString;
extern const MIDL_PROC_FORMAT_STRING __MIDL_ProcFormatString;


/* Object interface: IUnknown, ver. 0.0,
   GUID={0x00000000,0x0000,0x0000,
       {0xC0,0x00,0x00,0x00,0x00,0x00,0x00,0x46}} */


/* Object interface: IMyInterface, ver. 0.0,
   GUID={0xCE00560E,0x40F0,0x11D2,
       {0xBE,0xA0,0x00,0xC0,0x4F,0x8B,0x72,0xE7}} */


extern const MIDL_STUB_DESC Object_StubDesc;


extern const MIDL_SERVER_INFO IMyInterface_ServerInfo;

#pragma code_seg(".orpc")

static const MIDL_STUB_DESC Object_StubDesc =
    {
    0,
    NdrOleAllocate,
```

LISTING 11.6   Continued

```
    NdrOleFree,
    0,
    0,
    0,
    0,
    0,
    __MIDL_TypeFormatString.Format,
    0, /* -error bounds_check flag */
    0x20000, /* Ndr library version */
    0,
    0x303006e, /* MIDL Version 3.3.110 */
    0,
    0,
    0,   /* Reserved1 */
    0,   /* Reserved2 */
    0,   /* Reserved3 */
    0,   /* Reserved4 */
    0    /* Reserved5 */
    };

static const unsigned short
  IMyInterface_FormatStringOffsetTable[] =
    {
    0
    };

static const MIDL_SERVER_INFO IMyInterface_ServerInfo =
    {
    &Object_StubDesc,
    0,
    __MIDL_ProcFormatString.Format,
    &IMyInterface_FormatStringOffsetTable[-3],
    0,
    0,
    0,
    0
    };

static const MIDL_STUBLESS_PROXY_INFO IMyInterface_ProxyInfo =
    {
    &Object_StubDesc,
    __MIDL_ProcFormatString.Format,
    &IMyInterface_FormatStringOffsetTable[-3],
    0,
    0,
    0
    };


CINTERFACE_PROXY_VTABLE(4) _IMyInterfaceProxyVtbl =
```

LISTING 11.6 Continued

```
{
    &IMyInterface_ProxyInfo,
    &IID_IMyInterface,
    IUnknown_QueryInterface_Proxy,
    IUnknown_AddRef_Proxy,
    IUnknown_Release_Proxy ,
    (void *)-1 /* IMyInterface::Hello */
};

const CInterfaceStubVtbl _IMyInterfaceStubVtbl =
{
    &IID_IMyInterface,
    &IMyInterface_ServerInfo,
    4,
    0, /* pure interpreted */
    CStdStubBuffer_METHODS
};

#pragma data_seg(".rdata")

#if !defined(__RPC_WIN32__)
#error  Invalid build platform for this stub.
#endif


#if !(TARGET_IS_NT40_OR_LATER)
#error You need a Windows NT 4.0 or later to run this stub
#error because it uses these features:
#error    -Oif or -Oicf, more than 32 methods in the interface.
#error However, your C/C++ compilation flags indicate you
#error intend to run this app on earlier systems.
#error This app will die there with the
#error RPC_X_WRONG_STUB_VERSION error.
#endif



static const MIDL_PROC_FORMAT_STRING __MIDL_ProcFormatString =
    {
        0,
        {

  /* Procedure Hello */

      0x33,     /* FC_AUTO_HANDLE */
      0x64,     /* 100 */
/*  2 */ NdrFcShort( 0x3 ), /* 3 */
#ifndef _ALPHA_
/*  4 */ NdrFcShort( 0x8 ),
/* x86, MIPS, PPC Stack size/offset = 8 */
#else
```

LISTING 11.6   Continued

```
        NdrFcShort( 0x10 ),   /* Alpha Stack size/offset = 16 */
#endif
/*  6 */  NdrFcShort( 0x0 ),   /* 0 */
/*  8 */  NdrFcShort( 0x8 ),   /* 8 */
/* 10 */  0x4,      /* 4 */
        0x1,    /* 1 */

  /* Return value */

/* 12 */  NdrFcShort( 0x70 ),  /* 112 */
#ifndef _ALPHA_
/* 14 */  NdrFcShort( 0x4 ),
/* x86, MIPS, PPC Stack size/offset = 4 */
#else
        NdrFcShort( 0x8 ),  /* Alpha Stack size/offset = 8 */
#endif
/* 16 */  0x8,     /* FC_LONG */
        0x0,    /* 0 */

        0x0
          }
      };

static const MIDL_TYPE_FORMAT_STRING __MIDL_TypeFormatString =
      {
          0,
          {

        0x0
          }
      };

const CInterfaceProxyVtbl * _MyMidlExperiment_ProxyVtblList[]=
{
    ( CInterfaceProxyVtbl *) &_IMyInterfaceProxyVtbl,
    0
};

const CInterfaceStubVtbl * _MyMidlExperiment_StubVtblList[] =
{
    ( CInterfaceStubVtbl *) &_IMyInterfaceStubVtbl,
    0
};

PCInterfaceName const _MyMidlExperiment_InterfaceNamesList[] =
{
    "IMyInterface",
    0
};
```

LISTING 11.6 Continued

```c
#define _MyMidlExperiment_CHECK_IID(n)   \
  IID_GENERIC_CHECK_IID( _MyMidlExperiment, pIID, n)

int __stdcall _MyMidlExperiment_IID_Lookup( const IID * pIID,
                                             int * pIndex )
{

    if(!_MyMidlExperiment_CHECK_IID(0))
        {
        *pIndex = 0;
        return 1;
        }

    return 0;
}

const ExtendedProxyFileInfo MyMidlExperiment_ProxyFileInfo =
{
    (PCInterfaceProxyVtblList *) &
        _MyMidlExperiment_ProxyVtblList,
    (PCInterfaceStubVtblList *) &
        _MyMidlExperiment_StubVtblList,
    (const PCInterfaceName * ) &
        _MyMidlExperiment_InterfaceNamesList,
    0, // no delegation
    & _MyMidlExperiment_IID_Lookup,
    1,
    2
};
```

The Registration File

Listing 11.7 shows the registration file for COM+ classes that uses standard marshaling.

LISTING 11.7 Sample Registration File for Standard Marshaling

```
[HKEY_CLASSES_ROOT \ CLSID \ {my-proxy-stub-clsid}]
@="IMyInterface proxy/stub factory"

[HKEY_CLASSES_ROOT \ CLSID \ {my-proxy-stub-clsid} \
  InprocServer32]
@="{my-proxy-stub-module-path}"

[HKEY_CLASSES_ROOT \ CLSID \ {my-proxy-stub-clsid} \
  InprocServer32]
@="Both" or other
```

LISTING 11.7   Continued

```
[HKEY_CLASSES_ROOT \ Interface \ {my-interfaces-iid}]
@="IMyInterface"

[HKEY_CLASSES_ROOT \ Interface \ {my-interfaces-iid } \
   ProxyStubClsid32]
@="{my-proxy-stub-clsid}"

[HKEY_CLASSES_ROOT \ Interface \ {my-interfaces-iid } \
   NumMethods]
@="x"
```

Converting the MIDL Output Files

Now the important thing—how do you convert these MIDL output files into the proxy stub and register the proxy stub? Listing 11.8 shows the two commands that you should use to compile-link and register the proxy stub. Only one DLL file contains both proxy and stub. Hence, the same DLL should be present on the client and server. Also, ATL allows you to put the proxy/stub in the same DLL as the real COM objects in case of cross-apartment needs. If you want to register the proxy on another machine, you must copy the marshalserverps.dll to the machine and register it with Regsvr32.

LISTING 11.8   Compile-Link and Register the Proxy Stub

```
nmake /f marshalserverps.mk
regsvr32 marshalserverps.dll
```

Listing 11.9 is an interesting control program that can show the different results for when the proxy stub is not installed and when the proxy stub is installed.

LISTING 11.9   The Results of an Unregistered Proxy Stub

```
#include <windows.h>
#include <iostream>
#include "marshalserver\\marshalserver.h"
#include "marshalserver\\marshalserver_i.c"

char s[1024];

HRESULT GetUnknown(WCHAR * strProgID, IUnknown ** ppunknown)
{
  CLSID clsid;
  HRESULT hresult = ::CLSIDFromProgID(strProgID, &clsid);
  if (FAILED(hresult))
  {
```

LISTING 11.9 Continued

```cpp
    // CLSIDFromProgID failed
    std::cout << "CLSIDFromProgID failed = "
            << _ltoa(hresult, s, 16) << std::endl;
    ::DebugBreak();
    return hresult;
  }

  hresult = ::CoCreateInstance(clsid, NULL, CLSCTX_SERVER,
                          IID_IUnknown, (void **)ppunknown);
  if (FAILED(hresult))
  {
    // CoCreateInstance failed
    std::cout << "CoCreateInstance failed = "
            << _ltoa(hresult, s, 16) << std::endl;
    ::DebugBreak();
    return hresult;
  }

  return S_OK;
};

HRESULT GetInterface(IUnknown * punknown, REFIID riid,
                     IUnknown ** ppunknown)
{
  HRESULT hresult = punknown->QueryInterface(riid,
                                        (void **)ppunknown);
  if (FAILED(hresult))
  {
    // QueryInterface failed
    std::cout << "QueryInterface failed = "
            << _ltoa(hresult, s, 16) << std::endl;
    ::DebugBreak();
    return hresult;
  }

  return S_OK;
};

int main()
{
  CoInitialize(NULL);
  std::cout << "Start" << std::endl;

  IUnknown * punknown;
  HRESULT hresult = GetUnknown(L"MarshalClass.MarshalClass.1",
                                &punknown);
  if (FAILED(hresult))
  {
    // GetUnknown failed
```

LISTING **11.9**   Continued

```
    return hresult;
  }

  IMarshalClass * pmc;
  hresult = GetInterface(punknown, IID_IMarshalClass,
                         (IUnknown **)&pmc);
  if (FAILED(hresult))
  {
    // GetUnknown failed
    return hresult;
  }

  std::cout << "End" << std::endl;
  CoUninitialize();
  return 0;
}
```

If you run Listing 11.9 before registering the proxy stub, the call to
IUnknown::QueryInterface() will return 0x80004002 or E_NOINTERFACE. This is somewhat misleading because the interface exists, but the interface cannot be marshaled
between processes. If you've already registered your proxy stub and want to unregister
the proxy stub, run the Regsvr32 utility with the /U parameter. After you register your
proxy-stub DLL, the code in Listing 11.9 should run without error. Additional standard
marshaling code is available on the CD-ROM that accompanies this book. It can be
found in the marshaling subdirectory in the chapter11 directory.

Custom Marshaling

Generally, it is acceptable to use standard marshaling, but there are times when a more
efficient custom marshaler is required. A good example of when you would want to use
custom marshaling is when you are passing a value or when something is read-only and
will never change. In these cases, there is no need to call the real object anymore since
the proxy has stored its state. An object can implement custom marshaling by exposing
an IMarshal interface. Listing 11.10 shows the definition of the IMarshal interface.

LISTING **11.10**   Definition of the IMarshal Interface

```
interface IMarshal : IUnknown
{
  HRESULT GetUnmarshalClass([in] REFIID riid,
    [in, unique] void * pv,
    [in] DWORD dwDestContext,
    [in, unique] void * pvDestContext,
```

LISTING 11.10 Continued

```
    [in] DWORD mshlflags,
    [out] CLSID * pCid);
  HRESULT GetMarshalSizeMax([in] REFIID riid,
    [in, unique] void * pv,
    [in] DWORD dwDestContext,
    [in, unique] void * pvDestContext,
    [in] DWORD mshlflags,
    [out] DWORD * pSize);
  HRESULT MarshalInterface([in, unique] IStream * pStm,
    [in] REFIID riid,
    [in, unique] void * pv,
    [in] DWORD dwDestContext,
    [in, unique] void * pvDestContext,
    [in] DWORD mshlflags);
  HRSEULT UnmarshalInterface([in, unique] IStream * pStm,
    [in] REFIID riid, [out] void ** ppv);
  HRESULT ReleaseMarshalData([in, unique] IStream * pStm);
  HRESULT DisconnectObject([in] DWORD dwReserved);
}
```

The advantage of custom marshaling is that you can choose from a variety of inter-process or network communication protocols, including but not limited to Microsoft RPC, named pipes, TCP (streams), UDP (datagrams), and HTTP. In contrast, standard marshaling uses only Microsoft RPC.

The next example uses File I/O and synchronization events to perform marshaling between the proxy and server object (see Figure 11.2). I've created three components in this example to demonstrate custom marshaling: an ATL object server, an ATL proxy, and a Win32 client.

FIGURE 11.2

Custom proxy.

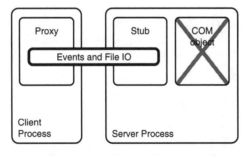

The ATL object server is more complex than it needs to be because I've implemented a lot of unnecessary code. For example, it was completely unnecessary to implement the IMyInterface interface because the marshaler is actually implementing the method calls. I implemented the COM+ object for the benefit of readability. The COM+ object in Figure 11.2 is crossed out to reflect that there is no reason to implement the COM+ object in the server.

Declaring the Object Class

Listing 11.11 shows the declaration of the object class. Two data members hold information necessary to do the marshaling. The m_szEventname member variable contains the name of the event that will trigger marshaling of data. The m_szFilename member variable contains the name of the file that will contain the data being marshaled.

LISTING **11.11**   Declaration of the Object Class

```
// myinterface.h: Definition of the MyInterface class
//
//////////////////////////////////////////////////////////////

#if !defined(AFX_MYINTERFACE_H)
#define AFX_MYINTERFACE_H

#if _MSC_VER >= 1000
#pragma once
#endif // _MSC_VER >= 1000

#include "resource.h"       // main symbols

//////////////////////////////////////////////////////////////
// MyInterface

struct OBJECTMARSHALDATA
{
  char szFilename[256];
  char szEventname[256];
};

class MyInterface :
  public IMyInterface,
  public CComObjectRoot,
  public CComCoClass<MyInterface,&CLSID_MyInterface>,
  public IMarshal
{
public:
  MyInterface() { m_recordnumber = 0; }
BEGIN_COM_MAP(MyInterface)
  COM_INTERFACE_ENTRY(IMyInterface)
  COM_INTERFACE_ENTRY(IMarshal)
END_COM_MAP()
//DECLARE_NOT_AGGREGATABLE(MyInterface)
// Remove the comment from the line above if you don't want
// your object to support aggregation.

DECLARE_REGISTRY_RESOURCEID(IDR_MyInterface)
```

LISTING **11.11** Continued

```
// IMyInterface
public:
  STDMETHOD(Next)(long *);
  STDMETHOD(get_propertythree)(/*[out, retval]*/ long *pVal);
  STDMETHOD(get_propertytwo)(/*[out, retval]*/ long *pVal);
  STDMETHOD(get_propertyone)(/*[out, retval]*/ long *pVal);
public:
  static long m_recordnumber;

// IMarshal
public:
  STDMETHOD(GetUnmarshalClass)(REFIID, LPVOID, DWORD, LPVOID,
                               DWORD, LPCLSID);
  STDMETHOD(GetMarshalSizeMax)(REFIID, LPVOID, DWORD, LPVOID,
                               DWORD, LPDWORD);
  STDMETHOD(MarshalInterface)(LPSTREAM, REFIID, LPVOID, DWORD,
                              LPVOID, DWORD);
  STDMETHOD(UnmarshalInterface)(LPSTREAM, REFIID, LPVOID *);
  STDMETHOD(ReleaseMarshalData)(LPSTREAM);
  STDMETHOD(DisconnectObject)(DWORD);
private:
  char m_szEventname[256];
public:
  static char m_szFilename[256];

};

#endif // !defined(AFX_MYINTERFACE_H)
```

The object server implements both the IMyInterface and IMarshal interfaces.

Defining the Object Class

Listing 11.12 shows the definition of the object class. I've intentionally left out the code that implements the IMyInterface interface because the code will never be called.

LISTING **11.12** Definition of the Object Class

```
// myinterface.cpp : Implementation of CObjectApp and DLL
// registration.

#include "stdafx.h"
#include "object.h"
#include "myinterface.h"
#include <fstream>
#include "..\\proxy\\proxy.h"
#include "..\\proxy\\proxy_i.c"
```

LISTING 11.12 Continued

```cpp
#include <process.h>

///////////////////////////////////////////////////////////
//

static long array[][3] = {{1,2,3}, {4,5,6}, {7,8,9}};

char MyInterface::m_szFilename[256] = {0};
long MyInterface::m_recordnumber = 0;


///////////////////////////////////////////////////////////
// Implementation of IMarshal

STDMETHODIMP MyInterface::GetUnmarshalClass(REFIID riid,
  LPVOID pv, DWORD dwCtx, LPVOID pvCtx, DWORD dwFlags,
  LPCLSID pClsID)
{
  ATLTRACE(_T("MyInterface::GetUnmarshalClass\n"));
  // The event and file are only known on the same machine.
  if (dwCtx & MSHCTX_DIFFERENTMACHINE)
  {
    return CO_E_CANT_REMOTE;
  }

  *pClsID=CLSID_marshalproxy;
  return S_OK;
}

STDMETHODIMP MyInterface::GetMarshalSizeMax(REFIID riid,
  LPVOID pv, DWORD dwDestCtx, LPVOID pvDestCtx, DWORD dwFlags,
  LPDWORD pdwSize)
{
  ATLTRACE(_T("MyInterface::GetMarshalSizeMax\n"));
  if (dwDestCtx & MSHCTX_DIFFERENTMACHINE)
  {
    return CO_E_CANT_REMOTE;
  }
  *pdwSize=sizeof(OBJECTMARSHALDATA);
  return S_OK;
}

void EventTrigger(void * marshaldata);

STDMETHODIMP MyInterface::MarshalInterface(LPSTREAM pstm,
  REFIID riid, LPVOID pv, DWORD dwDestCtx, LPVOID pvDestCtx,
  DWORD dwFlags)
{
  ATLTRACE(_T("MyInterface::MarshalInterface\n"));
  OBJECTMARSHALDATA marshaldata;
```

LISTING 11.12   Continued

```
if (dwDestCtx & MSHCTX_DIFFERENTMACHINE)
  {
    return CO_E_CANT_REMOTE;
  }

  strcpy(m_szFilename, "c:\\Hello.MAR");
  strcpy(marshaldata.szFilename, m_szFilename);
  strcpy(m_szEventname, "MY_EVENT");
  strcpy(marshaldata.szEventname, m_szEventname);
  std::ofstream os;
  os.open(m_szFilename, std::ios_base::out |
                        std::ios_base::trunc |
                        std::ios_base::binary);
  os << array[m_recordnumber][0] << " "
     << array[m_recordnumber][1] << " "
     << array[m_recordnumber][2];
  os.close();


  _beginthread(EventTrigger, 0, (void *)&marshaldata);

  return pstm->Write((void *)&marshaldata,
                     sizeof(OBJECTMARSHALDATA), NULL);
}

STDMETHODIMP MyInterface::UnmarshalInterface(LPSTREAM pstm,
  REFIID riid, LPVOID *pv)
{
  ATLTRACE(_T("MyInterface::UnmarshalInterface\n"));
  return E_NOTIMPL;
}

STDMETHODIMP MyInterface::ReleaseMarshalData(LPSTREAM pstm)
{
  ATLTRACE(_T("MyInterface::ReleaseMarshalData\n"));
  return E_NOTIMPL;
}

STDMETHODIMP MyInterface::DisconnectObject(DWORD dwReserved)
{
  ATLTRACE(_T("MyInterface::DisconnectObject\n"));

  char sz[256];
  strcpy(sz, m_szEventname);
  strcat(sz, "_STOP");
  HANDLE hevent = ::OpenEvent(EVENT_ALL_ACCESS, TRUE, sz);
  ::SetEvent(hevent);
  ::CloseHandle(hevent);
```

LISTING 11.12   Continued

```
  return S_OK;
}

void EventTrigger(void * marshaldata)
{
  SECURITY_ATTRIBUTES sa;
  SECURITY_DESCRIPTOR sd;
  sa.nLength = sizeof(SECURITY_ATTRIBUTES);
  sa.bInheritHandle = TRUE;
  sa.lpSecurityDescriptor = &sd;
  if(!InitializeSecurityDescriptor(&sd,
        SECURITY_DESCRIPTOR_REVISION))
  {
    ExitThread(1);
  }
  if(!SetSecurityDescriptorDacl(&sd, TRUE, (PACL)NULL, FALSE))
  {
    ExitThread(1);
  }
  OBJECTMARSHALDATA * p = (OBJECTMARSHALDATA*) marshaldata;
  HANDLE hevent = ::CreateEvent(&sa, FALSE, FALSE,
                                p->szEventname);
  char sz[256];
  strcpy(sz, p->szEventname);
  strcat(sz, "_ACK");
  HANDLE hack = ::CreateEvent(&sa, FALSE, FALSE, sz);
  strcpy(sz, p->szEventname);
  strcat(sz, "_STOP");
  HANDLE hstop = ::CreateEvent(&sa, FALSE, FALSE, sz);

  HANDLE harray[2] = {hevent, hstop};
  while (1)
  {
    DWORD dw = ::WaitForMultipleObjects(2, harray, FALSE,
                                        INFINITE);
    if (dw!=WAIT_OBJECT_0)
    {
      break;
    }
    std::ifstream is;
    is.open(MyInterface::m_szFilename,
          std::ios_base::in | std::ios_base::binary);
    long recordnumber;
    is >> recordnumber;
    is.close();

    if (recordnumber==-1)
    {
      MyInterface::m_recordnumber++;
```

LISTING 11.12 Continued

```
    if (MyInterface::m_recordnumber>2)
    {
      MyInterface::m_recordnumber = 0;
    }
    recordnumber = MyInterface::m_recordnumber;
  }
  else
  {
    (recordnumber)++;
    if ((recordnumber>2) || (recordnumber<0))
    {
      recordnumber = 0;
    }
    MyInterface::m_recordnumber = recordnumber;
  }

  std::ofstream os;
  os.open(MyInterface::m_szFilename,
          std::ios_base::out | std::ios_base::trunc |
          std::ios_base::binary);
  os << array[MyInterface::m_recordnumber][0] << " "
     << array[MyInterface::m_recordnumber][1] << " "
     << array[MyInterface::m_recordnumber][2];
  os << " " << recordnumber;
  os.close();

  ::SetEvent(hack);
}

::CloseHandle(hevent);
::CloseHandle(hack);
::CloseHandle(hstop);
}
```

When you attempt to create the out-of-process server, COM+ will call the
`MyInterface::GetMarshalSizeMax()`, `MyInterface::GetUnmarshalClass()`, and
`MyInterface::MarshalInterface()` methods. The `MyInterface::GetUnmarshalClass()`
method should return the `CLSID` of the proxy. The important call is to the
`MyInterface::MarshalInterface()` method. This method must initiate the marshaling
mechanism. In this case, I'm returning an `OBJECTMARSHALDATA` structure that holds the filename where I will marshal data elements and the event name that will trigger the methods.

Defining the Proxy Class

After returning from the `MtInterface::MarshalInterface()` method, COM+ then creates the proxy and calls the `marshalproxy::UnmarshalInterface()` method. The proxy

receives the `IStream` in which I saved the `OBJECTMARSHALDATA` structure. The proxy retrieves the data from the `IStream` object and saves the data of this structure in local storage for later use. The proxy class declaration is almost identical to the object class declaration.

Listing 11.13 shows the definition of the proxy class.

LISTING 11.13   Definition of the Proxy Class

```cpp
// marshalproxy.cpp : Implementation of CProxyApp and DLL
// registration.

#include "stdafx.h"
#include "proxy.h"
#include "marshalproxy.h"
#include "..\\object\\object_i.c"
#include "..\\object\\myinterface.h"
#include <fstream>

/////////////////////////////////////////////////////////////////
//

STDMETHODIMP marshalproxy::get_propertyone(long * pVal)
{
  ATLTRACE(_T("marshalproxy::get_propertyone\n"));

  std::ifstream is;
  is.open(m_szFilename, std::ios_base::in |
                        std::ios_base::binary);
  is >> *pVal;
  is.close();

  return S_OK;
}

STDMETHODIMP marshalproxy::get_propertytwo(long * pVal)
{
  ATLTRACE(_T("marshalproxy::get_propertytwo\n"));

  std::ifstream is;
  is.open(m_szFilename, std::ios_base::in |
                        std::ios_base::binary);
  is >> *pVal;
  is >> *pVal;
  is.close();

  return S_OK;
}
```

LISTING 11.13   Continued

```cpp
STDMETHODIMP marshalproxy::get_propertythree(long * pVal)
{
  ATLTRACE(_T("marshalproxy::get_propertythree\n"));

  std::ifstream is;
  is.open(m_szFilename, std::ios_base::in |
                        std::ios_base::binary);
  is >> *pVal;
  is >> *pVal;
  is >> *pVal;
  is.close();

  return S_OK;
}

STDMETHODIMP marshalproxy::Next(long * precordnumber)
{
  ATLTRACE(_T("marshalproxy::Next\n"));
  long recordnumber;
  if (precordnumber==0)
  {
    recordnumber = -1;
  }
  else
  {
    recordnumber = *precordnumber;
  }

  std::ofstream os;
  os.open(m_szFilename, std::ios_base::out |
                        std::ios_base::trunc |
                        std::ios_base::binary);
  os << recordnumber;
  os.close();

  HANDLE hevent = ::OpenEvent(EVENT_ALL_ACCESS, TRUE,
                              m_szEventname);
  ::SetEvent(hevent);
  ::CloseHandle(hevent);
  char sz[256];
  strcpy(sz, m_szEventname);
  strcat(sz, "_ACK");
  hevent = ::OpenEvent(EVENT_ALL_ACCESS, TRUE, sz);
  ::WaitForSingleObject(hevent, INFINITE);
  ::CloseHandle(hevent);

  if (precordnumber!=0)
  {
    std::ifstream is;
```

LISTING 11.13   Continued

```cpp
    is.open(m_szFilename, std::ios_base::in |
                          std::ios_base::binary);
    is >> recordnumber;
    is >> recordnumber;
    is >> recordnumber;
    is >> recordnumber;
    is.close();
    *precordnumber = recordnumber;
  }

  return E_NOTIMPL;
}

/////////////////////////////////////////////////////////////////
// Implementation of IMarshal

STDMETHODIMP marshalproxy::GetUnmarshalClass(REFIID riid,
  LPVOID pv, DWORD dwCtx, LPVOID pvCtx, DWORD dwFlags,
  LPCLSID pClsID)
{
  ATLTRACE(_T("marshalproxy::GetUnmarshalClass\n"));

  return E_NOTIMPL;
}

STDMETHODIMP marshalproxy::GetMarshalSizeMax(REFIID riid,
  LPVOID pv, DWORD dwDestCtx, LPVOID pvDestCtx, DWORD dwFlags,
  LPDWORD pdwSize)
{
  ATLTRACE(_T("marshalproxy::GetMarshalSizeMax\n"));

  if (dwDestCtx & MSHCTX_DIFFERENTMACHINE)
  {
    return CO_E_CANT_REMOTE;
  }
  *pdwSize=sizeof(OBJECTMARSHALDATA);
  return S_OK;
}

STDMETHODIMP marshalproxy::MarshalInterface(LPSTREAM pstm,
  REFIID riid, LPVOID pv, DWORD dwDestCtx, LPVOID pvDestCtx,
  DWORD dwFlags)
{
  ATLTRACE(_T("marshalproxy::MarshalInterface\n"));

  return E_NOTIMPL;
}

STDMETHODIMP marshalproxy::UnmarshalInterface(LPSTREAM pstm,
```

LISTING 11.13 Continued

```
  REFIID riid, LPVOID *pv)
{
  ATLTRACE(_T("marshalproxy::UnmarshalInterface\n"));

  OBJECTMARSHALDATA objectmarshal;

  pstm->Read((void *)&objectmarshal,
             sizeof(OBJECTMARSHALDATA), NULL);
  strcpy(m_szFilename, objectmarshal.szFilename);
  strcpy(m_szEventname, objectmarshal.szEventname);

  return InternalQueryInterface(this, _GetEntries(),
                                riid, pv);
}

STDMETHODIMP marshalproxy::ReleaseMarshalData(LPSTREAM pstm)
{
  ATLTRACE(_T("marshalproxy::ReleaseMarshalData\n"));

  return S_OK;
}

STDMETHODIMP marshalproxy::DisconnectObject(DWORD dwReserved)
{
  ATLTRACE(_T("marshalproxy::DisconnectObject\n"));

  return E_NOTIMPL;
}
```

The magic of the proxy is pretty transparent. In this example, the data was marshaled by saving to a file and unmarshaled by reading from it. The three proxy data accessors look into this file to read the data. The one proxy method, marshalproxy::Next(), saves the input data into the file and triggers the object server by calling the synchronization event. When the object server is finished, it signals the proxy server by calling a second synchronization event. The proxy is then able to read the output from the file.

The example here implements a very inefficient type of marshaling. File I/O does not compare in performance to the standard marshaler, and this type of marshaling will not work over the network, but the principles of how to do the marshaling should be well understood.

The server object is spawning a thread to listen to client requests, which are generated by the proxy. The proxy signals the event to get the result.

The Client

The last important part is the client, as shown in Listing 11.14. The client will instantiate the server object and then call its methods.

LISTING 11.14   The Client Code

```cpp
#include <windows.h>
#include <iostream>
#include "object\\object.h"
#include "object\\object_i.c"

char s[1024];

HRESULT GetUnknown(WCHAR * strProgID, IUnknown ** ppunknown)
{
  CLSID clsid;
  HRESULT hresult = ::CLSIDFromProgID(strProgID, &clsid);
  if (FAILED(hresult))
  {
    // CLSIDFromProgID failed
    std::cout << "CLSIDFromProgID failed = "
              << _ltoa(hresult, s, 16)
              << std::endl;
    ::DebugBreak();
    return hresult;
  }

  IClassFactory * pCF;
  hresult = ::CoGetClassObject(clsid, CLSCTX_SERVER, NULL,
                               IID_IClassFactory,
                               (void **)&pCF);

  if (FAILED(hresult))
  {
    *ppunknown = 0;
    std::cout << "CoGetClassObject failed = "
              << _ltoa(hresult, s, 16) << std::endl;
    ::DebugBreak();
    return hresult;
  }

  hresult = pCF->CreateInstance(NULL, IID_IUnknown,
                                (void **)ppunknown);
  pCF->Release();

  if (FAILED(hresult))
  {
    *ppunknown = 0;
    std::cout << "CreateInstance failed = "
```

LISTING 11.14   Continued

```cpp
                << _ltoa(hresult, s, 16) << std::endl;
    ::DebugBreak();
    return hresult;
  }

  return S_OK;
};

HRESULT GetInterface(IUnknown * punknown, REFIID riid,
                     IUnknown ** ppunknown)
{
  HRESULT hresult = punknown->QueryInterface(riid,
                                      (void **)ppunknown);
  if (FAILED(hresult))
  {
    // QueryInterface failed
    std::cout << "QueryInterface failed = "
              << _ltoa(hresult, s, 16) << std::endl;
    ::DebugBreak();
    return hresult;
  }

  return S_OK;
};

int main()
{
  CoInitialize(NULL);
  std::cout << "Start" << std::endl;

  IUnknown * punknown;
  HRESULT hresult = GetUnknown(L"Object.MyInterface.1",
                                &punknown);
  if (FAILED(hresult))
  {
    // GetUnknown failed
    return hresult;
  }

  IMyInterface * p_tor;
  hresult = GetInterface(punknown, IID_IMyInterface,
                         (IUnknown **)&p_tor);
  if (FAILED(hresult))
  {
    // GetUnknown failed
    return hresult;
  }

  long l[3] = {0};
```

LISTING 11.14 Continued

```
hresult = p_tor->get_propertyone(&l[0]);
hresult = p_tor->get_propertytwo(&l[1]);
hresult = p_tor->get_propertythree(&l[2]);
std::cout << l[0] << " " << l[1] << " " << l[2]
          << std::endl;
p_tor->Next(NULL);
hresult = p_tor->get_propertyone(&l[0]);
hresult = p_tor->get_propertytwo(&l[1]);
hresult = p_tor->get_propertythree(&l[2]);
std::cout << l[0] << " " << l[1] << " " << l[2]
          << std::endl;

std::cout << "End" << std::endl;
CoUninitialize();
return 0;
}
```

When the client calls `IClassFactory::CreateInstance()`, COM+ calls the
`MyInterface::GetMarshalSizeMax()`, `MyInterface::GetUnmarshalClass()`, and
`MyInterface::MarshalInterface()` methods in the object server, followed by
`marshalproxy::UnmarshalInterface()`in the proxy. After this code has been called,
the marshaling process should be set up, and it now becomes the proxy and server's
responsibility to marshal data between the client process and server process. Additional
code necessary to run the sample in this chapter is available on this book's CD-ROM as
custommarshal. It can be found in the custommarshal subdirectory in the chapter11
directory.

Summary

Marshaling is one of the most difficult and hidden parts of COM+, and you should take
great care in understanding it. In this chapter, you learned what marshaling is and what is
under the hood of marshaling. The basics of the RPC mechanisms are given for how
marshaling works behind the scenes.

The type libraries and differences among them were discussed. Reasons for using
each one were given, and from this you should be able to make the choice in any given
situation.

Standard and custom marshaling were then explained with sample code to demonstrate
their capabilities. This code provides the understanding necessary to jump in and get
started using the marshaling interface.

COM Security

CHAPTER 12

COM Versus DCOM Security

This chapter examines how to work with COM+ security in order to allow and deny access to a COM+ server. I'm covering plain vanilla COM security in this chapter because it's an important topic to master before some of the distributed topics are addressed (especially MTS and Transactions). Later, in chapter 18, "COM+ Security," the COM+-specific security issues are covered.

Before the release of DCOM, object security was not an important issue. Because objects could not access objects across the network, you only had to worry about objects on the same machine. Controlling objects on one machine is fairly easy, but managing them across a 200-workstation network is slightly more difficult than rocket science, unless you have built-in security as provided by DCOM.

A common misunderstanding is that DCOM provides security and that COM does not provide security. This is incorrect because the security added with the release of DCOM applies just as equally to legacy COM objects, distributed COM (DCOM) objects, and non-distributed COM objects. It is possible to disable distributed COM and enable COM objects to use the DCOM security. The DCOM security and distributed objects can be used independently of each other.

I use COM security and DCOM security as synonyms. They are in fact the same. When I refer to COM security prior to the introduction of DCOM security, I say exactly that, "COM security prior to DCOM." In order to understand that DCOM security and COM security are one and the same, think of the DCOM package as having introduced two subsystems to COM: a remoting subsystem and a security subsystem.

COM Security and SSPI

COM implements security using Microsoft's Security Support Provider Interface (SSPI). This enables COM to use any security provider that exposes itself with the SSPI interface. At this point, you might be asking, "Why doesn't COM just access the security protocol directly?" Microsoft's long-term strategy is to make COM available across a variety of platforms, including platforms that do not implement security, such as Macintosh and UNIX.

Another important reason why COM doesn't access security protocol directly is that COM is really just an object-oriented version of DCE RPC (Distributed Computing Environment Remote Procedure Call). DCE RPC is also designed in such a manner that it can take advantage of a variety of security providers.

Security, more appropriately called NT LAN Manager Security Service Provider (NTLMSSP), was the first security provider that exposed itself using an SSPI interface. The NTLMSSP provider is available on all NT workstations and servers and is, therefore, the primary candidate (and sometimes the only candidate) available for use with DCOM security. In order to continue the discussion of DCOM security, you begin by learning the security fundamentals.

The default protocol for network authentication in Windows 2000 is the Kerberos v5 authentication protocol. An emerging authentication standard, the Kerberos protocol provides a foundation for interoperability. It also enhances the security of enterprisewide network authentication. Key components of the protocol's implementation in Windows 2000 include the following:

- Integration of initial authentication with the Winlogon single sign-on architecture.
- Use of Active Directory, the directory service included in Windows 2000, in the Windows 2000 domain as the domain's security account database.
- Implementation of the Kerberos client as a Windows 2000 security provider through the Security Support Provider Interface (SSPI).

Windows Security

Windows provides security to a variety of object types: files, devices, processes, threads, semaphores, shared memory, registry keys, and more. In order to implement this security, every newly made object is created with a security descriptor. It would be very difficult to manage every object over every NT workstation, so NT simplifies security by dividing NT workstations into domains.

The combination of Owner (owning SID), list of principals (DACL), and list of principals to audit (SACL) is called a *security descriptor (SD)*. A security descriptor completely describes the security policy in terms of object owner, access, and auditing. The security descriptor (in its self-relative form) is a memory structure that references its elements (DACL, SACL, and so on) using offsets instead of pointers. This self-relative security descriptor can thus simply be written into a registry key and safely retrieved.

Developing Security with Domains

You can think of a domain as a group of networked machines. In the group of networked machines, one machine is nominated as the primary domain controller. This is the centrally managed authentication controller that authenticates access to networked resources.

Multiple domains can exist in a trust relationship. That is, if a security principal cannot be authenticated within a domain, the primary domain controller can attempt to authenticate the security principal against a trusted domain. This enables large network configurations to be managed on a smaller scale, with smaller domains.

Providing an authentication authority with the user identification and password confirms secured network access. Unless the authentication authority is specified, the network access will be verified using the local registration database and the domain registration database.

Security Descriptors

As mentioned earlier in this section, every newly made securable object is created with a security descriptor. The security descriptor is made up of two security IDs (SIDs) and two access control lists (ACLs). The two SIDs represent the securable object's owner and owner group. The two ACLs are the discretionary access control list (DACL) and the system access control list (SACL). You learn about ACLs, DACLs, and SACLs in more detail later in this chapter.

When you create a new securable object in NT, you should pass a SECURITY_ATTRIBUTES structure to the object. The SECURITY_ATTRIBUTES contains the SECURITY_DESCRIPTOR structure. The definition of both of these structures is shown in Listing 12.1.

LISTING 12.1   SECURITY_ATTRIBUTES and SECURITY_DESCRIPTOR Definitions

```
typedef struct _SECURITY_ATTRIBUTES
{
    DWORD nLength;
    LPVOID lpSecurityDescriptor;
    BOOL bInheritHandle;
} SECURITY_ATTRIBUTES, *PSECURITY_ATTRIBUTES, *LPSECURITY_ATTRIBUTES;

typedef struct _SECURITY_DESCRIPTOR
{
    UCHAR Revision;
    UCHAR Sbz1;
    SECURITY_DESCRIPTOR_CONTROL Control;
    PSID Owner;
    PSID Group;
    PACL Sacl;
    PACL Dacl;
} SECURITY_DESCRIPTOR, *PISECURITY_DESCRIPTOR;
```

You should not try to work directly with the SECURITY_DESCRIPTOR structure; instead, use the API functions that enable you to read and write to a security descriptor. The API functions will continue to work even while the structure of the SECURITY_DESCRIPTOR changes. These functions include

GetSecurityDescriptorDacl()

GetSecurityDescriptorSacl()

GetSecurityDescriptorGroup()

GetSecurityDescriptorLength()

GetSecurityDescriptorOwner()

InitializeSecurityDescriptor()

```
IsValidSecurityDescriptor()

MakeAbsoluteSD()

MakeSelfRelativeSD()

SetSecurityDescriptorDacl()

SetSecurityDescriptorSacl()

SetSecurityDescriptorGroup()

SetSecurityDescriptorOwner()
```

Two types of security descriptors are used in NT:

- The absolute security descriptor has pointers to the ACL structures.
- The self-relative security descriptor is self-contained with embedded ACL.

The advantage of the self-relative security descriptor is that it can be transmitted electronically (because of its flat format) or saved to a file or the registry. Two functions enable you to convert between the two types of security descriptors: `MakeSelfRelativeSD()` and `MakeAbsoluteSD()`.

Chapter 8, "COM and the Registry," showed how to save and load self-relative security descriptors in the registry. Another important task you must be able to perform is saving these self-relative security descriptors in files. Listing 12.2 shows how to do that.

Listing 12.2   Save a Security Descriptor in a File

```cpp
#include <windows.h>
#include <fstream.h>

//-------------------------
// SaveSecurityDescriptorToFile
//-------------------------
int SaveSecurityDescriptorToFile(PSECURITY_DESCRIPTOR pSD,
                                 ofstream & ofs)
{
    // convert the security descriptor to
    // self-relative security description
    PSECURITY_DESCRIPTOR pSRSD = NULL;
    DWORD cbSD = 0;
    if (!::MakeSelfRelativeSD(pSD, pSRSD, &cbSD))
    {
        DWORD dw = ::GetLastError();
        if( dw != ERROR_INSUFFICIENT_BUFFER )
        {
            if ( dw != ERROR_BAD_DESCRIPTOR_FORMAT)
            {
                std::cout << "Error ::MakeSelfRelativeSD "
```

LISTING 12.2   Continued

```
                        << dw << endl;
                return 0;
            }
            else
            {
                pSRSD = pSD;
            }
        }
        else
        {
            pSRSD = (PSECURITY_DESCRIPTOR)
                    ::LocalAlloc(LPTR, cbSD);
            if (!::MakeSelfRelativeSD(pSD, pSRSD, &cbSD))
            {
                std::cout << "Error ::MakeSelfRelativeSD "
                        << ::GetLastError() << endl;
                return 0;
            }
        }
    }

    // save the self-relative security description
    // in a file
    ofs.write((char *)pSRSD,
            ::GetSecurityDescriptorLength(pSRSD));

    if((pSRSD != NULL) & (pSRSD != pSD))
    {
        ::LocalFree((HLOCAL) pSRSD);
    }

    return 0;
}

int main(int , char **)
{
    const int cSD = 8096;
    UCHAR ucBuf[cSD] = {0};
    DWORD dw = cSD;
    PSECURITY_DESCRIPTOR psd = (PSECURITY_DESCRIPTOR)&ucBuf;

    HKEY hkey;
    LONG l = ::RegOpenKeyEx(HKEY_CLASSES_ROOT,
                        "MyObject.MyObject", 0,
                        KEY_READ, &hkey);

    l = ::RegGetKeySecurity(hkey,
                        OWNER_SECURITY_INFORMATION|
                        GROUP_SECURITY_INFORMATION|
```

LISTING 12.2   Continued

```
                        DACL_SECURITY_INFORMATION,
                        psd, &dw);

    ofstream ofs;
    ofs.open("C:\\HELLO.B", ios::binary+ios::trunc+ios::out);
    ::SaveSecurityDescriptorToFile(psd, ofs);
    ofs.close();

    return 0;
}
```

Listing 12.2 uses the RegGetKeySecurity() function to retrieve an existing security descriptor. Several other API functions enable you to create, retrieve, and save the security descriptor of various objects. Of special note is RegSetKeySecurity(), which saves self-relative security descriptors. They include the following:

CreateDirectory()	GetFileSecurity()
CreateDirectoryEx()	GetKernelObjectSecurity()
CreateEvent()	GetPrinter()
CreateFile()	GetPrivateObjectSecurity()
CreateFileMapping()	GetUserObjectSecurity()
CreateMailslot()	NetShareGetInfo()
CreateMutex()	NetShareSetInfo()
CreateNamedPipe()	QueryServiceObjectSecurity()
CreatePipe()	RegGetKeySecurity()
CreatePrivateObjectSecurity()	RegSetKeySecurity()
CreateProcess()	SetFileSecurity()
CreateProcessAsUser()	SetKernelObjectSecurity()
CreateRemoteThread()	SetPrinter()
CreateSemaphore()	SetPrivateObjectSecurity()
CreateThread()	SetServiceObjectSecurity()
CreateWaitableTime()	SetUserObjectSecurity()
DestroyPrivateObjectSecurity()	

Access Control Lists

An ACL is simply a list of zero or more access control entries (ACEs). Two types of ACLs are contained in a SECURITY_DESCRIPTOR structure. The first type is the discretionary ACL (DACL), which lists all the ACEs that deny and allow access to resources. The other is the system ACL (SACL), which specifies an auditing policy applied to resources. ACLs determine who has what type of access to a resource. The definition of the ACL structure is shown in Listing 12.3. The ACL structure is the header of an access-control list (ACL). A complete ACL consists of an ACL structure followed by an ordered list of zero or more access-control entries (ACEs).

LISTING 12.3 ACL Definition

```
typedef struct _ACL
{
    UCHAR AclRevision;
    UCHAR Sbz1;
    USHORT AclSize;
    USHORT AceCount;
    USHORT Sbz2;
} ACL, *PACL;
```

Access Control Entries

An ACE has three components: a type identifying the ACE as access-allowed or access-denied, an access mask, and an SID. Zero or more ACEs are contained in each ACL. This object specifies that a particular SID (which can be a user account or a group of users) has allow access or deny access (as identified by the type) for the access rights enumerated in the access mask. The definition of the ACE structure is shown in Listing 12.4.

LISTING 12.4 ACL and ACE Definitions

```
typedef struct _ACE_HEADER
{
    BYTE   AceType;
    BYTE   AceFlags;
    WORD   AceSize;
} ACE_HEADER, *PACE_HEADER;

#define ACCESS_ALLOWED_ACE_TYPE         (0x0)
#define ACCESS_DENIED_ACE_TYPE          (0x1)
#define SYSTEM_AUDIT_ACE_TYPE           (0x2)
#define SYSTEM_ALARM_ACE_TYPE           (0x3)

typedef struct _ACCESS_ALLOWED_ACE
{
    ACE_HEADER Header;
    ACCESS_MASK Mask;
    DWORD SidStart;
} ACCESS_ALLOWED_ACE, *PACCESS_ALLOWED_ACE;

typedef struct _ACCESS_DENIED_ACE
```

LISTING 12.4 Continued

```
{
    ACE_HEADER Header;
    ACCESS_MASK Mask;
    DWORD SidStart;
} ACCESS_DENIED_ACE, *PACCESS_DENIED_ACE;

typedef struct _SYSTEM_AUDIT_ACE
{
    ACE_HEADER Header;
    ACCESS_MASK Mask;
    DWORD SidStart;
} SYSTEM_AUDIT_ACE, *PSYSTEM_AUDIT_ACE;

typedef struct _SYSTEM_ALARM_ACE
{
    ACE_HEADER Header;
    ACCESS_MASK Mask;
    DWORD SidStart;
} SYSTEM_ALARM_ACE, *PSYSTEM_ALARM_ACE;
```

There are four types of ACEs: access allowed, access denied, system audit, and system alarm. Each ACE type is defined separately but has a common header.

Access Mask and Access Rights

An important member variable in the ACE structure is the access mask. The access mask is a 32-bit value where each bit is defined as follows:

0–15	Specific access rights
16–23	Standard access rights
16	DELETE
17	READ_CONTROL
18	WRITE_DAC
19	WRITE_OWNER
20	SYNCHRONIZE
24	ACCESS_SYSTEM_SECURITY
25	MAXIMUM_ALLOWED
26–27	Reserved
28–31	Generic access rights
28	GENERIC_ALL
29	GENERIC_EXECUTE
30	GENERIC_WRITE
31	GENERIC_READ

12

COM SECURITY

The generic and standard access rights apply to all objects, no matter what their object type. As their title implies, the specific access rights are specific to the securable object type. The specific access rights for the file object are shown in Table 12.1.

TABLE 12.1 Specific Access Rights for File Objects

File Object	*Access Rights*
FILE_READ_DATA	0x0001
FILE_WRITE_DATA	0x0002
FILE_APPEND_DATA	0x0004
FILE_READ_EA	0x0008
FILE_WRITE_EA	0x0010
FILE_EXECUTE	0x0020
FILE_READ_ATTRIBUTES	0x0080
FILE_WRITE_ATTRIBUTES	0x0100

The generic access rights can also be mapped to standard and specific access rights. The object type determines this mapping.

As with the SECURITY_DESCRIPTOR structure, you should not try to access the ACL structure directly, but instead use the API functions that enable you to read and write the structures. These functions include the following:

```
AddAccessAllowedAce()
AddAccessDeniedAce()
AddAce()
AddAuditAccessAce()
DeleteAce()
FindFirstFreeAce()
GetAce()
GetAclInformation()
InitializeAcl()
IsValidAcl()
SetAclInformation()
```

Listing 12.5 shows how you can read most of the values of a security descriptor, its ACLs, and its ACEs.

LISTING 12.5   Dump SECURITY_DESCRIPTOR Structure

```cpp
#include <windows.h>
#include <iostream>

int main(int, char **)
{
    const int   cSD = 8096;
    UCHAR       ucBuf[cSD] = {0};
    DWORD       dw = cSD;
    PSECURITY_DESCRIPTOR psd = (PSECURITY_DESCRIPTOR)&ucBuf;

    HKEY hkey;
    LONG l = ::RegOpenKeyEx(HKEY_CLASSES_ROOT,
                        "MyObject.MyObject", 0,
                        KEY_READ, &hkey);

    l = ::RegGetKeySecurity(hkey,
                    OWNER_SECURITY_INFORMATION|
                    GROUP_SECURITY_INFORMATION|
                    DACL_SECURITY_INFORMATION,
                    psd, &dw);

    l = ::RegCloseKey(hkey);
    std::cout << "SECURITY_DESCRIPTOR: " << psd << endl;

    BOOL bHasDacl, bDefaulted;
    ACL* pDACL=NULL;
    ::GetSecurityDescriptorDacl(psd, &bHasDacl, &pDACL,
                            &bDefaulted);
    std::cout << "ACL: " << pDACL << endl;
    if (pDACL)
    {
        ACE_HEADER* pAce=NULL;
        for (int i=0; i<pDACL->AceCount; i++)
        {
            ::GetAce(pDACL, i, (void**) &pAce);
            std::cout << endl << "ACE: " << pAce << endl;
            switch (pAce->AceType)
            {
            case ACCESS_ALLOWED_ACE_TYPE:
            case ACCESS_DENIED_ACE_TYPE:
            {
                TCHAR szUser[_MAX_PATH];
                TCHAR szDomain[_MAX_PATH];
                DWORD dwUserSize=sizeof(szUser);
                DWORD dwDomainSize=sizeof(szDomain);
                SID_NAME_USE use;
                ::LookupAccountSid( NULL,
                    &(((ACCESS_ALLOWED_ACE*)pAce)->SidStart),
                    szUser, &dwUserSize, szDomain,
```

LISTING 12.5   Continued

```
                        &dwDomainSize, &use);
            if (pAce->AceType==ACCESS_ALLOWED_ACE_TYPE)
            {
                std::cout << "AceType: "
                          << "ACCESS_ALLOWED_ACE_TYPE"
                          << endl;
            }
            else
            {
                std::cout << "AceType: "
                          << "ACCESS_DENIED_ACE_TYPE"
                          << endl;
            }
            std::cout << "User Name: " << szUser << endl;
            std::cout << "User Domain: " << szDomain
                      << endl;
            std::cout << "Access Mask: "
                      << ((ACCESS_ALLOWED_ACE*)pAce)->Mask
                      << endl << endl;
            break;
        }
        default:
            std::cout << "Unknown ACE type" << endl;
            break;
        }
    }
    }
    return 0;
}
```

Security IDs

Users and groups of users are identified in the security model by using security IDs.
These IDs are generated in such a manner that they are guaranteed to be unique across
space and time. Uniqueness across space means that no two NT machines can generate
the same security ID. The definition of the SID structure is shown in Listing 12.6.

LISTING 12.6   SID Definition

```
typedef struct _SID_IDENTIFIER_AUTHORITY
{
    BYTE  Value[6];
} SID_IDENTIFIER_AUTHORITY, *PSID_IDENTIFIER_AUTHORITY;

typedef struct _SID
{
    BYTE  Revision;
```

LISTING 12.6 Continued

```
   BYTE  SubAuthorityCount;
   SID_IDENTIFIER_AUTHORITY IdentifierAuthority;
   DWORD SubAuthority[ANYSIZE_ARRAY];
} SID, *PISID;
```

Some SIDs are referred to as *well-known SIDs* because they represent well-known security principals. The following list shows these.

Null SID	S-1-0-0
World	S-1-1-0
Local	S-1-2-0
Creator Owner ID	S-1-3-0
Creator Group ID	S-1-3-1
Creator Owner Server ID	S-1-3-2
Creator Group Server ID	S-1-3-3
(Non-unique IDs)	S-1-4
NT Authority	S-1-5
Dialup	S-1-5-1
Network	S-1-5-2
Batch	S-1-5-3
Interactive	S-1-5-4
Service	S-1-5-6
AnonymousLogon	S-1-5-7
Proxy	S-1-5-8
ServerLogon	S-1-5-8
(Logon IDs)	S-1-5-5-X-Y
(NT nonunique IDs)	S-1-5-21-...
(Built-in domain)	S-1-5-32

A few API functions enable you to use, query, and modify SIDs. They are

```
LookupAccountName()
LookupAccountSid()
IsValidSid()
EqualSid()
EqualPrefixSid()
```

```
AllocateAndInitializeSid()

FreeSid()

InitializeSid()

GetSidIdentifierAuthority()

GetSidSubAuthority()

GetSidSubAuthorityCount()

GetSidLength()

CopySid()
```

Access Tokens

When a user logs on to his NT machine, he is given an access token. This access token contains his user SID, a set of group SIDs, a default SID, and an ACL for creating new objects. When the user creates a new process or thread, the access token is copied to this new object. Eventually, a thread will attempt to access a securable object. At that point, the access tokens of the thread and the security descriptor of the resource are used by the authentication authority to allow or deny the access. The idea is to make the check only once—at the time of handle creation. It is possible to get two handles on the same object with different rights.

There is no definition for an access token structure, but a few API functions enable you to retrieve, query, and modify access tokens. They include the following:

```
OpenProcessToken()

OpenThreadToken()

DuplicateToken()

GetTokenInformation()

SetTokenInformation()

AdjustTokenPrivileges()

AdjustTokenGroups()
```

Listing 12.7 shows how to acquire the access token for the current process and dump all the SIDs in the access token. I've titled this piece of code the SID Viewer because it enables you to view all the SIDs in your access token.

LISTING 12.7   SID Viewer

```
#include <windows.h>
#include <strstrea.h>

strstream SidToString(PSID psid)
```

LISTING 12.7   Continued

```
{
    strstream str;
// is the sid valid?
    if(!::IsValidSid(psid))
    {
        return str;
    }
    // retrieve identifier authority
    PSID_IDENTIFIER_AUTHORITY pia =
        ::GetSidIdentifierAuthority(psid);
    // append prefix and revision number
    str << "S-" << SID_REVISION << "-";
    // append identifier authority
    if ( (pia->Value[0] != 0) || (pia->Value[1] != 0) )
    {
        str << (USHORT)pia->Value[0]
                << (USHORT)pia->Value[1]
                << (USHORT)pia->Value[2]
                << (USHORT)pia->Value[3]
                << (USHORT)pia->Value[4]
                << (USHORT)pia->Value[5];
    }
    else
    {
        str << ((ULONG)(pia->Value[5]      )   +
                (ULONG)(pia->Value[4] <<  8)   +
                (ULONG)(pia->Value[3] << 16)   +
                (ULONG)(pia->Value[2] << 24)   );
    }
    // retrieve count of sub authorities
    DWORD dw = *::GetSidSubAuthorityCount(psid);
    // append subauthorities
    for (int i=0 ; i < (int)dw ; i++)
    {
        str << "-" << *::GetSidSubAuthority(psid, i);
    }
    return str;
}

int main(int, char **)
{
    DWORD dwSize = 0;
    HANDLE hToken;

    // retrieve the current process' access token handle
    if (!::OpenProcessToken( ::GetCurrentProcess(),
                          TOKEN_QUERY, &hToken ))
    {
        std::cout << "Error ::OpenProcessToken "
```

LISTING 12.7 Continued

```
                        << ::GetLastError() << endl;
        return 0;
    }
    // retrieve the size of the token group structure
    if(!::GetTokenInformation(hToken, TokenGroups, NULL,
                              dwSize, &dwSize))
    {
        DWORD dw = ::GetLastError();
        if( dw != ERROR_INSUFFICIENT_BUFFER )
        {
            std::cout << "Error ::GetTokenInformation "
                      << dw << endl;
            return 0;
        }
    }
    // allocate the token group structure
    PTOKEN_GROUPS pTokenGroups = (PTOKEN_GROUPS)
                        ::GlobalAlloc( GPTR, dwSize );
    // retrieve the token group structure
    if(!::GetTokenInformation(hToken, TokenGroups,
                              pTokenGroups, dwSize,
                              &dwSize ))
    {
        std::cout << "Error ::GetTokenInformation "
                  << ::GetLastError() << endl;
    }
    else
    {
        // dump all the group sids
        for(int i=0; i<(int)pTokenGroups->GroupCount; i++)
        {
            std::cout
            << SidToString(pTokenGroups->Groups[i].Sid).str()
            << endl;
        }
    }

    // clean up
    if ( pTokenGroups )
    {
        ::GlobalFree( pTokenGroups );
    }
    return 0;
}
```

The previous code fails under Windows 95. The security API is only implemented by Windows NT and 2000. If you run the code in Listing 12.7, the output will be similar to the following:

S-1-5-21-1958420805-1419734996-339680022-513

S-1-1-0

S-1-5-32-544

S-1-5-5-0-5466

S-1-2-0

S-1-5-4

These SIDs represent, in order, my user account, the world, my administrator domain, my logon session, local user, and interactive user. You can match these SIDs using the well-known SIDs listed earlier in this section.

Authentication

COM has a function to enable the object's author to modify his module's security context. The CoInitializeSecurity() function enables the author to specify an alternative authentication service, authentication level, and impersonation level. It can be used by the server and the client. The following shows the parameters:

```
HRESULT CoInitializeSecurity(
  PSECURITY_DESCRIPTOR pVoid, //Points to security descriptor
  LONG cAuthSvc, //Count of entries in asAuthSvc
  SOLE_AUTHENTICATION_SERVICE * asAuthSvc, //Array of names to register
  void * pReserved1, //Reserved for future use
DWORD dwAuthnLevel, //The default authentication level for proxies
  DWORD dwImpLevel, //The default impersonation level for proxies
  SOLE_AUTHENTICATION_LIST * pAuthList, //Authentication information for each
                                        // authentication service
  DWORD dwCapabilities, //Additional client and/or server-side capabilities
  void * pReserved3 //Reserved for future use
  );
```

If this function is not called, COM calls the function with the legacy setting (system-wide defaults). The legacy settings are stored in the Windows system registry under the key HKEY_LOCAL_MACHINE\SOFTWARE\Microsoft\Ole. Chapter 8 discussed these default settings in the section "Legacy Security."

The authentication service will be one of NTLMSSP, Kerberos, Snego, SChannel, or others. As new authentication services become available, they will be added to this list.

- NTLMSSP is the security discussed earlier in this chapter. Kerberos authentication has replaced NTLM authentication in Windows 2000.

- Kerberos is a newer security package on the NT platform. This security package has many advantages over other security. One such advantage relates to COM in that Kerberos protocol allows impersonation delegation. With Windows NT using

NTLM, impersonation does not support delegation, and network resource access might fail. The Kerberos implementation on Windows 2000 is based on the Internet RFC 1510 Kerberos protocol definition.

- Snego is not really an authentication service. It is a virtual authentication service that uses a list of other authentication services.

- Secure Channel (SChannel) supports the secure socket layer (SSL) and private communication technology (PCT) protocols. This authentication service is targeted toward systems that require an Internet public-key security infrastructure. The authentication service provider uses a CAPI interface to enable the user to specify a variety of encryption and certificate implementations.

The authentication level is the amount of security requested. The authentication levels listed in Table 12.2 are available.

TABLE 12.2   Available Authentication Levels

Authentication Level	*Definition*
Default	In Windows NT 4.0, the default was Connect. In Windows 2000, a security blanket negotiation algorithm is used.
None	No authentication is performed.
Connect	Authentication is performed once when the client connects to the server.
Call	Authentication is performed on every RPC call.
Packet	Authentication is performed on every packet transmission.
Packet Integrity	Same as Packet. Also verifies that the packet has not been modified.
Packet Privacy	Same as Packet Integrity and encrypts the packet data.

Connect and call authentication levels are available only for connection-based protocols. Connectionless protocols must use one of the three packet authentication levels or no authentication.

Impersonation

The call to CoInitializeSecurity() also has an impersonation level parameter. The impersonation levels listed in Table 12.3 are available. Impersonation is the capability of a thread to execute in a security context that is different from the context of the process that owns the thread.

Remote access client impersonation occurs when a person takes over an existing authenticated connection. The intruder waits until the connection is authenticated and then obtains the connection parameters, disconnects the user, and takes control of the authenticated connection.

Remote server impersonation occurs when a computer appears to the remote access client as the remote access server. The impersonator appears to verify the remote access client credentials and then captures all the traffic from the remote access client.

TABLE 12.3   Impersonation Levels

Impersonation Level	*Description*
Default	Available in Windows 2000 only.
Anonymous	The server cannot use impersonation to read or use access rights.
Identity	The server cannot use impersonation to use access rights, but can read access rights.
Impersonate	The server can read and use access rights of the client.
Delegate	Available in Windows 2000 only, the server can read and use access rights of the client and enables cloaking.

When COM servers are launched, as when regular executables are launched, they normally assume the identity of the launching user. The user might not have access to a variety of resources. If you do not provide the capability to control the identity of the COM server, these access rights can prove to be lacking or overly generous. If the access rights are lacking, client calls to the server will result in access-denied errors. If the rights are overly generous, client calls to the server will result in security violations. It is possible to configure the server to launch with a set of access rights that is neither lacking nor overly generous. But what if some clients require some access rights that should not be available to other clients? In that case, you can require that the COM server change rights depending on the user. This was introduced to COM by implementation identity and impersonation. Not only can you use the client identity to validate access rights; you can also use the client identity to acquire rights in order to perform tasks on behalf of the client.

Cloaking

Cloaking capability determines what identity is presented to a server during impersonation. Cloaking provides a way for a server to project an identity, other than its own, to another server it is calling on behalf of the client. The impersonation level indicates how much authority the client has given the server.

Impersonation without cloaking works, but it might not be the best choice because, in some cases, the final server needs to know the identity of the initial caller. This cannot be achieved without using cloaking. Without cloaking, which presents the identity of the initial caller, it is difficult to ensure that only authorized clients can access a remote machine. When impersonation is used without cloaking, the identity presented to a downstream server is that of the immediate calling process.

Cloaking is not useful without impersonation either. Cloaking only makes sense when the client has set an impersonation level of impersonate or delegate. (With lower impersonation levels, the server cannot make cloaked calls.) Whether cloaking is successful depends on the impersonation level, which indicates how much authority the server has to act on behalf of the client and on the number of machine boundaries crossed. The following discussion explains how the choice of cloaking and impersonation level affect what happens during impersonation.

In some situations, it makes sense for the server to set cloaking when the client sets the impersonation level to `RPC_C_IMP_LEVEL_IMPERSONATE`. However, certain limitations are in effect. If the original client sets the impersonation level to `RPC_C_IMP_LEVEL_IMPERSONATE`, the intermediate server (acting as a client on the same machine) can cloak across only one machine boundary. This is because an impersonate-level impersonation token can only be passed across one machine boundary. After the machine boundary has been crossed, only local resources can be accessed. The identity presented to the server depends on the type of cloaking that is set. If no cloaking is set, the identity presented to a server will be that of the process making the immediate call.

To cloak over multiple machine boundaries, you must specify both an appropriate cloaking capability flag and delegate-level impersonation. With this type of impersonation, both the local and network credentials of the client are given to the server, so the impersonation token can cross any number of machine boundaries. Again, the identity presented to the server depends on the type of cloaking that is set. If no cloaking is set with delegate-level impersonation, the identity presented to a server is that of the process making the call.

For example, suppose Process A calls B, and B calls C. B has set cloaking, and A has set the impersonation level to impersonate. If A, B, and C are on the same machine, passing the impersonation token from A to B and then to C will work. But if A and C are on the same machine, and B is not, passing the token will work between A and B, but not from B to C. The call from B to C will fail because B cannot call C while cloaking. However, if A sets the impersonation level to delegate, the token can be passed from B to C, so the call can succeed.

CoImpersonateClient() and CoRevertToSelf()

CoImpersonateClient() allows the COM server to take on the identity of the calling client process. You'll want to do this when the COM server does not have sufficient access rights to perform a task on behalf of the calling client process. CoRevertToSelf() should be called when the COM server wants to discontinue impersonating the client and revert back to its own identity.

Listing 12.8 shows the implementation of these two helper functions.

LISTING 12.8   Implementation of CoImpersonateClient() and CoRevertToSelf()

```
WINOLEAPI CoImpersonateClient()
{
    IServerSecurity *pss;
    ::CoGetCallContext( IID_IServerSecurity, (void **) &pss);
    HRESULT hresult = pss->ImpersonateClient();
    pss->Release();
    return hresult;
}
WINOLEAPI CoRevertToSelf()
{
    IServerSecurity *pss;
    ::CoGetCallContext(IID_IServerSecurity, (void**)&pss);
    HRESULT hresult = pss->RevertToSelf();
    pss->Release();
    return hresult;
}
```

The functions CoImpersonateClient() and CoRevertToSelf() use the IServerSecurity interface that is implemented in the server. Listing 12.9 is the MIDL definition of this interface. It is important to note the IServerSecurity is almost always done at the stub level for standard marshaling. The only exception would be in response to custom marshaling.

IServerSecurity's CoGetCallContext() method is valid only for the current call as its name implies.

LISTING 12.9   MIDL Definition of the IServerSecurity Interface

```
interface IServerSecurity : IUnknown
{
    HRESULT QueryBlanket
    (
        [out] DWORD     *pAuthnSvc,
        [out] DWORD     *pAuthzSvc,
```

LISTING 12.9   Continued

```
        [out] OLECHAR **pServerPrincName,
        [out] DWORD    *pAuthnLevel,
        [out] DWORD    *pImpLevel,
        [out] void    **pPrivs,
        [out] DWORD    *pCapabilities
    );

    HRESULT ImpersonateClient();

    HRESULT RevertToSelf();

    BOOL IsImpersonating();
}
```

Another function is available to tell you whether the server is currently impersonating the client. This function is IServerSecurity::IsImpersonating(). No helper function exists for this method, but you can implement your own helper function, as shown in Listing 12.10. As you might notice from the code, we are in the server. This means the ImpersonateClient() has been previously called.

LISTING 12.10   Implementation of CoIsImpersonating()

```
BOOL CoIsImpersonating()
{
    IServerSecurity pss;
    CoGetCallContext(IID_IServerSecurity, (void**)&pss);
    BOOL b = pss->IsImpersonating();
    pss->Release();
    return b;
}
```

The last function of the IServerSecurity interface is the IServerSecurity::QueryBlanket() method. This method has a helper function called CoQueryClientSecurity() that is implemented as shown in Listing 12.11.

LISTING 12.11   Implementation of CoQueryClientSecurity()

```
WINOLEAPI CoQueryClientSecurity()
{
    IServerSecurity *pss;
    ::CoGetCallContext(IID_IServerSecurity, (void**)&pss);
    HRESULT hresult = pss->QueryBlanket();
    pss->Release();
    return hresult;
}
```

This function queries the security settings of the client that invoked the server.

Cloaking

The delegate impersonation level described previously is generally referred to as *cloaking*. This type of impersonation hides the server's true identity during calls to other servers by disguising the intermediate server's identity with the identity of the client.

Declarative Security

As you learned in Chapter 8, it is possible to declare the security for a COM server in the registry. This is sometimes called *declarative security* or *per-process security*. Note that declarative security and per-process security are not entirely the same. Declarative security consists of the settings in the Windows system registry that are used when a COM server is launched or accessed. Per-process security includes the registry settings but also includes other mechanisms of manipulating the COM server's settings for the entire process, such as the function `CoInitializeSecurity()`.

In Chapter 13, "Configuration and Error Handling," you learn how you can use two tools called `DCOMCNFG` and `OLEView` to configure the per-process security settings for your COM servers.

Programmatic Security

Earlier in this chapter, you learned two elements of programmatic security—the `IServerSecurity` interface that you used to impersonate the client and the `CoInitializeSecurity()` function used to set per-process security. The `CoInitializeSecurity()` function creates a security blanket for your process; that is, the security settings.

Security Blankets

So what is a security blanket? A security blanket is a set of security properties. Those security properties include the following:

- Authentication service
- Authorization service
- Principal name
- Authentication level
- Impersonation level
- Authentication identity
- Capabilities
- ACL

Both the client and server create their security blankets by calling the
CoInitializeSecurity() function. If either the client or server fails to call this function,
COM calls the function with default values on behalf of the process.

COM uses the client's and server's security blankets to negotiate the proxy's security
blanket. COM selects an authentication service (and an authorization service and principal name that work with the service) that is available on both the client and server. COM
selects the highest authentication level specified by the client or server. COM selects the
client's impersonation level, authentication identity (that works with the selected authentication server), and capabilities.

The security blanket is negotiated when the proxy is created. After the proxy is created,
the client has control over the proxy using the IClientSecurity interface described in
the next section.

IClientSecurity

Another interface called IClientSecurity allows the client to query and modify the
security settings of the interface proxies. Listing 12.12 is the MIDL definition of the
IClientSecurity interface.

LISTING 12.12 MIDL Definition of the IClientSecurity Interface

```
interface IClientSecurity : IUnknown
{
    HRESULT QueryBlanket
    (
        [in]  IUnknown            *pProxy,
        [out] DWORD               *pAuthnSvc,
        [out] DWORD               *pAuthzSvc,
        [out] OLECHAR             **pServerPrincName,
        [out] DWORD               *pAuthnLevel,
        [out] DWORD               *pImpLevel,
        [out] void                **pAuthInfo,
        [out] DWORD               *pCapabilites
    );

    HRESULT SetBlanket
    (
        [in]  IUnknown            *pProxy,
        [in]  DWORD               AuthnSvc,
        [in]  DWORD               AuthzSvc,
        [in]  OLECHAR             *pServerPrincName,
        [in]  DWORD               AuthnLevel,
        [in]  DWORD               ImpLevel,
        [in]  void                *pAuthInfo,
```

LISTING 12.12   Continued

```
        [in] DWORD                      Capabilities
    );

    HRESULT CopyProxy
    (
        [in]  IUnknown  *pProxy,
        [out] IUnknown  **ppCopy
    );
}
```

This interface has three helper functions: CoQueryProxyBlanket(),
CoSetProxyBlanket(), and CoCopyProxy(). These three helper functions are implemented as shown in Listing 12.13.

LISTING 12.13   Implementation of IClientSecurity Helper Functions

```
WINOLEAPI CoQueryClientSecurity(IUnknown * pProxy,
                    DWORD * pAuthnSvc,
                    DWORD * pAuthzSvc,
                    OLECHAR ** pServerPrincName,
                    DWORD * pAuthnLevel,
                    DWORD * pImpLevel,
                    RPC_AUTH_IDENTITY_HANDLE * ppAuthInfo,
                    DWORD * pCapabilities)
{
    IClientSecurity *pcs;
    pProxy->QueryInterface(IID_IClientSecurity, (void**)&pcs);
    HRESULT hresult = pcs->QueryBlanket(pProxy, pAuthnSvc,
                    pAuthzSvc, pServerPrincName,
                    pAuthnLevel, pImpLevel,
                    ppAuthInfo, pCapabilities);
    pcs->Release();
    return hresult;
}
HRESULT CoSetProxyBlanket(IUnknown * pProxy,
                    DWORD dwAuthnSvc,
                    DWORD dwAuthzSvc,
                    WCHAR * pServerPrincName,
                    DWORD dwAuthnLevel,
                    DWORD dwImpLevel,
                    RPC_AUTH_IDENTITY_HANDLE pAuthInfo,
                    DWORD dwCapabilities)
{
    IClientSecurity *pcs;
    pProxy->QueryInterface(IID_IClientSecurity, (void**)&pcs);
    pcs->SetBlanket(pProxy, dwAuthnSvc, dwAuthzSvc,
                pServerPrincName, dwAuthnLevel,
```

LISTING 12.13   Continued

```
                    dwImpLevel, pAuthInfo, dwCapabilities);
    pcs->Release();
}
HRESULT CoCopyProxy( IUnknown * pProxy, IUnknown ** ppCopy)
{
    IClientSecurity *pcs;
    pProxy->QueryInterface(IID_IClientSecurity, (void**)&pcs);
    pcs->CopyProxy(punkProxy, ppunkCopy);
    pcs->Release();
}
```

The `CoQueryProxyBlanket()` function queries the security settings that will be used to invoke COM object methods in the interface proxy.

The `CoSetProxyBlanket()` function modifies the security settings that will be used to invoke COM object methods in the interface proxy. If you set a parameter to the default value, `CoSetProxyBlanket()` will not change the security property even if the property is not set to the default value.

The `CoCopyProxy()` function enables the client to make a copy of the proxy so that future calls to `CoSetProxyBlanket()` do not affect security for other clients that are using the same proxy. Note that the caller of the `CoCopyProxy()` function or the `IClientSecurity::CopyProxy()` method is responsible for releasing the new proxy. Calling `CoCopyProxy()` can also be used to ensure that other clients do not modify the security of the new proxy (because they will be using the original proxy).

Access and Launch Security

Access permission determines whether users are allowed to invoke methods on the COM server's objects. Launch permission determines whether users are allowed to start the COM server. The two separate permissions make it possible to configure clients so that they can access objects in COM servers that have already been launched, but also to deny the same clients the capability to start the COM server.

These permissions are discussed in more detail in Chapter 8. In that chapter, you learn how to configure the system-wide default permissions and COM server-specific permissions.

In Chapter 13, you learn how to use a utility called DCOMCNFG to configure both access and launch permissions.

Summary

This chapter showed you how to work with COM security in order to allow and deny access to a COM server. Early in the chapter, you learned some fundamental concepts about Windows security with relation to COM.

Next, I tackled security descriptors. I accessed them programmatically and discussed their purpose. The different descriptor types were discussed and related registry entries listed.

We took a look at Access Control Lists (ACL) and the API functions to access them. Then, a special sample program was used to read through the ACLs on the current system.

The last major topics discussed were impersonation and cloaking. Understanding them is important if a comprehensive understanding of COM security is to be obtained.

COM security is a difficult subject. It's a topic that you should take your time learning because of its impact on your distributed programming.

Configuration and Error Handling

IN THIS CHAPTER

- Configuring a COM+ Object with DCOMCNFG *326*
- Using the OLEView Program *344*
- Error Handling *347*

Configuring a COM+ Object with DCOMCNFG

This chapter shows you how to configure a COM+ object on a systemwide basis using two advanced utilities called DCOMCNFG and OLEVIEW. You also learn different strategies for handling COM+ error codes.

> **Note**
>
> If you are not familiar with the COM+ registry settings, read Chapter 8, "COM and the Registry." That chapter is necessary in order to understand the registry lingo.

DCOMCNFG is installed in the system32 folder on your computer. This utility is the standard method for manually configuring COM+ security and remoting. The User Interface (UI) is a property sheet with four pages (see Figure 13.1).

FIGURE 13.1

The Applications page.

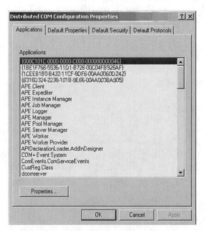

The Applications tab lists the COM+ servers that are registered on your system. Remember that in Chapter 7 the registry key `HKEY_CLASSES_ROOT\AppID` was used to identify COM+ servers. The list of subkeys in this registry key is nearly identical to the list of COM+ servers in this first tab. That's because DCOMCNFG uses the `HKEY_CLASSES_ROOT\AppID` registry key to generate the list of configurable COM servers.

Legacy COM Servers

Legacy out-of-process servers most often do not register their
`HKEY_CLASSES_ROOT\AppID\{my-clsid}` and, therefore, will not show up in the DCOM-
CNFG listing of configurable applications. In order for a server to appear in this listing,
you must add an `AppID` value name in the `HKEY_CLASSES_ROOT\CLSID\{my-clsid}` registry subkey and create an `AppID` registry subkey in the `HKEY_CLASSES_ROOT\AppID` key.
Confusing? Not really. The syntax of those entries follows. It was taken from the RGS
file (see Listing 13.1) of an out-of-process server that you will create later in this chapter.

```
[HKEY_CLASSES_ROOT \ CLSID \ {my-clsid-as-guid}] "AppID" =
➥{my-clsid-as-guid}

[HKEY_CLASSES_ROOT \ AppID \ {my-clsid-as-guid}] "" =
➥{Description of the server}
```

> **Note**
>
> The second registry entry has a key value of `""`. Whenever I specify a key value
> of `""`, I'm referring to the default key value.

LISTING 13.1 An Example of Registration Files

```
MyProject.RGS
HKCR
{
  NoRemove AppID
  {
    {E5A784C4-3498-11D2-9C2B-444553540000} = s 'MyProject'
    'MyProject.EXE'
    {
      val AppID = s {E5A784C4-3498-11D2-9C2B-444553540000}
    }
  }
}
MyObject.RGS
HKCR
{
  MyObject.MyObject.1 = s 'MyObject Class'
  {
    CLSID = s '{E5A784D3-3498-11D2-9C2B-444553540000}'
  }
  MyObject.MyObject = s 'MyObject Class'
  {
    CurVer = s 'MyObject.MyObject.1'
  }
  NoRemove CLSID
```

13

CONFIGURATION AND ERROR HANDLING

LISTING 13.1   Continued

```
    {
        ForceRemove {E5A784D3-3498-11D2-9C2B-444553540000} =
            s 'MyObject Class'

        {
            ProgID = s 'MyObject.MyObject.1'
            VersionIndependentProgID = s 'MyObject.MyObject'
            ForceRemove 'Programmable'
            LocalServer32 = s '%MODULE%'
            val AppID = s '{E5A784C4-3498-11D2-9C2B-444553540000}'
        }
    }
}
```

Visual C++ compiles these RGS files into the module's resources. When the server is started with the `RegServer` parameter, these RGS entries are automatically loaded into the registry. This is done in the call to `Module.UpdateRegistryFromResource(IDR_MyProject, TRUE);`. Listing 13.2 shows where to code the call to `UpdateRegistryFromResource()` and how to code the self-registering `RegServer` and `UnregServer` parameters in your main procedure. This listing was produced by the ATL AppWizard and ObjectWizard.

LISTING 13.2   A Self-Registering Executable

```
LPCTSTR FindOneOf(LPCTSTR p1, LPCTSTR p2)
{
    while (*p1 != NULL)
    {
        LPCTSTR p = p2;
        while (*p != NULL)
        {
            if (*p1 == *p++)
                return p1+1;
        }
        p1++;
    }
    return NULL;
}

extern "C" int WINAPI _tWinMain(HINSTANCE hInstance,
    HINSTANCE , LPTSTR lpCmdLine, int )
{
    lpCmdLine = GetCommandLine(); //necessary for _ATL_MIN_CRT
    HRESULT hRes = CoInitialize(NULL);
//  If you are running on NT 4.0 or higher you can use the
//  following call instead to make the EXE free threaded.
```

LISTING 13.2   Continued

```
//  This means that calls come in on a random RPC thread
//  HRESULT hRes = CoInitializeEx(NULL, COINIT_MULTITHREADED);
    _ASSERTE(SUCCEEDED(hRes));
    _Module.Init(ObjectMap, hInstance);
    _Module.dwThreadID = GetCurrentThreadId();
    TCHAR szTokens[] = _T("-/");

    int nRet = 0;
    BOOL bRun = TRUE;
    LPCTSTR lpszToken = FindOneOf(lpCmdLine, szTokens);
    while (lpszToken != NULL)
    {
        if (lstrcmpi(lpszToken, _T("UnregServer"))==0)
        {
            _Module.UpdateRegistryFromResource(IDR_MyProject,
                                                FALSE);
            nRet = _Module.UnregisterServer();
            bRun = FALSE;
            break;
        }
        if (lstrcmpi(lpszToken, _T("RegServer"))==0)
        {
            _Module.UpdateRegistryFromResource(IDR_MyProject,
                                                TRUE);
            nRet = _Module.RegisterServer(TRUE);
            bRun = FALSE;
            break;
        }
        lpszToken = FindOneOf(lpszToken, szTokens);
    }

    if (bRun)
    {
        hRes = _Module.RegisterClassObjects(
                                    CLSCTX_LOCAL_SERVER,
                                    REGCLS_MULTIPLEUSE);
        _ASSERTE(SUCCEEDED(hRes));

        MSG msg;
        while (GetMessage(&msg, 0, 0, 0))
            DispatchMessage(&msg);

        _Module.RevokeClassObjects();
    }

    CoUninitialize();
    return nRet;
}
```

Creating an Automation Server

The next few sections describe several experiments that you can do to understand how DCOMCNFG affects an automation server. These experiments use a simple out-of-process automation server that has one object and one property. The automation server is described in this section.

The out-of-process server is created in Visual C++ 6.0 by implementing the following steps:

1. Start Visual C++ and select File, New from the menu bar.

2. Select ATL COM+ AppWizard in the list view, type **MyProject** in the Project Name edit control, and click OK.

3. In the ATL COM+ AppWizard wizard, select the Executable radio button and click Finish. Visual C++'s main window reappears.

4. Select Insert, New ATL Object from the menu bar.

5. Name the object **MyObject** so that the interface is called IMyObject and the C++ object is called CMyObject. Again, you return to Visual C++'s main window.

6. Right-click the IMyObject interface and select Add Property from the pop-up menu. In the Property Type combo box, select Long, type **MyProperty** in the Property Name edit control, and deselect the Put radio button. (This will make the property read-only.)

The only thing left to do is write the code for the get_MyProperty handler function. I've attached the Microsoft Interface Definition Language (MIDL) and CPP files in Listings 13.3–13.5.

LISTING 13.3 Simple Local Server IDL

```
// MyProject.idl : IDL source for MyProject.dll
//

// This file will be processed by the MIDL tool to
// produce the type library (MyProject.tlb) and marshaling
// code.

import "oaidl.idl";
import "ocidl.idl";

    [
        object,
        uuid(E5A784D2-3498-11D2-9C2B-444553540000),
        dual,
        helpstring("IMyObject Interface"),
```

LISTING **13.3**   Continued

```
        pointer_default(unique)
    ]
    interface IMyObject : IDispatch
    {
        [propget, id(1), helpstring("property MyProperty")]
          HRESULT MyProperty([out, retval] long *pVal);
    };
[
    uuid(E5A784C3-3498-11D2-9C2B-444553540000),
    version(1.0),
    helpstring("MyProject 1.0 Type Library")
]
library MYPROJECTLib
{
    importlib("stdole32.tlb");
    importlib("stdole2.tlb");

    [
        uuid(E5A784D3-3498-11D2-9C2B-444553540000),
        helpstring("MyObject Class")
    ]
    coclass MyObject
    {
        [default] interface IMyObject;
    };
};
```

LISTING **13.4**   Simple Local Server Object Header

```
// MyObject.h : Declaration of the CMyObject

#ifndef __MYOBJECT_H_
#define __MYOBJECT_H_

#include "resource.h"        // main symbols

/////////////////////////////////////////////////////////
// CMyObject
class ATL_NO_VTABLE CMyObject :
    public CComObjectRootEx<CComSingleThreadModel>,
    public CComCoClass<CMyObject, &CLSID_MyObject>,
    public IDispatchImpl<IMyObject, &IID_IMyObject,
                    &LIBID_MYPROJECTLib>
{
public:
    CMyObject()
    {
    }
```

LISTING 13.4   Continued

```
DECLARE_REGISTRY_RESOURCEID(IDR_MYOBJECT)

BEGIN_COM_MAP(CMyObject)
    COM_INTERFACE_ENTRY(IMyObject)
    COM_INTERFACE_ENTRY(IDispatch)
END_COM_MAP()

// IMyObject
public:
    STDMETHOD(get_MyProperty)(/*[out, retval]*/ long *pVal);
};

#endif //__MYOBJECT_H_
```

LISTING 13.5   Simple Local Server Object Implementation

```
// MyObject.cpp : Implementation of CMyObject
#include "stdafx.h"
#include "MyProject.h"
#include "MyObject.h"

/////////////////////////////////////////////////////
// CMyObject

STDMETHODIMP CMyObject::get_MyProperty(long * pVal)
{
    // TODO: Add your implementation code here
    *pVal = 10;

    return S_OK;
}
```

The previous code is not created by the developer but by the Wizard. The only code you must write yourself is the *pVal = 10 to the CMyObject::get_MyProperty() method in Listing 13.5.

Listing 13.3 is the IDL source for MyProject.dll. In it, you can see the interface declaration.

Listing 13.4 contains the declaration for the CMyObject class. This is the class that implements the IMyObject interface. You can see the CComSingleThreadModel class as well.

Listing 13.5 shows the implementation code for the CMyObject class. There isn't much to it because there's only a single method, which acts as a property get method.

Default Properties

The second tab of the DCOMCNFG Property Sheet dialog is the Default Property tab (see Figure 13.2). This page enables you to change four separate selections that I have already discussed in Chapter 8. They can be found in the AppID structure of the registry.

FIGURE 13.2

The Default Properties page.

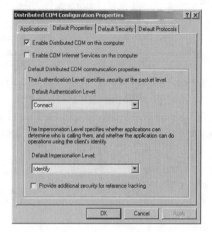

The Enable Distributed COM+ on This Computer check box enables and disables distributed objects by setting the `EnableDCOM+` registry value in the `HKEY_LOCAL_MACHINE\SOFTWARE\Microsoft\Ole` key. This controls whether client applications can launch or connect to remote COM+ objects—that is, objects that are not on the same computer.

The Default Authentication Level drop-down combo box sets the authentication level used by the security provider. Both the Connect and Call authentication levels are not available to connectionless protocols like UDP. By default, most DCOM+ installations use the connectionless UDP protocol. COM+ will bump the authentication level to the next acceptable level when the current level is not available. DCOM+ for Windows 95 uses the connection-based TCP protocol by default. If the authentication level is set to None, COM+ security is disabled, causing all connections, calls, and packets to be accepted no matter what the individual security settings.

The Default Impersonation Level drop-down combo box sets the impersonation level used by COM+ security. The default is Identity.

The last control, the Provide Additional Security for Reference Tracking check box, enables and disables security for calls to `AddRef()` and `Release()`. Enabling this additional security slows down COM. This check box should not be checked unless for some reason the additional security is necessary.

13

CONFIGURATION AND ERROR HANDLING

These last three settings are equivalent to the `LegacyAuthenticationLevel`, `LegacyImpersonationLevel`, and `LegacySecureReferences` settings in the `HKEY_LOCAL_MACHINE\SOFTWARE\Microsoft\Ole` registry key. These were discussed in Chapter 8. The settings are called legacy settings because newer COM+ objects should call `CoInitializeSecurity()` to set these settings. Legacy COM+ objects created before DCOM+ did not call this function because it was not available. COM+ uses these legacy settings when calling `CoInitializeSecurity()` on behalf of these legacy objects.

Default Security

The third tab of the DCOMCNFG property sheet dialog is the Default Security property page, shown in Figure 13.3. There are three categories that this tab brings to view: Default Access Permissions, Default Launch Permissions, and Default Configuration Permissions. They all work together to form the default security for COM+ objects.

FIGURE 13.3

The DCOMCNFG Default Security page.

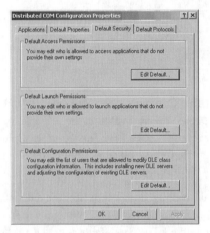

Setting the Access Permissions

When you click Edit Default in the Default Access Permissions box, you can modify the `DefaultAccessPermission` value in the `HKEY_LOCAL_MACHINE\SOFTWARE\Microsoft\Ole` registry key. This setting determines who can call objects that do not specify custom access permissions.

Let's go from the theoretical to the practical. Earlier in this chapter, in the section "Creating an Automation Server," you created and installed a COM+ server that can be used as an example. Listing 13.6 shows you how changes in configuration using DCOM-CNFG reflect in successful and unsuccessful calls to the COM+ API.

LISTING 13.6 Create and Access Test Object

```c
#include <windows.h>

HRESULT LaunchAndAccess()
{
    // HRESULT returned from last automation call
    HRESULT hresult;
    // IDISPATCH interface pointer for the existing object
    LPDISPATCH pdisp = NULL;
    // hold exception info here
    EXCEPINFO excepinfo;
    // hold argument error here
    UINT uArgErr;

    // Convert the progid to a clsid
    CLSID clsid;
    hresult = ::CLSIDFromProgID(OLESTR("MyObject.MyObject.1"),
                                &clsid);
    if (hresult)
    {
        // CLSIDFromProgID failed
        return hresult;
    };

    // Create the instance of the object
    LPUNKNOWN punk;
    hresult = ::CoCreateInstance(clsid, NULL, CLSCTX_SERVER,
                        IID_IUnknown, (LPVOID FAR *) &punk);
    if (hresult)
    {
        // CoCreateInstance failed
        return hresult;
    };

    // Retrieve the interface pointer
    hresult = punk->QueryInterface(IID_IDispatch,
                                   (LPVOID FAR *)&pdisp);
    if (hresult)
    {
        // QueryInterface failed
        return hresult;
    };

    // Release the IUnknown reference.
    hresult = punk->Release();

    // return an exception if the dispatch pointer is NULL
    if (pdisp==NULL)
    {
        return E_UNEXPECTED;
```

13

CONFIGURATION
AND ERROR
HANDLING

LISTING **13.6**   Continued

```cpp
    }

    // Retrieve the dispatch id for the function name
    DISPID dispid;
    BSTR bstr = ::SysAllocString(OLESTR("MyProperty"));
    hresult = pdisp->GetIDsOfNames(IID_NULL, &bstr, 1,
                                   LOCALE_USER_DEFAULT,
                                   &dispid);
    ::SysFreeString(bstr);
    if (hresult)
    {
        // GetIDsOfNames failed
        return hresult;
    };

    // Invoke the property GET
    DISPPARAMS dispparams = {0};
    VARIANTARG variantarg;
    VariantInit(&variantarg);
    ::memset(&excepinfo, 0, sizeof(EXCEPINFO));
    uArgErr = 0;
    hresult = pdisp->Invoke(dispid, IID_NULL,
                            LOCALE_USER_DEFAULT,
                            DISPATCH_PROPERTYGET,
                            &dispparams, &variantarg,
                            &excepinfo, &uArgErr);
    if (hresult)
    {
        // Invoke failed
        return hresult;
    };

    pdisp->Release();

    if (variantarg.lVal!=10)
    {
        // Wrong result
        return E_UNEXPECTED;
    };

    return S_OK;
};

int main(int, char **)
{
    CoInitialize(NULL);
    LaunchAndAccess();
    CoUninitialize();
    return 0;
}
```

Looking at the code, you'll notice that the object is instantiated with `CoCreateInstance()` and the interface is retrieved. Next, the `"MyProperty"` property is invoked with the `Invoke()` method. In summary, this code instantiates the object and accesses the property.

If you run the test source code with the default security settings, the automation server launches and is accessed without any problems.

Now deny access permission. In the Default Access Permissions dialog box, add Deny Rights for your user account. If you run the test source code with these settings, the server should launch without error, but an error will be reported when you attempt to access the object with the call to `CoCreateInstance()`. By checking the task list, you can verify that the server launched correctly.

Now, what if you set authentication level to None? Go back to the previous property page, the Default Properties page shown in Figure 13.2. Set the default authentication level to None. This time the code listing (refer to Listing 13.6) completes with no errors. Setting the authentication level to None disables the security, as mentioned in the previous section. Reset the authentication level to the default after you've completed this small test.

Setting the Launch Permissions

Clicking Edit Default in the Default Launch Permissions section on the Default Security page (refer to Figure 13.3) modifies the `DefaultLaunchPermission` value in the `HKEY_LOCAL_MACHINE\SOFTWARE\Microsoft\Ole` registry key. This setting determines who can launch objects that do not specify custom launch permissions.

Now deny launch permissions. However, before you attempt the next experiment, don't forget to remove the Deny Access permissions that you created in the previous experiment.

In the Default Launch Permissions section of the Default Security dialog box, add Deny rights for your user account. If you run the test source code from Listing 13.6 with these settings, the server should not launch, and the error will be reported when you attempt to create the object with the call to `CoCreateInstance()`.

If you launch the server manually from the command line or from Explorer, a repeat of the same test will succeed. The call to `CoCreateInstance()` will not launch the server because it is already launched.

Setting the Configuration Permissions

Clicking Edit Default in the Default Configuration Permissions section of the Default Security page (refer to Figure 13.3) enables you to modify the registry security permissions in the `HKEY_CLASSES_ROOT` subkeys. This setting determines who can modify the configuration for objects that do not specify custom configuration permissions.

13

CONFIGURATION AND ERROR HANDLING

I would never suggest changing these settings. The last thing you want to do is exclude somebody from modifying this registry key because applications must have access to this registry key in order to install themselves. So, unless you have specific needs, such as installing applications remotely or prohibiting users from installing COM+ objects, modifying this registry key's security permissions is not advisable.

Configuring a COM+ Server

Click the Applications tab to return to the listing of all the COM+ servers. If you select a COM+ server from this listing and click the Properties button, a separate property sheet dialog appears that enables you to configure the COM+ server (see Figure 13.4).

FIGURE 13.4

The DCOMCNFG application properties.

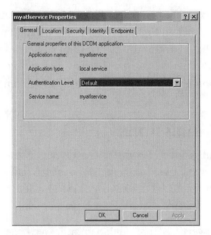

Four properties appear on the General page: the Application Name, Application Type, Application Level, and Service Name. DCOMCNFG does not enable you to change these settings. These settings are also found in the registry. The application name is the key value of the `HKEY_CLASSES_ROOT\AppID\{my-clsid}` registry subkey.

The application type is one of the following:

- In-process handler
- In-process server
- Local service
- Local server
- Remote server

DCOMCNFG searches the `HKEY_CLASSES_ROOT\CLSID\{my-clsid}` and `HKEY_CLASSES_ROOT\AppID\{my-clsid}` registry subkeys of the object. The setting it finds first, in the order listed previously, is used as the object's application type. For in-process handlers, in-process servers, and local servers, the setting is found in the `HKEY_CLASSES_ROOT\CLSID\{my-clsid}` registry subkey. For local services and remote servers, the setting is found in the `HKEY_CLASSES_ROOT\AppID\{my-clsid}` registry subkey. Return to Chapter 8 for more details in the section discussing the AppID registry tree.

The application location is the value name in the registry of the application type registry subkey discussed in the previous paragraph. For local servers, in-process servers, and in-process handlers, this is the module's local path. For a local service, this is the service's name. For a remote server, this is the remote server's name.

Server Location

The Location tab in DCOMCNFG has three check boxes, as shown in Figure 13.5.

FIGURE 13.5

Selecting the DCOMCNFG server location.

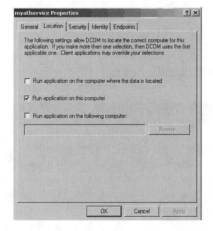

13

CONFIGURATION AND ERROR HANDLING

The first check box enables and disables activation at storage. This is equivalent to the `ActivateAtStorage` registry setting. Activation at storage means that the COM+ object is launched on the machine in which the data file is located.

The second check box tells COM+ to launch and connect to the COM+ server on the local machine. The third check box tells COM+ to launch and connect to the COM+ server on a remote machine. Checking this button writes the `RemoteServer` registry setting in the `HKEY_CLASSES_ROOT\AppID\{my-clsid}` subkey and enables the edit box and browse button controls. These controls enable you to specify the remote server name using an Explorer-style browser.

Server Security

The Security tab in DCOMCNFG has three sets of radio buttons, as shown in Figure 13.6. These radio buttons enable you to switch the security between systemwide defaults and custom security for the COM+ object.

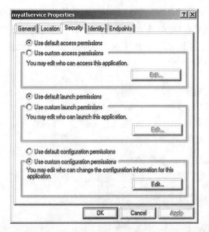

FIGURE 13.6

DCOMCNFG server security.

Note

Before you attempt the next experiment, don't forget to remove the Deny Launch permissions and Deny Access permissions that you created in the last two experiments. You should also kill any running instances of your server because any that are currently running will retain their settings. After you revert back to the default permission, run Listing 13.6. Everything runs correctly without error, as it should with the default launch and access permissions.

Setting Access Permissions

The first set of controls on this page is the access permissions radio buttons and Edit control. They modify the `AccessPermission` registry setting in the `HKEY_CLASSES_ROOT\AppID\{my-clsid}` subkey.

Again, before you attempt the next experiment, don't forget to remove the Deny Launch permissions and Deny Access permissions that you created in the last three experiments. You should also kill any running instances of the server.

Select Use Custom Access Permissions and click Edit. The Registry Value Permissions dialog appears. Change the setting to deny your user account access rights. Now when you run Listing 13.6, the `CoCreateInstance()` call fails because your user account cannot launch the server.

Setting Launch Permissions

The second set of controls on this page is the launch permissions radio buttons and edit control. They modify the `LaunchPermission` registry setting in the `HKEY_CLASSES_ROOT\AppID\{my-clsid}` subkey.

Select Use Custom Launch Permissions and click Edit. The Registry Value Permissions dialog will appear. Change the setting to Deny Your User Account Launch Rights. When you run Listing 13.6, the `CoCreateInstance()` call fails because your user account does not have launch permissions.

If you launch the server manually and run Listing 13.6, `CoCreateInstance()` succeeds. As before, the call to `CoCreateInstance()` did not need to launch the server because it was already running.

Setting Configuration Permissions

The last set of controls on this page is the configuration permissions radio buttons and Edit control. They modify the registry security permissions of the `HKEY_CLASSES_ROOT\AppID\{my-clsid}` subkey. This setting determines who can modify the configuration of the object.

Select Use Custom Configuration Permissions and click Edit. The Registry Key Permissions dialog appears. If you haven't changed COM+'s default configuration permissions, the next dialog box that appears should be similar to that shown in Figure 13.7.

FIGURE 13.7

Registry key permissions.

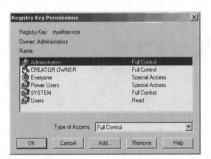

Make certain that you have administrative passwords before you attempt the next steps. You can demonstrate the effects of changes in custom configuration permissions by removing the Everyone entry. Log on to your computer as a non-administrative user. Open REGEDIT and REGEDT32 and try to view the `HKEY_CLASSES_ROOT\AppID\{my-clsid}` registry subkey for the COM+ server. You should see screens similar to those shown in Figures 13.8 and 13.9.

Figure 13.8
REGEDIT showing the AppID *subkey.*

Figure 13.9
REGEDT32 showing the AppID *subkey.*

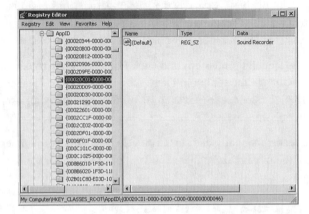

The REGEDIT editor reports an error because it was created without knowledge of system registry security features. The REGEDT32 editor correctly processes the security and grays the registry key that is not available to the user.

Server Identity

The Identity tab in DCOMCNFG has four radio buttons, as shown in Figure 13.10. These radio buttons enable you to change the identity used by the COM+ object for security validations.

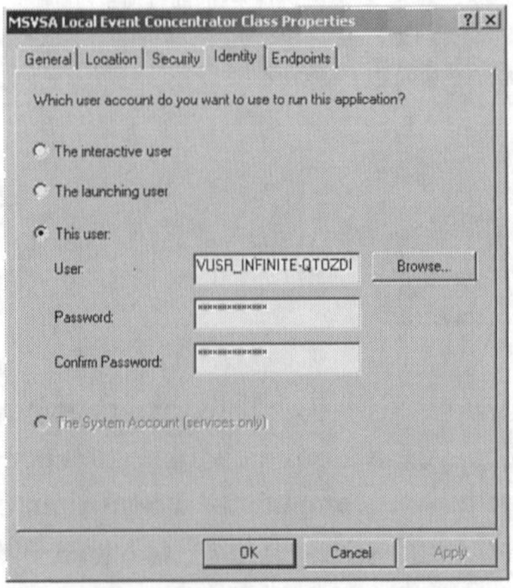

Figure 13.10
The DCOMCNFG server Identity page.

Again, before you attempt the next experiment, don't forget to remove the Deny Launch permissions and Deny Access permissions that you created in the previous experiments. You should also kill any running instances of the server.

This is an experiment you won't soon forget. Modify and recompile the COM+ server you built in the beginning of the chapter. Modify Listing 13.5 with the change in Listing 13.7. Run the code once and you'll note that the current username is output to the C:\USER.LOG log file.

LISTING 13.7 Test the `RunAs` Property

```cpp
// MyObject.cpp : Implementation of CMyObject
#include "stdafx.h"
#include <fstream.h>
#include "MyProject.h"
#include "MyObject.h"


/////////////////////////////////////////////////////
// CMyObject


STDMETHODIMP CMyObject::get_MyProperty(long * pVal)
{
    // TODO: Add your implementation code here
    char sz[256];
    DWORD l = 255;
    ::GetUserName(sz, &l);
    ofstream of;
    of.open("C:\\USER.LOG", ios::out | ios::app);
    of << sz << endl;
    *pVal = 10;

    return S_OK;
}
```

Now, change the identity of the user by setting the user to some non-administrator local account other than your current user account. Now run Listing 13.6. Oops! This account does not have sufficient rights to access the object. Oh, well, kill it from the process list and restart the experiment. Oops! The current user does not have sufficient rights to kill the process. So, how do you kill the process? Reboot? No. In order to kill it, you must log off and log on as the user who launched the process.

This time before you run the listing, add Custom Access Permissions (under Server Security\Setting Launch Permissions) to the COM+ server for Everyone. If you run the code Listing 13.6 again, the C:\USER.LOG file will contain the username of the RunAs user, not the current user.

Using the OLE2View Program

OLE2View is not installed during your installation. You can find the utility by visiting Microsoft's Web site. This utility provides nearly the same functionality as DCOMC-NFG, although some differences make this utility a welcome addition to my collection. The UI uses a tree view on the left pane of a splitter window (see Figure 13.11). As you select objects in the left pane, they display in the right pane.

FIGURE **13.11**

OLE2View 2.0.

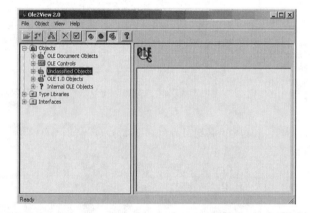

You'll find that OLE2View enables you to set a very similar group of configuration items as DCOMCNFG. In addition, OLE2View displays all the registry entries for the given COM+ object and displays all the registered type libraries and interfaces.

Disadvantages of OLE2View

The misfortune of OLE2View is that it is not installed on most systems, and it is not possible to install this utility on demand. I have found that many configurations can cause the OLE2View program to be very unstable, and the installation program does not install all required modules.

Configuring a COM+ Object with OLE2View

To configure a COM+ object with OLE2View, open the Object Classes, All Objects branch. This lists all the objects registered on your system by ProgID. After you've selected the COM+ object, you'll see five property pages in the right pane. The property pages are Registry, Implementation, Activation, Launch Permissions, and Access Permissions. The Registry property page displays all the settings in the other four pages, and therefore I will not discuss this page.

I have found that some versions of OLEView (including the latest at the time of writing) have a bug. Local servers acquire the `InProcServer32` registry subkey if you select an in-process server, select a local server, and switch between the local server and in-process server tabs in the Implementation property page. To work around this, I have tried deleting the module path for the in-process server in the Implementation property page, but the in-process server module path was substituted with the local server module path. As you might have guessed by now, I'm not the greatest fan of OLEView as a utility for configuring DCOM+ implementation.

Specifying the Surrogate for Remote In-Process Servers

In addition to enabling you to specify the in-process server, local server, and in-process handler module paths, you can also specify the surrogate for remote in-process servers (see Figure 13.12).

FIGURE 13.12

You can specify the surrogate.

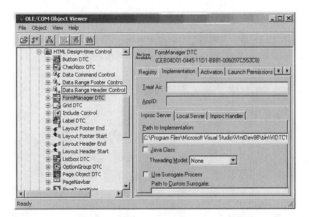

It should be obvious that you really cannot have remote in-process servers. In order for a COM+ object to be in-process, it would, at minimum, require that it be loaded into the same process. A lot of COM+ objects have already been written as in-process servers. In order to take advantage of these legacy objects, the concept of using a surrogate process was established.

In order to configure the client and server to use a surrogate for an in-process server, you must manually create an `AppID` entry in the COM+ object's `HKEY_CLASSES_ROOT\CLSID\{my-clsid}` registry subkey. You must also create an `AppID` registry subkey on both the client and server. In the `HKEY_CLASSES_ROOT\AppID\{my-clsid}` registry subkey of the client, you should have a `RemoteServerName` registry entry that identifies the

server in which the surrogate and in-process server will be launched. In the
HKEY_CLASSES_ROOT\AppID\{my-clsid} registry subkey of the server, you should have a
DllSurrogate registry entry. This last entry can be created using OLEView and the Use
Custom Surrogate check box and Path to Custom Surrogate edit control. Checking the
Use Surrogate Process check box creates the DLLSurrogate value name. If you do not
select a custom surrogate, the default surrogate (DllHost.exe) is used.

You can also use a surrogate to launch an in-process server locally but in a separate
process. In order to do this, you must set the DLLSurrogate value name in the client
machine's registry. You can do this with OLEView.

In order to launch a remote in-process server (or local in-process server in a separate
process), you call CoCreateInstanceEx() with the CLSCTX_LOCAL_SERVER flag. Because
the object does not contain a LocalServer32 entry, COM+ will check the
HKEY_CLASSES_ROOT\AppID\{my-clsid} registry subkey for a DllSurrogate or
RemoteServerName value.

Activation

The Activation property page enables you to specify At Storage activation, launching as
an interactive user and on a remote machine (see Figure 13.13).

FIGURE 13.13

*The OLEView
Activation page.*

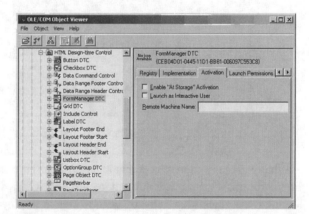

The Enable "At Storage" Activation check box is similar to the ActivateAtStorage registry setting described in Chapter 8. Activation at storage means that the COM+ object is
launched on the machine in which the data file is located.

Launch Permissions

The Launch Permissions property page enables you to specify custom launch permissions for the object (see Figure 13.14).

FIGURE 13.14

The OLEView Launch Permissions page.

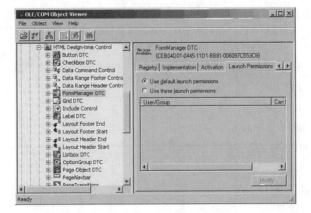

For more information on using custom launch permissions, read the sections earlier in this chapter on using DCOMCNFG.

Access Permissions

The Access Permissions property page enables you to specify custom access permissions for the object (see Figure 13.15).

FIGURE 13.15

The OLEView Access Permissions page.

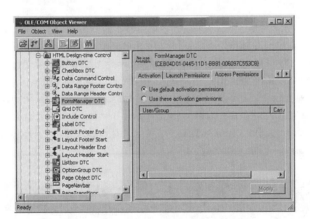

For more information on using custom access permissions, read the sections earlier in this chapter on using DCOMCNFG.

Error Handling

COM+ functions and object methods typically return an HRESULT (handle to a result). The HRESULT is actually a 32-bit value that represents success, warning, or error codes.

The high-order bit of the HRESULT is the severity code. A zero severity represents success (SEVERITY_SUCCESS) and a one severity represents failure (SEVERITY_FAILURE). The next four high-order bits are reserved (always set to zero). The sixth through sixteenth high-order bits represent the facility. The facility can be any of the following:

FACILITY_WINDOWS	8
FACILITY_STORAGE	3
FACILITY_SSPI	9
FACILITY_SETUPAPI	15
FACILITY_RPC	1
FACILITY_WIN32	7
FACILITY_CONTROL	10
FACILITY_NULL	0
FACILITY_MSMQ	14
FACILITY_MEDIASERVER	13
FACILITY_INTERNET	12
FACILITY_ITF	4
FACILITY_DISPATCH	2
FACILITY_CERT	11

The low-order 16 bits represent the status code field as well as the specific error or warning. Microsoft has reserved the exclusive right to define status codes for all the facilities except FACILITY_ITF. Developers, other than Microsoft, can only define status codes for the FACILITY_ITF facility. In order to minimize the conflict of error codes, the interface developers are responsible for defining all the status codes for their interfaces. This means that one FACILITY_ITF status code returned from two different interfaces can have two different meanings, but one FACILITY_ITF status code returned from two calls to the same interface can have only one common meaning.

> **Note**
>
> It is sometimes convenient to simply return error codes received by an intermediate COM+ server to the calling client. By intermediate COM+ server, I mean a COM+ server that is called by one client and that calls a second COM+ server. This strategy is not recommended if the returned error code is of type FACILITY_ITF, unless your intermediate interface specifically identifies these error codes as its own. The correct method is to return E_UNEXPECTED when unexpected error codes are received.

COM+ provides a few useful macros for working with HRESULTs, as shown in Table 13.1.

TABLE 13.1 Macros for Working with HRESULTs

Macros	Definition
SUCCEEDED()	Returns TRUE if the severity is success (zero) and FALSE if the severity is failure (one).
FAILED()	Opposite of SUCCEEDED().
HRESULT_FACILITY()	Returns the facility code of the HRESULT.
HRESULT_SEVERITY()	Returns the severity bit of the HRESULT_CODE().
HRESULT_CODE()	Returns the status code of the HRESULT.
MAKE_HRESULT()	Builds an HRESULT from its three components (facility, severity, status code).

Error-Handling Strategies

There are three strategies for handling HRESULT values. The first strategy is to simply test for S_OK, zero, and nonzero values. As you remember, earlier in this chapter you encountered the E_ACCESSDENIED HRESULT from the CoCreateInstance() function. In order to test for an error condition, you tested the HRESULT for a nonzero value. This caught the error adequately and terminated the program somewhat appropriately. This error-handling strategy is acceptable for some situations that do not require clean error handling.

The preferred method is to test the HRESULT using the SUCCEEDED() and FAILED() macros. This strategy is no harder to implement and is a better strategy for production-quality applications. Listing 13.8 is an example of using this strategy. Notice in the code that the FAILED() macro is used to test for an error.

LISTING 13.8 Using FAILED() for Error Handling

```
hresult = ::CoCreateInstance(clsid, NULL, CLSCTX_SERVER,
                    IID_IUnknown, (LPVOID FAR *) &punk);
if FAILED(hresult)
{
    // CoCreateInstance failed
    return hresult;
};
```

The third strategy is to test using specific HRESULTS. The difference between the second and third strategies is the difference between testing with an if statement and testing with a case statement. Listing 13.9 is an example of using the third strategy.

LISTING 13.9 Using Specific HRESULTS for Error Handling

```
hresult = ::CoCreateInstance(clsid, NULL, CLSCTX_SERVER,
                    D_IUnknown, (LPVOID FAR *) &punk);
switch (hresult)
{
case E_ACCESSDENIED:
    // CoCreateInstance failed because of access denied
    return hresult;
case S_OK:
    // CoCreateInstance succeeded
    break;
default:
    // CoCreateInstance failed for unexpected reason
    return E_UNEXPECTED;
};
```

Notice that the previous code doesn't stop at simply using the FAILED() macro to test for an error. I go through and check for specific error values such as E_ACCESSDENIED. You could add more if the need arises.

HRESULTs are convenient identifiers for returning limited error information to the client. But what if you want to pass back more than an identifier? You might remember seeing a check box in the ATL object wizard called Support ISupportErrorInfo. This is another form of error handling that enables COM+ servers to pass very rich error information to the client.

Passing Information with ISupportErrorInfo

The ISupportErrorInfo interface and its two cousins, ICreateErrorInfo and IErrorInfo, allow COM+ classes to pass additional information back to the client. The mechanism for implementing and using these interfaces is quite simple. Your COM+ class must implement the ISupportErrorInfo interface. Your COM+ class must set the error using ICreateErrorInfo, and your client must retrieve the error using IErrorInfo.

Not another three interfaces? Fortunately ATL has covered two of these interfaces well enough that I need only tell you about ISupportErrorInfo (see Listing 13.10).

LISTING 13.10 IDL for ISupportErrorInfo

```
interface ISupportErrorInfo: IUnknown
{
    HRESULT InterfaceSupportsErrorInfo(
            [in]  REFIID riid);
}
```

This isn't much of a task either. Start by creating a new ATL COM+ class using the ATL Object Wizard. From Developer Studio's menu bar, select Insert, New ATL Object. In the first wizard page, select the Objects category, the Simple Object object, and click the Next button. In the second wizard page, type the short name Oops and move to the Attributes property page. Now here's the tough part. Select Support ISupportErrorInfo and click OK. That's it.

Your COM+ class now supports this rich error information, but because your class doesn't do anything, it can't report any errors. You'll learn the power of this error-handling support by adding one method, conveniently enough called Throw, to the IOops interface. Listing 13.11 shows the declaration of the COops class.

LISTING 13.11   Declaration of COops, the class that implements IOops

```
// Oops.h : Declaration of the COops

#ifndef __OOPS_H_
#define __OOPS_H_

#include "resource.h"       // main symbols

/////////////////////////////////////////////////////////////////////////////
// COops
class ATL_NO_VTABLE COops :
    public CComObjectRootEx<CComMultiThreadModel>,
    public CComCoClass<COops, &CLSID_Oops>,
    public ISupportErrorInfo,
    public IDispatchImpl<IOops, &IID_IOops, &LIBID_SERVERLib>
{
public:
    COops()
    {
    }

DECLARE_REGISTRY_RESOURCEID(IDR_OOPS)

DECLARE_PROTECT_FINAL_CONSTRUCT()

BEGIN_COM_MAP(COops)
    COM_INTERFACE_ENTRY(IOops)
    COM_INTERFACE_ENTRY(IDispatch)
    COM_INTERFACE_ENTRY(ISupportErrorInfo)
END_COM_MAP()

// ISupportsErrorInfo
    STDMETHOD(InterfaceSupportsErrorInfo)(REFIID riid);

// IOops
```

LISTING **13.10**   Continued

```
public:
    STDMETHOD(Throw)();
};

#endif //__OOPS_H_
```

In the COops::Throw() method, you'll return rich error information by using the CComCoClass::Error() method (see Listing 13.12.

LISTING **13.12**   Definition of COops

```
// Oops.cpp : Implementation of COops
#include "stdafx.h"
#include "Server.h"
#include "Oops.h"

/////////////////////////////////////////////////////////////////////////////
// COops

STDMETHODIMP COops::InterfaceSupportsErrorInfo(REFIID riid)
{
    static const IID* arr[] =
    {
        &IID_IOops
    };
    for (int i=0; i < sizeof(arr) / sizeof(arr[0]); i++)
    {
        if (InlineIsEqualGUID(*arr[i],riid))
            return S_OK;
    }
    return S_FALSE;
}

STDMETHODIMP COops::Throw()
{
    Error(_T("Another error"), IID_IOops);

    return E_FAIL;
}
```

Note that in the definition of COops in Listing 13.12, there are two methods. The COops::InterfaceSupportsErrorInfo() method has a very simple implementation that returns S_OK if a REFIID supports the rich error information and S_FALSE if it doesn't. For now, there is only one IID (interface ID), so you only return S_OK for that interface. If you had a second interface, say IID_IOops2, the implementation of the COops::InterfaceSupportsErrorInfo() method would change to that in Listing 13.13.

LISTING 13.13 Multiple Interface Support

```
STDMETHODIMP COops::InterfaceSupportsErrorInfo(REFIID riid)
{
    static const IID* arr[] =
    {
        &IID_IOops,
        &IID_IOops2
    };
    for (int i=0; i < sizeof(arr) / sizeof(arr[0]); i++)
    {
        if (InlineIsEqualGUID(*arr[i],riid))
            return S_OK;
    }
    return S_FALSE;
}
```

The implementation of the `COops::Throw()` method in Listing 13.14 simply calls the `CComCoClass::Error()` method and returns `E_FAIL`.

LISTING 13.14 IErrorInfo Client

```
// controller.cpp : Defines the entry point for the console application.
//

#include "stdafx.h"

#import "..\server\server.tlb"

int main(int argc, char* argv[])
{
    ::CoInitialize(NULL);
    {
        SERVERLib::IOopsPtr p(__uuidof(SERVERLib::Oops));
        try
        {
            p->Throw();
        }
        catch(_com_error e)
        {
          std::cout << "Error: " << e.Error() << " - "
                              << (char *)e.Source() << " - "
                              << (char *)e.Description() << std::endl;
        }
    }
    ::CoUninitialize();
    return 0;
}
```

13

CONFIGURATION
AND ERROR
HANDLING

In this case, I used Visual C++'s support for importing type libraries. When Visual C++ encounters the #import statement, it generates a class for your COM+ object, thus allowing you very intuitive access to your COM+ object.

Don't be fooled into thinking that COM+ actually throws an exception. The exception was thrown by a wrapper class that was generated by the #import statement. If you are working with COM+ interface pointers, the method returns without throwing an exception. It is then the programmer's responsibility to fetch the rich error information (see Listing 13.15).

LISTING 13.15 Another IErrorInfo Client

```
// controller2.cpp : Defines the entry point for the console application.
//

#include "stdafx.h"
#include "../server/server.h"
#include "../server/server_i.c"

class WideToAnsiBuffer
{
public:
    WideToAnsiBuffer()
        : s(0) {};
    ~WideToAnsiBuffer()
        { del(); };
    void del()
        { delete [] s; };
    char * s;
};

inline char * WideToAnsi(const WCHAR * pwchar)
{
    long l = ::wcslen(pwchar)+1;
  static WideToAnsiBuffer s;
    s.del();
    s.s = new char[l+1];
  ::WideCharToMultiByte(CP_ACP, 0, pwchar, -1, s.s, l, NULL, NULL);
    return s.s;
}

HRESULT GetUnknown(WCHAR * strProgID, IUnknown ** ppunknown)
{
  CLSID clsid;
  HRESULT hresult = ::CLSIDFromProgID(strProgID, &clsid);
  hresult = ::CoCreateInstance(clsid, NULL, CLSCTX_SERVER,
                        IID_IUnknown, (void **)ppunknown);
    return S_OK;
```

LISTING **13.15** Continued

```cpp
};

HRESULT GetInterface(IUnknown * punknown, REFIID riid,
                     IUnknown ** ppunknown)
{
  HRESULT hresult = punknown->QueryInterface(riid,
                                             (void **)ppunknown);
  return S_OK;
};

int main()
{
  ::CoInitialize(NULL);

  IUnknown * punknown = 0;
  IOops * poops = 0;

  HRESULT hresult = GetUnknown(L"Server.Oops.1",
                              &punknown);
  hresult = GetInterface(punknown, IID_IOops,
                  (IUnknown **)&poops);
  hresult = poops->Throw();
  if (FAILED(hresult))
  {
      IErrorInfo * perrorinfo;
      ::GetErrorInfo(0, &perrorinfo);
      BSTR bstr = 0;
      perrorinfo->GetDescription(&bstr);
      std::cout << "We had an error\nDescription: " <<
      ➥WideToAnsi(bstr);
      perrorinfo->GetSource(&bstr);
      std::cout << "\nSource: " << WideToAnsi(bstr);
  }

  punknown->Release();

  ::CoUninitialize();
  return 0;
}
```

If you look near the end of Listing 13.15, you'll see that I called the GetErrorInfo()
function to retrieve the IErrorInfo interface. The IErrorInfo interface has a few members that enable you to retrieve different properties of the error (see Listing 13.16).

LISTING 13.16   IDL for `IerrorInfo`

```
interface IErrorInfo: IUnknown
{
    HRESULT GetGUID([out] GUID * pGUID);
    HRESULT GetSource([out] BSTR * pBstrSource);
    HRESULT GetDescription([out] BSTR * pBstrDescription);
    HRESULT GetHelpFile([out] BSTR * pBstrHelpFile);
    HRESULT GetHelpContext([out] DWORD * pdwHelpContext);
}
```

I used the `IErrorInfo::GetDescription()` and `IErrorInfo::GetSource()` methods to retrieve only the most basic information. All the source code for the `IErrorInfo` sections is included on the CD-ROM as errorinfo. It can be found in the errorinfo subdirectory in the chapter13 directory. If you step through the code of the two clients provided, you have a better feel for the power of these three error handling interfaces.

Summary

This chapter gives you a solid basis for understanding how to configure DCOM and to handle errors. You first learned how to use the DCOMCNFG utility so the COM+ works correctly on client machines. The sections in the registry that pertain to COM+ configuration were discussed, and you learned what to look out for when examining the registry. Several examples using Visual C++ were shown—these will help you write special utilities to automate some configuration operations.

Client COM+ errors were discussed along with ways to fix the client configuration so that the errors are fixed. This is an important section because the client configuration must be correct or all your COM+ development will have been in vain.

COM Internet
Services

CHAPTER 14

COM Internet Services (CIS) was created to provide support for Tunneling Transmission Control Protocol (TCP). This protocol allows COM to operate over TCP port 80 (the normal HTTP port). As a result, clients and servers can communicate in the presence of most proxy servers and firewalls. This enables a new class of COM-based Internet scenarios.

In addition to the new COM protocol, CIS also provides a new type of simple moniker—the OBJREF moniker—that facilitates the use of COM in Internet scenarios. The OBJREF moniker represents a reference to a running object and has a display name that can, for example, be embedded in an HTML page and bound by an ActiveX control or client applet.

This chapter explains what the COM Internet Services are, how they work, and how to configure computers running Microsoft Windows to use the services.

A New COM+ Transport Protocol

In many Internet situations, the network connectivity between a client and a server is subject to a number of restrictions. For example:

- A proxy server that filters outbound network traffic might gate the client connection to the Internet. This is often the case for applications running in a corporate environment, but it can also apply to applications run by a user connecting to the Internet through an ISP.

- A firewall often controls incoming Internet traffic, defining what combinations of network ports, packets, and protocols are accepted to protect the server (or client) network environment.

In practice, the net effect of such restrictions is that a client and a server will probably have a very narrow set of protocol and port combinations available to carry out a conversation. Because COM+ dynamically selects network ports in a range (1024–65535) on which Internet-to-intranet network traffic is typically not allowed, it is not possible to reliably use the often used COM+ ports (which consist largely of RPC calls) over the Internet (although they are perfectly suitable for intranets). Moreover, firewalls are often set up to restrict access to port 135, upon which COM+ depends for a variety of services. Port 135 is usually used by COM+ for RPC authentication and will need to be specifically configured to be open for this authentication because things such as Proxy Server normally block this port. As with all other ports besides 80, it represents a potential security risk and is closed by default.

The Tunneling TCP protocol introduces a special handshake at the beginning of each COM+ connection that allows it to pass through most firewalls and proxies. After this handshake (which is handled transparently by CIS), the wire protocol is simply COM over TCP. Aside from the caveats listed later in this chapter, this means

- The protocol is transparent to both client and server. Neither the client code nor the server code needs to be modified to use CIS.
- All the COM+-over-TCP protocol services are available—including COM+ security and lifetime management (that is, "pinging") services.

Limitations of the Tunneling TCP Protocol

The Tunneling TCP protocol is subject to the following limitations:

- It requires that Internet Information Server version 4.0 or higher be installed on the server-side machine hosting CIS-accessible COM+ objects because part of CIS functionality is implemented using an ISAPI filter.
- Because Tunneling TCP consists of non-HTTP traffic after the initial handshake, CIS requires that proxy servers and firewalls permit such traffic over a port opened to HTTP.

> **Note**
>
> Because of these limitations, in practice, CIS does not support callbacks. This means, for example, that your applications cannot perform notifications using the connection point or advise sink mechanisms. However, if the CIS client can function as a CIS server and is configured as discussed later in this chapter, nothing prevents the client from receiving COM+ calls—including callbacks.

Tunneling TCP Protocol Overview

If the client configuration indicates that HTTP traffic to the server should be routed through a proxy, the client COM+ runtime environment establishes a TCP/Internet Protocol (IP) connection to that proxy. It then sends the HTTP CONNECT method to the proxy requesting connection to port 80 on the server host. Figure 14.1 shows a diagram of the Tunneling TCP flow.

The proxy establishes a TCP/IP connection with the server host. This assumes that the proxy is configured to enable the HTTP CONNECT method on the port connected by the client. This port configuration on the proxy is sometimes referred to as "enabling SSL tunneling."

14

COM INTERNET SERVICES

FIGURE 14.1

The Tunneling TCP flow.

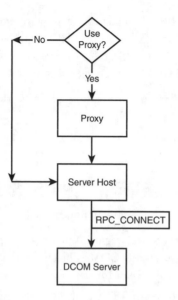

If the client configuration does not use a proxy, the COM+ runtime environment establishes a TCP/IP connection to port 80 on the server host. After this step, whether the client uses a proxy, the client has a connection to port 80 on the server host (perhaps mediated by a proxy). The client now sends the RPC_CONNECT command to the server requesting connection to the DCOM server on the server host.

In response to the RPC_CONNECT, the server RPC runtime environment (implemented in part by an ISAPI filter/extension pair) establishes a local connection to the COM+ server.

Client and server have now established a mediated TCP/IP connection and engage in a COM+-over-TCP conversation.

Configuring the Tunneling TCP Protocol

The Tunneling TCP protocol is supported on the operating systems listed in Table 14.1. Installation instructions are provided in the operating system or service pack release notes, as appropriate.

TABLE 14.1 Operating System Support for Tunneling TCP

Operating System	*Client*	*Server (Requires IIS 4.0 or greater)*
Windows 95 with DCOM95 1.2	Yes	No
Windows 98 with DCOM98 1.3	Yes	No
Windows NT 4.0 Workstation with SP4	Yes	No
Windows NT 4.0 Server with SP4	Yes	Yes
Windows 2000 Workstation	Yes	No
Windows 2000 Server	Yes	Yes

Client Configuration for Windows 95 and Windows 98

CIS requires that DCOM95 1.2 or a later version be installed on your Windows 95 machine. DCOM95 1.2 is available for download from the Microsoft COM Home Page, www.microsoft.com/com/default.asp. DCOM must be installed so that Windows 95 machines can participate in distributed applications. By default, the RPC capabilities needed are not present.

On Windows 98, you must have DCOM98 1.3 or later installed. DCOM98 1.3 ships with Windows 98 OSR1 and can also be downloaded from the Microsoft COM Home Page. Once again, as with Windows 95, you must install DCOM so that the RPC capabilities are present.

> **Note**
>
> You can download DCOM95 and DCOM98 from http://www.microsoft.com/Com/resources/downloads.asp.

One additional program you'll have to install is the DCOM98 configuration utility. In spite of its name, the same utility is used for both Windows 95 and Windows 98. When you run this program, it extracts the ciscnfg program to your computer into the Windows\System directory.

To enable CIS client support, run the CISCNFG utility from the command line with the following parameter (see Figure 14.2):

```
CISCNFG tcp_http
```

FIGURE 14.2

The ciscnfg utility.

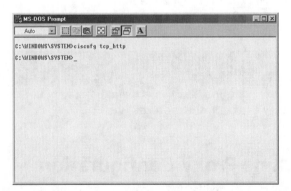

14

COM INTERNET SERVICES

CISCNFG configures the protocols that DCOM uses and can be used with the following arguments:

- tcp (DCOM over TCP only)
- http (Tunneled TCP only)
- tcp_http (DCOM over TCP is attempted, and then Tunneled TCP)

You will normally use tcp_http because this selects both tcp and http. After running CISCNFG, you must reboot your system.

> **Note**
>
> If you depend on DCOM98 functionality, you have two options: redistribute the updated system files (DCOM98) with your application, or point users to the DCOM98 Web release. Pointing users to the Web release is recommended if your application will be downloaded from the Web because DCOM98 is fairly large and many users might already have it.

Client Configuration for Windows NT 4.0 SP4 and Windows 2000

CIS support is included with Windows NT 4.0 Service Pack 4 and Windows 2000.

To enable CIS, you need to add the Tunneling TCP protocol to the DCOM protocol list. You can modify the protocol list by implementing the following steps to run DCOMC-NFG:

1. Select the Default Protocols tab.
2. Use the Add button to add Tunneling TCP/IP.
3. Reboot the system to have this change take effect.

> **Note**
>
> If multiple protocols are configured, an attempt is made to use them in the order in which they appear in the protocol list.

Client Machine Proxy Configuration

Let's say that your client is located behind a proxy server. If this is the case, you need to ensure that your client machine is correctly configured to use the proxy server to access the Web. To configure your client to use the proxy server, open the Connection tab of the Internet Properties dialog as shown in Figure 14.3, or go to Internet Options from Internet Explorer. This can also be set via a registry key as described in the later section "Registry Keys Affecting CIS." Note that this configuration is shared with the RPC run-time environment by other applications that use HTTP, most notably Microsoft Internet Explorer.

Proxy configuration must be set for all client machines behind proxy servers, regardless of operating system.

FIGURE 14.3

HTTP proxy configuration.

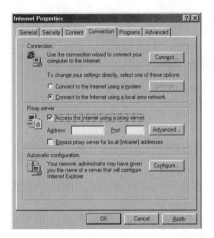

Server Configuration on Windows NT Server 4.0

CIS requires that Service Pack 4 be installed on your Windows NT Server 4.0 computer. CIS also requires that Internet Information Server 4.0 (including the Internet Service Manager) be running. IIS 4.0 is part of the Windows NT 4.0 Option Pack.

> **Caution**
>
> CIS should not be installed on a machine running Microsoft Proxy Server. CIS conflicts with the Microsoft Proxy Server port configuration.

Create an RPC subdirectory under your Inetpub directory. For example, at the command prompt, type the following:

```
md c:\inetpub\rpc
```

14

COM INTERNET
SERVICES

This directory will be referred to as %inetpub%\rpc in the following instructions.

Copy rpcproxy.dll from the Windows system directory to %inetpub%\rpc. For example, at the command prompt, type the following:

```
copy %windir%\system32\rpcproxy.dll c:\inetpub\rpc
```

Create a virtual root for the directory you created. To do this, implement the following:

1. From the Start menu, select Programs, point to Windows NT 4.0 Option Pack, Microsoft Internet Information Server, and then click Internet Server Manager.

2. In the console tree (the left pane), select Console Root/IIS/<machine name>/Default Web Site.

3. Right-click Default Web Site, click Create New, and then click Virtual Directory. In the New Virtual Directory Wizard, enter the following:

    Alias to be used to access virtual directory

    RPC

    Physical path

    %inetput%\rpc

    Permissions

    Execute Access

Don't close Internet Service Manager. Change the Connection Timeout for the Default Web Site to 5 minutes. To do this

1. In the console tree (the left pane), select Console Root/IIS/<machine name>/Default Web Site.

2. Right-click Default Web Site, and then click Properties.

3. In the Default Web Site Properties dialog box, select the Web Site tab.

4. Change the Connection Timeout to 300.

5. Click OK. Do not close Internet Service Manager.

6. Install the RPC Proxy ISAPI Filter. Select Console Root/IIS/<machine name> in the console tree (the left pane), right-click the machine name, click Properties, select Edit for the Master WWW Service Properties, select the ISAPI Filters tab, select Add, and then enter the following:

    Filter name

    Rpcproxy

    Executable

    %inetput%\rpc\rpcproxy.dll

You can close Internet Service Manager now. At a command prompt, stop and restart the Internet Information Server with the following commands:

```
net stop iisadmin
```

```
net start w3svc
```

Enable CIS on the server as described later in this chapter in the section "Enabling CIS."

> **Note**
>
> In previous versions of IIS, you could stop the entire Web service by typing at the command line **net stop w3svc**. This would terminate all the Web services on the computer, and shut down the Inetinfo.exe process. As a result of the new multiple–Web site architecture, there is another service, Iisadmin, that keeps running, even when W3SVC is shut down. The same is true for starting and stopping services from Control Panel. If you truly want to unload the Inetinfo.exe process and make sure that all the extensions are unloaded properly, you should now type **net stop iisadmin**, rather than **net stop w3svc**. Typing **net start w3svc** or **net start msftpsvc** automatically starts Iisadmin.

Configuring the RPC Proxy on Windows 2000 Server

On the Windows 2000 Server, CIS requires that the Internet Information Services (including the Internet Services Manager) be running.

On Windows 2000 Server, CIS has its own optional network setup (it is not installed by default). It can be installed just like other optional network components.

From the Control Panel, select Add/Remove Programs, click Add/Remove Windows Components, and then click the Components button. This will start the Windows Components Wizard. From the wizard, complete the following:

1. Select Networking Services, and click the Details button.
2. Select the COM Internet Services Proxy check box.

You can add CIS during the initial Windows 2000 Server install, or add it later to an existing system. On an upgrade from a Windows NT 4.0 (SP4) Server that already has CIS installed to Windows 2000, you will need to reinstall CIS as described previously.

Enabling CIS

To enable CIS on the server, you need to add the Tunneling TCP protocol to the DCOM protocol list. You do this by running DCOMCNFG from the Windows\System directory (using either a command prompt or the run box), and then follow the next steps:

1. Select the Default Protocols tab.
2. Use the Add button to add Tunneling TCP/IP.
3. Reboot the system to have this change take effect.

In addition, it is possible to control whether CIS is enabled by changing the value of a DCOM property. This setting, which defaults to disabled, can act as a coarse-grained security control to disable potential Internet access to DCOM. Note, however, that even when CIS is enabled, the usual DCOM security checks remain in effect. Run DCOMC-NFG to set this property by implementing these steps:

1. Select the Default Properties tab.
2. Select or unselect the Enable COM Internet Services on this computer check box.
3. Reboot the system for the change to take effect.

Proxy Server Configuration

If the client is configured to access the Internet through a proxy, the proxy server must be configured to enable the HTTP CONNECT method for the port to which the client connects (port 80 by default). This port configuration is sometime referred to as "enabling SSL tunneling." Consult the documentation for your proxy server for details on how to configure a port for the HTTP CONNECT method.

Configuring Microsoft Proxy Server

If you are using Microsoft Proxy Server, enabling HTTP CONNECT is achieved by manipulating a registry key (for example, using regedt32.exe) to indicate what ports should allow HTTP CONNECT. In the default configuration, two ports are enabled: 443 (https) and 563 (snews). The registry key of interest is

```
HKEY_LOCAL_MACHINE\system\CurrentControlSet\services\w3proxy\parameters\
➥SSLPortListMembers
```

The key value consists of a list of pairs of ports. For the default proxy configuration (handling HTTP traffic on port 80), add the pair **80 80** to the existing registry values. After making this modification, you will need to stop and restart the Microsoft Proxy Server for the new settings to take effect. You can view the Microsoft Proxy Server in Figure 14.4.

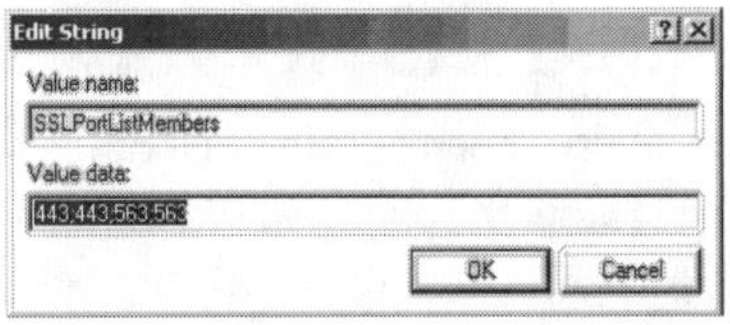

FIGURE 14.4

*Configuring
Microsoft Proxy
Server with
regedit.*

Firewall Configuration

The only configuration requirement placed by CIS on the firewall is that it allows TCP/IP traffic through port 80 unimpeded. Because port 80 is usually open to HTTP traffic, this is the standard scenario. In some rare cases, however, a firewall performs so-called application-level filtering on incoming traffic that might result in CIS traffic being rejected.

Configuration Tips and Known Issues

There are a few things that can go wrong when you configure CIS. I've found a number of them that are documented in TechNet.

Incorrect Proxy Server Settings on the CIS Client

The proxy server setting on the client should not contain any leading forward slash (/). For example, the reference myproxy:80 is correct but http://myproxy is not. Note that the proxy server setting (set using Internet in the Control Panel) is stored in the registry as the value of the

```
HKEY_CURRENT_USER\Software\Microsoft\Windows\CurrentVersion\Internet Settings\
➥ProxyServer
```

Caution

CIS server side should not be installed on a machine hosting Microsoft Proxy Server because of the port control conflicts.

The RPC proxy, RpcProxy.dll, does not function properly when installed on a machine hosting Microsoft Proxy Server.

14

COM INTERNET
SERVICES

Issue with a Multihomed CIS Server

A client of a multihomed CIS server activating an object using one of the server IP addresses can cause failure. To work around this limitation, the client should use the server name (for example, the DNS name). For example, instead of 209.42.234.81, use www.sourceDNA.com.

MTS Use of Callbacks

When a client and a server share a transaction in a Microsoft Transaction Server (MTS) scenario, the MTS infrastructure makes a callback to the client. This scenario is not supported with CIS unless the client machine is configured as a CIS server. Note, however, that this limitation does not hinder the most common transaction scenario for a base client, the case of a client not in a transaction calling a component that requires one.

Issue with HTTP Caching Devices

HTTP caching devices (for example, Cisco LocalDirector) might need to be tweaked or disabled.

Intelligent routers such as Cisco's LocalDirector allow a group of servers to appear as a single virtual server. The IP address of the virtual server is registered with the DNS server, whereas the IP addresses of the servers themselves remain unpublished. When the virtual server receives incoming requests, the router distributes the requests to one of them. The entire group of servers thus appears to the client as a single server.

When Cisco's LocalDirector is used in combination with IIS for session-aware load-balancing in a Web farm, it is important to make sure that the interval for the router matches or exceeds the timeout interval for the Session object. By default, the Session object timeout is set to 20 minutes. The timeout interval can be changed to 15 minutes by adding the following line to the Global.asa file:

```
<% Session.Timeout = 15 %>
```

Registry Keys Affecting CIS

The information in Table 14.2 shows you the registry keys that affect CIS.

TABLE 14.2   Registry Keys that Affect CIS Operation

Registry Key	Description
HKEY_CURRENT_USER\ Software\Microsoft\ Windows\CurrentVersion\ Internet Settings\ ProxyServer	The value of this client-side setting indicates the \<proxy server>:\<port> that CIS uses \<proxy server> should not contain leading forward slashes (/). Note that this configuration is shared with the RPC runtime environment by other applications that use HTTP, such as Internet Explorer. Proxy Server configuration can also be set in the Control Panel by opening the Internet icon.

TABLE 14.2 Continued

Registry Key	Description
HKEY_LOCAL_MACHINE\ SOFTWARE\Microsoft\Rpc\ DCOM Protocols	Client and server setting indicating which DCOM protocols to use. This can also be set with CISCNFG on Windows 95 and Windows 98 and DCOMCNFG for Windows NT 4.0.
HKEY_LOCAL_MACHINE\ SOFTWARE\Microsoft\Ole\ EnableDCOMHTTP	The value of this server-side setting indicates whether CIS is enabled for the machine. Possible values are Y and N. This property can be set with DCOMCNFG.

OBJREF Moniker

To allow clients to establish connections to an object already running on a remote server, CIS provides a new type of simple moniker known as the OBJREF moniker. This moniker provides a simple mechanism for embedding references to remote objects in an HTML page.

OBJREF monikers represent references to local or remote objects running on a distributed system. The OBJREF moniker represents a particular running instance on a particular server. If the object instance terminates, the OBJREF moniker is invalid.

If a moniker is created from a proxy to a remote object and bound on a different machine, the moniker will bind to the original object in keeping with the DCOM shortcut semantics. If the object cannot be located during an attempt to bind, no new objects will be launched.

In many ways, the semantics of the OBJREF moniker are similar to that of a pointer moniker and essentially represent a remote pointer to a running object. However, the display name of an OBJREF moniker might be embedded in an HTML page and bound by a client applet or ActiveX control.

Knowing When To Use CIS

An Active Server Page (or some other means of generating dynamic HTML content) might place the display name of an OBJREF moniker in a parameter to an applet or ActiveX control. The applet or control can then use the moniker to connect to the running object instance on the remote server.

To use OBJREF monikers, the server code generating the moniker must use the CreateObjrefMoniker function to create the monikers, passing an interface to the object that the moniker will bind.

14

COM INTERNET
SERVICES

Necessary Programming Changes

There are a few things you need to keep in mind when using the Tunneling TCP protocol. This section presents those.

OBJREF monikers represent a reference to an object instance that is running on an out-of-process server, either locally or remotely. The moniker identifies the object instance and the computer the object is running on. An OBJREF moniker is similar in many ways to a pointer moniker, except that the running object is out-of-process. A client can call `IMoniker::BindToObject()` on an OBJREF moniker and use the pointer it obtains to access the running object, regardless of its location.

An important distinction from a pointer moniker is that the display name of an OBJREF moniker can be embedded in an HTML page, and the running object represented by the moniker can be bound by a client script, applet, or ActiveX control.

The primary use for an OBJREF moniker is to obtain access to a running object instance over the Internet. An Active Server Page or some other means of generating dynamic HTML content places the display name of an OBJREF moniker in a parameter to an applet or an ActiveX control. The code of the applet or control calls `CreateObjrefMoniker()` to create an OBJREF moniker based on the display name, and it then calls `IMoniker::BindToObject()` on the resulting OBJREF moniker to get access to the running object instance. The Active Server Page then marshals a pointer to the running object back to the page's client. Table 14.3 shows the IMoniker functions with explanations.

TABLE 14.3   The IMoniker Functions and Comments Regarding CIS

IMoniker Function	Comments
`IMoniker::BindToObject()`	For OBJREF monikers, the `pmkToLeft` parameter must be `NULL`. Because the OBJREF moniker represents a running object, no activation takes place. If the represented object is no longer running, `BindToObject()` fails with `E_UNEXPECTED`.
`IMoniker::BindToStorage()`	This method obtains a marshaled pointer to the requested interface on the storage that contains the running object. Because the OBJREF moniker represents a running object, no activation takes place. If the represented object is no longer running, `BindToStorage()` fails with `E_UNEXPECTED`.
`IMoniker::Reduce()`	This method returns `MK_S_REDUCED_TO_SELF` and passes back the same moniker.

TABLE 14.3 Continued

IMoniker Function	Comments
IMoniker::ComposeWith()	If pmkRight is an anti-moniker, the returned moniker is NULL. If pmkRight is a composite whose left-most component is an anti-moniker, the returned moniker is the composite with the left-most anti-moniker removed. If pmkRight is neither an anti-moniker nor a composite moniker whose left-most component is an anti-moniker, the method checks the fOnlyIfNotGeneric parameter. If it is FALSE, the method combines the two monikers into a generic composite; if it is TRUE, the method sets *ppmkComposite to NULL and returns MK_E_NEEDGENERIC.
IMoniker::Enum()	This method returns S_OK and sets ppenumMoniker to NULL.
IMoniker::IsEqual()	This method returns S_OK if *pmkOther is an OBJREF moniker and the paths for both monikers are identical (using a not–case-sensitive comparison). Otherwise, the method returns S_FALSE.
IMoniker::Hash()	This method calculates a hash value for the moniker.
IMoniker::IsRunning()	Because OBJREF monikers represent a running object instance, this method returns TRUE unless the object is known to be no longer running because a recent call failed. The method ignores pmkToLeft.
IMoniker::GetTimeOfLastChange()	This method returns E_NOTIMPL.
IMoniker::Inverse()	This method returns an anti-moniker, such as the results of calling CreateAntiMoniker().
IMoniker::CommonPrefixWith()	If the two monikers are equal, this method returns MK_S_US and sets *ppmkPrefix to NULL. If the other moniker is not an OBJREF moniker, this method passes both monikers to the MonikerCommonPrefixWith() function. This function correctly handles the case in which the other moniker is a generic composite. If there is no common prefix, this method returns MK_E_.
IMoniker::RelativePathTo()	This method returns E_NOTIMPL.
IMoniker::GetDisplayName()	This method obtains the display name for the OBJREF moniker. The display name is a 64-bit encoding that encapsulates the machine location, process endpoint, and interface pointer ID (IPID) of the running object. For future compatibility, the display name is restricted to characters that can be specified as part of a URL.
IMoniker::ParseDisplayName()	If pmkToLeft is not NULL, this method returns MK_E_SYNTAX.
IMoniker::IsSystemMoniker()	This method returns S_OK and passes back MKSYS_OBJREFMONIKER.

14

COM INTERNET SERVICES

Summary

If you deal with a distributed technology that relies on COM+, and it lives behind a fire-wall, you might need to seriously consider using CIS. It's a solution to the problem of closed ports behind a firewall, many of which can prevent COM+ from functioning correctly.

CIS isn't hard to install or configure, and it's already part of the operating system. CIS gives you a solution that you'll be seeking when you deal with firewalls and closed ports.

MTS

CHAPTER 15

One of the goals of COM+ is to simplify the development of distributed applications. For this reason, COM+ services provide the infrastructure that MTS offers in an easier-to-user and more manageable process. But although this has simplified the tasks of most developers, it has foiled the tasks of others. COM+ doesn't offer the fine granularity of control that MTS offers, and there are times when a developer will want to drop down to MTS from COM+ to gain this control.

That's one reason this chapter was included in a COM+ book. MTS is underneath COM+ and as such can still be called upon in times of need.

Another reason to learn about MTS is that it can be beneficial to understand the fundamental technology to gain a better overall knowledge of the subject. This is the case here—learning MTS will help you in your quest to understand COM+.

Business Transactions

Most enterprise applications involve two distinct types of items, payment and goods or services. A customer might order an item such as a CD via a Web page. The customer then might enter his credit card number to pay for the CD. An invoice or receipt, which can be printed out, is generated in the Web browser. The Web application then indicates that the transaction is a success.

In database applications, a transaction is an action taken by a program that affects at least two pieces of shared data bound by a business rule. For example, in a client/server database application, a business rule might state that for each item removed from an inventory table in a relational database, a record for the money received must be added to one of the account tables in that database or in another database.

From a programming perspective, transactions must follow four criteria, known as the ACID rules. According to the principles of ACID, transactions must be the following:

- Atomic transactions—Must be all-or-nothing operations. For example, if inventory is reduced, an increase in revenue must occur. The application cannot simply reduce inventory without adding revenue. Along the same lines, the application cannot add revenue and not reduce inventory. Changes are permanent only when all the pieces have completed successfully.

- Consistent—After a transaction completes, the data in the database must be valid as specified by the rules of referential integrity. This means that even if individual changes break the database rules, when all updates have been made, the data must be valid.

- Isolated—Multiple transactions occurring simultaneously must affect the data as if all transactions were running one at a time and in sequence. A transaction is not allowed to use the uncommitted changes of another transaction. If transaction A, for example, reduces the number of books in inventory, transaction B cannot use the uncommitted total of books until transaction A is finalized.

• Durable—All commits in a transaction are final. After a program receives confirmation that a transaction has succeeded, if the operating system crashes, or if the network dies, when the system is restored, the changes must remain.

Coordinating Transactions

A common problem with distributed applications is coordinating transactions involving more than one data source in multiple servers that might be vastly different from one another. For transactions to be atomic, the servers must be coordinated. In other words, one server cannot be triggered to commit a transaction, only to discover that another server cannot continue the transaction. For a transaction to complete successfully, the servers must both commit the transaction.

To accomplish this, transaction systems employ the services of a transaction manager that executes a protocol known as the two-phase commit. The two-phase commit is a protocol in which, prior to committing a transaction, a data source or resource manager is asked whether it is ready to commit. After all the RMs reply positively, they are instructed to commit.

The term resource manager denotes a system that manages durable data (or resources). An example of a resource is a database. Microsoft SQL Server is an example of a resource manager. Other examples of resources include message queues, files, and so on.

To simplify coordinating transactions using the two-phase commit, you can use Microsoft Distributed Transaction Coordinator (MS DTC). MS DTC was first shipped in April 1996 with SQL Server 6.5. Later, MS DTC was separated from SQL Server and is now part of the Microsoft Windows NT core services.

MS DTC coordinates transactions that occur across multiple resource managers, which can operate on separate computers.

Transactions and COM

In the past, organizations created fat clients or two-tier solutions around specific database systems. In a client/server system, the database resided on a server computer and clients connected to the server via the network. Clients ran applications that contained code to display data and code to manipulate the data directly with the database system following a particular set of rules (business rules). These applications normally accessed the database server through a series of proprietary API functions designed for that particular database. These APIs often offered methods to begin, commit, and abort transactions. Thus, the client determined the length of a transaction.

15

MTS

Fat clients use a lot of memory, drive space, and have many dependencies. To improve performance and scalability, the fat client was split to allow it to run from different computers. The database manipulation code and business rules code were separated from the front end and became known as the middle tier.

Developers in Windows environments turned to COM as the standard for building middle-tier components. With COM, you can create separate components that specialize in multiple business tasks. For example, an application can have one component for updating inventory, another for calculating commissions, and so on. However, it is difficult to coordinate transactions among different COM objects, especially if these transactions involve multiple databases in more than one server.

To make it easier to write middle tiers in COM, Microsoft introduced MTS.

What Is MTS?

MTS is a container for COM-based middle-tier components. MTS serves as a transaction processing (TP) monitor. A TP monitor is a piece of software that manages transactions. TP monitors facilitate the implementation of the ACID rules and use transaction managers to execute the two-phase commit protocol in transactional distributed applications. In short, a TP monitor is the software location in which transactions occur—think of it as the marketplace. MTS enlists the services of MS DTC to coordinate transactions among COM objects that might involve different database resources in various computers.

MTS also serves as an object request .broker (ORB). An ORB is a piece of software that can manage the lifetime of middle-tier components. You will learn in this chapter, however, that MTS is much more than a TP monitor and an ORB. In many ways, MTS is an enhancement to classic COM.

Benefits of Using MTS

So far this chapter has defined MTS in terms of transaction processing (after all, the product is called Transaction Services). However, MTS can do much more than help coordinate transactions. MTS can enhance and change the way that components behave.

To provide many of its services seamlessly, MTS uses a mechanism known as interception. Interception allows MTS to monitor every call made into an object before and after the call occurs.

Because MTS can monitor and intercept calls, it can perform more functions than just coordinating transactions. For example, MTS uses interception to implement a role-based security mechanism more sophisticated than that provided by DCOM. Intercepting the calls allows MTS to block calls made from clients that do not have permission to use the object. This feature of MTS minimizes the need for the component to handle DCOM security APIs directly. You can simply use MTS Explorer to create security groupings (or roles) and assign these groupings to different interfaces in a component.

Role-based security is one example of how the behavior of a component or even an application can be affected by changing a few settings with MTS Explorer without modifying the actual component. This type of configuration in which external attributes control a component's behavior is declarative programming.

A COM object that lives in MTS, and thus can have its behavior modified by declarative properties, is said to be a configured component. Because MTS hosts COM objects and can use interception to control the behavior of those objects, MTS provides you with several benefits as discussed in the following sections.

Surrogate Process for Components

MTS eliminates the need to create out-of-process servers (such as Microsoft ActiveX executables). COM objects that reside in MTS are always part of in-process servers (ActiveX DLLs). When a client instantiates a COM object found in a different computer, MTS launches a surrogate process (Mtx.exe) to host the COM objects that communicate with the client. For a complete discussion of surrogates, refer to the MSDN ActiveX SDK documentation.

> **Note**
>
> COM+ ships with another surrogate process called Dllhost.exe.

Role-Based Security

MTS eliminates the need to access COM security APIs directly. In addition, MTS enhances the security model provided by DCOM. In a default configuration of DCOM, you can control launching and access security only for a group of components declared to be part of one application under an AppID. In the MTS environment, you can create groupings (or roles) that can be assigned to each component within an application, and even to each interface within a component.

> **Note**
>
> In COM+, you can also assign roles to each method within an interface.

Just-In-Time Activation

Because MTS can intercept calls to each configured component, MTS can delay activation of an object when one of its methods is being called for the first time. This is known as Just-In-Time Activation and will be covered in more detail in Chapter 20.

MTS Explorer

MTS Explorer is a user-friendly tool in the form of an MMC snap-in that allows you to configure COM objects running under MTS.

The UI of this tool is much easier to use and more robust than Dcomcnfg.exe, the tool used to configure DCOM servers.

Transaction Coordination

As mentioned previously, one of the main jobs of MTS is to coordinate transactions among components. MTS uses a democratic system of transactions. In other words, objects are not able to explicitly begin, commit, or abort a transaction. Instead, objects vote on whether the transaction should continue. The client originates the transaction when it makes a call to the first component marked as transactional.

MTS Integration with Microsoft Internet Information Server

Although not discussed in detail in this chapter, Microsoft Internet Information Server (IIS) is tightly integrated with MTS. This is a real advantage since a Web page can initiate a transaction, thus providing additional flexibility for enterprise applications. An Active Server Page (ASP) can participate in a transaction simply by specifying `Transaction=required` in its header, as shown in the following code:

```
<%@ TRANSACTION=Required LANGUAGE="VBScript" %>
```

MTS Integration with Microsoft Message Queuing Services

Microsoft Message Queuing Services (MSMQ) is a means for distributed applications to communicate through messaging. An application can send and receive an MSMQ message as part of a transaction. For example, an object might send a message, but the message will not be truly sent until the transaction has been committed.

Now that you are aware of the benefits of using MTS, take a look at how MTS is organized.

MTS Structures

This section explains the hierarchy of MTS objects and how MTS works internally. We'll start off by learning about packages, the MTS administrative units. Then, components and contexts will be discussed—these are important for the COM+ chapters that come later in the book. Activities and roles are then talked about to round out this section.

Packages

A package is a group of objects with a common goal; a package can often be considered to be the middle tier of an application. Two types of packages—server and library—exist in MTS. A server package runs in its own process; a library package is loaded into the process space of the client.

> **Note**
>
> Because this chapter focuses on the older technology of MTS and COM, it is advisable to be aware of any new terms that the COM+ technology uses in relation to transactional technologies. In COM+, packages are known as applications.

An object cannot be part of more than one package. As mentioned previously, MTS provides a surrogate process Mtx.exe to host COM objects found in a DLL. When you add a COM class to a server package, MTS modifies the registry settings for that class. COM classes store configuration settings in the registry under HKEY_CLASSES_ROOT\CLSID.

Each coclass has a GUID, also known as a CLSID. When a client wants to create a class, it invokes the COM API CoCreateInstance() or CoGetClassObject().

CoCreateInstance() and CoGetClassObject() use the SCM to get an instance of the class. A client specifies in the APIs what class to create with a CLSID. The SCM looks through the registry for that particular CLSID, and when it finds the CLSID, it looks in the InProcServer32 subkey for the name and path of the DLL that contains the class. The SCM then loads the DLL, and calls into a well-known entry point, DllGetClassObject.

The DllGetClassObject function gives the SCM a pointer to the intended class. When you create a package and add your components to this package, MTS changes the value of the InProcServer32 key. If the component is added to a server package, MTS deletes the value in the InProcServer32 subkey and adds a LocalServer32 subkey. (The LocalServer32 subkey specifies the path to out-of-process servers.) In the LocalServer32 subkey, MTS writes code similar to the following:

```
D:\WINNT\System32\mtx.exe /p:{4B118EAB-8BA8-11D3-81D8-000000000000}
```

15

MTS

The first half of the string is the name and path to the MTS surrogate process (Mtx.exe). The second half of the string is a command-line argument for the executable—it specifies the GUID for the package that contains the original server name. In other words, clients are able to continue requesting the same CLSID, and the application will transparently instantiate the object in the MTS surrogate process. MTS also adds the package GUID to the registry under HKEY_LOCAL_MACHINE\SOFTWARE\Microsoft\Transaction Server\Packages.

In the example shown, the exact package entry would be HKEY_LOCAL_MACHINE\SOFTWARE\Microsoft\Transaction Server\Packages\{4B118EAB-8BA8-11D3-81D8-000000000000}. Under this key, you will find all configuration settings for the package, and a component subkey with additional subkeys for each component in the package.

In addition to creating instances of the requested COM object, Mtx.exe loads the MTS Executive (Mtxex.dll). The MTS Executive (or MTS runtime) is in charge of creating a context wrapper for your object. You will learn more about context wrappers in the next section.

> **Note**
>
> If the component is added to a library package, MTS changes the value of InProcServer32 to point to the MTS Executive (Mtxex.dll).

Components and Context

Packages store components. An MTS component is equivalent to a COM class or coclass. An MTS object is the in-memory instance of an MTS component.

Before MTS creates an object it creates a context wrapper for the object (MTS destroys the context wrapper before it destroys the object). The context wrapper contains information about the object's execution environment—it stores security settings, transaction information, and so on. MTS inserts the context wrapper between the stub (in the proxy/stub layer) and the object. With the context wrapper in place, MTS can intercept each call made to the object both before and after it takes place. For all practical purposes, think of the context wrapper as the place where an MTS object lives.

Later in this chapter, you will learn how to ensure that the relationship between the context wrapper and object is maintained at all times. To take full advantage of MTS, you will also learn how to get access to your object's context wrapper and invoke its methods. Each object instance from an MTS configured component has a context wrapper associated with it. Each object has at most one context wrapper associated with it. Object instances from non-configured components (non-MTS components) created by configured components do not have their own context wrappers but can access the context wrapper of their creator.

Activities

An activity is a group of objects that have the same concurrency requirements. In MTS 2, only one concurrency model that cannot be set through properties exists. (This aspect of MTS 2 will become more important in Microsoft Windows 2000 with COM+ because an administrator might change an object's concurrency requirements.) The only concurrency model MTS 2 supports is serialized; only one client can make a call into an activity at a time. MTS begins a new activity when a client creates a new MTS object. The client creating the object is called the base client; the object that the base client creates to begin the activity is known as the root of the activity. The root object can invite other objects to be part of the same activity with a special MTS API function, `CreateInstance()` (you will learn how to do this later). `CreateInstance()` is a function in the `IObjectContext` interface. Henceforth, any other object in the activity can use this API to invite other objects into the activity. An activity can involve components from one or more packages, and even from components in packages in other computers. Only objects in the same activity can participate in the same transaction.

Roles

An examination of the MTS structures would not be complete without discussing roles. As mentioned earlier, roles are user-defined groups that define user access to a package, component, or interface. For instance, if you wanted all users in the accounting group to have access to a component, but not the users in the engineering group, you would put all of the accounting users in an MTS role for the given component.

Configuring MTS

There are normally two types of environments for MTS: production and development. When configuring the server in a production environment, you might want to restrict the users who can modify properties for a component. MTS provides a system package that you can configure to restrict access to various features in the server. This package has two predefined roles: Administrator and Reader. However, these two roles do not have any users assigned to them. In a production environment, you will want to assign users to these roles and ensure that security is turned on for this package.

To make sure that security is active, do the following:

1. Start MTS Explorer.
2. In the left pane, open the Packages Installed folder under My Computer.
3. Right-click the System package, and then select Properties.
4. Click the Security tab, and then select the Enable Authorization Checking check box.

By default, your MTS Explorer is set to view only the properties for the current computer. However, you can administer another computer's MTS settings on a network through a single computer.

To view another computer in MTS Explorer, do the following:

1. Right-click the Computers folder, point to New, and then select Computer.
2. In the Add Computer dialog box, type the name of the computer that you want to administer and click OK. You must have access to this computer, and you must be a member of Reader to view settings, or Administrator to change properties.

Note

You cannot remotely administer a computer running Windows 95 from a computer running Windows NT.

Administering Your MTS Server Programmatically

MTS provides a series of scriptable objects that allow you to administer your server programmatically. These objects are based on IDispatch, and although it is definitely possible to use Visual C++ to write programs to use these objects, most people agree that using the IDispatch interface is best left to scripting clients. The MTS administration objects are as follows:

- Catalog Root object—Allows you to connect to a local or remote catalog and retrieve a collection
- CatalogObject—Allows you to get and set object properties
- CatalogCollection—Enumerates, adds, deletes, and modifies catalog objects
- PackageUtil—Allows you to install and export a package
- ComponentUtil—Installs a component in a specific collection and imports components registered as in-process servers

- `RemoteComponentUtil`—Allows you to pull remote components from a package on a remote server

- `RoleAssociationUtil`—Associates roles with a component or interface

Listing 15.1 creates a new package named mcsdpackage in the Packages Installed folder. This example is written in VBScript. The code first creates an instance of the Catalog object and uses the `GetCollection()` method to retrieve the Packages collection. The code then calls the `Add()` method of the collection.

To run this code with Windows Scripting Host (WSH) installed, type the code from Listing 15.1 into a Notepad file and save it with a .vbs extension. To run it, double-click the file.

LISTING 15.1   Retrieve and Use a Package

```
' First, create the catalog object
Dim catalog
Set catalog = CreateObject("MTSAdmin.Catalog.1")
' Next, get the packages collection
Dim packages
Set packages = catalog.GetCollection("Packages")
packages.Populate

' Add a new package
Dim newPackage
Set newPackage = packages.Add
newPackage.Value("Name") = "mcsdpackage"
' Commit new package
packages.SaveChanges
' Refresh packages
packages.Populate
```

MTS Objects

It is difficult to give general guidelines for building middle-tier components because they vary depending on each situation. However, there are several tips that apply to most projects.

First, when creating components for database applications, you should not attempt to do the work of the database in your middle-tier components. Database work, such as searching for a record and joining two tables, is best done with queries.

Second, you should not attempt to write general-purpose components that work inside as well as outside MTS. MTS creates a context wrapper for each object. MTS objects can gain access to the context wrapper and obtain various properties. For instance, if your

15

MTS

object is dependent on MTS running on a transaction, you should first verify that the administrator has not changed the configuration of your object before you change the database. Similarly, if your object must have tight security, you should be aware that an administrator could turn off security for your package. You must check the context to ensure that security is indeed turned on. MTS objects also follow a different lifetime path than classic COM objects.

Developing Objects for MTS

MTS components are COM classes that have the following requirements:

- MTS components must reside within in-process servers.
- Classes must implement IClassFactory.
- Type-library marshaling or standard fully-interpreted marshaling must be used.
- All component interfaces and coclasses must be included in the type library.

In-Process Server Location

MTS requires that objects exist in in-process servers (DLLs). MTS objects can exist inside a library package or a server package. When a client asks MTS to create an object in a library package, the objects are loaded into the address space of the client. When the client asks MTS to create an object in a server package, MTS loads the objects into the address space of an MTS-provided surrogate Mtx.exe. If you are used to creating out-of-process servers, consider that the code necessary to run an out-of-process server is usually insignificant when compared to the business code in your component. MTS handles the infrastructure needed to run your component.

IClassFactory Implementation

Every COM DLL has a standard entry point called DllGetClassObject that COM uses to obtain an instance of a COM class. This class must implement IClassFactory. MTS creates objects using the IClassFactory::CreateInstance method.

Type-Library or Standard Fully-Interpreted Marshaling

An object can use one of two marshaling mechanisms: type-library marshaling or standard marshaling. MTS does not allow custom marshaling. If a proxy-stub DLL is required, the DLL source must be generated with the /Oicf MIDL compiler flag. This will generate a proxy-stub DLL that is "fully-interpreted." Also, if you use a proxy-stub DLL, the source must be generated with MIDL 3.00.44 or later, and you must link the DLL with the Mtxih.lib library provided by MTS.

The Mtxih.lib library must be the first file that you link into your proxy-stub DLL.

Component Interfaces and Coclasses in a Type Library

MTS reads a server's type library to display the names of the classes, interfaces, and methods in MTS Explorer. To create an MTS-compatible COM server with ATL, do the following:

1. Open Visual C++ 6.0. On the File menu, click New.

2. On the Projects tab of the New dialog box, select ATL COM AppWizard, type a name for the project, and click OK.

3. In the ATL COM AppWizard, select Dynamic Link Library (DLL) under Server Type and select the Support MTS check box.

4. Click Finish, and then click OK.

Projects generated with this procedure add two libraries to the linking step aside from the "traditional libraries." The two libraries are Mtx.lib (which is an import library for the MTS runtime, Mtxex.dll, containing various MTS API functions such as `CreateInstance` and `SafeRef`) and Mtxguid.lib (which contains all the GUIDs for the various classes and interfaces in MTS). In addition, the project is linked with the Delayimp.lib library. This library allows the server to delay-load a DLL, in this case Mtxex.dll. A small problem with the project files generated is that it adds the self-registration step as a custom-build step, which is not desirable because registering the server will change the registry settings back to their original state (prior to adding the DLL to a package).

To create COM objects that can access their context wrapper objects, remember this: The ATL Object Wizard allows you to create COM objects that are MTS compatible and that can take advantage of MTS runtime features. You do this by selecting MS Transaction Server Component from the Objects group in the ATL Object Wizard. However, if you want to modify an existing component to run in MTS, you can replicate the features of the ATL Object Wizard by performing the following steps:

1. Start with the equivalent of an ATL simple object shown in the previous code.

2. Add the following code: `#include <mtx.h>`

3. Add the macro `DECLARE_NOT_AGGREGATABLE` inside your class declaration in the header file for your class. MTS classes cannot be aggregatable.

By including mtx.h you gain access to several MTS API functions and several MTS interface definitions. One of these API functions is `GetObjectContext()`.

With this API, you can reach the context wrapper object associated with your object instance. The use of this API is shown in the following code:

```
IObjectContext *pObjectContext = NULL;
HRESULT hr = GetObjectContext(&pObjectContext);
if (SUCCEEDED(hr))
```

15

MTS

```
{
    // do something with the context wrapper here
    ...
    // release the context wrapper when done
    pObjectContext->Release();
}
```

Interception

For MTS to do its magic, it must perform interception. As you already know, interception occurs through the context wrapper. The client talks to the context wrapper and thinks of the context wrapper as the object. It is important that a client, or even another object, never gets a reference to your object directly, thus bypassing the context wrapper and interception. Therefore, never send a reference to your object to another object. For example, consider an example in which your object is implementing a callback interface, as follows:

```
ISomeObject *pObject;
HRESULT hr = CreateSomeObject(&pObject);
pObject->RegisterCallback(this);
```

The last line in the previous code is sending a direct reference to the object. Instead, you must use the SafeRef() function. SafeRef() gives you a reference to the context wrapper. You would then hand this reference to the client or other objects. The following code shows the correct way to share your object in a callback:

```
ISomeObject *pObject = NULL;
HRESULT hr = CreateSomeObject(&pObject);
IMyInterface *pIMe = NULL;
pIMe = SafeRef(IID_IMyInterface, (IUnknown*)this);
pObject->RegisterCallback(pIMe);
```

MTS 2 uses a feature known as Just-In-Time (JIT) activation. In JIT when a client creates an object, MTS creates the object and a context wrapper. It inserts the wrapper between the stub and the object, but does not bind the context wrapper to the object until activation. Activation occurs when the client makes its first method call. In the same fashion, before an object is destroyed, MTS performs deactivation. In deactivation, MTS destroys the context wrapper. Next, the object is destroyed.

JIT implies that all objects in MTS 2 have four phases in their life cycle: creation, activation, deactivation, and destruction. Therefore, in MTS 2, creation and destruction occur as they do without MTS; in other words, your object is created when another developer creates your object, and destroyed when all references are released. However, the object cannot gain access to the context wrapper until activation.

Similarly, an object cannot gain access to the context wrapper in its destructor because the context wrapper has already been disconnected at that point. (MTS 2 makes virtually no distinction between deactivation and destruction, except that the context wrapper is still available in the deactivation phase.) COM+ introduces the concept of object pooling, in which an object can control whether releasing all references truly deletes the object, or whether the object is instead stored in an object pool.

To implement `IObjectControl` for receiving JIT notifications, do the following:

1. Add `IObjectControl` to the inheritance list of your MTS-compatible class.
2. Add the interface to your query interface map as follows:
   ```
   COM_INTERFACE_ENTRY(IObjectControl)
   ```
3. Implement the three methods in `IObjectControl`—`Activate`, `CanBePooled`, and `Deactivate`:
   ```
   HRESULT Ctestobj1::Activate()
   {
   }

   BOOL Ctestobj1::CanBePooled()
   {
       return FALSE;
   }
   void Ctestobj1::Deactivate()
   {
   }
   ```

Object pooling is not available in MTS 2; therefore, the previous code should return FALSE.

> **Note**
>
> In reality, you can also return TRUE. Some people suggest answering TRUE so that object pooling can start working as soon as it is available. However, this is not recommended unless the implications of object pooling have been carefully considered.

Creating Packages to Host Components

After you have created your middle-tier components, you will want to create packages to host your components.

To create a package in MTS, do the following:

1. In MTS Explorer, open the Computers branch.
2. Open the computer branch where you want the package to be installed.

15

MTS

3. Right-click the Packages Installed branch, point to New on the shortcut menu, and then click Package. The Package Wizard dialog box appears.

4. Click the Create An Empty Package button. (You will learn how the Install Pre-Built Packages button is used in the "Importing a Package" section later in this chapter.)

5. Type a name for the new package (the name can include spaces). Click Next.

6. Set the package identity. You can change the identity later in the Package. During development, you want to use the Interactive User. This setting uses the credentials of the logged on user. A side effect of using the Interactive User is that all output appears in the current WinStation. A problem with this setting is that it requires someone to be logged on for the package to execute.

7. In a production environment, you should select the This User option. When you select This User, you can type in a particular user's credentials, which will be implemented when the server needs to access shared resources such as files. Be aware that you should never display output with this setting. The output will not appear in the current WinStation. For example, if you attempt to display a message box, the message would not be visible and your program will appear frozen as it waits for user interaction.

8. Click Finish.

Adding Objects to a Package

Although you can add objects to a package using a variety of mechanisms, you can most easily accomplish this by using a drag-and-drop operation to move the DLL that contains the classes into the Components folder underneath your package.

To add objects to a package using drag-and-drop, do the following:

1. Make sure that the Components folder is selected.

2. In Windows Explorer, drag the DLL file into the right pane of the MTS Explorer window. MTS will add all the objects described in the type library.

You can also add objects to a package without drag-and-drop.

To add classes to the package without a drag-and-drop operation, do the following:

1. Expand the package branch where you want to insert components. Right-click the Components folder, point to New on the shortcut menu, and then select Component.

2. Click Install New Component(s) if you want to add every component in a certain DLL. This option is similar to using the drag-and-drop operation and does not require that the DLL be preregistered.

3. If you want to select a component by its ProgID from the list of registered components, click Import Component(s) That Are Already Registered. This procedure is the only way to add individual components from a DLL. Use this method if you want to add some components to one package and some components to another package.

When creating packages, make sure to add any type libraries on which your objects depend, as well as your proxy-stub DLL if you need one. This will come in handy when deploying your package on another computer.

Package Properties

A package has many properties of which you need to be aware. You can right-click a package and select Properties from the shortcut menu to view the Package Properties dialog box.

On the General tab, notice that you can type a description for a package. This is useful when importing a package in another computer. The Security tab contains a check box for enabling security for a package. Notice that the default is No Security. This tab also contains the authentication level for calls made between a client and a package.

The Advanced tab provides a setting called Server Process Shutdown, which is used to determine when to shut down the server process. This is an optimization in MTS that you can use after all references to your objects have been released. After the server has deleted all instances of objects in a package, the server will remain loaded for the amount of time specified in the Server Process Shutdown setting. This improves performance for clients initiating a conversation with the server within the specified amount of time.

Note

During development, you should set the Server Process Shutdown setting as low as possible because you will be unable to rebuild your code when the server is running and the server DLL is loaded.

The Advanced tab also has two permission settings: Disable Deletion and Disable Changes. By enabling these settings, you are locking the package from users of MTS explorer. If you make the Disable Changes option available, users will not be able to modify this package. All the options in the property dialog box, except for the permission settings, will be made unavailable. To make modifications later, you must unlock the package; clearing the permission options unlocks the package.

15

MTS

The Identity tab allows you to choose the Security Identifier (SID) that MTS will use when accessing shared resources, such as files on the network. This is the user ID and password that your server will impersonate when making outbound calls. For example, your code might access files on another computer.

You might use a specific user ID and password to access that other computer, or you might use the interactive user—the user currently logged on. However, your server might not have anyone logged on, which will render your server unusable; or the logged-on user might not have security to access the shared resource.

Therefore, in a production environment, you should use a specific user with enough security to reach shared resources. Probably the most important property you can set for a package is the activation type, found on the Activation tab. The choices are Library Package or Server Package. A library package is simply a package to be used in-process. A server package is one that will be loaded into the MTS surrogate process Mtx.exe. A library package has a few limitations over a server package; the most notable is that library packages do not control security. The process that is loading them determines their security.

Object Properties

Objects also have a series of declarative properties. Perhaps the most important of these properties is transaction support.

MTS is in charge of initiating a transaction and calling on the services of MS DTC to enlist resource managers and control the flow of the transaction. Components dictate when MTS starts a transaction through declarative settings. An administrator can change the transaction requirements of a component by changing the Transaction properties of the component.

To do so, right-click the component you want to modify and select Properties on the shortcut menu. Next, click the Transactions tab. On the Transactions tab, you can choose from four options: Requires a Transaction, Requires a New Transaction, Supports Transactions, and Does Not Support Transactions.

MTS starts a transaction when an object marked as Requires a New Transaction or Requires a Transaction is created and activated (after the first method call).

The object that makes MTS begin the transaction is known as the root of the transactions.

Other objects can participate in the same transaction if they are created from within an object already in the transaction. For an object to participate in the same transaction, it must be part of the same activity. In other words, it must be created with the CreateInstance() function of the IContextObject() interface. The component must also be marked as Requires a Transaction or Supports Transactions.

If the secondary component is marked as Requires a New Transaction, MTS will create a new transaction for the object; the object will not be able to participate in the transaction of the creator. Components marked as Does Not Support Transactions cannot participate in the same transaction.

As you can see, changing the Transaction property setting in a component can have a huge impact on how your application behaves. Just imagine what would happen if you had coded object B with the idea that it would be in the same transaction as object A, and an MTS administrator decided to mark object B as Requires a New Transaction. You cannot do much to prevent an administrator from doing this. However, you can set a default transaction setting for each of your components in the type library. To do so, first include the file Mtxattr.h in the top of your IDL file as follows:

```
#include <mtxattr.h>
```

This file declares certain attributes that you can use as coclass attributes. These attributes are TRANSACTION_REQUIRED, TRANSACTION_SUPPORTED, TRANSACTION_NOT_SUPPORTED, and TRANSACTION_REQUIRES_NEW. To use these attributes, simply add them to the coclass attributes as follows:

```
[
    uuid(01C72192-8CB0-11D3-81E1-0050BAA1DBA9),
    helpstring("ctxobj1 Class"),
    TRANSACTION_REQUIRED
]
coclass ctxobj1
{
    [default] interface Ictxobj1;
};
```

These attributes do not prevent an administrator from changing the property; they only give MTS the default transaction setting for the component. That is, when the component is added to a package, the transaction setting will be set according to the default setting.

Deploying MTS-Based Objects

MTS provides a mechanism for exporting a package definition along with its components and importing the package in another server. MTS also provides a way to generate a setup program that will install the necessary registry information to activate a server component in client computers that do not have MTS installed.

15

MTS

> **Note**
>
> A client machine does not need to have the DLLs that implement the server objects installed in order to create instances of the objects, nor does it need MTS installed. The only things the client requires are the class ID GUID (CLSID) and the interface GUIDs (IIDs) in the registry. The client also needs the type library for the server so that the type library marshaler can marshal the interfaces between the two machines when the server uses type library marshaling or the proxy/stub DLL when the server requires standard marshaling. The setup program generated from exporting the package takes care of installing the type library, or the proxy/stub DLL, and adding the necessary keys to the registry. It creates a subdirectory called Remote Applications under the Program Files directory and installs the type library or proxy/stub DLL there. However, in the case in which the server has the type library embedded as a resource in the DLL, make sure to also add the type library file (TLB) to the package as a separate DLL. Otherwise, MTS will add the server files to the client setup instead of simply adding the type library file.

Exporting a Package

When you are ready to move your application to a production server, you will want to export your package.

To export a package, do the following:

1. In MTS Explorer, right-click the package you want to export, and select Export. The Export Package dialog box appears.

2. Type the exact path and name for the package. If you want to export the user IDs for each role, select the Save Windows NT User IDs Associated With Roles check box. This check box refers only to the users in the roles. If you do not select this check box, the role information will still be exported, but the actual user IDs within the role will not be included. This is normally what you want to do when moving from development to deployment. Click Export.

3. If this is not the first time you're exporting a package to the same location, the Overwrite Files dialog box will prompt you to overwrite the old package and DLL. Click OK.

4. The Export Package dialog box closes. When the export is complete, MTS Explorer reappears with a message box telling you that the package was exported successfully. Click OK.

You should now have an exported package in a .pak file. The .pak file is a text file containing the settings necessary to recreate the package in another server.

Importing a Package

After exporting the package, you can import it into another MTS server.

To import a package into another MTS server, do the following:

1. In MTS Explorer, open the Computers branch, and then open My Computer.
2. Right-click the Packages Installed folder, point to New on the shortcut menu, and then select Package. The Package Wizard dialog box appears.
3. Instead of clicking the Create An Empty Package button, click the Install Pre-Built Packages button. The Select Package Files dialog box appears.
4. Click the Add button, locate the package you want to install, and then click Next.
5. In the Set Package Identity dialog box, specify the account under which the package will run. Remember that when you are developing, it is more convenient to select Interactive User, but in a production environment, you will want to select This User and specify the user's credentials. Click Next.
6. In the Installation Options dialog box, type the directory where you want to copy the component files. This directory is the location in which the components will be registered.
7. Click Finish.

Many times, you might want to distribute an application with a UI to the clients, but not install the server components. For example, it does not make sense to install all the components on each client computer. All that is needed in client applications is the registry information for the classes in a package. When you export a package, MTS creates a client subdirectory that contains a small executable which simply writes the registry information to the client computer.

Advanced MTS Techniques

MTS security is built on top of DCOM, so it is no surprise that many of its elements are based on DCOM paradigms. However, MTS extends DCOM security by doing two things. First, because MTS provides a container application (Mtx.exe), it takes charge of controlling security for out-of-process activation and allows programmers to worry less about programming directly to the COM security APIs. Second, because MTS provides more security checkpoints, it provides higher granularity in security. DCOM provides only two security checkpoints: launching the server and accessing the server. In addition to those two levels, MTS provides checkpoints at the component level and the interface level. What's more, MTS provides several simple methods for extending security to the method level.

Making Security Available for a Package and a Component

A role is a group of users. Roles are assigned on a per-package basis. When you create a new package, security is unavailable by default. You can make security available for a package or for a component by performing the following steps.

To make security available for a package, do the following:

1. In MTS Explorer, right-click the package and select Properties on the short-cut menu. The Properties dialog box appears.

2. On the Security tab, select the Enable Authorization Checking check box and click OK.

To make security available for a component, do the following:

1. In MTS Explorer, right-click the component and select Properties on the shortcut menu. The Properties dialog box appears.

2. On the Security tab, select the Enable Authorization Checking check box and click OK.

> **Note**
>
> Security checking is available by default at the component level. In other words, as soon as you make security available at the package level, you must create roles and assign them to each component. Otherwise, every user will be denied permission to the package.

Creating a Role for a Package

Under DCOM, security is affected programmatically per process. The same is true under MTS; each package is run in a separate process. If you view the Task Manager, you will see that each time a client instantiates a component in a different package, MTS runs a separate instance of Mtx.exe (the surrogate process for the component). Because each package runs in a different process, roles are created in a per-package basis. This is also the reason why a library package cannot use the MTS role-based security. A library package loads in the process space of the caller, and is then bound to the process security model. Therefore, this library package can be secured or unsecured. A library package is secured when the Mtx.exe process loads it; that is, when the package is created by an MTS COM object. A non-MTS process that creates a library package automatically renders it unsecured.

To create a role for a package, do the following:

1. In MTS Explorer, select and open the package for which you want to set up roles.
2. Right-click the Roles folder, point to New on the shortcut menu, and then select Role.
3. In the New Role dialog box, type the role's name and click OK.
4. Open the New Role branch. Right-click the Users folder, point to New on the shortcut menu, and then select User.
5. You will be presented with the Add Users And Groups To Role dialog box.

Select the users you want to add to the role and click OK. You can add individual users or Windows NT security groups.

Assigning a Role to a Component or an Interface

After you have created a role, you can assign the role to specific components and interfaces in a package.

To assign a role to a component or an interface, do the following:

1. In MTS Explorer, select and open the object for which you want to assign roles.
2. Right-click the Role Membership folder, point to New on the shortcut menu, and then select Role.
3. The Select Roles dialog box containing a list of all the package roles appears. Select as many roles as you want, and click OK.

Affecting Security Programmatically

MTS also allows you to programmatically control security at the method level. To do so, you can use two methods in the `IObjectContext` interface: `IsSecurityEnabled()` and `IsCallerInRole()`. `IsSecurityEnabled()` helps you decide if security is activated for this package. If security is not activated, this function returns `FALSE`. This function is important for two reasons. First, if you are working in a library package, the function returns `TRUE` if the package was loaded from within an MTS object living inside Mtx.exe, and it returns `FALSE` if a client outside MTS created the component directly. Second,

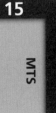

15

MTS

when security is turned off for a package, `IsCallerInRole()` always returns TRUE. Therefore, before using `IsCallerInRole()`, you must check to see if security is available. Listing 15.2 shows you how to test for security at the method level.

LISTING 15.2 Testing for Security at a Method Level

```
HRESULT MyObj::SecuredMethod()
{
    IObjectContext *pContext=NULL;
    HRESULT hr = GetObjectContext(&pContext);
    if (SUCCEEDED(hr))
    {
        if (!pContext->IsInTransaction())
            return E_ACCESSDENIED;
        BSTR bstrAdmin = SysAllocString(L"Admins");
        BOOL bInRole=FALSE;
        if (!pContext->IsCallerInRole(bstrAdmin,&bInRole))
        {
            SysFreeString(bstrAdmin);
            return E_ACCESSDENIED;
        }
     pContext->Release();
    }
    // Add your security code here
    return S_OK;
}
```

Direct Caller Versus Original Caller

MTS performs role-based security when a client outside MTS communicates with an object inside MTS. When an object inside MTS makes a method call on another MTS object, MTS does not check security. Consider an example in which a client has access to method1 in objectA, but does not have access to method1 in objectB. If the client calls method1 in objectA, objectA has access to method1 in objectB and could potentially call it. Because MTS does not check security for MTS objects calling other MTS objects, the client will not be stopped from performing this type of sequence. This could pose a security problem.

However, MTS does provide several APIs to help you determine the identity of a client. MTS distinguishes between the original caller (the client that accessed the first COM object in the chain) and the direct caller (the caller that made the method call). You can obtain the security identifiers for both the Original Caller and the Direct Caller using the methods in the `ISecurityProperty` interface. This interface has five methods: `GetDirectCreatorSID`, `GetOriginalCreatorSID`, `GetDirectCallerSID`, `GetOriginalCallerSID`, and `ReleaseSID`. To reach this interface, call `QueryInterface` on the context object.

Listing 15.3 demonstrates how to use the `ISecurityProperty` interface.

LISTING 15.3 The ISecurityProperty Interface

```
IObjectContext* pContext = NULL;
ISecurityProperty* pISecProp = NULL;
PSID pSid = NULL;
HRESULT hr = S_OK;
// Get the object context
hr = GetObjectContext(&pContext);
if (SUCCEEDED(hr))
{
    // Get a reference to the ISecurityProperty interface
    hr = pContext->QueryInterface( IID_ISecurityProperty,
        (void**)&pISecProp);
    // Obtain the creator's security ID
    hr = pISecProp->GetDirectCreatorSID(&pSid);
    // Add your security code here
    // Release the security ID
    pISecProp->ReleaseSID(pSid);
    // Release the interface
    pISecProp->Release();

    // Release the context
    pContext->Release();
}
```

Load Balancing

This section discusses load balancing, and suggests a technique for programmatically performing load balancing. Chapter 20, "Load Balancing and Pooling," goes into the nitty gritty details with a sample application. The basic goal behind load balancing is to improve server performance. Performance can be measured in many ways, but for the sake of this discussion, it means two things: more users and faster response.

There are two types of load balancing: dynamic and static. Dynamic load balancing occurs when the operating system can choose, based on performance statistics, which server will be most suited to run the components requested by the client. Static load balancing occurs when a program determines which server should handle a request based on fixed quantities (for example, if there are more than 50 users making requests, use server B).

Because MTS and Windows NT Server 4 cannot perform dynamic load balancing, the simplest way to perform load balancing is to make your distributed applications more scalable by having multiple servers export the same package and then letting the clients decide on which server they want to run. A more complicated and robust technique might involve creating a load-balancing package.

Using this technique, every client communicates with the load balancing package. The load balancing package's job is to then create instances of middle-tier components based on either an algorithm or a round-robin approach.

Microsoft offers several products that can help with load balancing, including Microsoft Cluster Server (MSCS). MSCS allows several Windows NT Enterprise Server computers to act as a single unit. Although a full discussion of MSCS is beyond the scope of this chapter, you can find more information about this product by visiting the Microsoft Web site, `www.microsoft.com/Windows/server/Technical/management/ClusterArch.asp`.

Creating MTS-Based Applications

One of the key goals in transaction-based applications is to perform a transaction as quickly as possible. When the transaction is occurring, database systems place locks on the data to prevent other applications from looking at intermediate data.

Locking prevents concurrency, which is a detriment to scalability. To improve scalability, you must design your objects so that they do not spend much time in the actual transaction. Essentially, this can be best accomplished by method calls with finer granularity. Granularity is discussed at length in Chapter 20, and transaction optimization is discussed in Chapter 16, "COM+ as a Component Manager."

Two aspects determine the longevity of a transaction. One involves the interception mechanism in MTS, specifically JIT. The other involves the timeout feature in MTS that automatically aborts a transaction in a specified amount of time. To understand these two forces, you must first understand how transactions operate in MTS.

Recall that activities are groups of objects with the same concurrency requirements. In MTS 2, when a base client creates an MTS object, MTS creates a new activity and puts the object instance in it. This object can, in turn, invite other objects to be part of the activity using the `CreateInstance()` function in the `IObjectContext` interface (recall that you obtain `IObjectContext` from the `GetObjectContext()` API).

Also, remember that only objects which are part of the same activity can vote on a transaction. Transactions have a single entry point and begin when an object marked as Requires a Transaction or Requires a New Transaction is activated.

You might recall also that an object is activated when a client makes the first method call. Thus, an object is first created when the client requests to create the object, but is not activated until the first method call. The vote an object makes is stored in the context wrapper. Therefore, voting begins when the object is activated and ends when the object is deactivated.

When the root of the transaction is destroyed, MTS will either commit the transaction or abort it. If an object needs, more precisely, to be part of the transaction, it must be created from within the first object and it must be invited into the same activity. Because MTS 2 was built after COM was released, an object in an activity cannot use the standard COM APIs to create an MTS component within the same activity. If you were to use CoGetClassObject() or CoCreateInstance(), the object would be part of a separate activity. To create an object that is part of the same activity, use the CreateInstance() method in the IObjectContext interface.

The following example shows how to invite an object CLSID_FriendObject into the same activity.

```
IObjectContext *pContext;
HRESULT hr = GetObjectContext(&pContext);
if (SUCCEEDED(hr))
{
    IFriendObject *pFriendObject;
    pContext->CreateInstance(CLSID_FriendObject,
        _uuidof(pFriendObject),
    (void **)&pFriendObject);
}
```

When an object's context wrapper is gone, the vote cannot be changed. A context wrapper keeps track of the vote status on what is commonly called the "happy" flag. A vote of yes means the object is "happy," a vote of no means the object is "unhappy." If the context wrapper gets destroyed in an unhappy state, the transaction will be doomed. Two styles of voting can occur. One style is to make a temporary vote; another style is to make a final vote. With a temporary vote, an object is indicating that it can change its mind. ("I'm unhappy but perhaps if you make another method call, I can be persuaded to be happy.") With a permanent style, an object says, "I'm unhappy (or happy) and there is nothing anyone can do to change my mind." The object controls the state of happiness by calling one of two methods in the IObjectContext interface: EnableCommit() and DisableCommit(). EnableCommit() sets the state of the "happy" flag to happy, and DisableCommit() sets the state to unhappy. The following code shows how to call these methods:

```
IObjectContext *pContext;
HRESULT hr = GetObjectContext(&pContext);
if (SUCCEEDED(hr))
{
    pContext->EnableCommit();
    pContext->Release();
}
```

EnableCommit() and DisableCommit() do a temporary vote—they do not affect the lifetime of the context wrapper; they only affect the state of the happy bit. If the object is destroyed and the context wrapper with it, at that point the last vote will be final.

15

MTS

If your object reaches a state in which it is definitely done with its part of the transaction, the object can request deactivation from MTS. As a result, the object will also be destroyed. Remember that the transaction does not end until the root object is deactivated. However, when a subordinate object is destroyed, the object notifies the application that it has completed voting. To deactivate itself, an object can call one of two methods in the `IObjectContext` interface: `SetComplete()` or `SetAbort()`. `SetComplete()` and `SetAbort()` tell MTS that the object has completed doing its job.

In other words, when the method call finishes and passes through the context wrapper, MTS will deactivate the context wrapper and destroy the object. `SetComplete()` tells MTS that it wants to be deactivated in a happy state; `SetAbort()` tells MTS that it wants to be deactivated in an unhappy state. Deactivation occurs when the call returns through the context wrapper. The following code demonstrates calling the `SetComplete()` method:

```
IObjectContext *pContext;
HRESULT hr = GetObjectContext(&pContext);
if (SUCCEEDED(hr))
{
    pContext->SetComplete();
    pContext->Release();
}
```

> **Note**
>
> In COM+, the object will have a choice to be destroyed or pooled. Based on the previous rules for voting, you can infer the following rules:
>
> - If an object says that it is unhappy with `DisableCommit`, it can change its mind and become happy with `EnableCommit`. An object can change its mind until it is destroyed.
> - If one object calls `SetAbort` within a method call and does not change its mind—ending the method call with `SetComplete`, for example—when the call ends and goes through the context wrapper, MTS will destroy the object, and the transaction will be doomed.
> - If the root object is destroyed, any objects that are part of the transaction will also be destroyed.

Designing with MTS

Many developers like to call `SetAbort()` at the beginning of the method code, and then call `SetComplete()` when they are sure that the code has executed properly. In this way, if an unexpected error occurs and the method exits prematurely, changes will not be committed.

You should try to spend as little time as possible in a transaction. When designing your application, observe the following guidelines.

First, try to use `SetComplete()` and `SetAbort()` instead of `EnableCommit()` and `DisableCommit()`. Using `SetComplete()` and `SetAbort()` could mean that your object would be continually destroyed and recreated on a per-call basis. This could have an enormous impact on your system—your objects will be stateless. (In fact, you should write your object with the assumption that it will be stateless. Write any initialization code in the Activate method, perform your operation in the method call, and clean up in the Deactivate method.)

Second, after a subordinate object is destroyed in an unhappy state, either explicitly with `SetAbort()` or implicitly when all its references are gone, the transaction will be doomed. There is no point in continuing it; therefore, to make the system perform as quickly as possible, you should eliminate the root object as soon as you have determined that the transaction is doomed in it. Similarly, you should almost never call `EnableCommit()` or `DisableCommit()` from within the root object. It is not good design practice for middle-tier components to let the client make the decision of when the transaction will end.

If you call `EnableCommit()` instead of `SetComplete()`, the transaction continues until the client eliminates all references to the object. Letting the client decide means that the system will perform slower and the transaction has a greater chance of failing. This is because MTS sets a timeout for transactions. If you were to return a code to the client so that the client could make a decision, the system might timeout before the user gets around to answering. Instead, you should let the transaction fail and return an error code indicating that the user should retry the operation. A well-designed UI should allow the user to retry a transaction without having to retype all the information, or to type in a compensating transaction if an error was committed.

Scaling Applications with MTS

When people use the term "scaling an application," they usually mean adding more users. Computers can handle only a certain number of users running concurrently. The answer to adding more users after a certain time is to add more servers. In MTS applications, it is possible to run certain components in separate computers. You might have noticed from looking at the `CreateInstance()` method in `IObjectContext` that there is no way to specify a server computer where the object should be created. It is possible, however, to create objects from another server and have them be part of the same activity. To do so, you must tell one MTS server through MTS Explorer that the object is going to be created remotely.

You can do so in the manner as demonstrated in the following subsections.

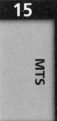

Remote Administration

An administrator can tell MTS Explorer to execute various components remotely.

To run components remotely with MTS Explorer, do the following:

1. Ensure that the remote computer is a Windows NT 4 Workstation, Server, or Windows 2000 and MTS is installed.

2. Verify that the Packages directory under the MTS installation directory on the remote computer is shared with read access to the administrator.

3. The package must be installed in the remote computer. If you are exporting from your local computer, use the package exporting procedure.

4. The components you are configuring to run remotely must not be installed in the local computer.

5. Right-click the Remote Components folder in the local computer, point to New on the shortcut menu, and then select Remote Components. The Remote Components dialog box appears.

6. Select the computer in which you want to run the components, and the package you want to use. The Remote Components dialog box lists the components in the package. Click the components you want to use, and then click Add.

Summary

In programming, transactions are actions that affect shared data. A transaction must follow the ACID rules: atomic, consistent, isolated, and durable. When more than one database system is involved in a transaction, transaction systems use an algorithm known as the two-phase commit. It is difficult to build an infrastructure to make COM components available to share a transaction, to guarantee the ACID rules, and to use the two-phase commit algorithm by hand. Microsoft provides that infrastructure through MTS, which serves as a TP monitor—software that can manage the flow of a transaction—and serves as an ORB—software that can create and manage the lifetime of middle-tier components.

MTS uses interception to monitor all calls going to and from an object. By using interception, MTS is able to provide its clients with more services than just transaction management. For example, interception allows MTS to provide role-based security. As mentioned earlier, components residing in MTS are configured components.

MTS uses declarative attributes to change the behavior of an object. MTS provides interception by inserting a context wrapper object between the stub and the object. Objects that have the same concurrency requirements run as part of an activity.

MTS uses a transactional system in which components can vote on the outcome of a transaction. A transaction occurs within the confines of an activity. Only components in the same activity can participate in the transaction. To ensure that a subordinate component becomes part of the same activity, use the `CreateInstance()` method of the `IObjectContext` interface. If you were to use `CoCreateInstance()`, MTS would treat the request as a separate client, and the object would become part of a different activity. Objects can vote on the outcome of a transaction using four methods: `EnableCommit()`, `DisableCommit()`, `SetComplete()`, and `SetAbort()`. `SetComplete()` and `SetAbort()` also tell the system to deactivate the component when the method call completes. When designing a distributed application, always try to destroy the components as soon as possible so that you can ensure a higher level of concurrency.

Component Management and Transactions

PART III

IN THIS PART

CHAPTER 16

COM+ as a Component Manager

COM+ has the basic function of providing object dispatch and management services to a host of clients in a distributed enterprise. In this way, COM+ is much like a Common Object Request Broker Architecture Object Request Broker (CORBA ORB). It supplies shared state management and process management services. Objects instantiated through COM+ services look just like normal objects to COM clients, but offer several advantages. One of the most important is scalability.

This chapter and the next three chapters provide comprehensive coverage of the critical aspects of COM+ component development. This chapter covers issues of scalability and fundamental COM+ component design and programming. Chapter 17, "COM+ as a Transaction Coordinator," covers transactions and COM+ integration with data access services. Chapter 18, "COM+ Security," covers security and COM+ role management. Chapter 19, "The COM Transaction Integrator," presents a view of COM+ transaction integration with the mainframe world and also gives you a look at COMTI.

In this chapter, you'll look at the essence of COM+ programming. You'll learn the most fundamental aspects of COM+ and expand into the critical design issues germane to scalable COM+ applications and how they differ from other types of DCOM programs.

Programming COM+ and Other Component-Based Services

In order to master just about any new component-based service on the Windows platform, you must answer the following three questions:

- What are the classes and interfaces exposed?
- How does the service typically interact with applications?
- How does the service integrate with external services?

These questions have increasingly complex answers in most cases. This is true with COM+. Discovering the COM+ classes and their respective interfaces is often as simple as scanning through all the methods and properties in the help system and then boning up on the calls that are important to your endeavor. It is a far more three-dimensional affair to understand the object instance scenarios a service employs and expects of your application and to know how to orchestrate the various method calls involved in solving a given problem. The answer to the second question is also difficult to express simply, and so it is often inadequately treated in most references. Usually, examples come to the rescue when trying to answer question number two. The last question's answer is often shrouded in secrecy and only vague glimpses of how things really interact are ever presented. Usually snippets discovered in the notes at the bottom of unrelated API help pages are the only fuel to burn.

In light of the preceding observations I will cover less of what can be easily derived in half a paragraph of the Help on an interface method and focus more on the not so obvious elegance of the COM+ model and how it interacts with other services. COM+ is probably the most revolutionary aspect of Windows application development since the event-driven GUI, and it's surprisingly easy to miss the point of it. Most developers who bumble into COM+ for the first time (I shan't name names) produce completely left-field components that don't even come close to functioning properly within the COM+ environment. These first attempts miss out on the true power of COM+. I will try to save you that pain as you explore COM+.

COM+ Scalability Features

COM+ supplies several key features that greatly enhance the scalability of component services. Each of these features attempts to reduce internal server overhead in a way transparent to external client applications. To a client, a COM+ component looks just like a standard COM component.

One of the keys to highly scalable applications is effective resource management. Applications that create all the resources they need, but no more, have a reduced memory footprint and can support exceedingly large numbers of clients as long as all the clients are not active concurrently.

Another valuable technique is that of limiting the frequency with which resources are set up and torn down. Reusing previously allocated resources has the benefit of reducing memory segmentation from constant allocation and deallocation. Also, fewer page faults (transfers of data from disk to memory) are incurred in applications that have a stable working set (collection of in-memory pages). Re-initialization of resources is often faster than strict initialization in many scenarios as well.

In order to obtain these benefits, COM+ supplies the following scalability features:

- Just-in-time activation
- Early deactivation
- Object pooling
- Resource pooling

Just-in-time (JIT) activation enables COM+ to create objects only when they are needed. *Early deactivation* allows objects to be deleted as soon as their current activity is complete. In this way, COM+ can keep the total number of objects down to just the number that are actually being used. *Pooling* is the process of maintaining resources in a temporary collection and reusing them as requests for such resources come in. COM+ provides facilities to pool component objects that support pooling. COM+ also defines a model for resource dispensers that can provide pooled resources of any type, such as database connections.

> **Note**
>
> MTS does not actually pool component objects. All the provisions are in place. MTS makes all the calls that would be expected in a pooling scenario, but it deletes the objects when the client finishes with them. COM+ is the first object-pooling, COM-based application server.

COM+ and Standard COM Components

In this section, you'll look at the pros and cons of using standard COM components in the COM+ environment. You'll begin by building a standard COM component and examining its features. Then you'll deploy and test the COM component under COM+. Finally, you'll explore the pros and cons facing a standard COM component operating within the COM+ runtime.

A Standard COM Component

To get started working with COM+, you can build a normal COM component with no specific COM+ support and see how it operates under COM+ control. To try this demonstration, you will need to create a basic ATL DLL project called Stateful. Next, add a simple ATL COM class to the project naming it Sum. (Right-click the project icon in the class view and choose New ATL Class; specify a simple object with the default interface of ISum). You'll use a dual interface in order to support a VBScript client.

> **Note**
>
> Dual interfaces are generally problematic. COM classes can have multiple interfaces, which is one of the high points of COM+ programming. Declaring more then one implementation of the same interface is a dangerous proposition because inter-apartment marshaling will only see a need to set up proxies for the first instance of a given interface. Three dual interfaces present the client with three drastically different implementations of IDispatch. Developers should generally choose between programming with COM interfaces or building classes that supply a single IDispatch interface to support scripting (the only popular modern client environment that can't handle COM interfaces directly). We use dual interfaces here for simplicity but be warned that real applications relying on dual interfaces will have serious problems evolving under the impact of new requirements.

COM+ as a Component Manager

CHAPTER 16

411

16

COM+ AS A
COMPONENT
MANAGER

Finally, add two methods to the ISum interface, Accumulate() and Add(). (Right-clicking the interface in the Class View window and choosing Add Method is the easiest way to do this.) Use Listing 16.1 as a guide to define and implement your Sum class methods—the header and .cpp files are provided. Note that the Accumulate() method uses an integer property named m_iTotal, which you must add to the class definition and initialize to zero in the constructor.

LISTING 16.1   Simple COM Object Example

```
// Sum.h : Declaration of the CSum
#include "resource.h"        // main symbols

/////////////////////////////////////////////////
// CSum
class ATL_NO_VTABLE CSum :
    public CComObjectRootEx<CComSingleThreadModel>,
    public CComCoClass<CSum, &CLSID_Sum>,
    public IDispatchImpl<ISum, &IID_ISum, &LIBID_STATEFULLib>
{
public:
    CSum()
    {
        m_iTotal = 0;
    }

DECLARE_REGISTRY_RESOURCEID(IDR_SUM)
DECLARE_PROTECT_FINAL_CONSTRUCT()
DECLARE_NOT_AGGREGATABLE(CSum)

BEGIN_COM_MAP(CSum)
    COM_INTERFACE_ENTRY(ISum)
    COM_INTERFACE_ENTRY(IDispatch)
END_COM_MAP()

// ISum
public:
    STDMETHOD(Sum)(int iValue1, int iValue2, int *piTotal );
    STDMETHOD(Accumulate)(int iValue, int * pTotal);

// Attributes (unmanaged state, yikes!)
private:
    int m_iTotal;
};


// Sum.cpp : Implementation of CSum
#include "stdafx.h"
#include "Stateful.h"
```

LISTING 16.1 Continued

```c
#include "Sum.h"

/////////////////////////////////////////////////
// CSum

STDMETHODIMP CSum::Accumulate(int iValue, int *piTotal)
{
    if ( NULL == piTotal )
        return E_INVALIDARG;

    m_iTotal += iValue;
    *piTotal = m_iTotal;

    return S_OK;
}

STDMETHODIMP CSum::Sum(int iValue1, int iValue2, int *piTotal)
{
    if ( NULL == piTotal )
        return E_INVALIDARG;

    *piTotal = iValue1 + iValue2;

    return S_OK;
}
```

As you can see, one of the class methods, `Accumulate()`, requires object state information (an object attribute), whereas the other, `Sum()`, uses only transient state (stack variables). Both of these methods work fine outside MTS. Later, you'll test them within the MTS runtime. Compile your DLL. (You can find the compiled `.dll` and the project in the Chapter16\Stateful directory on the CD-ROM.)

So once again, you are faced with the pesky task of building client-side software. To keep your focus, just throw together a simple VBScript to do the job. Listing 16.2 is the sample client listing. (You can find the `.vbs` file in the Chapter16 directory of the CD-ROM.)

LISTING 16.2 Sum Client Example

```vbscript
' SumClient.vbs
'
' Simple COM+ Client VB Script

'Application Entry Point

'Create Sum Object
```

COM+ as a Component Manager

CHAPTER 16

413

16

COM+ AS A
COMPONENT
MANAGER

LISTING 16.2 Continued

```
Set obSum = CreateObject("Stateful.Sum.1")
Total = 0

do
    'Set up menu
    Menu = "COM+ Client Menu" & vbCr & _
           "0 - Exit" & vbCr & _
           "1 - Accumulate a value" & vbCr & _
           "2 - Add two values" & vbCr & vbCr & _
           "Current Cumulative Total: "

    'Get selection
    Choice = InputBox(Menu & Total)

    'Execute command
    Select Case Choice
        Case "":
            'This interprets the cancel button as a quit request
            Choice = "0"
        Case "0":
        Case "1":
            Value = InputBox("Enter a value to accumulate:")
            Total = obSum.Accumulate(Value)
        Case "2":
            Value1 = InputBox("Enter the first value to add:")
            Value2 = InputBox("Enter the second value to add:")
            MsgBox obSum.Sum(Value1,Value2), 0, "Transient Total"
        Case Else:
            MsgBox "Bad choice"
    End Select

Loop While Choice <> "0"
'End of Application
```

Test your component. Make sure that your client script operates as expected and success-fully creates a Sum object using the in-process COM server created previously. To run the client script simply double-click the .vbs source file in the view pane of an Explorer window. You can see the script in operation in Figure 16.1.

Using Standard COM Components with COM+

Now try it with COM+. You'll need to create a new application called Sum and then add your Stateful component into the new application.

To create a new application simply right-click the COM+ Applications icon in the Component Services Console and choose New, Application.

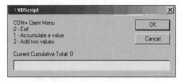

Step through the wizard dialogs to create a new application named Stateful; accept the defaults throughout. To add your Stateful.dll to the package, simply select the new application's Components folder, right-click and select New/Component, and then add the registered component. This causes COM+ to adjust the registry entries to run the component within the mtx.exe runtime.

Selecting the Components folder for the Stateful package in the Component Services Console and choosing Status View enables you to monitor object activity. Double-click the .vbs source file to test the component under COM+. Voilá! You didn't even need to modify your client. COM+ has taken care of everything.

Want to try using the new application in a distributed configuration? No problem, just right-click the application and choose Export, and then provide an export pathname. A client installer can be found in the export path client subdirectory when the export is complete. Simply run this installer on the remote client machine, and you're finished. Running your script on the client invokes a DCOM connection to the COM+ server process supporting the component on the server system.

There are two additional concerns when building components and testing them under COM+ on a single machine. First, remember that COM+ server processes don't shut down immediately by default. You need to shut down your package (right-click it and choose Shutdown) in order for the linker to overwrite the component DLL with a new build. Failing to do this produces a link error because the target DLL is still in use by the COM+ server process. Second, remember that each time you build a component in Visual C++, it tries to reregister the component as a standard COM component. You then need to refresh the registry with the COM+ application configuration by right-clicking the computer in the Component Services Console and choosing Refresh All Components.

Security Problems

Your non-COM+ component has some problems. Some of the problems are obvious now, and others will become obvious as the component use increases. One glaring point is that your component is now running under a server process, likely having a relatively powerful access token, as opposed to its previous home in the client process. Anytime you start distributing components across process boundaries, security concerns arise. It's hard to decide what a client is allowed to do in a vacuum, and unless you are intimately familiar with the deployment environment's account structure, knowing who clients are doesn't really help you to decide what they should be allowed to do. COM+ supplies a powerful role system to shore up this security gap, as you shall see in Chapter 18.

Transaction Problems

An important topic related to non-COM+ specific components is that of transactional behavior. It's important to note that, if the component is not using transactions outside COM+, it probably won't miss them inside COM+. But what *does* happen if you configure the non-COM+ component to use a transaction? The answer is predictable, but it is not good. The problem is that MS DTC (which must be running in order for COM+ to support transactions) keeps transaction-related statistics. If COM+ sees that your class requires a transaction, it will create one for each object of that class when a method is called. If an object is destroyed quickly, DTC assumes the transaction is complete and commits it if possible. If an object hangs around past the transaction timeout deadline (set in the Component Services Console Computer Properties dialog) without explicitly committing the transaction, the transaction will abort. This random behavior is hardly appropriate for applications requiring robustness of transactions.

You might want to try experimenting with automatic transactions on your Stateful component. To make your Stateful component transactional, simply right-click the component in the Component Services Console and choose Properties. In the Properties window, select the Transaction tab and choose Requires a Transaction. Watching the transaction statistics display in the Component Services Console enables you to track the commit and abort rate of your object's transactions. Deactivating your object within the transaction timeout (by quitting the VBScript client) commits the implied transaction. Maintaining the object longer (by leaving the client running) aborts the transaction. Although legacy components might appear to work acceptably within a transaction (as yours does), at least one component in a COM+ call chain should use the COM+ transaction facilities to ensure proper transaction completion behavior. You'll take a look at the right way to build transactional components in Chapter 17.

Scalability Problems

As you have seen, COM+ has no problem using your COM+-oblivious component. The script process communicates with the COM+ server process without a hitch. The problems come when you try to use this component in a heavily used, high-performance environment. This component supplies no support for early deactivation or pooling. Because the component is not COM+-aware, COM+ cannot delete it during long intervals of inactivity. Indeed, doing so would most certainly break the stateful Accumulate() method because it relies on the object state m_iTotal value stored in the object's memory. About the only thing COM+ can do to improve the scalability of this object is to leave the server process running after it has been started (which it does within the timeout constraints set in the Component Services Console). The default inactivity period before a server is shut down is three minutes, but you can configure the application to remain running indefinitely.

Another problem is that each copy of your object maintains a copy of the total. This might not be appropriate in a multiuser, server-based application. As you can see, maintaining stateful values has several weighty ramifications when designing COM+ components.

What would happen if you let COM+ know that your operations are complete? To do this, you'll need to get ahead of yourself just a little and add a bit of COM+-specific code (discussed in detail later in this chapter) to your application. At the end of each of the two ISum methods, just before the return, add the following code:

```
//Tell COM+ that our work is complete
HRESULT hr;
IObjectContext * pOC;
hr = GetObjectContext( &pOC );
if ( FAILED(hr) )
    return hr;
pOC->SetComplete();
pOC->Release();
```

This is a boilerplate block of code that informs COM+ that your object has completed its task in full. Making this statement is, of course, a lie in the case of your component, and COM+ duly punishes such insubordination. Your object is never really done with its work until the client releases it. Why? Because the object is responsible for the state of the m_iTotal value and must remain in context as long as the client requires it. Try compiling this new version to see what happens. In order to work directly with the COM+-related MTS APIs and interfaces, you need to add the mtx.h header to your source and link against the mtx.lib and mtxguid.lib libraries.

Rebuild your component. Before testing the component, you probably need to reregister it with COM+ because Visual C++ registers the DLL as an in-process server automatically after completing a successful build. To reregister your component, simply right-click the My Computer icon in the Component Services Console and choose Refresh All Components. Test the Add function of your component. Works fine, right? Try executing the Accumulate() routine two or three times. Not so good, huh? The Accumulate() routine always returns the current value only.

To discover what's going on here, add a descriptive message box to your component's constructor, displaying Object Created. It should be something like this:

```
Csum::CSum ()
{
    m_iTotal = 0;
    MessageBox(    NULL,
```

COM+ as a Component Manager

CHAPTER 16

417

16

COM+ AS A
COMPONENT
MANAGER

```
        _T("Sum Object Created"),
        _T("Statful.dll"),
        MB_OK );
}
```

Create a similar message in a destructor for the class. Build, reregister, and run your application again. Ah ha! As you can see, COM+ is snuffing your object between calls. Watching the status view of your package's component folder tells the tale. COM+ knows that there is one outstanding object. However, now that the object methods inform COM+ when they have completed an operation, COM+ feels free to delete the objects immediately upon return to the client. So you lose your total after each call! But, hey, the object is much more scalable now. If you could support 10 clients before, but the clients only used the object 10% of the time, you might be able to support as many as 100 clients now. This is because COM+ only maintains the number of objects needed to handle the *active* calls.

> **Note**
>
> This example is designed to be demonstrative and is therefore necessarily trivial. This component has such a small memory footprint that it's probably just as much of a burden to create it over and over as it is to just leave it in memory. The important thing to gain from this example is how to enable COM+ to deactivate your components before the client is finished with them on operational (perhaps transactional) boundaries. Only careful testing under loads simulating real-world operation can tell you if your specific component can benefit from an early-deactivation–capable design.

COM+ Benefits for Standard COM Components

As you have seen, even generic COM objects acquire some scalability improvements through persistent COM+ server processes and COM+ resource pooling (such as pooled ODBC connections). Administration is greatly simplified through the use of easy-to-configure and easy-to-export applications. Reliability is improved through process isolation (running components in a separate process defined by application settings) and, in some creative cases, automatic transactions. When all is said and done, even standard COM components have much to gain from the COM+ application server environment.

The Road to COM+ Components

Like most things, COM+ didn't just fall out of the sky. It is the product of a steady and continuing evolution of application design and implementation techniques. The following discussion leads you into an understanding of what and why COM+ exists today. I'm sure my selection of demonstrative languages and technologies in the following section will leave the UNIX/Corba/Java contingent in a foaming lather. Because this book focuses on C++ level COM development, I have drawn from the most relative technology sets, not necessarily those at the genesis of any particular construct.

Software Reuse

At the dawn of computing, programmers settled for anything that would run to completion, but soon they sought greater benefits. As data storage technologies advanced, it became possible to easily store and reuse basic blocks of code from one application to the next. These blocks of code were also generally more reliable than new code because of prior testing and debugging. Several evolutionary steps took place in the course of the unending search for the ultimate software design methodology.

Modules: Separating Units of Behavior (Modularity)

Early programming languages presented structured programming as their champion and broke large applications into "reusable" modules. And so it was that developers conceived ways in which they could organize their applications' functions into reusable groups. This enabled several programmers to work on separate modules concurrently, but it required that they carefully design the interfaces that they would present to the other developers. The C programming language boasted extreme modularity and has arguably had a greater impact on software development than any language ever invented. (Or was it Java? Lisp? No, Forth?) Windows presented a binary version of the reusable module in the form of DLLs. The chief problem in reusing and testing generic modules has to do with the fact that modules are designed from a functional viewpoint. Decomposing problems into functional modules generally fails to encompass the critical aspects and integration requirements related to data structures and their instantiation. Thus, in the early years, developers paid little heed to the importance of data and state. The functional approach did, however, map well onto the way CPUs did things and provided a performance-friendly compromise between code structure and execution speed.

Classes: Binding Data to Behavior (Encapsulation)

Okay, so now that you have a little more horsepower to burn and memory has reached per-megabyte costs significantly lower than the per-square-foot price of a Manhattan condo, you've got some breathing room. The obvious next step is to make your applications larger and slower. Of course, these are just the side effects of the elusive reuse quest. As databases grew ever more critical, it became obvious that the structures of most applications are more closely bound to the information they managed than to the processing they purvey.

Enter the object and object class. Classes presented a way to bind a set of routines to a set of related data. The routines provide an external interface, similar to that pioneered by the module. Instances of classes could be created on-the-fly by constructing objects. Objects had one private copy of the class-defined data structures, representing their state, and they shared the class member functions with other objects of the same class. In addition to enabling designs to model the entities in the problem space as objects, this approach provided better modularity than modules! Modules had no predefined data management provisions and represented a set of behavior that could only be bound into an application once.

Reusing a module often required management of global data structures that could be easily corrupted. The class changed the focus to a more holistic approach that placed the entity (data and functionality) in the forefront of design considerations. Data and state became important concerns, if not the primary ones. Many objects of a single class could be created, and the objects provided a natural way to partition the global namespace, so often polluted in modular applications. Thus encapsulation and instancing became key issues in object-oriented data management. Inheritance enabled you to reuse preexisting classes, implementation and all. This proved problematic in many scenarios because implementation behavior variance was the primary reason that designers had shifted their focus to data structures. Code was more reusable, but, even so, code was more often recycled rather than strictly reused.

I've created a component named Rectangle and a client program named UseRectangle. The Rectangle (highlights shown in Listing 16.3) component draws a filled rectangle in its windows according to a color that's a class member. Each time the client application (highlights shown in Listing 16.4) instantiates the class, it sets the class member variable to a different color. This illustrates the concept of data encapsulation.

LISTING 16.3   Component with a Color Class Member

```
// Rect.cpp : Implementation of CRect

#include "stdafx.h"
#include "Rectangle.h"
#include "Rect.h"


/////////////////////////////////////////////////////////////////////////////
// CRect


STDMETHODIMP CRect::get_RectColor(long *pVal)
{

    *pVal = (long) m_RectColor;
```

LISTING 16.3   Continued

```
    return S_OK;
}

STDMETHODIMP CRect::put_RectColor(long newVal)
{

    m_RectColor = (COLORREF) newVal;

    return S_OK;
}
// Rect.h : Declaration of the CRect

#ifndef __RECT_H_
#define __RECT_H_

#include "resource.h"        // main symbols
#include <atlctl.h>

// Rect.cpp : Implementation of CRect

#include "stdafx.h"
#include "Rectangle.h"
#include "Rect.h"


/////////////////////////////////////////////////////////////////////////////
// CRect


STDMETHODIMP CRect::get_RectColor(long *pVal)
{

    *pVal = (long) m_RectColor;

    return S_OK;
}

STDMETHODIMP CRect::put_RectColor(long newVal)
{

    m_RectColor = (COLORREF) newVal;

    return S_OK;
}
```

LISTING 16.4   Using the Rectangle Component

```
// Machine generated IDispatch wrapper class(es) created by
// Microsoft Visual C++
```

COM+ as a Component Manager
CHAPTER 16
421

16

COM+ AS A
COMPONENT
MANAGER

LISTING 16.4   Continued

```
// NOTE: Do not modify the contents of this file.  If this class is
// regenerated by Microsoft Visual C++, your modifications will be
// overwritten.


#include "stdafx.h"
#include "rect.h"

/////////////////////////////////////////////////////////////////////////////
// CRect1

IMPLEMENT_DYNCREATE(CRect1, CWnd)

/////////////////////////////////////////////////////////////////////////////
// CRect1 properties

/////////////////////////////////////////////////////////////////////////////
// CRect1 operations

long CRect1::GetRectColor()
{
    long result;
    InvokeHelper(0x1, DISPATCH_PROPERTYGET, VT_I4, (void*)&result, NULL);
    return result;
}

void CRect1::SetRectColor(long nNewValue)
{
    static BYTE parms[] =
        VTS_I4;
    InvokeHelper(0x1, DISPATCH_PROPERTYPUT, VT_EMPTY, NULL, parms,
        nNewValue);
}

// UseRectangleView.h : interface of the CUseRectangleView class
//
/////////////////////////////////////////////////////////////////////////////

#if !defined(AFX_USERECTANGLEVIEW_H__8C04473E_1A26_11D4_B9F9_
➥00105AA721BE__INCLUDED_)
#define AFX_USERECTANGLEVIEW_H__8C04473E_1A26_11D4_B9F9_00105AA721BE__
➥INCLUDED_

#if _MSC_VER > 1000
#pragma once
#endif // _MSC_VER > 1000

#include "rect.h"
```

LISTING 16.4 Continued

```cpp
class CUseRectangleView : public CView
{
protected: // create from serialization only
    CUseRectangleView();
    DECLARE_DYNCREATE(CUseRectangleView)

// Attributes
public:
    CUseRectangleDoc* GetDocument();

// Operations
public:

    CRect1 m_Rectangle[8];
    BOOL m_bRectanglesCreated;

// Overrides
    // ClassWizard generated virtual function overrides
    //{{AFX_VIRTUAL(CUseRectangleView)
    public:
    virtual void OnDraw(CDC* pDC);  // overridden to draw this view
    virtual BOOL PreCreateWindow(CREATESTRUCT& cs);
    protected:
    //}}AFX_VIRTUAL

// Implementation
public:
    virtual ~CUseRectangleView();
#ifdef _DEBUG
    virtual void AssertValid() const;
    virtual void Dump(CDumpContext& dc) const;
#endif

protected:

// Generated message map functions
protected:
    //{{AFX_MSG(CUseRectangleView)
    //}}AFX_MSG
    DECLARE_MESSAGE_MAP()
};

#ifndef _DEBUG  // debug version in UseRectangleView.cpp
inline CUseRectangleDoc* CUseRectangleView::GetDocument()
   { return (CUseRectangleDoc*)m_pDocument; }
#endif

/////////////////////////////////////////////////////////////////////////////
```

COM+ as a Component Manager

CHAPTER 16

423

16

COM+ AS A
COMPONENT
MANAGER

LISTING 16.4   Continued

```
//{{AFX_INSERT_LOCATION}}
// Microsoft Visual C++ will insert additional declarations
// immediately before the previous line.

#endif // !defined(AFX_USERECTANGLEVIEW_H__8C04473E_1A26_11D4_B9F9_
➥00105AA721BE__INCLUDED_)

// UseRectangleView.cpp : implementation of the CUseRectangleView class
//

#include "stdafx.h"
#include "UseRectangle.h"

#include "UseRectangleDoc.h"
#include "UseRectangleView.h"

#ifdef _DEBUG
#define new DEBUG_NEW
#undef THIS_FILE
static char THIS_FILE[] = __FILE__;
#endif

/////////////////////////////////////////////////////////////////////////////
// CUseRectangleView

IMPLEMENT_DYNCREATE(CUseRectangleView, CView)

BEGIN_MESSAGE_MAP(CUseRectangleView, CView)
    //{{AFX_MSG_MAP(CUseRectangleView)
    //}}AFX_MSG_MAP
END_MESSAGE_MAP()

/////////////////////////////////////////////////////////////////////////////
// CUseRectangleView construction/destruction

CUseRectangleView::CUseRectangleView()
{

    m_bRectanglesCreated = FALSE;

}

CUseRectangleView::~CUseRectangleView()
{
}

BOOL CUseRectangleView::PreCreateWindow(CREATESTRUCT& cs)
{
    return CView::PreCreateWindow(cs);
```

LISTING 16.4   Continued

```cpp
}

/////////////////////////////////////////////////////////////////////////////
// CUseRectangleView drawing

void CUseRectangleView::OnDraw(CDC* pDC)
{
    CUseRectangleDoc* pDoc = GetDocument();
    ASSERT_VALID(pDoc);

    if( !m_bRectanglesCreated )
    {
        for( int i=0; i<8; i++ )
        {
            RECT Rect;
            Rect.top = 10;
            Rect.bottom = 40;
            Rect.left = 10 + i * 30;
            Rect.right = 10 + i * 30 + 25;
            m_Rectangle[i].Create( "", WS_VISIBLE, Rect, this, 0x1001 + i );
            m_Rectangle[i].SetRectColor( RGB( ( rand() & 255 ),
➡( rand() & 255 ), ( rand() & 255 ) ) );
        }
    }

}

/////////////////////////////////////////////////////////////////////////////
// CUseRectangleView diagnostics

#ifdef _DEBUG
void CUseRectangleView::AssertValid() const
{
    CView::AssertValid();
}

void CUseRectangleView::Dump(CDumpContext& dc) const
{
    CView::Dump(dc);
}

CUseRectangleDoc* CUseRectangleView::GetDocument() // non-debug
➡version is inline
{
    ASSERT(m_pDocument->IsKindOf(RUNTIME_CLASS(CUseRectangleDoc)));
    return (CUseRectangleDoc*)m_pDocument;
}
#endif //_DEBUG

/////////////////////////////////////////////////////////////////////////////
// CUseRectangleView message handlers
```

COM+: Separating Interface from Implementation

The next evolutionary example follows the course of distributed computing. If one small computer is one-tenth as fast as a mainframe, 20 should be twice as fast, right? Sure, as long as you can find some handy way to wire all those little devils together with zero overhead. Of course, the driving factor in most things left to management is price. So the era of distributed computing began, performance woes and all.

Because you're already working with objects, it would be very convenient if you could just bounce them around the various computers available. The problem here, waiting for a solution, is this: How does an object on one system talk to an object on another system? The answer, of course, is through the objects' public interface. Unfortunately, in most languages, an object's public interface is inseparable from the object's implementation and is not implemented or even declared on the caller's system in a generic, easily consumable way. Many developers began to realize that the most important and likely element of a class that you could reuse was the interface. Creating C++ classes with nothing but pure virtual functions became a standard technique for building interfaces that could be reused much more readily than implementation classes. Languages such as Java directly support pure interface definition, but these still have the drawback that the interface is language specific.

Now if the interface were declared in some generic language, you could publish interfaces separately from implementation and support objects constructed in any language. The heavy part of the object (the interface implementation) could be separated from the light part of the object (the interface declaration). Thus, in the Windows world, COM presented a solution that enabled any language to declare its object interfaces in a generic way through Interface Definition Language (IDL). This promoted the binary reuse of object implementations, but, more often, the reuse of interfaces. COM then would manage the interface to the caller and the object being called, making the location of clients and servers transparent. Transparent, that is, if you are oblivious to the distributed application performance vortex that you just introduced.

The distributed-object, cross-network transactions were often the least of the overhead concerns. Consider the fact that each object created on a server has its own private set of data maintaining its state. One hundred clients mean one hundred copies of the server object in memory. All the same, as long as you can simply add more computers to the mix, things will be OK, for a while. Objects maintaining database connections and using other elements of shared state shut down the infinite scalability philosophy rather quickly. Regardless, COM did introduce reusable, somewhat distributable, binary components, while ushering in the era of the interface and the greatest promise of reuse yet.

Performance, Scalability, and Robustness

So, reuse and reliability were long-sought goals, partially met through objects and interfaces. But what good is it all if you just have to rewrite everything from scratch in order to supply effective performance in the world's high-demand, Internet-powered computing superstructure. Well, no good at all, I reckon. So how do you make things faster and more scalable? The answer is carefully managed state.

COM+: Separating State from Behavior

Consider this: What would happen if, in response to a client's request to create an object, the COM runtime simply returned with a success code (as it often does). Creating objects would be a pretty rapid affair, not to mention the reduced network overhead and the fact that the server would not have to construct and maintain the object's state. Of course, when you call one of the object's methods, the server must produce the object. What if the server kept a pool of the objects about and simply handed one to you when you needed it, and then gave it to another client after you were finished? A thousand clients could be supported with one hundred objects assuming only 10% of the clients use the server objects at a time. This presents a tenfold resource benefit! You might have noticed the hitch, what happens when the object you get already has state (data set up) from the last client. Yikes! In order for this whole business to work correctly, the objects in question need to carefully manage their state. This entails keeping track of the required per-client state, which would optimally be none. Such is the principal requirement of true COM+ components.

As an enterprise application server, COM+ makes provisions for just-in-time (JIT) object creation, early object destruction, object pooling, and many other performance and scalability benefits. In order to operate in this advanced application server environment, components must eliminate all state assumptions and recover any required data on a transaction-by-transaction basis.

Your average COM developer wouldn't think twice about adding a big, hairy data structure to a given object class, although a COM+ developer would focus on a few more things. Performance, robustness, and scalability are all provided by COM+ components through carefully managed state. No object can be created, dispatched, and destroyed faster than a stateless object (an object with no attributes). No object can execute across a cluster of CPUs more transparently than a stateless object. No object presents a more robust life cycle than a stateless object. A client executing a method in a stateless object can just try again if the object blows up, but, if the object was tracking the totals of your last seven operations when it blows up, you've got some real clean up to do. Unfortunately, state is a necessary evil in many situations. For this reason COM+ provides an array of means to manage data in stateful objects.

COM+ as a Component Manager

CHAPTER 16

427

16

COM+ AS A
COMPONENT
MANAGER

So as you can see, the programming world has moved through an initial era of collecting things together into closely coupled units to aid the concerns of reuse and manageable structure in monolithic applications. We are currently embroiled in a new era where distributed (often Internet-based) applications are the brass ring of the development world. In this new era, entity identification and relationships are still important, but a second design wave must also ensue. This critical second step focuses on separating reusable interfaces from semi-reusable implementation behavior and from nonreusable state. This separation of interface, behavior, and state is the key to massively scalable, distributed, n-tier applications. Because you're reading this, I'll assume you've got a handle on the interface and implementation issues, so let's take a look at state.

COM+ and State

State consists of those elements that describe a particular object and its current condition in an object-oriented application. The gas tank can be in the full or empty state. To be more generic, *state* consists of the values ascribed to relevant data items at a given point in time. In general, the values of a programmatic object's attributes describe its state.

Properly managing application state is one of the most critical aspects of COM+ application design. The great thing about the few restrictions that COM+ applies to your state model is that, if you're designing a scalable server application and are not following these rules beforehand, you probably should be. In this way, your existing applications will experience relatively little impact or a great improvement in scalability, even if this entails a bit of extra work, when migrating to COM+.

Well-described objects often have several legal states. The launch object can have a Ready state, a Failsafe state, and a Fire state. Some state transitions on objects might be illegal, for example, going from Failsafe to Fire. Objects left in an illegal state are the leading cause of application failure. For example, it would be bad to simultaneously have the Door attribute set to Closed and the Ignition attribute set to True. When it all boils down, no one really cares if your algorithm is wrong, as long as the data it manipulates is always right! Reducing the total set of routines that can tamper with object state (for example, information hiding or encapsulation) is, therefore, one of your most important software reliability tactics.

Types of State

State is a little like baggage—you can't just leave it lying around. You must carry it with you or check it somewhere safe. Some things, like your name, you keep around all the time; other things, like your lunch, you only keep with you for a short while. Identifying the durability of a certain piece of state is an important step in establishing how that state will need to be managed in COM+. Although many state life-span variations exist, the three types discussed in the following sections are very common.

Transient State

Transient state includes items that require only interim storage. Transient state is often maintained on the call stack. For example, method parameters and local variables constitute transient state. COM+ object methods invoked by a particular client always complete their execution in a sequential way, and so transient state requires no special handling. This is a form of *nondurable state* because it is not protected by a persistent storage mechanism.

Object-Bound State

Object-bound state includes those elements of state tied to the lifetime of the object. Unfortunately, if you want to design an application platform that will support thousands of corporate users or tens of thousands of Web users, you can't very well maintain an object in memory for each user. Standard object attributes usually fall into the category of semidurable state. Object state outlives the client's call, and in COM+ perhaps even the physical object, but not the logical object (the object that the client perceives). COM+ can dispatch various physical objects to service the requests of a client against a single logical object. We don't want to lose the information while the client is using the logical object, but in most cases we don't actually want to squirrel it away in a database to keep for all time either.

Durable State

Durable state is information that you maintain over long periods of time, often across several executions of an application. In many cases, durable state is data that you simply can't afford to lose. Usually this is the type of information that you carefully maintain in a database, and that you modify within a transaction and always back up.

State Storage

So obviously, you should minimize your component's state as much as possible to reduce resource retention on the server. Not all objects can operate in the void of statelessness, however. So if you really need to build components that maintain state and yet require scalability, you need to select a mechanism for storing your durable and semidurable state. The sections that follow present various possibilities for state storage and their respective trade-offs. The key factors that constantly play against one another are the burden of maintaining state and the burden of transmitting it. If you need state, your choices are to retain it or retrieve it from where it is stored.

COM+ as a Component Manager

CHAPTER 16

429

16

COM+ AS A
COMPONENT
MANAGER

Client Temporary Storage

Client applications run on the client's computer. This is one of the big advantages of the whole client/server thing. Add a client; add another client processor to bear the load. If you're in the midst of trying to reduce the burden on the relatively few servers you have, it makes perfect sense to make the client keep track of any state the object might require. Client Web pages can maintain memory variables or standard HTML-style parameters to preserve needed state. Traditional clients can create memory structures to manage necessary information. This data can then be passed back to the COM+ object with each call. This approach works well for managing object (semidurable) state. The advantages of client temporary storage are that the approach scales well and distributes the state maintenance burden to the client. The more clients, the more client machines there are to manage client state. Also, when a client crashes, it only takes out its own state. The drawback is that you are required to pass necessary state data in with every method call. This can produce excessive call overhead and additional client code, and might not even be feasible in some cases.

Client Persistent Storage

Client systems are not generally within the protected circle of the corporate data center and are, therefore, rarely trusted with critical data storage tasks. However, client preferences and other noncritical state information can be effectively stored persistently on the client machine. This state can be stored in the form of Web cookies, registry settings, or disk files, among other methods. Client persistent storage has the same basic pros and cons listed for client temporary storage, with the added feature of increased durability.

Server Temporary Storage

At this point you're probably wondering how to manage the necessary state of your components without slowing down the already lethargic Internet and without rewriting all your client code (as these two situations often require). Well, if you're looking to just maintain some client-specific object state between object activations, the MTS Shared Property Manager (SPM) might be your solution. The SPM is a high-speed repository for property data and is designed specifically to maintain shared object semidurable state. You could, of course, design your own system to retrieve state, but you'd have to have a pretty specific need to exceed the features supplied by the SPM. One of the first COM+ components you will build in this chapter will demonstrate use of the SPM. Alternatively, you could create a stateful object that COM+ must retain in memory until the object client releases it, or the object itself concedes to be deactivated.

Server Persistent Storage

All the state management options discussed previously fail to meet the rigorous requirements and large storage capacity generally required by a significant enterprise application. For years, organizations have trusted their critical information to databases. Fortunately, COM+ integrates data access services into its runtime environment. COM+ supports pooled resources, such as database connections, which reduce the overall connection counts against the database and improve data access turnaround. Sophisticated data stores, such as databases, can also be enlisted into MTS transactions to provide robust data manipulation services that avoid inconsistent durable state (partially committed transactions, for example). Databases also have the significant advantage of distribution-supporting data access from various hosts in a network. The stateful objects and Shared Property Manager approaches instance data on a per-server-process basis, disallowing shared state across multiple servers. Of course, there is always a trade-off, and in the case of the database, it is performance, because databases are one of the most expensive data stores available.

As you can see, each of these state storage options has its place and can be useful in several scenarios. Which techniques will work best for you depend entirely upon your application.

COM+ Component Requirements

Now that you've explored the critical state management concerns of COM+, look at the more tangible COM+ physical component requirements. The following list presents the eight mandatory requirements of COM+ components:

- COM+ components require standard class objects with standard `IClassFactory` interfaces. Because COM+ controls object life span to enhance application, scalability components cannot use unorthodox object-creation techniques. Remember that COM+ intercepts all object-creation requests and can perform any number of performance-enhancing shortcuts. Only COM+ directly invokes the class factory of a COM+ object.

- COM+ requires an `IClassFactory::CreateInstance()` that returns one new object for each call. COM+ creates objects as its needs demand. `CreateInstance()` methods that fail to produce precisely one new object with each call confound the life cycle management mechanisms employed by COM+. *Singletons* (produced by class factories that construct only one object and that return interface pointers to this single object over and over) are explicitly illegal.

- COM+ components must be implemented within a DLL with a `DllGetClassObject()` routine that returns a class object. This DLL export is the routine through which COM+ gains initial access to component class factories.

- COM+ components require standard COM reference counting. COM+ cannot manage object lifetimes if the standard `AddRef()` and `Release()` routines do not increment and decrement a reference counter once per call.

- COM+ components cannot aggregate with non-COM+ objects. Because COM+ intercepts method invocation in order to support several of its advanced features, all aggregate elements of a single logical object must be entirely within or entirely without the COM+ management infrastructure. This keeps subobjects from manipulating direct interface pointers to COM+ objects.

- COM+ components must support a complete `DllRegisterServer()` implementation. The COM+ administration system manages components within applications down to the method level. The only way COM+ can effectively perform these administration tasks is to have access to ProgID, CLSID, Interface, and TypeLib information directly through calls to `DllRegisterServer()`.

- COM+ components must use standard or type library marshaling. COM+ supplies no support for custom marshaling and will never call a component's `IMarshal` interface. Interfaces using only automation types (tType lLibrary marshaling) can be marshaled by COM's Oleaut32.dll using type library information. Interfaces using an MIDL-generated proxy/stub DLL (standard marshaling) will also operate correctly under COM+.

- Components using standard marshaling must compile their IDL with MIDL.exe version 3.00.44 or later, using `/Oicf` switches, and link their proxy stubs to mtxil.lib as the first library in the search list. Only components using standard marshaling will be concerned with this point.

As you can see, most plain vanilla ATL components and all VB and VJ components meet the needs of COM+ structurally. The real trick is ensuring that your designs and implementation code meet the required and strongly recommended architectural guidelines of COM+.

Building COM+ Components

Now that we've dealt with the significant and critical design requirements of COM+, let's examine the implementation details. Here's the good news—the COM+ API only has two functions, `SafeRef()` and `GetContextObject()`. Of course, one of these functions returns a COM interface pointer that enables you to call several more methods, some of which return additional interfaces pointers, and, well, you get the idea.

So before you develop your first COM+-aware component, you need to get a handle on the various objects and interfaces available to COM+ constituents. The next discussion examines the nature of IObjectContext, the most important interface implemented by COM+, and IObjectControl, which is the only COM+-specific interface that a component can itself implement.

Context Objects

Context is the stuff that gives you your bearings and makes the outcome of two executions of the same operation produce different results. Can you take the corkscrew at Laguna Seca going 50 miles an hour? Depends on the context. Is it raining? Am I in a car or on a motorcycle? Do I have new Dunlop 207s on my rims?

Stateless components scale very well, but sometimes they need a little context, something to tell them who's calling them and why, or if a transaction is active. For this reason COM+ maintains a context object to shadow each COM+ object. Figure 16.2 depicts the relationship between COM+ objects and their COM+ context objects.

FIGURE 16.2

Context objects.

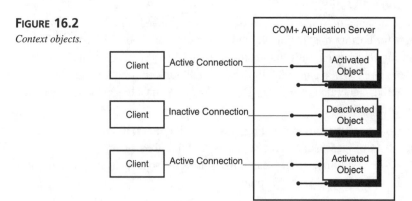

COM+ context objects are opaque and are accessed through methods of the IObjectContext interface. An object can retrieve an interface pointer to its context object's IObjectContext interface by calling the MTS GetObjectContext() function. Table 16.1 provides a list of the IObjectContext methods.

COM+ as a Component Manager

CHAPTER 16

433

16

COM+ AS A
COMPONENT
MANAGER

TABLE 16.1 IObjectContext Methods

Method	What It Does
CreateInstance()	Creates an object within the current context.
DisableCommit()	Declares that the object's transactional updates are in an inconsistent state. (The object retains its state across method calls.)
EnableCommit()	Declares that the object's transactional updates are in a consistent state. (The object retains its state across method calls.)
IsCallerInRole()	Indicates whether the object's caller is in a specified role.
IsInTransaction()	Indicates whether the object is executing within a transaction.
IsSecurityEnabled()	Indicates whether security is enabled.
SetAbort()	Aborts the current transaction. (The object can be deactivated upon return.)
SetComplete()	Declares that the object's transactional updates can be committed. (The object can be deactivated upon return.)

Object Control

What if you want to take advantage of the just-in-time activation and early deactivation features of COM+? In so doing, you agree to be deleted between method calls. Even better, what if you want to take advantage of object pooling by letting COM+ assign your object to whichever client happens to be requesting service currently? Both of these scenarios have severe impact on object state. Deleting an object constitutes destroying its state, and reassigning an object constitutes handing one user's object state over to another user. In order for objects to operate correctly in this performance turmoil, they must either be stateless or be provided some way of saving and retrieving important state information persistently.

The IObjectControl interface is defined by COM+ and implemented by COM+ components. COM+ queries objects for IObjectControl and, if it is discovered, COM+ invokes the three IObjectControl methods at appropriate times during the object's life cycle. Table 16.2 describes the three methods of IObjectControl.

TABLE 16.2 IObjectControl Methods

Method	When It Is Invoked
Activate()	Called by COM+ when an object is activated, before any other methods are called on the object in the current context
CanBePooled()	Called by COM+ to determine whether an object can be pooled for reuse
Deactivate()	Called by COM+ when an object is deactivated, after which no other methods are called on the object in the current context

As you recall, the Stateful object example from the beginning of the chapter lost its state between calls when we enabled early deactivation through a call to `SetComplete()`. As you can see, `IObjectControl` is the solution to your ill-functioning Stateful object. Now you have a way to support early deactivation and just-in-time activation without losing state. The `Activate()` call enables you to retrieve any needed state for client interactions, and the `Deactivate()` call enables you to store any object state needed for later client calls. You might ask why the class constructor and destructor will not suffice. There are two specific reasons. First, some operations (such as accessing the object's context) cannot take place until after the object is completely constructed. These methods sidestep this issue by executing after construction and before destruction. The second and most important reason is that, if the object supports pooling, it can be reused instead of being destroyed and re-created.

Returning true from `CanBePooled()` informs COM+ that your object supports pooling. This enables COM+ to maintain a pool of objects that can be quickly dispatched to service client requests without the overhead of object construction and destruction. MTS versions 2.0 and earlier do not actually pool objects, but they still make the calls to `IObjectControl` as if they were doing it for future compatibility's sake. COM+ actually implements object pooling. If you're interested in optimum scalability, you should try testing components that support early deactivation, just-in-time activation, and pooling. Only careful design and testing will uncover the optimal solution for a given component.

The `Activate()` call wouldn't be of much use without the benefit of context information. Being activated out of the blue doesn't help you understand who is calling and what state you might need to recover in order to perform the tasks requested. For this reason, most component designs use the `Activate()` method as a queue to retrieve context information from COM+ (using `GetObjectContext()`) and context-specific state information from wherever it might be stored.

Using ATL to Build COM+ Components

ATL makes it easy to construct COM+-ready components. All the COM+ examples from here out have been developed using Visual C++ 6 and its associated ATL elements. Let's construct a basic ATL DLL that you can use to work through several of the examples that follow. Although there's not a lot involved in constructing a COM+-ready ATL component, the ATL COM App Wizard takes care of the few details for you. Visual C++ 6 can create MTS components, not COM+ components. For this reason, the steps we'll take will create an MTS component. It will operate in the COM+ environment, though.

First, reconstruct the Stateful DLL and its `Sum` class within an MTS component. As you move forward in the chapter, you'll fix each of the problems exposed in your earlier

COM+ as a Component Manager

CHAPTER 16

435

16

COM+ AS A
COMPONENT
MANAGER

experimentation. To create an MTS component project simply choose File, New from the Visual C++ main menu and select the ATL COM App Wizard. Give your project a name and directory; then, at the first wizard dialog, choose the MTS support check box. MTS components are always DLLs, which enables MTS to supply a complete runtime environment. If you maintain the same project and class names used in the previous example, you won't have to create a new COM+ application or modify the client application.

The DSP file is the only file that is modified from those generated for a normal ATL DLL project. MTS components are linked against the MTS support libraries, mtx.lib and mtxguid.lib. It is also worth noting that VC 6 introduces a new performance feature that enables your build to flag certain DLLs for delayed (just-in-time) loading. This keeps the size of the application image in memory to a minimum and speeds up initial program load times. ATL links to the mtxex.dll (the MTS Executive) in this way, using the /delayload linker switch. Use of the /delayload switch requires helper functions to load the DLL on-the-fly. You can roll your own or link in the presupplied routines found in delayimp.lib, as ATL does.

Next, add a new ATL object to the project by right-clicking the project icon in the Class View pane and selecting New ATL Object. Select the MS Transaction Server Component type and choose Next. Give your class a name (like Sum) and then click the MTS tab in the ATL Object Wizard Properties dialog to configure MTS-specific settings.

Checking support for IObjectControl causes the ATL Wizard to add interface support and starter code for all the IObjectControl methods. Checking Can Be Pooled causes ATL to generate a CanBePooled() method that returns true.

After creating the class, you'll note that ATL adds a smart pointer attribute to reference the MTS IObjectContext interface. ATL adds code to initialize the pointer in the Activate() method and release it in the Deactivate() method. The generated code should look something like this:

```
HRESULT CSum::Activate()
{
    HRESULT hr = GetObjectContext(&m_spObjectContext);
    if (SUCCEEDED(hr))
        return S_OK;
    return hr;
}

BOOL CSum::CanBePooled()
{
    return TRUE;
}

void CSum::Deactivate()
```

```
{
    m_spObjectContext.Release();
}
```

Add the ISum::Add() and ISum::Accumulate() methods from the previous example. In
your new class, you can replace the large SetComplete() block of code with a simple
call to SetComplete() through the object context smart pointer. The Activate() and
Deactivate() methods ensure that all other methods have free access to your MTS context object.

```
STDMETHODIMP CSum::Accumulate(int iValue, int *piTotal)
{
    if ( NULL == piTotal )
        return E_INVALIDARG;

    m_iTotal += iValue;
    *piTotal = m_iTotal;

    //Tell MTS that our work is complete
    m_spObjectContext->SetComplete();

    //Return success
    return S_OK;
}
```

Testing your new COM+ component should demonstrate the same functionality and
problems that you experienced earlier.

Although you currently still lose state between calls, the object is now equipped with
several ways to save and retrieve the m_iTotal state. The Activate() method provides a
way for your object to recover state before it is needed, and the context information provided by IObjectContext enables you to identify which client is calling. By the same
token, the Deactivate() method can be used to save the object state before it is
destroyed. Or, as in your case, the total could be stored, and retrieved only when needed
to improve performance. Your new multiuser COM+ object also needs to make sure that
all users have access to the total. This task is easily solved using the MTS Shared
Property Manager.

The Shared Property Manager

The need to save semidurable object state across multiple objects and activations is quite
common. So common in fact, that MTS provides a resource dispenser called the Shared
Property Manager (SPM) for exactly this purpose.

The Shared Property Manager is instantiated up to once per MTS server process, providing all objects within the process access to shared state under its control. The SPM provides concurrency management to ensure that shared state elements are not corrupted by

writes and reads from more than one object at a time. Shared properties are managed through named groups, reducing the potential for name collisions. Monolithic applications often make use of global variables when requiring shared state. The SPM solves the two biggest problems associated with global variables, access control and global namespace pollution. For more information about SPM, see Chapter 15.

SPM Shortcomings

It is important to keep several things in mind when designing components to use the SPM. Most important, the SPM is instantiated only once per server process. This means that any properties stored in the SPM are available to all components within the server process and to no components without it. For this reason, it is generally a bad idea to share properties between components using the SPM. Should an administrator redeploy a component in another server process (application), the shared properties can no longer be shared, and each server process maintains its own set of property data. Load-balancing scenarios that enable clients to connect to the same class of objects running on different computers present the same problem. A proper database is the most plausible solution when application-wide shared state is required.

SPM Interfaces

Components using the SPM need to include the mtxspm.h header. This header defines three interfaces which provide access to the Shared Property Manager resources:

- `ISharedPropertyGroupManager`
- `ISharedPropertyGroup`
- `ISharedProperty`

The `ISharedPropertyGroupManager` interface provides access to the top-level SPM behavior, including named property group creation, retrieval, and enumeration. The only way to purge the SPM of any existing groups or properties is to shut down the server process in which the SPM is running. The `ISharedPropertyGroup` interface provides methods that enable you to create and retrieve properties by name or position within the referenced group. The `ISharedProperty` interface allows property values to be set and retrieved as variants.

Adding SPM Features to a Component

Now you can update your existing COM+ component using the SPM. Previously, the Stateful component maintained object state in an attribute. There are several problems with this approach. First, there is no way to share this information among the various objects that might be executing within your distributed multiuser application. This can be good or bad depending on the design, but, for this example, assume you want all users to be able to add to the cumulative total. Totaling all sales by all salespeople for the day might work in this way. As discussed previously, this makes the rash assumption that all clients will use a single COM+ server process for this class.

As soon as you make the total available to all objects in the COM+ process, you introduce synchronization problems. You cannot allow multiple objects to access the total simultaneously. You also need to make sure that your total does not conflict with other property names in the shared namespace. As a final point, in making your component more scalable you have sacrificed attribute persistence between calls.

The SPM solves all these problems by presenting a named group property store with built-in synchronization services for multithreaded access. Using the SPM to store your total, your new stateless Sum class has no need for stateful attributes and has thus eliminated the m_iTotal property. Listing 16.5 shows the updated Sum::Accumulate() routine.

LISTING 16.5   SPM Example

```
STDMETHODIMP CSum::Accumulate(int iValue, int *piTotal)
{
    if ( NULL == piTotal )
        return E_INVALIDARG;

    //SPM, Group and Property interface pointers
    ISharedPropertyGroupManager * pSPGM = NULL;
    ISharedPropertyGroup * pGroup = NULL;
    ISharedProperty * pProp = NULL;

    //Get interface pointer to SPM
    m_spObjectContext->CreateInstance(
            CLSID_SharedPropertyGroupManager,
            IID_ISharedPropertyGroupManager,
            (void**) &pSPGM );
    if ( NULL == pSPGM )
        return E_FAIL;

    //Create or open the property group
    BSTR bstrGroupName = SysAllocString( L"SumProperties" );
    long lIsoMode = LockMethod;
    long lRelMode = Process;
    VARIANT_BOOL fExists = VARIANT_FALSE;
    pSPGM->CreatePropertyGroup(    bstrGroupName,
                                    &lIsoMode,
                                    &lRelMode,
                                    &fExists,
                                    &pGroup );
    SysFreeString(bstrGroupName);
    pSPGM->Release();
    if ( NULL == pGroup )
```

COM+ as a Component Manager

CHAPTER 16

439

16

COM+ AS A
COMPONENT
MANAGER

LISTING 16.5 Continued

```
            return E_FAIL;


        //Open the property
        BSTR bstrPropName = SysAllocString(L"Total");
        pGroup->CreateProperty(      bstrPropName,
                                    &fExists,
                                    &pProp);
        SysFreeString(bstrPropName);
        pGroup->Release();
        if ( NULL == pProp )
            return E_FAIL;


        //Update the total
        VARIANT vtTotal;
        vtTotal.vt = VT_I4;
        vtTotal.lVal = 0;
        pProp->get_Value(&vtTotal);
        vtTotal.lVal += iValue;
        *piTotal = vtTotal.lVal;
        pProp->put_Value(vtTotal);
        pProp->Release();

        //Tell MTS that our work is complete
        m_spObjectContext->SetComplete();

        //Return success
        return S_OK;
}
```

The Shared Property Group Manager

As illustrated here, three steps are commonly involved in using the SPM. The first step is to get an interface pointer to the `ISharedPropertyGroupManager`. Although it's perfectly acceptable to use `CoCreateInstance()` in constructing the SPM, your example uses the context object's `CreateInstance()` method. In the case of the SPM, both work fine. The details of `IContextObject::CreateInstance()` are discussed in the following section. Regardless of how you retrieve the `ISharedPropertyGroupManager` interface pointer, only a single instance of the SPM will ever be created per process.

SPM Property Groups

The next step is to open the group of interest. Each SPM group has a unique name. Group names act a lot like a C++ namespace in that they partition the global space into named groups. Your group has been arbitrarily named `SumProperties`. Much like the `CreateInstance()` call used to access the SPM, the `CreatePropertyGroup()` call creates the group if it doesn't exist and opens it if it does, simplifying your program logic. One important point about your group is that you need it to maintain your total, even after your call completes and your object is deactivated. The Process release mode flag indicates that your group should be maintained for the life of the server process. The alternative is Standard, which releases the group as soon as all outstanding group interface pointers are released.

SPM Properties

The final step is opening the property and updating it. SPM properties are nothing more than named variants. One important aspect of the property update code is that it requires isolated access to the total property across two property calls. First, it needs to read the total, and then it needs to write it with the updated value. Allowing other objects to write to the total between these two calls would cause a loss of information. To solve this problem, you can open the group in LockMethod isolation mode. This locks the SPM at the group level for the duration of the method, providing exclusive access to the total during the read and write. The alternative is LockSetGet, which reduces group contention between components by locking at the property level, and only for the duration of successive get and put calls.

Note that you cannot trust the SPM to maintain state between client sessions, although it might on a busy system that never allows the server process to time out. Slow nights, weekends, a process crash, or any number of other situations could conspire to terminate the server process and the SPM with it. The SPM is most certainly not a durable data store. State information that is durable or that needs to be shared across several servers should be stored in a database or some such distributed and reliable data store. You will learn about transactional, durable data access in Chapter 17.

Referencing Objects Within COM+

Your non-COM+ component at the beginning of this chapter exhibited poor scalability, but no processing flaws. Unfortunately, many normal COM components actually fail in some way when operating within COM+. The most common issue related to normal COM component failure is that COM+ manages object lifetimes in the COM+ runtime, where traditional component implementations allow the client to control the object's lifespan. Every object created within a COM+ server process is provided with a proxy object that acts as a front end to the actual object and a context object that maintains information regarding the calling client and the call itself. This enables COM+ to intercept client calls, especially those to IUnknown, and then to selectively delegate only those calls that are necessary. In situations where objects support early deactivation, COM+ can even release an object before a client has finished using it. What all this means is that the client really requires a connection to the COM+ proxy object, not the actual object itself.

Holy COM+ backdoors, Batman! What happens when you give a client a direct reference to your object and then COM+ deletes said object after its current operation completes? I'll let you ponder the consequences. Okay, stop pondering. The result is that the object is gone, and yet the reference you handed out behind the back of COM+ is still in the hands of the client! This means that you must not, I repeat, *must not*, return a COM+ object reference (interface pointer) to a client outside the current object context. The solution to this problem is the COM+-supplied `SafeRef()` API, as shown here:

```
void* SafeRef ( REFIID riid UNKNOWN* pUnk );
```

The `SafeRef()` call enables an object to produce an interface pointer that is safe to pass to clients outside the current context. Failing to do this gives the client direct COM/DCOM access to the object, which foils most, if not all, the mechanisms of COM+, causing nasty fireworks. `SafeRef()` works pretty much like `QueryInterface()`, in that it takes the interface ID of the interface you want and the `IUnknown` of the object that you want it on (which must be the current object), and finally returns the safe interface pointer to that interface. Safe references must be released just as normal references are. Note that `QueryInterface()` calls and `SafeRef()` calls made on a safe reference always return another safe reference. The only serious complication possible here is that two non-equal `IUnknown` interface pointers can actually refer to the same object within the context of a COM+ object's method call (one to the safe reference and one to the actual object).

Creating Objects Within COM+

Another important weakness of non-COM+ components is that they often attempt to construct wildcat objects not configured to run within a COM+ package using `CoCreateInstance()`. These objects, of course, execute wherever the registry has them configured to execute. This might be okay, or it might be very bad. In general, after a method call enters the COM+ environment, it should stay there if the various benefits and rules of COM+ are to be maintained. COM+ has no control over components running outside the package environment. You might run across scenarios in which external objects are required. If so, you must make sure that out-of-context referencing rules and other application-specific considerations are attended to.

So how do you create a new object within the current context? The answer to that question is by using your context object, of course. The `IObjectContext` interface supplies a `CreateInstance()` method that operates like `CoCreateInstance()` with the exception that it creates objects within the current context. The new object inherits the current activity (logical thread of control across COM+ servers), security settings, and possibly even the active transaction. In Chapter 17, you will examine the `ITransactionContextEx` interface, which also supplies a `CreateInstance()` method. Using the `ITransactionContextEx`

CreateInstance() method is much the same as the IObjectContext version, with the exception that it enables the creator to control the transaction context of the new object.

Summary

The sample application developed in this chapter is, at best, trivial. Aren't you glad? You focused on building a highly scalable, stateless COM+ component, and it was a snap. This is exactly what COM+ is all about. You write the business logic, and COM+ handles the high-end, mainframe-style performance and robustness issues. If COM+ wasn't easy to use, it would be far less valuable. The real trick is adjusting your brain to focus on matters of state. The most important things to take away from this chapter are the concept of state, behavior, and interface separation, along with the scalability guidelines of the COM+ system. This chapter covered the key concepts behind basic COM+ component development as well as the implementation issues related to IObjectContext and IObjectControl. Now that you've mastered the art of high performance, MTS component design, Chapter 17 will examine transactions, the key to highly reliable state management and robust applications.

CHAPTER 17

COM+ as a Transaction Coordinator

A *transaction*, or *commitment control*, is the capability to define a set of a logically related operations as a single unit of work. That way, if one of those operations should fail, the work done by all those operations can be "undone," or *rolled back*, with a single function call. Performing transactions is one of the oldest challenges facing the computer industry. A tremendous percentage of the actual server-centric operations taking place in enterprise applications requires the protection of transactions. At the onset, transaction technology was the domain of mainframes alone, but as critical applications have migrated to workstations and finally to the PC platform, transactional technology has paved the way. In fact, transactions are the enabler for many of the most critical applications, making a platform with no transaction support an anathema to such applications.

COM+ supplies transaction services similar to those offered by traditional mainframe transaction processing monitors, as well as those found in the UNIX workstation world. The real beauty and uniqueness of COM+ has to do with the component nature of its framework. The COM foundation, upon which COM+ is built, makes constructing distributed component-based enterprise applications a dream. In Chapter 16, "COM+ as a Component Manager," I discussed the basic nature of COM+ as a scalable, distributed component runtime environment. In this chapter, you'll learn about the mainframe-level reliability features afforded COM+ components through distributed transaction services.

The Need for Transactions

You might be wondering how the average person benefits from transactions. Answering that is best done with an example.

Suppose you're planning a trip to Kansas. You need an airline ticket, hotel reservations, and a rental car reservation. Of course, each one of these must be paid for with a credit card at the time of booking. You call the airline and book a ticket for a time that's convenient, and pay for it with your credit card. You then call the car rental agency and reserve your favorite car for the week, and, of course, guarantee payment with a credit card. But when you call the hotel, you find that you can't get a room for the period of time that matches your airline and car reservations.

You're going to have to arrive in Kansas one day later than you originally planned. Two phone calls later, and your airline and car reservations match the hotel reservations. It would have been nice if you could have done it all in one easy step, and only finalized the reservations when all three were in agreement.

One alternative would have been to let a travel agent handle the entire thing for you. All you would have had to do is call and give her your needs. She would have called you back to let you know of the hotel availability problem. When presented with the alternative plan, you could have given the green light that everything was okay, and the travel agent could place all the reservations for you.

COM+ transactions give your applications the capability to avoid situations analogous to what I just described. A travel reservation system is a perfect example of where a distributed application that supports transactions is most effective. A travel agent can enter a customer's information into a computer and then submit the order. If any part of the order such as the hotel reservation doesn't past muster, then all other parts of the order (transaction) are also aborted. This saves the travel agent (or you) from having to call the airline and the car rental agency to change plans when the hotel turns out to have no vacancy when you plan to arrive.

There are some other complications that transactions can help with, too. Suppose the travel agent is using an application that accesses three different servers. What happens if, when the order is placed, the car reservation agency server is down? It could mean that the airline and hotel reservations are completed without confirmation of the car reservation. When the down server comes back online, there might not be any cars available on the dates that correspond to those of the airline and hotel reservations. If the travel agent is using an application that uses transactions, the down server is not be able to give a thumbs up, and the transaction can't be committed.

Continuing in the footsteps of MTS, COM+ gives developers the transaction capability that helps avoid these unpleasant situations. And this chapter will help you take advantage of the capability in your applications.

Transactions Defined

Generally speaking, transactions are atomic operations in which no one part of the operation can succeed unless all parts of the operation succeed. A successful transaction is committed, and any changes it has made to data stores becomes permanent. Unsuccessful transactions are rolled back so that all data stores are returned to their state prior to the transaction's inception. This transactional approach to data modification helps developers guarantee that data stores maintain a consistent state. This means that there are no surprises. If the account balance database can never have negative values unless the credit database has a corresponding approved record, you must make sure that only legal combinations prevail. If you want to perform a money transfer by deducting funds from one account and crediting another, you need a guarantee that both or neither operation takes place. Transactions enable multiple changes like these to be treated atomically.

Transactions are usually committed in two parts (not to be confused with the two-phase transactions discussed later in this chapter). In the first part, each of the participants votes to commit or abort the transaction. Although database servers are the most common transaction participants, any transaction-aware software component can participate. If any participant votes to abort the transaction, the transaction is rolled back in part two, and the states of all data stores involved are returned to their pretransaction form. If all participants vote to commit, the transaction is committed in part two. This does not mean that the operations are completed; it just means that the participants are committed to completing their parts of the transaction sooner or later.

So far I've talked about transactions in generic terms. Transactions have been around for decades in environments such as mainframes exist in. But the Microsoft Distributed Transaction Coordinator (MS DTC) has been instrumental in moving transaction infrastructure to the Windows operating system. We'll talk about MS DTC shortly, and then go on to talk about Resource Managers (which manage many of the transactional resources).

ACID

Transactions have several integral facets, known as the ACID properties:

- Atomicity
- Consistency
- Isolation
- Durability

The *atomicity* property refers to the fact that all elements of a transaction are treated as an indivisible unit. A transaction is an all-or-nothing proposition. In a transaction where three database tables are updated, all the tables will be updated or none of them will be updated.

The *consistency* property promises that data stores will remain stable. Manipulation of data will not corrupt or be corrupted by other concurrent operations. Thus, your writes to the database will not collide with those of other objects in the system.

Transactional operations are *isolated*, or independent, from other users of the data stores involved. Therefore, no other elements of the system will ever view a partial transaction. They will see state before or after the transaction only. This means that no object will ever retrieve records from a table reflecting part of another object's transactional updates.

Finally, transactions are *durable*, indicating that, after a transaction is committed, an operation will complete. A transactional message queue server might need to attempt message delivery for several hours during network outages. Regardless, the message queue server is committed to delivering transaction messages.

Microsoft Distributed Transaction Coordinator (MS DTC)

MS DTC is Microsoft's Distributed Transaction Coordinator. It was introduced with SQL Server 6.5 as a means to manage distributed transactions involving several SQL databases. In this way, MS DTC acts as a transaction processing (TP) monitor on the Windows platform. The DTC creates a transaction object supporting the ITransaction interface to represent each new distributed transaction. Other interfaces support the two-phase commit process, allowing enlisted resource managers to vote on the success of the their parts of the overall operation. One dissenting resource manager causes the whole transaction to abort, in which case DTC notifies the constituent resource managers that all bets are off. If all the resource managers agree to commit the transaction, the DTC commits the distributed transaction, once again notifying all the interested parties. COM+ components are insulated from the complexities of distributed transaction management and, in most cases, never need to invoke the interfaces of DTC directly. In fact, COM+ provides automatic DTC transaction creation, automatic resource manager DTC transaction enlistment, and a simple IObjectContext interface used by objects to commit or abort transactional operations.

IObjectContext

This section focuses on the transactional features of IObjectContext. Chapter 18, "COM+ Security," will wrap up coverage of the IObjectContext interface with a look at security features. Most of the methods available through IObjectContext are transaction-related. Table 17.1 shows the IObjectContext methods.

TABLE 17.1 IObjectContext Methods

Method	What It Does
CreateInstance()	Creates an object within the current context.
DisableCommit()	Declares that the object's transactional updates are in an inconsistent state. (The object retains its state across method calls.)
EnableCommit()	Declares that the object's transactional updates are in a consistent state. (The object retains its state across method calls.)
IsCallerInRole()	Indicates whether the object's caller is in a specified role.
IsInTransaction()	Indicates whether the object is executing within a transaction.
IsSecurityEnabled()	Indicates whether security is enabled.
SetAbort()	Aborts the current transaction. (The object can be deactivated upon return.)
SetComplete()	Declares that the object's transactional updates can be committed. (The object can be deactivated upon return.)

The CreateInstance() method is the preferred way to construct new objects within MTS. When using IObjectContext::CreateInstance(), newly created objects that support or require transactions inherit the current transaction. Calling `CoCreateInstance()` to create objects passes none of the current context information on to the new object. For this reason, `CoCreateInstance()` should be used only when explicitly creating objects outside the current COM+ activity.

`DisableCommit()` is a useful call that enables a method to safeguard against accidental transaction commit behavior. For example, an object method that begins a transactional operation and then errantly or intentionally returns to the client before completing the transactional operation has its transaction committed if the client then releases the object within the transaction timeout. Object shutdown defaults to commit. `DisableCommit()` disables the transaction and only an explicit call to the `SetComplete()` method can commit the operation. Thus, should a client ever release an object maintaining a disabled transaction, MTS has no choice but to abort the transaction. Should the client make another method call to the object to complete the transaction, the object can call `EnableCommit()` to re-enable the transaction or simply call `SetComplete()`, which overrides the `Disable` call and commits the transaction if possible.

`EnableCommit()` re-enables a transaction, enabling the transaction to complete implicitly. This is the default state of a newly issued transaction. I don't know about you, but I have little use for implicit behavior in my mission-critical server components. Disabling the current transaction at the top of every external method call until the transaction is explicitly committed with `SetComplete()` has stood me in good stead.

`SetComplete()` is the method used by objects when they are happy with the various operations they have performed and would like to commit changes to any resource managers involved in the transaction. Object methods invoking `SetComplete()` should return `S_OK` to indicate success. Unfortunately calling `SetComplete()` is just the object's vote to complete the transaction and should any one resource manager vote to abort, the transaction fails completely. In this case, COM+ replaces the root object method's return value (if it's a success code) with `CONTEXT_E_ABORTED`. Regardless, an object method calling `SetComplete()` is a signal to MTS that the object can be deactivated. Stateful objects should never call `SetComplete()` unless they can safely be destroyed.

`SetAbort()` is the method used by objects that want to abort their current transaction. This is a no-nonsense call that ensures the rollback of all transactional modifications to any resource managers involved. Objects voting to abort the current transaction can return any value they choose to the client application and are generally deactivated immediately after returning.

`IsInTransaction()` simply returns `True` or `False` depending on whether there is an active transaction in context. This is handy for aborting in cases where a transaction is required, but none exists.

COM+ as a Transaction Coordinator

CHAPTER 17

449

17

COM+ AS A
TRANSACTION
COORDINATOR

A Simple Transaction Example

To make it easy for you to understand what I've talked about so far, and to give you a picture of how to implement transactions in your COM+ code, I've written a very simple example. I made a point of keeping it as simple as possible so that you can easily understand the important points that relate to transactions.

The component was written in Visual C++ using ATL, and the client program was written in Visual Basic. Both can be found in the Chapter17\SimpleTrans directory on the CD-ROM.

Listing 17.1 shows you the important code from the COM+ component, and Listing 17.2 shows you the Visual Basic code for the client application. An explanation follows the code listings.

LISTING 17.1 A Very Simple Transaction Component

```
// First.cpp : Implementation of CFirst
#include "stdafx.h"
#include "SimpleTrans.h"
#include "First.h"


/////////////////////////////////////////////////////////////////////////////
// CFirst


STDMETHODIMP CFirst::DoIt()
{
    AFX_MANAGE_STATE(AfxGetStaticModuleState())

    // Get the object context.
    IObjectContext *pObjectContext = NULL;
    HRESULT hRes = GetObjectContext( &pObjectContext );

    // Make sure we didn't get an error while getting
    // the object context.
    if( FAILED( hRes ) )
    {

        if( hRes == E_INVALIDARG )
            m_strTransactionResult = "Invalid argument.";
        else if( hRes == E_UNEXPECTED )
            m_strTransactionResult = "Unexpected error.";
        else if( hRes == CONTEXT_E_NOCONTEXT )
            m_strTransactionResult = "No context associated with object.";
        else
            m_strTransactionResult = "Object context could not be obtained.";
```

LISTING 17.1 Continued

```
return( hRes );
    }

    // Here we'll decide to be successful based on the system time.
    // If it is an even minute, we'll be succcessful. Otherwise
    // the transaction will abort.

    // Get the system time.
    SYSTEMTIME st;
    GetSystemTime( &st );

    // Even
    if( ( st.wMinute & 1 ) == 0 )
    {
        // Success.
        pObjectContext->SetComplete();

        m_strTransactionResult = "Transaction completed.";

    }

    // Odd
    else
    {
        // Failure and we abort.
        pObjectContext->SetAbort();

        m_strTransactionResult = "Transaction aborted.";

    }

    // Release the object context.
    pObjectContext->Release();

    return S_OK;
}

STDMETHODIMP CFirst::get_TransactionResult(BSTR *pVal)
{
    AFX_MANAGE_STATE(AfxGetStaticModuleState())

    // Return the string that alerts caller to the
    // transaction result.
    *pVal = m_strTransactionResult.AllocSysString();

    return S_OK;
}
```

LISTING 17.2 The Visual Basic Client Application That Uses the Simple Transaction Component

```
Private Sub Command1_Click()
    Label2.Caption = "Executing Transaction"

    Dim obj As Object
    Set obj = CreateObject("SimpleTrans.First.1")

    Res = obj.DoIt()

    Label2.Caption = "Result of DoIt():" & obj.TransactionResult

    Set obj = Nothing

End Sub
```

The component has a class named CFirst with a method named DoIt() that does the work. The first thing that happens in the DoIt() method is `GetObjectContext()` is called. The object context must be obtained in order to either commit (with `SetComplete()`) or abort (with `SetAbort()`) the transaction.

Some error checking comes next to make sure the `IObjectContext` pointer was retrieved without an error. We wouldn't want to perform operations on a NULL or invalid `IObjectContext` pointer.

For this example, the decision to commit or abort is based on the system time. If the system time returns a minute that's an even number, the transaction succeeds. If the minute is an odd number, the transaction aborts.

In order to commit the transaction, a simple call to `SetComplete()` is made. To abort, a call to `SetAbort()` is made. The `IObjectContext` is freed with a call to `Release()`, and the method then returns to the caller.

Notice that a `CString` class member named `m_strTransactionResult` is set during the method so that the calling program can easily get a text string describing the outcome of the method call.

The Visual Basic program (Listing 17.2) is easy to understand. It simple instantiates the component, calls the `DoIt()` method, and then sets a label in the form with the result string.

It's very important to note here that in order for this to work, the component must be in the COM+ catalog as part of an application. Its attributes must also be set correctly. I talk about setting COM+ component attributes later in the chapter.

Transaction Protocols

Of course, transactions have been around a long time and have cropped up somewhat independently on various platforms. This complicates matters somewhat. The COM+ programming environment provides support for several different transaction protocols, discussed in the next sections.

OLE Transactions

Microsoft bases almost all its services and architectures on COM these days. Thus COM is the basis for the OLE transaction standard. OLE transactions are native to MS DTC, SQL Server, and just about any other transactional Microsoft product.

XA Transactions

The X/Open UNIX standards body promotes its XA transaction standard. XA transactions are used extensively in many distributed environments, especially UNIX. Because this is the preferred transaction mechanism used by some of the largest database companies in the world (Oracle, Informix, Sybase, and others), it would be a tragedy to leave out XA transaction support in any product seeking to become the enterprise-enabling, transactional component runtime of the millennium. Thus DTC supplies support for XA transactions.

As you might have guessed, there is, regrettably, a little more to it than that. Because Microsoft is more inclined to integrate and fully test the services of SQL Server than, say, Oracle 8, XA transaction configuration can take some work. Be sure to examine the COM+ Help system supplied with your version to ensure that you have the correct driver revisions before attempting to use XA transactions in a COM+ system. The `TestOracleXAConfig.exe` command line utility enables you to check for correct Oracle database transaction support. Check your database vendor's Web site and the Microsoft Web site for the latest support.

CICS and IMS Transactions

Okay, now you're moving into alien territory. Not only do mainframes support their own unique transaction protocols, but they often also operate in a completely different network infrastructure. They were here first, so you can't blame them for that. Mainframes are the center of the transaction processing world because of their legendary reliability. So it really would be nice to allow a slick Web-based client that calls a component running in a COM+ middle-tier server to interact with the big iron. Fortunately, DTC supports LU 6.2 Sync Level 2, and with the help of SNA Server and COMTI, transactions can be distributed into the mainframe environment. Chapter 19, "The COM Transaction Integrator," discusses the nature of CICS and IMS transaction integration with COM+.

The COM+ Transaction Programming Model

One of the greatest things about the COM+ transaction programming model is that most things are automatic, and those that aren't are pretty darn easy to code. Once again, COM+ comes through with a very complex set of services in an easy-to-use package; however, certain rules remain invariant no matter how easy the programming task becomes. In fact, it's very easy to build a really bad COM+ component. In light of this fact, take a hard look at design issues as you work your way through the programming features and the design-specific section at the end of the chapter.

The basic design premise to consider when structuring your components is that transactions are expensive. Avoid them if you can. If you can't avoid transactions, keep your transactions as fine-grained as possible. Reserving expensive resources for extended periods of time only exacerbates the transactional overhead. This means that you should complete all transactions as quickly as you can.

Here's a sketch of a typical COM+ transaction sequence:

1. A client calls a transactional COM+ object method.
2. COM+ receives the call and allocates a DTC transaction to attach to the object's context. It then forwards the call to the object, creating and activating the object if necessary.
3. The object method performs a behavior, invoking the services of other objects and resource managers, which are automatically enlisted in the transaction.
4. Upon completion the object assesses the results of the various functions and either commits or aborts the transaction. (Resource managers subsequently make permanent or roll back the transactional changes.)
5. The object returns status to the client, and COM+ deactivates the object.

This execution sequence, which is illustrated in Figure 17.1, demonstrates one of the most powerful features of component-based transactions. Each of the objects involved in the transaction performs its task in a well-encapsulated way. The calling component does not need details regarding the implementation of the objects it calls. Should the called object make transactional updates to a resource manager, those updates are automatically enlisted in the existing transaction. This automatic transaction propagation ensures that fragments of the overall operation fail or succeed with the whole, regardless of the base object's knowledge of the subordinate object's specific behavior.

FIGURE **17.1**

*Component-based
transaction.*

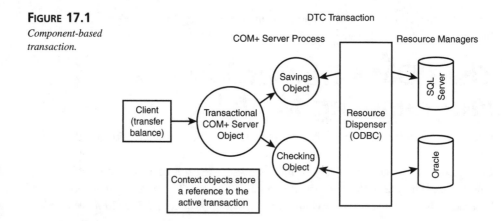

FIGURE **17.1**

*Component-based
transaction.*

Creating Transactions

Creating transactions in COM+ is most often a declarative process. You can generate transactions procedurally, but this is not generally necessary. Transactions are automatically created by COM+ in much the same way that transactions automatically propagate from object to object and from object to resource manager. Usually the only manual part of the process is the final step in which the object chooses to commit or abort the operation.

This sometimes happens behind the scenes depending on the Resource Dispenser (RD) in question. Some RDs expose this functionality in their own API. (ODBC simply added support behind the scenes of such calls as ::SQLConnect(), ::SQLDriverConnect(), and so on.) Other RDs require that you explicitly enlist in a transaction.

Automatic Transactions

Automatic transactions are created or propagated by COM+ any time a method of a transactional object is invoked. The one exception to this rule occurs when a transactional object retains a transaction for more than one method call. In this case, successive calls use the existing transaction. Objects can be configured to use transactions through the Component Management Console. Simply right-click the class in question and choose properties. The Transactions tab of the Class Properties dialog box supplies the five transaction settings listed here (see Figure 17.2):

- Disabled
- Not Supported
- Supported
- Required
- Requires New

FIGURE **17.2**

Class transaction settings.

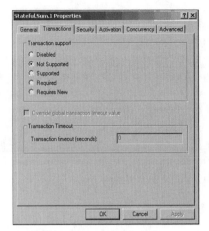

Disabled

This option eliminates transaction-related overhead that never access a resource manager. This simulates the transaction behavior of an unconfigured COM object.

Not Supported

Not Supported is the default setting for any standard COM object installed into a COM+ application. Objects of this type never maintain a transaction in their context; neither do they pass any prior transactions on to objects that they create. Objects of this type are generally legacy components not specifically designed for COM+.

Supported

The Supported transaction setting is for the whimsical classes that don't really care whether there's a transaction around or not but can pass one along to the next object if need be. If an object of this type is called by a client having a transaction, then the context of the current object is set with the client's transaction. In this way, the current object can pass the transaction along to other objects that it creates and which might need the transaction, even though the current object itself really has no interest in the transaction. If an object with this setting is created by a transactionless client, then the current object is also transactionless.

Required

The most commonly used setting by far is Required. This setting ensures that all method calls (outside IUnknown) operate within the protection of a transaction. If the object calling the current object already has a transaction, the current object inherits the existing transaction. This effectively blankets all the various objects invoked, directly or indirectly, from a base transactional object in the same transaction.

Requires New

The Requires New transaction setting is used for components that must operate in an isolated transaction of their own. For example, if you created an `OrderEntry` object for a sweater factory, a side effect of placing an order might be that you order new boxes when the supply gets low. You need a transaction for your box order, but you don't want the existing customer order to fail just because your box order has problems. This scenario could be managed by creating a separate class to handle the box order and setting it to require a new transaction. Now when the `OrderEntry` object calls the `BoxOrder` object, the `OrderEntry` object's transaction does not propagate to the `BoxOrder` object. MTS provides the `BoxOrder` object with a brand new transaction.

ITransactionContextEx

The `TransactionContextEx` interface provides access to the three external methods of the `TransactionContextEx` object. Perhaps you won't be surprised to hear that all `TransactionContextEx` objects require a new transaction. This provides client and server objects alike with an easy way to partition the transaction space or create a transaction where there was none before. You must include the `txctx.h` header to use the `ITransactionContextEx` interface. Table 17.2 lists the methods of the `ITransactionContextEx` interface.

TABLE 17.2 `ITransactionContextEx` Methods

Method	*What It Does*
`Abort()`	Rolls back all transactional operations performed in the current transaction on return from the current method.
`Commit()`	Attempts to commit all transactional operations performed in the current transaction on return from the current method. (If any of the objects participating in the transaction have called `SetAbort()` or `DisableCommit()`, the transaction will be aborted.)
`CreateInstance()`	Creates a new object within the `TransactionContextEx` object's transaction. (If the object class created does not support transactions, the object will still be created, but it will not inherit the transaction.)

A transactionless object could easily construct a `TransactionContextEx` object (thus creating a transaction) and then use the `CreateInstance()` method of the `ITransactionContextEx` interface to create other objects within the new transaction. This is an important feature because an object without a transaction cannot directly create an object that requires a transaction without creating a new transaction every time.

Using the `TransactionContextEx` object, a client can create a pair of transaction-required savings and checking objects within the same transaction using the `ITransactionContextEx::CreateInstance()` method. A single transaction protecting a transfer between the two objects would then be possible. A sample `TransactionContextEx` object creation call can be found in Listing 17.3.

LISTING 17.3   `TransactionContextEx` Object Creation Example

```
#include <txctx.h>

ITransactionContextEx * pTransactionContext;

CoCreateInstance(   CLSID_TransactionContextEx,
                    NULL,
                    CLSCTX_INPROC,
                    IID_ITransactionContextEx,
                    (void**)&pTransactionContext);
```

The `Commit()` and `Abort()` methods of the `ITransactionContextEx` interface simply enable the client to vote to commit or roll back the effects of the transaction upon task completion. All three of these methods are actually just slight variations of the `SetAbort()`, `SetComplete()`, and `CreateInstance()` methods of the `IObjectContext` interfaces.

IDL

Building an IDL file describing your interfaces is a powerful tool in the process of architecting truly scalable and reusable software components. IDL provides an implementation-independent environment in which developers are forced to focus on the virtues of their interfaces. This is critical because interfaces are the most binding contracts in a distributed COM+ system. A C++ component developer cannot often avoid the IDL coding process. ATL and various other toolkits generate much of the modern COM+ interface definition code, but developers are still left with the task of tuning the interfaces and hand-coding elements too esoteric for the subordinate wizards to manage. If more systems began the software construction process in the IDL world, the clarity of many distributed object models would be greatly improved.

COM+ embraces IDL and makes extensive use of type information in the various Component Management Console component display trees. COM+ also adds new coclass attributes to the IDL fray. You can use these COM+ specific attributes to indicate the transactional requirements of your COM+ classes. The following list presents the COM+ transaction attributes available to components:

- `TRANSACTION_REQUIRED`
- `TRANSACTION_REQUIRES_NEW`
- `TRANSACTION_SUPPORTED`

The default transactional value of a class is Not Supported, and any of the other three values can be specified explicitly with the previously mentioned attributes. These values are defined in the `mtxattr.h` header, which must be included in your IDL before using the transactional flags. The great benefit of these transactional type library attributes is that the Component Management Console uses them as defaults when your component is added to a package. As a developer, you probably understand very well what transactional requirements your components have. An administrator, on the other hand, might or might not have this understanding. When you add a class with a transactional attribute to a package, the Component Management Console automatically applies the type library–specified transactional setting. If the COM+ administrators know what they're doing, they can change the transaction attribute to whatever they please, as the type library value is just a helpful default. There's no reason not to brand every COM+ specific transactional component with a suitable default transactional value.

Listing 17.4 shows the IDL code from the `OrderEntry` component that enables clients to place orders within a transaction.

LISTING 17.4   IDL Code from the `OrderEntry` Component

```
import "oaidl.idl";
import "ocidl.idl";
#include <mtxattr.h>
    [
        object,
        uuid(E8482A00-A2F6-11D2-A512-00600893FB20),
        dual,
        helpstring("IMTSOrder Interface"),
        pointer_default(unique)
    ]
    interface IMTSOrder : IDispatch
    {
        [id(1), helpstring("method PlaceOrder")]
        HRESULT PlaceOrder(    long AccountNumber,
                               long ProductID,
                               long Quantity);
    };

    [
        uuid(E84829F4-A2F6-11D2-A512-00600893FB20),
        version(1.0),
        helpstring("OrderEntry 1.0 Type Library")
    ]
    library ORDERENTRYLib
    {
        importlib("stdole32.tlb");
        importlib("stdole2.tlb");

        [
```

LISTING 17.4   Continued

```
        uuid(E8482A01-A2F6-11D2-A512-00600893FB20),
        helpstring("MTSOrder Class"),
        TRANSACTION_REQUIRED
    ]
    coclass MTSOrder
    {
        [default] interface IMTSOrder;
    };
};
```

Completing Transactions

Transactional components must explicitly commit or abort an outstanding transaction. Failing to do so leaves the transaction up in the air, in which case it will commit if the object is released by the client within the transaction timeout. If the object is not released and the transaction times out, then the transaction is aborted. Leaving things to chance is hardly appropriate behavior for a mission-critical server component, and for this reason all correctly designed transactional components explicitly commit or abort their transactions. Keep in mind that all objects involved in a transaction are deactivated at the completion of the transaction. Transactions are managed through an object's `ObjectContext`.

ObjectContext

Every COM+ object has an `ObjectContext` associated with it. The `ObjectContext` maintains the implicit COM+ state information associated with the object. Of particular interest here is the fact that the `ObjectContext` tracks information related to the current transaction, if any exists. A COM+ object can manipulate its `ObjectContext` by calling the COM+ API function `GetObjectContext()`, which returns an `IObjectContext` interface pointer.

An object's `ObjectContext` should never be accessed in the object's constructor or destructor, or during any `IUnknown` method call. In general, this is because COM+ has either not created the context or has already destroyed it during these object calls. It is important to note that calling an object's `IUnknown` methods does not activate the `ObjectContext`. `ObjectContext` references (interface pointers to `IObjectContext`) should never be passed to other objects as they are generally invalid outside the owning object.

IObjectContext Revisited

Listing 17.5 is an example of the one and only method for the transactional `OrderEntry` object.

LISTING 17.5 PlaceOrder Method for the OrderEntry Object

```
STDMETHODIMP CMTSOrder::PlaceOrder(     long AccountNumber,
                                        long ProductID,
                                        long Quantity)
{
    //Ensure that we have a transaction
    if ( ! m_spObjectContext->IsInTransaction() )
        return CONTEXT_E_TMNOTAVAILABLE;

    //Disable commit to keep an accidental
    //  return in the body of our code from
    //  committing the transaction on client
    //  object shutdown
    m_spObjectContext->DisableCommit();

    //Compute total price and deduct account balance within
    //  the current transaction (all sweaters are $20)
    double lfTotalPrice = Quantity * 20.0;
    HRESULT hr = ChargeAccount( AccountNumber, lfTotalPrice );
    if ( FAILED(hr) )
    {
        //Abort transaction and return error
        m_spObjectContext->SetAbort();
        return hr;
    }

    //Reduce our inventory within the current transaction
    hr = ReduceInventory( Quantity );
    if ( FAILED(hr) )
    {
        //Abort transaction and return error
        m_spObjectContext->SetAbort();
        return hr;
    }

    //Commit transaction and return success
    m_spObjectContext->SetComplete();
    return S_OK;
}
```

There are several points of interest in this code. The most important of which is the fact that, aside from some sanity checking and defensive programming at the top of the routine, and the SetComplete()or SetAbort() calls tied to the returns, the code is devoid of cryptic transaction instructions. Note that the two routines ChargeAccount() and ReduceInventory() could directly modify a database or create a new component and have it do so. It matters little because the transaction automatically propagates to any new objects or resources managers that support transactions. The complete example on the CD-ROM simply uses OLE DB to modify two tables in a SQL Server database. Note that it is not a problem if you charge the account and then find that you're out of stock because the transaction simply aborts when `ReduceInventory()` returns a failure code. This returns the account in question to its state prior to the attempted transactional updates.

Because you wouldn't want to try this kind of operation without a transaction, the first line of code in the routine makes sure that a transaction is available. If you find that you are without a transaction, you return the MTS code indicating that the transaction manager (TM) is not available. It is important to note that if you are operating outside MTS, the `IObjectControl` methods that you rely on to acquire and release your `IObjectContext` pointer are never invoked, causing bad scoobies any time you try to use the ATL-provided `m_spObjectContext`. Checking this pointer before using it is not a bad idea, especially if you continually switch your component between MTS and straight COM+.

The sample routine immediately disables implicit transaction commitment. This allows you the security of knowing that, no matter what happens, if you don't call `SetComplete()`, the transaction aborts. This is generally the idea with transactional methods, although not always. Finally, if the gauntlet of `SetAbort()` calls is survived, you assume everything went well and call `SetComplete()` to vote for committing the transaction.

At this point the client receives one of three values: `S_OK`, `CONTEXT_E_ABORTED`, or something else. It's the "something else" that's bothering you, isn't it? Well, here's the rotten truth about things—anything can fail. If all's well, the client gets `S_OK`. If the transaction couldn't be committed, the client gets `CONTEXT_E_ABORTED` or an application-defined error. And, if either of the two previous values are returned, but there's a network failure in your DCOM call, your client gets a network related `HRESULT`. Thus it's possible for the transaction to commit and yet have the client receive an obscure COM communications error. If this is not satisfactory, you'll have to come up with an application-specific way for the client to discover the result of a transactional call suffering just such a failure. No hints here. It's as ugly as it sounds. The best bet is to build clients that don't care about the transactions result, if at all possible. You always have the reassurance that the call either worked or it didn't and all in one big transactional piece.

The preceding example uses two subroutines, `ReduceInventory()` and `ChargeAccount()`. Both manipulate COM+-compliant resource managers (SQL Server in this case) to perform their functions.

Travel Agency Example

It's time to take a look at an example that models the travel agency example given early in the chapter. I've created a component with a class named CSubmitOrder (seen in Listing 17.6). The class checks to see if the hotel, airline, and car reservations are okay, and then writes the information to a database.

A Visual Basic program (in Listing 17.7) is the client application that uses the component.

After the code listings, there is an explanation.

LISTING 17.6   The CSubmitOrder Class Acts on Behalf of the Travel Agent

```cpp
// SubmitOrder.cpp : Implementation of CSubmitOrder
#include "stdafx.h"
#include "Travel.h"
#include "SubmitOrder.h"

#include "dboAirlineReservations.h"
#include "dboCarReservations.h"
#include "dboHotelReservations.h"


/////////////////////////////////////////////////////////////////////////////
// CSubmitOrder


STDMETHODIMP CSubmitOrder::DoIt()
{
    AFX_MANAGE_STATE(AfxGetStaticModuleState())

    // Get the object context.
    IObjectContext *pObjectContext = NULL;
    HRESULT hRes = GetObjectContext( &pObjectContext );

    // Make sure we didn't get an error while getting
    // the object context.
    if( FAILED( hRes ) )
    {

        if( hRes == E_INVALIDARG )
            m_strStatus = "Invalid argument.";
        else if( hRes == E_UNEXPECTED )
            m_strStatus = "Unexpected error.";
        else if( hRes == CONTEXT_E_NOCONTEXT )
            m_strStatus = "No context associated with object.";
        else
            m_strStatus = "Object context could not be obtained.";
```

LISTING 17.6 Continued

```
        return( hRes );
    }

// Check and store the hotel information below.
CdboHotelReservations Hotel;

// Check to make sure the hotel reservations are valid.
if( !HotelReservationOK() )
{
    m_strStatus = "Problem with hotel reservations.";
    pObjectContext->SetAbort();
    return( S_OK );
}

// Attempt to open the Hotel table.
hRes = Hotel.Open();
if( FAILED( hRes ) )
{
    m_strStatus = "Hotel did not open.";
    pObjectContext->SetAbort();
    return( hRes );
}

// Store the information into the Hotel
// class and then update the database.
strcpy( Hotel.m_Date, m_strStartDate );
strcpy( Hotel.m_Type, m_strHotelType );
strcpy( Hotel.m_Name, m_strCustomerName );
Hotel.SetData();
Hotel.Insert();


// Check and store the car information below.
CdboCarReservations Car;

// Check to make sure the Car reservations are valid.
if( !CarReservationOK() )
{
    m_strStatus = "Problem with Car reservations.";
    pObjectContext->SetAbort();
    return( S_OK );
}

// Attempt to open the Car table.
hRes = Car.Open();
if( FAILED( hRes ) )
{
    m_strStatus = "Car did not open.";
    pObjectContext->SetAbort();
```

LISTING 17.6 Continued

```
        return( hRes );
    }

    // Store the information into the Car
    // class and then update the database.
    strcpy( Car.m_Date, m_strStartDate );
    strcpy( Car.m_Type, m_strCarType );
    strcpy( Car.m_Name, m_strCustomerName );
    Car.SetData();
    Car.Insert();


    // Check and store the airline information below.
    CdboAirlineReservations Airline;

    // Check to make sure the Airline reservations are valid.
    if( !AirlineReservationOK() )
    {
        m_strStatus = "Problem with Airline reservations.";
        pObjectContext->SetAbort();
        return( S_OK );
    }

    // Attempt to open the Airline table.
    hRes = Airline.Open();
    if( FAILED( hRes ) )
    {
        m_strStatus = "Airline did not open.";
        pObjectContext->SetAbort();
        return( hRes );
    }

    // Store the information into the Airline
    // class and then update the database.
    strcpy( Airline.m_Date, m_strStartDate );
    strcpy( Airline.m_Type, m_strAirlineType );
    strcpy( Airline.m_Name, m_strCustomerName );
    Airline.SetData();
    Airline.Insert();

    m_strStatus = "Transaction completed.";

    // Commit the transaction.
    pObjectContext->SetComplete();

    // Release the object context.
    pObjectContext->Release();

    return S_OK;
```

COM+ as a Transaction Coordinator

CHAPTER 17

465

17

COM+ AS A
TRANSACTION
COORDINATOR

LISTING 17.6   Continued

```
}

BOOL CSubmitOrder::CarReservationOK( void )
{

    // Perform checks here to make sure the
    // car reservation is OK.

    // This method always returns true for the
    // purposes of this example.

    return( TRUE );

}

BOOL CSubmitOrder::AirlineReservationOK( void )
{

    // Perform checks here to make sure the
    // airline reservation is OK.

    // This method always returns true for the
    // purposes of this example.

    return( TRUE );

}

BOOL CSubmitOrder::HotelReservationOK( void )
{

    // Perform checks here to make sure the
    // hotel reservation is OK.

    // This method always returns true for the
    // purposes of this example.

    return( TRUE );

}

STDMETHODIMP CSubmitOrder::put_CustomerName(BSTR newVal)
{
    AFX_MANAGE_STATE(AfxGetStaticModuleState())

    m_strCustomerName.SetSysString( &newVal );

    return S_OK;
}
```

LISTING 17.6 Continued

```
STDMETHODIMP CSubmitOrder::put_StartDate(BSTR newVal)
{
    AFX_MANAGE_STATE(AfxGetStaticModuleState())

    m_strStartDate.SetSysString( &newVal );

    return S_OK;
}

STDMETHODIMP CSubmitOrder::put_EndDate(BSTR newVal)
{
    AFX_MANAGE_STATE(AfxGetStaticModuleState())

    m_strEndDate.SetSysString( &newVal );

    return S_OK;
}

STDMETHODIMP CSubmitOrder::put_AirlineType(BSTR newVal)
{
    AFX_MANAGE_STATE(AfxGetStaticModuleState())

    m_strAirlineType.SetSysString( &newVal );

    return S_OK;
}

STDMETHODIMP CSubmitOrder::put_CarType(BSTR newVal)
{
    AFX_MANAGE_STATE(AfxGetStaticModuleState())

    m_strCarType.SetSysString( &newVal );

    return S_OK;
}

STDMETHODIMP CSubmitOrder::put_HotelType(BSTR newVal)
{
    AFX_MANAGE_STATE(AfxGetStaticModuleState())

    m_strHotelType.SetSysString( &newVal );

    return S_OK;
}

STDMETHODIMP CSubmitOrder::get_Status(BSTR *pVal)
{
    AFX_MANAGE_STATE(AfxGetStaticModuleState())
```

LISTING 17.6 Continued

```
    *pVal = m_strStatus.AllocSysString();

    return S_OK;
}
```

LISTING 17.7 A Good Part of the Client Code Sets the Object Properties

```
Private Sub Command1_Click()
    Label2.Caption = "Executing Transaction"

    Dim obj As Object
    Set obj = CreateObject("Travel.SubmitOrder.1")

    obj.CustomerName = "Rick Leinecker"
    obj.HotelType = "Suite"
    obj.AirlineType = "First Class"
    obj.CarType = "Red Mustang Convertible"
    obj.StartDate = "10/10/2001"
    obj.EndDate = "12/15/2002"

    Res = obj.DoIt()

    Label2.Caption = "Result of DoIt():" & obj.Status

    Set obj = Nothing

End Sub
```

Before I created this component, I added a database to SQL Server 7.0 with three tables. One table to record the hotel information, one for the airline information, and one for the car rental information. To make things easier, I created an ODBC connection to the database.

The easiest way for me to add access to the database tables was to insert ATL data consumer objects into the project. I did this and created three classes named CdboAirlineReservations, CdboHotelReservations, and CdboCarReservations. These three classes were then ready to be used in the main component class.

As with the simple example earlier in the chapter, the CSubmitOrder class obtains an IOBjectContext pointer before it does any real work. And again, error checking makes sure that the pointer was obtained without any errors.

I created three dummy methods named AirlineReservationOK(), HotelReservationOK(), and CarReservationOK(). These three methods all simply return TRUE. In these three methods, though, the business logic has to decide if these three things pass muster—based on them, can the transaction proceed?

After it's decided that the airline, car, and hotel reservations can go through, each set of information is written to its respective database table. At the end of the method the `SetComplete()` method is called, and then the `IOBjectContext::Release()` method is called.

Monitoring Transactions

The Component Management Console supplies transaction monitoring facilities, called To Whom It May Concern, to aid administrators and developers in tracking transaction execution times and in balancing transaction loads across several servers (see Figure 17.3). The Transaction List view provides a list of the in-doubt transactions that are operating on the current machine. *In-doubt* transactions occur when some element of the transaction framework, such as a remote database, stops responding. You can right-click these problem transactions in the Transaction List to manipulate them. The Transaction Statistics view displays various important pieces of transaction information, including critical values such as response time figures and abort counters.

FIGURE 17.3

Transaction Statistics view.

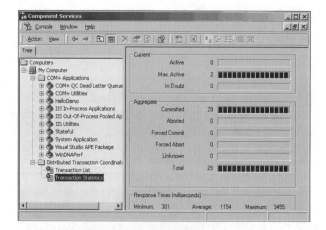

Design Considerations

Okay, so that's a look at COM+ transactions. To wrap it up, consider some of the critical design issues involved with COM+ transactional component construction.

Prefer Fine-Grained Components

Don't maintain transactions across method calls. Objects operating at a granularity of one transaction per method call perform much better than coarser-grained components. Requiring several client method calls to complete an operation produces objects that scale poorly because transaction resources (DTC Transaction objects, database connections, COM+ object state, and so on) have to be maintained by COM+ during the interim.

Fine-grained solutions are not only highly scalable but also much easier to debug. If each method call stands on its own, complex method interactions often drop out of the picture during debugging sessions. Upon the completion of a transaction, all object state is destroyed reducing the potential for error carry-over. Each method should begin with data in a consistent state and end with data in a consistent state. Failures in this setting require repair of only a single method activity.

Therefore, stateless solutions are the optimal COM+ component implementation. If you must make several method calls to complete an operation, a compromise can be achieved by maintaining a stateful object between calls, but committing transactions on a call-by-call basis. For example, try creating a transactionless, stateful base object that creates an object requiring a new transaction for each successive method call. In this way, COM+ only has to maintain the minimal memory footprint of the stateful base object, committing or aborting each subordinate object's transaction on a method-call-by-method-call basis.

Locate Components Close to Their Data Source

The closer a server process is to the resource manager it uses, the faster it can complete transactions involving that resource manager. If you configure your data access components to run in a package on the same system as the database they access, you generally acquire a significant performance edge over remote packages. In this scenario, it is critical to ensure proper server memory configurations as excessive page faults can easily rob applications of any potential performance benefit.

Put Components Using the Same Resources Together in the Same Application

Resource dispensers pool resources on a per-process basis. This means that components running in separate packages cannot share the same resource pool. Because COM+ manages thread creation and concurrency issues within application server processes, scaling multiple components is not a problem and can improve overall performance by more effectively utilizing pooled resources, such as database connections. It is important to note that this is an opposing administrative operation to that of fault isolation. The more components in a single process, the more exposed the entire process is to a single-component fault. Separating components into different applications improves fault isolation but degrades inter-component communications and resource sharing.

Summary

In this chapter, you examined the nature of transactions and how the COM+ system marries component technology with mainframe-style transaction services. Although the COM+ transaction programming syntax is trivial, the critical concepts involved in designing truly robust software components are a delicate affair, carefully considered throughout this chapter. Chapter 18, "COM+ Security," covers the principles of security within the COM+ framework.

COM+ Security

In this chapter, you learn the nature of COM+ security. Most serious multiuser applications have some security considerations, if not a bevy of them. For this reason, COM+ provides powerful but simple security features enabling system users and groups to be mapped into COM+-centric application roles. Many of the COM+ security features are available to the administrator and the programmer alike. As past experience would predict, COM+ makes security programming, usually a black art, relatively easy.

Although users authenticate to a server, there are scenarios in which network resources are involved that aren't handled by local- or domain-based authentication. In an enterprise application, it's important that a user or machine can be validated across network boundaries in addition to the normal logon authentication.

COM+ Security Concepts

COM+ security is designed to suit the needs of a middle-tier, multiuser, enterprise-scale component system. This is a tricky apex of security considerations. You have the client world on one side, which might include HackUBill coming in over the Web, and the data center on the other side, which generally includes your business-critical data stores. Many e-commerce solutions simply rule out any behavior that is not completely benign and suitable for unidentified public consumption. Still other solutions work an application-specific security mechanism into their systems with user IDs and PINs. Both of these scenarios plot a relatively clear security course—no security at all versus develop everything yourself. Although both of these have their place in the world, what happens if you're in a secure enterprise environment where administrators have already spent years developing an infrastructure of users and groups and secure resources? I doubt they'll take too kindly to tangential security psychosis.

So the challenge before you is to build a powerful application security system that is flexible enough to suit the needs of your components and yet fits into the existing account system of your enterprise.

Another wrench in the gears is the fact that real enterprises don't run without sophisticated MIS staff. COM+ makes developing serious component applications a lot easier from the developer's perspective, but it drops a lot of new problems into the lap of the local system administrator. For example, COM+ is a component-based system, not a traditional monolithic application environment. As previously discussed, that means that administrators can reorganize components and applications to suit their performance needs on a given strata of back-office equipment. Start shuffling components between processes (which, of course, are the built-in security perimeters on most systems) and what happens to your security model? This is a very new and, let's say, interesting question for most administrators.

So once again COM+ presents a basket of new goodies to ponder and concepts to master for both the developer and the administrator. Also, as before, a powerful yet simple interface has prevailed in both the configuration environment and the programming domain. Now take a look at the parts of the COM+ security model.

Roles

Roles are the most central concept in the entire COM+ security fabric. A *role* represents a type of usage. For example, people in the clerk role check out customers, and people in the accounting role balance the books. The role icons found in the Component Management Console are depicted as a bunch of hats. The same person might do the books and check out customers, in which case he's acting in a dual role, or wearing two hats.

Roles are defined on an application-by-application basis. Roles can be defined by the administrator based on the needs of the enterprise, or by developers based on the needs of the system, or by both. In this way, developers can ensure that the security needs of the program are well-addressed without knowing a whole lot about the account structure of the deployment environment. Administrators assign system users and groups to the various roles created for an application in order to mesh the program with their account structure.

After roles are properly laid out by the system architects and configured by the system administrators deploying the components, two systems provide security checking. Built-in NT security can be used to satisfy security configurations assigned by administrators. As an example, an administrator might make the modification interface of a class unavailable to all telemarketing staff. Components can provide their own internal logic to control access as well. For example, a program might allow calls to all routines in an interface except Delete(), in which case the caller must be an administrator. Procedurally, one simple function performs the majority of COM+ security checking: IObjectContext::IsCallerInRole().

COM+ maintains context data describing the roles of the caller for every COM+ object. By checking the caller's role, the component can determine whether the caller, whoever it is, should be allowed to perform the task or to what degree his or her capabilities should extend.

This can be done with the IObjectContext::IsCallerInRole() method, as shown in the following code:

```
IObjectContext objContext = null;

objContext = MTX.GetObjectContext(); // Find out if Security is enabled.
```

```
if( objContext.IsSecurityEnabled() )
{
  //Then find out if the caller is in the right role.
  if( !objContext.IsCallerInRole( "Manager" ) )
     {
          // If not, do something appropriate here.
     }
}
else
{
    // If security's not enabled, do something appropriate here.
}
```

COM+ simplifies some of the complexity involved in dealing with security in a distributed object environment by limiting permissions to roles. There are, however, still some fine points to consider. For example, if a client, Bob, calls an object running in a COM+ server process with the identity administrator, it's obvious that the Bob's account will be the determining principle in the role look-up proceedings. What happens if this first COM+ object then calls another object that requires a certain role? The answer is, it depends. If the second object runs in the same process as the first, the client identity is used. If the second object runs in a separate process from the first object, the first object's process identity is used for role checking. This behavior occurs because the IsCallerInRole() routine, used automatically for administrator-assigned security and called procedurally by developers, checks the role of the direct caller, not the original caller. To clarify this point, let's examine the nature of direct and original callers.

Direct Caller

An object's direct caller in a COM+ call sequence is identified as the identity of the process that called into the current process. So if a client calls object A, running in a COM+ server process, the direct caller is the client. If object A calls object B, and B in turn calls C, and A, B, and C all run in the same process, the direct caller for all three objects is the client. If a client calls object A in a COM+ server process, and A calls object B, which runs in another server process, A's direct caller is the client's process, and B's direct caller is object A's server process.

You might remember learning how to use the ISecurityProperty::GetDirectCallerSID() and ISecurityProperty::GetDirectCreatorSID() methods in Chapter 12, "COM Security." They allow you to identify the direct caller.

Original Caller

The *original caller* is the identity of the process running outside COM+ that calls into COM+ to begin an activity. Remember that a COM+ activity is a logical thread of execution tracing the call sequence from an external client through a set of COM+ objects running in one or more COM+ processes. Figure 18.1 depicts the caller identity relationships.

FIGURE 18.1
Caller identity.

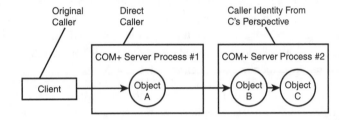

As you can see, the identity of Process #1 in Figure 18.1 is of critical concern. If Process #1 is not allowed to invoke Object B, you have a security breakdown. Setting an application's identity through application properties is often a mandatory step in composing successful server-to-server communications under COM+ security control.

Security Responsibilities

So as you can see, COM+ security involves two practical elements, the application design (which can include a role model and code to enforce it) and the enterprise account structure. There is also an administrator to map system accounts to application roles and possibly define security requirements at a class and interface level. Next we'll examine the two basic approaches to COM+ security, declarative and procedural security.

- *Declarative security* is the part of COM+ security that you declare through administrative means. That is, the part where administrators assign user and group accounts to application roles. Administrators can also assign required roles to classes and interfaces, limiting which roles can use the protected elements.

- *Procedural security* is the part of COM+ security managed programmatically by component code. Some applications can get by with nothing more than declarative security. It is important to note that procedural security enables developers to choose alternative logic at the sub-method level, whereas declarative security only applies down to the interface level.

Because the security responsibilities involved in a COM+ system are split in this way, it is very important for developers to communicate their role model and component requirements, if any, to administrators. You can make a good start by providing complete applications with roles defined and helpful description fields for each application, component, and interface. Failing to provide declarative support for procedural requirements dooms your security operations. For example, if your program requires the clerk role, and administrators fail to provide it, your program is not going to work. I'm holding out for a type library–style role definition that could accompany components on their road to deployment, much like IDL transactional attributes do, but no such feature now exists.

User authentication on a local machine or domain effectively guards resources so that only authorized users can access them. This falls short in a Distributed Computing Environment (DCE), where there is communication across a disparate set of topologies and machines. For this reason, the Remote Procedure Call (RPC) was given a security API all its own to provide the extra security a DCE requires.

COM+ is designed and implemented as a layer on top of Microsoft's RPC implementation supporting complex interactions between independently created software objects. While it reuses many of RPC's advanced features, including authentication and privacy services, COM+ also adds another layer of security to the RPC API.

SSPI

The Microsoft Security Support Provider Interface (SSPI) is the well-defined common API for obtaining integrated security services for authentication, message integrity, message privacy, and security quality of service for any distributed application protocol. Application protocol designers can take advantage of this interface to obtain different security services without modification to the protocol itself.

The SSPI provides an abstraction layer between application-level protocols and security protocols. The following are some of the ways to use SSPI services:

- Traditional socket-based applications can call SSPI routines directly and implement the application protocol that carries SSPI security-related data, using request and response messages.

- COM+ applications provide the best level of integrated security features. Applications can use DCOM to call security options, which are implemented using authenticated RPC and SSPI at lower levels. Applications do not call SSPI APIs directly.

- Winsock 2.0 extends the Windows Sockets interface to enable transport providers to expose security features. This approach integrates the SSPI security provider into the network stack and provides both security and transport services through a common interface.

WinInet is an application protocol interface that is designed to support Internet security protocols, such as Secure Sockets Layer (SSL), over Internet protocols. The implementation of WinInet security support uses the SSPI interface to the Secure Channel (Windows NT implementation of SSL) security provider.

Declarative COM+ Security

It is possible to take a bunch of components that are completely bereft of security and package them into a highly secure program. This is what declarative security is all about, configuring security on components and interfaces through the Component Management Console.

Declarative security is performed via the COM+ catalog (using the Component Services Administrator). COM+ security can also be defined programmatically. However, dealing with the definition of the activation and access control, you typically want to define this at a higher level than a single component for several reasons. First, you want to set up a security environment that COM+ could handle automatically for you. Second, it greatly reduces the amount of security-related code that needs to be written. And third, it ensures that the security settings are enforced systemwide because COM+ runtime is responsible for the enforcement.

Many security settings deal with the machine as a whole (for example, settings such as default authentication and impersonation levels, whether DCOM can be used on that machine, whether CIS is enabled, and so on). It would be better to put these settings into one section of the catalog and then go into a "Defining Component Identity" section of the catalog where different things, like which user can execute an application, are defined.

Figure 18.2 illustrates the layout of security features in a COM+ application. Each application has a Roles folder in which administrators can create roles for the application. Roles are specific to a particular application and its components. Both components and component interfaces have Role Membership folders. Adding a role to a Role Membership folder enables callers in that role to use the element in question. Users not found to be in a membership role are rejected by the COM+ security system. This enables administrators to set up roles and define access down to the interface level within a given application.

FIGURE 18.2

COM+ application roles.

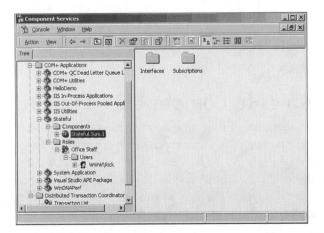

18

COM+ SECURITY

Keep in mind that declarative security settings can also be configured procedurally using the COM+ administrative components.

> **Note**
>
> Interface-based declarative security does not function with dual interfaces when the interfaces are accessed via IDispatch. However, class-level security is still applicable.

Creating Roles

Creating roles is as easy as right-clicking the Roles folder and choosing New, Role (see Figure 18.3).

FIGURE 18.3
Creating roles.

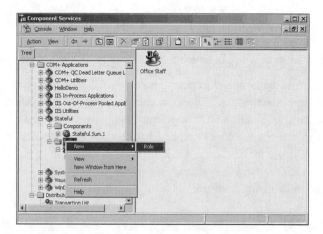

Each Roles object has a Users folder. You can add system users and groups to the role by right-clicking the Users folder and choosing New, User.

Adding Roles to Components and Interfaces

Some applications can manage their own security, checking to see whether callers are in the appropriate role procedurally. Other applications can perform some security checking, and still others might leave the whole business up to the administrator. COM+ administrators can configure security restrictions on components and component interfaces. Elements of these types have Role Membership folders. When security is enabled, COM+ only enables calls in the specified roles to use the protected resources.

Enabling Security

COM+ does not perform application security checking unless you enable security on the application. To enable application security, choose the Security tab in the Application Properties display and click the Enable access checks for this application box. Components work the same way. You must enable checking on a component in order for COM+ to check authorization on components and their interfaces.

It is important to keep in mind that declarative security checking is performed only at COM+ server process (application) boundaries. Calls internal to a COM+ application are not scrutinized by COM+, although objects are free to procedurally perform all the checking they want. Security checking in library applications is always disabled because libraries run in the caller's process.

In order to use COM+ security, clients should have DCOM security settings set to identify impersonation levels and connect authentication levels. These setting can be made with DCOMConfig.exe. These are the recommended settings, although other more inclusive settings might work as well. For a more complete explanation, refer to Chapter 10, "Using NT Services."

In addition to applications, the COM+ administration system itself has some security dependencies. In order to use COM+ securely, you should examine and modify the configuration of security settings for the COM+ system application. The COM+ system application contains components used to maintain and manage applications on the COM+ machine in question. Two roles are configured for this application, Administrator and Reader. Users mapped to the Administrator's role can use any Component Management Console feature. Users mapped to the Reader role can view COM+ settings, but cannot modify the current COM+ configuration. COM+ Administrator accounts for systems installed on Domain Controllers must have Domain Administrator privileges in order to properly manage COM+.

Authentication

Authentication can be done both declaratively and programmatically. Applications supply a security property, which lets you configure the application authentication level. The default is Packet, which works quite well. Table 18.1 shows a list of authentication levels and their implications. As you might expect, the further down the table you go, the more overhead the security system creates.

TABLE 18.1   Authentication Levels

Level	Description
None	No security checking occurs on communication to or from this application.
Connect	Security checking occurs only upon the initial connection.
Call	Security checking occurs on every call.
Packet	The sender's identity is encrypted.
Packet Integrity	The sender's identity and signature are encrypted (guaranteeing integrity).
Packet Privacy	The entire packet is encrypted (guaranteeing privacy).

Procedural COM+ Security

You've seen how an administrator can completely secure an application down to the interface level. I've also introduced some of the concerns, especially the importance of administrator competency. It is no small task to configure a free-form component program, consisting of applications and components that change machines and processes over time.

In order to reduce the declarative burden on administrators or simply to get more granular control of the security mechanism, developers might want to code in their own security features. In this section, you'll combine some declarative features with some low-level security operations in code.

The example used throughout is a security-aware version of your Stateful Sum class. In order to follow along with the examples, you need to create a new application called SecureSum. Add the Stateful component to the application and add two roles, Admins and Accumulators. Add one user account to Admins and another to Accumulators, so that you can test both roles.

Identifying Users

Your security endeavors here are limited to the Accumulate() method in your Sum class. One of the first tasks that I'd like you to perform is that of ensuring that each user has his own private copy of the accumulated total. In a multiuser enterprise, this is easier said than done. Your object supports deactivation, so you probably still need to use the Shared Property Manager to maintain state information between calls. However, you need to name the property in such a way as to make it unique among all users. Of course,

Windows NT and Windows 2000 have this feature built in. It's known as a Security Identifier, or SID. SIDs are assigned to all users (and groups, computers, and so on) to provide a unique reference to a specific security principle. SIDs are opaque structures accessed through WIN32 system calls, but they can be represented in text form.

> **Note**
>
> Keep in mind that the proliferation of Web-based applications introduces application designs in which the actual end user might not have an SID and might even be anonymous.

CoInitializeSecurity() Function

The CoInitializeSecurity() function initializes the security layer and sets the specified values as the security default. If the process does not call CoInitializeSecurity(), COM+ calls it automatically the first time an interface is marshaled or unmarshaled, registering the system default security. No default security packages are registered until then. The function prototype can be seen here:

```
HRESULT CoInitializeSecurity( PSECURITY_DESCRIPTOR pVoid,
➥//Points to security descriptor
    LONG cAuthSvc, //Count of entries in asAuthSvc
    SOLE_AUTHENTICATION_SERVICE * asAuthSvc, //Array of names to register
    void * pReserved1, //Reserved for future use
    DWORD dwAuthnLevel, //The default authentication level for proxies
    DWORD dwImpLevel, //The default impersonation level for proxies
    SOLE_AUTHENTICATION_LIST * pAuthList,
        ➥//Authentication information for each authentication service
    DWORD dwCapabilities, //Additional client and/or server-side capabilities
    void * pReserved3 //Reserved for future use
);
```

When the EOAC_APPID flag is set in dwCapabilities, pVoid points to an AppID, and all other parameters to CoInitializeSecurity() are ignored (and must be zero). CoInitializeSecurity() looks for the authentication level under the AppID key in the registry and uses it to determine the default security. If pVoid is NULL, CoInitializeSecurity() looks up the application .exe name in the registry and uses the AppID stored there. This gives the same security settings as if the process had not called CoInitializeSecurity().

If the EOAC_ACCESS_CONTROL flag is set, pVoid is a pointer to an IAccessControl object, which determines who can call the process. COM+ calls AddRef() for the IAccessControl and Release() when CoUninitialize() is called. The state of the

18

COM+ SECURITY

IAccessControl object should not be changed. If EOAC_ACCESS_CONTROL is specified, the dwAuthnLevel cannot be NULL.

The CoInitializeSecurity() function returns an error if both the EOAC_APPID and EOAC_ACCESS_CONTROL flags are set.

If neither the EOAC_APPID nor the EOAC_ACCESS_CONTROL flag is specified in dwCapabilities, pVoid must be a pointer to a Win32 SECURITY_DESCRIPTOR. A security descriptor contains two ACLs: the discretionary ACL (DACL), which indicates who is (and who is not) allowed to call the process, and the system ACL (SACL), which contains audit information. COM+ looks for the COM_RIGHTS_EXECUTE flag in the DACL to find out which callers are permitted to connect to the process's objects. The SACL must be NULL. A DACL with no ACEs allows no access. A NULL DACL allows calls from anyone.

If pVoid is a security descriptor, the owner and group of the SECURITY_DESCRIPTOR must be set—applications should call AccessCheck (not IsValidSecurityDescriptor) to ensure that their security descriptor is correctly formed prior to calling CoInitializeSecurity(). COM+ copies the specified security descriptor. If the application passes a NULL security descriptor, COM+ constructs one that allows calls from anyone.

When a CAPI handle is specified for the SSL entry in pAuthList, the CAPI handle must not be freed until CoUninitialize() is called. If the list is specified but there is no entry for SSL, COM+ tries to find a default identity the first time COM+ negotiates SSL as the authentication service. If that succeeds, COM+ saves that identity as the default. Otherwise, the client is anonymous for SSL.

ISecurityProperty Interface

COM+ provides the ISecurityProperty interface as a means to discover various caller process SIDs. ISecurityProperty is obtained through a QueryInterface() call on an object's ObjectContext. Each ISecurityProperty method call returns the respective SID pointer. Because you are getting back a system-allocated resource, you must release the resource when you're finished with it by calling ReleaseSID(). Table 18.2 shows the methods.

TABLE 18.2   ISecurityProperty Methods

Method	*What It Does*
GetDirectCallerSID()	Retrieves the security ID of the external process that called the currently executing method
GetDirectCreatorSID()	Retrieves the security ID of the external process that directly created the current object
GetOriginalCallerSID()	Retrieves the security ID of the base process that initiated the call sequence from which the current method was called

TABLE 18.2 Continued

Method	What It Does
GetOriginalCreatorSID()	Retrieves the security ID of the base process that initiated the activity in which the current object is executing
ReleaseSID()	Releases the security ID returned by one of the other ISecurityProperty methods

Listing 18.1 shows a new internal Sum class method that discovers the direct caller's SID.

LISTING 18.1 Discovering the Direct Caller's SID

```
void CSum::GetDirectCallerSID( BSTR * pbstrSid )
{
    //Initialize the security interface pointer,
    //  the binary SID and the string SID
    ISecurityProperty * pSecurityProperty = NULL;
    PSID pSID = NULL;
    * pbstrSid = NULL;

    //Get the security property interface
    //  from the ObjectContext
    m_spObjectContext->QueryInterface( IID_ISecurityProperty,
                                       (void**)&pSecurityProperty );
    if ( NULL == pSecurityProperty )
        return;

    //Get the direct callers' binary SID
    HRESULT hr = pSecurityProperty->GetDirectCallerSID( &pSID );
    if ( FAILED(hr) )
        return;

    //Convert the binary SID to a text string and release
    //  the binary SID and security property interface
    SidToString( pSID, pbstrSid );
    pSecurityProperty->ReleaseSID(pSID);
    pSecurityProperty->Release();
}
```

As you can see, the steps are quite simple. You get the security property interface and make the GetDirectCallerSID() call. The catch here is that COM+ gives you a binary SID. If you want to use this SID to create a SPM property, you'll have to convert it to text (all SPM properties have text names). The helper function SidToString() does the dirty work. Unfortunately, this is not a system call. Listing 18.2 shows the code.

18

COM+ SECURITY

LISTING 18.2   Converting a Binary SID to Text

```
bool CSum::SidToString(    PSID pSid,                //Binary Sid
                           BSTR * pbstrSid )    //String Sid
{
    //Test Sid for validity
    if(!IsValidSid(pSid))
        return false;

    //Test BSTR for validity
    if(NULL == pbstrSid )
        return false;

     //Set up working buffer and initialize input BSTR
     WCHAR wsSid[128];
     * pbstrSid = NULL;

    //Obtain SidIdentifierAuthority
    PSID_IDENTIFIER_AUTHORITY psia = GetSidIdentifierAuthority(pSid);

    //Prepare S-SID_REVISION-
    DWORD dwSidLength = swprintf( wsSid, L"S-%lu-", SID_REVISION );

    //Prepare SidIdentifierAuthority
    if ( (psia->Value[0] != 0) || (psia->Value[1] != 0) )
     {
        dwSidLength += swprintf(wsSid + dwSidLength,
                    L"0x%02hx%02hx%02hx%02hx%02hx%02hx",
                    (USHORT)psia->Value[0],
                    (USHORT)psia->Value[1],
                    (USHORT)psia->Value[2],
                    (USHORT)psia->Value[3],
                    (USHORT)psia->Value[4],
                    (USHORT)psia->Value[5]);
    }
     else
     {
        dwSidLength += swprintf(wsSid + dwSidLength,
                    L"%lu",
                    (ULONG)(psia->Value[5]      ) +
                    (ULONG)(psia->Value[4] <<  8) +
                    (ULONG)(psia->Value[3] << 16) +
                    (ULONG)(psia->Value[2] << 24) );
    }

    //Loop through SidSubAuthorities
    DWORD dwSubAuthorities = *GetSidSubAuthorityCount(pSid);
    for(DWORD dwCounter=0; dwCounter<dwSubAuthorities; dwCounter++)
     {
        dwSidLength += swprintf(wsSid + dwSidLength,
                        L"-%lu",
```

LISTING 18.2   Continued

```
                                *GetSidSubAuthority(pSid, dwCounter) );
    }

    //Copy text SID into callers BSTR
    * pbstrSid = SysAllocString(wsSid);

    //Return success
    return true;
}
```

This routine basically just retrieves each of the parts of the SID and translates them into text values. The SID text representation is relatively standard and is composed of the SID revision number, the SID identifier authority, and the SID sub-authorities in that order. For more information on SIDs, check Chapter 12, "COM Security," in this book or the Windows Platform SDK.

Authorizing Users

Now that you've got all this great security information, you can do something constructive with it. As a demonstration of authorization checking at the programmatic level, assume that you have two possible roles calling the Accumulate() method—Admins and Accumulators. Admins can add values to the cumulative total and retrieve the value of the total. Accumulators, on the other hand, can only add values and must never see the actual total.

If you were going to stick with declarative security, you would have no choice but to create an entirely new interface for the Accumulator-specific behavior. You might ask, "Why not just a new method?" Well, because declarative security stops at the interface level. If you left it up to the administrators, they would not be able to apply roles down to the method level.

Because you definitely don't want two interfaces and actually would just as soon have only one method, you'll take control at the programmatic level. Two methods of the IObjectContext interface are of interest here, IsSecurityEnabled() and IsCallerInRole(). You can use the first to ensure that security is operating and the second to discover the direct callers' capabilities with your application.

> **Note**
>
> When running on Windows 9x, the IsCallerInRole() method will always return TRUE. As mentioned previously, Windows 9x makes a relatively poor server platform because of its lack of security, scalability, and portability, among other things. Serious COM+ applications should be tested and deployed on Windows NT and Windows 2000 platforms.

18

COM+ SECURITY

Table 18.3 shows the ever-present IObjectContext interface methods list for your reference.

TABLE 18.3   IObjectContext Methods

Method	What It Does
CreateInstance()	Creates an object within the current context.
DisableCommit()	Declares that the object's transactional updates are in an inconsistent state. (The object retains its state across method calls.)
EnableCommit()	Declares that the object's transactional updates are in a consistent state. (The object retains its state across method calls.)
IsCallerInRole()	Indicates whether the object's caller is in a specified role.
IsInTransaction()	Indicates whether the object is executing within a transaction.
IsSecurityEnabled()	Indicates whether security is enabled.
SetAbort()	Aborts the current transaction. (The object can be deactivated upon return.)
SetComplete()	Declares that the object's transactional updates can be committed. (The object can be deactivated upon return.)

Examine the fully secure version of your Accumulate() method in Listing 18.3. Before testing this code, make sure that you have created an application with an Admin's role and an Accumulator's role, both having appropriate user members.

LISTING 18.3   The Secure Accumulate() Method

```
STDMETHODIMP CSum::Accumulate(int iValue, int *piTotal)
{
    //Make sure the security system is running
    if ( ! m_spObjectContext->IsSecurityEnabled() )
        return E_FAIL;

    //Ensure that caller is in required role
    //  Admins and Accumulators can add to the total
    BOOL bInAdminsRole = FALSE;
    BOOL bInAccumulatorsRole = FALSE;
    HRESULT hr;
    hr = m_spObjectContext->IsCallerInRole(L"Admins",
                                                & bInAdminsRole );
    if ( FAILED(hr) )
        return E_FAIL;
    hr = m_spObjectContext->IsCallerInRole(L"Accumulators",
                                            &bInAccumulatorsRole );
    if ( FAILED(hr) )
```

LISTING 18.3 Continued

```
    return E_FAIL;
if ( ! bInAdminsRole && ! bInAccumulatorsRole )
    return E_FAIL;

//Check input argument
if ( NULL == piTotal )
    return E_INVALIDARG;

//SPM, Group and Property interface pointers
ISharedPropertyGroupManager * pSPGM = NULL;
ISharedPropertyGroup * pGroup = NULL;
ISharedProperty * pProp = NULL;

//Get interface pointer to SPM
m_spObjectContext->CreateInstance(
                            CLSID_SharedPropertyGroupManager,
                            IID_ISharedPropertyGroupManager,
                            (void**) &pSPGM );
if ( NULL == pSPGM )
    return E_FAIL;

//Create or open the property group
BSTR bstrGroupName = SysAllocString( L"CallerTotals" );
long lIsoMode = LockMethod;
long lRelMode = Process;
VARIANT_BOOL fExists = VARIANT_FALSE;
pSPGM->CreatePropertyGroup(    bstrGroupName,
                               &lIsoMode,
                               &lRelMode,
                               &fExists,
                               &pGroup );
SysFreeString(bstrGroupName);
pSPGM->Release();
if ( NULL == pGroup )
    return E_FAIL;


//Create or open the caller's private total property
BSTR bstrSID;
GetDirectCallerSID( &bstrSID );
pGroup->CreateProperty(    bstrSID,
                           &fExists,
                           &pProp);
SysFreeString(bstrSID);
pGroup->Release();
if ( NULL == pProp )
    return E_FAIL;
```

18

COM+ SECURITY

LISTING 18.3 Continued

```
    //Update the total
    VARIANT vtTotal;
    vtTotal.vt = VT_I4;
    pProp->get_Value(&vtTotal);
    vtTotal.lVal += iValue;
    pProp->put_Value(vtTotal);
    pProp->Release();

    //Only admins can see the total
    if ( bInAdminsRole )
        *piTotal = vtTotal.lVal;
    else
        *piTotal = 0;

    //Tell COM+ that our work is complete
    m_spObjectContext->SetComplete();

    //Return success (after which COM+ deactivates us)
    return S_OK;
}
```

The top of this routine establishes basic security information. First, you check to see that security is up and running in your application, and then you check to see whether the caller is in one or both of the authorized roles. Failing any of these things, you bail out. Next, you work your way down to the property level in the SPM and create/open a per-user property using the caller's SID (constructed using the two previously covered functions). After adding the new value to the total, you check the user's roles and return the current total only if he is in the role of Admins (otherwise, he gets zero).

Summary

The topics covered in this chapter are not too difficult as security topics go, and you've actually made a pretty complete COM+ security circuit. You've examined fundamental security architecture topics and then perused the declarative and programmatic mechanisms available for enabling COM+ security. The chapter examined the various security-related methods and interfaces and presented a sample procedure that exemplified several key COM+ security features.

Chapter 19, "The COM Transaction Integrator," takes a look at transaction integration between COM and the mainframe world.

The COM Transaction Integrator

IN THIS CHAPTER

CHAPTER

19

This chapter examines COMTI, which extends COM+ to the mainframe world via Microsoft Systems Network Architecture (SNA) Server. The chapter is divided into five major parts. The first and second sections cover mainframes and their role in Windows DNA. The third and fourth sections deal with the visual interfaces of COMTI (Component Builder, COBOL wizards, and the COMTI/MTS MMC). The final section explores the COMTI runtime using a hypothetical, but thorough, COMTI and SNA Server configuration. The next product in the line is Host Integration Server 2000 (code named Babylon).

It's important to note here that the COMTI was intended to support mainframes. Models such as S/38, AS/400, and RS6000 are really midrange and, as such, aren't addressed by COMTI.

> **Note**
>
> If you do not intend to work with mainframe or other legacy systems, you should skip this chapter because COMTI is specifically created to bridge the gap between COM+ and mainframes (via SNA Server) within the Windows DNA model. COMTI is not useful outside this realm.

COMTI Requirements

I assume you are familiar with SNA Server 4.0 and have a working connection to an IBM mainframe. The mainframe should be operating under MVS v4.3 or later with Advanced Program to Program Communication (APPC) for LU6.2 capability. Currently, COMTI supports two IBM mainframe systems for running transaction programs: the Customer Information Control System (CICS) v4.0 and Information Management System (IMS) v4.0 or higher. This chapter focuses only on CICS programs.

COMTI does not work without an SNA Server somewhere in the network. In addition, all examples described here are shown in COBOL because it is currently the only language supported by the COMTI wizards in the Component Builder.

> **Note**
>
> COMTI consists of a development environment and a runtime module. Both ship with Windows SNA Server 4.0 as part of the Development Environment. Note that COMTI is unchecked by default during the typical SNA Server installation process. If SNA Server has already been installed and the COMTI icons under the SNA group are missing, rerun the SNA installation program and add only the COMTI option.

Although I will not go into the details of SNA Server setup and administration, I will give a brief overview of SNA Server and mainframes in general to benefit readers new to legacy applications. However, to take full advantage of COMTI, the reader should have the sufficient SNA Server skills and background knowledge to configure and administer an SNA Server. This chapter is not a substitute for the many excellent SNA Server and COMTI resources found on the Microsoft SNA Web site (www.microsoft.com/sna).

> **Note**
>
> SNA Server has a steep learning curve, especially for non-mainframe program-mers. SNA Server has many undocumented pitfalls and frustrations, but after the system is configured and the development process is smooth, SNA Server is quite possibly the most powerful legacy-accessing tool ever created for the Windows operating system.

> **Caution**
>
> It is not an overstatement to mention that mainframes and PCs live in different worlds. If you have never developed in a mainframe system, you will be sur-prised to find many discrepancies in common NT terminology.
>
> In mainframes, simple issues such as compiling, working with files, or just plain human-computer interaction are so different from PCs that mainframes almost look alien at first. Many of the technical terms that you might be familiar with (interface, transactions, client, server) mean very different things to a mainframe developer. If you should take only one thing from this chapter, it is to be aware of the techno-logical communication barrier that exists between the mainframe and PC worlds.

Mainframes and Windows DNA

Before you can learn COMTI, you must learn the Microsoft SNA Server. And before that, you must delve into a little history of mainframes: why they are the way they are, and why it is still important to develop software for them in the year 2000 and beyond.

> **Note**
>
> Apologies in advance to seasoned mainframe veterans; this short section will not do justice to the machines that have changed civilization as we know it. However, I do not claim to be an expert in the mainframe field and am only reporting on recent experiences.

19

THE COM
TRANSACTION
INTEGRATOR

One of the main reasons for the popularity of mainframes in the past and present is their tremendous resilience and robustness. They're analogous to Maytag appliances in the information technology world. A mainframe will crash about as often as Haley's comet flies by.

But why? What makes mainframes so reliable? Why aren't there more of them? If mainframes are so reliable, why can't software giants such as Sun and Microsoft incorporate the same resilience into their PC operating system kernels?

There are many answers to those questions, but one seems to predominate: tight integration. Mainframes do not have hundreds of third-party video or sound cards to choose from. There are no ergonomic keyboards, joysticks, pointing devices, or digital cameras to accommodate. There is no virus-checking software, and not even a decent GUI to track upclicks and window painting events. No Web browsers, no multimedia, no 3D games, no ActiMate Barney, no fun.

Mainframes are just pure and simple raw computing and storage power, the like of which no PC user could ever possibly imagine.

Mainframes were built and designed with reliability in mind and thus have become tightly coupled to enforce this. Mainframe manufacturers do not have to contend with thousands of competing hardware vendors who believe their products are better. They do not have to accommodate extra driver layers between the CPU and I/O or intricate security and networking layers to meet the demands of heterogeneous network and platform environments. It is this reduced complexity that makes mainframes so resilient when compared to PCs.

Mainframes even have hardware support—at the instruction level—for facilitating multi-user operating environments. The writer of a mainframe kernel is working alongside the computer engineer designing the processor's instruction set. The price for all this, of course, is a very rigid and inflexible environment. For storing and retrieving data, this is fine. It is this firm, coupled structure that gives mainframes their strength, scalability, and fault-tolerance. But obviously, mainframes are lacking in many areas and, even today, are prohibitively expensive. This is where PCs and SNA Server come in.

Tight Coupling: A House of Cards

Coupling was covered in detail in Chapter 2, "Multitiered Component Architectures," but I will use a fresh analogy to describe it here because it is critical to understanding mainframe resilience.

What is coupling? A tightly coupled system is a monolithic one, with few or no independent parts. A loosely coupled system, on the other hand, consists of objects or components that can be interchanged without affecting the whole.

Consider, for example, a house built of playing cards. It is very fragile and delicate, but simple to build. It can withstand its own weight and is visually appealing. The strength in the house's structure comes from the dependencies created from the bottom cards all the way to the top. Each card can hold several times its own weight, and with clever arrangement, possibly much more.

However, the strength of a house of cards is also its weakness. If one card collapses, there is a high probability the entire house of cards will fall. It is also not very feasible to make changes to a house of cards after it has been completed. Replacing or adding cards could cause the whole structure to crumble. This is a tightly coupled system (mainframe).

Contrast this technique for building structures with LEGOs. Each LEGO piece can be viewed as a single interoperable component with known interfaces and methods. A house built of LEGOs can withstand much more structural abuse and is easy to modify. Additional LEGOs can be connected to it long after the structure was completed without affecting the whole. This is a loosely coupled system (PC).

SNA Server

SNA Server is a protocol bridge between the robust mainframe systems and the PC world—particularly the Windows DNA framework. As discussed in the first chapters of this book, Windows DNA is inherently component-based and prefers products compliant with the COM standard. It's no surprise that COMTI is the ideal link between SNA Server and all the other tiers in the DNA architecture. SNA Server was around for many years before DNA was ever dreamed of, but it is still a powerful part of today's DNA technology. Figure 19.1 shows this relationship.

19

THE COM
TRANSACTION
INTEGRATOR

Note

Configuring an SNA Server can be a very challenging task. Two completely different worlds collide under SNA: mainframe and Windows. Expert knowledge in both areas is required for a successful configuration.

FIGURE **19.1**

COMTI and main-frame unite via SNA Server.

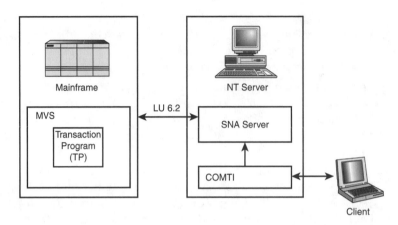

During the configuration phase, SNA Server will not always accurately describe a configuration problem, and many times it will be unclear whether a problem exists. What appears to be a healthy connection might turn out to be corrupt when COMTI kicks in. Dozens of properties and values have to be set on both sides (mainframe and Windows), and a trial-and-error approach is not feasible if time is a constraint.

Caution

Without a proactive person working on each side (mainframe and PC) before and after the configuration phase, it is nearly impossible for COMTI to work correctly.

Before proceeding to the configuration phase of SNA Server, it is vital to identify a mainframe contact person who will be responsible for setting up the mainframe connection and security accounts. This contact person should devote at least two or three days to the procedure to assure a smooth installation.

When you are setting up SNA Server, a network path must be routed and configured to physically connect to a mainframe. This can be accomplished in hundreds of ways, but the most popular is to connect through an Ethernet DLC network link because most environments support some form of Ethernet. Fortunately, SNA Server has several helpful wizards to assist in managing the network configuration process. Some of the wizards even generate worksheets to be filled by the mainframe operators. The worksheets are then used to configure SNA Server properly and to ensure that all link and security values match.

> **Note**
>
> In addition to a network link, COMTI requires an LU6.2 connection. The APPC/LU6.2 Connection Wizard in particular should prove invaluable here.

Before COMTI

Before COMTI was available, there were many techniques for communicating data from mainframes to PCs and vice versa. These techniques ranged from manual ASCII FTP transfers to the awkward but automated screen-scrapers (snapshotting mainframe output windows and "scraping" data out from known x,y coordinates). These techniques were error prone, did not scale well, and were unpredictable under distributed heterogeneous environments (such as Windows DNA).

By encapsulating much of the plumbing involved in communicating with a mainframe, COMTI eliminates these error-prone techniques by directly executing programs on the mainframe and presenting a scalable and familiar COM interface to all clients in the PC world.

For example, one of the most popular uses for mainframes today is data storage. As you will learn in the next section, COMTI enables you to read and write to a mainframe's data store easily and without any hassles.

COMTI

With the help of COMTI, SNA Server enables Windows DNA to access mainframe programs and resources (DB2 data, for example) as if they were distributed objects in the network.

On the surface, COMTI works by creating a proxy of a mainframe program on the PC. This proxy looks, acts, and behaves like a regular COM component and can, therefore, benefit from all COM's features. The proxy exports interfaces and methods that represent transaction programs (TPs) running on a mainframe. The client of a COMTI component is unaware that a mainframe even exists. All the complex interactions between COMTI, SNA Server, and the mainframe are completely encapsulated. Figure 19.1 illustrates this process.

> **Note**
>
> With COMTI, Windows DNA objects (such as ASP pages, Visual Basic ActiveX controls, and even Word documents) can access mainframe data and programs as if they were COM Automation objects. Never has such an elegant bridge been built between two entirely different worlds of technology!

Figure 19.2 shows where COMTI fits in the Windows DNA framework (the business and presentation components are absent to emphasize COMTI). To see a more complete description of Windows DNA in general, please refer to Chapter 1, "COM+: The Glue for Windows DNA."

FIGURE 19.2

Legacy data and Windows DNA coexist via COMTI.

COMTI Caveats

The three-tiered architecture depicted in Figure 19.2 is not a Windows DNA exclusive. It is also not a new idea. Some mainframe applications written in the 1970s were designed with three tiers in mind. Unfortunately, they are rare. Most mainframe programs have hardcoded terminal output screens along with their business logic and data access code. This monolithic structure is very difficult for COMTI to work with.

COMTI excels at communicating with a mainframe program or database, but there are some caveats and limitations. For a TP to work correctly with COMTI, it must not have any screen output or user interaction. COMTI components usually pass a list of arguments to a TP (of variable or fixed length) and expect a result back.

MTS/DTC Transactions Versus Mainframe Transactions

In Microsoft jargon, a transaction is described as an atomic unit of work. It is a protocol that enables information to persist in a consistent and reliable manner. In MTS and the DTC, changes made during a transaction can be undone (rolled back) or made permanent (committed) depending on certain rules and criteria.

In the mainframe world, transactions are CICS programs or TPs. You run a transaction program that might or might not employ a two-phase commit protocol such as Sync Level 2. (That's up to the programmer to include.)

Keep this information in mind when communicating with mainframe peers. It will prevent many misunderstandings during the development cycle.

If COMTI must interface with an interactive TP (one that relies on screen I/O), the TP must be modified, stripped of its terminal logic, or rewritten to do logic only.

This is a good example of how a three-tiered architecture approach would alleviate this problem. If the TP were written in three tiers, all the terminal I/O could be easily substituted for a Windows DNA presentation tier, leaving COMTI to transparently communicate with the mainframe's business logic and data stores without modifications.

CICS and CICS-LINK

This section covers the details of passing data to and from mainframe TP programs and their operating environment, Customer Information Control System (CICS). The next section covers the COMTI Component Builder development tool required to help you gain access to TP programs from a PC. COMTI, then, enables you to bring the reliability of mainframes into the distributed PC world via SNA Server. This is done in a sequential multistep process. First, I define the CICS operating environment.

CICS is IBM's transaction manager for MVS. The CICS subsystem contains regions that, in turn, contain mainframe programs (TPs). Resource and security management can also be contained within regions. Because each TP runs in its own address space, a fault or memory corruption within a region does not bring down the entire system, enhancing reliability.

COMTI can call and execute these regional TPs and pass information back and forth between a PC and mainframe. A typical TP might gather and update data from DB2 tables, check security, or perform business rules. Some TPs might even execute other TPs, all within the same transactional context if needed. Note that although CICS manages transactions transparently when required, the transactions are not automatic and must be specified at the region or TP level.

The two most popular methods of executing TPs on a mainframe are CICS and CICS-LINK. The main difference between CICS and CICS-LINK programs is how they communicate parameter information across calls. Some advantages and limitations of each are discussed later in this chapter.

19

THE COM TRANSACTION INTEGRATOR

Note

There are many types of COMTI components: transactional, non-transactional, fixed-length, variable-length, IMS, CICS, and CICS-LINK. This section covers only non-transactional CICS and CICS-LINK because they are the most popular. For all other transactional components, refer to the excellent online help in COMTI.

In a CICS TP, the program's logic must execute a `CICS RECEIVE INTO` statement to receive parameterized data and must issue a `CICS SEND FROM` to send data back to the caller. CICS programs run under unique transaction IDs. Listing 19.1 shows a fragment of a COBOL program that uses CICS to return a parameter (`END-IT`) back to COMTI. Notice the `EXEC CICS RETURN END-EXEC` command, which signals the end of the CICS session.

LISTING 19.1   Code Fragment Illustrating `SEND FROM` and `SEND RETURN`

```
350700 999-NOMAP.
350800     EXEC CICS SEND FROM(END-IT) LENGTH(0) ERASE END-EXEC.
350900     EXEC CICS RETURN END-EXEC.
```

On the other hand, CICS-LINK TPs are like proxies. CICS-LINK programs are mirrored by a special region called CICS Mirror Transaction (CSMI), which passes control to a TP via an `EXEC CICS LINK` command. The TP then receives any input parameters from the caller into its runtime COMMAREA. All output parameters are also stored in the COMMAREA, and are returned to the caller. CICS-LINK programs run under the CSMI transaction ID. Listing 19.2 illustrates this idea.

LISTING 19.2   A Function Uses the CICS-LINK Protocol to Pass Parameters Via the COMMAREA

```
YR2KP     9999-GSTDATE.
YR2KP         EXEC CICS LINK PROGRAM('GSTDATE')
YR2KP         COMMAREA(GSTDATE-REC)
YR2KP         LENGTH(GDT-LEN)
YR2KP         END-EXEC.
YR2KP     9999-GSTDATE-EXIT.
```

> **Note**
>
> Because most existing mainframe COBOL programs are already structured to work with a COMMAREA, they do not require any additional modifications for COMTI. Thus, CICS-LINK is the preferred method of creating COMTI components. However, if variable-length recordsets must be used, CICS-LINK will not work because all incoming and outgoing data must be defined in the COMMAREA before starting or ending the program.

Using a CICS-LINK object, the CSMI program receives and sends parameters via the COMMAREA (short for DFHCOMMAREA) and does not require any extra commands as CICS does. Listing 19.3 shows the DFHCOMMAREA of a program you will use in a later section. Notice how each line clearly defines the name, type, and size of a variable. It is for this reason that variable-length parameters cannot be used in CICS-LINK.

LISTING 19.3 The Linkage Section of a CICS-LINK TP Contains the COMMAREA Used to Pass Parameters to and from COMTI

```
003300****************************************************************
003400*      L  I  N  K  A  G  E      S  E  C  T  I  O  N
003500****************************************************************
003600 LINKAGE SECTION.
003700 01   DFHCOMMAREA.
003800      05   CA-RETURN-CODE          PIC S9(9) COMP.
003900      05   CA-DATA.
004000           10   CA-DT              PIC X(10).
004010           10   CA-REP-MO          PIC XXX.
004020           10   CA-REP-YR          PIC X(4).
004031           10   CA-CLOSE-OUT       PIC X(10).
004040           10   CA-OBJ-CAR         PIC S9(4) COMP.
004041           10   CA-CR-PAC          PIC S9(4) COMP.
004042           10   CA-OBJ-TRK         PIC S9(4) COMP.
004043           10   CA-TR-PAC          PIC S9(4) COMP.
004044           10   CA-OBJ-TOT         PIC S9(4) COMP.
004045           10   CA-TOT-PAC         PIC S9(4) COMP.
004050           10   CA-REP-DAYS        PIC S9(4) COMP.
004060           10   CA-SA-CAR          PIC S9(4)V9 COMP-3.
004061           10   CA-SA-PU           PIC S9(4)V9 COMP-3.
004062           10   CA-SA-TRK          PIC S9(4)V9 COMP-3.
004063           10   CA-SA-TOT          PIC S9(4)V9 COMP-3.
004070           10   CA-DS-LAST-RTL     PIC S9(9) COMP.
004080           10   CA-SELL-DAYS       PIC S9(4) COMP.
004090           10   CA-MAX-LINES       PIC S9(4) COMP.
004200           10   CA-LINES OCCURS 30 TIMES.
004300                15   CA-RTL-MTD              PIC S9(9) COMP.
004400                15   CA-CURR-STK             PIC S9(9) COMP.
004500                15   CA-IN-TRANS             PIC S9(9) COMP.
004600                15   CA-ON-ORD               PIC S9(9) COMP.
004700                15   CA-PIPELINE-DS          PIC S9(9) COMP.
004800                15   CA-RTL-YTD              PIC S9(9) COMP.
004900                15   CA-RTL-60D              PIC S9(9) COMP.
005000                15   CA-INV-MTD              PIC S9(9) COMP.
005100                15   CA-WHLSL-MTD            PIC S9(9) COMP.
005200                15   CA-WHLSL-YTD            PIC S9(9) COMP.
005300           10   CA-MESSAGE-OUT          PIC X(50).
005400
```

19

THE COM
TRANSACTION
INTEGRATOR

Caution

CICS-LINK programs do not support the use of unbounded recordsets or multiple sends and receives in their parameter communication protocol. CICS programs, on the other hand, do support multiple sends and receives because they can request data at any time via mainframe CICS SEND and RECEIVE commands. I will not cover multiple sends and receives here, but keep this support issue in mind when choosing a method of communication.

It is important to identify the type of TP program you will be working with (CICS or CICS-Link) because the next section discusses how to create COM objects to interact with each type.

Figure 19.3 builds on the architecture diagram in Figure 19.1 and illustrates a more realistic configuration with multiple TPs (CICS or CICS-LINK) running on the mainframe. Also, here the client interacts with MTS server, and not with COMTI directly (as shown in Figure 19.1).

Figure 19.3

A more realistic COMTI configuration.

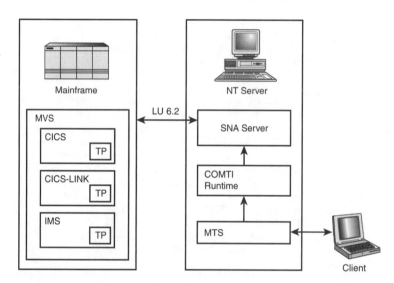

The COMTI Component Builder

The Component Builder is a COM programmer's tool for extracting parameter I/O information out of mainframe COBOL programs. COMTI can parse a TP's source code, create COM interfaces and methods (with appropriate OLE data types), and register a component with an MTS package. After the component is under the umbrella of MTS, it can be used throughout a distributed environment. In addition, the Component Builder can specify transactional and mainframe region properties, too.

It's important to note, however, that although the Component Builder is an essential tool for developing mainframe components for COMTI, all its features can be carried out manually using standard COM tools such as the MIDL compiler, OLE View, and Regedit. The Component Builder just makes the process much easier and more reliable.

> **Note**
>
> This section gives a general overview of how the Component Builder works and how to use its wizards to quickly create COMTI components. This section is by no means a reference guide or substitute for the COMTI documentation provided with the product. You are strongly encouraged to explore the COMTI documentation for a more thorough discussion on the Component Builder.

Figure 19.4 shows the main explorer view of the Component Builder.

FIGURE 19.4

The COMTI Component Builder.

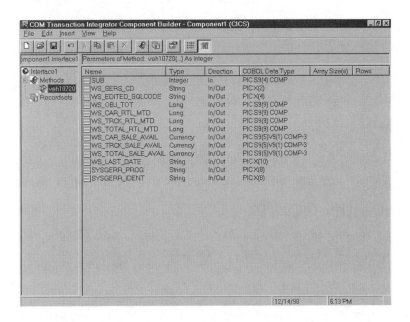

There are two ways to create components within the COMTI Component Builder: manually or with a wizard. I will focus on the wizard-driven approach because it is very effective and easy to learn. However, the manual approach is recommended for finer-grained control over the interfaces created by COMTI.

The Component Builder COBOL Wizard

The COBOL Wizard in the Component Builder is the easiest way to quickly and correctly set up a COMTI component. It involves a multistep process that begins with identifying the TP type and source code on the mainframe. I will cover two types of TPs: CICS and CICS-LINK (the previous section highlighted the differences in each).

19

THE COM
TRANSACTION
INTEGRATOR

> ### Caution
>
> Before continuing with the examples, make sure that the version of the COMTI Component Builder is v1.01, or a higher version is being used. This version is included in SNA Server 4.0 Service Pack 1. (At the time of this writing, there is only one service pack for SNA Server 4.0.)
>
> To verify which version is installed, run the COMTI Component Builder and select About from the Help menu. The version should be v1.01 (build 0524) (SP1) or higher, as shown in Figure 19.5.

FIGURE 19.5

Be sure SNA Server 4.0 SP1 is installed.

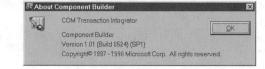

CICS TP

A CICS TP requires special commands to tell the mainframe it can receive parameters or that it has parameters to send back to the caller. These commands do not appear in the Component Builder and must be added to the source code of the mainframe TP.

Identify CICS TP

Before you can create a COMTI proxy of the mainframe TP, you must know what the TP does, what arguments (if any) it expects as input, and what arguments (if any) it returns on exit. You can then create an aptly named COM object, interface, and method to represent it on the PC side. This creation is done by selecting New from the File menu, which will create a new Component Library. You add methods to the library in step 2.

> ### Caution
>
> Be sure to select CICS in the Remote Environment Type drop-down box (see Figure 19.6).

If this component will participate in transactions, you can click the Supports Transactions radio button at this time. This can later be changed under MTS.

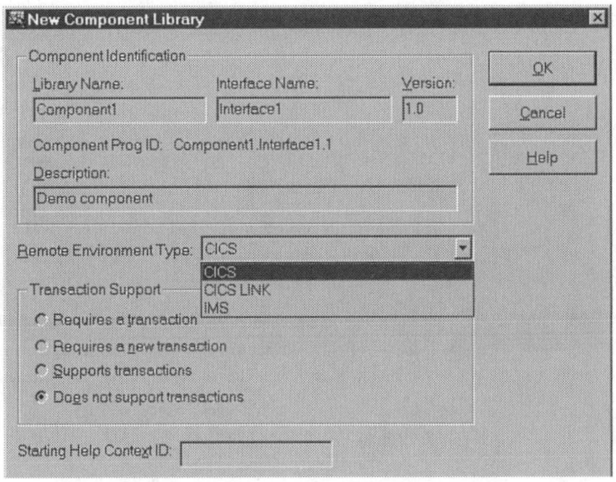

FIGURE **19.6**

The New Component Library dialog is the first step in creating COMTI components.

Import TP COBOL Source Code

After a new CICS object is created and given a name, you're ready to build a method that will access a TP on the mainframe. Remember, for COMTI to work properly, the data types that the mainframe expects (integers, floats, arrays, and so on), and the data types that COM understands (BSTRs, ints, variants, objects, and so on) must be properly translated. The translation happens at runtime by the COMTI proxy, but the data types must be defined at compile time. This is where the COBOL Wizard comes in.

> **Note**
>
> You must download the TP's COBOL source code from the mainframe for this step. FTP, email, and terminal emulation methods are useful for this.

From the File menu, select Import, and then select COBOL Wizard. This will bring up the COBOL Wizard (see Figure 19.7), which will prompt for the TP COBOL source code.

Locate and load the code and review it. Make sure the code being viewed is the same code used to compile the TP program on the mainframe (see Figure 19.8).

> **Note**
>
> Do not underestimate this advice! I once spent an entire day chasing down a bug due to inconsistent source code. The mainframe TP program was one version older than the source code I imported into COMTI. The COMMAREA was off by a single byte, throwing off all the variables and creating garbage values.

FIGURE **19.7**

*The COBOL
Import Wizard
greatly simplifies
data type defini-
tion.*

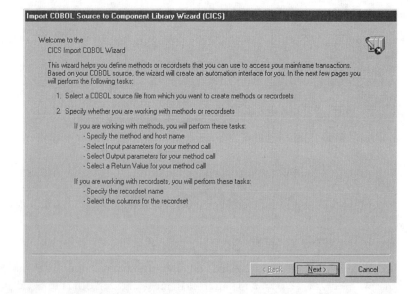

Caution

There is a bug in the Component Builder (v1.01) that does not scale dialogs for
the COBOL Wizard below 800×600. You must be in 1024×768 or higher to correctly view the wizard dialogs.

FIGURE **19.8**

*Begin by import-
ing the COBOL
code.*

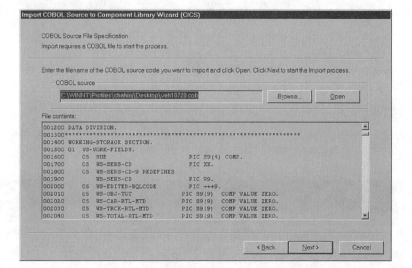

Continuing through the wizard, you see the Import options. For this example, you can select Create a New Method and continue. (Recordsets are left as an exercise for you.) In the next dialog, you have the opportunity to name the method that will activate this TP in the mainframe host (see Figure 19.9). It is critical to name the TP exactly as it is named on the mainframe (it is case-sensitive); otherwise, the TP will not be found and the component will fail.

FIGURE 19.9

Enter the exact name of the mainframe TP.

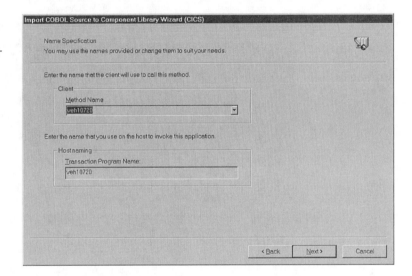

Next, you specify where the data will change hands. Select 01 Level Working Storage for the input (see Figure 19.10), output (see Figure 19.11), and return value (see Figure 19.12). Listing 19.4 shows the complete working storage area for the sample code shown in Figure 19.10. The working storage is synonymous with a variable declaration section of a C or Pascal program.

LISTING 19.4   The Working Storage Delineates Heap Memory the Program Will Use at Runtime

```
001100************************************************************
001200 DATA DIVISION.
001300************************************************************
001400 WORKING-STORAGE SECTION.
001500 01  WS-WORK-FIELDS.
001600     05  SUB                      PIC S9(4) COMP.
001700     05  WS-SERS-CD               PIC XX.
001800     05  WS-SERS-CD-9 REDEFINES
001900         WS-SERS-CD               PIC 99.
002000     05  WS-EDITED-SQLCODE        PIC +++9.
002010     05  WS-OBJ-TOT               PIC S9(9)  COMP VALUE ZERO.
```

LISTING 19.4   Continued

```
002020    05  WS-CAR-RTL-MTD        PIC S9(9)    COMP VALUE ZERO.
002030    05  WS-TRCK-RTL-MTD       PIC S9(9)    COMP VALUE ZERO.
002040    05  WS-TOTAL-RTL-MTD      PIC S9(9)    COMP VALUE ZERO.
002060    05  WS-CAR-SALE-AVAIL     PIC S9(5)V9  COMP-3 VALUE ZERO.
002070    05  WS-TRCK-SALE-AVAIL    PIC S9(5)V9  COMP-3 VALUE ZERO.
002080    05  WS-TOTAL-SALE-AVAIL   PIC S9(5)V9  COMP-3 VALUE ZERO.
002090    05  WS-LAST-DATE          PIC X(10).
002100
```

FIGURE 19.10

CICS requires an 01 Level working storage for inputs.

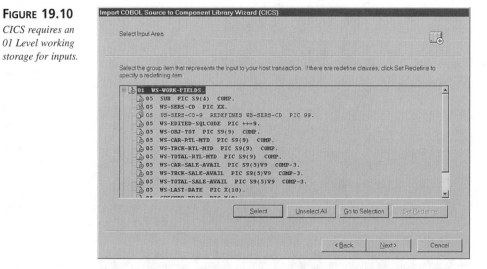

FIGURE 19.11

CICS also requires an 01 Level WS for outputs.

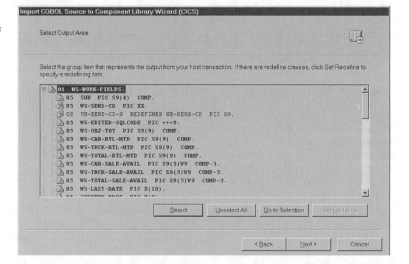

FIGURE 19.12

Finally, choose a variable to contain the return value of the TP.

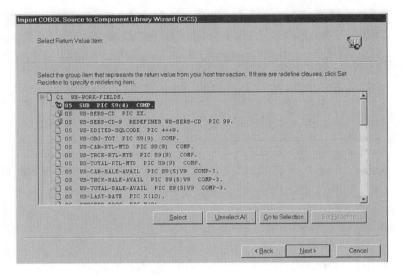

The wizard page shown in Figure 19.12 prompts for a return value. If your TP program is to return a status code or computed result, this is where it should be specified. If your TP does not return a value, you may skip this step. It is highly recommended that all TP programs return at least one value to indicate success or failure. This makes it much easier to debug the TP later.

When completed, the wizard evaluates the source code and creates the method signatures for this TP (see Figure 19.13).

FIGURE 19.13

A successful import.

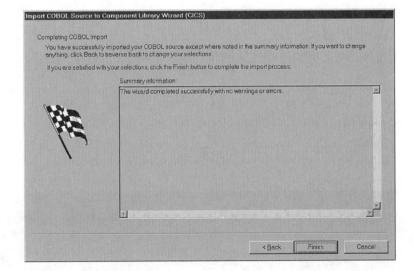

> **Caution**
>
> On some correct COBOL source code, the COBOL Wizard will display an error and fail (see Figure 19.14). If this happens, try different methods of formatting the COBOL code (with or without line numbers, binary or text FTP transfers, and so on). I have not been able to determine exactly what causes this bug, and Microsoft has not acknowledged nor confirmed this to be a bug.

FIGURE 19.14

Bug: Correct COBOL sometimes produces this error.

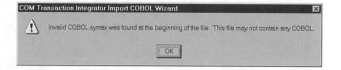

Add Component to an MTS Package

With the COBOL code imported and method signatures created, the component can be added and registered to an MTS COMTI package. From the toolbar (or, alternatively, from the Tools/Add To Package menu), select the Package icon. This activates the Package Export Wizard.

The wizard prompts for a remote environment. This is very important because it tells COMTI where to find the TP. (Remote environments are configured in SNA Server.) If you do not specify a remote environment, your component is stored in a special area called Unassigned Components in the COMTI MMC.

Test the Component

Test the component with a COM-compliant language such as VB or VC++ and make sure the data types you pass to the methods match those specified in the COMTI wizard. Test for error codes if your TP supports them. If errors do occur, you must examine the NT log using the Event Viewer. (Look under the Applications section for any red markers associated with COMTI or SNA Server.) This is the only way the COMTI runtime can communicate failures to the developer.

Figure 19.15 shows a common problem that arises when the COMTI MMC cannot locate an SNA Server and tries to access information on remote environments.

> **Note**
>
> If you do not get correct results when working with CICS TPs, go back to the mainframe and make sure there is explicit use of EXEC CICS RECEIVE INTO commands to receive the data into the working storage. Likewise, to return data to the PC, you must explicitly issue an EXEC CICS SEND FROM command. These commands manipulate the data used by the TP in its 01 Level Working Storage.

FIGURE 19.15

A common COMTI runtime error.

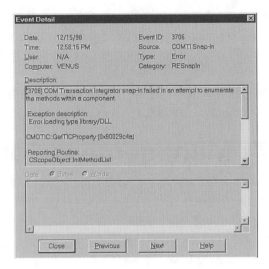

CICS-LINK

The steps involved in creating COMTI components for CICS-LINK TPs are similar to the steps described for CICS except for a few minor details. When choosing a remote environment, select CICS-LINK, not CICS.

Instead of choosing a 01 Level Working Storage, select the DFHCOMMAREA. This ensures that parameters are passed to the program's runtime when it executes and does not require any additional EXEC statements (like CICS TPs). Listing 19.3 shows the COMMAREA for our example.

For output parameters, select the lines of code in the COMMAREA that will serve as outputs. If the COMMAREA in your imported COBOL program is returning or accepting group tables (OCCURS statements), these must be selected as inputs or outputs as well. For a return value, choose a variable that will hold the TP's return value and select the Retval button.

19

THE COM
TRANSACTION
INTEGRATOR

> **Note**
>
> Return values are very important, even for TPs that are write-only. Error and status output codes should accompany all TPs because they simplify the debugging process when working with COM. When something goes wrong without return codes, it is very difficult to pinpoint where the silent failure occurred. Did the TP execute? Did the mainframe fail? Was the SNA Server down? A return value can reduce the time to debug a COMTI configuration.

Remember, CICS-LINK programs do not require explicit mainframe EXEC commands to send or receive parameters. All parameters are passed from the client (COMTI) to the mirror transaction CSMI. CSMI runs on the mainframe host and links to the specified TP, passing any parameters via the DFHCOMMAREA.

Next I will cover the COMTI MMC, a snap-in for the MTS MMC that enables you to configure security, transaction support, and DCOM for COMTI packages.

The COMTI Management Console

Fortunately, the COMTI console is a snap-in for the familiar Microsoft Management Console (MMC). There are a few minor changes, but otherwise, it works and feels just like the MTS MMC.

At the root of the COM Transaction Integrator branch (see Figure 19.16) are two COMTI-specific folders: Remote Environments and Unassigned Components.

Remote Environments contains the mainframe connections configured under SNA Server. If you have not yet set up your SNA Server, this folder will be empty.

Each configured remote environment connection houses the components and packages that do the actual invocation of the mainframe TPs. Figure 19.16 shows two environments with CICS-Link expanded.

> ### Caution
>
> Without these environments, COMTI cannot access a mainframe. If everything is configured properly, the environments in this folder should match the ones listed in the SNA Manager.
>
> When working with the Package Export Wizard in the Component Builder, a key question is the remote environment under which the component will operate. If a remote environment is not present, the package is sent to the Unassigned Components folder and will not function.

The Unassigned Components folder holds any components created by the Component Builder that have not yet been assigned to remote environment or a COMTI package. These components will not work and must be configured properly to be of use.

Notice that when selecting a COMTI component, the right pane of the MMC shows a list of property columns. Here you can quickly see at a glance which components are CICS, CICS-LINK, or IMS. You can also see the transactional properties of each component by selecting

its properties (by right-clicking, using the toolbar Properties icon, or choosing from the
Action menu). This is the same technique used for MTS components throughout the MMC.

FIGURE 19.16

*Notice the familiar
MTS look and feel
of the COMTI
MMC.*

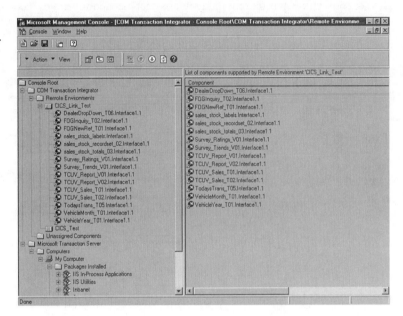

To aid the developer, Microsoft has chosen the MMC as the standard explorer for most
Windows DNA server-side products. Figure 19.17 shows the SNA Server MMC, which
is also a snap-in like COMTI.

FIGURE 19.17

*The SNA Server
MMC.*

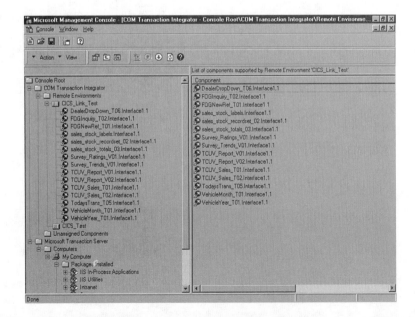

19

**THE COM
TRANSACTION
INTEGRATOR**

The COMTI Runtime

This section brings together all the previous sections and illustrates a complex, but certainly feasible configuration architecture of COMTI.

Consider Figure 19.18. This figure has many parts. At the lower center is the mainframe, which houses all the data you are interested in and which can support hundreds of concurrent users. In this example, the mainframe has access to DB2 and VSAM databases. All this data will be made available to PC clients through the magic of COMTI.

FIGURE 19.18

A complex, but correct COMTI configuration.

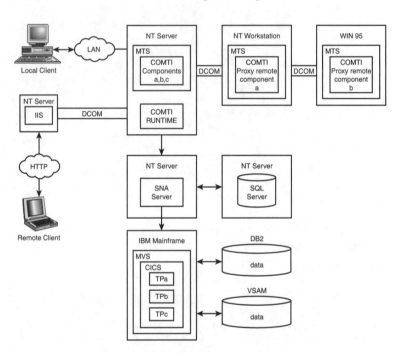

At the far left are the browser-based dumb clients that do not understand COM, but can still use its services via Active Server Pages or other forms of server-side scripting. The client requests a Web page, which in turn activates a COMTI component that gathers any necessary mainframe data and returns an HTML result.

At the top right are the Windows 95 and NT clients. These clients are connected via DCOM and have remote MTS proxy copies of the COMTI components. The COMTI components live in the middle machine and have a direct connection to SNA Server. Look at the process, in detail, of how the Win95 machine (far right) might get data from the mainframe:

1. The Win95 client instantiates a COMTI COM component. The component is looked up in the Registry and found to live within MTS. MTS knows this is a remote component and also knows where the real component lives. A DCOM connection is established to the remote machine and initiates a conversation with the remote component. This causes a generic COMTI class factory to be created on the remote client. (Remember, COMTI components are proxies themselves.)

2. The Win95 client calls one of the methods in the component that represents a TP program in the mainframe. The TP program executes a business rule and makes note of it in a mainframe log. A return value of 0 denotes success; any other return denotes failure.

3. The remote component (living under MTS) is activated and ready. A request via DCOM comes in for a method. Any arguments from the Win95 client are marshaled and passed to the method.

   When the remote COMTI component receives the method request, the dispatch ID for the method is located and the COMTI state machine is started. The state machine is in charge of managing transactions outside the DTC context (the mainframe) and allowing for timeouts and errors on the mainframe side. For more information on the COMTI state machine, see the COMTI documentation.

   If transactions are supported, COMTI enlists with the DTC.

4. The component is intercepted by the COMTI runtime and calls are made to the mainframe via the LU6.2 connection provided by the SNA Server (the remote environment).

5. The TP program runs under its region and returns a result via working storage or DFHCOMMAREA (CICS or CICS-LINK, respectively).

6. The COMTI state machine is waiting for a response from the TP and when one arrives, it is marshaled and translated into OLE data.

7. The LU6.2 connection is closed, the COMTI resources are freed, and the result is marshaled over DCOM to the Windows 95 client, where the request originated.

8. The Win95 client receives the response and releases the component.

There's a lot going on in these steps, but these are only the tip of the iceberg. Many other subtle mechanisms are employed in both worlds (security, memory management, and so on). For the other clients in the diagram, the story is basically the same. DCOM might not always be involved, but that is only an intermediate step.

Despite all these numerous interactions across networks and platforms, in practice, the whole process is incredibly fast. A typical call to a small mainframe TP executes and returns in less than a second.

As COMTI programmers, however, we know this is not magic, but only the careful configuration of COMTI components.

Summary

This chapter introduced you to mainframes and the COM Transaction Integrator. Mainframes (and their operating systems) are very resilient and powerful computers that get their strength from their tight integration and strict OS licensing standards. This reduces compatibility complexity and increases robustness. Compared to PCs, mainframes are tightly coupled. PCs are much easier and more fun to use, but they have little control over their environment (untested third-party hardware and tools). OS licensing agreements are very relaxed and prone to instability from third parties.

COMTI is a very powerful tool for communicating with mainframe programs and accessing their resources, thus bridging the gap between the two worlds (Windows DNA on PCs and legacy applications on mainframes).

COMTI supports two methods for communication: CICS and CICS-LINK. CICS requires mainframe programs (TPs) to make explicit SEND and RECEIVE calls when data needs to be transferred to COMTI. CICS-LINK, on the other hand, automatically uses a special communications area (the COMMAREA) to read and write variables that COMTI intercepts.

The COMTI Component Builder is a great tool for setting up components to work with mainframe TPs. The COBOL Wizard can import COBOL source code, generate method signatures for TPs, and register the results with MTS.

Finally, you examined a complex but realistic architecture of a COMTI environment and looked at its operation from a high level.

Component Load Balancing

CHAPTER 20

If you develop enterprise applications, you have two opposing forces at work. On one side is your marketing department. It wants as many simultaneous users on the application as possible. This drives its commerce model and makes money. On the other side is the hardware implementation team, who tells you there's a limit to the number of users that the hardware will support. What is a developer to do?

There's more to the problem than just limited bandwidth. What happens when the application server goes down? All your customers are out of luck, and you can hear the marketing staff down the hall when they realize that all their carefully crafted plans are out the window until the server is back up.

The answer, as you've probably guessed by the title of this chapter, is to implement COM+ load balancing. It's a solution that's easy to implement and requires no change in your programming model for almost all cases.

Before you get too far into this chapter, I need to warn you that as of the writing of this book, component load balancing is not part of COM+. I cover the reasons for this at the end of the chapter and talk about its future.

Component Load Balancing Defined

Load balancing, simply put, is the distribution of work among several computers. Many times these computers are referred to as *cluster machines*. There is always one central point that distributes the work among the cluster machines. This is known as the *load-balancing server*, or the router. The router can also act as one of the cluster machines. Conceivably a machine could be managing and assigning requests as a router, while satisfying some of the requests as a cluster machine.

The term *unit of work* is used when discussing load balancing. The unit of work is a chunk of work performed by a cluster machine. Usually the designers of a technology determine the unit of work. In this case the engineers from Microsoft have done just that. I discuss the unit of work at greater length in the section "Parallelism and Granularity."

Granularity, as referenced in this chapter, is the size of the work chunks that are distributed. The greater the chunk of work doled out to a cluster machine, the coarser is its granularity. The smaller the chunk of work doled out to a cluster machine, the finer is its granularity.

The Need for Component Load Balancing

Before going too much further I'm going to present some of the challenges to enterprise applications. This will give you a better understanding of the compelling need for load balancing. Essentially, load balancing provides an application the capability to work within and satisfy the unique requirements of an enterprise.

Scalability

Scalability is the term used to describe the capability of an enterprise system to easily grow in response to ever-increasing demands. Scalability has been the Holy Grail of enterprise developers for many years. Early on, the most common methods of scaling an application were to get bigger and faster machines, or to upgrade machines so that they had more available resources. And although bigger and faster machines are good and help service more traffic, there comes a point when even the biggest and best machine won't handle the load.

Current enterprise applications are about traffic. In most cases the greater the traffic, the greater the financial payoff. This usually holds true for subscription services, e-commerce situations, and free services where money is made in other ways such as exposure and advertising.

With the increased traffic comes a host of difficulties. The first problem you must solve is how to deal with the extra traffic. The hardware on which your application runs might be overloaded to the point that it either doesn't function adequately, or stops functioning altogether. I can think of a very recent example when *Encyclopaedia Britannica* went online, offering users the ability to access its entire encyclopedia's contents. Within a matter of hours, the site's entire system crashed because of the heavy demand. It was three weeks before it was operational again. Needless to say, you want to avoid a similar situation.

Imagine being part of a team that develops a Web-based application. The goal is to get as many users as possible to visit to and use the Web site. Yet, if your only recourse, when traffic grows beyond capacity, is beefing up the Web server, then you are in trouble. A single Web server, no matter how powerful, will not suffice indefinitely.

Static Component Load Balancing

From the developer's point of view, the easiest way to solve a scalability problem is with static load balancing. This can be done by simply telling half the clients to use server A and the other half to use server B. However, this classic approach has a number of problems. First, the administrative work of pointing each client at the right server is expensive and hard to implement correctly. Suppose you have 100 clients on one server that is too slow, so you add another. You probably want to even out the server usage, with 50 clients using each server. Now you have to tell 50 users about the new server you want them to use, and they have to go to their UI and enter the name of the new server in an options dialog. What happens if they don't get around to it? What happens if they do it incorrectly? What happens if the wrong users do it? Not only does the process cost you time and money, it costs the users time and money. And you have no control over when, how, or even whether the assignment of clients to the new server gets implemented. And when you are up to 200 subscribers and need to add a third server, you have to do it all over again. What would you want to do to a phone company that made you change area codes twice in a year? We want our load-balancing algorithm to be deterministic and easy to use for clients and servers. The static approach is neither.

The second problem of static load balancing is that the assignment of clients to servers does not vary as the client load varies. Suppose a blizzard in one state causes school to be canceled, and all the homebound kids want to hit your site. If you've assigned clients to the server closest to their geographical location, the server for the blizzard area might become heavily loaded, whereas a server for another location becomes an expensive paperweight. The same thing happens with international time zones. Australian and Japanese users are most active when users on the east coast of the United States are winding down. The static load-balancing algorithm cannot track even coarse-grained variations of user load. The wasted server sits around, spinning its disks while users on the heavily loaded servers fume. This is how you feel when you see a bank clerk filing her nails while you wait in line for the one teller who's actually working. We'd really like our load-balancing mechanism to respond to the actual, rather than a hypothetical, load on the system at any given time. The static approach doesn't do this. What is needed is dynamic load balancing, in which each resource is used equally. I talk about this shortly.

Availability

Another factor to consider is *availability*, meaning whether a given system can service client requests. If a machine is down or not functioning, it is not available. What if you rely on a single Web server? What happens when it goes down? Your operation is shut down until the problem is fixed. With a single machine, availability can be an issue.

Availability is especially an issue if you are creating an application on contract. You tell your client that the application is reliable. You cite the hours and hours of stress testing that the application has undergone. But if a hard drive fails or something else goes wrong and the server goes down, your client will not be too happy.

Here again Microsoft's load balancing technology can help. Not only does it distribute work so that applications are scalable, but distribution of work among several machines increases the rate of the availability of an application. If an enterprise application has eight machines and one goes down, the other seven can still probably perform up to an acceptable level.

The third problem of static load balancing is that it doesn't easily handle a downed server. Splitting the server resources among several boxes is supposed to afford the system some degree of continuity and robustness. If you have four boxes and one goes down, you would really like the other three to pick up the load as best they can. But this doesn't work with static load balancing. All the clients that are pointed at the malfunctioning server are disabled themselves. You could give them each a backup server name to try, as many online servers do with dial-up numbers, but the same administrative problems described previously will come back to bite you. The last thing you want is your clients having to worry about the location of a server. You'd really like your load-balancing mechanism to dynamically track the available hardware, assigning incoming clients to all the available server boxes while bypassing those that are nonfunctional.

Flexibility

Flexibility is another good thing in today's market. Load balancing technology enables you to easily add and subtract hardware as you want. This gives you great flexibility at a relatively low cost because you can add a variety of hardware. And the hardware variety can be in terms of type, cost, and capability.

Parallelism and Granularity

In this chapter, I have mentioned the unit of work and granularity. In this section I will talk more about these subjects. You will learn how the unit of work is defined, and how its granularity affects load balancing and performance. These subjects fall under the broader topic known as parallelism. *Parallelism* is the capability of a system to operate on several different machines in parallel.

A unit of work begins when a client calls `CoCreateInstance()`. The request is forwarded to the load-balancing router, which decides to which cluster machine the request will be delegated. The router returns a reference to the client, ending its involvement in that particular request. From that point on, the client and the selected cluster server continue the conversation.

Although the client holds on to the object reference, it is bound to the assigned server. During the entire lifetime of the object reference, the assigned server maintains the object and all related activities. When the client finally releases the reference (with a call to `Release()`), the unit of work ends. Figure 20.1 shows this process.

FIGURE 20.1

An overview of request routing.

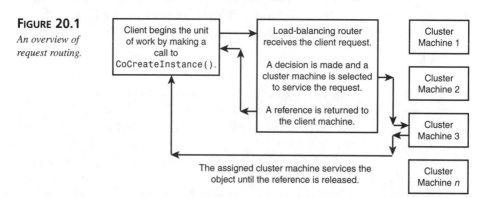

Granularity is a relative measure of how small a unit of work is. A finer degree of granularity indicates fewer tasks for each unit of work. A coarser degree of granularity indicates more tasks for each unit of work. That means that an object with a fine degree of granularity is instantiated with `CoCreateInstance()`, but then does very little, and can only make a handful of method calls. It is then is destroyed with a call to `Release()`. An object with a coarse granularity starts with a `CoCreateInstance()` and ends with a `Release()`, but probably makes many method calls (or at least makes method calls that consume large amounts of time and energy).

Parallelism Illustrated

To illustrate granularity, let me present both extremes. On one side we have a very finely grained object that makes a single method call between the time it's created and the time it's released. On the other side is a coarsely grained object that remains alive for weeks, in which time thousands or millions of method calls are made.

You're probably asking which one is better in a situation when good load balancing is desired. The answer is, "It depends."

It should be pretty obvious that the most even load balancing can be achieved with fine granularity. Let's say you have an application that's composed of coarsely grained objects. Client requests are satisfied, and everything is well-balanced. But the client machines might stay connected for days or weeks. If this is the case, then you are vulnerable to some of the same weaknesses that static load balancing has. The load can become unbalanced if a large number of client machines drop off because of a power failure in their building.

Okay, then fine granularity it is. Right? Actually, no. Fine granularity might be easier to load balance, but it carries much more overhead than coarse granularity does. Fine granularity requires many more calls to `CoCreateInstance()` and `Release()`. These don't perform any real work with regard to the business problems your application is designed to solve.

If both coarse and fine granularity carry their respective baggage, how does a developer decide which route to take? Microsoft's recommendation is this: "Don't change the programming model in order to optimize load balancing." Microsoft's position is that COM+'s load-balancing capabilities are designed to function under a wide range of situations. They advise against changing any programming model that you are using because the benefits of a well-designed programming model probably outweigh any benefits gained from trying to optimize the load-balancing process with changes to the programming model

The Dynamic Load-Balancing Algorithm

I want to spend some time talking about how the load-balancing server implements load balancing as an algorithm. If you think for a minute, you will come up with two candidate methods. The first would be based on the current load of each cluster server. The router would keep track of the load on each cluster machine. When a new request is made, the router assigns the request to the cluster machine with the lowest current load. This is called a *response time algorithm*.

The second method that presents itself as an obvious choice is a *round-robin* approach. The router maintains a list of cluster servers through which it cycles when assigning cluster servers to requests.

Microsoft has implemented these two methods into a single hybrid algorithm. The router polls the cluster machines at a given interval, called the *polling interval*. When the cluster machines are polled, the response time is recorded. Based on this response time, the router determines which of the cluster machines are most heavily loaded and which are most lightly loaded. An ordered list is assembled from the most lightly loaded to the most heavily loaded cluster machines. The router then simply goes through the ordered list in a *round-robin* fashion. The ordered list remains intact during the polling interval.

> **Note**
>
> The polling interval has a significant effect on which of the two implementation methods have the most effect. For instance, if the polling interval is very small, then the router might not make it completely through the list before the next ordered list is assembled. In this case the algorithm is more heavily based on response time. At the other extreme is a longer polling interval. In this case the ordered list might be gone through many times before it is reordered. This means that before long, as the load on each cluster server changes, response time has less effect, and implementation simply becomes a round-robin scheme.

COM+ performs load balancing only when an object is initially created. If the object supports just-in-time activation (JIT), subsequent JIT activations of a specific object instance are always performed on the server on which the object was first created. Here's how JIT activation works: When the computer is deactivated, the actual object is destroyed on the server, but the client-side proxy, the server stub, and the channel connecting them stay in place. The connection between the client in the specific machines is not destroyed, even though the actual server-side component is. You can demonstrate this feature with the sample by configuring the load-balancing sample component to use JIT activation. You'll have to set the component for Auto Done as well, because the component does not set the deactivate on return bit on its own. Clicking the Create button creates the object, invoking COM+ load balancing. Clicking the Call button calls the components GetMachineName method. Each time you do this, the object is activated just in time. You can see that the location of the component doesn't change when you repeatedly click the call button. Clicking the release button causes the client to release the component, destroying the actual component, the proxy stub, and the channel. If you click the Create button again, the creation operation invokes the load-balancing mechanism again. I talk more about JIT in Chapter 21, "Optimizing Windows DNA Applications," when we use the DNA Performance Kit.

Component Load-Balanced Component Design

When designing a component that can support load balancing, it is essential that you avoid any sort of location dependency because the component never knows ahead of time which machine it will be running on. For example, you can't depend on the location of specific files, such as C:\mydirectory\somefile, unless you are positive that every server machine has the same file in the same location.

Location dependencies can be subtle. If an object on server A enters a foreign exchange deal into a database at 0900 hours and an object on server B enters a local dealer at 0901 hours, which entry actually happens first? It depends on the time zones the two servers are using. If the servers are or might someday be in different physical locations, you probably want to write your component to use a single time standard for all of its work, regardless of the time zone setting of the machine on which it finds itself running. Barclays Bank, headquartered in London, probably runs all its servers on Greenwich mean time, regardless of their physical location, whereas the L.L.Bean order servers will probably run on the eastern U.S. time used in Freeport, Maine.

Because you don't know on which machine's components objects will next be created, you must be very careful about state management when designing load balance of the components. For example, the object might retrieve its initial state from parameters passed by the client, or it might retrieve its initial state from a database outside the machine on which it runs. Objects can retrieve a machine-dependent state, such as the DSN for a specific machine, by using object constructor strings.

Component Load-Balanced Client Design

A client application doesn't do anything different when creating a component that is load balanced than it does when creating one that isn't. The client application simply creates an object, specifying the load-balancing router as the host. The client doesn't know whether the object that resulted from the call is running on a machine it specified or on one to which the writer delegated the object creation. In general, you probably don't want your clients to have to care whether their components are load balanced or not.

A client should be aware that, if a component is load balanced, the death of a server doesn't necessarily mean that the client is useless until the server comes back up. The application cluster might contain other servers that can take over the load. Suppose a client creates an object that, after load balancing, actually resides on server A. The client makes a few calls on the object, but then server A blows its power supply and dies. In this case, the next time the client makes a call on the object, the call times out, and the client receives an error code indicating that the server has, in fact, died. The client should, at this point, release its object and try to re-create it; the router routes the creation request to a server that is still running. A client that thinks it might be using a load-balanced component should release and re-create the object when it encounters a server failure.

The Bad News

I got pretty excited about the prospects of load balancing while using the Windows 2000 release candidate 2. Everything seemed on track, and I expected load balancing to be in everybody's enterprise development toolkit. But, when the third release candidate came to my doorstep, load balancing was missing. It seems that there were problems Microsoft didn't feel it could solve before the release of Windows 2000. I found the following on the Web that explains Microsoft's position:

> On September 13, 1999, Microsoft announced the redeployment of the COM+ load-balancing feature, known as Component Load Balancing (CLB), from Windows 2000 to the upcoming Microsoft AppCenter Server. This change is effective with Windows 2000 Beta 3 Release Candidate 2. CLB was previously part of Windows 2000 Advanced Server and Datacenter Server. This packaging change will not affect the ship schedule or quality of Windows 2000. Network Load Balancing and Windows Clustering remain core components of Windows 2000 Advanced Server and Datacenter Server and are not affected by this change.

> Feedback from customers evaluating CLB as part of the Windows 2000 beta program has been very positive, but it indicated there was a need for additional functionality around CLB in the areas of management, monitoring, and deployment. In response to this feedback, Microsoft is developing AppCenter Server, the high-availability deployment and management solution for Web applications built on the Microsoft Windows 2000 operating system. AppCenter Server will include CLB as part of its core functionality in direct response to this customer feedback.

> Microsoft is committed to delivering a set of clustering features for the Windows 2000 platform that enable the creation of highly scalable and available multitier networks. These clustering features include Network Load Balancing and Windows Clustering in addition to CLB. Network Load Balancing acts as a front-end cluster, distributing incoming IP traffic across a cluster of up to 32 servers, and is ideal for enabling incremental scalability and outstanding availability for e-commerce Web sites. The Cluster service acts as a back-end cluster, providing high availability for applications such as databases, messaging, and file and print services. Windows 2000 Advanced Server supports 2-node clusters with the Cluster service, and Datacenter Server supports 4-node clusters.

> With Release Candidate 2, customers building distributed solutions can create scalable multitiered clustered solutions using Network Load Balancing and Windows Clustering. The new addition to Microsoft's expanding clustering feature set, CLB complements these solutions by load balancing on the middle or business logic tier. When formally released with AppCenter Server, CLB will form a key part of the Windows clustering solution.

As I'm writing this book, Windows 2000 no longer has a load-balancing capability, and AppCenter Server is still a few months from being released. This leaves the question of load balancing open for a while. This is not good news.

Component Load Balancing Without AppCenter Server

Some of you might be in need of a solution right now and can't wait for AppCenter Server to obtain a solution to your component load-balancing needs. I've developed my own system that you should consider for your load-balance–hungry applications.

Working with the SCM

The solution in this section mimics the COM+ load-balancing service. The goal is to have clients configured to send object creation requests to a single server, which delegates the requests to a cluster of servers. The first problem to solve is how to work around the windows Service Control Manager (SCM). The SCM was not designed to forward creation requests for remote clients to remote servers. We could consider a new implementation of the SCM, but that would require a great deal of work.

It would be, however, much easier to change things on the server side. The SCM locates the server code it needs to execute and fulfill a creation request first by looking for class objects in its Class Table. Next, it searches the registry for the executable code that puts the right class object in its Class Table. You can trick the SCM by launching a server in advance that registers an implementation of a class object to execute your own given executable code. If you edit the registry for any given class, you can cause the SCM to launch your server as well.

Using this method, the SCM executes code that performs the desired load balancing. It does so by forwarding creation requests to other servers. We begin with a special class object as follows:

```
class ClassObjectShim : public IClassFactory

 {

   CLSID m_clsid;

 public:

   ClassObjectShim(CLSID clsid) : m_clsid(clsid) {}

   virtual ~ClassObjectShim() {}

   // IUnknown
   STDMETHODIMP QueryInterface(REFIID riid,
                               void **ppv);
```

```
STDMETHODIMP_(ULONG) AddRef();
STDMETHODIMP_(ULONG) Release();

// IClassFactory
STDMETHODIMP CreateInstance(IUnknown *pUnkOuter,
  REFIID riid,
  void **ppv);
STDMETHODIMP LockServer(
  BOOL bFlag);
};
```

One thing to note is that the implementation stores a CLSID. This can be used with classes dynamically. The `CreateInstance()` method does most of the work for the class. The implementation is as follows:

```
STDMETHODIMP ClassObjectShim::CreateInstance(
    IUnknown *pUnkOuter, REFIID riid,void **ppv)
{
    *ppv = 0;

    COSERVERINFO csi = { 0, OLESTR("MyServer"), 0, 0 };
    MULTI_QI mqi = { riid, 0, 0 };

    hr = CoCreateInstanceEx(m_clsid, 0,
                            CLSCTX_REMOTE_SERVER, &csi,
                            1, &mqi);
    if (SUCCEEDED(hr))
    {
        (*ppv = mqi.pItf)->AddRef();
        mqi.pItf->Release();
    }

    return hr;
}
```

Anytime an implementation of this class is registered for a CLSID, the creation request would be forwarded to `MyServer`. The following is a simple example of an executable server that does this:

```
// LoadBalancer.exe
 int WINAPI WinMain(HINSTANCE, HINSTANCE, LPSTR, int)
 {
   HRESULT hr = CoInitialize(0);
   if (SUCCEEDED(hr))
   {
     ClassObjectShim cos(CLSID_Balanced);

     DWORD dwReg;
     hr = CoRegisterClassObject(CLSID_Balanced, &cos,
       CLSCTX_LOCAL_SERVER, REGCLS_MULTIPLEUSE, &dwReg);
```

```
    if (SUCCEEDED(hr))
    {
      MSG msg;
      while (GetMessage(&msg, 0, 0, 0))
        DispatchMessage(&msg);

      CoRevokeClassObject(dwReg);
    }

    CoUninitialize();
  }

  return hr;
}
```

If this executable were pre-started on the server MyCLBS, all client requests to create Balanced objects would be serviced by the instance of ClassObjectShim initialized with CLSID_Balanced. Based on the implementation of CreateInstance shown previously, the requests would be forwarded to the SCM on MyServer and serviced there locally. If the Balanced class is registered on MyCLBS and the LocalServer32 key pointed to the LoadBalancer.exe, shown in the previous code, the server would auto-start as well. This implementation is slightly slower than the mechanism in COM+ because an extra LRPC call from the SCM on the CLBS to the COM server providing the forwarding class objects is necessary. But this is a small price to pay for a load-balancing infrastructure that works without the COM+ implementation.

The Problem with CoCreateInstance

If clients create objects by calling CoGetClassObject() and IClassFactory::CreateInstance(), the approach I just outlined works great. For example, this client code ends up calling to an instance of Balanced running on MyServer:

```
HRESULT hr;
 COSERVERINFO csi = { 0, OLESTR("MyCLBS"), 0, 0 };

 IClassFactory *pcf = 0;
 hr = CoGetClassObject(CLSID_Balanced,
   CLSCTX_REMOTE_SERVER, &csi,
   IID_IClassFactory, (void**)&pcf);
 if (SUCCEEDED(hr))
 {
   IBalanced *pb = 0;
   hr = pcf->CreateInstance(0, IID_IBalanced,
     (void**)&pb);
   pcf->Release();
   if (SUCCEEDED(hr))
```

20
COMPONENT LOAD BALANCING

```
   {
   .
   .
   .
     // use object on MyServer
     pb->Release();
   }
 }
```

If, however, the client code were rewritten to use `CoCreateInstance()` or `CoCreateInstanceEx()`, it won't work.

```
HRESULT hr;

 COSERVERINFO csi = { 0, OLESTR("MyCLBS"), 0, 0 };
 MULTI_QI mqi = { &IID_Ibalanced, 0, 0 };

 IBalanced *pb = 0;
   hr = CoCreateInstanceEx(CLSID_Balanced, 0,
     LSCTX_REMOTE_SERVER, &csi, 1, &mqi);
 if (SUCCEEDED(hr))
 {
   (pb = reinterpret_cast<Ibalanced*>(mqi.pItf))->
     AddRef();
   mqi.pItf->Release();
   .
   .
   .

     // use object on MyServer

   pb->Release();
 }
```

Unfortunately, the current implementation of `CoCreateInstance()` and `CoCreateInstanceEx()` doesn't support returning an object reference to an object living on a server other than the one targeted by `CoCreateInstance()` or `CoCreateInstanceEx()`. In other words, if a client on a user's machine calls `CoCreateInstance()` or `CoCreateInstanceEx()` with the remote server named MyCLBS, and the class object running on MyCLBS attempts to return an interface pointer to an object it created on MyServer, the client's call always fails and returns `RPC_E_INVALID_OXID`, "The object exporter specified was not found."

An *OXID* is a machine-relative identifier of an apartment in which objects live. When an interface pointer is marshaled for transmission between contexts, it's represented by a low-level data type called an *OBJREF*, which is context-neutral and can be passed on the wire. Most objects rely on the standard COM marshaling plumbing to do the right thing when their interface pointers are passed between contexts. When their interface pointers are marshaled, the resulting standard OBJREF includes their OXID. When an OBJREF is unmarshaled into a destination context, the receiving machine translates the OXID into a set of RPC string bindings by calling back to the machine where the OXID exists, the address of which is also encoded in a standard OBJREF. The string bindings can be used to build an RPC binding handle that can be used to make remote calls back to the OXID's process on the original machine.

The server side of `CoCreateInstance()` and `CoCreateInstanceEx()` (it is a cross-context call) checks to ensure that the OXID in the OBJREF it is returning is valid on the machine where it is executing. (This is also the machine that the client originally targeted with its call.) If the OXID isn't on that machine, `CoCreateInstance()` and `CoCreateInstanceEx()` complain that the OXID is invalid, hence `RPC_E_INVALID_OXID` is returned. Although there are undoubtedly good reasons for the implementation to work this way, it feels incorrect to the COM philosophy because all object references should be equal. Because it is valid for a class object to return an object reference from another context on its own machine (this is how you do round-robin, single-threaded, and apartment-thread pools in MTS, ATL, and Visual Basic), it should be able to return an object reference from a context on another machine. But it can't, and this fact isn't going to change any time soon.

This wasn't a problem when a client used `CoGetClassObject()` because that method returned an object on the machine the client called. Unfortunately, the vast majority of COM clients are written using `CoCreateInstance()` and `CoCreateInstanceEx()`, or the Java and scripting languages, which are new in Visual Basic. So, the fact that `CoGetClassObject()` works is largely irrelevant.

Creating an Envelope

`CoCreateInstance()` seeks to know the OXID of the object reference being returned. This information can be hidden by placing the object reference into another object and returning a reference to that object instead. Here's the interface for `IEnvelope`:

```
[
   uuid(5E7F74C0-E165-11D2-B72C-00A0CC212296), object
]
interface IEnvelope : IUnknown
{
   [propput] HRESULT Letter([in] IUnknown *pUnk);
};
```

I modified my special class object's implementation of `CreateInstance` to hide the object it wants to return in an envelope it creates locally.

If the envelope used standard marshaling, `CoCreateInstance()` would succeed because the envelope lives in a context on the machine the client called. Clients, however, would end up with references to objects of the wrong type running on the wrong machine, in this case the CLBS. What clients want, of course, is a reference to the underlying object running on the ultimate destination server, `MyServer`. This can be achieved through the use of custom marshaling.

The first thing the remoting layer does when it attempts to marshal an interface pointer is check to see whether the object implements custom marshaling by calling `QueryInterface` and asking for `IMarshal`. If the object implements this interface, the remoting layer delegates to it the task of writing its context-neutral OBJREF. The envelope could custom marshal and carry as its payload the standard OBJREF for the remote object living on `MyServer`.

If the envelope uses custom marshaling, `CoCreateInstance()` still succeeds because it only checks OXIDs for standard-marshaled OBJREFs. Clients still end up with objects of the wrong type, although now they are running inside the clients' processes. This problem can be solved using some clever sleight-of-hand.

When an object custom marshals, the remoting layer asks it for a CLSID identifying a class that is capable of interpreting the payload it will write into the custom OBJREF. When a custom OBJREF is received in a destination context, an instance of this class is instantiated and asked to interpret the data and return a reference to an object. Although it is often the case that the object interpreting the custom payload returns a reference to itself (typical when implementing marshal-by-value), this isn't a requirement.

The object doing the unmarshaling can return a reference to any object it likes, and therein lies the key. If the envelope custom marshals, when it unmarshals back in the client's process, it can strip itself away simply by unmarshaling the standard OBJREF it hid in its payload and then returning a reference to the resultant proxy for the real remote object. This is why the `IEnvelope` interface shown previously uses a write-only property. There's no need for a `propget` method because the envelope opens itself.

The envelope returns its own CLSID in `GetUnmarshalClass` to indicate that another instance of this class will interpret its custom payload. In `GetMarshalSizeMax()` and `MarshalInterface()`, the envelope uses the marshaling APIs to delegate (to the letter) which standard marshals, so it will write a standard OBJREF as the custom marshal data. In `UnmarshalInterface()`, which is called in the client process when the envelope is returned from `CoCreateInstance()` or `CoCreateInstanceEx()`, the envelope unmarshals its payload and returns a reference to the resultant object. In this case, a proxy refers to the real remote object, wherever it runs.

Making the envelope trick work requires registering the envelope class on the CLBS machine and on each client machine. This is an additional burden, but a very cheap price to pay for making `CoCreateInstance()` and `CoCreateInstanceEx()` work with the forwarding class object.

Actually, there is one additional cost. The custom marshaling interface `IMarshal` includes the method `ReleaseMarshalData()`, which is called by the remoting architecture if it fails to unmarshal the custom payload in the receiver's context. This method call gives a custom-marshaling object a chance to clean up any extant server-side resources. If, for instance, an object was custom marshaling using sockets to pipe data, this would give the object a chance to close the socket it set up in `MarshalInterface()`.

Unfortunately, with objects that marshal by value (such as the envelope), this method isn't called because the server-side copy of the object has already been destroyed. For most marshal-by-value objects this is not a big deal because they don't carry references to objects. But the envelope does carry an object reference, and if it fails to unmarshal, the reference leaks. Luckily, the COM+ garbage collector kicks in and cleans up these leaked references within six minutes, so this shouldn't be a problem.

Algorithms

With a surrogate server hosting the forwarding class object and the envelope implementation in place, the basic framework needed to implement load balancing is complete. All that's missing is an algorithm for selecting remote machines. The astute observer will have noticed that all my code thus far always forwards creation requests to `MyServer`. There are lots of ways to choose a server to send work to, including (but not limited to) random, round-robin, CPU load, method invocation time, and expense of access over the network. This wide range of options suggests that the load-balancing algorithm is a prime candidate for being implemented as a pluggable component.

For my own pluggable algorithms, I defined the following interface:

```
[
   uuid(741F3750-E3B1-11d2-8117-00E09801FDBE), object
]
interface ILoadBalancingAlgorithm : IUnknown
{
   HRESULT CreateInstance([in] REFCLSID rclsid,
      [in] REFIID riid, [out, iid_is(riid)] void **ppv);
}
```

Assuming there is a precreated instance of an implementation of this interface, the forwarding class object's `CreateInstance` method can be rewritten.

It is up to the specific implementation of ILoadBalancingAlgorithm to decide how to implement CreateInstance(). Given a list of available servers (m_rgwszServers) and a count (m_nCount) as data members, a random algorithm could be implemented this way:

```
STDMETHODIMP CRandom::CreateInstance(REFCLSID rclsid,
    REFIID riid, void **ppv)
{
    *ppv = 0;

    COSERVERINFO csi = {0};

    csi.pwszName =
      m_rgwszServers[rand() % m_nCount];

    MULTI_QI mqi = { &riid, 0, 0 };

    HRESULT hr = CoCreateInstanceEx(rclsid, 0,
      CLSCTX_REMOTE_SERVER, &csi, 1, &mqi);
    if (SUCCEEDED(hr))
    {
      (*ppv = mqi.pItf)->AddRef();
      mqi.pItf->Release();
    }

    return hr;
}
```

The implementation of the round-robin algorithm is similar, but I really wanted COM+-style load balancing, so the algorithm I wanted was method timing. Remember that on Windows 2000, method timing is built in to the interceptors that wrap each object executing in the COM+ runtime environment. Achieving the same thing requires reaching deep down into the COM+ bag of tricks.

Timing Methods

COM+ supports an undocumented feature called channel hooks. Well, they are semi-documented in the Win32 header files. Microsoft does not officially support channel hooks on either Windows NT 4.0 or Windows 2000, and, if you're shy about these things, now is the time to flip to the next chapter. If you're still reading, then you've acknowledged that disclaimer, and I can get into the details.

A *channel hook* is an object registered into a COM+ process that is given the chance to piggyback data on the request and response messages sent by the RPC plumbing as part of every remote COM call. To support method timing, I built a channel hook that doesn't send any data, but does record the start time of a call into a server and, upon completion of the call, measures the time that the method took to complete.

The channel hook maintains timing data in a stack of CALLINFO structures:

```
struct CALLINFO
{
    time_t tStart;         // start time of call
    GUID guidCausality;    // current causality
    struct CALLINFO *pNext; // pointer to next callinfo
                            // on stack
};
```

which it stores in thread local storage (TLS). Whenever a call comes into the server, the channel hook's ServerNotify method is called. It creates a new CALLINFO structure, initializes it with the current time and causality, and adds it to the stack in TLS.

Whenever a call is about to leave the server, the channel hook's ServerFillBuffer() method is called (actually ServerGetSize() is called, but because it specifies a nonzero size, ServerFillBuffer() is called). The ServerFillBuffer() implementation pops the top CALLINFO off the stack and searches the remaining nodes to see whether there is another CALLINFO with the same causality. If it doesn't find one, the CALLINFO it just popped off the stack represents a top-level call. ServerFillBuffer() calculates the difference between the CALLINFO's tStart time and the current time and aggregates this data into two global variables, g_nCount and g_nTime (more about these later). If ServerFillBuffer() does find a CALLINFO with a matching causality, the one it just popped off the stack represents a nested call, so it is ignored. The time the nested call took to complete is automatically included in the time it took its top-level call (represented by the CALLINFO with the same causality deeper in the stack) to complete.

For this implementation of method timing to work, the channel hook has to be loaded into a server process. Because I didn't want to make any changes to server code, I opted to load the channel hook via a proxy/stub DLL. This does require a minimal amount of work; proxy/stub code has to be linked against some additional code that provides a new DLL entry point called NewDllMain.

NewDllMain() creates an instance of a class called Loader, which is implemented by the channel hook DLL. Creating the object causes the hook DLL, which must be registered on any machine where the proxy/stub DLL is registered, to load. In its implementation of DllMain(), the code creates and registers the channel hook object. When that's done, the loader object is released; there is no need to hold it because the channel hook DLL's implementation of DllCanUnloadNow() always returns FALSE.

The last thing this code does is delegate to the DllMain() function provided by the proxy/stub infrastructure in the dlldata.c file generated by the MIDL compiler. This function must be called to give the proxy/stub DLL a chance to initialize itself. The /entry linker switch is used to remap the proxy/stub DLL's entry point to the

NewDllMain() function in place of the original DllMain(). The makefile also compiles and links MethodTimeHookPS.cpp, which contains the code for the new entry point.

By default, dual and oleautomation interfaces rely on the Universal Marshaler to build proxies and stubs on-the-fly, based on the information in their typelibs. These interfaces can be made to work with the method-timing channel hook simply by building a standard proxy/stub DLL for them instead. ATL makes this easy because the wizards emit interface definitions outside the ATL-created IDL file's library statement. The MIDL compiler generates proxy/stub code for any interfaces defined outside a library, so the code is already there, just waiting to be used. Visual Basic generates typelibs directly, but the IDL can be reverse-engineered using OleView or an equivalent tool. At installation time, dual and oleautomation interface proxy/stub DLLs need to be registered after the servers with embedded typelibs so that typelib registration doesn't overwrite their registration.

All of this grungy proxy/stub work can be avoided simply by linking the method-timing channel hook DLL directly into a server process, but this requires inserting the key portion of NewDllMain() into the server's startup sequence, which I was trying to avoid.

```
HRESULT hr = CoCreateInstance(CLSID_Loader, 0,
  CLSCTX_INPROC_SERVER, IID_IUnknown, (void**)&pUnk);
if (SUCCEEDED(hr)) pUnk->Release();
```

The Method-Timing Algorithm

The previous section explained how the method-timing channel hook collects data about COM calls. This information acts as input for a method-timing algorithm encapsulated by a MethodTiming class implementing the pluggable algorithm interface, ILoadBalancingAlgorithm. It keeps a list of available servers and periodically picks the one that is least loaded. To make this decision, the algorithm needs to collect the timing data stored on each server. Notice that the global variables that the channel hook's ServerFillBuffer() method updates are declared inside a special segment that is mapped into shared memory.

```
#pragma data_seg("Shared")

long g_nCount = 0;
long g_nTime = 0;

#pragma data_seg()

#pragma comment(linker, "/section:Shared,rws")
```

This means the data stored in g_nCount and g_nTime is shared across all processes that load the channel hook DLL on a given machine.

Retrieving this information from a particular server is simply a matter of instantiating an object in a process on that server that loads the channel hook code. The object then returns the data in response to a method call. The Loader class exposed by the channel hook DLL is designed to do this. Here's its interface, `ILoader`:

```
[
    uuid(233108A2-E3CD-11D2-8117-00E09801FDBE), object
]
interface ILoader : IUnknown
{
    HRESULT GetAverageMethodTime(
        [out, retval] long *pnAvg);
};
```

To enable a Loader object to be created remotely, I configured the channel hook DLL to support activation using the standard COM surrogate process, dllhost.exe.

The implementation of the MethodTiming() class uses remote Loader objects on each server in an application cluster to collect timing data. Each time the data is retrieved, the algorithm uses the new information about each machine's current state to decide which one to send work. It sends all creation requests to that machine until it finds another with better timing statistics. All this work is done on a separate thread to not slow down the handling of client creation requests.

The actual process of analyzing timing data and selecting a machine deserves a little more attention. I wasn't able to find a documented algorithm for load balancing based on method timing, so I cooked one up on my own. It isn't as tuned as I would like it to be, but it is better than what I started with. In essence, the Loader object hooks the timing data to return "task-seconds" per interval, where task-seconds is the total time of all measured COM calls ending in the interval. The interval is controlled by the algorithm object's thread, which sleeps for half a second between polling the servers. The `Loader` also changes the signal slightly as the data is represented as longs, and the implicit integer division means fractional values would be dropped.

As noted previously, all the data collection and analysis work is done on a separate thread so as not to interfere with client creation requests. This separate thread is started when a MethodTiming object is initialized and executes the `MethodTimeMonitor` function. The function is passed a pointer to the MethodTiming object that created it. Every half second the thread wakes up and polls each of the machines in the object's list of servers. The list is maintained as an array of HostTimeInfo structures, each of which contains a machine's name, a reference to a remote Loader object running on that machine, and a current average method time value:

```
typedef struct HostTimeInfo
{
    OLECHAR *wsz;          // name of machine
```

```
    ILoader *pl;          // Loader on machine
    long nAvgMethodTime; // timing data for machine
} HostTimeInfo;
```

The thread walks the array (m_rghti), calls to each server's Loader to get the latest timing data, and stores the lowest value as an index (m_phti). (A more sophisticated implementation would do this polling on separate threads.)

Notice that it softens the impact of dramatic timing changes by only applying a quarter of the delta between the current timing value and the value from the previous reading. When a forwarding class object calls to a MethodTiming object's CreateInstance() method:

```
STDMETHODIMP CMethodTiming::CreateInstance(
  REFCLSID rclsid, REFIID riid, void **ppv)
{
  COSERVERINFO csi = {0};

  csi.pwszName = m_phti->wsz;

  MULTI_QI mqi = { &riid, 0, 0 };

  HRESULT hr = CoCreateInstanceEx(rclsid, 0,
    CLSCTX_REMOTE_SERVER, &csi, 1, &mqi);
  if (FAILED(hr)) return hr;

  (*ppv = mqi.pItf)->AddRef();
  mqi.pItf->Release();

  return hr;
}
```

the creation request is forwarded to the server that is currently least loaded, as identified by the m_phti pointer.

All the decisions I made about frequency of polling and my recipe for cooking the data are based entirely on simple empirical study on my set of hosts using my test client and server. Mileage in other situations can vary.

Making It Real

The prototype load-balancing service I implemented uses all the techniques described here, but there are a few other things worth noting. The heart of my infrastructure is a Windows NT service installed on a CLBS that registers forwarding class objects for load-balanced classes. The service is configured to use a particular algorithm and list of servers; both settings are defined in the registry under

```
HKEY_LOCAL_MACHINE\Software\DevelopMentor\LoadBalancing\RoutingServer
```

(`RoutingServer` was the earlier name for a CLBS.) Subkeys under the `RoutingServer` key specify servers in the application cluster.

The DefaultAlgorithm–named value specifies the ProgID or CLSID of a class that implements `ILoadBalancingAlgorithm`. Four implementations are provided: random, round-robin, method timing (which I described), and CPU load (based on Performance Monitor statistics gathered via the Performance Data Helper library).

Finally, because it needs to make calls to remote machines, the load-balancing service can't run as System. It must be configured to execute as a discriminated user account instead.

As with COM+, classes must be configured to support load balancing. Classes indicate their desire to be load balanced by registering on the CLBS under a new class category, Load Balanced Classes. The classes must also be registered as having the same AppID as the load-balancing service to avoid problems with activation identity. If they aren't, the service's attempts to register class objects succeeds, but client attempts to access the class objects fail, returning `CLASS_E_CLASSNOTREGISTERED`. As with COM+, clients must be configured to send creation requests to a CLBS where the load-balancing service is running.

Other Balancing and Clustering Technologies

There are a couple of general topics that are relevant to both the COM+ load-balancing infrastructure and to any scratch-built implementation. First, it's helpful to understand the relationship between these services and load balancing and clustering technologies.

The NLB Service is a little-known add-on to Windows NT Server Enterprise Edition that Microsoft purchased from Valence Research (the original product was called Convoy). It provides load balancing for TCP services across a cluster of up to 32 machines, which all appear, from a client's perspective, to have the same IP address. All the machines see a client's connection request arrive, but only one of them services it as determined by an undocumented algorithm. That node handles further work until the connection is broken and a new one is established.

Windows Clustering Server (WCS) provides redundancy by configuring a pair of machines as reflections of one another addressed via a common IP address. Both machines are attached to a shared hard disk that lives on a common bus. If one fails, the other takes its place, with fast access to the same persistent data.

Both NLB and WCS are similar to the component load-balancing services I've examined here. All three have clients sending requests to a single IP address; they all service those requests using multiple machines. There are, however, a couple key differences.

First, the component load-balancing mechanisms offer finer-grained control than NLB because their behavior is parameterized based on CLSID. The NLB has no notion of the purpose of a given connection, meaning it can't differentiate between URLs being sent in HTTP requests, so it treats all requests and all clustered machines as identical.

Next, the component load-balancing mechanisms, such as the NLB, can spread work across more than two nodes, whereas WCS cannot. On the other hand, WCS nodes share a disk, which is important for storage services like databases or groupware messaging stores but provides little benefit to the majority of COM servers.

Finally, and most importantly, although all three infrastructures use a single IP address for client requests, machines in an NLB or WCS cluster share that IP address, and machines in a component load-balancing cluster do not. In the latter case, the IP address identifies a single machine (the CLBS). If that machine fails, the entire service collapses. Adding the CLBS to an NLB or WCS cluster can solve this problem.

JIT Activation

It's also useful to understand the relationship between the COM+ load-balancing infra-structure or any scratch-built implementation and the just-in-time (JIT) activation capa-bilities of MTS and COM+. In either runtime environment, an object can agree to be deactivated by setting its done bit (via `SetComplete()`, `SetAbort()`, or in the future, `SetDeactivateOnReturn()`) during a call.

When the call completes, the interception layer releases the object. The object is replaced on-the-fly the next time a client makes a call (hence the name JIT). Because the intercep-tion layer stays in place, the new object is always re-created in the same context in the same process on the same machine in perpetuity; load balancing does not occur.

Load balancing happens at connection creation time, not at object activation time. In order to support load balancing at object activation time, the underlying remoting layer would have to be able to update all extant proxies with a new network address to send work. The records kept by the OXID Resolver on each machine with an extant proxy would also have to be updated so that the distributed garbage collection pinging protocol continued to work. Both are nontrivial tasks. But beyond the complexity is the potential performance hit, especially for objects that continually deactivate themselves. Doing all this work on each method call would make method calls very expensive.

The solution is to have a client release its proxy, tear down its connection, and re-create it by issuing another creation request and giving the load balancer a chance to kick in again. At first this seems like an unpleasant burden for clients, but they should already be prepared to do this in case they lose communication with a particular server. Some form of smart proxy could hide this detail from a client, but for now that task is left to developers.

Summary

Load balancing can solve many of the problems with enterprise applications. It provides scalability, availability, and flexibility. Load balancing should not require any change in the program model, so well-designed components are ready for load balancing out of the gate.

Unfortunately, Windows 2000 has not shipped with the load-balancing service. This is because Microsoft could not address all the issues surrounding load balancing before the shipment of Windows 2000. AppCenter Server will have the load-balancing service and will make load balancing more of an administrative task than anything. Until then, you'll have to rely on your own resources as you have in previous enterprise development.

But if you're able to get access to AppCenter Server when you read this book, you're in luck. The principles and techniques you learned in this chapter will serve you well.

Optimizing Windows DNA Applications

IN THIS CHAPTER

Developing an enterprise application is difficult because many months go into the effort. After the arduous development stage, though, you might go through a sequence of testing procedures only to find that the application bogs down under heavy loads.

The first thing that comes to mind in order to fix the problem is to give the servers substantial upgrades so that the application can handle the projected usage. But that is expensive in terms of hardware and network administration, and the servers will all have some down time. This is not what your client wants to hear.

If you're lucky, you'll easily find some performance-gaining steps you can take. You might even find something with a relatively small amount of investigation time. Some simple items such as changing from a File to a System DSN can make all the difference.

This scenario plays out in most software development shops at one time or another. A simple change can make an enormous difference in performance and save the day. Even more frustrating is the situation in which an application is deployed with great expectations, only to find that it can't handle heavy usage situations. This chapter addresses many of the Windows Distributed interNet Architecture (Windows DNA) performance issues, and shows you how to test your applications before you go live.

I'll start off with some Windows DNA performance topics, and give you some optimization techniques that you can apply right away. I'll also talk about using the Microsoft Windows DNA Performance Kit to benchmark your Windows DNA applications. Since COM+ is such a big part of Windows DNA, the DNA kit helps test your components within the Windows DNA framework.

Assessing Your Needs

Before you dive headlong into the Windows DNA optimization morass, you need to ascertain your goal. It's possible that your application is ready even without any optimization. The most important hard number you'll need is the number of transactions per second (TPS) that the application must support. Two variables determine this: the application Think Time and the number of current users.

Think Time is the amount of human interaction time for each transaction. This includes reading and viewing screens, making decisions, and making selections or typing input. If your application is an order-entry system, the Think Time is the amount of time it takes for a user to view the catalog, decide what to buy, and select the desired items in the user interface.

To calculate the required TPS, divide the number of users by the Think Time as shown in the following formula:

Optimizing Windows DNA Applications

CHAPTER 21

543

21

OPTIMIZING
WINDOWS DNA
APPLICATIONS

$$\text{Transactions Per Second} \quad = \quad \frac{\text{Number of Users}}{\text{Think Time (in seconds)}}$$

With a target TPS value in hand, you can determine if your application can handle the projected load. The determination might be a result of your own testing, or a result of using the Windows DNA Performance Kit (more on this in the second half of this chapter). The story isn't over, though, when you test and find out that everything works well enough for the next 12 months. Consider the following:

- Will traffic increase at any time to outpace the capacity of the application before it's upgraded?
- Will you rely on any of the components in the current version for the next version of the application?
- Will other applications be deployed to the same server reducing its capabilities for this application?

On the first point, I've found it rare that traffic increases past expectations. That doesn't mean it won't happen, but management and marketing have a way of spinning everything so that projections are always rosy. As a matter of fact, I'm still waiting for throughput to meet the expectations of management on any project.

As for the second point, management always thinks you can reuse components in the next version without alteration. They don't realize that what delivered adequate performance last year can turn out to be a bottleneck in the next version of the application. This is usually a result of newer components being based on newer, more efficient technology outpacing the components built on older technology. You have to decide before deploying a component if it will be expected to serve in a new version of the application, and if it can handle the increased demands. You might or might not decide that modifications are needed based on the constraints of the project.

The third point is difficult as well. A server that's humming along is easy prey for overutilization. When someone's budget is short, the first things targeted are servers that can accommodate an additional application. If another application is installed on the server where your application is performing perfectly, you might suddenly be faced with a performance hit that it can't sustain. Plan for this eventuality in advance. I have been burned this way several times.

Optimization Tips

In this section, I'll talk about some specific ways to optimize your Windows DNA applications. Check out some helpful optimization hints, such as implementing user or system

DSNs instead of file DSNs, avoiding Registry access, using just-in-time (JIT)activation, and a host of other tips that will enhance the performance of your DNA applications.

Implement User or System DSN Instead of File DSN

As mentioned earlier, a User or System DSN gives better performance than a File DSN. That's because a File DSN requires more resources, including RAM and CPU cycles. In Microsoft's DNA Performance Kit, the documentation contains a graph showing the results when changing from a File DSN to a System DSN. The performance in its example increased 577%. For this reason, avoid File DSNs whenever possible.

Optimize Algorithms, Especially Iterative Loops

It is amazing how much difference a simple algorithmic change can make. This is especially evident inside of loops. Compare, for example, the two code fragments for similar loops in the following:

Loop—Version One:

```
for( i=0; i<10000; i++ )
  {
    for( j=0; j<10000; j++ )
    {
      nValue = ( 10000 - i - 1 ) * 50 + j;
    }
  }
```

Loop—Version Two:

```
for( i=0; i<10000; i++ )
  {
    nTemp = ( 10000 - i - 1 ) * 50;
    for( j=0; j<10000; j++ )
    {
     nValue = nTemp + j;
    }
  }
```

I created a COM+ object with two classes, CVersionOne and CVersionTwo. CVersionOne implements the first loop in a method named Perform(). CVersionTwo implements the second loop in a method also named Perform(). Each class also has a property named Milliseconds that contains the number of milliseconds it took to execute the method. After calling both methods from a Visual Basic program on a 350Mhz Pentium II, I found the second code fragment that uses a temporary variable to reduce the amount of computations inside of the inner loop to be significantly faster as Table 21.1 shows.

Optimizing Windows DNA Applications

CHAPTER 21

545

21

OPTIMIZING
WINDOWS DNA
APPLICATIONS

TABLE 21.1 Results of the Two Loops

Class	Milliseconds	Percent Performance Increase
CVersionOne	2975	n/a
CVersionTwo	2063	30.65

The ATL and Visual Basic projects can be found in the Chapter21 directory on the CD-ROM.

> **Note**
>
> If you compile the Algorithm COM object in anything but debug mode, the efficient compiler that comes with Visual C++ sees that nothing is actually being done. The code reduces to nothing as the compiler optimizes the `Perform()` method to practically nothing. The Visual Basic program then simply gets a value of zero milliseconds for the time it takes to call each method.

Avoid Registry Access

For standalone applications, Registry access is fast enough. That's because most standalone applications make a minimum number of trips to the Registry. A component that's part of a middle tier is an entirely different matter. Although the trip to the Registry exacts a small price in itself, it quickly compounds with a large-scale application.

I wrote a COM object that opens and reads a single Registry string 10,000 times to find out a hard number for how expensive Registry access really is. The code fragment that does the work is shown in Listing 21.1.

LISTING 21.1 Reading a Registry String 10,000 Times

```
void CWorker::ReadRegistryString( HKEY Key, DWORD dwSize,
  const char *pszKeyname, const char *pszDataname, void *pRetbuffer )
{
  HKEY hKey;

  if( RegOpenKeyEx( Key, pszKeyname, 0, KEY_ALL_ACCESS, &hKey )
    != ERROR_SUCCESS )
    return;

  RegQueryValueEx( hKey, pszDataname, NULL, NULL,
    (unsigned char *) pRetbuffer, &dwSize );
```

LISTING 21.1   Continued

```
  RegCloseKey( hKey );

}

STDMETHODIMP CWorker::Perform()
{
  char szBuffer[500];

  DWORD dwStart = GetTickCount();

  for( int i= 0;i<10000; i++ )
  {
    ReadRegistryString( HKEY_LOCAL_MACHINE, sizeof( szBuffer ),
      "SOFTWARE\\RefillMinder\\RefillMinder",
      "DrugInfoDatabase", szBuffer );
  }

  m_dwMilliseconds = GetTickCount() - dwStart;

  return S_OK;
}
```

From a Visual Basic program, I called the `Perform()` method. It took 802 milliseconds for the call to `Perform()`. This equates to about .08 milliseconds per Registry access. Although this is small, avoiding it might save you a great deal of time under heavy traffic situations.

The ATL and Visual Basic projects can be found in the Chapter21 directory on the CD-ROM.

Use Just-in-Time Activation Whenever Possible

One of the general techniques of optimization is to use resources as late as possible and release as early as possible. This ties up resources for the shortest period of time. Tight resources can steal performance from components as quickly as anything else. This can be caused by several things, but the first and most likely cause is that the system performs virtual memory swapping when RAM gets low. Resources can also be pooled more efficiently when their usage time is short.

Just-in-time activation (JIT) allows MTS and COM+ to manage objects so that they can be easily reused and pooled. This means that even if an object is created, it won't tie up resources until it's needed.

There's a program in the Windows DNA Performance Kit named MTCLIENT (I'm ahead of myself already) that makes a great case for this argument. You can turn JIT on and off with command-line arguments when executing the program. In my test, I found JIT increased the performance by more than sixteen times, from 5174 TPS to 86882 TPS, as shown in Table 21.2.

TABLE 21.2 JIT Performance Increases

Uses JIT	TPS	Percent Performance Increase
No	5174	n/a
Yes	86882	1679.2

Fix Resource Leaks

Resource leaks, even small ones, can slow a server to an absolute crawl over time. Suppose, for example, that a component fails to deallocate 1024 bytes. After 1024 instantiations of the component, you have 1MB (megabyte) of locked RAM. Before long, that 1MB becomes 2MB, and so on. Even with lots of memory, the server starts to slow down as it relies on the swap file for virtual memory. Worse yet, the server will probably eventually crash.

I have personally learned how costly component memory leaks can be. I wrote a component that did some special email handling for a Web application. It had a memory leak of 12 bytes per instance. Over a two-month period, the server bogged down and then crashed. Of course, the system administrator was the one worrying over it. I was obliviously leading my life as if nothing were wrong. But six months after the component was in use, they had tracked the slowdown and crashing problems to the component. Needless to say, I had to do some talking just to get out of the system administrator's office alive.

The point is this: a resource leak of any kind, no matter how small, degrades performance over time. Testing for and eliminating resource leaks should be a high priority when you or your team members develop components.

The code in Listing 21.2 illustrates how easily it can happen. If the file doesn't open, a return is made before the char buffer is deallocated.

LISTING 21.2 An Easy-To-Miss Memory Leak

```
void MyMethod( void )
{
  char *pszBuffer;
  HFILE hFile;
```

LISTING 21.2   Continued

```
pszBuffer = new char [1024];

hFile = _lopen( "TestFile.txt", OF_READ );
if( hFile == HFILE_ERROR )
  return;

_lread( hFile, pszBuffer, 1024 );
_lclose( hFile );

delete [] pszBuffer;

}
```

You might be looking at that simple code example and saying, "I never do that, I'm more careful." Sure you are. Don't forget that the more complex the code, though, the more room for error. Everyone must be eternally vigilant to prevent memory leaks.

Balance Object-Oriented Component Architecture with Practicality

This topic is an invitation for dissent regardless of what I say. The debate over this rages on. In one camp, are those who take a pragmatic approach and almost forsake object-oriented (OO) principles in the name of performance. In the other camp are the OO purists who say that good software design carries the day in any situation.

One point to consider is that OO components are typically slower and larger than their non-OO counterparts. This means that under MTS and COM+, you have to worry about whether they consume too much in the way of resources, and chew up too many CPU cycles. Microsoft seems to be backpedaling from pure OO design in its effort to achieve scalability. Its emphasis is shifting to using many small classes that each do very little. Although this helps in the scalability arena, it hurts in the maintainability arena.

I had a recent experience in which I took over a VB project that was developed by someone else. The application concept was pretty simple and straightforward: Although a single method call with one or two arguments would have sufficed, there were 20 properties to look through and understand in the code. This cost an additional 40% of my time to make the required modifications to the application over what a less object-oriented code base would have yielded. The person who wrote the original code was fresh out of school, and he hadn't been on the receiving end of an application such as this. He'll have his day.

Many find that OO hierarchies give extremely poor performance in VB components. These same developers have broken those classes out into separate components. One of the reasons is that smaller, discreet components work better because of the load time of the component being shorter. Many classes, even if they are simple, in a VB project produce larger compiled components. For MTS and COM+, this is bad. It's better to have more smaller components; in fact, in VB they should be compiled for small size preferred over faster code.

You can't throw away OO principles. They have tremendous merit. When your application grows into a huge enterprise application, OO is a good thing because of the organization it provides. But you can't forget performance and the resource issues, either. Everything I do now is a balance of the two. I keep things object-oriented when I can, and don't worry so much about OO architecture when it hurts performance and resource allocation past an unacceptable level.

The Right Language for the Job

Obviously you must decide on a language with which to develop a component. Visual Basic allows for quick and robust component development. Visual C++ takes longer, is more prone to bugs, but gives better performance. I haven't used Visual J++ in any real-life settings, but many choose it for a variety of tasks. (Visual J++ is usually chosen because it is very easy to develop components with, and unlike Visual Basic, it is truly object-oriented.)

Avoid Middle Tier State

To achieve scalability and performance, you shouldn't use stateful components. Specific issues exist with using the Session and Application objects to store state of any kind. Not the least of these issues is the current inability to scale such objects across multiple servers. This becomes especially problematic (even in single-server deployments) when someone attempts to cache object instances, such as database connections in Session or Application objects.

Avoid Data Access in the Middle Tier

Developers (especially those under a tight deadline) sometimes directly perform tasks on data from the middle tier where the business logic resides. I know that rules can be hard and inflexible, and there are times when they should be broken, but it would be unusual to find a justification for breaking this one. Direct data access in a middle tier while in a Windows DNA application is likely to perform more poorly than it would otherwise.

For example, it would be a mistake to retrieve multiple data sets from different tables and then join, sort, or search the data in middle-tier objects. The database is designed to handle this kind of activity and removing it to a middle tier is almost certainly a bad practice. True, there might be circumstances in which doing so is called for because of the nature of the data store, but as much of this as possible should happen in the database before the dataset is returned to the middle tier.

Using the Microsoft Windows DNA Performance Kit

Now that you have encountered several optimization tips, you will learn about using the Microsoft Windows DNA Performance Kit to test your own applications. It's a great way to test components under simulated conditions. And you get a pretty accurate indication of how the application components will perform in a live situation.

You might be smugly saying to yourself, "My components are already optimized. I know how to write tight code." I've said that myself a time or two, only to be wrong. The first time was in 1991 when some of us still wrote graphics functions in assembly language. I had carefully calculated the number of machines cycles for each line of code and just knew I couldn't get the function any faster. Still, the performance wasn't what I would have liked. Then I read Michael Abrash's very next column, and learned a brilliant way to do the same thing with a 25 percent reduction in execution time. So much for calculating machine cycles!

The other point I'd like to make is that real-life situations can throw you curves you don't expect. For instance, when resources get tight during heavy traffic conditions, virtual memory swapping may make your component slower than you ever imaged it could be. That's why testing is so important. Until the rubber hits the road and your component is in action in a real-life situation or a simulation thereof, you can't be sure it's as fast as it can be.

First, you need to get and install the Perfomance Kit. To download the setup program, go to `http://www.microsoft.com/Com/resources/WinDNAperf.asp` and click on the "Windows DNA Performance Kit Beta" link. The installation is a simple setup process as Figure 21.1 shows.

Getting Ready to Use the Kit

Almost all the Kit's functionality requires SQL Server 6.5 or 7.0. Before you go any further, make sure that the system you're going to use as a test machine has a proper SQL Server installation, and that it is running properly.

The Kit needs a database with a number of tables. There's a batch file that comes in the Kit that creates the database device, database, and tables for you. At a command prompt, go to the \WinDNAPerf\Source\Scripts directory. Get everything set up in the database, and type the following:

```
buildall c:\ c:\ . 10
```

FIGURE 21.1

*Installing the
Windows DNA
Performance Kit is
simple.*

The process takes several minutes, depending on the speed of your computer. You'll see
the various machinations it goes through, as shown in Figure 21.2.

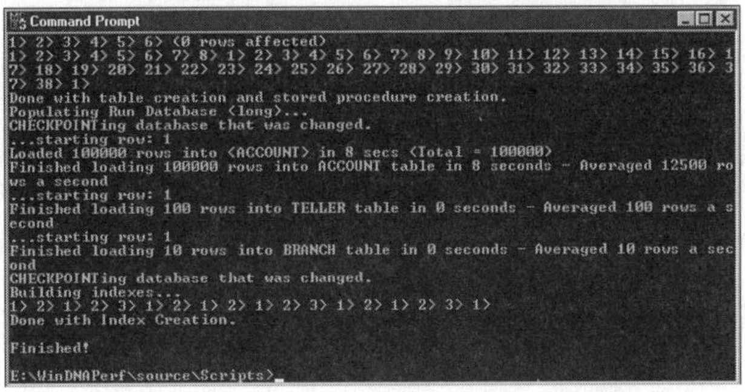

FIGURE 21.2

*Building the data-
base objects.*

Two of the tables are especially important for your tests because the Kit looks at these
tables to get much of the information is uses for the tests. For instance, you can specify
the component that you want tested by changing the ProdID field in the
ComConfiguration table.

A .vbs file comes with the Kit that provides some default values for the
ComConfiguration table. Among these default values are those necessary to test the
IBank component that comes with the Kit. Run the populate.vbs script from the
\WinDNAPerf\Source\Scripts directory.

After you've populated the ComConfiguration table, you can run your first test. Change
to the \WinDNAPerf\Bin directory. From the command line, enter the following:

```
WinDNALoadController -Ftest.ini
```

By default, an instantiation of the IBank component is tested. The default configuration
specifies a ramp up time of 150 seconds, a normal runtime of 90 seconds, and a ramp
down time of 20 seconds. The ramp up and ramp down times enable the testing to simulate a situation that's closer to what actually happens in real circumstances. You can see
this default test running in Figure 21.3.

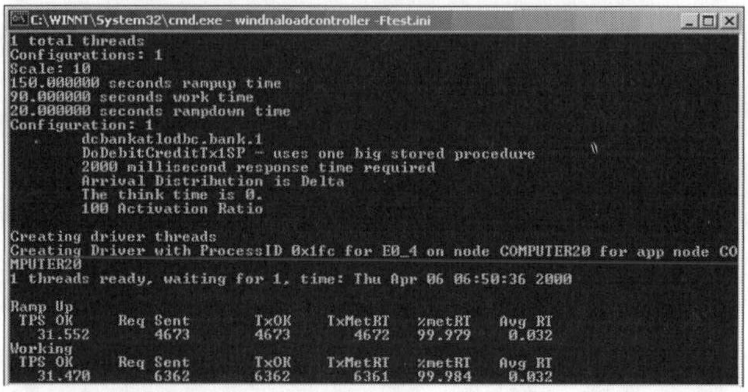

FIGURE 21.3

This default test shows the screen output of the Kit's controller.

Before you edit the ComConfiguration table so that you can test your own components, you'll need to know what fields are in the tables and what each one contains. The ComConfiguration database table can be seen in Figure 21.4; its corresponding fields are shown in Table 21.3.

FIGURE 21.4

The ComConfiguration table.

TABLE 21.3 The ComConfiguration Fields

Field Name	Type	Description
ConfigID	Int	A unique identifier for a Configuration.
ArrivalDist	Int	The random number distribution to be used in calculating the Think Time. A 0 indicates a Delta distribution, a 1 indicates a Uniform distribution, a 2 indicates an Exponential distribution, and a 3 indicates a Normal distribution.
ThinkTimeMean	Int	The average Think Time.
ThinkTimeMax	Int	The maximum Think Time.
ThinkTimeMin	Int	The minimum Think Time.

TABLE 21.3 Continued

Field Name	Type	Description
ThinkTimeSTDDev	Int	The standard deviation of the Think Time. This parameter only has an effect for the Normal distribution.
ActivationRatio	Int	The percentage of method calls that are not accompanied by an object creation. A value of 100 indicates that all calls should use just-in-time activation.
ResponseTimeMax	Int	The maximum response time allowed for a method call to be considered successful.
InterfaceID	Int	A number indicating what interface the component supports. For example, 1 indicates that the IBank interface should be used.
ProgID	Varchar(64)	The ProgID of the component to be tested.
Method	Int	A number indicating which method should be tested.
RespTimeThreshold	Int	Reserved for future use.
Throttle	Int	Reserved for future use.
OutstandingRequests	Int	Number of unfulfilled requests.

The Scenario table can be seen next in Figure 21.5, and its corresponding fields are shown in Table 21.4. Notice that it gives you the ability to set the test characteristics such as the RampUp and RampDown times.

FIGURE 21.5

The Scenario table.

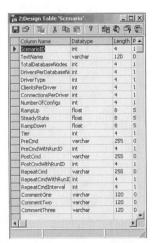

TABLE 21.4 The Scenario Fields

Field Name	Type	Description
ScenarioID	Int	A unique identifier for a test.
TestName	Varchar(120)	The name of the test.
TotalDatabaseNodes	Int	The total number of database nodes to be used in the test.
DriversPerDatabaseNode	Int	The number of Drivers used per database node. The total number of drivers is this number times TotalDatabaseNodes.
DriverType	Int	A number to indicate what type of driver to use. For example, a 1 indicates a COM driver, whereas a 2 indicates a Web driver.
ClientsPerDriver	Int	The number of clients used for each driver node. The total number of clients for a test is TotalDatabaseNodes× DriversPerDatabaseNode×ClientsPerDriver. This value only applies to the COM driver.
ConnectionsPerDriver	Int	The number of connections to use for the Web driver.
NumberOfConfigs	Int	The number of configurations from the Configuration table to be used.
RampUp	Float	The number of seconds the experiment should stay in Ramp Up. Statistics will not be kept for this period.
SteadyState	Float	The number of seconds the experiment should stay in Steady State. Statistics will be kept for this period.
RampDown	Float	The number of seconds the experiment should stay in Ramp Down. Statistics will not be kept for this period.
Tier	Int	The number of tiers to use in a test.
PreCmd	Varchar(255)	A command that the Controller should run at the beginning of the test.
PreCmdWithRunID	Int	Whether the pre-command should be passed the Token, RunID, DatabaseName, UserName, and the Database NodeName of the test. A 1 indicates that they should be passed; a 0 indicates that they should not be passed.

Optimizing Windows DNA Applications
CHAPTER 21

555

21

OPTIMIZING
WINDOWS DNA
APPLICATIONS

TABLE 21.4 Continued

Field Name	Type	Description
PostCmd	Varchar(255)	A command the Controller should run after a test.
PostCmdWithRunID	Int	Whether the post-command should be passed the Token, RunID, DatabaseName, UserName, and the NodeName of the test. A 1 indicates that they should be passed; a 0 indicates that they should not be passed.
RepeatCmd	Varchar(255)	A command the Controller should run periodically during a test.
RepeatCmdWithRunID	Int	Whether the repeat command should be passed the Token, RunID, DatabaseName, UserName, and the NodeName of the test. A 1 indicates that they should be passed; a 0 indicates that they should not be passed.
RepeatCmdInterval	Int	The interval, in seconds, that the controller should wait
CommentOne	Varchar(120)	A comment about the test.
CommentTwo	Varchar(120)	A comment about the test.
CommentThree	Varchar(120)	A comment about the test.

Viewing the Results of a Test

Of course, after you run a test, you'll want to see and understand the results. It's easy to get the basics, such as transactions per second and requests sent, because you can see these statistics in the command window while the test is being run, as you saw in Figure 21.3. These numbers are saved to an .out file that you can read with any text editor.

Summary

Large-scale, enterprise applications are complex. Getting them to perform at an acceptable level can be an enormous challenge, especially when the application load is heavy.

The first thing you must do is to assess your needs. An application that performs up to snuff doesn't need optimization, and you don't want to waste time doing so.

Some relatively simple considerations can make a big difference. On the list of things to note are DSN types, algorithm efficiency, using JIT, Registry use, avoiding memory leaks, language considerations, and middle-tier architecture. And some of these can make a difference of more than 1000%.

Asynchronous Component Programming

PART
IV

IN THIS PART

CHAPTER 22

Programming Loosely Coupled Systems

The more dissimilar two systems are, the less likely they are to operate effectively when rigidly connected. Operations that take a considerable amount of time on one system can often be dispatched quickly by another. The process of communicating between two heterogeneous systems can also require lengthy translation. This mismatch severely limits the effectiveness of traditional function call semantics. This chapter examines the benefits of messaging as a means to creating loosely coupled systems in an enterprise setting.

What Is Messaging?

Messaging is the process of sending a completely encapsulated set of data between two application components. These messages provide a loose communications channel between the two components, as shown in Figure 22.1. Messages can travel in one or both directions. Messaging components can exist on the same thread, on different threads in the same process, in different processes on the same computer, or even in different processes on different computers with completely different architectures.

FIGURE 22.1
Message-based communication.

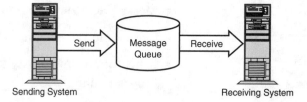

Sending System   Receiving System

Windows messaging is a testament to the power and flexibility of message passing. The entire event-driven Windows user interface operates through messages, queues, and message processing procedures. This same concept can be extended to the enterprise to allow application components to collaborate across networks.

Messaging Strengths

Messaging systems provide several unique advantages over traditional functionally coupled applications. The following list highlights some of these strengths:

- Communications between dissimilar systems
- Communications between highly dynamic components
- Asynchronous communications
- Fully offline communications
- Broadcast communications
- Efficient use of bandwidth

Enhancing Large-Scale Application Development with Messaging

Messaging can solve several critical problems that arise in large-scale application development. Messaging systems are often used to communicate between two nodes that are not always available at the same time. Comparing the postal system to the phone system is a good way to contrast message-oriented services with online communications. For example, sending a letter is a good way to reach someone who never answers the phone. Further, mail can be tracked as it is received; it can be translated and forwarded among other things. Mail will, perhaps unfortunately, still be waiting for you when you get home from vacation. In fact, mail has several advantages over a direct phone conversation in the right environment.

Software messaging takes this same concept and applies it to application development and distributed component communications. Through messaging, client components gain the capability to send messages at their convenience. Servers can collect the queued messages at any later point in time. Messages can be translated during transmission between dissimilar systems such as PCs and mainframes. Messages can also be sent and immediately queued when a client is not connected to its network, in which case final delivery takes place later when the client is reconnected to its network.

Utilizing Communication Resources with Messaging

Messaging tends to better utilize communications resources than do tightly coupled approaches. Tightly coupled systems bind the client and server together through synchronous communications, usually in the form of function calls. For example, DCOM uses RPC to invoke functions synchronously in remote objects. In most tightly coupled scenarios, a connection, or session, between two systems must be maintained whether or not the systems are constantly using the connection. Messaging systems transmit messages to queues where they are stored intermediately. In this way, messaging systems use the full available bandwidth of the communications channel to transmit the message, and then free the channel for other transmissions. This queuing approach also allows messages to be stored temporarily in scenarios in which the source and destination are disconnected, either because of network outages or planned disconnects (such as a ship leaving port or a salesperson taking a laptop on a plane). Messaging also supports multipoint delivery enabling a developer to transmit a message once and yet have several peers receive copies of the message. Function call semantics imply that the caller will wait until the callee completes the call, thus defeating all the preceding loosely coupled advantages.

Unifying Dissimilar Systems with Messaging

Messaging can be unifying. Messaging allows dissimilar systems with varying transmission capacity to communicate. I was discussing some business with a customer in Spain the other day, and I marveled at how she preferred email to a phone call. The messaging approach allowed her to take her time translating my English to Spanish and her Spanish to English. (To quote Korben Dallas, Bruce Willis' character from *The Fifth Element*, "I only speak two languages, English and Bad English.") It also kept me from having to get up at some crazy time in the morning to reach her during business hours in her country. You can directly compare this scenario to a PC-based application that must communicate with a piece of software running on a mainframe. A messaging system enables you to translate between the two systems' native formats (say ASCII and EBCDIC) and enables the online PC system to work interactively while the batch mainframe system stores messages for processing at midnight.

As a final point, messaging systems produce a much more accessible pivot point in systems that are highly fluid or volatile. For example, it would be very easy to direct a message from one component to the bit bucket if the component that previously received the message simply wasn't needed anymore. This would have no impact on the remaining component as long as it did not expect an acknowledgement (which could be hoaxed up pretty easily). You might say, "Wow, that sounds like a pretty serious hack." Well, yes and no. In the real world, things evolve. Pieces of large systems become redundant or require extensive modification. When these elements are connected via messaging, even the most traumatic changes to one component will often have only a small impact on others.

Consider a piece of code running on a mainframe that is critical to the financial stability of some business. Suppose that this code has been refined and tested to perfection over the course of five years. It sends a message to a PC-based system, and the message no longer contains enough information to perform the PC-based task. Do you really want to modify that mainframe code? There might be times when it's unavoidable, but you'd probably pass in most cases. So what to do? In a loosely coupled system such as this, you could add a piece of software (on the mainframe or on the PC) to accept the original message, add the needed information, and pass it along to the target PC. Neither of the existing well-tested pieces of software need to be modified, and only the components downstream from the inserted message modification must be retested. This is the essence of loose coupling.

Messaging Weaknesses

So what's the down side of messaging? Well, in my opinion, the advent of messaging and the transaction-based application server (MTS/COM+) on the Windows platform make the most significant step forward in enterprise application support since the release of Windows NT itself. Of course, every technology has its place, and messaging might not fit into the model at every turn. The following are examples of the weaknesses of messaging:

- Typically slower end-to-end processing.
- Asynchronous execution complicates cross-component synchronization.

Extended Processing Time

Messaging might not always be the best way to go. By human standards, electronic messaging can be very fast. However, it is inevitably slower for round-trip data transactions than an interactive communications session. Calling a function in a remote object and getting back a return value, or creating a TCP connection with another process and transmitting requests and receiving responses, usually works best for highly interactive application components .

Another thing to consider is the impact that marshaling has on the processing time. Although we often talk of the performance hit incurred when marshaling data to out-of-process servers on the same machine, this pales in comparison to the performance hit when marshaling distributed data.

Asynchronous Execution

Messaging also lacks the self-synchronizing aspects of function-call interactions. When the routine you called returns, you generally know it has completed its work. Messages, on the other hand, are generally delivered asynchronously; and thus you have no idea about when or whether the message was handled. Synchronizing behavior across loosely coupled systems tends to be much more complex and expensive than it would be in a naturally synchronous environment, such as RPC, RMI, or IIOP.

Synchronous Versus Asynchronous Programming

Loosely coupled systems are asynchronous whereas tightly couple systems are synchronous. Most of us have no problem developing synchronous applications because they're simpler than their asynchronous counterparts, and we all cut our programming teeth on them. This section shows you the differences, and points out some considerations you need to keep in mind when developing asynchronous systems.

Every aspect of technology has its collateral lingo to deal with. I've always been one to avoid 25-cent words and high-tech jargon unless they really pay off. My auto shop teacher pointed out to me that you'd be hard pressed to discuss a vehicle with a carburetor problem without using the word *carburetor*. Two or three passes with the replacement phrase, "the multiported mechanism that mixes fuel with air," would give you all the reason in the world to go back to *carburetor*. Messaging technology has its share of carburetors. In particular, you will frequently run into the following phrases when dealing with message-oriented software:

- Tightly coupled systems—Applications using components that operate in lock step, through synchronous, function-call–style interactions

- Loosely coupled systems—Systems that are not rigidly (synchronously) connected and that operate in a largely independent fashion

- Asynchronous programming—Coding with components that operate independently of synchronization

- Overlapped communications—Using I/O in parallel with normal application code execution

- Non-blocking I/O—I/O requests that can be submitted without causing the thread of execution to yield the CPU

- No-wait operations—Operations (usually I/O) that can be executed without causing the thread to wait for the operations completion

All of these phrases, except the first, apply to programming techniques in which one component can communicate with another without yielding the CPU. Thus, component A could send a message to component B and then immediately go on about its business.

The benefits of messaging are tremendous in many scenarios. The overall scalability and performance of systems that are loosely coupled almost always outdistance that of tightly coupled systems. So wait a minute: Didn't I just finish highlighting the fact that tightly coupled systems, although less flexible, are faster end-to-end? Yes, indeed, they are exclusively faster in some cases, and temporarily so in other cases. The issue lies in the fact that loosely coupled messaging systems scale and distribute in a far more linear manner than call-based systems.

In some cases, you can simulate a synchronous operation with Windows mechanisms such as a semaphore. This doesn't work in all cases, but can in some.

Look at an example from the WinSock world. It's a well-known fact that overlapped WinSock network I/O is faster than synchronous WinSock network I/O; but why? Well, if you prepare a buffer to write to the network and then call send() to submit the I/O request in a blocking fashion, your thread will inevitably have to wait for the I/O operation to complete. This means the kernel will take the CPU away from your thread and give it to some other thread that is ready to run. Your I/O continues along in the space of short interrupts occurring in the background, but your application thread is blocked waiting for the I/O operation to finish. There are two levels of performance to consider here (as there always are):

- Application performance
- System performance

Obviously, both factors must be kept within bounds. In the preceding scenario, both suffer from your blocking I/O call. First, the application's task stops running to wait for the I/O to complete. Is there really nothing else you could be doing? Second, the system is required to take the CPU away from your thread and locate a new thread to run. This can seem harmless, but a rather extensive set of operations is involved, including the following:

- Saving the context information for your application thread in such a way that it can safely be restarted later
- Setting up system structures that indicate what your thread is waiting for, so it can be reactivated when the wait completes
- Locating the next properly prioritized thread that is ready to run
- Restoring the selected thread's context

Note that during this process, nothing useful or even comprehensible to the system users is taking place. Context switching between threads is one of the great performance bandits on modern multithreaded systems. So how do you avoid this? Well, we will look at each performance vantage point in turn.

First, you'd like to speed up your own application. Often, attending to this solves the system performance problems before you have a chance to address them. In order to improve the performance of the application, you want to postpone releasing the CPU as long as possible—no need to worry about starving other applications in a preemptive environment such as Win32. What you're trying to achieve is context switching that fits naturally into your application's internal processing. So how do you do I/O and keep using the CPU? The technique you're looking for is known as overlapped I/O. It occurs when you submit an I/O request and then continue using the CPU while the I/O system processes the request at interrupt time in the background. Using overlapped I/O, you could write code to prepare a second buffer while the first is being written to the network, keeping the I/O system and the CPU constantly busy. Compare the thread execution graphs shown in Figures 22.2 and 22.3.

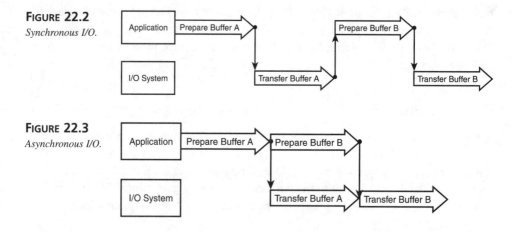

FIGURE 22.2

Synchronous I/O.

FIGURE 22.3

Asynchronous I/O.

In the second example, the thread completes its task much faster and reduces system overhead by eliminating the need for an arbitrary context switch. This tactic can be directly applied to component communications in a distributed system if you favor asynchronous messaging over synchronous function calls. Messaging systems accept message transfer requests from applications and then immediately return control to the caller.

Scalability

Overlapped or asynchronous I/O can be achieved between two application components using messaging. Instead of calling a function in some other component and then giving up the CPU until the function processing in the (possibly) remote component returns, you can simply send a message and go on about your business. If you require a response, you can poll a response queue from time to time to check for replies. This kind of approach effectively decouples the two application components involved. This decoupling reduces interapplication component dependencies, allowing components to operate at varying rates in very diverse environments and at varying physical and logical distances. Every time you increase the distance between two synchronous components, you increase the overhead required for their communications. Because of the synchronous nature of function calls, network latency of this sort impacts every element in that call chain from the end component all the way back to the call originator.

In a loosely coupled system, you take a fire-and-forget strategy. The component that must communicate simply sends a message to the target component and goes to its next task. Of course, you have the overhead of the messaging software responsible for delivering this message (which has been noticeably glossed over), but the component itself is largely unimpacted by the expense of the communication. If you further assume that your message queue can grow as you overwhelm the remote component in times of high traffic and that the queue can shrink in times of low traffic, you introduce new efficiencies. Perhaps only one server component can service a particular kind of message, but many client components can post the message. Decoupling the two types of components enables you to provide rapid response in the client space by creating many client components. Your server-side latency increases accordingly, but because your client components are not directly coupled to the performance of your server, you have a system that scales well within the limits of your server component providing rapid response to client requests.

The real trick to designing very scalable and interoperable applications is to decompose the problem in such a way to allow the pieces to operate as independently as possible. A loosely coupled approach avoids the "weakest link in the chain" situation. Loose coupling supports independence that enables components to work at their own pace and across several systems. Although this is a deep issue, I'll throw in as many tips as I can throughout this chapter to help you take advantage of this powerful technique.

Message-Oriented Middleware

Okay, I'm sure you've been wondering, "What's the catch?" What mystical piece of software is behind the cornucopia of messaging? The answer is Message-Oriented Middleware (MOM). Several popular MOM systems are available on various platforms today. This discussion takes you into the world of the Microsoft Message Queue Server (MSMQ) in particular. MOM systems supply the communications glue that makes it easy for distributed components to send and receive messages. Standard MOM systems consist of several elements:

- A programming interface (API)
- A set of system software components
- Administrative tools

MOM APIs

MOM APIs usually contain several basic functions that enable application developers to easily send and receive messages. It is very easy to get up and running with a good messaging system in a short period of time, as you shall soon see. Various additional arcane MOM API routines are often provided to allow administration and management functions to be performed, including security, performance tuning, and timed delivery, among others.

MOM System Software

MOM systems also include software responsible for moving messages throughout a network of computers. These messages must be stored in queues until they can be transmitted to the next node in the system. This might sound easy, but there are actually several very complex database-oriented tasks involved.

First, it would be very confusing to a message recipient if more than one copy of a given message were received. This could easily happen if the message were transmitted from one queue to the next but before the acknowledgment could be returned to the sender, the line dropped. The sender would have no choice but to resend the message when the line restabilized. Another problem appears when two or more servers can handle a particular message type. What happens if both servers retrieve the same message concurrently? Finally, what would happen if a set of messages arrived in the wrong order?

All these problems could be catastrophic if not planned for. Implementing application logic to avoid these problems would be redundant, however, because these problems were solved by database systems years ago. For this reason, most MOM systems use database technology to implement robust and even transactional messaging environments for their application developers. The MOM system software can thus allow ease of application development to be married with mainframe reliability.

Administrative Tools

As you can see, a MOM system makes the developer's life easier but, much like a distributed database, adds a new management concern to the list for the system administrator. Where are the queues to be created? Who can read and write the queues? Which routes should queues use to communicate? How should components and queues be deployed to best utilize the available computing power? All these questions must be answered to effectively deploy a distributed messaging system. For this reason, commercial MOM environments ship with administrative tools and utilities that support queue-based configuration and monitoring tasks.

Microsoft Message Queue Server (MSMQ)

Microsoft Message Queue Server (MSMQ) is Microsoft's MOM product for Windows-based application development. MSMQ provides two distinct APIs. The first consists of a flat C-style function call API. The second API is COM-based and consists of a set of ActiveX components. Each can prove effective in different situations, as you will see later. MSMQ also consists of a set of system components that use database technology to manage robust queue behavior and networking facilities that provide protocol-independent communications between queues. Finally, MSMQ provides a Microsoft Management Console (MMC) snap-in for administering and configuring the queues, clients, and servers throughout the network.

MSMQ Connector

Real distributed applications are frequently required to integrate very diverse systems. Fortunately, messaging systems have the word "interoperability" engraved in their charter. Microsoft has designed the MSMQ Connector to allow third parties to wire into MSMQ. Microsoft uses this technology internally to enable MSMQ to easily interoperate with Exchange Mail. Level8 Systems has also used this technology with FalconMQ Bridge. The FalconMQ bridge has been licensed by Microsoft and allows MSMQ messages to move into the IBM MQSeries message space and vice versa. As COM programmers, MSMQ is the messaging system of choice, but it's nice to know that you're not painting yourself into a corner.

MSMQ and Other APIs

If you're familiar with Messaging API (MAPI), RPC, or WinSock, you might be wondering why you should learn to program MSMQ. Obviously, there will be some overlap between MSMQ and any other communications programming interface. One particularly compelling advantage of MSMQ is its capability to support communications with a peer that is not running. No other general IPC programming environment allows one application to queue requests that can be picked up by a peer at a later time. APIs such as MAPI support messaging but with a much stricter programming model (largely targeting email).

MSMQ and Email

Ah, yes, email. As you might expect, MSMQ is a likely environment for email programming. To this end, Microsoft has supplied specific support for email programming and interoperability. Various MSMQ API routines support the composition and parsing of email messages. MSMQ can be quite effective for applications that must receive and process email forms. MSMQ mail messages have their own format, but they can be easily transferred to Exchange Servers and MAPI clients through MSMQ connectors. MSMQ Mail programming is covered in detail in Chapter 25, "Advanced MSMQ Programming."

Summary

In this chapter, you learned the scalability and performance benefits of loosely coupled systems. You looked at the strengths and weaknesses of messaging systems and learned a new class of middleware designed specifically to support message-oriented interapplication communications. You also learned about Microsoft Message Queue Server (MSMQ) and reviewed some basic MSMQ features. Chapter 23, "MSMQ Administration and Architecture" provides a detailed look at the architecture of MSMQ. Chapters 24 and 25 present basic and advanced MSMQ programming concerns, respectively.

CHAPTER 23

MSMQ Administration and Architecture

IN THIS CHAPTER

Now much you tell me, and yet more I perceive.
—Melian the Maia

This chapter describes the various parts of an MSMQ enterprise and how to configure and manage them. You'll get a chance to look at the tools used to create, destroy, monitor, and configure queues. You'll also examine the applications and components that depend on queues.

Because I discuss provisional programming issues here as well, I should point out that there are two basic approaches to building MSMQ applications, the MSMQ API and the MSMQ ActiveX Components. You can choose one or the other or mix and match. The API provides the lowest-level support, exposing all the various MSMQ services and requiring a little more code in most cases. The ActiveX approach is designed to be generic enough to service any development environment and provides sufficient power with a simplified, object-oriented COM programming model. Throughout this chapter, when I refer to programming issues, I will provide descriptions of both environments.

A basic MSMQ exchange involves three parties:

- The sending application
- The target queue
- The receiving application

Client applications use MSMQ by sending messages to the queues that the MSMQ servers monitor. If the target queue is not local to the sender, the sender's local servers are responsible for forwarding the message through the MSMQ enterprise. The message is passed from queue to queue until it finally reaches its destination. The message body format is arbitrary from the perspective of MSMQ, but must obviously be understood by the end points sending and receiving the messages. Queues act as intermediaries, enabling the applications involved to run at different points in time and on any system within a distributed MSMQ enterprise. The decoupling effect provided by the queues makes the client and server elements of an MSMQ system very independent. Most operations occur asynchronously, enabling applications to adopt a fire-and-forget mentality when sending messages.

MSMQ Objects and Properties

An MSMQ system is defined in terms of several key object types:

- Messages
- Queues
- Machines

These objects exist within an administration unit defined as an MSMQ Enterprise. Messages are the objects that carry information throughout the enterprise. Messages have a flexible structure and can contain some data or nothing at all; in the latter case, the receipt of such an empty message might be all the communication required between two applications. On the other hand, messages can include up to 4MB of data. Queues act as the destination for all messages in an MSMQ enterprise. Messages are sent to queues, not to applications. The intermediary nature of queues provides a layer of independence between peers involved in a messaging scenario, thus supporting loosely coupled application development. MSMQ machines run a process known as the Queue Manager. MSMQ machines are the computer systems designated to supply certain queuing services within the MSMQ enterprise.

All these objects are described by properties, such as labels, types, sizes, timeouts, and priorities. Variable-length property lists allow developers to work with unspecified objects in a generic way. Some applications might require objects with tons of properties, and other applications might require no property information at all. Some object properties are set by MSMQ, others can be set by MSMQ administrators, and still others can be set only procedurally. Some properties can be written to only when creating the object in question, and persist as read-only attributes thereafter.

The MSMQ Explorer enables administrators to create objects and manage object properties throughout the MSMQ enterprise. The MSMQ Explorer runs as a standalone application in early versions of MSMQ and as a Microsoft Management Console (MMC) based snap-in in more recent releases.

When assigned procedurally, properties are configured through variable-length property arrays. This allows new properties to be defined by MSMQ over time and enables a flexible programming interface. MSMQ uses this model extensively, as does OLE DB and other modern COM systems. All the basic MSMQ objects described previously support any number of properties. With the exception of a few mandatory properties that might be required in certain circumstances, the properties you set and get will be defined by the needs of your application. Listing 23.1 shows how you would procedurally configure a queue property structure with one property.

LISTING 23.1   Procedurally Configuring a Queue Property

```
//Set up properties (we only need the path name property)
QUEUEPROPID aPropId[1];                    //Property id array
PROPVARIANT aVariant[1];                    //Property value array
aPropId[0] = PROPID_Q_PATHNAME;            //Set the ID
aVariant[0].vt = VT_LPWSTR;                //Set the value type
aVariant[0].pwszVal = L"Svr1\\Orders";     //Set the value data
```

23

MSMQ ADMINISTRATION AND ARCHITECTURE

LISTING 23.1   Continued

```
//Set up the property struct
MQQUEUEPROPS QueueProps;              //Queue properties struct
QueueProps.cProp = 1;                 //Number of properties
QueueProps.aPropID = aPropId;         //Properties id array
QueueProps.aPropVar = aVariant;       //Properties value array
QueueProps.aStatus = NULL;            //No prop error reports
```

As you can see, this extensible structure allows any number of properties to be passed to MSMQ through the same MQQUEUEPROPS structure. Variants are used to store property values, enabling many different programming environments to access property settings. There are similar MQMSGPROPS and MQQMPROPS structures for messages and machines (also known as Queue Managers), respectively.

Messages

Messages are the *raison d'être* (reason for being) for everything else that is MSMQ; they represent the atomic units of information that move around an MSMQ enterprise. As it turns out, messages are simply a set of property values. This being the case, messages have a large set of properties to choose from. In general, applications are most interested in the Body property of a message. The Body property is the one property that has a clearly understood function. The Body property can be any size (up to 4MB). Several other message properties will frequently be set and examined by sophisticated applications.

Message Properties

Table 23.1 presents a list of the possible MSMQ message properties.

TABLE 23.1   MSMQ Message Properties

Property	Description
PROPID_M_ACKNOWLEDGE	Types of acknowledgment messages MSMQ sends
PROPID_M_ADMIN_QUEUE	Queue used for acknowledgment messages
PROPID_M_ADMIN_QUEUE_LEN	Length of the acknowledgment queue
PROPID_M_APPSPECIFIC	Application-generated information such as single integer values or application-defined message classes
PROPID_M_ARRIVEDTIME	The maximum amount of time the message has to reach the queue
PROPID_M_AUTH_LEVEL	Indicates that the message needs to be authenticated when read

TABLE 23.1 Continued

Property	Description
PROPID_M_AUTHENTICATED	Indicates that the message was authenticated by MSMQ
PROPID_M_BODY	The body of the message
PROPID_M_BODY_SIZE	The size of the message body
PROPID_M_BODY_TYPE	The type of message body (string, array of bytes, or object)
PROPID_M_CLASS	The type of message (for example, a message can be a normal, acknowledgment, or report message)
PROPID_M_CONNECTOR_TYPE	Indicates that some message properties were generated external to MSMQ
PROPID_M_CORRELATIONID	The correlation identifier of the message (original message ID)
PROPID_M_DELIVERY	How the message is delivered (optimize throughput or recoverability)
PROPID_M_DEST_QUEUE	The queue where the message will reside (where the message is sent)
PROPID_M_DEST_QUEUE_LEN	The length of the destination queue
PROPID_M_DEST_SYMM_KEY	The symmetric key required when sending encrypted messages to foreign queues
PROPID_M_DEST_SYMM_KEY_LEN	The length of the symmetric key
PROPID_M_ENCRYPTION_ALG	The algorithm used to encrypt the message body
PROPID_M_EXTENSION	Additional unformatted information
PROPID_M_EXTENSION_LEN	The length of the unformatted information
PROPID_M_HASH_ALG	The hash algorithm used when authenticating messages
PROPID_M_JOURNAL	Indicates that a copy of the message is stored in the machine journal
PROPID_M_LABEL	Application-defined label for the message
PROPID_M_LABEL_LEN	The length of the message label
PROPID_M_MSGID	The MSMQ-generated identifier
PROPID_M_PRIORITY	The priority of the message
PROPID_M_PRIV_LEVEL	Indicates that the message is encrypted
PROPID_M_PROV_NAME	The name of the cryptographic provider
PROPID_M_PROV_NAME_LEN	The length of the cryptographic provider name
PROPID_M_PROV_TYPE	The type of cryptographic provider
PROPID_M_RESP_QUEUE	The queue for sending responses to the message

23

**MSMQ
ADMINISTRATION
AND ARCHITECTURE**

TABLE 23.1   Continued

Property	Description
PROPID_M_RESP_QUEUE_LEN	The length of the response queue
PROPID_M_SECURITY_CONTEXT	Security information for authenticating the message
PROPID_M_SENDER_CERT	The security certificate used to authenticate the message
PROPID_M_SENDER_CERT_LEN	The length of the sender certificate buffer
PROPID_M_SENDERID	The user who sent the message
PROPID_M_SENDERID_LEN	The length of the sender identifier
PROPID_M_SENDERID_TYPE	The type of sender identifier found in PROPID_M_SENDERID; currently, the only type of sender identifier available to MSMQ is a security identifier (SID)
PROPID_M_SENTTIME	The date and time that the message was sent by the source queue
PROPID_M_SIGNATURE	The digital signature for authenticating the message
PROPID_M_SIGNATURE_LEN	The length of the digital signature used to authenticate the message
PROPID_M_SRC_MACHINE_ID	The computer where the message originated
PROPID_M_TIME_TO_BE_RECEIVED	How long the receiving application has to remove the message from the queue
PROPID_M_TIME_TO_REACH_QUEUE	How long the message has to reach the queue
PROPID_M_TRACE	The route of the message is traced
PROPID_M_VERSION	The version of MSMQ used to send the message
PROPID_M_XACT_STATUS_QUEUE	The format name of the transaction status queue
PROPID_M_XACT_STATUS_QUEUE_LEN	The length of the transaction status queue's format name buffer

Queues

Message queues are the buffering mechanism that makes MSMQ an effective tool for developing loosely coupled applications. Queues store a message until an appropriate application sees fit to retrieve the message. Queues make it possible for various components to communicate, even though they execute at different times and at various locations within an enterprise.

Queue Types

Although all queues provide the same basic functionality, acting as a temporary store for messages, several types of queues are used by MSMQ and MSMQ applications:

- Message queues
- Administration (acknowledgement) queues
- Response queues
- Journal queues
- Dead Letter queues
- Report queues

Applications or application administrators create the first three application queue types. An application might use several queues or use a single queue in various capacities. For example, the same queue can be used by a server for administration and response messages. The next three types of queues are known as system queues. Journal and Dead Letter queues are created and maintained by MSMQ. The message `Class` property is used to identify acknowledgement and report messages found in Administration, Dead Letter, and Report queues. Applications can receive but not send messages to the three system queue types.

Message Queues

Well, you guessed it. These are the kinds of queues that store plain old application messages. They are the targets of most messages, and the place from which standard messages are received. Message queues are usually created by applications; however, some applications might require that the MSMQ administrator create specific queues. Application Message queues can be public or private. Public queues are registered in the active directory (or an interim substitute on Windows NT 4) and are available throughout the MSMQ enterprise. Private queues are visible only on the MSMQ machine on which they were created. Applications can pass the names of private queues to remote applications in order to support response messages.

Administration Queues

Administration queues are just like normal Message queues with one exception; they are specified as the target for MSMQ acknowledgement messages. Why they aren't called Acknowledgement queues I can't say, but that's what they are. They are created by an application in order to receive status messages sent by MSMQ. The status messages can indicate that a message has reached its target queue, a message was actually received by an application, or the non-acknowledgement of either of these cases (because of timeouts and other failures). Applications flag requests for acknowledgement on a message-by-message basis. Administration queues cannot be transactional.

Response Queues

Response queues are just like normal Message queues with one exception—they are specified as the target queue for response messages. The PROPID_M_RESP_QUEUE message property is the "courtesy of a reply requested" field of the MSMQ world. Applications receiving a message that requires a response can look up the Response queue in the PROPID_M_RESP_QUEUE property of the inbound message. These queues can be private because the sending application targeting a Response queue does not need to look up the queue name; instead, it is supplied with the original message.

Journal Queues

The two types of Journal queues are machine journals and queue journals. As you might expect, machine journals maintain a record of important messages transported by that machine, and queue journals maintain a record of important messages transported by the associated queue. Every MSMQ machine has a machine journal queue, and every MSMQ application-created queue has a queue journal. Queues with the PROPID_Q_JOURNAL property set copy all messages to their journal upon delivering the messages. Messages not using a journal queue, but with their PROPID_M_JOURNAL property set, are copied to the machine journal upon successful transmission to the next enterprise queue or end application. MSMQ never clears journal messages, although journal queues can have a quota. Obviously, administrators or applications should examine and purge these queues on a regular basis if they are to be used. After a queue's quota is reached, no new messages can be sent to that queue.

Dead Letter Queues

Dead Letter queues store application messages that cannot be delivered. Each MSMQ machine maintains two Dead Letter queues, one for transactional dead letters and one for non-transactional dead letters. Messages are copied to the Dead Letter queue of the last machine in the chain of queues that successfully received the message. Only journaled, non-transactional messages will be copied to either a Journal or Dead Letter queue. Failed transactional messages, on the other hand, are always copied to the Transactional Dead Letter queue on the machine that last successfully received the message.

Report Queues

Report queues can be created at the MSMQ Administrator's discretion. Report queues receive progress reports about a message that is making its way through an MSMQ enterprise. Report messages are generated by MSMQ each time a message flagged for tracking passes through a source, routing (intermediate), or destination server. Report messages have the MQMSG_CLASS_REPORT class and are requested by setting the PROPID_M_TRACE message property to the name of the target report queue.

The MQIS—Message Queue Information Service

MSMQ enterprise, site, and queue information is stored in the Message Queue Information Service (MQIS) database. This database resides in the Active Directory on Windows 2000 systems and operates on top of Microsoft SQL Server in earlier versions of Windows. You can install the MSMQ service on a pre-Active Directory system with an existing SQL Server database, or use the limited SQL Server implementation that ships with pre-Active Directory MSMQ.

Local Queue Storage (LQS)

MSMQ stores private queue information as well as cached information about local public queues in the Local Queue Storage (LQS). The MSMQ LQS is usually located in the \program files\msmq\storage\lqs directory.

Queue Properties

Queues have several properties, some of which are read/write, some of which are set by MSMQ and are read-only, and still others that can only be configured at queue creation, as shown in Table 23.2.

TABLE 23.2   Queue Properties

Property	Description
PROPID_Q_AUTHENTICATE	Indicates that the queue accepts only authenticated messages
PROPID_Q_BASEPRIORITY	Queue's priority in MSMQ message routing
PROPID_Q_CREATE_TIME	Time and date of queue creation
PROPID_Q_INSTANCE	Queue GUID set by MSMQ on queue creation
PROPID_Q_JOURNAL	Indicates that the queue journals all messages
PROPID_Q_JOURNAL_QUOTA	Maximum size in KB of queue journal
PROPID_Q_LABEL	Queue display caption
PROPID_Q_MODIFY_TIME	Last queue property modification date and time
PROPID_Q_PATHNAME	Queue's full pathname (the machine name, plus \, plus the queue name)
PROPID_Q_PRIV_LEVEL	Queue requires messages to be encrypted
PROPID_Q_QUOTA	Maximum size in KB of queue
PROPID_Q_TRANSACTION	Queue is transactional
PROPID_Q_TYPE	A GUID used to categorize queues

Priorities

MSMQ transfers messages with the highest routing priority first. To determine a message's routing priority, MSMQ combines the base priority of the next queue in the message's path with the message's priority property (PROPID_M_PRIORITY). A queue's base priority can be used by MSMQ administrators to control the routing of messages and apply costs to different routes. Queue base priorities can range from –32,768 to 32,767— the default being 0. Message priorities can range from 0–7. The default priority for normal messages is 3, whereas the default and only priority available for transactional messages is 0. Messages are ordered within their queue based on message priority alone.

Transactional Queues

Transactional queues are used in conjunction with transactional messages. Only transactional messages can be sent to a transactional queue. Queues must be configured as transactional or non-transactional at creation time, and these settings cannot be changed later. Transactional queues supply additional assurances in the areas of reliability and message ordering. As mentioned earlier, all transactional messages are either delivered or copied to the Transaction Dead Letter queue.

Furthermore, several messages can be managed within a single transaction, in which case MSMQ ensures that either all the messages are delivered or none of the messages are delivered. Messages within the same transaction, destined for the same queue, will also always be queued in the order that they were sent. All messages sent within a single transaction have their timeouts set to the value specified in the first message sent within the transaction. In addition, their priority is set to zero. These settings are necessary in order to meet the basic unifying criteria set forth by messaging transactions.

Transactional messages are not actually transferred until the transaction is committed, and delivery of all messages in the transaction can be rolled back at any time prior to commitment.

Identifying Queues

What's in a name? Well, when it comes to MSMQ queues, that depends on which name you're talking about. Queues have several identifying properties. Queues can also be collected into categories. This makes it easy to look them up using the Active Directory. The MSMQ API routines MQLocateBegin(), MQLocateNext(), and MQLocateEnd(), and the MSMQQuery ActiveX object allow applications to search for public queues using almost any criteria.

Pathnames

Perhaps the most commonly used identifying queue property is the pathname
(`PROPID_Q_PATHNAME`). A queue's pathname consists of the MSMQ machine name that
hosts the queue, a backslash, and the queue's name. For example, the queue used to store
new orders on the host Sauron might have the pathname `Sauron\NewOrders`. Local
queues can also be referred to with a dot in place of the hostname like `.\NewOrders`.
Don't forget to escape the backslash in C and C++ string constants.

Format Names

Unfortunately, most MSMQ routines can't open a queue using the pathname (that would
be too easy). Instead, MSMQ prefers to use the queue's format name. Several MSMQ
API routines provide format name lookup services:

- `MQPathNameToFormatName()`
- `MQHandleToFormatName()`
- `MQInstanceToFormatName()`

The `MSMQQueueInfo` ActiveX object provides similar format name resolution services.
Format names are Unicode strings composed of a GUID and some ancillary text. Listing
23.2 is a list of the general formats for various format name types. Each listed item provides a description, a template, and an example for a specific format name type.

LISTING 23.2 Format Name Types

```
Public queues
PUBLIC=QueueGUID
PUBLIC={9792EFBA-9549-11d2-8285-00A0C9929FD0}

Journal for a public queue
PUBLIC=QueueGUID;JOURNAL
PUBLIC={9792EFBA-9549-11d2-8285-00A0C9929FD0};JOURNAL

Private queue
PRIVATE=MachineGUID\QueueNumber
PRIVATE={7FC4449A-955B-11d2-8285-00A0C9929FD0}\0000000b

Journal for a private queue
PRIVATE=MachineGUID\QueueNumber;JOURNAL
PRIVATE={7FC4449A-955B-11d2-8285-00A0C9929FD0}\0000000b;JOURNAL

Public queue direct format
DIRECT=AddressSpecification\QueueName
DIRECT=TCP:208.167.209.145\NewOrders
```

23

MSMQ
ADMINISTRATION
AND ARCHITECTURE

LISTING 23.2   Continued

```
Private queue direct format
DIRECT=AddressSpecification\PRIVATE$\QueueName
DIRECT=TCP:208.167.209.145\PRIVATE$\NewOrders

Journal for a machine
MACHINE=MachineGUID;JOURNAL
MACHINE={DF0EDE5A-955E-11d2-8285-00A0C9929FD0};JOURNAL

Dead letter queue for a machine
MACHINE=MachineGUID;DEADLETTER
MACHINE={DF0EDE5A-955E-11d2-8285-00A0C9929FD0};DEADLETTER

Transaction dead letter for a machine
MACHINE=MachineGUID;DEADXACT
MACHINE={DF0EDE5A-955E-11d2-8285-00A0C9929FD0};DEADXACT

Foreign queue
CONNECTOR=ForeignCNGUID
CONNECTOR={32CDC6FA-955F-11d2-8285-00A0C9929FD0}

Foreign transactional queue
CONNECTOR=ForeignCNGUID:XACTONLY
CONNECTOR={32CDC6FA-955F-11d2-8285-00A0C9929FD0};XACTONLY
```

In most cases, public and private format names are used to open public and private queues, respectively. Direct format names can be used to open queues in a foreign MSMQ enterprise or in order to deliver a message in one transfer, avoiding standard MSMQ message routing. Direct format name/address specifications must be a re-solvable hostname or a TCP/IP (shown in the preceding example) or IPX/SPX address specification. MSMQ machine queues can be opened using the machine GUID. The MQGetMachineProperties() API routine and the MSMQApplication ActiveX object can both produce a machine GUID. The final connector format names are used to access MSMQ connectors to send messages to external services.

Instance Identifiers

Every public MSMQ queue is assigned a standard 128-bit globally unique identifier (GUID). The queue GUID is stored in the queue's PROPID_Q_INSTANCE property. Queue instance identifiers can be used to look up the queue's format name or even manually construct it.

Labels

A queue's PROPID_Q_LABEL property can be set and managed procedurally or through the MSMQ Explorer. The queue label property provides a possible, albeit vague, search criteria using human-readable text strings.

Types

The PROPID_Q_TYPE queue property provides an exacting mechanism that can be used to identify the service type of queue in question. Developers and administrators can set a queue's type to any GUID. This allows application developers to use GUIDGen.exe or uuidgen.exe to create unique identifiers that distinguish a class of queue used within the application. This provides a less human-readable but more precise type identification mechanism than does the label property.

Private Queues

Private queues are queues created for exclusive use by an application. Private queues are not registered with the Active Directory and are instead tracked in the host machine's LQS. Private queues are created using a pathname with PRIVATE$ inserted between the machine name and queue name as shown here: Sauron\PRIVATE$\NewOrders. Private queues cannot be discovered by searching the Active Directory but can be used by an application when provided as a Response queue.

Machines

MSMQ machines host Message queues and are configured by an MSMQ administrator. There is, unfortunately, no programmatic way to add machines to the MSMQ system. In the MSMQ world, messages move around between queues within an enterprise. This MSMQ enterprise is usually a direct reflection of an Active Directory enterprise consisting of a forest or collection of Active Directory domain trees. MSMQ enterprises are partitioned into sites. Sites organize a set of MSMQ resources connected through high-speed, reliable links (usually LANs) into a management unit. Clients in a particular site will use servers in that same site to improve messaging performance and simplify administrative tasks. Sites can then interoperate throughout the enterprise using less reliable and slower (often WAN) links. This model requires a way for clients and servers within a site to discover information regarding the available queues. By the same token, servers within a site require a way to discover the general makeup of the enterprise as a whole. MSMQ maintains queue, site, and enterprise configuration information in the Active Directory.

Machine Properties

MSMQ machines or queue managers have several properties, as shown in Table 23.3.

TABLE 23.3   MSMQ Machine (Queue Manager) Properties

Property	Description
PROPID_QM_CONNECTION	Identifies the connected network (CN) list of the computer
PROPID_QM_ENCRYPTION_PK	Identifies the public encryption key of the computer
PROPID_QM_MACHINE_ID	Identifies the computer
PROPID_QM_PATHNAME	Identifies the MSMQ pathname of the computer
PROPID_QM_SITE_ID	Identifies the MSMQ site where the computer is defined

The MSMQ Enterprise

An MSMQ enterprise is maintained by various MSMQ controller servers. Controller servers allow multiple MSMQ sites to be connected to form an enterprise. A site is a set of MSMQ servers that can readily and reliably communicate. Each site can consist of one or more connected networks. Connected networks can also span several logical sites. An MSMQ enterprise is woven together through site links managed by MSMQ administrators.

Site Links

Administrators establish site links that allow message traffic to flow between sites. Site links have costs assigned by administrators that allows MSMQ to choose the most efficient route for a message in an MSMQ enterprise.

Connected Networks

All MSMQ machines on the same LAN segment, using the same protocol, are said to exist on the same connected network. MSMQ administrators name the connected networks in use by MSMQ servers in order to simplify enterprise administration.

MSMQ Controllers

MSMQ controller servers are the designated infrastructure management servers. All controllers act as routing servers responsible for moving messages throughout the enterprise. At the top of the controller food chain is the primary enterprise controller (PEC). The PEC acts as a primary site controller (PSC) for its site, supporting intersite communications and site link management. The PEC also acts as the principal machine in the maintenance of MSMQ enterprise settings and configuration, tying information together from all the connected MSMQ sites. Each additional MSMQ site in the MSMQ enterprise must have a single primary site controller (PSC) responsible for the configuration information in its site. Backup site controllers can be added to a site to act as additional routing servers and distribute the PSC's load across several machines. MSMQ machines can also be configured as noncontroller routing servers to provide additional intersite communication support.

MSMQ Clients

MSMQ client machines use queue managers to send and receive messages. The MSMQ queue manager is implemented as a background service running on all independent client computers and servers. Queue managers communicate with queue servers when sending and receiving public queue messages. Private queues are maintained by the queue manager itself and are usually available only to applications running on the queue manager's machine. Dependent clients do not run the MSMQ queue manager service and must be synchronously connected to a server in a site with an operational PSC to function. Independent clients can send messages while disconnected from the MSMQ enterprise. Messages sent while disconnected are queued for later delivery. Independent clients can also attach to the MSMQ enterprise using different sites with little or no reconfiguration.

MSMQ Administration

MSMQ administration is accomplished through the MSMQ Explorer or the Active Directory Manager in domains with Active Directory support. The MSMQ Explorer provides a graphical display of the MSMQ enterprise and allows administrators to create and configure sites and servers within the enterprise. Modern MSMQ systems leverage the Active Directory and the Microsoft Management Console, although older NT 4–based implementations use SQL Server and an MMC look-alike designed specifically to support MSMQ.

MSMQ administrators can add queues, remove queues, and configure messages, queues, machines, sites, and other aspects of the MSMQ enterprise through actions and object properties accessible through the MSMQ management console. MSMQ machines also provide a control panel applet used to configure local MSMQ storage and other machine-specific issues.

The process of installing MSMQ on a system can vary depending on the flavor of Windows you're using and the version of MSMQ you are applying. Presently, MSMQ servers can be installed through any one of the following packages:

- Windows NT 4 Option Pack
- Windows NT 4 Enterprise Edition
- Windows 2000 Server Distribution

23

MSMQ
ADMINISTRATION
AND ARCHITECTURE

The installation process walks you through adding your server to an existing MSMQ enterprise or creating a new enterprise. The installation process enables you to configure an MSMQ client installation share on your newly created server. The client installation share can be used to quickly configure other Windows systems as MSMQ clients in your enterprise.

Summary

So, those are the basics. In this chapter, you've seen an overview of the parts of an MSMQ enterprise. You have been introduced to MSMQ queues, messages, and machines as well as their several properties. MSMQ object property configuration and theory were also investigated. The final parts of this chapter examine how it all fits together and provide an orientation to the various administrative tasks and tools associated with MSMQ. The next two chapters get into the good stuff—how to develop programs that use it all.

Programming the MSMQ

IN THIS CHAPTER

There are two basic options when it comes to MSMQ programming: using the MSMQ API directly or using the MSMQ ActiveX components. The MSMQ API is the superset that provides access to all the various MSMQ features and intricacies.

As you might guess, the API approach makes programming with MSMQ a little more cumbersome than it might be otherwise. The ActiveX angle has one tremendous advantage, COM+. The native MSMQ API is a C programming language style interface based on a set of functions and structures. The ActiveX MSMQ programming interface is, obviously, a set of COM+ interfaces and objects. The ActiveX approach is thus universally available to anything from Java to Visual Basic Scripting Edition.

In order to be certified as "safe for consumption" in the scripting world, components generally provide a necessarily simplified set of services, as do the MSMQ ActiveX components. Don't let this sway you prematurely; my guess is that about 95% of your standard MSMQ applications need nothing more than the features presented by the MSMQ ActiveX components.

In the next two sections, you'll take a look at both the native MSMQ Library API and the ActiveX MSMQ components. You'll build the same application using each technique in turn, thus giving you a chance to evaluate the pros and cons of each. There is, of course, no reason to limit yourself to one interface or the other. You could quite easily use the ActiveX components for most of your application work and then access the native API calls when some nitty-gritty operations are required.

All the character and string manipulations in the samples use Unicode storage. This is a transitional time, somewhere between the widespread use of Unicode and the waning popularity of ANSI eight-bit characters. For this reason, I recommend using the generic character formats and macros (TCHAR and what have you) in most applications. I've used Unicode throughout these examples to narrow the focus on MSMQ and streamline the COM+ side of things. In general, both MSMQ and COM+ interfaces take only Unicode (also known as wide) characters. You might be interested to know that Windows NT and Windows 2000 use Unicode internally, so ANSI takes a performance hit where it is used.

The MSMQ Library API

What am I doing? Am I examining a big, flat, functional messaging API in a book about COM+? MSMQ is relevant to COM+ because it is a set of services and technologies, not just a programming interface. As you will soon see, MSMQ is one of the most exciting additions to the COM+ service smorgasbord. COM+ and MSMQ are related in many critical ways. MSMQ provides support for transporting asynchronous COM+ calls and moving persistent COM+ objects between applications; it features transactional queues that can participate in MTS/COM+ transactions and several other significant COM+

interactions. MSMQ is *the* COM+ message-oriented middleware system and thus is extremely relevant to any large-scale COM+ endeavor.

To get started, I'll show you how to build something simple that demonstrates all the basics. There are more than 25 different MSMQ library calls, but you'll only need a few to begin. You'll continue to construct more complete examples that tie in all the really powerful features of MSMQ as you move along.

I don't know about you, but I'd rather cut and paste boilerplate starter code than type it. So what could be more helpful to the professional programmer than a clean, concise, generic example. A 50Mb island coffee-roasting Web monster is about the last thing you have time to sort through. It makes matters worse when you finally locate the behavior you've been looking for, but then it takes you five hours to whack off all the fat so that you can use it! I will do my best to make sure that you don't have that problem here.

You will now write a program that creates a queue, sends a message to the queue, gets a message from the queue, and finally deletes the queue. You'll make it menu-driven so that you can use two copies of the application to communicate through messaging across a network. In fact, after completing any two of the several MSMQ API and ActiveX component versions of this example, you can use them together to prove interoperability.

Building an MSMQ Application with the MSMQ Library API

Before you can get started writing your first MSMQ application, you need to get a handle on the native MSMQ build environment. The previous chapter discussed setting up MSMQ and administering queues manually. The next step is to get the programmatic perspective on the same chores.

Setting up a middleware development environment can be a trying affair. One of the things that I really enjoy about developing in the Microsoft world is the absence of this concern. The only thing necessary to develop MSMQ applications is to install Visual C++, Version 6 (or a more recent version).

In order to compile applications with MSMQ, you'll need to include the MSMQ header, `MQ.H`, in your source. You'll also need to add the MSMQ library, `MQRT.LIB`, to the linker's library search list to successfully link your application. This is done in the Visual Studio shell by selecting [Project]Settings, choosing the link tab, and adding the library name to the Object/library modules: edit box. As a final point, you'll need to install MSMQ on your test system to actually run the application.

Format Names

You'll construct this first Hello-MSMQ program as a simple MSMQ API console application and communicate with a single queue. As you will see, all the MSMQ library calls begin with the MQ prefix. Your application will construct a queue at the behest of the user on the local machine.

All queues are uniquely defined by a GUID, which is assigned by MSMQ when the queue is constructed. Many MSMQ library calls require a queue format name, which is stored as a NULL-terminated Unicode string, such as PUBLIC=f5271149-8634-11d2-a4f0-ab19dda7f755. Format names are basically just the target queue's disposition and its GUID. They can be up to 44 characters in length for public queues and up to 54 characters in length for private queues.

Pathnames

Queues are created with a pathname that defines the queue display name and the machine that will host the queue, such as Tempest\BasicQueue. You can use a . to represent the local machine's queue server in this way: .\BasicQueue.

Looking Up Format Names

It isn't very useful to persist queue format names because this generates an instance dependency. In other words, if the queue is destroyed and recreated, the second instance will have a different format name. For this reason, MSMQ provides several ways to look up a queue's format name. Your first application looks up the format name using the pathname, which, for our example, will always be consistent. Table 24.1 shows the various format name lookup techniques.

TABLE 24.1   Format Name Lookup Functions

Lookup Function	*Description*
MQPathNameToFormatName()	Constructs a format name from a queue pathname.
MQInstanceToFormatName()	Constructs a format name from a queue GUID.
MQHandleToFormatName()	Constructs a format name from an open queue handle.

It's quite common to have information regarding a queue's pathname because this is the more human-readable of the unique queue descriptors. (This is similar to a ProgId for a COM object's GUID.) It's a simple matter to retrieve the format name by using the pathname, as the following code example demonstrates:

```
//Get the format name of the queue using the pathname
HRESULT hr;                           //Return status
WCHAR wcsFormatName[64];              //Queue format name
DWORD dwFormatNameLen = 64;          //Format name buf size
hr = MQPathNameToFormatName(     L".\\BasicQueue",
                                  wcsFormatName,
                                  &dwFormatNameLen );
```

Now you will take a closer look at some key parts of this application. Remember that building with Visual C++ 6, including the MQ.H header, and linking against the MQRT.LIB library are the only extraneous steps that you take to enable MSMQ development. The program is broken into four generic, reusable routines: CreateQueue(), SendMessage(), ReceiveMessage(), and DestroyQueue(). Begin by taking a look at the CreateQueue() routine.

Working with Properties

Before you can actually create the queue, you must set up a MQQUEUEPROPS structure that specifies the properties your new queue will have. The MQQUEUEPROPS structure is defined in MQ.H as follows:

```
typedef struct tagMQQUEUEPROPS
{
    DWORD cProp;
    QUEUEPROPID aPropID[];
    PROPVARIANT aPropVar[];
    HRESULT aStatus[];
} MQQUEUEPROPS;
```

The cProp field is used by MSMQ to determine how many properties you have specified. Each of the other three structure members is an array with one element for each property. The aPropID field is an array of unique MSMQ-defined property identifiers indicating the property at that index location. The aPropVar field is an array of variants used to store property values. The aStatus field is an array of HRESULTs used to store error and success codes associated with each property submitted. Queue managers and messages use the same kind of property structures.

In your CreateQueue() routine, you only need a single property, PROPID_Q_PATHNAME, to specify the queue pathname. Although several properties can be set at queue creation, the pathname is the only required property. The following code excerpt demonstrates the process of declaring and initializing the ID and value arrays. This example ignores property-based errors and can thus pass a NULL pointer in the aStatus field of the queue properties structure.

```
//Set up properties (we only need the path name property)
PROPVARIANT aVariant[1];              //Property value array
```

24

PROGRAMMING
THE MSMQ

```
QUEUEPROPID aPropId[1];                 //Property id array
aPropId[0] = PROPID_Q_PATHNAME;
aVariant[0].vt = VT_LPWSTR;
aVariant[0].pwszVal = L".\\BasicQueue";

//Set up the property struct
MQQUEUEPROPS QueueProps;                //Queue properties struct
QueueProps.cProp = 1;                   //Number of properties
QueueProps.aPropID = aPropId;           //Properties id array
QueueProps.aPropVar = aVariant;         //Properties value array
QueueProps.aStatus = NULL;              //No error reports
```

Creating a Queue

The next step is to call the MQCreateQueue() library routine with the initialized
MQQUEUEPROPS structure to create the queue. The MQCreateQueue() call can optionally
return the format name assigned to the newly created queue. Much like other COM+
services, all characters passed through the MSMQ API are stored in Unicode format.
This simple application uses Unicode characters internally, so all our library routine
calls will be wide versions as well. The format name buffer should be at least 44
Unicode characters for public queues and at least 54 Unicode characters for private
queues. If an undersized buffer is presented, the MQCreateQueue() call will return
MQ_INFORMATION_FORMATNAME_BUFFER_TOO_SMALL (recently awarded grand prize for
world's longest symbol), placing the required buffer size in the dwFormatNameLen parameter (if you provide one):

```
//Create queue
HRESULT hr;                             //Return status
WCHAR wcsFormatName[64];                //Queue format name
DWORD dwFormatNameLen = 64;             //Format name size
hr = MQCreateQueue( NULL,               //Security descriptor
                    &QueueProps,        //Queue properties
                    wcsFormatName,      //Receive buffer
                    &dwFormatNameLen ); //Size of buffer
```

Destroying a Queue

Next, take a look at the destroy side. All you need to destroy a queue is the format name
and the permission to do so. The trick here is how to get the format name. As discussed
earlier, you can discover the queue format name by passing the queue pathname to the
MSMQ MQPathNameToFormatName() library call:

```
//Get the format name of the queue using the pathname
HRESULT hr;                                  //Return status
WCHAR wcsFormatName[64];                      //Queue format name
DWORD dwFormatNameLen = 64;                   //Format name size
hr = MQPathNameToFormatName(    L".\\BasicQueue",
                                wcsFormatName,
                                &dwFormatNameLen );
```

It's always harder to create than to destroy and, as you can see from the queue deletion example that follows, MSMQ presents no exception:

```
//Destroy queue
hr = MQDeleteQueue(wcsFormatName);
```

Opening a Queue

As is the Windows way, you need to get a handle to any system resource before you can make use of it. Queue handles are returned by calling the MSMQ MQOpenQueue() library routine with the format name of the queue in question, along with access and sharing parameters. Tables 24.2 and 24.3 present the access and sharing options available. Access permissions cannot be changed while the queue is open.

TABLE 24.2 Queue Access Permissions

Access Flags	*Permission Granted*
MQ_PEEK_ACCESS	Messages can be examined but not removed.
MQ_SEND_ACCESS	Messages can be sent.
MQ_RECEIVE_ACCESS	Messages can be examined or removed.

TABLE 24.3 Queue Sharing Disposition

Sharing Flag	*How Shared*
MQ_DENY_NONE	The queue is available to all processes.
MQ_DENY_RECEIVE_SHARE	Only the calling process can retrieve messages from the queue.

Opening a queue is just like opening most other Win32 objects. Here is a sample:

```
//Open the queue with send access
QUEUEHANDLE hQueue;                        //Handle to queue
hr = MQOpenQueue(   wcsFormatName,         //Queue format name
                    MQ_SEND_ACCESS,        //Access requested
                    MQ_DENY_NONE,          //Share mode
                    &hQueue);              //Queue handle
```

Sending a Message

Now, take a look at sending messages. Sending a message is a lot like creating a queue because the main task is creating a set of properties and passing them to a MSMQ library call. The difference is that the properties are message properties stored in a MQMSGPROPS structure, as opposed to queue properties stored in a MQQUEUEPROPS structure. MSMQ

24

PROGRAMMING
THE MSMQ

messages are simply a collection of message properties. There are almost 50 different properties that apply to MSMQ message objects. In this basic example, you will use only three: `PROPID_M_LABEL` (specifies a label of the message), `PROPID_M_BODY_TYPE` (indicates the type of body the message contains), and `PROPID_M_BODY` (contains the body of the message).

Message labels can be up to 249 characters in length and, like all MSMQ strings, message labels are stored in Unicode format. Labels are optional and are generally used as a display string when enumerating messages in a queue. The message body is an arbitrary byte vector that has meaning only to the applications processing the message unless you set a type property to describe the data field. To send a message, an application calls the `MQSendMessage()` routine with three parameters: the handle of the queue in question, the message properties, and an optional transaction object pointer. I'll examine transactions in detail in the next chapter. Listing 24.1 demonstrates sending a simple byte-array message through MSMQ.

LISTING 24.1   A Simple String Message

```
//Allocate message property objects
MQMSGPROPS MsgProps;                 //Message properties struct
MSGPROPID aMsgPropId[3];             //Message property id array
PROPVARIANT aMsgPropVar[3];          //Message property value array

#define MSGLABELSIZE    64
#define MSGBODYSIZE     128

//Set up message label
static int s_cMessageNumber = 0;     //Message label counter
WCHAR wcsLabel[MSGLABELSIZE];        //Message label buffer
swprintf(wcsLabel,L"Message number %d", ++s_cMessageNumber);
aMsgPropId[0] = PROPID_M_LABEL;
aMsgPropVar[0].vt = VT_LPWSTR;
aMsgPropVar[0].pwszVal = wcsLabel;

//Set up message body
WCHAR wcsBuf[MSGBODYSIZE];
wprintf(L"Enter message body: ");
_getws(wcsBuf);
aMsgPropId[1] = PROPID_M_BODY;
aMsgPropVar[1].vt = VT_VECTOR | VT_UI1;
aMsgPropVar[1].caub.pElems = (LPBYTE)(wcsBuf);
aMsgPropVar[1].caub.cElems = (wcslen(wcsBuf) + 1) * sizeof(WCHAR);

//Set up the body type
aMsgPropId[2] = PROPID_M_BODY_TYPE;
aMsgPropVar[2].vt = VT_UI4;
aMsgPropVar[2].ulVal = VT_BSTR;
```

LISTING 24.1 Continued

```
//Set up message property struct
MsgProps.cProp = 3;              //Number of properties
MsgProps.aPropID = aMsgPropId;   //Ids of properties
MsgProps.aPropVar = aMsgPropVar; //Values of properties
MsgProps.aStatus = NULL;         //No error reports

//Send message
MQSendMessage(    hQueue,        //Queue handle
                  &MsgProps,     //Message properties
                  NULL );        //Transaction
```

Notice that the application could be constructed with only the PROPID_M_BODY property.
The PROPID_M_LABEL is a frill, but there is an ulterior motive behind the inclusion of the
PROPID_M_BODY_TYPE. Our application knows that message bodies always contain wide
character strings. The MSMQ ActiveX components, on the other hand, don't. In particu-
lar the ActiveX components only support the following types: VT_I2, VT_UI2, VT_I4,
VT_UI4, VT_R4, VT_R8, VT_CY, VT_DATE, VT_BOOL, VT_I1, VT_UI1, VT_BSTR, VT_ARRAY,
VT_STREAMED_OBJECT, and VT_STORED_OBJECT. Anything else will be treated as a raw
byte stream by the ActiveX components. Adding the VT_BSTR type property enables our
API application to easily interoperate with the ActiveX component applications.

Receiving a Message

Next, you will add some code to receive a message. The ReceiveMessage() routine
begins by looking up the target queue's format name and getting a handle to it just as it
did in the SendMessage() routine. The next step is to construct a MQMSGPROPS object to
act as a buffer for the properties you want to receive. You are not required to receive all
or any of the properties originally queued with the message. MSMQ discards any properties that you do not provide for in your inbound message structure. This can save unnecessary memory copying. To receive messages, you must also provide MSMQ information
regarding the size of the property buffers you are presenting. This is a simple matter of
providing property length properties for each variable length property buffer. The code
example in Listing 24.2 uses four properties compared to the send example's two,
and it demonstrates a simple message receive scenario. The two additional properties
are PROPID_M_LABEL_LEN and PROPID_M_BODY_SIZE. If any of the output buffers
prove too small for the queued data, MSMQ responds with an error such as
MQ_ERROR_BUFFER_OVERFLOW (a popular error indicating that the message body buffer is
too small).

LISTING 24.2 Receiving a Message

```
//Allocate message property objects
MQMSGPROPS MsgProps;                      //Message properties struct
MSGPROPID aMsgPropId[4];                  //Message property id array
PROPVARIANT aMsgPropVar[4];               //Message property value array

#define MSGLABELSIZE    64
#define MSGBODYSIZE     128

//Set up message label and length
WCHAR wcsLabel[MSGLABELSIZE];             //Message label buffer
aMsgPropId[0] = PROPID_M_LABEL;
aMsgPropVar[0].vt = VT_LPWSTR;
aMsgPropVar[0].pwszVal = wcsLabel;
aMsgPropId[1] = PROPID_M_LABEL_LEN;
aMsgPropVar[1].vt = VT_UI4;
aMsgPropVar[1].ulVal = MSGLABELSIZE;

//Set up message body and length
WCHAR wcsBody[MSGBODYSIZE];               //Message body buffer
aMsgPropId[2] = PROPID_M_BODY;
aMsgPropVar[2].vt = VT_VECTOR | VT_UI1;
aMsgPropVar[2].caub.pElems = (LPBYTE) wcsBody;
aMsgPropVar[2].caub.cElems = MSGBODYSIZE * sizeof(WCHAR);
aMsgPropId[3] = PROPID_M_BODY_SIZE;
aMsgPropVar[3].vt = VT_UI4;
aMsgPropVar[3].ulVal = MSGBODYSIZE * sizeof(WCHAR);

//Set up message property struct
MsgProps.cProp = 4;                       //Number of properties
MsgProps.aPropID = aMsgPropId;            //Ids of properties
MsgProps.aPropVar = aMsgPropVar;          //Values of properties
MsgProps.aStatus = NULL;                  //No error reports

//Get first message
hr = MQReceiveMessage(    hQueue,         //Queue to receive from
                          0,              //Timeout
                          MQ_ACTION_RECEIVE,  //Receive or peek
                          &MsgProps,      //Message properties
                          NULL,           //Overlapped structure
                          NULL,           //Callback function
                          NULL,           //Queue cursor
                          NULL );         //Transaction
```

The last step is to call the MSMQ `MQReceiveMessage()` library routine. The `MQReceiveMessage()` call takes several additional parameters. Of particular interest is the timeout parameter. `MQReceiveMessage()` supports asynchronous and synchronous calls. The synchronous versions might be blocking or nonblocking depending on the timeout value. A timeout value of zero produces a polling behavior, which we will use in our example. Values from one to the symbolic constant INFINITE cause the routine to block until either a message is available or the number of milliseconds specified transpires. Overlapped structure and callback function fields are used for asynchronous behavior, which we'll take a look at in the next chapter.

The next MQReceiveMessage() call parameter field of interest is the action field. Table 24.4 lists the available action options.

TABLE 24.4   Receive Message Actions

Receive Action	*Receive Behavior*
MQ_ACTION_RECEIVE	Reads the current message and removes it
MQ_ACTION_PEEK_CURRENT	Reads the current message without removing it
MQ_ACTION_PEEK_NEXT	Reads the next message without removing it

Because a queue might have more than one message available, MSMQ provides cursors that enable an application to scan through the queue, much like cursors used in database programming. The current example will set the MQReceiveMessage() cursor handle field to NULL, thus limiting you to reading from the front of the queue. Because you do not require a transaction, the transaction object is also set to NULL.

Closing a Queue

Standard resource management requires us to release any handle we acquire, and MSMQ is no exception. The following code sample demonstrates the MQCloseQueue() routine.

```
//Close queue
MQCloseQueue(hQueue);
```

That's all there is to it. Listing 24.3 shows the complete code for the MSMQ library version of your simple application.

LISTING 24.3   MSMQ Library Programming Example

```
// HelloMSMQ.cpp
//
// Simple MSMQ API Application


//Dependencies
#include <windows.h>
#include <stdio.h>
#include <conio.h>
#include <mq.h>
```

LISTING 24.3   Continued

```c
//Symbols
#define FORMATNAMESIZE    64
#define MSGBODYSIZE       128
#define MSGLABELSIZE      64
#define QUEUEPATHNAME     L".\\BasicQueue"


//Prototypes
void CreateQueue();
void SendMessage();
void ReceiveMessage();
void DestroyQueue();


//Application entry point
int main()
{
    int iChoice;      //User input buffer

    //User command processing loop
    do
    {
        //Display menu
        wprintf(L"Choose a command:\n");
        wprintf(L"0 - Exit\n");
        wprintf(L"1 - Create the Queue\n");
        wprintf(L"2 - Send a Message\n");
        wprintf(L"3 - Receive a Message\n");
        wprintf(L"4 - Destroy the Queue\n");
        wprintf(L"\n>> ");

        //Get selection
        iChoice = getch();
        wprintf(L"%c\n\n",iChoice);

        //Execute command
        switch ( iChoice )
        {
        case '0':
            break;

        case '1':
            CreateQueue();
            break;

        case '2':
            SendMessage();
            break;
```

LISTING 24.3   Continued

```
        case '3':
            ReceiveMessage();
            break;

        case '4':
            DestroyQueue();
            break;

        default:
            wprintf(L"Bad choice.\n\n");
            break;
        }
    } while ( iChoice != '0' );

    //Return success
    return 0;
}

void CreateQueue()
{
    //Set up properties (we only need the path name property)
    PROPVARIANT aVariant[1];            //Property value array
    QUEUEPROPID aPropId[1];             //Property id array
    aPropId[0] = PROPID_Q_PATHNAME;
    aVariant[0].vt = VT_LPWSTR;
    aVariant[0].pwszVal = QUEUEPATHNAME;

    //Set up the property struct
    MQQUEUEPROPS QueueProps;            //Queue properties struct
    QueueProps.cProp = 1;               //Number of properties
    QueueProps.aPropID = aPropId;       //Properties id array
    QueueProps.aPropVar = aVariant;     //Properties value array
    QueueProps.aStatus = NULL;                  //No error reports

    //Create queue
    HRESULT hr;                                 //Return status
    WCHAR wcsFormatName[FORMATNAMESIZE];        //Queue format name
    DWORD dwFormatNameLen = FORMATNAMESIZE;     //Size of format name
    hr = MQCreateQueue( NULL,           //Security descriptor
                        &QueueProps,    //Queue properties
                        wcsFormatName,  //Format name buffer
                        &dwFormatNameLen ); //Format name size

    //Check results
    if ( FAILED(hr) )
        wprintf(L"Error creating queue: %x\n\n",hr);
    else
        wprintf(L"Queue created with format name: %s\n\n",wcsFormatName);
}
```

24

PROGRAMMING
THE MSMQ

LISTING 24.3 Continued

```
void SendMessage()
{
    //Get the format name of the queue using the pathname
    HRESULT hr;                                    //Return status
    WCHAR wcsFormatName[FORMATNAMESIZE];           //Queue format name
    DWORD dwFormatNameLen = FORMATNAMESIZE;        //Size of format name
    hr = MQPathNameToFormatName(    QUEUEPATHNAME,
                                    wcsFormatName,
                                    &dwFormatNameLen );

    //Check results
    if ( FAILED(hr) )
    {
        wprintf(L"Error looking up queue format name: %x\n\n",hr);
        return;
    }

    //Open the queue with send access
    QUEUEHANDLE hQueue;                            //Handle to queue
    hr = MQOpenQueue( wcsFormatName,               //Queue format name
                      MQ_SEND_ACCESS,     //Access requested
                      MQ_DENY_NONE,       //Share mode
                      &hQueue);           //Queue handle

    //Check results
    if ( FAILED(hr) )
    {
        wprintf(L"Error opening queue: %x\n\n",hr);
        return;
    }

    //Allocate message property objects
    MQMSGPROPS MsgProps;                 //Message properties struct
    MSGPROPID aMsgPropId[3];             //Message property id array
    PROPVARIANT aMsgPropVar[3];          //Message property value array

    //Set up message label
    static int s_cMessageNumber = 0;                //Message label counter
    WCHAR wcsLabel[MSGLABELSIZE];                   //Message label buffer
    swprintf(wcsLabel,L"Message number %d", ++s_cMessageNumber);
    aMsgPropId[0] = PROPID_M_LABEL;
    aMsgPropVar[0].vt = VT_LPWSTR;
    aMsgPropVar[0].pwszVal = wcsLabel;

    //Set up message body
    WCHAR wcsBuf[MSGBODYSIZE];
    wprintf(L"Enter message body: ");
    _getws(wcsBuf);
```

LISTING 24.3   Continued

```
    aMsgPropId[1] = PROPID_M_BODY;
    aMsgPropVar[1].vt = VT_VECTOR | VT_UI1;
    aMsgPropVar[1].caub.pElems = (LPBYTE)(wcsBuf);
    aMsgPropVar[1].caub.cElems = (wcslen(wcsBuf) + 1) * sizeof(WCHAR);

    //Set up the body type
    aMsgPropId[2] = PROPID_M_BODY_TYPE;
    aMsgPropVar[2].vt = VT_UI4;
    aMsgPropVar[2].ulVal = VT_BSTR;

    //Set up message property struct
    MsgProps.cProp = 3;                        //Number of properties
    MsgProps.aPropID = aMsgPropId;             //Ids of properties
    MsgProps.aPropVar = aMsgPropVar;           //Values of properties
    MsgProps.aStatus = NULL;                   //No error reports

    //Send message
    MQSendMessage(    hQueue,                  //Queue handle
                      &MsgProps,               //Message properties
                      NULL );                  //Transaction

    //Check results
    if ( FAILED(hr) )
        wprintf(L"Error sending message: %x\n\n",hr);
    else
        wprintf(L"Message sent\n\n");

    //Close queue
    MQCloseQueue(hQueue);
}

void ReceiveMessage()
{
    //Get the format name of the queue using the pathname
    HRESULT hr;                                      //Return status
    WCHAR wcsFormatName[FORMATNAMESIZE];             //Queue format name
    DWORD dwFormatNameLen = FORMATNAMESIZE;          //Size of format name
    hr = MQPathNameToFormatName(    QUEUEPATHNAME,
                                    wcsFormatName,
                                    &dwFormatNameLen );

    //Check results
    if ( FAILED(hr) )
    {
        wprintf(L"Error looking up queue format name: %x\n\n",hr);
        return;
    }

    //Open the queue with send access
```

24

LISTING 24.3   Continued

```
QUEUEHANDLE hQueue;                        //Handle to queue
hr = MQOpenQueue( wcsFormatName,           //Queue format name
                  MQ_RECEIVE_ACCESS,       //Access requested
                  MQ_DENY_NONE,            //Share mode
                  &hQueue);                //Queue handle

//Check results
if ( FAILED(hr) )
{
    wprintf(L"Error opening queue: %x\n\n",hr);
    return;
}

//Allocate message property objects
MQMSGPROPS MsgProps;                   //Message properties struct
MSGPROPID aMsgPropId[4];               //Message property id array
PROPVARIANT aMsgPropVar[4];            //Message property value array

//Set up message label and length
WCHAR wcsLabel[MSGLABELSIZE];                     //Message label buffer
aMsgPropId[0] = PROPID_M_LABEL;
aMsgPropVar[0].vt = VT_LPWSTR;
aMsgPropVar[0].pwszVal = wcsLabel;
aMsgPropId[1] = PROPID_M_LABEL_LEN;
aMsgPropVar[1].vt = VT_UI4;
aMsgPropVar[1].ulVal = MSGLABELSIZE;

//Set up message body and length
WCHAR wcsBody[MSGBODYSIZE];                       //Message body buffer
aMsgPropId[2] = PROPID_M_BODY;
aMsgPropVar[2].vt = VT_VECTOR | VT_UI1;
aMsgPropVar[2].caub.pElems = (LPBYTE)wcsBody;
aMsgPropVar[2].caub.cElems = MSGBODYSIZE * sizeof(WCHAR);
aMsgPropId[3] = PROPID_M_BODY_SIZE;
aMsgPropVar[3].vt = VT_UI4;
aMsgPropVar[3].ulVal = MSGBODYSIZE;

//Set up message property struct
MsgProps.cProp = 4;                        //Number of properties
MsgProps.aPropID = aMsgPropId;             //IDs of properties
MsgProps.aPropVar = aMsgPropVar;           //Values of properties
MsgProps.aStatus = NULL;                   //No error reports

//Get first message
hr = MQReceiveMessage(    hQueue,           //Queue to receive from
                          0,                //Timeout
                          MQ_ACTION_RECEIVE,//Receive or peek
                          &MsgProps,        //Message properties
                          NULL,             //Overlapped structure
```

LISTING 24.3 Continued

```
                                    NULL,           //Callback function
                                    NULL,           //Queue cursor
                                    NULL );         //Transaction
    //Check results
    if ( FAILED(hr) )
    {
        wprintf(L"Error receiving message: %x\n\n",hr);
        MQCloseQueue(hQueue);
        return;
    }

    //Display message
    wcsBody[(aMsgPropVar[3].ulVal)/sizeof(WCHAR)] = L'\0';
    wprintf(L"Retrieved message label:\n\t%s\n",wcsLabel);
    wprintf(L"Retrieved message body:\n\t%s\n\n",wcsBody);

    //Close queue
    MQCloseQueue(hQueue);
}

void DestroyQueue()
{
    //Get the format name of the queue using the pathname
    HRESULT hr;                                 //Return status
    WCHAR wcsFormatName[FORMATNAMESIZE];         //Queue format name
    DWORD dwFormatNameLen = FORMATNAMESIZE;      //Size of format name
    hr = MQPathNameToFormatName(    QUEUEPATHNAME,
                                    wcsFormatName,
                                    &dwFormatNameLen );

    //Check results
    if ( FAILED(hr) )
    {
        wprintf(L"Error looking up queue format name: %x\n\n",hr);
        return;
    }

    //Destroy queue
    hr = MQDeleteQueue(wcsFormatName);

    //Check results
    if ( FAILED(hr) )
        wprintf(L"Error destroying queue: %x\n\n",hr);
    else
        wprintf(L"Queue destroyed\n\n");
}
```

24

PROGRAMMING
THE MSMQ

The MSMQ ActiveX Control API

ActiveX components are a distribution mechanism for COM+ class behavior operating behind COM+ interfaces in the context of dynamically constructed COM+ objects. That means the behavior of MSMQ ActiveX components is well encapsulated, and the way it was developed has nothing to do with the way it is used. In Visual C++ alone, there are several ways to make use of the MSMQ components, including raw COM+ interfaces, Class Wizard dispatch wrappers, and ATL-style smart pointers. A multitude of additional techniques is available in other languages. For example, you'll try three different approaches: raw COM, smart pointers with ATL, and finally a Visual Basic script to ensure low-level programmer humility.

The first example using the MSMQ ActiveX components will use raw COM+ interfaces. All COM+ components expose COM+ interfaces. COM+ consumers, on the other hand, can use any level of abstraction available in programming against COM+ objects. The lowest and, often, the most powerful approach is to use the COM+ interfaces directly. This usually means quite a bit of work for the developer, along with several easy-to-step-into snares. For example, a script using an object doesn't have to remember to release the object; the scripting engine takes care of that. A low-level COM+ interface developer who fails to release an interface pointer has a resource leak on his hands.

As you've probably determined by now, this is a hard-core COM+ book, so of course it looks at the bottom layer of things. Even if you decide to adopt one of the other styles of MSMQ development presented here, the ensuing discussion of what's going on beneath the covers will probably make your high-level efforts that much easier.

Your second COM+ cut at the "Hello World" MSMQ application will be with the Active Template Library–derived smart pointer technique. C++ developers have always enjoyed the power of their language but at the same time have envied the ease with which many applications, especially those related to COM, could be constructed in higher-level environments like Visual Basic. ATL has made serious inroads in simplifying the C++ COM+ programming model. ATL has also become more than just a set of templates you can use for common coding tasks. Visual C++ 5 featured the `#import` statement, which provided the capability to generate "compilable" (is that a word?) type information directly from a COM+ component on-the-fly. Visual C++ 6 improves the studio and debugging tools that work with ATL. Perhaps the most exciting ATL-derived technology is the attribute COM+ programming techniques to be introduced with Visual C++ 7. Attributes such as `coclass` (for automatically turning a C++ class into a COM+ class by generating ATL-based code during the build process) are quite enticing. In the second MSMQ ActiveX component example, you'll take a look at how much easier COM+ programming can be using smart pointers and a bit of ATL.

In the final example, you'll write a Visual Basic script that performs the same behavior as the previous applications. No, it isn't here to depress you. You know that it's well worth typing a few extra lines of code to gain performance in a critical application with an extended life span. But what about a system administrator who needs to glue some *ad hoc* stuff into his enterprise? Or how about presenting a scriptable message-based interface to your server-side application without writing any client proxies? In these contexts, a Visual Basic script would make the most sense. This final example will complete our high-level view of MSMQ programming.

MSMQ ActiveX Classes

There are 10 different COM+ classes in the MSMQ ActiveX component set. There are also 10 additional object types dedicated to MSMQ email support. This might seem like a lot compared to the meager 26 total functions in the MSMQ library API. The important thing to remember about a good COM+ programming model is that it simplifies the process of development by modeling the entities in the system, not necessarily by reducing the total object count. It's much easier to understand and work with a set of objects that map directly to the mechanisms in the problem domain rather than work with a smaller set of arbitrarily reduced components with nonintuitive interfaces. This is especially the case when working with high-level programming systems that have trouble dealing with more than one interface per object, such as VBScript. In fact, the MSMQ ActiveX component set has been tailored to fit well into any programming environment, particularly those at higher levels.

MSMQ COM+ classes all begin with the MSMQ prefix. Each MSMQ COM+ class supplies one dual interface named for the class with the traditional I prefix. A basic application like yours will require the use of three of the MSMQ classes and their subordinate interfaces:

MSMQQueueInfo	IMSMQQueueInfo
MSMQQueue	IMSMQQueue
MSMQMessage	IMSMQMessage

The first class is MSMQQueueInfo. This object type is used to create and destroy queues and also to open existing queues. The next class you will work with is the MSMQQueue class. The queue class is used to represent actual queues (instances of queues) in the MSMQ system providing support for browsing and retrieving messages from queues. The final class in the introductory suite is the MSMQMessage class. MSMQMessage instances are used to represent individual messages that are sent or received through the queue objects.

Building an MSMQ Application with Raw COM+ Interfaces

Building COM+ applications with native COM+ calls provides many powerful and previously documented COM+ advantages. It, of course, carries with it the overhead of maintaining the generic nature of COM+ interfaces, required IUnknown features, and various initialization and shutdown issues. The great part is that you only have to learn COM+ once, and yet the issues it contends with occur over and over again in a myriad of programming situations. So without further ado, you will build a MSMQ application with native COM.

Your COM+ application versions will not need any explicit linkage adjustments in the project settings. After all, one of the hallmarks of COM+ programming is dynamic interface resolution. Next, note that you will need to present the compiler with different support, depending on how you want to tackle your problem. In the low-level COM+ example, you will need to include a header generated from the MSMQ component type library. The header in question is MQOAI.H, and it is provided with Visual C++. This header defines the various interfaces and class IDs needed to access the MSMQ COM+ objects.

Defining Interfaces and GUIDs

There is one "gotcha." The MQOAI.H header can be used standalone because it includes the other necessary COM+ elements. One of the most important of these indirectly included header files is objbase.h. The problem lies in the fact that GUIDs defined within MQOAI.H appear something like this:

```
DEFINE_GUID(IID_IMSMQMessage,0xD7D6E074L,
          0xDCCD,0x11D0,0xAA,0x4B,0x00,0x60,0x97,0x0D,0xEB,0xAE);
```

Defining things—that is, actually allocating storage—through statements in a header file can lead to several flavors of linker trauma. The use of precompiled headers complicates the issue somewhat. For this reason, objbase.h uses the following statement to define DEFINE_GUID:

```
#ifndef INITGUID
#define DEFINE_GUID(name, l, w1, w2, b1, b2, b3, b4, b5, b6, b7, b8) \
    EXTERN_C const GUID FAR name
#else

#define DEFINE_GUID(name, l, w1, w2, b1, b2, b3, b4, b5, b6, b7, b8) \
        EXTERN_C const GUID name \
                = { l, w1, w2, { b1, b2,  b3,  b4,  b5,  b6,  b7,  b8 } }
#endif // INITGUID
```

As you can see, INITGUID must be defined precisely once to generate the actual GUIDs. If you fail to define INITGUID, you'll end up with unresolved references to all your MSMQ GUIDs. If you define it in more than one module, you'll end up with duplicate GUIDs and more linker errors. Your simple application exists within a single source file that enables you to use the following simplified include approach:

```
//MSMQ ActiveX component header
//  ( We need to define INITGUID to force the definition
//     of the MSMQ GUIDs )
#define INITGUID
#include <mqoai.h>
```

Initializing COM

Any use of COM+ beyond CoGetMalloc() requires proper initialization. The following lines set up and shut down your single-threaded application's single-threaded apartment. With the exception of these additions, the main() routine is otherwise identical to that of the previous example. Calling CoInitialize() would have the same effect as the call to CoInitializeEx().

```
//Initialize COM
CoInitializeEx(NULL,COINIT_APARTMENTTHREADED);

//body of main function
...

//Uninitialize COM+ and return success
CoUninitialize();
```

CoInitialize() is deprecated in modern COM+ development, however. If you have trouble compiling the call to CoInitializeEx(), you might try defining the symbol _WIN32_DCOM. CoInitializeEx() is conditionally declared based on either the _WIN32_DCOM symbol or a value in _WIN32_NT greater than or equal to 0x0400. NT 5 beta 2, for instance, has problems with CoInitializeEx() that can be solved simply by including _WIN32_DCOM in your project symbol list (Project[Settings] C/C++ tab).

Creating a Queue

In order to create a queue, you'll need to get a pointer to the IMSMQQueueInfo interface of a MSMQQueueInfo object. The IMSMQQueueInfo interface supplies a Create() method that creates new queues. Because you have migrated from a functional API to a component-oriented interface, property and object affinity will play an important part in the code required by this application. In particular, values are often set and retrieved as properties of the various object types, as opposed to using inquiry function calls. Here is a sample call to `CoCreateInstance()` that will give you the object and interface you need:

```
//Get an interface pointer to a QueueInfo object
HRESULT hr;
IMSMQQueueInfo * pQInfo;
hr = CoCreateInstance(   CLSID_MSMQQueueInfo,
                         NULL,
                         CLSCTX_SERVER,
                         IID_IMSMQQueueInfo,
                         (LPVOID *)&pQInfo );
```

VARIANTs

As you have learned previously, queues can be created with transactional and/or global attributes. Your basic requirements call for no special features, so you can simply set the required pathname and pass in false queue attributes to the `IMSMQQueueInfo::Create()` call. Because the MSMQ interfaces were designed to support high-level application programming environments, most method parameters will take the form of `BSTR`s and `VARIANT`s. `VARIANT`s are used heavily by automation because of their support for untyped scripting environments. `VARIANT`s have a `vt` field used to flag the type stored and a field in the form of a union of all the supported variant types. Here's the code to set up the required variants and create the queue:

```
//Create a default queue
VARIANT varTransactional;
   varTransactional.vt = VT_BOOL;
   varTransactional.boolVal = FALSE;
VARIANT varWorldReadable;
   varWorldReadable.vt = VT_BOOL;
   varWorldReadable.boolVal = FALSE;
pQInfo->put_PathName(L".\\BasicQueue");
   hr = pQInfo->Create( &varTransactional, &varWorldReadable );
```

BSTRs

After successful queue creation, the format name of the created queue is stored as an attribute of the queue info object. Retrieving the format name requires that you make use of a `BSTR`. `BSTR`s are Basic (Visual Basic) formatted strings and are always stored using Unicode characters. `BSTR`s are basically `WCHAR` pointers with a twist: The two bytes before the first character pointed to are used to store the string's length. An important aspect of `BSTR` usage in COM+ is that servers often allocate the memory for `BSTR`s, and clients are expected to release the memory. COM+ methods that require a pointer to a `BSTR` are usually interested in passing a `BSTR` buffer back to the client, thus handing off control of the buffer. Because of the prefixed nature of `BSTR`s, it is easier to allocate and de-allocate them with the system `SysAllocString()` and `SysFreeString()` calls. Here is the code that retrieves the newly created queue's format name:

```
//Display format name
BSTR bstrFormatName;
pQInfo->get_FormatName(&bstrFormatName);
wprintf(L"Queue created with format name: %s\n\n",bstrFormatName);
SysFreeString(bstrFormatName);
```

Notice the get_ and put_ methods used to operate on the properties of the MSMQ
COM+ objects in the two preceding blocks of code. These are the low-level COM+ property accessors. Wrapper versions of these same routines with the prefix form Get and
Put, will be used in your smart pointer example. Be sure to distinguish between these
two because the low-level versions return HRESULTs, whereas the wrappers throw exceptions. Unexpected exceptions are never fun.

Unlike so many other higher level forms of COM+ programming, down here in the thick
of it you need to be sure to release all your interface pointers when you are finished with
them. Releasing the IMSMQQueueInfo interface pointer completes the CreateQueue()
function:

```
//Release the QueueInfo object
pQInfo->Release();
```

Destroying a Queue

Destroying a queue is almost exactly the same procedurally as creating a queue. You simply create a MSMQQueueInfo object, set the target queue pathname, and then invoke the
MSMQQueueInfo::Delete() method. Here's an example.

```
//Setup queue info path & destroy queue
BSTR bstrPathName;
bstrPathName = SysAllocString(L".\\BasicQueue");
pQInfo->put_PathName(bstrPathName);
SysFreeString(bstrPathName);
hr = pQInfo->Delete();
pQInfo->Release();
```

Opening a Queue

In order to send and receive messages, you will need to open a target queue. An
MSMQQueueInfo object will provide you with the means to get an interface pointer to a
queue, given the pathname. The queue will be represented as a MSMQQueue object. After
creating a MSMQQueueInfo object, you invoke the IMSMQQueueInfo::Open() method,
which returns the queue interface pointer as its last parameter if successful. The
MSMQQueue class provides a convenient Handle property, which can be conveniently used
to bail out of the COM+ world in order to use features available only through MSMQ
API functions. Here's an example:

```
//Setup queue info path & get interface pointer to queue
IMSMQQueue * pQueue;
```

```
BSTR bstrPathName;
bstrPathName = SysAllocString(L".\\BasicQueue");
pQInfo->put_PathName(bstrPathName);
SysFreeString(bstrPathName);
hr = pQInfo->Open( MQ_SEND_ACCESS, MQ_DENY_NONE, &pQueue );
pQInfo->Release();
```

Sending a Message

In order to send a message to a queue, you'll need to get interface pointers to three separate objects. An `MSMQQueueInfo` object to open the queue, an `MSMQQueue` object to send the message to, and an `MSMQMessage` object to represent the message. Your application needs to create a message with a label and a text body to send. As you might guess, this is done by creating a message object and setting its properties. Here is an example:

```
//Get an interface pointer to a message object
IMSMQMessage * pMsg;
    hr = CoCreateInstance(   CLSID_MSMQMessage,
                             NULL,
                             CLSCTX_SERVER,
                             IID_IMSMQMessage,
                             (LPVOID *)&pMsg );


//Set up message label
static int s_cMessageNumber = 0;                //Message label counter
WCHAR wcsLabel[MSGLABELSIZE];                    //Message label buffer
swprintf(wcsLabel,L"Message number %d", ++s_cMessageNumber);
BSTR bstrLabel = SysAllocString( wcsLabel);
pMsg->put_Label(bstrLabel);
SysFreeString(bstrLabel);

//Set up message body
WCHAR wcsBody[MSGBODYSIZE];
wprintf(L"Enter message body: ");
_getws(wcsBody);
BSTR bstrBody = SysAllocString(wcsBody);
VARIANT varBody;
varBody.vt = VT_BSTR;
varBody.bstrVal = bstrBody;
pMsg->put_Body(varBody);
```

The last step is to transmit the message to the target queue. The `IMSMQMessage::Send()` method requires an interface pointer to the target queue and transaction information. You will not be using transactions until the next chapter, so you can simply pass in a `FALSE` Boolean type variant. Notice that when programming with C++ at the native COM+ level, you must provide all method parameters even though COM+ supports optional parameters in higher-level programming environments. Here is an example of the `IMSMQMessage::Send()` call:

```
//Send message
VARIANT varTransactional;
varTransactional.vt = VT_BOOL;
varTransactional.boolVal = FALSE;
hr = pMsg->Send( pQueue, &varTransactional );
    pQueue->Release();
    pMsg->Release();
    SysFreeString(bstrBody);
```

Receiving a Message

Receiving a message is always a little bit tougher than sending one because of the potential for unknown buffer sizes and such. Unlike the `IMSMQMessage::Send()` method, the `Receive()` method is a member of the `IMSMQQueue` interface. The first step in retrieving a message is to open a queue for receive access:

```
//Setup queue info path & get interface pointer to queue
IMSMQQueue * pQueue;
BSTR bstrPathName;
bstrPathName = SysAllocString(L".\\BasicQueue");
pQInfo->put_PathName(bstrPathName);
SysFreeString(bstrPathName);
hr = pQInfo->Open( MQ_RECEIVE_ACCESS, MQ_DENY_NONE, &pQueue );
pQInfo->Release();
```

The `IMSMQQueue::Receive()` method takes several parameters. The first specifies transactional status, which you will once again set to false. The second parameter sets an `IMSMQQueueInfo` interface pointer describing the original message destination queue in the returned message object. This makes it possible to determine the original destination of a message retrieved from a Dead Letter or other such queue. The third parameter specifies whether to retrieve the message body or not. The fourth parameter is the timeout value, which specifies whether the function will wait for a message or return immediately. Last, but not least, an interface pointer for the returned message object must be supplied.

The message object provides various attributes of interest. A receive call that times out is not strictly considered an error. If no messages are available, the `IMSMQMessage` interface pointer parameter will be set to NULL. For this reason, you should check the value of your message interface pointer against NULL before using it. Listing 24.4 is an example of a simple, nonblocking synchronous receive scenario.

LISTING 24.4   A Simple Nonblocking Synchronous Receive

```
//Receive message using nonblocking synchronous call
IMSMQMessage * pMsg;
VARIANT varTransaction;
```

24

LISTING 24.4 Continued

```
varTransaction.vt = VT_BOOL;
varTransaction.boolVal = FALSE;
VARIANT varWantDestQueue;
varWantDestQueue.vt = VT_BOOL;
varWantDestQueue.boolVal = FALSE;
VARIANT varWantBody;
varWantBody.vt = VT_BOOL;
varWantBody.boolVal = TRUE;
VARIANT varTimeout;
varTimeout.vt = VT_I4;
varTimeout.lVal = 0;
hr = pQueue->Receive(    &varTransaction,
                         &varWantDestQueue,
                         &varWantBody,
                         &varTimeout,
                         &pMsg );

pQueue->Release();

//Get message label
BSTR bstrLabel;
pMsg->get_Label( &bstrLabel );
wprintf(L"Retrieved message label:\n\t%s\n",bstrLabel);
SysFreeString(bstrLabel);

//Get message body
VARIANT varBody;
pMsg->get_Body( &varBody );
wprintf(L"Retrieved message body:\n\t%s\n\n", varBody.bstrVal );
VariantClear(&varBody);

//Release message object
pMsg->Release();
```

Closing a Queue

As you have probably noticed in the previous examples, there is no explicit MSMQ-defined mechanism to close a queue or any other object for that matter. This behavior is, of course, already built into COM+ in the form of the IUnknown::Release(). The final release of an MSMQ ActiveX object's interface causes it to perform any necessary shutdown operations. Closing a queue from the COM+ perspective is, therefore, as simple as this:

```
pQueue->Release();
```

As you can see, the native COM+ approach to MSMQ programming can be a bit more cumbersome than using the MSMQ API directly. The intuitive programming model is the most significant strength of this approach. The benefits provided by COM+ will increase as your applications grow larger and more distributed. The COM+ MSMQ angle is also significantly easier to program as you move up the COM+ client food chain.

In Listing 24.5, you'll notice a lot of error-handling code. Functional approaches to API development generally require a check for every return value. This application is no different, but I have made an exception in the area of put and get methods operating on properties. These are indeed function calls and could fail, but the loss of clarity involved with adding the additional checks caused me to leave them out because there are many HRESULT checking examples elsewhere throughout the code. Getting and setting properties on in-process objects is a pretty reliable affair, but a real production system should never take this kind of shortcut. Listing 24.5 shows the complete code for the native COM+ MSMQ "Hello World" application.

LISTING 24.5 MSMQ Raw COM+ Programming Example

```
// HelloMSMQ.cpp
//
// Simple MSMQ Raw COM+ application


//MSMQ ActiveX component header
//   ( We need to define INITGUID to force the definition
//     of the MSMQ GUIDs )
#define INITGUID


//Standard Dependencies
#include <windows.h>
#include <stdio.h>
#include <conio.h>
#include <mqoai.h>


//Symbols
#define MSGBODYSIZE        128
#define MSGLABELSIZE        64
#define QUEUEPATHNAME    L".\\BasicQueue"


//Prototypes
void CreateQueue();
void SendMessage();
void ReceiveMessage();
void DestroyQueue();


//Application entry point
```

LISTING 24.5   Continued

```c
int main()
{
    int iChoice;                    //User input buffer

    //Initialize COM
    CoInitializeEx(NULL,COINIT_APARTMENTTHREADED);

    //User command processing loop
    do
    {
        //Display menu
        wprintf(L"Choose a command:\n");
        wprintf(L"0 - Exit\n");
        wprintf(L"1 - Create the Queue\n");
        wprintf(L"2 - Send a Message\n");
        wprintf(L"3 - Receive a Message\n");
        wprintf(L"4 - Destroy the Queue\n");
        wprintf(L"\n>> ");

        //Get selection
        iChoice = getch();
        wprintf(L"%c\n\n",iChoice);

        //Execute command
        switch ( iChoice )
        {
        case '0':
            break;

        case '1':
            CreateQueue();
            break;

        case '2':
            SendMessage();
            break;

        case '3':
            ReceiveMessage();
            break;

        case '4':
            DestroyQueue();
            break;

        default:
            wprintf(L"Bad choice.\n\n");
            break;
        }
```

LISTING 24.5   Continued

```
    } while ( iChoice != '0' );

    //Uninitialize COM+ and return success
    CoUninitialize();
    return 0;
}

void CreateQueue()
{
    //Get an interface pointer to a QueueInfo object
    HRESULT hr;
    IMSMQQueueInfo * pQInfo;
    hr = CoCreateInstance(     CLSID_MSMQQueueInfo,
                               NULL,
                               CLSCTX_SERVER,
                               IID_IMSMQQueueInfo,
                               (LPVOID *)&pQInfo );

    //Check result
    if ( FAILED( hr ) )
    {
        wprintf(L"Error creating queue info object: %x\n\n",hr);
        return;
    }

    //Create a default queue
    VARIANT varTransactional;
    varTransactional.vt = VT_BOOL;
    varTransactional.boolVal = FALSE;
    VARIANT varWorldReadable;
    varWorldReadable.vt = VT_BOOL;
    varWorldReadable.boolVal = FALSE;
    pQInfo->put_PathName(QUEUEPATHNAME);
    hr = pQInfo->Create( &varTransactional, &varWorldReadable );

    //Check result
    if ( FAILED(hr) )
    {
        wprintf(L"Error creating queue: %x\n\n",hr);
        pQInfo->Release();
        return;
    }

    //Display format name
    BSTR bstrFormatName;
    pQInfo->get_FormatName(&bstrFormatName);
    wprintf(L"Queue created with format name: %s\n\n",bstrFormatName);
    SysFreeString(bstrFormatName);
```

24

LISTING 24.5   Continued

```
    //Release the QueueInfo object
    pQInfo->Release();
}

void SendMessage()
{
    //Get an interface pointer to a QueueInfo object
    HRESULT hr;
    IMSMQQueueInfo * pQInfo;
    hr = CoCreateInstance(    CLSID_MSMQQueueInfo,
                              NULL,
                              CLSCTX_SERVER,
                              IID_IMSMQQueueInfo,
                              (LPVOID *)&pQInfo );

    //Check result
    if ( FAILED( hr ) )
    {
        wprintf(L"Error creating queue info object: %x\n\n",hr);
        return;
    }

    //Setup queue info path & get interface pointer to queue
    IMSMQQueue * pQueue;
    BSTR bstrPathName;
    bstrPathName = SysAllocString(QUEUEPATHNAME);
    pQInfo->put_PathName(bstrPathName);
    SysFreeString(bstrPathName);
    hr = pQInfo->Open( MQ_SEND_ACCESS, MQ_DENY_NONE, &pQueue );
    pQInfo->Release();

    //Check queue open result
    if ( FAILED( hr ) )
    {
        wprintf(L"Error opening queue object: %x\n\n",hr);
        return;
    }

    //Get an interface pointer to a message object
    IMSMQMessage * pMsg;
    hr = CoCreateInstance(    CLSID_MSMQMessage,
                              NULL,
                              CLSCTX_SERVER,
                              IID_IMSMQMessage,
                              (LPVOID *)&pMsg );

    //Check result
    if ( FAILED( hr ) )
    {
```

LISTING 24.5 Continued

```
        wprintf(L"Error creating message object: %x\n\n",hr);
        pQueue->Release();
        return;
    }

    //Set up message label
    static int s_cMessageNumber = 0;              //Message label counter
    WCHAR wcsLabel[MSGLABELSIZE];                 //Message label buffer
    swprintf(wcsLabel,L"Message number %d", ++s_cMessageNumber);
    BSTR bstrLabel = SysAllocString( wcsLabel);
    pMsg->put_Label(bstrLabel);
    SysFreeString(bstrLabel);

    //Set up message body
    WCHAR wcsBody[MSGBODYSIZE];
    wprintf(L"Enter message body: ");
    _getws(wcsBody);
    BSTR bstrBody = SysAllocString(wcsBody);
    VARIANT varBody;
    varBody.vt = VT_BSTR;
    varBody.bstrVal = bstrBody;
    pMsg->put_Body(varBody);

    //Send message
    VARIANT varTransactional;
    varTransactional.vt = VT_BOOL;
    varTransactional.boolVal = FALSE;
    hr = pMsg->Send( pQueue, &varTransactional );
    pQueue->Release();
    pMsg->Release();
    SysFreeString(bstrBody);

    //Check result
    if ( FAILED(hr) )
        wprintf(L"Error sending message: %x\n\n",hr);
    else
        wprintf(L"Message sent\n\n");
}

void ReceiveMessage()
{
    //Get an interface pointer to a QueueInfo object
    HRESULT hr;
    IMSMQQueueInfo * pQInfo;
    hr = CoCreateInstance(    CLSID_MSMQQueueInfo,
                              NULL,
                              CLSCTX_SERVER,
                              IID_IMSMQQueueInfo,
                              (LPVOID *)&pQInfo );
```

LISTING 24.5   Continued

```
//Check result
   if ( FAILED( hr ) )
   {
       wprintf(L"Error creating queue info object: %x\n\n",hr);
       return;
   }

   //Setup queue info path & get interface pointer to queue
   IMSMQQueue * pQueue;
   BSTR bstrPathName;
   bstrPathName = SysAllocString(QUEUEPATHNAME);
   pQInfo->put_PathName(bstrPathName);
   SysFreeString(bstrPathName);
   hr = pQInfo->Open( MQ_RECEIVE_ACCESS, MQ_DENY_NONE, &pQueue );
   pQInfo->Release();

   //Check queue open result
   if ( FAILED( hr ) )
   {
       wprintf(L"Error opening queue object: %x\n\n",hr);
       return;
   }

   //Receive message using non-blocking synchronous call
   IMSMQMessage * pMsg;
   VARIANT varTransaction;
   varTransaction.vt = VT_BOOL;
   varTransaction.boolVal = FALSE;
   VARIANT varWantDestQueue;
   varWantDestQueue.vt = VT_BOOL;
   varWantDestQueue.boolVal = FALSE;
   VARIANT varWantBody;
   varWantBody.vt = VT_BOOL;
   varWantBody.boolVal = TRUE;
   VARIANT varTimeout;
   varTimeout.vt = VT_I4;
   varTimeout.lVal = 0;
   hr = pQueue->Receive(    &varTransaction,
                            &varWantDestQueue,
                            &varWantBody,
                            &varTimeout,
                            &pMsg );
   pQueue->Release();

   //Check result
   if ( FAILED(hr) )
   {
       wprintf(L"Error receiving message: %x\n\n",hr);
       return;
```

LISTING 24.5 Continued

```
    }
    else if ( NULL == pMsg )
    {
        wprintf(L"No messages in queue\n\n");
        return;
    }

    //Get and display message label
    BSTR bstrLabel;
    pMsg->get_Label( &bstrLabel );
    wprintf(L"Retrieved message label:\n\t%s\n",bstrLabel);
    SysFreeString(bstrLabel);

    //Get and display message body
    VARIANT varBody;
    pMsg->get_Body( &varBody );
    wprintf(L"Retrieved message body:\n\t%s\n\n", varBody.bstrVal );
    VariantClear(&varBody);

    //Release message object
    pMsg->Release();
}

void DestroyQueue()
{
    //Get an interface pointer to a QueueInfo object
    HRESULT hr;
    IMSMQQueueInfo * pQInfo;
    hr = CoCreateInstance(    CLSID_MSMQQueueInfo,
                              NULL,
                              CLSCTX_SERVER,
                              IID_IMSMQQueueInfo,
                              (LPVOID *)&pQInfo );

    //Check result
    if ( FAILED( hr ) )
    {
        wprintf(L"Error creating queue info object: %x\n\n",hr);
        return;
    }

    //Setup queue info path & destroy queue
    BSTR bstrPathName;
    bstrPathName = SysAllocString(QUEUEPATHNAME);
    pQInfo->put_PathName(bstrPathName);
    SysFreeString(bstrPathName);
    hr = pQInfo->Delete();
    pQInfo->Release();
```

LISTING 24.5   Continued

```
    //Check queue open result
  if ( FAILED( hr ) )
      wprintf(L"Error destroying queue object: %x\n\n",hr);
  else
      wprintf(L"Queue destroyed\n\n");
}
```

Building an MSMQ Application with Smart Pointers

The last C++ endeavor in this chapter will take a smart pointer/ATL approach to building the "Hello World" MSMQ application. The primary goal of ATL technology is to simplify COM+ development in C++ without removing any power or speed. This was originally effected through templates alone but has moved into the arena of compiler technology. Visual C++ and ATL are tightly coupled and provide many powerful features designed to make the job of the COM+ developer quite a bit easier. As you step though the basics here, you might want to reflect on the raw COM+ example and consider what is really going on behind the scenes.

Defining Interfaces and GUIDs

One of the first differences between the raw COM+ example and the smart pointer/ATL example is the way that interfaces and GUIDs are defined. In the raw COM+ example, you used a pregenerated header output as a result of midl.exe parsing the MSMQ type library. This is, of course, handled for you at the factory, and the header can be found in the Visual C++ include subdirectory.

#import

ATL applications more often use the #import alternative introduced with Visual C++ 5. The #import directive takes the actual COM+ component housing the type library as a parameter. During your build process, the compiler will parse the mqoa.dll type library and emit two files. Both files have the component name with the new extensions .tlh and .tli. Here's the import directive for the MSMQ ActiveX component:

```
#import <mqoa.dll> no_namespace
```

Many important things take place because of this directive. As mentioned, two new files will be generated and included in the source compilation. In this case, the emitted files are mqoa.tlh and mqoa.tli. The no_namespace attribute used here imports the declarations into the global C++ namespace. Omitting the no_namespace attribute would cause the imported elements to be imported into the MSMQ namespace. This is convenient if you have some potential name conflicts.

`.tlh` Files

The `mqoa.tlh` file contains the C++ equivalent of the information in the type library. This, of course, means that you cannot include the pregenerated `mqoai.h` header used in the raw COM+ example because it contains the same information. The advantage of the `import` directive here is that it will always generate matching type information, even as you upgrade your target components. This is unlike the static header shipped with the latest version of Visual C++. You can, of course, use this approach to include interface and GUID definitions in your raw COM+ applications as well, and as you might expect, this is the trend. The `.tlh` file also includes definitions for smart pointers to each COM+ class defined. The following are examples of the `MSMQQueueInfo`-related declarations generated in the `mqoa.tlh` header.

Interface Declarations

Here is a line of code from the `mqoa.thl` file that declares an MSMQ component interface:

```
struct __declspec(uuid("d7d6e07b-dccd-11d0-aa4b-0060970debae"))
/* dual interface */ IMSMQQueueInfo;
```

This is the declaration of the `IMSMQQueueInfo` COM+ interface. The beautiful part about this declaration is the way the `uuid declspec` enables you to wire the GUID to the interface at the compiler level. Because this is not a preprocessor statement, you also avoid the potential duplicate GUID definitions that were discussed in the `INITGUID` scenario of the raw COM+ application.

Class Declarations

Here is a line of code from the `mqoa.thl` file that declares an MSMQ component class:

```
struct /* coclass */ MSMQQueueInfo;
```

This is the declaration of the `MSMQQueueInfo` class. No surprises here.

Smart Pointer Declarations

Here is a line of code from the `mqoa.thl` file that declares an MSMQ component interface smart pointer:

```
_COM_SMARTPTR_TYPEDEF(IMSMQQueueInfo, __uuidof(IMSMQQueueInfo));
```

If you were to unravel the nontrivial set of defines and templates that this line of code invokes, you would discover that it creates a powerful interface pointer wrapper. These

24

PROGRAMMING THE MSMQ

smart pointer wrappers take care of most of the IUnknown issues involved with interface operations. Smart pointers also simplify the error-handling operations of the interface by generating exceptions for failed HRESULTs on standard methods. Note that the __uuidof keyword is used to retrieve the GUID attached to the interface in the previous declaration. You will see several blocks of code that make use of smart pointers in this application.

There is one pitfall that comes up from time to time when using smart pointers. There are always dangers inherent in using a sophisticated set of pregenerated code below your actual source level; that is, code generated behind the scenes so that it is visible to the compiler but not to you. This danger exists especially in cases in which you haven't examined the macros and templates carefully. The most popular difficulty is that the source looks as if it does one thing, and the emitted code actually does something else. Because smart pointers implement the client side of a COM+ interface, attempting to override portions of the smart pointer behavior is not a particularly compelling solution. Smart pointers provide some dangerous cast operators that might make the wrong assumptions in regard to IUnknown::AddRef() and IUnknown::Release() calls. This is one of the few prevailing arguments against smart pointers.

Interface Definitions

The next block of code found in the .tlh file is the interface definitions block. Listing 24.6 is an example of the definition for the IMSMQQueueInfo interface.

LISTING 24.6 The IMSMQQueueInfo Interface

```
struct __declspec(uuid("d7d6e07b-dccd-11d0-aa4b-0060970debae"))
IMSMQQueueInfo : IDispatch
{
    //
    // Property data
    //

    __declspec(property(get=GetPathName,put=PutPathName))
    _bstr_t PathName;
    __declspec(property(get=GetFormatName,put=PutFormatName))
    _bstr_t FormatName;
    __declspec(property(get=GetIsTransactional))
    short IsTransactional;
...

    //
    // Wrapper methods for error-handling
    //

    _bstr_t GetPathName ( );
```

LISTING 24.6 Continued

```
    void PutPathName (
        _bstr_t pbstrPathName );
    _bstr_t GetFormatName ( );
    void PutFormatName (
        _bstr_t pbstrFormatName );
    short GetIsTransactional ( );
...

    HRESULT Create (
        VARIANT * IsTransactional = &vtMissing,
        VARIANT * IsWorldReadable = &vtMissing );
    HRESULT Delete ( );
    IMSMQQueuePtr Open (
        long Access,
        long ShareMode );
    HRESULT Refresh ( );
    HRESULT Update ( );

    //
    // Raw methods provided by interface
    //

     virtual HRESULT __stdcall get_PathName (
        BSTR * pbstrPathName ) = 0;
    virtual HRESULT __stdcall put_PathName (
        BSTR pbstrPathName ) = 0;
    virtual HRESULT __stdcall get_FormatName (
        BSTR * pbstrFormatName ) = 0;
    virtual HRESULT __stdcall put_FormatName (
        BSTR pbstrFormatName ) = 0;
    virtual HRESULT __stdcall get_IsTransactional (
        short * pisTransactional ) = 0;
...

    virtual HRESULT __stdcall raw_Create (
        VARIANT * IsTransactional = &vtMissing,
        VARIANT * IsWorldReadable = &vtMissing ) = 0;
    virtual HRESULT __stdcall raw_Delete ( ) = 0;
    virtual HRESULT __stdcall raw_Open (
        long Access,
        long ShareMode,
        struct IMSMQQueue * * ppq ) = 0;
    virtual HRESULT __stdcall raw_Refresh ( ) = 0;
    virtual HRESULT __stdcall raw_Update ( ) = 0;
};
```

24

PROGRAMMING
THE MSMQ

Note that raw property accessors take the form get_PathName() and put_PathName().
The generated header also provides for equivalent wrapper methods taking the names

GetPathName() and GetPathName(), respectively. As you can see, the wrapper routines look more like standard functions than low-level COM+ calls.

Another advantage provided by smart pointers is the introduction of optional call parameters. Raw COM+ interfaces do not present default or named parameters in C++. Smart pointer method declarations reintroduce optional parameters. The following `IMSMQQueuePtr::Receive()` method example demonstrates this:

```
IMSMQMessagePtr Receive (
        VARIANT * Transaction = &vtMissing,
        VARIANT * WantDestinationQueue = &vtMissing,
        VARIANT * WantBody = &vtMissing,
        VARIANT * ReceiveTimeout = &vtMissing );
```

Also note that the VARIANT vtMissing, which has a runtime type of VT_ERROR, is defined to represent fields that you are not interested in supplying.

.tli Files

The big difference between raw MSMQ COM+ programming and ATL-style MSMQ COM+ programming revolves around the use of smart pointers and the wrapper functions previously declared. Wrapper functions are defined in .tli files. The mqoa.tli file contains wrapper routines similar to the following:

```
inline _bstr_t IMSMQQueueInfo::GetLabel ( ) {
    BSTR _result;
    HRESULT _hr = get_Label(&_result);
    if (FAILED(_hr)) _com_issue_errorex(_hr, this, __uuidof(this));
    return _bstr_t(_result, false);
}
```

One of the strengths of these wrapper routines is that they reduce the functional error-management overhead by converting failed HRESULTs into exceptions that can be managed in a structured way. The smart pointers implement similar behavior for stock COM+ calls like CoCreateInstance(), which is invoked by the smart pointer constructor method among others.

ATL Dependencies

Although the smart pointer templates and generated wrappers fall under the blanket of ATL technology, they don't really make use of the official ATL template library. ATL is, in general, the preferred mechanism for COM+ application construction in C++. You're really just writing a COM+ client application in these examples, but if you're going to buy into the smart pointer thing, you'll find other efficiencies in ATL proper that complement the approach. In order to simplify the application, I'll make use of the ATL

CComBSTR class instead of using raw BSTRs. Basic ATL dependencies are resolved by including atlbase.h as follows:

```
#include <atlbase.h>
```

Creating a Queue

You'll need to get an interface pointer to a MSMQQueueInfo object in order to create a queue. In the current example, you'll use smart pointers for this task. Smart pointers have the same name as the interface that they wrap, with the addition of a Ptr suffix. Smart pointers encapsulate various basic COM+ behaviors such as calls to CoCreateInstance() as well as error management. You can also do away with the several Release() calls of the previous example because the smart pointer destructors handle it for you. Furthermore, you can avoid some of the BSTR allocation and free business by using the CComBSTR ATL class.

```
try
{
    //Setup queue information using a smart pointer
    IMSMQQueueInfoPtr pQInfo("MSMQ.MSMQQueueInfo");
    pQInfo->PutPathName(L".\\BasicQueue");

    //Create the queue
    pQInfo->Create();

    //Display format name
    CComBSTR FormatName;
    FormatName.Attach( pQInfo->GetFormatName() );
    wprintf(L"Queue created with format name: ");
    wprintf(L"%s\n\n",BSTR(FormatName));
}
catch (_com_error &e)
{
    wprintf(L"Error creating queue: %x\n\n",e.Error());
}
```

Notice the way the preceding code distills the essence of the CreateQueue() function behavior presented in the previous raw COM+ example. All the error management is handled in a structured fashion using a catch block and the _com_error class. All the routines discussed in the following paragraphs operate within a similar try block, although the code has been omitted for brevity. As you are working with COM+ at a higher level of abstraction, you will also migrate to ProgIDs, MSMQ.MSMQQueueInfo, from the previous usage of CLSIDs. This is simply a preference as opposed to a requirement.

Destroying a Queue

As in previous examples, the destroy behavior is pretty straightforward:

```
//Setup queue information using a smart pointer
IMSMQQueueInfoPtr pQInfo("MSMQ.MSMQQueueInfo");
pQInfo->PutPathName(L".\\BasicQueue");

//Destroy the queue
pQInfo->Delete();
wprintf(L"Queue destroyed\n\n");
```

Opening a Queue

Opening a queue with smart pointers is almost as easy as opening a queue with the MSMQ Library API. All you need to do is get an interface pointer to a `MSMQQueueInfo` object, set the pathname in the `Info` object, and call the `IMSMQQueueInfo::Open()` method. An `IMSMQQueuePtr` smart pointer object receives the interface pointer returned by the open call:

```
//Setup queue information using a smart pointer
IMSMQQueueInfoPtr pQInfo("MSMQ.MSMQQueueInfo");
pQInfo->PutPathName(L".\\BasicQueue");

    //Open the queue
IMSMQQueuePtr pQueue =
                pQInfo->Open(MQ_SEND_ACCESS, MQ_DENY_NONE);
```

Sending a Message

Sending a message with smart pointers involves setting up a `MSMQMessage` object and sending it to the target `MSMQQueue` object. Listing 24.7 demonstrates sending a message with standard label and body properties.

LISTING 24.7   Sending a Message with Standard Label and Body Properties

```
//Set up message label
static int s_cMessageNumber = 0;     //Message label counter
WCHAR wcsLabel[MSGLABELSIZE];          //Message label buffer
swprintf(wcsLabel,L"Message number %d", ++s_cMessageNumber);

//Set up message body
WCHAR wcsBody[MSGBODYSIZE];
CComBSTR MessageBody;
VARIANT vtBody;
wprintf(L"Enter message body: ");
_getws(wcsBody);
MessageBody.Attach(SysAllocString(wcsBody));
```

LISTING 24.7   Continued

```
vtBody.vt = VT_BSTR;
vtBody.bstrVal = BSTR(MessageBody);

//Set up the message and send it
IMSMQMessagePtr pMsg("MSMQ.MSMQMessage");
pMsg->PutLabel(wcsLabel);
pMsg->PutBody(vtBody);
pMsg->Send( pQueue );
wprintf(L"Message sent\n\n");
```

Receiving a Message

Receiving a message with smart pointers is actually easier than sending one. Once again, you will need to create a MSMQMessage object. In receive mode, you use the IMSMQQueue::Receive() method to retrieve the message:

```
//Set up the message and send it
IMSMQMessagePtr pMsg("MSMQ.MSMQMessage");
VARIANT vtTimeout;
vtTimeout.vt = VT_I4;
vtTimeout.lVal = 0;
pMsg = pQueue->Receive( &vtMissing,
                        &vtMissing,
                        &vtMissing,
                        &vtTimeout );
wprintf(L"Retrieved message label:\n\t%s\n",
                        (const wchar_t *)pMsg->Label);
wprintf(L"Retrieved message body:\n\t%s\n\n",
                        (pMsg->Body).bstrVal );
```

Notice that you can use vtMissing to take the place of ignored arguments leading up to our field of interest, which is the timeout value. Because you want nonblocking behavior, you supply a four-byte integer variant with a value of zero. Note that C++ allows you to completely leave out trailing parameters that you're not interested in. As you can see, the smart pointer property accessors make this block of code very easy to put together. I should mention the fragile nature of your last print statement. You are making the strong assumption that the message body is a BSTR. You could avoid the danger inherent in assumptions by simply checking the variant type to be sure that it is a BSTR.

Closing a Queue

As you might expect, there's nothing to do here, but I'm a fan of symmetry. The smart pointer destructors handle the entire shutdown behavior involved with releasing interface pointers

24

PROGRAMMING
THE MSMQ

The coding effort involved with using MSMQ can be greatly reduced by smart pointers and ATL. There's almost always a price in performance when using generated (and thus somewhat generic) code. Smart pointer wrappers and templates are specifically designed to minimize this overhead. For many, the smart pointer tack embodies the perfect trade-off between performance and ease of use. Listing 24.8 shows the complete smart pointer example.

LISTING 24.8   MSMQ COM+ Smart Pointer Programming Example

```cpp
// HelloMSMQ.cpp
//
// Simple MSMQ Smart Pointer application


//Dependencies
#include <windows.h>
#include <stdio.h>
#include <conio.h>
#include <atlbase.h>
#import <mqoa.dll> no_namespace


//Symbols
#define MSGBODYSIZE        128
#define MSGLABELSIZE        64
#define QUEUEPATHNAME    L".\\BasicQueue"


//Prototypes
void CreateQueue();
void SendMessage();
void ReceiveMessage();
void DestroyQueue();


//Application entry point
int main()
{
    int iChoice;                  //User input buffer

    //Initialize COM
    CoInitializeEx(NULL,COINIT_APARTMENTTHREADED);

    //User command processing loop
    do
    {
        //Display menu
        wprintf(L"Choose a command:\n");
        wprintf(L"0 - Exit\n");
```

LISTING 24.8   Continued

```
            wprintf(L"1 - Create the Queue\n");
            wprintf(L"2 - Send a Message\n");
            wprintf(L"3 - Receive a Message\n");
            wprintf(L"4 - Destroy the Queue\n");
            wprintf(L"\n>> ");

            //Get selection
            iChoice = getch();
            wprintf(L"%c\n\n",iChoice);

            //Execute command
            switch ( iChoice )
            {
            case '0':
                break;

            case '1':
                CreateQueue();
                break;

            case '2':
                SendMessage();
                break;

            case '3':
                ReceiveMessage();
                break;

            case '4':
                DestroyQueue();
                break;

            default:
                wprintf(L"Bad choice.\n\n");
                break;
            }
    } while ( iChoice != '0' );

    //Uninitialize COM+ and return success
    CoUninitialize();
    return 0;
}

void CreateQueue()
{
    try
    {
        //Setup queue information using a smart pointer
        IMSMQQueueInfoPtr pQInfo("MSMQ.MSMQQueueInfo");
```

LISTING 24.8 Continued

```
        pQInfo->PutPathName(QUEUEPATHNAME);

        //Create the queue
        pQInfo->Create();

        //Display format name
        CComBSTR FormatName;
        FormatName.Attach( pQInfo->GetFormatName() );
        wprintf(L"Queue created with format name: ");
        wprintf(L"%s\n\n",BSTR(FormatName));
    }
    catch (_com_error &e)
    {
        wprintf(L"Error creating queue: %x\n\n",e.Error());
    }
}

void SendMessage()
{
    try
    {
        //Setup queue information using a smart pointer
        IMSMQQueueInfoPtr pQInfo("MSMQ.MSMQQueueInfo");
        pQInfo->PutPathName(QUEUEPATHNAME);

        //Open the queue
    IMSMQQueuePtr pQueue =
                    pQInfo->Open(MQ_SEND_ACCESS, MQ_DENY_NONE);

        //Set up message label
        static int s_cMessageNumber = 0;      //Message label counter
        WCHAR wcsLabel[MSGLABELSIZE];          //Message label buffer
        swprintf(wcsLabel,L"Message number %d", ++s_cMessageNumber);

        //Set up message body
        WCHAR wcsBody[MSGBODYSIZE];
        CComBSTR MessageBody;
        VARIANT vtBody;
        wprintf(L"Enter message body: ");
        _getws(wcsBody);
        MessageBody.Attach(SysAllocString(wcsBody));
        vtBody.vt = VT_BSTR;
        vtBody.bstrVal = BSTR(MessageBody);

        //Set up the message and send it
        IMSMQMessagePtr pMsg("MSMQ.MSMQMessage");
        pMsg->PutLabel(wcsLabel);
        pMsg->PutBody(vtBody);
        pMsg->Send( pQueue );
```

LISTING 24.8 Continued

```
                wprintf(L"Message sent\n\n");
        }
    catch (_com_error &e)
    {
            wprintf(L"Error sending message: %x\n\n",e.Error());
        }
}

void ReceiveMessage()
{
    try
    {
            //Setup queue information using a smart pointer
            IMSMQQueueInfoPtr pQInfo("MSMQ.MSMQQueueInfo");
            pQInfo->PutPathName(QUEUEPATHNAME);

            //Open the queue
        IMSMQQueuePtr pQueue =
pQInfo->Open(MQ_RECEIVE_ACCESS, MQ_DENY_NONE);

            //Set up the message and send it
            IMSMQMessagePtr pMsg("MSMQ.MSMQMessage");
            VARIANT vtTimeout;
            vtTimeout.vt = VT_I4;
            vtTimeout.lVal = 0;
            pMsg = pQueue->Receive( &vtMissing,
                                    &vtMissing,
                                    &vtMissing,
                                    &vtTimeout );
            wprintf(L"Retrieved message label:\n\t%s\n",
                            (const wchar_t *)pMsg->Label);
            wprintf(L"Retrieved message body:\n\t%s\n\n",
                            (pMsg->Body).bstrVal );
        }
    catch (_com_error &e)
    {
            wprintf(L"Error receiving message: %x\n\n",e.Error());
        }
}

void DestroyQueue()
{
    try
    {
            //Setup queue information using a smart pointer
            IMSMQQueueInfoPtr pQInfo("MSMQ.MSMQQueueInfo");
            pQInfo->PutPathName(QUEUEPATHNAME);

            //Destroy the queue
```

LISTING 24.8 Continued

```
        pQInfo->Delete();
        wprintf(L"Queue destroyed\n\n");
    }
    catch (_com_error &e)
    {
        wprintf(L"Error destroying queue: %x\n\n",e.Error());
    }
}
```

Building an MSMQ Application with VBScript

I'll wrap up this introduction to MSMQ programming with a look at the Visual Basic side of things (sort of inevitable, right?). Visual Basic went from the HAM radio operator's best friend to an application development platform used to construct mission-critical enterprise applications, and in a very short time. Perhaps the most compelling facet of the Visual Basic phenomenon is the fact that it's everywhere. VB can be found in client-side and server-side Web applications, in the macro languages of many programs (VBA), in standalone applications, and now in host scripts. Because the standard shell script represents the lowest common VB denominator, I'll build an example as a standalone VB shell script.

I'll leave the code perusal to you with the exception of a few top-level observations. Notice as you look through the source, that it is very similar to the smart pointer example you just finished examining. In fact, many parts of the two applications track line for line. You'll also notice that Visual Basic is pretty hard to beat when it comes to string handling and variant operations. After all they're native types to VB. COM+ is also second nature to VB because many elements of VB and COM+ were developed in tandem. Consider the power this places in the hands of a script-aware system administrator. Your high-performance, enterprisewide application can send and receive messages directly with MIS managed scripts. Kind of good, kind of scary.

LISTING 24.9 MSMQ VBScript Programming Example

```
' HelloMSMQ.vbs
'
' Simple MSMQ VB Script application


'MSMQ constants
```

LISTING 24.9   Continued

```
MQ_DENY_NONE = 0
MQ_DENY_RECEIVE_SHARE = 1

MQ_RECEIVE_ACCESS = 1
MQ_SEND_ACCESS = 2
MQ_PEEK_ACCESS = 32


'Application Entry Point
do
    'Set up menu
    Menu = "MSMQ Script Menu" & vbCr & _
           "0 - Exit" & vbCr & _
           "1 - Create the Queue" & vbCr & _
           "2 - Send a Message" & vbCr & _
           "3 - Receive a Message" & vbCr & _
           "4 - Destroy the Queue"

    'Get selection
    Choice = InputBox(Menu)

    'Execute command
    Select Case Choice
        Case "":
            'This interperets the cancel button as a quit request
            Choice = "0"
        Case "0":
        Case "1":
            CreateQueue
        Case "2":
            SendMessage
        Case "3":
            ReceiveMessage
        Case "4":
            DestroyQueue
        Case Else:
            MsgBox "Bad choice"
    End Select

Loop While Choice <> "0"
'End of Application Entry Point


Sub CreateQueue()
    On Error Resume Next

    'Get a QueueInfo object and create our queue
    Set QInfo = CreateObject("MSMQ.MSMQQueueInfo")
    QInfo.PathName = ".\BasicQueue"
```

LISTING 24.9   Continued

```
    QInfo.Create
    If Err <> 0 Then
        MsgBox ("Error # " & CStr(Err.Number) & " - " & Err.Description)
        Err.Clear
    Else
        MsgBox "The queue's format name is: " & qinfo.FormatName
    End If
End Sub


Sub SendMessage()
    On Error Resume Next

    'Get a QueueInfo object and open our queue for sending
    Set QInfo = CreateObject("MSMQ.MSMQQueueInfo")
    QInfo.PathName = ".\BasicQueue"
    Set Queue = QInfo.Open(MQ_SEND_ACCESS, MQ_DENY_NONE)

    'Create a message, set up the message properties and send it
    Set Message = CreateObject("MSMQ.MSMQMessage")
    Message.Label = "Hello MSMQ from VB Script"
    Message.Body = InputBox("Enter a message to send:")
    Message.Send Queue
    Queue.Close
    If Err <> 0 Then
        MsgBox ("Error # " & CStr(Err.Number) & " - " & Err.Description)
        Err.Clear
    Else
        MsgBox "Message Sent"
    End If
End Sub


Sub ReceiveMessage()
    On Error Resume Next

    'Get a QueueInfo object and open our queue for receiving
    Set QInfo = CreateObject("MSMQ.MSMQQueueInfo")
    QInfo.PathName = ".\BasicQueue"
    Set Queue = QInfo.Open(MQ_RECEIVE_ACCESS, MQ_DENY_NONE)

    'Receive the message and display it
    Set Message = Queue.Receive
    Queue.Close
    If Err <> 0 Then
        MsgBox ("Error # " & CStr(Err.Number) & " - " & Err.Description)
        Err.Clear
    Else
        MsgBox "Received: " & vbCr & _
```

LISTING 24.9 Continued

```
                      "Label: " & CStr(Message.Label) & vbCr & _
                      "Body: " & CStr(Message.Body)
        End If
End Sub


Sub DestroyQueue()
    On Error Resume Next

    'Get a QueueInfo object and delete our queue
    Set QInfo = CreateObject("MSMQ.MSMQQueueInfo")
    QInfo.PathName = ".\BasicQueue"
    QInfo.Delete
    If Err <> 0 Then
        MsgBox ("Error # " & CStr(Err.Number) & " - " & Err.Description)
        Err.Clear
    Else
        MsgBox "Queue deleted"
    End If
End Sub
```

Summary

In this chapter, you have seen four equivalent examples implemented with varying MSMQ programming strategies. By way of these examples, this chapter has presented the fundamental concepts of generic MSMQ programming as well as the strengths and weaknesses of the programming models available. The skills you have gained here will be important in any MSMQ programming endeavor you undertake. The examples are tailored to help you choose your development approach. The next chapter will supplement the programming skills presented here with coverage of the various advanced add-on features available through MSMQ.

24

PROGRAMMING
THE MSMQ

Advanced MSMQ Programming

CHAPTER 25

This chapter delves into some of the more interesting and esoteric features of MSMQ. MSMQ is MOM, or Message-Oriented Middleware. The goal of any good piece of middleware is to solve some particularly nasty problem in a generic way so that it is usable by many final products. The application messaging tools required to complete many projects consist of nothing more than the basic features covered in the preceding chapter. Asynchronous message delivery throughout an entire enterprise is, after all, no small service. However, several common situations call for behavior that would incur extreme in-house development tolls, such as guaranteed in-order message delivery, support for highly scalable dequeuing mechanisms, and collaboration with peer COM+ services. For this reason, Microsoft has integrated MSMQ with several other key enterprise services.

This chapter covers the aspects of MSMQ that integrate with other critical enterprise development services. The following pages will give you a chance to examine advanced MSMQ features in the context of a simple messaging application. The sample application consists of the order entry system for a wholesale clothier selling nothing but sweaters that cost $20. No wading through Colombian Supremo inventory depreciation algorithms. This system will be constructed with three projects:

- Order Entry Client—Console front end for placing and browsing orders
- Order Entry DLL—COM+ component that accesses databases and shipping queues
- Shipping Server—Console application that processes shipping orders

The example is an order-processing system for a Scottish-owned sweater wholesaler. This is a pattern that you can readily apply to many enterprises (stay away from the Scottish sweater part, that's my idea). The client application places orders, which are processed by the OrderEntry COM+ component. OrderEntry houses the Order COM+ class responsible for reducing the customers' account balance in a SQL Server database and queuing a message to the shipping system to request that the order be shipped. The Shipping Server receives the sweater orders and then attempts to transmit them to your factory in Scotland. I like sunshine better than sheep, so with the location transparency of the Internet, we'll set up shop in California. As a proud Scot myself, I can assure you that we will keep our costs down, and transatlantic lines being more than pricey, our connection from the shop to the factory is not going to be very reliable. This means that we'll have to do the reliability part in software (heard that before?). Nothing wrong with a little context, right?

As you can see from Figure 25.1, the Order Entry Client and the Shipping Server are both standard console-style applications, although the COM+ Order Processing component is a default ATL COM+ DLL housing a default simple ATL COM+ class called Order (innovative, huh?). The messages being sent are a simple byte array in the form of an order structure. The order structure simply contains the account number, quantity, and product number for the order. A complete code listing of all three projects can be found at the end of this chapter. You can also find the projects in their entirety on the accompanying CD-ROM.

FIGURE 25.1

The architecture of the Order Processing system.

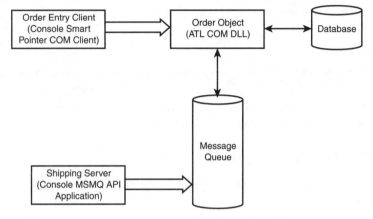

The Order Entry Client and component use COM+ to interact with MSMQ. The Shipping Server uses the MSMQ Library API to provide another perspective. I'll include examples of both API and ActiveX component techniques in the text, where the translation is not obvious. Some features presented by the MSMQ API are not available through the MSMQ ActiveX components. In particular, if a feature can't be easily represented through automation interfaces or consumed by Visual Basic (synonymous considerations), you won't find it in the MSMQ ActiveX components. Examples include multiple concurrent cursors for a single queue and queue security management.

This sample application will help you explore MSMQ cursors, transactions, scalable multithreaded message handlers, and other concerns. The project's goal is to provide just enough of an application without clouding the MSMQ programming focus. Most features are demonstrated in the OrderEntry component. In cases in which competing techniques would have been a little too obtuse to integrate, I have created branching projects, which are mentioned in the text covering them.

To wrap up, I'll add some coverage of the latest in MSMQ COM+ integration. Topics will include transmitting persistent COM+ objects through MSMQ messages and queuing COM+ calls through MSMQ in disconnected scenarios.

Cursors

Cursors are used by MSMQ to keep track of an application's place in a queue. An application can maintain and manipulate many cursors simultaneously using the MSMQ

Library. The MSMQ ActiveX queue objects maintain a single cursor behind the scenes. Both mechanisms enable messages to be examined and optionally removed as cursors are advanced through the queue. Because several applications can interact with a queue concurrently, cursors might not always point to a message. Such is the case when another application removes a message from a queue after your application has already advanced its cursor to that message, but before your application has a chance to actually remove the message.

Cursors are used only when you are interested in messages that are not at the front of the queue. Although most queue processing will probably operate in the established FIFO manner, some out-of-band operations might be necessary—for example, displaying the labels of all the pending messages in a particular queue for administrative purposes.

MSMQ API Cursors

The MSMQ Library API treats cursors as separate objects that must be created and released much like any other resource. This enables an application to create several cursors to track multiple locations in the same queue. The following API routines create and release cursor resources:

- `MQCreateCursor()`
- `MQCloseCursor()`

The `MQReceiveMessage()` routine, as you might have noticed, is one of the most complex functions in the MSMQ Library. Previously, you only worked with the timeout feature to acquire nonblocking synchronous behavior. You'll be learning many new uses for the `MQReceiveMessage()` routine in this chapter. First, be aware that `MQReceiveMessage()` can take an optional cursor handle, which supports three different actions:

- `MQ_ACTION_RECEIVE`
- `MQ_ACTION_PEEK_CURRENT`
- `MQ_ACTION_PEEK_NEXT`

Peek operations retrieve message data but, unlike the receive action, do not remove the message from the queue. If a `NULL` cursor handle is supplied to `MQReceiveMessage()`, only the message at the front of the queue can be operated on. The peek-next action requires a cursor, which is moved to a next location before the message is peeked. Receiving a message will automatically update the cursor to the next message in the queue. It is important to execute the `MQ_ACTION_PEEK_CURRENT` to initialize a cursor before attempting to use `MQ_ACTION_PEEK_NEXT`.

Listing 25.1 shows the routine from the Shipping Server that displays the pending orders using the MSMQ Library API.

LISTING 25.1   Using MSMQ API Cursors

```
void DisplayOrders()
{
    //Get the format name of the queue using the pathname
    HRESULT hr;                             //Return status
    WCHAR wcsFormatName[FORMATNAMESIZE];    //Queue format name
    DWORD dwFormatNameLen = FORMATNAMESIZE; //Size of format name
    hr = MQPathNameToFormatName(   QUEUEPATHNAME,
                                   wcsFormatName,
                                   &dwFormatNameLen );

    //Check results
    if ( FAILED(hr) )
    {
        wprintf(L"Error looking up queue format name: %x\n\n",hr);
        return;
    }

    //Open the queue with peek access
    QUEUEHANDLE hQueue;                     //Handle to queue
    hr = MQOpenQueue( wcsFormatName,        //Queue format name
                      MQ_PEEK_ACCESS,       //Access requested
                      MQ_DENY_NONE,         //Share mode
                      &hQueue);             //Queue handle

    //Check results
    if ( FAILED(hr) )
    {
        wprintf(L"Error opening queue: %x\n\n",hr);
        return;
    }

    //Create cursor
    HANDLE hCursor;
    hr = MQCreateCursor( hQueue, &hCursor );

    //Check results
    if ( FAILED(hr) )
    {
        wprintf(L"Error creating cursor: %x\n\n",hr);
        MQCloseQueue(hQueue);
        return;
    }

    //Allocate message property objects
    MQMSGPROPS MsgProps;                    //Message properties struct
```

LISTING 25.1   Continued

```
MSGPROPID aMsgPropId[4];                 //Message property id array
PROPVARIANT aMsgPropVar[4];              //Message property value array

//Set up message label and length
WCHAR wcsLabel[MSGLABELSIZE];            //Message label buffer
aMsgPropId[0] = PROPID_M_LABEL;
aMsgPropVar[0].vt = VT_LPWSTR;
aMsgPropVar[0].pwszVal = wcsLabel;
aMsgPropId[1] = PROPID_M_LABEL_LEN;
aMsgPropVar[1].vt = VT_UI4;
aMsgPropVar[1].ulVal = MSGLABELSIZE;

//Set up message properties struct
MsgProps.cProp = 2;                      //Number of properties
MsgProps.aPropID = aMsgPropId;           //Ids of properties
MsgProps.aPropVar = aMsgPropVar;         //Values of properties
MsgProps.aStatus = NULL;                 //No error reports

//Browse messages labels
DWORD dwAction = MQ_ACTION_PEEK_CURRENT;
while ( TRUE )
{
    hr = MQReceiveMessage(    hQueue,     //Queue to receive from
                             0,           //Timeout
                             dwAction, //Receive or peek
                             &MsgProps,//Message properties
                             NULL,        //Overlapped structure
                             NULL,        //Callback
                             hCursor,  //Queue cursor
                             NULL );     //Transaction
    //Check results
    if ( FAILED(hr) )
    {
        if ( MQ_ERROR_IO_TIMEOUT == hr )
        {
            wprintf(L"End of list\n\n");
            break;
        }
        wprintf(L"Error peeking message: %x\n\n",hr);
        MQCloseCursor(hCursor);
        MQCloseQueue(hQueue);
        return;
    }

    //Set next action to Peek Next
    dwAction = MQ_ACTION_PEEK_NEXT;

    //Display message
    wprintf(L"Found message label: %s\n",wcsLabel);
```

LISTING 25.1   Continued

```
    }

    //Close cursor and queue
    MQCloseCursor(hCursor);
    MQCloseQueue(hQueue);
}
```

In Listing 25.1, you quickly scan through the queue retrieving only the message labels to improve performance. (We'll talk about queues more later, especially with regard to finding queues.) Notice that you use an action variable, dwAction, which enables you to peek the current message in the first iteration of the loop and then change to peek-next operations until you reach the end of the queue. Reaching the end of the queue is flagged by a timeout in the receive operation.

MSMQ ActiveX Component Cursors

The MSMQ ActiveX components support cursor operations through the MSMQQueue class. There is no cursor object *per se* when dealing with the MSMQ COM+ interfaces. All MSMQ cursor behavior is wrapped inside an MSMQQueue object and accessed through several methods that manipulate the underlying message queue cursor:

- IMSMQQueue::Reset()
- IMSMQQueue::PeekCurrent()
- IMSMQQueue::PeekNext()

The Reset() method returns the cursor to the front of the queue and, as you might expect, the PeekNext() method advances the cursor to the next message in the queue. You must be sure to call PeekCurrent() to initialize the underlying cursor before you call PeekNext() just as discussed in the API approach. By calling Reset(), you can return the cursor to the front of the queue; by calling PeekCurrent() you can peek at the first message in the queue; and, finally, by calling PeekNext() you can iterate through all the other messages in the queue.

The order entry component provides a method that lists all the pending order labels in a BSTR buffer. The code shown in Listing 25.2 has been optimized to run faster than a normal receive operation by passing a FALSE in the vtWantBody flag to exclude the body of the message in the peek calls.

LISTING 25.2   Using MSMQ ActiveX Component Cursors

```
STDMETHODIMP COrder::GetPendingOrders(BSTR *pbstrOrderLabels)
{
    try
    {
```

LISTING 25.2 Continued

```cpp
            //Empty the output string and read buffer
            WCHAR wcsBuffer[WORKINGBUFFERSIZE] = L"";
            * pbstrOrderLabels = NULL;

            //Setup queue information using a smart pointer
            IMSMQQueueInfoPtr pQInfo("MSMQ.MSMQQueueInfo");
            pQInfo->PutPathName(SHIPPINGQUEUEPATHNAME);

            //Open the queue
            IMSMQQueuePtr pQueue =
                    pQInfo->Open( MQ_PEEK_ACCESS, MQ_DENY_NONE);

            //Peek at the first message
            IMSMQMessagePtr pMsg("MSMQ.MSMQMessage");
            VARIANT vtTimeout;
            vtTimeout.vt = VT_I4;
            vtTimeout.lVal = 0;
            VARIANT vtWantBody;
            vtWantBody.vt = VT_BOOL;
            vtWantBody.boolVal = false;
            pMsg = pQueue->PeekCurrent(&vtTimeout,&vtMissing,&vtWantBody);

            //Return pending if queue is empty
            if ( NULL == pMsg )
               return E_PENDING;

            //Add label to output string
            wcscpy( wcsBuffer, pMsg->GetLabel() );
            wcscat( wcsBuffer, L"\n" );

            //Loop through all messages
            while ( pMsg =
                    pQueue->PeekNext(&vtTimeout,&vtMissing,&vtWantBody) )
            {
                //Add label to output string
                if ( (wcslen(wcsBuffer)+wcslen(pMsg->GetLabel()) + 2) >
                                             WORKINGBUFFERSIZE )
                    return E_OUTOFMEMORY;
                wcscat( wcsBuffer, pMsg->GetLabel() );
                wcscat( wcsBuffer, L"\n" );
            }

            //Return label list to user
            * pbstrOrderLabels = SysAllocString( wcsBuffer );
        }
        catch (_com_error &e)
        {
            return e.Error();
        }

        //Return success
        return S_OK;
    }
```

As you can see, if you've got a handle on the receive process, there are not many surprises when peeking through a queue. As long as you make sure to call PeekCurrent() before attempting to call PeekNext() and check the IMSMQMessage pointer to ensure that you haven't reached the end of the list, you should have no difficulty.

Finding Queues

There might come a time when you're not sure of the queue that you're supposed to be sending to or receiving from. This presents a problem because it is not advisable or even possible to open a random queue and then start firing messages at it. Of course, the solution is to use services provided by MSMQ to enumerate the various queues available. There are several techniques an application can use to identify an acceptable target or source queue. In particular, all queues have a Service Type GUID slated for just this purpose. Application developers can generate a GUID with GUIDGen.exe or UUIDGen.exe and use the resulting GUID to tag all queues used by their applications. Labels can also be used, but this is obviously a far less precise approach. Listing 25.3 shows a sample routine that lists all available queues and their properties, and displays them in the console window.

LISTING 25.3   Finding and Examining Queues

```
void LookupQueues(void)
{
    try
    {
        //Create assorted objects
        IMSMQQueryPtr pQuery("MSMQ.MSMQQuery");
        IMSMQQueueInfosPtr pQInfos = pQuery->LookupQueue();
        IMSMQQueueInfoPtr pQInfo;

        for  (    pQInfos->Reset(), pQInfo = pQInfos->Next();
                  NULL != pQInfo;
                  pQInfo = pQInfos->Next() )
        {
            //Unpack values
            CComVariant CreateTime(pQInfo->GetCreateTime());
            CreateTime.ChangeType( VT_BSTR );
            BSTR bstrFormatName;
            pQInfo->get_FormatName(&bstrFormatName);
            BSTR bstrLabel;
            pQInfo->get_Label(&bstrLabel);
            CComVariant ModifyTime(pQInfo->GetModifyTime());
            ModifyTime.ChangeType( VT_BSTR );
            BSTR bstrPathName;
            pQInfo->get_PathName(&bstrPathName);
```

LISTING 25.3 Continued

```
                BSTR bstrQueueGUID;
                pQInfo->get_QueueGuid(&bstrQueueGUID);
                BSTR bstrTypeGUID;
                pQInfo->get_ServiceTypeGuid(&bstrTypeGUID);

                BSTR bstrPrivLevel = NULL;
                long lPL = pQInfo->PrivLevel;
                switch( lPL )
                {
                case MQ_PRIV_LEVEL_NONE:
                    bstrPrivLevel = SysAllocString(L"Non-encrypted only");
                    break;
                case MQ_PRIV_LEVEL_BODY:
                    bstrPrivLevel = SysAllocString(L"Encrypted only");
                    break;
                case MQ_PRIV_LEVEL_OPTIONAL:
                    bstrPrivLevel =
                     SysAllocString(L"Either Non-encrypted or Encrypted");
                    break;
                default:
                    bstrPrivLevel = SysAllocString(L"Unknown");
                    break;
                }

                //Display queue attributes
                wprintf(L"Found queue with the following properties:\n");
                wprintf(L"Authenticate:\t\t%ld\n",pQInfo->Authenticate);
                wprintf(L"Base Priority:\t\t%ld\n",pQInfo->BasePriority);
                wprintf(L"CreateTime:\t\t%s\n",CreateTime.bstrVal);
                wprintf(L"FormatName:\t\t%s\n",bstrFormatName);
                wprintf(L"IsTransactional:\t%hd\n",pQInfo->IsTransactional);
                wprintf(L"IsWorldReadable:\t%hd\n",pQInfo->IsWorldReadable);
                wprintf(L"Journal:\t\t%ld\n",pQInfo->Journal);
                wprintf(L"JournalQuota:\t\t%ld KB\n",pQInfo->JournalQuota);
                wprintf(L"Label:\t\t\t%s\n",bstrLabel);
                wprintf(L"ModifyTime:\t\t%s\n",ModifyTime.bstrVal);
                wprintf(L"PathName:\t\t%s\n",bstrPathName);
                wprintf(L"PrivacyLevel:\t\t%s\n",bstrPrivLevel);
                wprintf(L"QueueGUID:\t\t%s\n",bstrQueueGUID);
                wprintf(L"Quota:\t\t\t%ld KB\n",pQInfo->Quota);
                wprintf(L"TypeGUID:\t\t%s\n",bstrTypeGUID);
                wprintf(L"\n");

                //Clean up
                SysFreeString(bstrFormatName);
                SysFreeString(bstrLabel);
                SysFreeString(bstrPathName);
```

LISTING 25.3   Continued

```
            SysFreeString(bstrQueueGUID);
            SysFreeString(bstrPrivLevel);
            SysFreeString(bstrTypeGUID);
        }
    }
    catch (_com_error &e)
    {
        wprintf(L"Error %x, %s\n\n",e.Error(),e.ErrorMessage());
        return;
    }
}
```

Machine Properties

Just like messages and queues, machines in the MSMQ enterprise have properties.
Listing 25.4 demonstrates the MSMQ ActiveX component technique for retrieving a
machine's GUID. The MSMQ API equivalent, `MQGetMachineProperties()`, enables you
to retrieve the site ID, connected network list, pathname, and public key of the machine.

LISTING 25.4   Retrieving Machine Properties

```
void GetMachineId(void)
{
    try
    {
        //Get machine name from user
        WCHAR wcsName[64];
        wprintf(L"Enter the name of the machine to look up: ");
        _getws(wcsName);

        //Look up independent MSMQ client or MSMQ server
        IMSMQApplicationPtr pApp("MSMQ.MSMQApplication");
        BSTR bstrName = SysAllocString(wcsName);
        BSTR bstrId = pApp->MachineIdOfMachineName(wcsName);
        wprintf(L"Machine %d has the Id: %s\n\n",bstrName,bstrId);
        SysFreeString(bstrName);
        SysFreeString(bstrId);
    }
    catch (_com_error &e)
    {
        wprintf(L"Error %x, %s\n\n",e.Error(),e.ErrorMessage());
        return;
    }
}
```

Message Acknowledgment, Response, and Journals

Some situations call for more than just an open-ended message transmission. Sometimes it's nice to get a little feedback about what happened after you've sent your message. MSMQ provides three levels of feedback:

- None
- Acknowledgment
- Response

The first option, None, is pretty straightforward, and I think that I've already covered that sufficiently, so I'll move on to the other two. Acknowledgments are a form of confirmation regarding the status of a message that was sent. Acknowledgments come from the MSMQ system, not the receiving application. MSMQ provides a message Ack property that enables you to specify the type of confirmation messages that you would like to receive. Responses come from the actual receiving application. Applications on the receiving end of a message generally determine the need for a response by examining the message's Response Queue property, which supplies the format name of a designated response queue.

Administration Queues

There are two properties involved in setting up acknowledgments, the Ack property and the Administration Queue property. The Ack property can be set to any combination of the following settings:

- MQMSG_ACKNOWLEDGMENT_FULL_REACH_QUEUE—Whether the message reaches the queue
- MQMSG_ACKNOWLEDGMENT_FULL_RECEIVE—Whether the message is retrieved
- MQMSG_ACKNOWLEDGMENT_NACK_REACH_QUEUE—When the message cannot reach the queue
- MQMSG_ACKNOWLEDGMENT_NACK_RECEIVE—When the message is not retrieved
- MQMSG_ACKNOWLEDGMENT_NONE—No acknowledgment messages

Because these flags represent bits in the long Ack bit field, you need to bitwise AND the values that you would like to use together. As you can see, information is available on all deliveries or just failed deliveries. You can also choose between queue delivery and actual receipt of the message.

The next step is to set the Ack queue information so that MSMQ knows where to deliver the acknowledgments. This is done by setting the `AdminQueueInfo` property to a `QueueInfo` object. The `QueueInfo` object must have complete information regarding the Ack queue or else the Ack messages will not be delivered.

Several different acknowledgment messages can be returned by MSMQ. The acknowledgment message type is identified using the `Class` property of the acknowledgment message. Table 25.1 lists the possibilities.

TABLE 25.1   Acknowledgment Message Types

Property	Description
MQMSG_CLASS_ACK_REACH_QUEUE	The original message reached its destination queue.
MQMSG_CLASS_ACK_RECEIVE	The original message was retrieved by the receiving application.
MQMSG_CLASS_NACK_ACCESS_DENIED	The sender does not have send access rights to the destination queue.
MQMSG_CLASS_NACK_BAD_DST_Q	The destination queue is not available to the sender.
MQMSG_CLASS_NACK_BAD_ENCRYPTION‚	The destination Queue Manager could not decrypt a private message.
MQMSG_CLASS_NACK_BAD_SIGNATURE	MSMQ could not authenticate the original message.
MQMSG_CLASS_NACK_COULD_NOT_ENCRYPT	The source Queue Manager could not encrypt a private message.
MQMSG_CLASS_NACK_HOP_COUNT_EXCEEDED	The message hop count was exceeded. (A maximum hop count of 15 is set by MSMQ and cannot be modified.)
MQMSG_CLASS_NACK_Q_EXCEED_QUOTA	The message was not delivered because the destination queue is full.
MQMSG_CLASS_NACK_REACH_QUEUE_TIMEOUT	The message did not reach the destination queue.
MQMSG_CLASS_NACK_PURGED	This class indicates the message was purged before reaching the destination queue.
MQMSG_CLASS_NACK_NOT_TRANSACTIONAL_Q	A transaction message was sent to a nontransaction queue.
MQMSG_CLASS_NACK_NOT_TRANSACTIONAL_MSG	A nontransaction message was sent to a transaction queue.

25

ADVANCED MSMQ PROGRAMMING

TABLE 25.1   Continued

Property	Description
MQMSG_CLASS_NACK_Q_DELETED	The queue was deleted before the message could be read from the queue.
MQMSG_CLASS_NACK_Q_PURGED	The queue was purged, and the message no longer exists.
MQMSG_CLASS_NACK_RECEIVE_TIMEOUT	The message was not retrieved from the queue before its time-to-be-received timer expired.

Messages can be given a timeout value in seconds at the Queue Delivery or Receive level. Both values are set through standard message properties. When a message times out, it is destroyed, and any required acknowledgments are forwarded by MSMQ.

The process of working with acknowledgments is rather similar at the API level and with the MSMQ ActiveX components, so we'll just examine the ActiveX component side of things. It should be easy to extrapolate the API equivalent. The sample Ping application shown in Listing 25.5 creates a destination queue and an administration queue. Messages transmitted have Receive Time Out and full Acknowledgment properties set. You can test Acks and Nacks by simply letting the messages time out.

LISTING 25.5   Working with Acknowledgment Messages

```cpp
// Ping.cpp
//
// Simple MSMQ Smart Pointer application


//Dependencies
#include <windows.h>
#include <stdio.h>
#include <conio.h>
#include <atlbase.h>
#import <mqoa.dll> no_namespace


//Symbols
#define MSGBODYSIZE       128
#define MSGLABELSIZE    64
#define PONGPATHNAME        L".\\PongQueue"
#define PINGACKPATHNAME    L".\\PingAckQueue"


//Prototypes
```

LISTING 25.5   Continued

```
void CreateQueues();
void SendMessage();
void ReceiveMessage();
void DestroyQueues();


//Application entry point
int main()
{
    int iChoice;                    //User input buffer

    //Initialize COM
    CoInitializeEx(NULL,COINIT_APARTMENTTHREADED);

    //User command processing loop
    do
    {
        //Display menu
        wprintf(L"Choose a command:\n");
        wprintf(L"0 - Exit\n");
        wprintf(L"1 - Create Queues\n");
        wprintf(L"2 - Send a Message\n");
        wprintf(L"3 - Receive acknowledgment\n");
        wprintf(L"4 - Destroy Queues\n");
        wprintf(L"\n>> ");

        //Get selection
        iChoice = getch();
        wprintf(L"%c\n\n",iChoice);

        //Execute command
        switch ( iChoice )
        {
        case '0':
            break;

        case '1':
            CreateQueues();
            break;

        case '2':
            SendMessage();
            break;

        case '3':
            ReceiveMessage();
            break;

        case '4':
```

LISTING 25.5   Continued

```
                DestroyQueues();
                break;

            default:
                wprintf(L"Bad choice.\n\n");
                break;
        }
    } while ( iChoice != '0' );

    //Uninitialize COM and return success
    CoUninitialize();
    return 0;
}

void CreateQueues()
{
    try
    {
        //Set up queue information using a smart pointer
        IMSMQQueueInfoPtr pQInfo("MSMQ.MSMQQueueInfo");

        //Create the pong queue
        pQInfo->PutPathName(PONGPATHNAME);
        pQInfo->Create();

        //Create the ping queue
        pQInfo->PutPathName(PINGACKPATHNAME);
        pQInfo->Create();

        //Display success
        wprintf(L"Queues created\n\n");
    }
    catch (_com_error &e)
    {
        wprintf(L"Error creating queues: %x\n\n",e.Error());
    }
}

void SendMessage()
{
    try
    {
        //Set up queue information using a smart pointer and open queues
        IMSMQQueueInfoPtr pQInfo("MSMQ.MSMQQueueInfo");
        pQInfo->PutPathName(PONGPATHNAME);
        IMSMQQueuePtr pQueue = pQInfo->Open(    MQ_SEND_ACCESS,
                                                MQ_DENY_NONE);

        IMSMQQueueInfoPtr pAdminQInfo("MSMQ.MSMQQueueInfo");
```

LISTING 25.5 Continued

```
        pAdminQInfo->PutPathName(PINGACKPATHNAME);
        IMSMQQueuePtr pAdminQueue = pAdminQInfo->Open(MQ_SEND_ACCESS,
                                                      MQ_DENY_NONE);


        //Set up message label
        static int s_cMessageNumber = 0;        //Message label counter
        WCHAR wcsLabel[MSGLABELSIZE];           //Message label buffer
        swprintf(wcsLabel,L"Message number %d", ++s_cMessageNumber);

        //Set up message body
        WCHAR wcsBody[MSGBODYSIZE];
        CComBSTR MessageBody;
        VARIANT vtBody;
        wprintf(L"Enter message body: ");
        _getws(wcsBody);
        MessageBody.Attach(SysAllocString(wcsBody));
        vtBody.vt = VT_BSTR;
        vtBody.bstrVal = BSTR(MessageBody);

        //Set up the message and send it
        IMSMQMessagePtr pMsg("MSMQ.MSMQMessage");
        pMsg->PutLabel(wcsLabel);
        pMsg->PutBody(vtBody);
        pMsg->PutAck(    MQMSG_ACKNOWLEDGMENT_FULL_REACH_QUEUE |
                         MQMSG_ACKNOWLEDGMENT_FULL_RECEIVE);
        pMsg->PutRefAdminQueueInfo( pAdminQInfo );
        pMsg->PutMaxTimeToReceive(5);
        pMsg->Send( pQueue );
        wprintf(L"Message sent\n\n");
    }
    catch (_com_error &e)
    {
        wprintf(L"Error sending message: %x\n\n",e.Error());
    }
}

void ReceiveMessage()
{
    try
    {
        //Set up queue information using a smart pointer
        IMSMQQueueInfoPtr pQInfo("MSMQ.MSMQQueueInfo");
        pQInfo->PutPathName(PINGACKPATHNAME);

        //Open the queue
        IMSMQQueuePtr pQueue = pQInfo->Open(    MQ_RECEIVE_ACCESS,
                                        MQ_DENY_NONE);

        //Receive the acknowledgment and display the class
```

LISTING 25.5   Continued

```
            IMSMQMessagePtr pMsg("MSMQ.MSMQMessage");
            VARIANT vtTimeout;
            vtTimeout.vt = VT_I4;
            vtTimeout.lVal = 0;
            pMsg = pQueue->Receive( &vtMissing,
                                    &vtMissing,
                                    vtMissing,
                                    &vtTimeout );
            wprintf(L"Retrieved message label:\n\t%s\n",
                                (const wchar_t *)pMsg->Label);
            if ( MQMSG_CLASS_ACK_RECEIVE == pMsg->Class )
                wprintf(L"ACK: Message received\n\n");
            else if ( MQMSG_CLASS_NACK_RECEIVE_TIMEOUT == pMsg->Class )
                wprintf(L"NACK: Message receive timeout\n\n");
            else if ( MQMSG_CLASS_ACK_REACH_QUEUE == pMsg->Class )
                wprintf(L"ACK: Message reached queue\n\n");
        else if ( MQMSG_CLASS_NACK_REACH_QUEUE_TIMEOUT == pMsg->Class )
            wprintf(L"NACK: Message timed out before reaching queue\n\n");
        else if ( MQMSG_CLASS_NACK_ACCESS_DENIED == pMsg->Class )
            wprintf(L"NACK: Access denied on target queue\n\n");
        else if ( MQMSG_CLASS_NACK_BAD_DST_Q  == pMsg->Class )
            wprintf(L"NACK: Target queue not available\n\n");
        else if ( MQMSG_CLASS_NACK_HOP_COUNT_EXCEEDED  == pMsg->Class )
            wprintf(L"NACK: Exceeded hop count\n\n");
    }
    catch (_com_error &e)
    {
        wprintf(L"Error receiving message: %x\n\n",e.Error());
    }
}


void DestroyQueues()
{
    try
    {
        //Set up queue information using a smart pointer
        IMSMQQueueInfoPtr pQInfo("MSMQ.MSMQQueueInfo");

        //Destroy the pong queue
        pQInfo->PutPathName(PONGPATHNAME);
        pQInfo->Delete();

        //Destroy the ping queue
        pQInfo->PutPathName(PINGACKPATHNAME);
        pQInfo->Delete();

        //Display success
        wprintf(L"Queue destroyed\n\n");
    }
```

LISTING 25.5 Continued

```
    catch (_com_error &e)
    {
        wprintf(L"Error destroying queues: %x\n\n",e.Error());
    }
}
```

Response Queues

Response queues can be set using the message Response Queue property. The Response Queue property is set up the same way that the Administration Queue property was configured in the previous example. Response queues are used by receiving applications that want to set up a discourse with the sender. Response queues can be private queues, which would normally be unavailable to the receiver. Unlike acknowledgment messages, the messages sent to a response queue have no predefined format and can be standardized by the application developers involved.

Message IDs

MSMQ message ID properties have some nice features that are particularly useful when working with response and administration queues. The ID Message property is a 20-byte, read-only, unique message identifier assigned to every message by MSMQ. This can come in rather handy when sorting through messages. You can retrieve the message ID any time after sending or receiving a message. What makes the ID particularly useful is the fact that all messages also have a Correlation ID property. MSMQ automatically sets the Correlation ID of all Acks and Nacks to the ID of the original message. As a participant in a response scenario, you can do the same. The Correlation ID property is read/write.

Journals

Journals are system queues created by MSMQ that are used to keep copies of journal messages and all messages received from journal queues. Setting the Journal property of a queue through the QueueInfo object during the Queue Creation process causes MSMQ to copy all messages received from the queue into the queue journal. A separate queue journal exists for each Journal queue. Table 25.2 shows the Queue Journal property values.

TABLE 25.2 Queue Journal Property Values

Property Value	Description
MQ_JOURNAL	Messages removed from the queue are stored in the queue journal.
MQ_JOURNAL_NONE	Messages are not stored in a journal queue.

MSMQ machines maintain a machine journal. Individual messages can be configured as journal messages through the Message Journal property. MSMQ machines supply a Dead Letter and a Transaction Dead Letter queue for storing messages that cannot be delivered. Transactional messages are always copied to the Transaction Dead Letter queue when delivery fails. Nontransactional messages must have the `MQMSG_DEADLETTER` flag set in their Journal property in order to be copied to the normal Dead Letter queue. Regardless, MSMQ ensures that there is never more than one copy of any message on a given machine at a time. Table 25.3 shows the Message Journal property values.

TABLE 25.3 Message Journal Property Values

Property Value	Description
MQMSG_DEADLETTER	If the message is not delivered to the receiving application within a timeout period (either `time-to-be-received` or `time-to-reach-queue`), the message is sent to a Dead Letter queue on the computer where the message is located.
MQMSG_JOURNAL	If the message is transmitted, keep it in the machine journal on the originating machine.
MQMSG_JOURNAL_NONE	The message is not kept in the originating computer's machine journal.

Transactions

OK, here's the heavy stuff. If you've ever rolled your own transactional software, you know what I mean when I say, "You don't want to develop this stuff in house." Thanks to MSMQ you won't have to. MSMQ presents a complete set of transaction services that can be easily integrated into any project, especially projects making heavy use of COM+. The highly complex database-style behavior and extreme reliability required to provide messaging transactions has been completely hidden behind a few simple routines. The real trick is making sure that you understand the nature of this powerful concept and how to effectively apply it to your MSMQ applications. In this section, we'll examine several types of transactions and look at a number of programming techniques that you can use to apply them.

Transactions are atomic operations in which no one part of the operation can succeed unless all parts of the operation succeed. A successful transaction is committed, and any changes it has made to data stores become permanent. Unsuccessful transactions are rolled back so that all data stores are returned to their state prior to the transaction's inception. This transactional approach to data modification helps developers guarantee that data stores maintain a consistent state. This means that there are no surprises. If the account balance database can never have negative values unless the credit database has a corresponding approved record, we must make sure that only legal combinations prevail. Transactions allow multiple changes like this to be treated atomically.

Transactions are generally committed through a two-phase process. In the first phase, each of the participants votes to commit or abort the transaction. If any participant votes to abort the transaction, the transaction is rolled back and the states of all data stores involved are returned to their pretransaction form. If all participants vote to commit the transaction, the transaction is committed. This does not mean that the operations are completed, it just means that the participants are committed to completing their parts of the transaction.

Messaging Transactions

Messages can be sent and received within a transaction. It is important to note that the messages sent will not actually become available until the transaction is committed. This means that you can never send and then receive the same message within a transaction.

Messages sent within a transaction are guaranteed to be delivered only once. Messages will also be delivered in the order that they were sent within a transaction. This order guarantee is only valid when the messages are sent to the same queue within the same transaction.

Transactional Receive operations can only take place against local queues. Furthermore, transactional Receive calls must be synchronous, thus NULLs should be supplied for the lpOverlapped and fnReceiveCallback parameters when calling MQReceiveMessage().

Both API and ActiveX component flavors of MSMQ development support complete transaction behavior. MSMQ transaction behavior is accessed through the ITransaction interface. API developers need to include the transact.h header before the mq.h header to gain proper declarations for the ITransaction interface. API developers can get an interface pointer to a local MSMQ transaction object by calling MQBeginTransaction().

Developers guarantee application consistency by defining transactions within their applications. A set of MSMQ operations are grouped within a transaction by making a call to begin a transaction before any critical operations take place. When all the aspects of the transaction have returned successfully, the application calls a routine to commit the transaction. MSMQ transactions are started by calling MQBeginTransaction() or the BeginTransaction() method of either the IMSMQCoordinatedTransactionDispenser or

25

ADVANCED
MSMQ
PROGRAMMING

the `IMSMQTransactionDispenser` interfaces. Transactions are ended by calling the `commit()` or `abort()` methods of the `ITransaction` interface.

ITransaction

The `ITransaction` COM+ interface is used to end transactions and to retrieve transaction information regarding a given transaction. From the MSMQ API perspective, the `ITransaction` interface supports three methods:

- `Commit()`
- `Abort()`
- `GetTransactionInfo()`

MSMQ ActiveX components represent this interface through the `MSMQTransaction` class, which treats the last method as a property. Note that `ITransaction` is a COM+ interface and, therefore, inherits `IUnknown` and must be released when no longer needed. Be careful with Smart Pointers because they will take care of this for you.

The `commit()` method ends the transaction requesting that all queues make permanent and public any changes taking place in the transaction. The commit can fail, however. It is very important to examine the `HRESULT` returned by the commit operation. A failed commit is equivalent to an abort, and all queue operations in the transaction will be rolled back. The `abort()` method performs a transaction abort outright, rolling back all changes. Both commit and abort methods have three parameters, which can be used to configure advanced features such as asynchronous completion. These parameters are set to `0` to provide default behavior in most cases.

Creating Transactional Queues

Transaction messages can only be sent to transaction queues. By the same token, non-transaction messages can only be sent to nontransaction queues. Transaction queues are created just like normal queues with the addition of a `true` value in the transaction flag field. A queue's transactional attribute cannot be modified, so it must be set correctly at the time the queue is created. The sample Create routine for a transactional queue, shown in Listing 25.6, comes from our `EnterOrder` component.

LISTING 25.6 Creating a Transactional Queue

```
STDMETHODIMP COrder::CreateShippingQueue()
{
    try
    {
        //Set up queue information using a smart pointer
```

LISTING 25.6   Continued

```
    IMSMQQueueInfoPtr pQInfo("MSMQ.MSMQQueueInfo");
    pQInfo->PutPathName(SHIPPINGQUEUEPATHNAME);

    //Create the transaction queue
    VARIANT vtTransactional;
    vtTransactional.vt = VT_BOOL;
    vtTransactional.boolVal = true;
    pQInfo->Create(&vtTransactional);
}
catch (_com_error &e)
{
    return e.Error();
}

//Return success
return S_OK;
}
```

The API version is also little different from the basic queue creation examples of the previous chapter. Setting the `PROPID_Q_TRANSACTION` property with the `MQ_TRANSACTIONAL` value and bundling it in with the rest of the Create Queue properties will do the trick.

Types of Transactions

MSMQ supports three kinds of transactions:

- Single message
- Internal
- External

The next few pages discuss each of these transaction types in turn and provide sample code to demonstrate the programming techniques involved. The minimal application supplied with this chapter demonstrates the more complex types, internal and external. Figure 25.2 illustrates the transactional boundaries exercised by the sample application.

Single Message Transactions

Single message transactions are the only kind of transaction that do not require a preallocated transaction object. These are only used to send messages. The process of sending a message to a destination queue can be a dicey affair in a large enterprise. Using a single message transaction provides a very efficient means of guaranteeing message delivery. This type of transaction also makes it easy for normally nontransactional applications to deliver messages into a transactional queue framework. The `MQSendMessage()`

routine accepts the `MQ_SINGLE_MESSAGE` constant in the transaction pointer field in order to flag a single message transaction. If you use the ActiveX Component `IMSMQMessage::Send()` method, you can also use the `MQ_SINGLE_MESSAGE` constant, but it must be passed in the `lVal` field of a `VT_I4` variant. Here is a sample single message transaction:

```
//Set up the message and send it
IMSMQMessagePtr pMsg("MSMQ.MSMQMessage");
VARIANT vtTransaction;
vtTransaction.vt = VT_I4;
vtTransaction.lVal = MQ_SINGLE_MESSAGE;
pMsg->PutLabel(wcsLabel);
pMsg->PutBody(vtBody);
pMsg->Send( pQueue, &vtTransaction );
```

FIGURE 25.2

`OrderEntry` *transactional boundaries.*

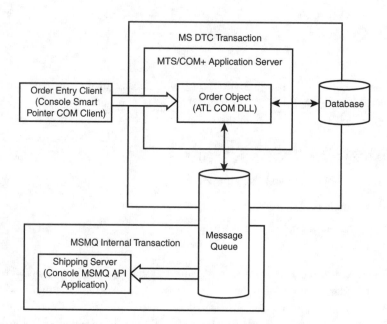

Internal Transactions

Internal transactions are MSMQ-specific transactions that allow multiple messaging operations to be treated as a unit. Internal transactions are more expensive than single message transactions, but much less expensive than external transactions.

Messaging transactions make several important covenants. First, transactional messages will be delivered only once. This might sound like an obvious point, but when you get down to the nitty-gritty coding aspects and all the potential error conditions in a multiqueue enterprise, it is certainly a nontrivial guarantee. Transactions also ensure that all messages destined for the same queue are delivered in order.

Internal transactions are created using the `MQBeginTransaction()` API call or through an `MSMQTransactionDispenser` ActiveX object `BeginTransaction()` method call. Listing 25.7 shows an API example used by the sample application's Shipping Server to ensure that messages are only dequeued if the orders can be successfully shipped.

LISTING 25.7   Using Internal Transactions

```
void Ship()
{
    //Get the format name of the queue using the pathname
    HRESULT hr;                             //Return status
    WCHAR wcsFormatName[FORMATNAMESIZE];    //Queue format name
    DWORD dwFormatNameLen = FORMATNAMESIZE; //Size of format name
    hr = MQPathNameToFormatName(    QUEUEPATHNAME,
                                    wcsFormatName,
                                    &dwFormatNameLen );

    //Check results
    if ( FAILED(hr) )
    {
        wprintf(L"Error looking up queue format name: %x\n\n",hr);
        return;
    }

    //Open the queue with receive access
    QUEUEHANDLE hQueue;                       //Handle to queue
    hr = MQOpenQueue( wcsFormatName,          //Queue format name
                      MQ_RECEIVE_ACCESS,      //Access requested
                      MQ_DENY_NONE,           //Share mode
                      &hQueue);               //Queue handle

    //Check results
    if ( FAILED(hr) )
    {
        wprintf(L"Error opening queue: %x\n\n",hr);
        return;
    }

    //Allocate message property objects
    MQMSGPROPS MsgProps;                //Message properties struct
    MSGPROPID aMsgPropId[4];            //Message property id array
    PROPVARIANT aMsgPropVar[4];         //Message property value array

    //Set up message label and length
    WCHAR wcsLabel[MSGLABELSIZE];       //Message label buffer
    aMsgPropId[0] = PROPID_M_LABEL;
```

LISTING 25.7 Continued

```
aMsgPropVar[0].vt = VT_LPWSTR;
aMsgPropVar[0].pwszVal = wcsLabel;
aMsgPropId[1] = PROPID_M_LABEL_LEN;
aMsgPropVar[1].vt = VT_UI4;
aMsgPropVar[1].ulVal = MSGLABELSIZE;

//Set up message body and length
WCHAR wcsBody[MSGBODYSIZE];            //Message body buffer
aMsgPropId[2] = PROPID_M_BODY;
aMsgPropVar[2].vt = VT_VECTOR | VT_UI1;
aMsgPropVar[2].caub.pElems = (LPBYTE)wcsBody;
aMsgPropVar[2].caub.cElems = MSGBODYSIZE * sizeof(WCHAR);
aMsgPropId[3] = PROPID_M_BODY_SIZE;
aMsgPropVar[3].vt = VT_UI4;
aMsgPropVar[3].ulVal = MSGBODYSIZE;

//Set up message property struct
MsgProps.cProp = 4;                   //Number of properties
MsgProps.aPropID = aMsgPropId;    //Ids of properties
MsgProps.aPropVar = aMsgPropVar;   //Values of properties
MsgProps.aStatus = NULL;           //No error reports

//Get messages
while ( TRUE )
{
  //Start MSMQ internal transaction
    ITransaction  *pTransaction;
  hr = MQBeginTransaction(&pTransaction);

    //Check results
    if ( FAILED(hr) )
    {
        wprintf(L"Error creating transaction: %x\n\n",hr);
        break;
    }

    hr = MQReceiveMessage(    hQueue,      //Receive queue
            0,                             //Timeout
            MQ_ACTION_RECEIVE,    //Receive or peek
            &MsgProps,            //Message properties
            NULL,                        //Overlapped struct
            NULL,                        //Callback function
            NULL,                        //Queue cursor
            pTransaction );       //Transaction
    //Check results
    if ( FAILED(hr) )
    {
        if ( MQ_ERROR_IO_TIMEOUT != hr )
            wprintf(L"Error receiving message: %x\n\n",hr);
```

LISTING 25.7   Continued

```
            pTransaction->Release();
            break;
    }

    //Display message
    ShippingRequest * psr = (ShippingRequest *) wcsBody;
    wprintf(L"Retrieved message label: %s\n",wcsLabel);
    wprintf(L"\tAccount: %ld, Product ID: %ld, Quantity: %ld\n",
                psr->Account,psr->Product,psr->Quantity);

    //Try to ship order
    if ( ExecuteSlowUnstableLinkShippingRequest(    psr->Account,
                                                    psr->Product,
                                                    psr->Quantity) )
    {
        hr = pTransaction->Commit(0,0,0);
        if ( FAILED(hr) )
        {
            wprintf(L"Transaction failed to commit\n\n");
            pTransaction->Release();
            break;
        }
    }
    else
    {
        pTransaction->Abort(0,0,0);
        wprintf(L"Shipping failed, order processing aborted\n\n");
        pTransaction->Release();
        break;
    }

    //Release the transaction and display success
    pTransaction->Release();
    wprintf(L"Order shipped\n\n");
}

//Close queue
MQCloseQueue(hQueue);
}
```

External Transactions

External MSMQ transactions are transactions that use Microsoft's Distributed
Transaction Coordinator (MS DTC) to manage transaction oversight responsibilities.
External transactions are used when MSMQ and other resource managers must collaborate to complete an atomic operation. A typical example would be sending a message
with MSMQ and updating a customer record in a database. Both or neither operations

must succeed. In order to provide interoperability with existing transaction infrastructures, MS DTC also supplies glue that enables MSMQ to operate within the context of MTS and XA transactions. You will get a close look at DTC and MTS transactions in this chapter's sample application. MTS transactions will be discussed in more detail in the MTS section of this book.

One of the sample `OrderEntry` components makes use of an MTS DTC transaction in order to update the customer account balance and queue the shipping order atomically. The transactional layout of this application is depicted in the previous model. DTC can also be used outside of MTS. There are actually few differences, as far as transactions are concerned, between MTS and straight DTC transactions. Although MTS provides more automatic features and several very powerful application server aspects, direct DTC transactions have the advantage of being able to run on systems where MTS is not available.

In the next two sections, we'll examine direct DTC transactions and MTS transactions in turn.

Dispensing DTC Transactions

External transaction dispensers are accessed through either the `DtcGetTransactionManager()` routine or the `MSMQCoordinatedTransactionDispenser` class. The DTC routine returns a raw `ITransactionDispenser` interface, and the MSMQ class provides a wrapper implementation. Both mechanisms give you access to the all-important `BeginTransaction()` method. The DTC and MSMQ `BeginTransaction()` routines return an `ITransaction` interface pointer and an `MSMQTransaction` object, respectively. It is the `ITransaction` interface pointer that you pass to any other application components that you want to enlist in the DTC transaction. Other than the severe case of carpal tunnel syndrome that you'll get typing these ridiculously long names, it's all pretty easy.

The `OrderEntry` project included on the CD-ROM demonstrates the MTS transaction approach, whereas the `DTCOrderEntry` project demonstrates the direct DTC approach. Here's the code that constructs the DTC transaction in our DTC-compliant `Order` class:

```
//Create external MS DTC transaction
IMSMQCoordinatedTransactionDispenserPtr pTransactionDispenser(
                    "MSMQ.MSMQCoordinatedTransactionDispenser");
IMSMQTransactionPtr pTransaction =
                    pTransactionDispenser->BeginTransaction();
```

No problems here. Just make sure that you have greater than 800×600 resolution so that your editor can display the type names.

Enlisting Message Transfers in a DTC Transaction

So now that you've got the transaction, how do you get someone to care? Well, because transactions are easier to deal with than people, this is pretty easy. Anything that you want to manage within the transaction has to be enlisted. Messages are enlisted at the transfer level, whereas databases are usually enlisted at the session level. Here's the code that enlists the MSMQ Send operation:

```
VARIANT vtTransaction;
vtTransaction.vt = VT_DISPATCH;
vtTransaction.pdispVal = pTransaction;

//Execute send within current external transaction
pMsg->Send( pQueue, &vtTransaction );
```

Notice the variant trick required in order to stuff the transaction interface into the ActiveX component Send call. I really do like Visual Basic, but this kind of VB catering at the C++ level does become cumbersome.

Enlisting Database Sessions in a DTC Transaction

MS DTC first appeared with the release of Microsoft SQL Server 6.5. MS DTC has grown well beyond its roll as minion of MS SQL to become the Windows platform transaction manager. Although other database platforms can certainly be included in DTC transactions, the mechanisms for enlisting them are varied.

OLEDB is the current darling in the Microsoft data access world and offers extreme flexibility because unlike ODBC, it is not limited to relational data stores. OLEDB also provides very generic mechanisms for accessing resources. The good thing is that we now have a single generic interface to access any data on any platform. The bad thing is that the OLEDB interface is rather large because of its support for everything ever invented that will store data. Table 25.4 shows some of the choices available for enlisting a SQL Server or other database into an external DTC transaction.

TABLE 25.4 Enlisting Databases to an External DTC Transaction

DB Library	dbenlisttrans()
Transact-SQL	Automatic Propagation
MTS	Automatic Propagation
ODBC	SQLSetConnectAttr(...) with second parameter set to SQL_COPT_SS_ENLIST_IN_DTC
OLEDB	ITransactionJoin::JoinTransaction()

Listing 25.8 demonstrates the process of enlisting an OLEDB provider session in a DTC transaction. This code is from the internal `ChargeAccount()` method of the `Order` class in the `OrderEntry` project. The sample application accesses a single table in a SQL Server database containing balance, account number, and email address fields. The application uses the ATL consumer templates to simplify the management of the several OLEDB interfaces involved.

LISTING 25.8   Enlisting an OLEDB Session to an External DTC Transaction

```
CDataSource OrderConnection;          //Accounts database connection
CSession OrderSession;                //Session for Order processing
HRESULT hr;                           //Call result

//Open database and create session
hr = OrderConnection.OpenFromInitializationString(
        L"DRIVER=SQL Server;SERVER=(local);"
        L"APP=Microsoft(R) Windows NT(R) Operating System;"
        L"WSID=WILANIR;DATABASE=Accounts;TranslationName=Yes;"
        L"QueryLogFile=Yes"    );
if ( FAILED(hr) )
    _com_issue_error(hr);
hr = OrderSession.Open(OrderConnection);
if ( FAILED(hr) )
    _com_issue_error(hr);

//Join the external transaction
ITransactionJoin * pTJ = NULL;
hr = (OrderSession.m_spOpenRowset)->QueryInterface(
                                    IID_ITransactionJoin,
                                    (void**)&pTJ);
if ( FAILED(hr) )
    _com_issue_error(hr);
hr = pTJ->JoinTransaction( pTransaction,0,0,NULL);
if ( FAILED(hr) )
    _com_issue_error(hr);
```

Notice that the process used to join the transaction has two steps. You have probably also noticed that I reverted to direct OLEDB operations here. At this stage of the game, the ATL templates are still a bit new and have no direct support for joining explicit DTC transactions. The direct OLEDB operation is not too painful in this case. Simply query for an `ITransactionJoin` interface using the session `IOpenRowset` interface pointer and call `JoinTransaction()`.

If you get back a NULL from your `ITransactionJoin` query, the provider is indicating that it cannot support external DTC transactions. I have also found that some providers which return a good interface pointer don't support external transactions either, or at least not correctly.

> **Note**
>
> The many possible features presented by various drivers for various databases and data stores is mind-boggling. The OLEDB property list reflects this and receives my award for the longest HTML help page of all time. Unfortunately for you, fortunately for me, we do not have time to deal with the inner complexities of OLEDB here. Somebody ought to write a book....

Ending a DTC Transaction

The final block of transaction-related code in the `IOrder::PlaceOrder()` method calls a subroutine that uses the transaction during an update to a SQL Server database. Assuming that no exceptions fly out of there, the transaction is committed. The `ITransaction` interface is rather Spartan, providing only `Commit()`, `Abort()`, and `GetTransactionInfo()` methods.

```
ChargeAccount( AccountNumber,
               lfTotalPrice,
               (ITransaction * )pTransaction->Transaction );
pTransaction->Commit();
```

There is one funky thing about this piece of code: the `ITransaction` interface passed to `ChargeAccount()`. This is a property of `MSMQTransaction` represented as a `long`, of all things. Casting it back to an `ITransaction` interface pointer looks scary but supplies the correct behavior. The smart `MSMQTransaction` pointer takes care of releasing the transaction object for us, and, unless we explicitly commit the transaction, it will roll back at this point. It is also important to note that you should always check the return value of the `Commit()` method because it will return an error if it finds it must abort the transaction. We actually are checking the result of the `Commit()` call here because it's really a Smart Pointer wrapper, which will throw a `_com_error` at us in case of failure.

Listing 25.9 shows the complete code for the DTC version of the `PlaceOrder()` method for the order entry application.

LISTING 25.9 DTC Version of the `PlaceOrder()` Method

```
STDMETHODIMP COrder::PlaceOrder(   long AccountNumber,
                                   long ProductID,
                                   long Quantity    )
{
    try
    {
```

LISTING 25.9   Continued

```
//Set up queue information using a smart pointer
IMSMQQueueInfoPtr pQInfo("MSMQ.MSMQQueueInfo");
pQInfo->PutPathName(SHIPPINGQUEUEPATHNAME);

//Open the queue
IMSMQQueuePtr pQueue =
            pQInfo->Open(MQ_SEND_ACCESS, MQ_DENY_NONE);

//Set up message label
WCHAR wcsLabel[SHIPPINGMSGLABELSIZE];
swprintf(wcsLabel,L"Order for Account #: %ld", AccountNumber);

//Set up message body as a byte array
VARIANT vtBody;
vtBody.vt = VT_ARRAY|VT_UI1;
vtBody.parray = SafeArrayCreateVector(
            VT_UI1,
            0,
            sizeof(ShippingRequest));
if ( NULL == vtBody.parray )
   _com_issue_error(E_OUTOFMEMORY);
ShippingRequest * psr =
         (ShippingRequest *) vtBody.parray->pvData;
psr->Account = AccountNumber;
psr->Product = ProductID;
psr->Quantity = Quantity;

//Create external MS DTC transaction
IMSMQCoordinatedTransactionDispenserPtr pTransactionDispenser(
     ""MSMQ.MSMQCoordinatedTransactionDispenser"");
IMSMQTransactionPtr pTransaction =
         pTransactionDispenser->BeginTransaction();

//Set up the message
IMSMQMessagePtr pMsg("MSMQ.MSMQMessage");
VARIANT vtTransaction;
vtTransaction.vt = VT_DISPATCH;
vtTransaction.pdispVal = pTransaction;
pMsg->PutLabel(wcsLabel);
pMsg->PutBody(vtBody);

//Execute send within current external transaction
pMsg->Send( pQueue, &vtTransaction );
SafeArrayDestroy( vtBody.parray );

//Compute total price and deduct account balance within
//  the current external transaction
double lfTotalPrice = Quantity * 20.0;
ChargeAccount( AccountNumber,
```

LISTING 25.9 Continued

```
            lfTotalPrice,
            (ITransaction * )pTransaction->Transaction );
    pTransaction->Commit();
}
catch (_com_error &e)
{
    return e.Error();
}

//Return success
return S_OK;
}
```

I suppose that something should be said about the SAFEARRAY business in Listing 25.9. This Automation beast is designed to support the needs of Visual Basic. The SAFEARRAY structure supplies fields allowing support for fully described multidimensional arrays. In this scenario, we just want to transfer a block of memory X bytes long. Well, in Visual Basic terms, this is an X-sized array of bytes and requires an Automation or "safe" array. The SAFEARRAY provides for dimension count, array of dimension sizes, element size, feature flags, a lock counter, and finally a pointer to the actual data. Any self-respecting C programmer would have, of course, just cut to the chase, dropped in the data pointer, and gone to lunch. We must take a more tempered approach here. It's hard to argue with the power and speed of Visual Basic for client and graphical front-end development. In order to use the MSMQ ActiveX components and maintain Automation compatibility, we've used a SAFEARRAY. There are many helpful routines in the Automation programmer's kit that simplify the allocation and initialization of SAFEARRAYs. In particular, single dimension (vector) arrays are only a function call away. Our SafeArrayCreateVector() call is matched with a call to SafeArrayDestroy(), which releases the resources the prior call allocates.

MTS Managed Transactions

One of my favorite things about MTS is that it handles some of the ugliest software programming tasks ever invented, and yet the interface it presents to the developer who uses it is remarkably compact. This is because MTS does many things declaratively through attributes (also because it is very well designed; hats off to you guys). If you want your COM+ object methods to be transactional, simply fire up the MTS Explorer, slap your object into a package, and set its Transaction Support property to Requires Transaction. That's honestly all you need to do. MTS will create a DTC transaction for every call and propagate it to other objects or resource managers that support distributed transactions.

So, wait a minute. What happens when you return from your method call to the client application running in a browser in Timbuktu? Well, if it can, MTS commits the transaction; if some resource manager dissents, it aborts. What if I want to abort the transaction myself because of a problem my code discovers? Well, I'm glad you asked. (It's lonely sitting in a dark room, typing all day. You start talking to yourself.) Every COM+ call carries with it some basic information or context. This might be information such as who called you plus all the security stuff discussed in Chapter 18, "COM+ Security." MTS ups the ante with even more context, including things such as transaction information. In fact, the MTS context supplies support for just about everything that a sane developer could need within a component method call. Using the MTS context interface, we can vote to commit or abort the current transaction.

This is not the MTS section of the book, so I'll limit the discussion here to the things you would need to simply queue messages in an MTS transaction. The first things you need are declarations for the various MTS interfaces and structures of interest. These are available through mtx.h. Next, you need a way to get the context information for the call. MTS maintains a Context object describing the specifics for each outstanding MTS call. The Context object supports the IObjectContext interface and can be retrieved through the MTS GetObjectContext() call. Because MTS tries to simplify the commit model for COM+ objects, the protocol for ending a transaction is a little different from what you've seen before. Objects have access to five routines relating to the state of their transaction, as shown in Table 25.5.

TABLE 25.5   Transaction State Access Routines

Routine	Description
IsInTransaction()	Identifies the existence of a transaction in the current context.
DisableCommit()	Causes subsequent attempts to commit to abort.
EnableCommit()	Re-enables a transaction after a call to DisableCommit().
SetAbort()	Aborts the transaction.
SetComplete()	Attempts to commit the transaction (implicitly enables commitment).

Listing 25.10 shows the complete code for the PlaceOrder() method of the MTS OrderEntry component. You'll note that we don't begin the transaction within the code; instead, we rely on an implicit transaction. Such transactions can be configured by the MTS administrator, or (as you'll see in the MTS section) configured through attributes in the components type library. In cases in which you find yourself executing with MTS without a transaction (sacrilege!), you can always roll your own with the ITransactionContextEx::CreateInstance() method call. You can create a TransactionContextEx object with CoCreateInstance(), and because it requires a

transaction, it and all the offspring you create with its `CreateInstance()` method will exist in the new transaction. `ITransactionContextEx` also supplies `Commit()` and `Abort()` methods that let you control the end point of the transaction.

As you examine Listing 25.10, note that it can be fine for many applications.

LISTING 25.10 Version of `PlaceOrder()` That Uses MTS Transactions

```
#include <mtx.h>

STDMETHODIMP COrder::PlaceOrder(long AccountNumber,
                                long ProductID,
                                long Quantity)
{
    //Get MTS context and disable commit
    //  Disabling commit will keep an accidental
    //  return in the body of our code from
    //  committing the transaction
    IObjectContext * pOC = NULL;
    HRESULT hr = GetObjectContext(&pOC);
    if ( FAILED(hr) )
        return hr;
    pOC->DisableCommit();

    try
    {
        //Set up queue information using a smart pointer
        IMSMQQueueInfoPtr pQInfo(""MSMQ.MSMQQueueInfo"");
        pQInfo->PutPathName(SHIPPINGQUEUEPATHNAME);

        //Open the queue
        IMSMQQueuePtr pQueue = pQInfo->Open(   MQ_SEND_ACCESS,
                                            MQ_DENY_NONE   );

        //Set up message label
        WCHAR wcsLabel[SHIPPINGMSGLABELSIZE];
        swprintf(wcsLabel,L""Order for Account #: %ld"", AccountNumber);

        //Set up message body as a byte array
        VARIANT vtBody;
        vtBody.vt = VT_ARRAY|VT_UI1;
        vtBody.parray = SafeArrayCreateVector(VT_UI1,
                                              0,
                                              sizeof(ShippingRequest));
        if ( NULL == vtBody.parray )
            _com_issue_error(E_OUTOFMEMORY);
        ShippingRequest * psr =
                (ShippingRequest *) vtBody.parray->pvData;
        psr->Account = AccountNumber;
        psr->Product = ProductID;
```

LISTING 25.10 Continued

```
        psr->Quantity = Quantity;

        //Set up the message
        IMSMQMessagePtr pMsg(""MSMQ.MSMQMessage"");
        VARIANT vtTransaction;
        vtTransaction.vt = VT_I4;
        vtTransaction.lVal = MQ_MTS_TRANSACTION;
        pMsg->PutLabel(wcsLabel);
        pMsg->PutBody(vtBody);

        //Execute send within current external transaction
        pMsg->Send( pQueue, &vtTransaction );
        SafeArrayDestroy( vtBody.parray );

        //Compute total price and deduct account balance within
        //  the current external transaction
        double lfTotalPrice = Quantity * 20.0;
        ChargeAccount( AccountNumber, lfTotalPrice );
    }
    catch (_com_error &e)
    {
        //Abort transaction and return error
        pOC->SetAbort();
        return e.Error();
    }

    //Commit transaction and return success
    pOC->SetComplete();
    return S_OK;
}
```

A few notes on Listing 25.10. Notice that I disable commitment of the transaction right off the bat. This is a habit I've gotten into which ensures that any unsavory bailouts within the transactional code will abort the transaction. The final call to SetComplete() implicitly re-enables the transaction and attempts to commit it. Another point of interest is that the default transaction type in the ActiveX component MSMQMessage::Send() routine is not NONE, it's MTS! So although you've explicitly requested the send operation enlist in the outstanding MTS transaction, you could have left the parameter out altogether just as easily. If there's a transaction, the MSMQ ActiveX components use it; if not, they go without.

MSMQ Email API

MSMQ provides a simple programming interface to the world of email. After all, what's an email system if it isn't just a big message queuing network? MSMQ supplies both

API routines and ActiveX components that make it easy to construct basic email services. The MSMQ Email interface does not support attachments, and it supplies limited interoperability. Microsoft presently supplies MSMQ services for Exchange Server and MAPI Client interaction. Other services, such as SMTP, might appear as time goes by. The two services provided by Microsoft have very different features.

The Exchange Server connector is an actual connector taking advantage of the MSMQ connector architecture. MSMQ applications address messages to the actual Exchange user, and the MSMQ Exchange connector acts as a gateway delivering the message to a target Exchange server for further processing.

The MAPI Provider is not a real inter-messaging system connector. It is more of a MAPI Client translator. Each MAPI user must have a queue, and MSMQ must be installed on each MAPI Client machine.

The MSMQ mail API and components are used to construct and parse email messages destined for external services. The MSMQ Library API supplies three routines related to Email operations:

- `MQMailComposeBody()`
- `MQMailFreeMemory()`
- `MQMailParseBody()`

The compose body routine takes an MSMQ Email message body structure and returns a formatted buffer and the buffer's size. This buffer can be set as the body of an MSMQ message destined for Exchange or a MAPI Client. The Email message can contain text, an Exchange form, and MAPI Transport-Neutral Encapsulation Format data, as well as delivery and nondelivery reports. Listing 25.11 shows the `MQMailEMail` structure.

LISTING 25.11 Definition of the `MQMailEMail` Structure

```
typedef struct   MQMailEMail_tag
{
   LPSTR                 szSubject;   //Subject of mail
   BOOL                  fRequestDeliveryReport;
   BOOL                  fRequestNonDeliveryReport;
   LPFILETIME            pftDate;     //Time sent
   LPMQMailRecip         pFrom;       //Sender
   LPMQMailRecipList     pRecips;     //List of recipients
   LPMQMailEMailType     iType;       //Type of Email
   union                              //Union of available Email types
   {
       MQMailFormData                form;
       MQMailMessageData             message;
       MQMailTnefData                tnef;
```

25

LISTING 25.11   Continued

```
        MQMailDeliveryReportData             DeliveryReport;
        MQMailNonDeliveryReportData          NonDeliveryReport;
    };
    LPVOID                    pReserved;   //Should be set to NULL.
} MQMailEMail, FAR* LPMQMailEMail;
```

Inbound messages go through the reverse of the compose process that is effected by the
MQMailParseBody() routine. The buffers created with the compose and parse functions
must be released with the MQMailFreeMemory() call.

The ActiveX Email Component set consists of several classes designed to provide
MSMQ Email access to Automation clients. Most of the classes are simple wrappers
around the various recipient and form structures found in the API. The MSMQMailEMail
class is representative of the MQMailEMail structure shown in Listing 25.11, providing
properties similar to each of the listed structure fields. The MSMQMailEMail class also
supplies ComposeBody() and ParseBody() methods that mimic the packing and cracking
behavior of the similarly named API routines.

Asynchronous Operations

Wait a minute. Isn't the whole MSMQ system asynchronous? Well, yes, with the exception of one call. The Receive operation, as you have seen, can be a blocking call, and it
provides a timeout setting for this reason. It is possible to queue a Receive operation for
later completion, just as you queue outbound messages for later delivery. The workings
of asynchronous Receive operations greatly complicate the simple nature of a basic synchronous Receive call. Several different approaches are provided that give developers the
flexibility to select a mechanism that works well within the framework of their application. Three factors often motivate developers to complicate their applications with this
asynchronous stuff:

- Performance
- Application Design
- Performance

Okay, so two really, but performance is by far the greatest persuader in this area.
Asynchronous operations, as their name indicates, don't wait for the entire call behavior
to complete. They touch off their operation and return to do other work as soon as possible. In this way, an application could start a Receive operation on three queues at once
and then wait for any one of them to actually complete the Receive operation. Can't you
do that with a polling approach by setting the Receive timeout to zero? Yes and no. You

can, but the process of continually checking Receive status on several queues over and over again in a tight loop will needlessly eat up CPU cycles. It is also very unlikely that a polling operation will occur immediately following the message's availability. So it's much better for overall system performance to use an asynchronous approach when the message load begins to get serious.

What about the application design bit? Because many applications are developed as graphical event-driven systems these days, it is actually pretty easy to work an event-driven MSMQ Receive approach into these programs.

Here are the various mechanisms for building asynchronous MSMQ Receive services:

- Automation events
- System event objects
- Callback functions
- System I/O completion port objects

Only API-level programmers can take advantage of all four of these options. Automation events are the one source of asynchronous operations supported by the MSMQ ActiveX components. I'll take a look at each of these methods in turn and build a few complete examples including one based on the big kahuna of asynchronous transfers, I/O completion ports. It is important to note that most designs using one of the four asynchronous techniques listed in the previous paragraph find themselves naturally working with multiple threads of execution within a single process. If you're not comfortable with multithreading techniques, you might want to supplement the upcoming sections with a little remedial thread theory.

Automation Events

The MSMQ ActiveX components provide an MSMQEvent object with two event routines, MSMQEvent_Arrived() and MSMQEvent_ArrivedError(). MSMQEvents are associated with queues by calling the IMSMQQueue::EnableNotification() method passing the MSMQEvent as a parameter. This call causes the queue to begin firing events as Receive operations become available. This approach is trivial to program in Visual Basic, but presents a bit of work at the C++ level. The main benefit of this technique is that it is available in all client languages. The drawback is that it does not provide the most efficient solution for very high-performance, multithreaded applications.

System Event Objects

Events are heavily used, system-synchronization objects provided by Win32. Events are an integral part of many Win32 overlapped I/O scenarios. Overlapped I/O is another term often used in referencing asynchronous I/O. Many Win32 calls accept an overlapped structure in order to perform asynchronous I/O. Overlapped structures have the following format:

```
typedef struct _OVERLAPPED
{
    DWORD  Internal;
    DWORD  InternalHigh;
    DWORD  Offset;
    DWORD  OffsetHigh;
    HANDLE hEvent;
} OVERLAPPED;
```

Notice that the overlapped structure maintains a handle to an event object used to signal I/O completion. The offset fields represent a 64-bit offset into the file object on which the I/O is performed. As we are working with messages in queues and not data streams, these fields are irrelevant. The internal fields are, well, internal. We're not supposed to use them, but from time to time, you will find the first 32 bits useful because they contain error codes during overlapped I/O failure.

So using events is as easy as creating an event, saving its handle in the overlapped structure, passing the structure to the Receive call, and then waiting for the I/O to complete. Events are created with the Win32 `CreateEvent()` call. For our purposes, a default event is fine. Therefore, we can supply the `CreateEvent()` call with all zero or NULL arguments.

Several routines can be used to wait for objects in Win32. Win32 synchronization objects have two states, signaled and nonsignaled. Waiting for a nonsignaled object will cause a thread to block. Signaled objects release waiting threads from their wait.

The following routines are the two most popular wait functions, enabling you to wait for one or many objects respectively:

- `WaitForSingleObject()`
- `WaitForMultipleObjects()`

Application code can cause events to become signaled and nonsignaled by calling the following two event API routines:

- `SetEvent()`
- `ResetEvent()`

Listing 25.12 demonstrates a simple application that uses events to synchronize MSMQ Receive operations. You'll note that I have created a Quit event to allow the main application thread to signal the worker thread to exit.

LISTING 25.12 Using Events to Synchronize MSMQ Receive Operations

```cpp
// Pong.cpp
//
// Async event message receiving application


//Dependencies
#include <windows.h>
#include <stdio.h>
#include <conio.h>
#include <mq.h>


//Symbols
#define FORMATNAMESIZE     64
#define MSGBODYSIZE        128
#define MSGLABELSIZE       64
#define PONGPATHNAME       L".\\PongQueue"


//Prototypes
DWORD WINAPI HandleMessages( LPVOID pv );


//Application entry point
int main()
{
    //Masthead
    wprintf(L"Pong messages receiving applications\n\n");

    //Create the quit event
    HANDLE hQuitEvent = CreateEvent(NULL,true,false,NULL);
    if ( NULL == hQuitEvent )
        return GetLastError();

    //Create the message handling thread
    DWORD dwThreadId;
    HANDLE hThread = CreateThread(     NULL,
                                       0,
                                       HandleMessages,
                                       hQuitEvent,
                                       0,
                                       &dwThreadId);
    if ( NULL == hThread )
            return GetLastError();
    wprintf(L"Created message handling thread %x\n",dwThreadId);

    //Wait for user to exit
    wprintf(L"\nPress any key to exit\n\n");
    getch();
```

Listing 25.12   Continued

```
    //Signal background thread to quit
    SetEvent(hQuitEvent);
    wprintf(L"\nWaiting for I/O thread to exit...\n");
    WaitForSingleObject(hThread,INFINITE);

    //Close thread and event handles and return success
    CloseHandle(hThread);
    CloseHandle(hQuitEvent);
    wprintf(L"Exiting...");
    Sleep(3000);
    return 0;
}


DWORD WINAPI HandleMessages( LPVOID pv )
{
    //Recover quit event handle
    HANDLE hQuitEvent = (HANDLE) pv;

    //Get the format name of the queue using the pathname
    HRESULT hr;                                 //Return status
    WCHAR wcsFormatName[FORMATNAMESIZE];        //Queue format name
    DWORD dwFormatNameLen = FORMATNAMESIZE;     //Size of format name
    hr = MQPathNameToFormatName(    PONGPATHNAME,
                                    wcsFormatName,
                                    &dwFormatNameLen );
    if ( FAILED(hr) )
        return hr;

    //Open the queue with receive access
    HANDLE hQueue;
    hr = MQOpenQueue( wcsFormatName,            //Queue format name
                      MQ_RECEIVE_ACCESS,        //Access requested
                      MQ_DENY_NONE,             //Share mode
                      &(hQueue) );              //Queue handle
    if ( FAILED(hr) )
        return hr;

    //Create the overlap event
    HANDLE hIOEvent = CreateEvent(NULL,false,false,NULL);
    if ( NULL == hIOEvent )
        return GetLastError();

    //Set up the Overlapped structure for async reads
    OVERLAPPED ol = {0,0,0,0, hIOEvent};

    //Set up array of wait handles
    HANDLE ah[2];
```

LISTING 25.12   Continued

```
ah[0] = hQuitEvent;
ah[1] = hIOEvent;

//Allocate message property objects
MQMSGPROPS MsgProps;                 //Message properties struct
MSGPROPID aMsgPropId[4];             //Message property id array
PROPVARIANT aMsgPropVar[4];          //Message property value array

//Set up message property struct
MsgProps.cProp = 4;                  //Number of properties
MsgProps.aPropID = aMsgPropId;       //Ids of properties
MsgProps.aPropVar = aMsgPropVar;     //Values of properties
MsgProps.aStatus = NULL;             //No error reports

//Set up message label and length
WCHAR wcsLabel[MSGLABELSIZE];            //Message label buffer
aMsgPropId[0] = PROPID_M_LABEL;
aMsgPropVar[0].vt = VT_LPWSTR;
aMsgPropVar[0].pwszVal = wcsLabel;
aMsgPropId[1] = PROPID_M_LABEL_LEN;
aMsgPropVar[1].vt = VT_UI4;

//Set up message body and length
WCHAR wcsBody[MSGBODYSIZE];          //Message body buffer
aMsgPropId[2] = PROPID_M_BODY;
aMsgPropVar[2].vt = VT_VECTOR | VT_UI1;
aMsgPropVar[2].caub.pElems = (LPBYTE)wcsBody;
aMsgPropVar[2].caub.cElems = MSGBODYSIZE * sizeof(WCHAR);
aMsgPropId[3] = PROPID_M_BODY_SIZE;
aMsgPropVar[3].vt = VT_UI4;

//Get messages
while ( TRUE )
{
    //We have to reset these because they are [in,out] params
    aMsgPropVar[1].ulVal = MSGLABELSIZE;
    aMsgPropVar[3].ulVal = MSGBODYSIZE;

    //Get message from queue
    hr = MQReceiveMessage(      hQueue,      //Queue to receive from
                                INFINITE,  //Timeout
                                MQ_ACTION_RECEIVE,//Receive or peek
                                &MsgProps, //Message properties
                                &ol,         //Overlapped structure
                                NULL,        //Callback function
                                NULL,        //Queue cursor
                                NULL );    //Transaction
    //Check results
    if ( FAILED(hr) )
```

LISTING 25.12   Continued

```
        {
            wprintf(L"Error receiving message: %x\n\n",hr);
            break;
        }
        if ( MQ_INFORMATION_OPERATION_PENDING == hr )
            wprintf(L"IO pending on thread %x\n",GetCurrentThreadId());

        //Wait for IO
        hr = WaitForMultipleObjects(2,ah,false,INFINITE);
        if ( WAIT_OBJECT_0 == hr )
        {
            wprintf(L"Got quit message on thread %x\n",
                                            GetCurrentThreadId());
            MQCloseQueue(hQueue);
            ExitThread(0);
        }
        else if ( WAIT_OBJECT_0+1 != hr )
        {
            wprintf(L"Wait error %x\n",GetLastError());
            break;
        }

        //Display message
        wcsBody[(aMsgPropVar[3].ulVal)/sizeof(WCHAR)] = L'\0';
        wprintf(L"Retrieved message label:\n\t%s\n",wcsLabel);
        wprintf(L"Retrieved message body:\n\t%s\n\n",wcsBody);
    }

    //Exit with error
    MQCloseQueue(hQueue);
    wprintf(L"Abort on thread %x\n",GetCurrentThreadId());
    return 1;
}
```

Callback Functions

Callback functions enable a developer to create a routine that is invoked asynchronously every time a Receive operation completes. The MSMQReceiveMessage() routine supplies a parameter for the pointer to a callback function:

```
HRESULT APIENTRY
MQReceiveMessage(    QUEUEHANDLE hSource,
                     DWORD dwTimeout,
                     DWORD dwAction,
                     MQMSGPROPS pMessageProps,
                     LPOVERLAPPED lpOverlapped,
                     PMQRECEIVECALLBACK fnReceiveCallback,
```

```
                              HANDLE hCursor,
                              Transaction *pTransaction  );
```

MSMQ callback routines must have the following prototype:

```
void APIENTRY ReceiveCallbackRoutine(    HRESULT hrStatus,
                                         QUEUEHANDLE hSource,
                                         DWORD dwTimeout,
                                         DWORD dwAction,
                                         MQMSGPROPS* pMessageProps,
                                         LPOVERLAPPED lpOverlapped,
                                         HANDLE hCursor);
```

There are lots of ways to design a callback I/O sequence. A popular approach is to kick off the I/O from a thread's entry point and then perpetuate the I/O by making the next I/O request from within the I/O completion routine itself.

Listing 25.13 shows a sample application that uses a callback routine to receive incoming MSMQ messages. This is one of the several Pong programs. I introduced the Ping application earlier in the chapter as a means to explore message acknowledgments and delivery timeouts. The various Pong applications pretty much only oblige the Ping side by receiving messages. The main thread creates a worker thread to handle the I/O work. When instructed to quit, the main thread signals an event to notify the waiting worker thread that it's time to go.

LISTING 25.13   Using a Callback Routine to Receive Messages

```
// Pong.cpp
//
// Message receiving application


//Dependencies
#include <windows.h>
#include <stdio.h>
#include <conio.h>
#include <mq.h>


//Symbols
#define FORMATNAMESIZE     64
#define MSGBODYSIZE        128
#define MSGLABELSIZE       64
#define PONGPATHNAME       L".\\PongQueue"


//Prototypes
DWORD WINAPI HandleMessages( LPVOID pv );
void APIENTRY ReceiveCallbackRoutine(    HRESULT hr,
```

LISTING 25.13 Continued

```
                                      QUEUEHANDLE hSource,
                                      DWORD dwTimeout,
                                      DWORD dwAction,
                                      MQMSGPROPS* pMessageProps,
                                      LPOVERLAPPED lpOverlapped,
                                      HANDLE hCursor  );


//Application entry point
int main()
{
    //Masthead
    wprintf(L"Pong messages receiving applications\n\n");

    //Create the quit event
    HANDLE hQuitEvent = CreateEvent(NULL,true,false,NULL);
    if ( NULL == hQuitEvent )
        return GetLastError();

    //Create the message handling thread
    DWORD dwThreadId;
    HANDLE hThread = CreateThread(    NULL,
                                      0,
                                      HandleMessages,
                                      hQuitEvent,
                                      0,
                                      &dwThreadId);
    if ( NULL == hThread )
            return GetLastError();
    wprintf(L"Created message handler thread %x\n",dwThreadId);

    //Wait for user to exit
    wprintf(L"\nPress and key to exit\n\n");
    getch();

    //Signal background thread to quit
    SetEvent(hQuitEvent);
    wprintf(L"\nWaiting for I/O threads to exit...\n");
    WaitForSingleObject(hThread,INFINITE);

    //Close thread and event handles and return success
    CloseHandle(hThread);
    CloseHandle(hQuitEvent);
    wprintf(L"Exiting...");
    Sleep(3000);
    return 0;
}
```

LISTING 25.13   Continued

```
DWORD WINAPI HandleMessages( LPVOID pv )
{
    //Recover quit event handle
    HANDLE hQuitEvent = (HANDLE) pv;

    //Get the format name of the queue using the pathname
    HRESULT hr;                                 //Return status
    WCHAR wcsFormatName[FORMATNAMESIZE];        //Queue format name
    DWORD dwFormatNameLen = FORMATNAMESIZE;     //Size of format name
    hr = MQPathNameToFormatName(    PONGPATHNAME,
                                    wcsFormatName,
                                    &dwFormatNameLen );
    if ( FAILED(hr) )
        return hr;

    //Open the queue with receive access
    HANDLE hQueue;
    hr = MQOpenQueue( wcsFormatName,              //Queue format name
                      MQ_RECEIVE_ACCESS,    //Access requested
                      MQ_DENY_NONE,              //Share mode
                      &(hQueue) );            //Queue handle
    if ( FAILED(hr) )
        return hr;

    //Allocate message property objects
    MQMSGPROPS MsgProps;                 //Message properties struct
    MSGPROPID aMsgPropId[4];             //Message property id array
    PROPVARIANT aMsgPropVar[4];          //Message property value array

    //Set up message property struct
    MsgProps.cProp = 4;                  //Number of properties
    MsgProps.aPropID = aMsgPropId;       //Ids of properties
    MsgProps.aPropVar = aMsgPropVar;     //Values of properties
    MsgProps.aStatus = NULL;             //No error reports

    //Set up message label and length
    WCHAR wcsLabel[MSGLABELSIZE];            //Message label buffer
    aMsgPropId[0] = PROPID_M_LABEL;
    aMsgPropVar[0].vt = VT_LPWSTR;
    aMsgPropVar[0].pwszVal = wcsLabel;
    aMsgPropId[1] = PROPID_M_LABEL_LEN;
    aMsgPropVar[1].vt = VT_UI4;
    aMsgPropVar[1].ulVal = MSGLABELSIZE;

    //Set up message body and length
    WCHAR wcsBody[MSGBODYSIZE];              //Message body buffer
    aMsgPropId[2] = PROPID_M_BODY;
    aMsgPropVar[2].vt = VT_VECTOR | VT_UI1;
    aMsgPropVar[2].caub.pElems = (LPBYTE)wcsBody;
```

LISTING 25.13   Continued

```
        aMsgPropVar[2].caub.cElems = MSGBODYSIZE * sizeof(WCHAR);
        aMsgPropId[3] = PROPID_M_BODY_SIZE;
        aMsgPropVar[3].vt = VT_UI4;
        aMsgPropVar[3].ulVal = MSGBODYSIZE;

        //Get first message from queue with async callback
        hr = MQReceiveMessage(    hQueue,           //Queue to receive from
                                  INFINITE,       //Timeout
                                  MQ_ACTION_RECEIVE,//Receive or peek
                                  &MsgProps,      //Message properties
                                  NULL,             //Overlapped structure
                                  ReceiveCallbackRoutine,//Callback function
                                  NULL,                   //Queue cursor
                                  NULL );                 //Transaction
        //Check results
        if ( FAILED(hr) )
        {
            //Exit with error
            wprintf(L"Receive error %x\n",hr);
            MQCloseQueue(hQueue);
            ExitThread(1);
        }

        //Wait for quit
        WaitForSingleObject( hQuitEvent, INFINITE );
        return 0;
}

void APIENTRY ReceiveCallbackRoutine(    HRESULT hr,
                                         QUEUEHANDLE hSource,
                                         DWORD dwTimeout,
                                         DWORD dwAction,
                                         MQMSGPROPS* pMessageProps,
                                         LPOVERLAPPED lpOverlapped,
                                         HANDLE hCursor  )
{
    //Id Thread
    wprintf(L"Processing message on thread %x\n",GetCurrentThreadId());

    //Check status
    if (FAILED(hr))
    {
        if ( MQ_ERROR_OPERATION_CANCELLED == hr )
        {
            //If IO was canceled we need to bail out
            MQCloseQueue(hSource);
            return;
        }
        else
```

LISTING **25.13**   Continued

```
            {
                //IO error, report status and Abort
                wprintf(L"I/O error %x\n",hr);
                ExitThread(2);
            }
        }
        else
        {
            //Display message
            (pMessageProps->aPropVar[2].caub.pElems)[
                (pMessageProps->aPropVar[3].ulVal)] = '\0';
            (pMessageProps->aPropVar[2].caub.pElems)[
                (pMessageProps->aPropVar[3].ulVal)+1] = '\0';
            wprintf(    L"Retrieved message label:\n\t%s\n",
                        pMessageProps->aPropVar[0].pwszVal);
            wprintf(    L"Retrieved message body:\n\t%s\n\n",
                        pMessageProps->aPropVar[2].caub.pElems);
        }

        //We have to reset these because they are [in,out] params
        pMessageProps->aPropVar[1].ulVal = MSGLABELSIZE;
        pMessageProps->aPropVar[3].ulVal = MSGBODYSIZE;

        //Get next message from queue with this async callback
        hr = MQReceiveMessage(      hSource,        //Queue to receive from
                            INFINITE,       //Timeout
                            MQ_ACTION_RECEIVE,//Receive or peek
                            pMessageProps,//Message properties
                            NULL,           //Overlapped structure
                            ReceiveCallbackRoutine,//Callback function
                            NULL,                   //Queue cursor
                            NULL );                 //Transaction
        //Check results
        if ( FAILED(hr) )
        {
            //If we can't schedule receive operations we have to abort
            MQCloseQueue(hSource);
            wprintf(L"Error receiving message: %x\n\n",hr);
            wprintf(L"Abort on thread %x\n",GetCurrentThreadId());
            ExitThread(3);
        }
}
```

Completion Ports

I/O completion ports (IOCPs) are a powerful multithreaded I/O mechanism introduced
with Windows NT 3.5. Successful I/O completion port implementations begin with good

25

**ADVANCED
MSMQ
PROGRAMMING**

multithreaded application design. If you aren't too keen on threads (threads are the actual units of execution within a process), you probably will want to breeze through this section until such time as you do become keen on threads. Furthermore, I/O completion ports require use of the MSMQ API and are not supported through the ActiveX components. On the other hand, IOCPs are probably one of the fastest ways to perform massive concurrent I/O processing on Windows.

Completion ports are system objects that can be associated with one or more I/O files, such as disk files, pipes, sockets, and MSMQ queues. A thread can schedule several asynchronous I/O operations and then wait on an I/O completion port. You might already know that NT has always had a `WaitForMultipleObjects()` routine that can perform the same sort of task. So what makes I/O completion ports so special? The magic here lies in the fact that NT knows about I/O completion ports and that you use them when implementing multiple threads to service a set of logical I/O devices. This information enables the NT scheduler to optimize its behavior and improve your application performance and, in fact, the overall system performance.

When confronted with a set of threads waiting on an I/O completion port, Windows NT will limit the total number of threads executing to a value you specify when creating the IOCP. You can allow this value to default to the number of system CPUs. If NT basically treats all threads at the same priority level equally, wouldn't it be better to have as many threads as possible? Not by a long shot. First of all, you might get a slightly larger percentage of the overall available CPU time by slamming the system with a thread-creation frenzy. You will, unfortunately, drag the entire system down (your threads included) in the process, most often defeating your greedy intentions. Keep in mind that switching between threads doesn't get anything done as far as applications are concerned. Also remember that most threads have a one-megabyte stack reservation and a set of system resources to account for. Sure, it's really easy to code one thread per client (or queue if you will), but it's not the fastest approach in heavy-use applications.

The next thing to consider is that you might actually want a few more threads than you have CPUs. If you have only four CPUs, you can run only four threads concurrently, right? Why have more? Well, depending on your design, threads can enter a wait operation not based on the completion port. For instance, a message comes in from a queue, and the thread that receives it subsequently camps out on a rather slow database operation. If another message arrives in the queue, and your other three threads are busy with clients of their own, you have a CPU open but nothing to run on it. If you had created six threads, NT would have a couple of spares to work with in just such a situation. You might ask what happens when all the threads are available. This is an interesting question and demonstrates one of the most powerful aspects of ICOPs. Normal waiting threads are scheduled in a FIFO fashion as their objects of desire become available. This is only fair in generic thread scheduling, but in the context of IOCPs, it's a context-switching nightmare. One of the best things you can do to improve overall system performance is to let any thread that is running continue to run. Saving the current thread and then selecting and loading a new thread is not a cheap operation, nor is faulting all the new thread's resources back into memory. In the case of an IOCP application, we don't care which thread runs, just as long as the messages get handled. For this reason, NT schedules threads waiting on IOCPs in LIFO order. Threads that have been waiting the shortest period of time (sometimes not at all) are the most likely to have all their necessary state in cache or at least main memory.

Okay, how do we use these miraculous IOCPs? I'm sure that you'll like the fact that there are only three functions directly associated with IOCPs:

- `CreateIoCompletionPort()`
- `PostQueuedCompletionStatus()`
- `GetQueuedCompletionStatus()`

`CreateIoCompletionPort()` creates a new IOCP, as you might expect. It is also the routine used to associate logical device (file) handles with the port. Simply call `CreateIoCompletionPort()` to create the IOCP and get a handle to it; then pass the handle back in on subsequent calls with the handle of the logical device to associate with the port.

When creating a thread within, the process can start several asynchronous I/O operations and then wait on the IOCP by calling `GetQueuedCompletionStatus()`. If an asynchronous I/O completes while your threads are waiting on the IOCP, the NT scheduler will select the best thread to wake up, leaving the threads that are switched to disksleeping. The `GetQueuedCompletionStatus()` supplies a key to your application when it returns. This key is set when you originally called `CreateIoCompletionPort()` and can be different with each `CreateIoCompletionPort()` call. Developers often use this to identify which logical device has complete I/O.

The final routine, `PostQueuedCompletionStatus()`, is used to send I/O completion messages to waiting threads. This is most handy for waking up the I/O threads when it's time to quit.

The sample program in Listing 25.14 is a variation on the Shipping Server for our sweater company that makes use of four threads and I/O completion ports to improve message processing speed. The main routine creates the IOCP and associates it with the shipping queue. The main function goes on to create four threads and set them about retrieving orders. At this point, the main routine waits for you to instruct it to exit the process. When you do, it sends a message to the shipping threads indicating they should quit, and then it waits for them to do so before exiting.

The threads in the Ship() routine set up their message buffer as usual and prepare to receive. The MQReceiveMessage() call used here is a little different from the usual in that it is asynchronous. You are thus obliged to pass it an overlapped structure that has been initialized to the defaults. Because your Receive call is asynchronous, you can wait for the completion port. When the completion port routine returns, you check status and then continue processing the message. When you're done, it starts all over again. Have a look.

LISTING 25.14   Using I/O Completion Ports to Process MSMQ Messages

```
// Shipper.cpp
//
// Order shipping application


//Dependencies
#include <windows.h>
#include <stdio.h>
#include <conio.h>
#include <transact.h>
#include <mq.h>


//Symbols
#define FORMATNAMESIZE      64
#define MSGBODYSIZE        128
#define MSGLABELSIZE        64
#define QUEUEPATHNAME     L".\\ShippingQueue"
#define THREADCOUNT          4
#define QUITKEY              0
#define MSMQKEY              5

//Data structures
struct ShippingRequest
{
    long Account;
    long Product;
    long Quantity;
};
struct ThreadInfo
{
    QUEUEHANDLE hQueue;
    HANDLE hIOCP;
};

//Prototypes
```

LISTING 25.14   Continued

```
DWORD WINAPI Ship( LPVOID pv );
bool ExecuteSlowUnstableLinkShippingRequest( long, long, long );



//Application entry point
int main()
{
    ThreadInfo ti; //Thread information structure used by IO threads

    //Masthead
    wprintf(L"I/O Completion Port Sweater Shipping Application\n\n");

    //Get the format name of the queue using the pathname
    HRESULT hr;                                 //Return status
    WCHAR wcsFormatName[FORMATNAMESIZE];         //Queue format name
    DWORD dwFormatNameLen = FORMATNAMESIZE;      //Size of format name
    hr = MQPathNameToFormatName(    QUEUEPATHNAME,
                                    wcsFormatName,
                                    &dwFormatNameLen );
    if ( FAILED(hr) )
        return hr;

    //Open the queue with receive access
    hr = MQOpenQueue( wcsFormatName,             //Queue format name
                        MQ_RECEIVE_ACCESS,       //Access requested
                        MQ_DENY_NONE,            //Share mode
                        &(ti.hQueue) );          //Queue handle
    if ( FAILED(hr) )
        return hr;

    //Create IOCP that lets SYSTEM_PROCESSORS many threads run
    ti.hIOCP = CreateIoCompletionPort(ti.hQueue,NULL,MSMQKEY,0);
    if ( NULL == ti.hIOCP )
        return GetLastError();

    //Create I/O threads
    HANDLE ahThreads[THREADCOUNT];
    for ( int i = 0; i < THREADCOUNT; i++ )
    {
        DWORD dwThreadId;
        ahThreads[i] = CreateThread(NULL,0,Ship,&ti,0,&dwThreadId);
        if ( NULL == ahThreads[i] )
            return GetLastError();
        wprintf(L"Created thread %x\n",dwThreadId);
    }

    //Wait for user to exit
    wprintf(L"\nPress and key to exit\n\n");
    getch();
```

25

ADVANCED
MSMQ
PROGRAMMING

LISTING 25.14   Continued

```
//Notify threads that supper's ready and wait for them to quit
    for ( i = 0; i < THREADCOUNT; i++ )
        PostQueuedCompletionStatus(ti.hIOCP,0,QUITKEY,NULL);
    wprintf(L"\nWaiting for I/O threads to exit...\n");
    WaitForMultipleObjects(THREADCOUNT,ahThreads,true,INFINITE);

    //Close completion port and queue and return success
    CloseHandle(ti.hIOCP);
    MQCloseQueue(ti.hQueue);
    wprintf(L"Exiting...");
    Sleep(3000);
    return 0;
}


DWORD WINAPI Ship( LPVOID pv )
{
    HRESULT hr;
    ThreadInfo * pti = (ThreadInfo *) pv;

    //Create the overlapped event
    HANDLE hEvent = CreateEvent(NULL,false,false,NULL);
    if ( NULL == hEvent )
        return GetLastError();

    //Set up Overlapped structure for async reads
    OVERLAPPED ol = {0,0,0,0, hEvent};
    LPOVERLAPPED pol = &ol;

    //Allocate message property objects
    MQMSGPROPS MsgProps;                //Message properties struct
    MSGPROPID aMsgPropId[4];            //Message property id array
    PROPVARIANT aMsgPropVar[4];         //Message property value array

    //Set up message property struct
    MsgProps.cProp = 4;                 //Number of properties
    MsgProps.aPropID = aMsgPropId;      //Ids of properties
    MsgProps.aPropVar = aMsgPropVar;    //Values of properties
    MsgProps.aStatus = NULL;            //No error reports

    //Set up message label and length
    WCHAR wcsLabel[MSGLABELSIZE];              //Message label buffer
    aMsgPropId[0] = PROPID_M_LABEL;
    aMsgPropVar[0].vt = VT_LPWSTR;
    aMsgPropVar[0].pwszVal = wcsLabel;
    aMsgPropId[1] = PROPID_M_LABEL_LEN;
    aMsgPropVar[1].vt = VT_UI4;

    //Set up message body and length
```

LISTING 25.14   Continued

```
WCHAR wcsBody[MSGBODYSIZE];              //Message body buffer
aMsgPropId[2] = PROPID_M_BODY;
aMsgPropVar[2].vt = VT_VECTOR | VT_UI1;
aMsgPropVar[2].caub.pElems = (LPBYTE)wcsBody;
aMsgPropVar[2].caub.cElems = MSGBODYSIZE * sizeof(WCHAR);
aMsgPropId[3] = PROPID_M_BODY_SIZE;
aMsgPropVar[3].vt = VT_UI4;

//Get messages
while ( TRUE )
{
    //We have to reset these because they are [in,out] params
    aMsgPropVar[1].ulVal = MSGLABELSIZE;
    aMsgPropVar[3].ulVal = MSGBODYSIZE;

    //Get message from queue
    hr = MQReceiveMessage(pti->hQueue,    //Queue to receive from
                          INFINITE,       //Timeout
                          MQ_ACTION_RECEIVE,//Receive or peek
                          &MsgProps,      //Message properties
                          &ol,            //Overlapped structure
                          NULL,           //Callback routine
                          NULL,           //Queue cursor
                          NULL );         //Transaction
    //Check results
    if ( FAILED(hr) )
    {
        wprintf(L"Error receiving message: %x\n\n",hr);
        break;
    }

    if ( MQ_INFORMATION_OPERATION_PENDING == hr )
        wprintf(L"IO pending on thread %x\n",GetCurrentThreadId());

    //Wait for IO
    DWORD dwBytesIn;
    DWORD dwKey;
    BOOL b = GetQueuedCompletionStatus( pti->hIOCP,
                                        &dwBytesIn,
                                        &dwKey,
                                        &pol,
                                        INFINITE);
    if ( !b )
    {
        wprintf(L"IO Port error %x\n",GetLastError());
        break;
    }

    //Check for quit message from main thread
```

LISTING 25.14   Continued

```
        if ( QUITKEY == dwKey )
        {
          wprintf(L"Got quit message thread %x\n",GetCurrentThreadId());
          ExitThread(0);
        }

      //Display message
      ShippingRequest * psr = (ShippingRequest *) wcsBody;
      wprintf(L"Received message on thread %x\n",GetCurrentThreadId());
      wprintf(L"Message label: %s\n",wcsLabel);
      wprintf(L"\tAccount: %ld, Product ID: %ld, Quantity: %ld\n",
                  psr->Account,psr->Product,psr->Quantity);

      //Try to ship order
      if ( ! ExecuteSlowUnstableLinkShippingRequest(
                    psr->Account,psr->Product,psr->Quantity) )
      {
          wprintf(L"Shipping failed thread %x\n",GetCurrentThreadId());
          //We should retry the shipping operation or requeue here
          continue;
      }

        //Release the transaction and display success
        wprintf(L"Order shipped on thread %x\n",GetCurrentThreadId());
    }

    //Exit with error
    wprintf(L"Abort on thread %x\n",GetCurrentThreadId());
    return 1;
}


bool ExecuteSlowUnstableLinkShippingRequest( long, long, long )
{
    Sleep(4000);
    return ( (rand()%4) > 0 );
}
```

An important point to note about this application is that you have had to give up your transaction. Transactions only operate with synchronous calls. The threads in this application operate independently of each other for the most part. It is important that you synchronize the shutdown process, however. Exiting the main thread is an implicit `ExitProcess()` and would kill the shipping threads. For this reason, you have created the special `QUITKEY`, which is queued to the IOCP once for each thread you need to shut down. Having done this, the main thread waits for the shipping threads to clean up and then exits. Also, look at two other changes in the `MQReceiveMessage` call loop. The first is the timeout value of INFINITE. This is important because you do not want your pending I/O operation to timeout. That causes you to return from the GetQueuedCompletionStatus() call with an error. The last issue is that the Receive call modifies some of the size properties to reflect the data actually retrieved. It is very important to reset these in a loop so that MSMQ doesn't think your buffer is shrinking. An undersize buffer will return an error, but from GetQueuedCompletionStatus()! This is problematic because the error code you want to see is the one delivered by MQReceiveMessage() not GetQueuedCompletionStatus(). Note that the original I/O error message can be found in the internal field of the overlapped structure.

Queue Security

The MSMQ ActiveX components supply support for security context information, which is available through properties and methods of the MSMQMessage and MSMQQueueInfo classes. Basic MSMQ queue security features are configured when the queue is created through MSMQQueueInfo object settings. Queues can be configured to accept only authenticated messages through the Authenticate property. Queues can be set as world readable during the IMSMQQueueInfo::Create() call enabling any application to receive messages from the queue, as opposed to just the owner. The QueueInfo object also supplies a Privacy Level property that allows queues to accept messages that are encrypted, unencrypted, or both.

The examples you have looked at create queues with default security. Creating queues in this way sets the creating process user and group as the queue's user and group. The discretionary access control list is initialized to provide full control for the creator as well as property read, security read, and send access to others. No system access control list for auditing is provided.

MSMQ queues are administrator visible enterprise objects secured with standard NT security descriptors. As I discussed in the Chapter 20, "Component Load Balancing," security features can be managed through the MSMQ Explorer. It is also possible to manage queue security through the MSMQ API call interface. Managing queue security requires knowledge of the Windows/COM+ security services discussed in Chapter 18, "COM+ Security." Several routines supply MSMQ security support:

- MQCreateQueue()
- MQGetQueueSecurity()
- MQSetQueueSecurity()
- MQFreeSecurityContext()
- MQGetSecurityContext()

Queue security features can be created, retrieved, and modified with the first three routines. Queues maintain standard permissions as well as queue-specific permissions such as Peek Message, Receive Message, Send Message, and Receive Journal. Queues also support read and write access to queue permissions and properties. Security context settings are used to manage message authentication through certificates. Servers impersonating another user must make use of the MSMQ security context system to send messages in the impersonation context.

Message Security

Messages have several security provisions of their own. Messages can be digitally signed with various hash algorithms and encrypted with various encryption techniques.

The message Authentication Level property specifies whether the message requires the receiving queue to authenticate the message using its digital signature. Authentication-enabled messages can have their Hash Algorithm property set to specify a nondefault signing method. MSMQ supplies several signing choices through the `MSMQ_CALG` enumeration. Messages also provide a Sender Certificate property, enabling applications to provide their own certificates and authentication management.

A message's Privacy Level property indicates whether the message should be encrypted. The Encrypt Algorithm property specifies the type of encryption to be used on the message. If this property is not set, MSMQ uses a default value. Currently RC2 and RC4 algorithms are supported through public key security implemented by the underlying RSA provider.

Summary

In this chapter, you have examined the advanced features of MSMQ in gory detail. You have learned how to build transactional MSMQ applications with message-based, internal, DTC, and MTS-managed transactions. You have also examined the mutually exclusive asynchronous techniques for managing MSMQ queues. The sample Ping/Pong and `OrderEntry` applications have provided a simple base for exploration into cursors and the various properties offered by messages and queues. If you made it this far, you're definitely bucking for MSMQ guru.

Loosely Coupled Events

A common need of any component-based system is the capability to enable a component to notify other components that an event they care about has transpired. An example might be a stock ticker component that needs to be updated when a given stock changes prices or a backorder fulfillment component that needs to know when certain parts have been received into inventory.

In fact, this is such a common programming task, that the authors of Design Patterns explicitly named this task and provided a generic means of programmatically addressing it. This pattern is called the Observer pattern, and it defines a mechanism by which a component can publish the fact that it has knowledge which might be of importance to other components. Other components can then subscribe to the events they care about. For this reason, many people often refer to this pattern as the publish/subscribe pattern.

In this chapter, you will learn how COM+ addresses this issue by way of the COM+ Event Service so that your programmatic requirements for implementing a solution to this common problem are minimal. The chapter starts out by explaining the different technologies available to deal with event notification and why loosely coupled events (and specifically the COM+ Event Service) address this issue well. From there, you will learn the roles of the publisher and subscriber components in the Event Service architecture. After that, you will see how to code a simple application that fires an event and another application that receives notification of that event's firing. After you've learned the basics of handling loosely coupled events, the chapter moves into the advanced issues of dealing with the IEventSubscription interface and using the COM+ Event Service administrative interfaces to register and unregister transient subscriptions. Finally, the chapter wraps up with a section on how to programmatically filter the subscriber's incoming events.

Some Basic Terminology Defined

Before continuing, I will take a moment to clarify some basic nomenclature regarding loosely coupled events, the COM+ Event Service, and this chapter:

- Design patterns
- Publisher
- Subscriber
- COM+ Event Service

Design Patterns

A design pattern is defined as a documented solution to a recurring problem. In 1997, Erich Gamma, Richard Helm, Ralph Johnson, and John Vlissides produced a much-publicized book entitled *Design Patterns: Elements of Reusable Object-Oriented Software*. What this book did was to provide generic designs for addressing these common tasks. As an example, most programmers have run across the common problem of needing to ensure that a given object only be instantiated once within the context of a given system. Say that you are writing a database manager. You might want to design your system so that a database client component lives on each client machine and a database server component lives on the network's server. In this case, you would certainly want to make sure that only one instance of the database server component ever existed at a time to ensure that all the database client components are communicating with the same component. This particular design problem is addressed with the Singleton pattern.

In this chapter, you'll learn about a very specific problem and how to address that problem using the COM+ implementation of the Observer pattern.

Publisher

A publisher is a component that basically states it has information which might be of interest to other components. By virtue of being a publisher, the component is also implying that it will notify any interested parties of certain events if they would like.

Subscriber

A subscriber is a component that indicates to a publisher it is interested in receiving (asynchronous) notification when a given event has transpired.

COM+ Event Service

Because providing a mechanism by which one component can provide information that changes over time (or alert that an important event has transpired) is such a critical piece of developing component-based systems, the designers of COM+ decided to build this functionality into the COM+ runtime. This service is called the COM+ Event Service, and it is the focal point of this chapter.

Comparing the Options for Publish-Subscribe

As mentioned previously, the task of enabling a component to notify other components of changes to data, or transpired events, is a common problem in component-based development. The basic flow works like this:

1. Component A publishes the fact that it can notify any component of a given event (such as inventory being received).

2. Component B makes it known that it wants to be included in the list of components that are notified of this change by virtue of subscribing to this event.

3. When the change does occur, Component A notifies all subscribing components of the change.

Now that you have a basic outline of the problem, the players involved, and how they would interact, we will take a look at some options available to us which address this issue.

Polling

By far, the simplest way to address this problem is through a process known as *polling*. Using this approach, the developers of the publisher and the subscriber each agree on a calling convention by which the subscriber will (at some agreed upon interval) poll the publisher, asking it if anything of note has transpired. Figure 26.1 illustrates how this would look graphically.

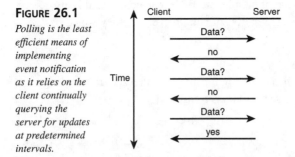

FIGURE 26.1

Polling is the least efficient means of implementing event notification as it relies on the client continually querying the server for updates at predetermined intervals.

One obvious problem with this approach is that it is analogous to you calling your recruiter every hour to know if she's found you a potential job yet. Obviously, in doing this, both the subscriber and the publisher waste a lot of time performing meaningless work and tying up valuable resources. This might not be such a bad approach if both components are running on a single machine and there's very little contention for such resources as memory and CPU utilization. However, in most applications (and certainly, distributed applications), the disadvantages of poor resource utilization far outweigh the advantages of quicker implementation.

A second problem with this approach is that it doesn't lend itself to reuse. Look at the distribution example in which a backorder fulfillment component (subscriber) needs to know when certain parts have been received into inventory. In this case, the publisher and subscriber components would have to agree on a contract by which the subscriber would ask the publisher "Has part x been received yet?" The publisher would then respond it had or had not received the part. As you can see, this code would then be too specific to the problem domain to allow for reuse.

What you really want is for the publisher to initiate the notification; not for the subscriber to continually request if there's been any changes. We will look at some of publisher-initiated options next.

Tightly Coupled Events

One approach to handling the issue of asynchronous notification can be seen in the way that ActiveX controls fire events to their containers. In this case, the container (subscriber) calls a standard method implemented by the ActiveX control (publisher) to communicate that is interested in being notified of a given event. With this call, the container passes an interface to the control that the control subsequently uses when it wants to communicate back to the container. Figure 26.2 shows this relationship.

FIGURE 26.2

A tightly coupled events solution can work well for applications in which the lifetimes of both components run concurrently. However, it isn't a very good choice for distributed systems.

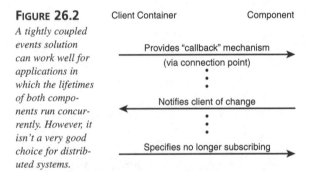

Alas, although using tightly coupled events is exponentially better than polling, this approach has several drawbacks that limit its effectiveness in a distributed environment:

- Too tightly coupled
- Need for concurrent lifetimes
- Inability to filter noise

Too Tightly Coupled

One problem of using tightly coupled events can be seen in the name itself. Tightly coupled events are so called because the subscriber is very intimate with its publisher in terms of the publisher's ID, and the mechanism used to communicate with it. Using the ActiveX control and container example, the container specifically refers to the ActiveX control's `CLSID` (class identifier) while using the control's `IConnectionPointContainer` and `IConnectionPoint` interfaces. As we've all been taught, the more coupled one component is with another, the less likely the solution is generalized for use across the problem domain.

Need for Concurrent Lifetimes

Another problem with tightly coupled events is that the lifetimes of both the publisher and subscriber must overlap at key times. For example, the publisher must be running when the subscriber attempts to provide it with the "callback" interface. Also, the subscriber needs to be running when the publisher attempts to give the requested notification of the transpired event or data change. This need for concurrent lifetimes isn't a problem with ActiveX controls simply because there aren't any times when the control would be active and its container wouldn't be. However, in a distributed environment, requiring both the publisher and subscriber to be active at the same time isn't a viable option most of the time and certainly isn't a limitation that you want to place on your system if you don't have to.

Inability to Filter Noise

Tightly coupled events such as the ActiveX control/container example, do not provide a mechanism to define a filter so that unwanted information (noise) doesn't get passed. When the backorder fulfillment component tells the receiving component that it wants to know when a part is received, it certainly doesn't want to be notified upon receipt of every single part. Another way of looking at it would be if you were to ask your recruiter to call you upon hearing of a good job opportunity. If you're a Visual C++ developer, chances are that you don't want to be notified of every RPG or COBOL position that becomes available. Therefore, along with the fact that you need a generic, loosely coupled asynchronous notification mechanism, you also need the ability to filter out the notifications that although they are the types you care about, they don't pertain to the data you care about.

Loosely Coupled Events

Therefore, how can you get around some of the problems you've seen so far? Well, look at how you could decouple the publisher and the subscriber. When talking about providing a generic means for two entities to communicate, you usually wind up with a generic seam that exists between the two components. The seam can have generic interfaces that allow it to communicate with both the publisher and the subscriber and therefore, be used in any publish/subscribe scenario regardless of the specifics of the problem domain involved. Figure 26.3 shows an example of what that would look like.

FIGURE 26.3

Generic approach to asynchronous event handling.

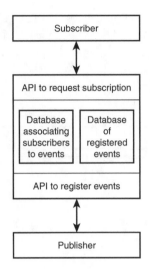

Using this approach, you could maintain a database that contains a list of all the publishers and events on the system that might be of interest to any subscribers. Any subscribers could then read through that list and pick and choose the events they care about. The subscriber would then write out to another database that it is subscribing to a given publisher/event. Finally, when the publisher wants to fire an event, it would read through the subscriber/event database, searching for all subscribers who have indicated a desire to be notified of the event being fired. The publisher would then notify the subscriber.

So what would this accomplish? First, it would decouple the publisher and subscriber because nowhere in either component's code is there a specific mention of the other component. Second, it would be a generic approach because all publishers and subscribers could communicate through these databases. Third, it would work even in scenarios in which the lifetimes of the components involved do not run concurrently.

Therefore, the only thing you have to do is develop these databases and write the code that reads and writes to them. Obviously, I say this tongue-in-cheek because this entire system would be far from trivial to implement to any degree of sophistication. Lucky for us, not only have the designers of COM+ recognized the need for this type of asynchronous event notification system, but also they even included it in a COM+ service called the Event Service.

COM+ Event Service

In a nutshell, the COM+ Event Service is a feature that is built into Windows 2000 and handles the task of connecting publishers and subscribers. As you can see in Figure 26.4, the COM+ Event Service brings into play the COM+ catalog that you've seen used in several different contexts throughout this book. In this context, the COM+ catalog is being used to provide the database seam expounded upon in the previous section.

FIGURE 26.4

*The COM+ cata-
log acts as a kind
of "middle man"
in connecting pub-
lishers with sub-
scribers.*

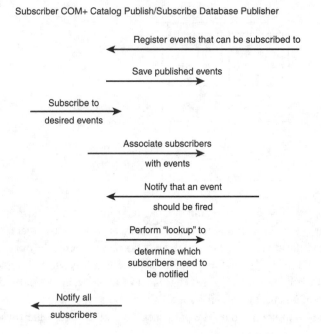

Up until now, I've used the term event to signify a particular happening in a system such as parts being received into inventory or a stock price change. However, COM+ has a slightly different usage of the term. With regards to the COM+ Event Service, the term event represents the actual call (using a COM interface) from the publisher to the subscriber in notification of a data change. This requires that the subscriber implement a predefined COM interface (more on this shortly) and, as such, acts as a COM server to the publisher, which acts as a COM client. If you're at all familiar with COM, you'll recognize this as being a standard and straightforward means of having the publisher and subscriber communicate with each other. The only new entity added to the mix is the Event Service itself that acts as a layer of abstraction. This layer of abstraction is exactly what makes this whole mechanism the kind of loosely coupled system that is desirable in a distributed application.

Now that you know an event is the call itself, it's important to understand that the act of calling this event is known as firing an event. In this case, this term is being used exactly as before in the tightly coupled event example in which I discussed the pros and cons of using the ActiveX mechanism for asynchronous notification.

If you look back at Figure 26.4, you'll see the first thing that happens is the publisher has to register itself with the COM+ catalog. This is done via a special system-provided class called the event class. It is the event class that implements the interfaces necessary to enable the publisher to fire events. On the subscriber side, the subscriber is obliged to implement the event class in order to receive events (incoming notifications from the publisher of a data change).

You tell COM+ which interfaces and methods you want a particular event class to contain by providing COM+ with a type library. These defined event classes are then stored in the COM+ catalog by means of being placed there directly by a publisher or by using the Component Services snap-in.

The subscriber then tells the COM+ catalog which events its interested in by providing and defining a subscription and passing it to the COM+ catalog. A subscription is a data structure that defines such things as the recipient of the event (the subscriber), the event class (defined and registered by the publisher), and which interface or method within the event class that the subscriber cares about. Much like event classes, subscribers can place the subscriptions directly into the COM+ catalog, or this can be done via the Component Services snap-in.

At this point, you've seen a 50,000-foot view of how to define events (and the event's publisher), how to define subscriptions (and its subscriber), and how to associate the two. Now, you will look at how the event actually gets fired.

In order for the publisher to fire the event, it first uses the standard COM object creation function `CoCreateInstance` (in Visual C++) or `CreateObject` in (in Visual Basic) to create an instance of the event class. The publisher can then call the desired event method in order to notify subscribers that a data change has occurred.

When the publisher calls the desired event method, the COM+ catalog performs a lookup for all subscribers that have subscriptions naming the event class and event method used. After the COM+ catalog has located the subscribers that have to be notified, it sets about connecting to them and calling the specified method.

One limitation that is extremely important to realize is event methods cannot use the [out], [in, out] or [out, retval] attributes on any of their parameters when defining the event class' IDL.

Now that I've talked a good deal about the COM+ Event Service and how it solves many problems associated with the asynchronous notification of data changes in a distributed application, I will take a moment to discuss some of its shortcomings.

Firstly, the subscription mechanism (in which the subscriber basically defines for the COM+ catalog which event interfaces and event methods are of importance to it) is not distributed. What this means is that if one developer creates a subscription on one computer, the rest of the network does not inherently know that subscription. In other words, there is no central repository of subscriptions for an entire network. The obvious workaround is to do all your work of creating event classes and subscriptions on one central server. This would mean that all notifications would then have to come from one machine, which has several drawbacks:

- If a specific server is down, any part of your system that depends on these notifications will not work.

- If all your event classes and subscriptions were on one machine, by definition, it wouldn't be load balanced to intelligently use your particular network's topology.

- Performance takes a hit when the publisher is not on this central event server because the publisher would first have to instantiate the event class on that server.

The second issue (and one that is easily overlooked until it nails you between the eyes) is that the notification mechanisms used by the COM+ Event Service are DCOM and COM+ Queued Components (QC). The problem is that these technologies weren't built with the idea of what amounts to broadcasting information to multiple clients in mind. In other words, both of these technologies are one-to-one communications in which a single entity communicates with another single entity either synchronously (DCOM) or asynchronously (Queued Components). What this means is because each subscriber needs to be notified one at a time, the delivery time increases in relation to the number of subscribers that need to be notified. Figuring out exactly how many subscribers your system can handle without becoming unusable is sometime referred to as the "threshold of pain". Generically defining this threshold for everyone is impossible because it is dependent on factors such as your network topology, network traffic, CPU utilization on key machines (such as the event server), and so on.

If you're familiar with any type of communications programming such as NetBIOS or TCP/IP, you might be wondering why there isn't a mechanism to send out what would amount to a datagram. Actually, this is a very good question and hopefully one that Microsoft will address in subsequent versions of the COM+ Event Service. For now, if you know that the number of subscribers is going to force you to either find a solution for this limitation or not use the COM+ Event Service, I would highly recommend writing a single (base) subscriber that acts as an "event broadcaster". This event broadcaster would be responsible for receiving the events via DCOM or Queued Components and then sending the incoming data to all subscribers via a datagram. As you work through the examples in this chapter and start to get a feel for how useful this service is, you'll understand that the trouble you go through to implement your own event broadcaster is more than offset by the benefits derived from using the COM+ Event Service.

Event Service Demo

In this demo, you will see how easy it is to use the COM+ Event Service by means of a simple application that fires events based on the receipt of inventory. Figure 26.5 shows what the publisher application will look like when finished. After coding this publisher application, the next step is then to code a subscriber application that would, upon receiving notification of newly received inventory, attempt to satisfy any open backorders. Whereas it's a very simple demo, the key is realizing how easy it is to write applications, which—although reaping the rewards of the COM+ Event Service—do not require intrinsic knowledge of the underlying mechanics that make it all happen. In fact, as you're about to see, we can do almost every thing necessary to take advantage of the COM+ Event Service simply by making a couple of administrative entries into the COM+ catalog.

FIGURE 26.5

As you can see from this demo (available on the book's CD-ROM), regardless of the complexity of your application, taking advantage of the COM+ Event Service is a very simple task.

As you saw back in Figure 26.4, the first step to utilizing the COM+ Event Service is to register an event class. Also remember that you can install an event class either programmatically from the publisher or manually through an administrative application such as the Windows 2000 Component Services snap-in. Since I first want to show you the shortest route to using events, we'll use the latter method.

Therefore, at this point, open the Component Services and create a new COM+ application called EventTestApp. After you've created the COM+ application that will contain the server-side COM+ component, you need to register an event class. You can do this by right-clicking the EventTestApp and selecting the Add Component menu option from the context menu (which will result in the wizard you see in Figure 26.6).

FIGURE 26.6

*The COM
Component Install
Wizard enables
you to add a
component to a
COM+ applica-
tion from different
sources.*

At this point, click the Install new event class(es) button. Doing this will present you
with a dialog that allows you to define your event class. As you just learned, COM+
learns about your class by reading the class' type library. Therefore, the next dialog
(shown in Figure 26.7) you will see allows you to specify where the type library is
located.

FIGURE 26.7

*To create an event
class from
Component
Services, the class
must be defined in
a self-registering
DLL and be
accompanied by
the class' type
library.*

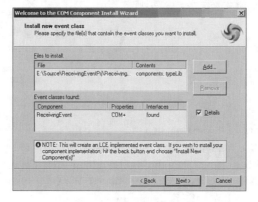

So that you can focus on the task of working with events, I've included an ATL component on the book's CD-ROM called ReceivingEvent. However, because an ATL project
cannot have the same name as the component itself, the project is named Receiving and
can be located in a folder on the CD-ROM called ReceivingEventPrj. This project contains the definition of the interface that the publisher will utilize when signaling that
inventory has been received. Actually, the specific interface is called IReceivingEvent,
and it contains the method InventoryReceived. The COM+ Event Service will use the
type library and the self-registration code from this component to acclimate the component into the system for use by both the publisher and the subscriber.

After you have either typed in the fully qualified path to the event class' type library or DLL, click the Next or Finish button to allow COM+ to read the file and discern its viability as a valid event class. For those of you who are curious about what happens "under the covers," Component Services calls the administrative function `ICOMAdminCatalog::InstallEventClass`. As mentioned earlier, you could have also written a simple application to do the same. I just took this (slightly more manual) route so that you could get an idea of what's going on with regard to installing a new event class.

After you've finished with the Add Component wizard, your new component will be listed under the EventTestApp COM+ application. Now, right-click the newly created `ReceivingEvent` class and when the context menu appears, select the properties menu option. If you've created other COM+ components, you'll recognize this tabbed dialog. However, there are some very important differences on the Advanced tab (see Figure 26.8) that deal specifically with events.

FIGURE 26.8

Advanced properties of an event class.

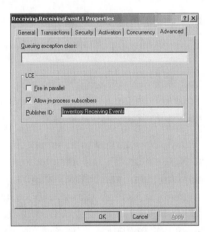

The key field to concentrate on here is the Publisher ID field. The value you type in here is what you'll see when you create the subscription later. Remember that I said when you create a subscription entry into the COM+ catalog, you are marrying a subscriber to a specific event class. For purposes of this demo, I used the value `ReceivingID`. This value is also used by the publisher when it wants to create an instance of the event class in order to fire the event.

Now that the event class has been registered, we will add a subscriber to the mix. Once again, I've provided a demo component for you on the book's CD-ROM. You can locate this component in a folder called BackOrders. For simplicity, simply add a new component to the existing EventTestApp COM+ application. You probably won't want to mix your components like this all the time, but for purposes of this demo, it's not an issue.

After you've added the BackOrders component to Component Services, take a look at
the two folders that have been created for you. You've probably noticed, and maybe have
even used, the Interfaces folder. However, the folder of interest here is the Subscriptions
folder. This is the folder used to define a component's subscription to an event method.
Therefore, right-click the Subscriptions folder and click the Add Subscription menu
option. Doing so will invoke the New Subscription wizard shown in Figure 26.9.

FIGURE 26.9

*As with most
Component
Services tasks, a
wizard allows you
to easily define a
component's sub-
scription to an
event method.*

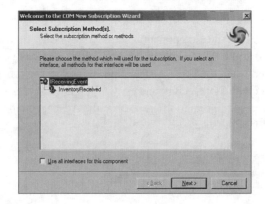

As you look at Figure 26.9, realize that although you probably only have the one event
class displayed, all the event classes that you define will show up in this wizard (along
with their defined event methods listed beneath the class name).

The way you subscribe to a method is fairly obvious now. You simply click on the desired
interface or method and then click the Next button. It's important to note that a single subscription can subscribe to an entire interface (all of its methods) or to a single method.
However, the only way to subscribe to multiple methods (and not all methods) of an interface is to create a subscription for each desired set of event methods. In our little demo, the
only component we have that cares about new inventory is the BackOrders component.
However, in a real distribution, there will probably be numerous components that have the
same need to be notified of a change. Some examples would be a Purchasing component
that needs to update the fact that the bought SKU has been received and an Inventory
Transaction component that keeps logs of all changes to inventory.

After you've clicked the Next button (after selecting the desired event method), you will
see the page shown in Figure 26.10. Because multiple components can implement the
same interface, this page is needed to allow you to specify which component you need.
Notice that you can also click on the check box entitled Use All Event Classes that
Implement the Specified Interface.

FIGURE 26.10

*Although this dia-
log might seem
redundant at first,
realize it is needed
because multiple
components can
implement the
same interface.*

After you've selected the desired event class (use the `ReceivingEvent` for this demo), click Next to display the dialog shown in Figure 26.11.

FIGURE 26.11

*The last dialog of
the New
Subscription wiz-
ard gives you the
option of naming
the subscription
and enabling/dis-
abling it.*

Now, enter a name for your subscription; `BackOrdersToReceiving Inventory` is the name I used. The naming convention, `<subscriber component>To<event method>` is simply my own convention. You're free to use whatever makes the most sense to your particular system.

Finally, click the Enable this Subscription Immediately check box so that you can use the subscription. Once you've done that, click the Finish button so that Component Services can create and enable the new subscription.

At this point, the only thing we need to do is to have an application that would actually fire the event. As mentioned before, firing an event amounts to nothing more than standard COM calls. However, that's the beauty of the COM+ Event Service. It's not as though you need to learn this whole new, elaborate set of interfaces.

Two demo applications (one in Visual C++ and the other in Visual Basic) are provided on the CD-ROM. These demos do the exact same thing and only co-exist to illustrate how to accomplish this task in the two different development environments. These demos can be found in the EventDemoVc and EventDemoVb folders. All these applications do is to create an instance of the ReceivingEvent event class and call its InventoryReceived method. Because you used Component Services to create a subscription between the BackOrders component and the InventoryReceived method, it will then be incumbent upon the COM+ Event Service to step in and make sure that the BackOrders component is dutifully notified.

Using the Visual Basic Immediate Window

One thing you should learn when working with COM is that, without a doubt, the easiest and quickest way to test COM components is through a VBA (Visual Basic for Applications) interface. This can be accomplished through any application that supports VBA such as any Microsoft Office application, Microsoft Outlook, or even Visual Basic itself. Even though I program almost exclusively in Visual C++ (aside from my Web work on www.sourcedna.com), I still use the Visual Basic Immediate Window (which gives access to VBA from within the Visual Basic development environment) to test my components because it's so easy and beats having to create a complete Visual C++ application for each little test.

As mentioned in the tip on using the Visual Basic Immediate Window, it is much easier to use this already available tool in order to test your COM components and interfaces rather than having to write a new Visual C++ application for each test. Therefore, the first thing you need to do is to fire up Visual Basic. When it has started, open the Immediate window by clicking Ctrl+G. Now you have a complete VBA environment at your disposal without having to create a new project and provide needless dialogs and buttons simply to instantiate and test a COM component. Now, type in the code you see in Listing 26.1.

LISTING 26.1 Simple Script to Instantiate a COM Component and Call One of Its Methods

```
Set obj = CreateObject("ReceivedEvent.Events")

Obj.InventoryReceived "abcd", 42
```

I told you it was easy. These two lines of code enabled you to instantiate a COM component and call one of its methods *sans* a project or user interface. Now you see why even the most ardent Visual C++ supporters keep Visual Basic installed.

Now, receiving notification will require an application because we need to have something that can be notified from another process. Therefore, at this point either open the CD-ROM's EventDemoVb project or create a new Visual Basic project and do the following:

1. Add the following code in the general section of the default form. This is needed because the subscriber must implement the interface on which it wants to receive calls from the actual event component.

   ```
   Implements ReceivingEvent
   ```

2. Now code the event handler by adding the following subroutine:

   ```
   Private Sub ReceivingEvent_InventoryReceived(ByVal strSKU as String, _
   ByVal iQuantity as integer)
     ' display msg that you received notification of new inventory
     MsgBox "New inventory has been received for SKU '" _
            & strSKU _
            & "'. Quantity received=" _
            & iQuantity, _
            vbOKOnly, _
            "Inventory Received Notification"
   End Sub
   ```

Obviously, if there were an actual Backorder fulfillment component, we'd be doing a lot more work. However, this snippet of code does serve to illustrate how easy it is to receive an asynchronous event notification from the COM+ Event Service.

After you run the code, the results should be similar to what you see in Figure 26.12.

FIGURE 26.12

For simple or complex applications, setting up events can be a very basic task.

Advanced COM+ Event Service Issues

Now that you've seen how easy it is to get the basics of loosely couple events to work, we will look at a couple of more advanced COM+ Event Service issues.

Subscriptions and the `IEventSubscription` Interface

Because the first thing you'll probably want to play with after you get beyond the basics of asynchronous events is the subscription interface, we will take a look at what you can do with it.

As mentioned before, a subscription is an entity that, once created, resides within the COM+ catalog. Actually, the only subscriptions that live in the COM+ catalog are persistent subscriptions. I'll get into the distinction between persistent and transient subscriptions in the next section.

However, regardless of whether the subscription is persistent or transient, the subscription itself is nothing more than a data structure containing the members needed to define a subscription and how it should be handled by the COM+ Event Service at runtime. These members can be seen in Table 26.1. Although most of these members—or properties—can be modified using Component Services, some can only be manipulated through the administrative methods supplied by the `IEventSubscription` interface.

TABLE 26.1 `IEventSubscription` Interface Methods

Method Name	Method Description.
Description	Arbitrary text field used to document the subscription. Can be useful for your own documentation, but not used by the Event Service.
Enabled	Enables or disables the subscription.
EventClassID	Used to define the event class that the subscription is associated with. This is generally not used in favor of the InterfaceID property.
MachineName	Name of the machine on which the subscription resides.
MethodName	Name of the method that the subscription points to. This is relative to the InterfaceID property.
OwnerSID	Security identifier of the applications that created the subscription.
PerUser	Takes a Boolean value, indicating that the subscription will only receive events if the user is identified with the OwnerSID property.
PublisherID	Identifies the publisher responsible for firing the event.
PublisherProperty	Probably the most likely method to be used when dealing with subscriptions, this method allows you to set a collection of properties in order to filter whether an event should fire.
SubscriberCLSID	CLSID of the subscriber component. You would almost never touch this value because it is used by the event class in order to create the subscriber object.

TABLE 26.1 Continued

Method Name	*Method Description.*
`SubscriberInterface`	The COM IUnknown pointer on which the subscriber wants to receive incoming event calls.
`SubscriptionID`	Uniquely identifies a subscription within the event system.
`SubscriptionName`	Name given by the user for a subscription upon creation.

Before I talk about how to use the `IEventSubscription` interface, I will take a moment to discuss the types of subscriptions that can be created. At this point, there are two of them: Persistent and Transient. The basic difference between the two is that a persistent subscription survives across an IPL boundary.

However, there are several other distinctions between the two subscription types as shown in the following:

- **Subscription creation**—Because persistent subscriptions actually reside in the COM+ catalog, they can be created either programmatically or via Component Services. Transient subscriptions, on the other hand, can only be created programmatically.

- **Mapping of registered events**—Persistent subscriptions map registered events to objects that are created automatically whenever an event is fired. However, transient subscriptions are a bit more dynamic in this regard in that they map registered events to specific interface pointers. Because of this, transient subscriptions are typically used when a currently running application dynamically wants to subscribe to a specific event as opposed to a persistent subscription in which the mapping is more global and static in nature.

- **Components they work with**—Because persistent subscriptions are defined within the context of the COM+ catalog, they are always associated with configured COM components. Conversely, transient subscriptions can work with components that are either configured or nonconfigured.

- **Subscription longevity**—As mentioned previously, persistent subscriptions, by definition, reside in the COM+ catalog and therefore, exist across IPL boundaries. Transient subscriptions, on the other hand, are more of a dynamic entity and only exist in the scope in which they are created.

Working with Transient Subscriptions

In the previous demo, you learned how to use Component Services to register an event class and subscription. You then saw some very simple VBA to fire the event and some

Visual Basic code to receive notification of this event's firing. However, that demo dealt only with persistent subscriptions. We will look at how you would perform the task of registering and unregistering transient subscriptions. One thing to also keep in mind is that whether you register either a persistent or transient subscription, the act of firing the event and handling the event works in exactly the same way. In other words, the publisher and the subscriber should be abstracted from this knowledge.

Registering Transient Subscriptions

The first thing you'll need to see is how to register a transient subscription with the Event Service because this task cannot be done via Component Services. To do this, simply perform the following steps:

1. Create an instance of a COMAdminCatalog object.

2. Use the ICOMAdminCatalog::GetCollection interface in order to retrieve a collection of the COM+ catalog's transient subscriptions.

3. Use ICaalogCollection::Add to add a new transient subscription.

4. Use ICatalogObject::pub_Value to assign the values discussed in the previous section regarding subscription properties.

5. Finally, save the subscription to the COM+ catalog using the ICatalogCollection::SaveChanges method.

Now, take a look at a bit of Visual C++ code (shown in Listing 26.2) to see exactly how this would work. This code (as well as a Visual Basic equivalent) can also be located on the book's CD-ROM in folders named TransientSubscriptionVC and TransientSubscriptionVB, respectively.

LISTING 26.2   Registering a Transient Subscription in Visual C++

```
HRESULT hr;
ICOMAdminCatalog* pAdminCatalog;

// retrieve the COM+ catalog object
hr = ::CoCreateInstance(CLSID_COMAdminCatalog, NULL,
                        CLSCX_SERVER,
                        IID_ICOMAdminCatalog,
                        (void**)&pAdminCatalog);
if (SUCCEEDED(hr))
{
  ICatalogCollection* pCatalogCollection;

  // allocate bstr for catalog name
  BSTR bstrCatalogName = ::SysAllocString(L"TransientSubscriptions"));
```

LISTING 26.2 Continued

```
// retrieve catalog collection for transient subscriptions
hr = pAdminCatalog->GetCollection(bstrCatalogName,
                                  (IDispatch**)&pCatalogCollection);

// free bstr
::SysFreeString(bstrCatalogName);

if (SUCCEEDED(hr))
{
 ICatalogObject* pCatalogObject;

 // get new, initialized catalog object (not in catalog yet!)
 hr = pCatalogCollection->Add((IDispatch**)&pCatalogObject);
 if (SUCCEEDED(hr))
 {
  // use the pCatalogObject->put_Value to set the
  // subscription values

  // when finished setting values, release catalog object
  pCatalogObject->Release();

  // save object into COM+ catalog
  LONG lResult;
  hr = pCatalogCollection->SaveChanges(&lResult);

  // check lResult for success
 }
}
 pCatalogCollection->Release();
}
```

Unregistering Transient Subscriptions

Now that you've seen how to register a transient subscription, I will show you how to unregister a transient subscription. Although some of the setup work (such as instantiating the COMAdminCatalog object and retrieving the ICatalogCollection interface) is the same, enough differences exist to warrant looking at a snippet of Visual C++ code (Listing 26.3) to see how this is done programmatically.

LISTING 26.3 Unregistering a Transient Subscription in Visual C++

```
HRESULT hr;
ICOMAdminCatalog* pAdminCatalog;

// retrieve the COM+ catalog object
hr = ::CoCreateInstance(CLSID_COMAdminCatalog, NULL,
                        CLSCX_SERVER,
```

LISTING 26.3   Continued

```
                                IID_ICOMAdminCatalog,
                                (void**)&pAdminCatalog);
if (SUCCEEDED(hr))
{
 ICatalogCollection* pCatalogCollection;

 // allocate bstr for catalog name
 BSTR bstrCatalogName = ::SysAllocString(L"TransientSubscriptions"));

 // retrieve catalog collection for transient subscriptions
 hr = pAdminCatalog->GetCollection(bstrCatalogName,
                                   (IDispatch**)&pCatalogCollection);

 // free bstr
 ::SysFreeString(bstrCatalogName);

 if (SUCCEEDED(hr))
 {
  // fill out collection
  hr = pCatalogCollection->Populate();

  if (SUCCEEDED(hr))
  {
   IEnumVariant* pEnumVariant;
   hr = pCatalogCollection->get__NewEnum((IUnknown**)&pEnumVariant);

   if (SUCCEEDED(hr))
   {
    VARIANT var;
    VariantInt (&var);
    int nIdx = 0;

    while (S_OK == pEnuVariant->Next(1, &var, NULL)
    {
     ICatalogObject* pCatalogObject =
      (ICatalogObject*)var.pdispVal;
     if (/* compare to name you want to remove */)
     {
      hr = pCatalogCollection->Remove(nIdx);
      if (SUCCEEDED(hr))
      {
       long lResult;
       pCatalogCollection->SaveChanges(&lResult);
      }

      VariantClear(&var);
      break;
     }
```

LISTING 26.3   Continued

```
      VariantClear(&var);
      nIdx++;
    }
    pEnumVariant->Release();
   }
  }
  pCatalogCollection->Release();
 }
 pCatalogCollection->Release();
}
```

Event Filtering

The last thing we'll focus on in this chapter is the issue of event filtering. You might remember from early on that a major problem with tightly coupled event systems is that they do not allow for a generic means of filtering out the events you don't care about. After all, where would this code go in a tightly coupled event system? You can't put it in the publisher because the publisher might have many different subscribers, all of whom have different (possibly dynamic) filtering needs. You certainly don't want to put the event filtering logic in the subscriber because that would mean the subscriber would still incur the overhead of having to receive every notification of a given type before it could decide whether it even cared about that event. Not only does this waste the subscriber's resources, but also, in a network environment, it means needless network traffic.

Therefore, in this section, we'll first look at how you can use the COM+ catalog to define a filter for a given subscription. By defining the filter in the COM+ catalog, this allows you to alleviate both the subscriber and publisher from having to programmatically deal with the task of filtering out noise, or unwanted data. After that, you'll see how to programmatically add filter strings to the COM+ catalog. This is useful if you want to write an administrative application instead of allowing your users to use the Component Services snap-in.

Creating a Filter String Administratively

In this example, we'll assume that our application wants to filter on a specific part number. Obviously, in the scenario of a backorder fulfillment application, we would want to set up this type of information dynamically (shown in the next section). However, this section will serve to illustrate how to set up a filter from Component Services.

First, select the desired subscription that will have the filter applied to it and invoke its Properties dialog. After you've done that, click on the Options tab (shown in Figure 26.13).

FIGURE 26.13

Using the Component Services, you can define a single filter for a given subscription. This isn't very practical most of the time, however, because filters are typically dynamic in nature.

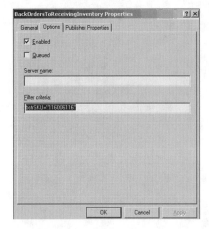

From here, the options are fairly obvious. Simply name the filter and then specify the desired filter using a property and valid value as a name/value pair. A simple example of wanting inventory updates for a SKU numbered "1234" would look like the following:

```
bstrSKU="1234"
```

You would probably never want to filter something as fine-grained as a single SKU. However, a particular "suggested buy" component might want to filter on a specific class of SKU. For example, in an auto parts distribution system, you might have multiple subscriptions for entire classes of parts such as "glass," "body," and "mechanical." Obviously, from this point, your particular choice of how to filter is very much application-specific. However, do keep in mind that you can use standard Boolean operators (listed in Table 26.2) to aid in the definition of your system's filter strings.

TABLE 26.2   Filter Syntax

Operator(s)	Meaning
=, ==	Equal to
!=, ~=, <>	Not equal to
&	Boolean "AND"
|	Boolean "OR"
!, ~	Boolean "NOT"

Creating a Filter String Programmatically

Now that you've seen how to use Component Services to create a filter string, I will show you how to perform the same task using Visual C++ and the COM+ Event Service admin interface (see Listing 26.4). This application can be found on the CD-ROM in a folder named FilterStringVC (a Visual Basic alternative is located in FilterStringVB). Once again, we're filtering for a part whose SKU is "1234".

LISTING 26.4   Programmatically Creating an Event Filter String

```
HRESULT hr;
ICOMAdminCatalog* pAdminCatalog;

// retrieve the COM+ catalog object
hr = ::CoCreateInstance(CLSID_COMAdminCatalog, NULL,
                        CLSCX_SERVER,
                        IID_ICOMAdminCatalog,
                        (void**)&pAdminCatalog);
if (SUCCEEDED(hr))
{
 ICatalogCollection* pCatalogCollection;

 // allocate bstr for catalog name
 BSTR bstrCatalogName = ::SysAllocString(L"TransientSubscriptions"));

 // retrieve catalog collection for transient subscriptions
 hr = pAdminCatalog->GetCollection(bstrCatalogName,
                                   (IDispatch**)&pCatalogCollection);

 // free bstr
 ::SysFreeString(bstrCatalogName);

 if (SUCCEEDED(hr))
 {
  BSTR bstrPropName = ::SysAllocString(L"FilterCritera"));

  // notice the handling of the quotes for an embedded string
  BSTR bstrValue = ::SysAllocString(L"bstrSKU=\"1234\""));

  VARIANT var;
  var.vt = VT_BSTR;
  var.bstrVal = bstrValue;

  hr = pCatalogCollection->put_Value(bstrPropName, var);
  // check hr for success

  ::SysFreeString(bstrValue);
  ::SysFreeString(bstrPropName);
 }
}
```

Summary

In this chapter, you learned how COM+ addresses the issue of event notification via loosely coupled events and the Event Service. After learning the roles of the publisher and subscriber components in the Event Service architecture, you saw a simple application that fires an event and another application that receives notification of that event's firing. After that, you discovered some of the more advanced issues of the COM+ Event Service such as dealing with the IEventSubscription interface and using the COM+ Event Service admin interfaces to register and unregister transient subscriptions. Finally, you learned how to programmatically filter the subscriber's incoming events. At this point, you've learned quite a bit about using asynchronous event handling under COM+, and hopefully this information will enable you to write more dynamic, distributed applications.

Queued Components

CHAPTER 27

This chapter is separated into four sections to make the learning of Queued Components easier and to give you, the reader, the flexibility to jump to the sections that make sense to you. After an initial section giving an overview of the purpose of Queued Components, the second section introduces the concept of distributed computing and how it relates to Queued Components. The reason this section precedes the section describing Queued Components is one of practical use. I, for one, can't stand reading through several pages of how great a given technology is only to find out that after the limitations are listed, my application isn't a viable candidate for implementing it. Therefore, even if you're familiar with the concepts of distributed computing (especially with regard to MTS and MSMQ), I would recommend reading this section.

After deciding if Queued Component is a good option for your application, the third section then presents and looks at the Queued Components architecture. Finally, in the fourth and last section of this chapter, you will put your new-found knowledge to work by writing a server-side component and client-side application, testing it and then exporting the COM+ Application for distribution to client machines.

> **Note**
>
> Many developers want to jump into the code as quickly as possible. After all, one of the main responsibilities of our jobs is to evaluate the different technologies and programming techniques and to decide if they will work for a particular application. Sometimes we simply don't have time to read about all the intricacies of a given technology, and instead we want to test it out before deciding if it warrants further investigation as to how it works internally.
>
> Therefore, for those of you with itchy fingers, I would recommend reading the second section ("Distributed Computing and Queued Components") and then proceeding directly to the demo applications in the fourth section. That way, you can immediately see how easy it is implement a component and client application using Queued Components. After you've done that, you can then return to the third section ("Queued Component Architecture") to find out exactly what happened "under the covers."

Queued Components Overview

Ten years ago, salespeople who roamed the great outdoors on a full-time basis, visiting customers, vendors, and suppliers were accustomed to the fact that any work they did would have to be "uploaded" when they got back to their hotel. Actually, those were the advanced ones because they could at least communicate from the road. In those days, many systems wouldn't get updated until the employee either physically returned to the home office or faxed in the order and it was manually input into the company's system. This wasn't such a bad thing, however, because that's how everyone did business. Therefore, customers came to expect this period of latency between placing an order and the order being processed.

However, the last decade has brought us such technological advancements as small, powerful notebook and laptop computers (which now make up over half of all computer sales), handheld computers, such as the Cassiopeia and the PalmPC, and wireless remote PCs. As is the case with all new technologies, they only serve to raise the bar insofar as what the customer demands. Ten years ago, you might have gotten away with telling a customer that you'd input his order in a day or two when you got back into the office, but even hinting at something like that today would be akin to professional suicide. Your customers might not know the geeky names of all the technologies available, but they do know one thing: their competitor just placed a major order, and it was processed immediately. Therefore, in an increasingly competitive world, if you want to keep your customers, you had better be prepared to meet or exceed your competitor's abilities to satisfy such demands.

Luckily for you, this is where Queued Components come into the picture. Queued Components allow you to develop componentized, distributed systems in which even though your components live on one or more servers, your remote machines can still function even when completely disconnected from the server.

One thing I should add here is that Queued Components bring more to the table than the support of disconnected users. These other benefits include the following:

- The scaling of large systems through the ability to easily load balance components across multiple servers

- Better user feedback through the asynchronous communications inherent in a queue-based system

- The ability to prioritize tasks so that the more urgent tasks, such as new orders, take precedence over tasks of less urgency (such as backorder fulfillment)

Distributed Computing and Queued Components

Now that you've seen a brief overview of what Queued Components can do for your application, we will take a look at some limitations of using the Queued Components service and what that means to you with regard to deciding when using a technology is the right choice.

Because by definition, Queued Components are meant to ease the development of distributed systems, the first thing you have to consider when making a decision on using Queued Components (or MSMQ) is whether your application is truly a candidate for being a distributed system. The reason I bring this up so early in the chapter is that Queued Components have one very clearly documented (and logical) rule about how the queued interfaces of a component can be defined. The rule is that any communications with Queued Components must be unidirectional.

From a logical perspective, it means that when you are designing your client application(s) and component(s), you need to be aware that the callee will not be able to respond to the caller. With Queued Components, you cannot mark a specific method as being queued. You must first mark the components of the COM+ Application as being queued and then specify which interfaces of that component you want queued. Therefore, from a technical standpoint, you cannot use the [in,out],[out,retval] or [out] IDL attributes when describing a method that will belong to an interface you want queued.

However, is this a major limitation of Queued Components? The types of information that the component would normally attempt to convey back to a calling client would be things such as the following:

- Server requests more data
- Confirmation of data received
- Confirmation of work performed
- Need for "lookup" data

In the next few paragraphs, I'll discuss each item, give examples of each, and then I'll address whether it can be accommodated within the scope of Queued Components.

Confirmation of Data Received

This is the easiest one to address. Say that you have an Order component with a standard set of methods such as AddLineItem and ProcessOrder. Being a conscientious programmer, you might want to design the client in such a way that it verifies that the server received the request.

However, if you're thinking (and designing) like this, you're not putting yourself in the right mindset. Queued Components (and its underlying MSMQ queuing) guarantee delivery of each message that gets queued. Once queued, at some point, upon connection to the server, the message will make its way to the server and be processed.

Therefore, the only return value you need with regard to an attempt to queue information is a value indicating whether the message was successfully queued.

Server Requests More Data

One example of this would be some sort of variation on the Challenge/Response security built into Windows NT. Using this mechanism, a client requests something. The server responds by challenging the client to identify himself in some way that validates his authority to make the original request. The client then responds by sending the requested information, whereupon the server validates that information and carries out the requested task.

In this example, you could change your design to send all the necessary data to the component. In fact, if your application is truly distributed and message queuing is the right alternative, you (as a component designer) will never know when you are going to receive the request. In other words, keep in mind that the whole concept of queuing is built on the precept that the client using it requests a task be performed and then goes on about its business, knowing that there's no guarantee for when the server will process the request. In fact, if the component could respond to the client in this environment (say two hours later), how would the client understand the context of the component's request?

The work-around is simple: When designing components that are going to be queued, you need to keep in mind that all transactions are atomic. Another way of putting it is that when a client calls a component's method in order for it to perform a given task, the client and the component need to be designed in such a way that all the data which needs to be sent in order to carry out that task is sent in a single call.

Confirmation of Work Performed

Once again, I will use the Order component example. In a standalone application, when the client is finished adding the line items and calls the ProcessOrder method, the Order component would probably return some sort of value indicating that the order had been successfully processed. However, with Queued Components, you won't get that confirmation. One obvious reason is that by the time the server receives the order information and processes it, the client might not even be connected any more. And even if the client is still connected, will it be in a context in which it will understand the returning value?

Obviously, the issue of confirming the successful completion of work is an important one. However, because we are talking about a distributed, queued environment in which a request for an asynchronous task was requested, the solution would be that the component "respond" to the client in the same asynchronous fashion. Designing a component (named, for example, ConfirmOrder) that would run on the client would address this issue.

Now, the data flow would go something like this: The client would acquire a new order number from the system (more on how that would be done in the next section, "Writing a Queued Components Demo Application"). The client would then create an Order object, call its `SetOrderNumber` method followed by multiple calls to `AddLineItem` and finally a call to `ProcessOrder`. The client would then keep track of outstanding orders that have been submitted, but not verified as having been completed. After the server-side component had completed the processing of the order, it could then turn around and, using the same queuing mechanism, instantiate a ConfirmOrder component and call its `SetOrderNumber` method. When the client reconnects to the server, it would receive its messages for the ConfirmOrder component specifying which orders had been completed since the last time the machine had been connected to the server.

Need for Lookup Data

Another common misconception about using queuing with a distributed (and possibly) disconnected system is that of lookup tables (also known as, master tables). Say that you have an invoicing application. You would certainly expect to communicate with the server in order to complete the invoice. However, what about the validation of certain fields on the invoice such as ZIP Code and customer ID? Also, many users want applications that provide some sort of "auto fill" feature in which they type in a customer's name and the address fields are filled out automatically.

Even in a fully connected, yet distributed environment, you would not want to make round-trips to the server for each of these items because not only would performance on the client machine be poor (can you imagine fetching data from the server as you tab from field to field?), but also any amount of users would produce such a tremendous amount of round-trips across the network that overall network performance would be adversely affected. The common way to work around this is to load certain key lookup tables on the client machines (for example; customers, vendors, suppliers, and so on) so that the validation and auto-fill features of the client would be performed without incurring network traffic.

However, what about larger tables such as items? Certainly any decent sized company can't overload each salesperson's computer with their entire inventory. Once again, a little forethought into the design of the client will go a long way. In this case, it is quite common to have the salesperson download onto his laptop a subset of the inventory master table that represents the item information which is most likely to be needed. As a supplement, the salesperson would then take along a catalog of the company's items and would have to manually enter the information of any items that were not downloaded.

The last example of this type would be this: How does the salesperson get a unique order number if his machine is disconnected from the server? In this case, the system could be designed in such a way to allow for the allocation of a block of order numbers before the salesperson leaves the office. That way, these order numbers could be kept in a local table, and when the client connects to the server, the server would process the new orders. You could go as far as designing the server to call a client-side component in order to automatically send down another block of allocated order numbers if the trip has been longer than expected or the salesperson had an exceedingly good sales day.

To Queue or Not to Queue

A good starting point for considering whether to queue-enable your application is to think about how your system would work in an environment with the following traits:

- Communication is always asynchronous with no guarantee of exactly when the requested task will be completed.
- There is no synchronous manner of reporting back the success or failure of a requested task.
- Calls to queued interfaces are limited to unidirectional communications.
- All data necessary to carry out a given request must be passed on the requesting call.

As you can see, writing a distributed system, especially one that works asynchronously via queuing, takes a lot of forethought in terms of the design of both the client and component. My advice would be if you find the aforementioned items too restricting or simply impossible to live with regarding your system, it might not be a good candidate for queuing.

Queued Component Architecture

When detailing an architecture such as Queue Components, it is often easier to illustrate key points using a standard example. Therefore, I'll use the example of a simple remote order entry system that supports disconnected sales people via Queued Components. Figure 27.1 shows a high-level view of how the client would interact with this component. As you wind your way through this section, I will focus more and more on exactly how the component is marked as queued and how the data flows from the client to the component.

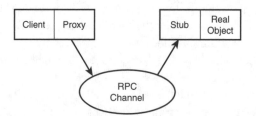

FIGURE 27.1
At this point, we only know that a client needs to communicate with a component on the server.

Creating and Defining a Component as Queued

The process of creating a component varies only slightly from that of creating any other COM component. Using the remote order entry example, you might want to create a component called Order with an interface called ICreate. The ICreate interface would then contain two methods (for the purposes of this example anyway) called AddLineItem (which takes as its arguments an item number and a value representing the quantity ordered) and ProcessOrder.

Although a COM component you want to mark as queued can be created with any language that supports the creation of COM components (such as Visual C++, Visual Basic, and Visual J++), you have to obey the following rules regarding the definition of your COM component if you want it to be queued:

- All methods within an interface that you want queued must not be defined in the IDL as having the attributes [out], [in,out], and [out,retval].

- Because the client and component of a Queued Components relationship might exist on different machines and run at different times, the data that is passed from the client to the component must be passed by value.

> **Tip**
>
> By default, Visual Basic passes all parameters "by reference." Therefore, the fact that all methods within an interface will be marked as queued must mandate that the passing of data by value can be problematic for Visual Basic programmers. To get around this, simply use the Visual Basic attribute ByVal when specifying the parameters of any methods as in the following example:
>
> ```
> Public Sub AddLineItem(ByVal lItemNumber As Long, ByVal lQuantity As Long)
> ```

After you've created your component, the only thing left on the server side is to mark it as queued. This is a simple four-part administrative process that usually takes no more than a minute to complete.

1. Assuming that you're adding this component to a new (not an existing) COM+ Application, you would use the Component Services snap-in to create a new, empty COM+ Application. This application acts as a surrogate process for the COM component.

2. After creating the COM+ Application, you would mark the application itself as being queued. When you do that, Queued Components automatically creates for your application a queue of the same name as your chosen application name. This is the queue that will be used by MSMQ to route messages from the client to the application's components.

3. After you've marked the COM+ Application as being queued, you then add any number of COM components to that COM+ application.

4. Finally, for any of the COM component's interfaces that you want queued, you would simply go about manually selecting them from a list in Component Services and marking them as being queued. If any method in an interface you want to mark as queued is not unidirectional, Component Services will not allow you to mark the interface as queued. It's really an all-or-nothing proposition.

That's it on the server side. There's absolutely nothing from a code perspective that you need to explicitly do in order to mark a component as queued.

The Client Side of Queued Components

On the client side, things are even easier. In fact, the client doesn't even know that the component it's using is queued. Here's how that works. In Visual C++, the client uses a function called ::CoGetObject (in Visual Basic, you would use GetObject) to retrieve a proxy for the opponent. Actually, what the client is receiving is a very special kind of Queued Component object called a *Recorder* object.

However, the key point is that this Recorder object can be used in every way just as if the client had a reference to the actual server-side component. The advantage of this is that the client code doesn't have to be written differently for a standalone versus a queued environment.

Once the client acquires this Recorder object, it can call the methods of the desired server-side component. However, each time the client calls a method, the Recorder simply buffers the call. The data is not sent until the client deactivates the object (either by explicitly releasing the object or letting it go out of scope). The client simply calls the AddLineItem repeatedly to add each item the customer ordered, calls ProcessOrder to signify that the order is ready for processing, and then deactivates the object. Listing 27.1 shows how easy this is to code from a Visual Basic application. Once again, don't worry too much about the specifics of the GetObject call because it will be explained in detail when you get to the demo section of this chapter.

LISTING 27.1 This Visual Basic Snippet Should Begin to Give You an Idea of How Incredibly Easy It Is to Use a Queued Component

```
Dim order
Set order = GetObject("queue:/new:Order.Create")

order.AddLineItem 384, 2
order.AddLineItem 380, 5
order.AddLineItem 289, 1

order.Process
```

When the Recorder object is deactivated, the data is sent to the local MSMQ queue. When the client machine is connected to the server, MSMQ sends the data to the server-side queue for processing. You can see this data flow in Figure 27.2.

FIGURE 27.2

The Queued Components Recorder object acts as a proxy for the server-side component so that the client can use the component without worrying about whether the component is queued.

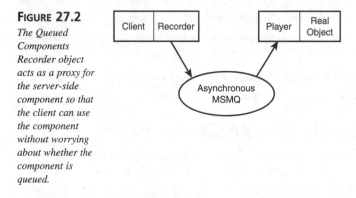

The Server Side of Queued Components

On the server side, each COM+ Application has defined for it a set of default Queued Components called ListenerHelper and Player. When a message is sent via MSMQ to a queue belonging to a given COM+ Application, that application's `ListenerHelper` object reads the message. For each message read, the `ListenerHelper` object then creates an instance of the Player object and passes the message data to it.

The Player object is then responsible for opening the message and detecting which component needs to be created to handle the request. After the target component is created, the Player object translates the message into actual COM method calls to the component. Figure 27.3 shows how this intimate little dance between the different objects results in the component finally receiving the client's calls.

Figure 27.3

The server-side component is also abstracted away from the details of queuing so that it can be used in a queued or non-queued environment without change.

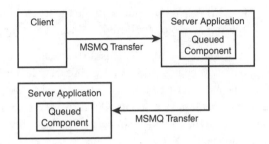

Writing a Queued Components Demo Application

It's finally time to put what you've learned here to the test. In this section, you will write a very simple component that has one interface and one method. The one method simply displays, via a message box, a string that is passed to it from a client application. Obviously, this demo won't win you too many awards for programming ingenuity, but what it will do is illustrate how to perform the following functions that are necessary when utilizing the COM+ Queued Components service. In fact, because the following steps need to be done when using Queued Components regardless of the complexity of the component itself, I've purposely kept the demo as simple as possible so that the elements specific to Queued Components can be focused on. The steps for creating the demo are as follows:

1. Writing a component (using Visual C++ and ATL)
2. Installing the component and marking it as queued
3. Writing a client application using Visual C++
4. Testing the Component and Client Code
5. Exporting the COM+ Application

Writing a Queued Component with Visual C++ and ATL

In this first example, we're going to use Visual C++ and ATL to create a simple component that we'll call QCCompVC. In order to create this component, simply fire up the Visual C++ 6 development environment and create a new Visual C++/ATL project called

QCCompVC. When the ATL COM AppWizard starts up, you will see a dialog similar to what's shown in Figure 27.4. From here, you will need to select the following options:

- Specify the Server Type as being a DLL—This is done because, like most components, this test component will be housed in a DLL. In fact, when using Queued Components, your components must be inserted into a COM+ Application. In order to do that, the component must reside in a DLL. After creating this component, you'll see how to create the COM+ Application that basically acts as a surrogate process for the component's DLL.

- Select the option to allow merging of proxy/stub code—This option is available for DLL projects only and is used because, by default, the proxy/stub code would be marshalling code contained in a separate DLL from the component.

- Check the Support MFC check box—This will be purely optional in your own applications. However, we need it here simply because the demo component uses some MFC-specific classes and functions such as `CString` and `AfxMessageBox`.

FIGURE 27.4

Visual C++ ATL COM AppWizard—It is extremely important to create your ATL correctly in order to use a COM+ Application.

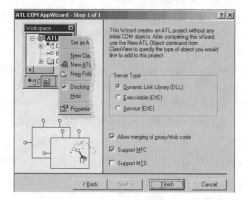

After you have chosen the settings described previously for your ATL component, click the Finish button and then click OK on the New Project Information confirmation dialog.

It's important to realize that you don't have a component at this point. You simply have a Visual C++ ATL project that, when built, creates a DLL capable of housing ATL components. Therefore, the next step is to define the actual ATL component itself. To do that, click the ClassView tab in the Workspace dialog bar and right-click the QCCompVC Classes entry. This will cause a context menu to appear. From there, select the New ATL Object menu option, which will result in the dialog you see in Figure 27.5.

FIGURE 27.5

Adding an ATL component to a project is as simple as point and click.

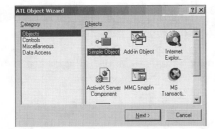

Because this component will be the most bare bones, simple component possible, select the Simple Object icon from the dialog's listview and click the Next button. The next dialog (Figure 27.6) allows you to enter the information that will dictate several key names and files. For the purposes of this demo, type Interaction into the Short Name field. When you do this, you will see that its interface is named `IInteraction`.

FIGURE 27.6

Typically when adding ATL components to a project, set the Short Name value and let the other values—such as CoClass, Interface name, and C++ class name—default to a conjugated version of what you entered.

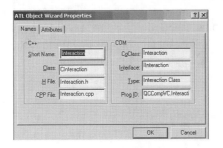

Now, click the Attributes tab of this dialog. This tab (shown in Figure 27.7) enables you to specify some key attributes associated with your ATL component. However, for this demo, the only important attribute is the Free Threaded Marshaler option. For those of you with inquiring minds, take a look at the sidebar entitled "A Glimpse at the Free Threaded Marshaler" for a short synopsis on why you would want to specify the Free Threaded Marshaler.

FIGURE 27.7

The Attributes tab allows you to set the more advanced attributes of your ATL component's definition.

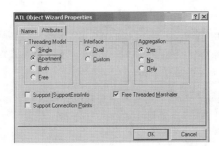

27

QUEUED
COMPONENTS

A Glimpse at the Free Threaded Marshaler

Specifying the Free Threaded Marshaler option aggregates the COM Free Threaded Marshaler to your new class. The generated class accomplishes this in its `FileConstruct` method (defined in the object's header file) by calling the `CoCreateFreeThreadedMarshaler` function.

Basically stated, this function enables objects that are thread-safe to bypass the standard marshaling that occurs whenever cross-apartment interface methods are invoked. Doing this enables threads running in one apartment to access interface methods in another apartment as though they were in the same apartment. The result is a much more efficient code path and therefore, increased performance.

After the ATL component has been created, it's time to add the one and only method that will be used in this demo. To do that, right-click the `IInteraction` interface and select the Add Method option from the context menu. The ensuing dialog (shown in Figure 27.8) will allow you to specify the method's characteristics such as name, return type, and help strings.

FIGURE 27.8

Visual Studio provides a dialog for quickly adding methods to an ATL component.

From the Add Method To Interface dialog, specify a Method Name of `DisplayMessage`. Then, in the Parameters field, specify the value `[in] BSTR bstrMessage`. What you're doing here is simply creating a method named `DisplayMessage` that takes as its only parameter a value of type `BSTR` called `bstrMessage`.

Note

If you read the section covering the architecture of Queued Components and its limitations, you will remember that queued components can't return values. Therefore, you might be wondering how it is that we're creating a method which returns a HRESULT. After all, if this component is used as a queued component (the purpose of this demo), the client application will never see the value returned from this method. Why then is the method defined as returning a value?

The fact is that in accordance with COM rules, all methods (except the IUnknown methods) must return an HRESULT. However, don't be misguided into thinking that you can simply return any value because the client will never see it anyway. One of the biggest advantages of using Queued Components is that the component itself is completely unaware of whether it is being used in a queue environment. Therefore, even if you think this component will never be used in a nonqueued environment, it is good practice to code it as thought it might be and to abide by COM rules with regard to returning the correct information.

If you need more cajoling than that, think back on how many bugs you've had to fix because of another programmer's short-sightedness in deciding not to implement something correctly because, "Nobody will ever use it like that."

At this point, click the OK button to create the DisplayMessage method. Now, open the Interaction.cpp file and the code to display the message that it receives (via the bstrMessage parameter). When you're finished, the code should resemble Listing 27.2.

LISTING 27.2 Component's DisplayMessage Method

```
STDMETHODIMP CInteraction::DisplayMessage(BSTR bstrMessage)
{
 CString strDlgString; // string to display

 AFX_MANAGE_STATE(AfxGetStaticModuleState())

 // convert from BSTR to something we can display in a dlg
 USES_CONVERSION;
 strDlgString = OLE2T(bstrDlgString);

 // display string
 AfxMessageBox(strDlgString);

 return S_OK;
}
```

This code is fairly self-explanatory. We simply create a CString object on the stack, use the ATL OLE2T string conversion macro to convert the incoming BSTR to a CString, and then display the message.

After you've finished modifying the DisplayMessage method, select the build project option in order to create the DLL that contains the ATL component.

Installing a Queued Component

At this point, you might be wondering "Where the heck is the Queued Components part?" The reason you haven't seen anything relating to Queued Components in this demo so far is because the component developer never has to worry about the aspect of defining the component as queued. That's a task typically left up to the person installing the application. However, it would be a misnomer to state that the component developer doesn't have to think about the ramifications of the component being queued because that directly affects the component design.

To further illustrate this in an example, Say that you're developing a component to handle customer orders. The issues that you have to deal with regarding the design of this component are things like, "Can this component live in an isolated environment?" Remember, when this component is processing on the server, it might not have the capability to request more information from the client or to send back a confirmation for the simple reason that the client might not be connected any longer. Besides, the client application certainly won't be in the context it was when it sent the message to begin with. Can you get around that? Definitely. As explained in the earlier section entitled "Returning Information to the Client," there are ways around this issue. However, the point is still valid that the component developer needs to take these issues into account when designing and developing the component.

It's the actual defining of the component as being queued that the component developer doesn't have to deal with and that's the subject of this section.

Defining a COM+ Application

The first thing we need to do to install the component as a queued component is to create a COM+ Application to act as the component's surrogate process. This is done via the Windows 2000 administrative tool, Component Services. Therefore, click the Windows Start button and then Programs, Administrative Tools, Component Services.

After the Component Services has started, expand the tree view until you locate the COM+ Applications folder (located beneath the My Computer folder).

> **Tip**
>
> There's a bit of strangeness when dealing with the Component Services snap-in. Normally, when you right-click an item in a tree view, the application first selects the item and then displays that item's corresponding context menu. However, in the case of Component Services, the application appears to select the item (it is highlighted), but then displays the context menu of the previously selected item. Therefore, you need to make sure to click the desired item with the left mouse button in order to select it and then right-click the item in order to display its context menu.

From the COM+ Application's context menu, select the New, Application menu option. When the COM+ Application installation wizard begins, click the Next button. The next page you will see (see Figure 27.9) enables you to specify whether you are installing a prebuilt application or creating a new, empty COM+ Application. Because our COM+ Application doesn't exist yet, select the latter.

FIGURE 27.9
You can add pre-built COM+ Applications to your system as well as create new, empty applications.

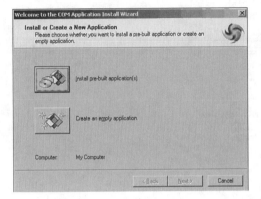

In the next dialog (see Figure 27.10), you need to specify the name of the application as well as the Activation Type.

FIGURE 27.10
Most COM+ Applications that you create will be of the Activation Type, Server Application.

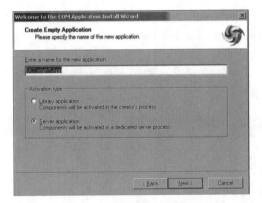

Everyone has their own naming convention for creating COM+ applications. However, because our application will only contain the one component, we'll simply use that name as the root of the application name in order to keep things easy. Therefore, name the application QCCompVCApp. Then, select the Server Application option. Selecting the Library Application option would result in the component being activated in the client's process (which is something we obviously don't want for a queued component).

After clicking the Next button, you will see a dialog that is used to define the application's "identity." This is used for security purposes. For this demo, we'll use the Interactive User option. After selecting the Application Identity, click the Next button and on the last page of the COM+ Application wizard, click the Finish button.

At this point, your new COM+ Application will be created and be listed with any other system applications (see Figure 27.11).

FIGURE 27.11

After a COM+ Application has been added to Component Services, you can set its properties and view its components and defined security roles.

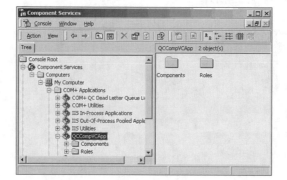

Marking a COM+ Application as Queued

Now that the COM+ Application has been created, you need to mark it as being queued. Once again, this is done via a Component Services wizard. Select the QCCompVCApp application and right-click it to invoke its context menu. Then, select the Properties option. When the QCCompVCApp properties dialog appears, select the Queuing tab. As you can see in Figure 27.12, Component Services makes it easy to define an application as having queued components.

FIGURE 27.12

In almost all cases, you will check both the Queued and Listen options when marking a COM+ Application as queued.

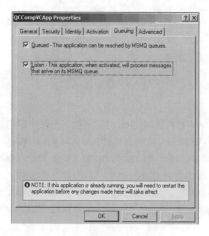

The first option must be checked for a queued component, and it simply states that client applications will communicate with this application via MSMQ.

The listen option is something you only need to check if your component will be using the standard Queued Components feature. When the application is started using this feature, a server-side object is automatically created that reads in any messages intended for it. Therefore, click this option as well and then click the OK button.

Adding Components to a COM+ Application

Now that you've created and marked as queued the COM+ Application, you need to add the component you created earlier. To do this, select Components folder for the QCCompVCApp application and right-click it to invoke its context menu. Then, click the New, Component menu option. When the first page of the wizard appears, click the Next button in order to see the installation options shown in Figure 27.13.

FIGURE 27.13
Several different components can be added to a COM+ Application.

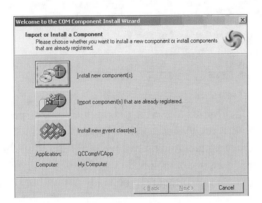

Now, click the Install New Components button to display a standard file selection dialog. At this point, browse to the location of the DLL you created in the previous section and select it. When you select the DLL and click the Open button, you will see the Install New Components dialog. Although it isn't useful in this particular demo, the reason for this demo is that you can have a DLL with more than one component in it. This dialog, therefore, gives you the ability to select which components you want added to the current COM+ Application. As you can see on the dialog, you can also iteratively select other DLLs/components to add to the current COM+ Application. However, because this demo only uses one DLL with a single component, you can click the Next button to proceed. After that, click the Finish button to complete the process of adding the QCCompVC component to the QCCompVCApp application.

Marking a COM Interface as Queued

Now that the component has been added to the COM+ Application, the last thing you need to do is to mark its interface(s) as being queued. To do that, expand the QCCompVCApp Components folder. From there, expand the QCCompVC.Interaction.1 folder. Finally, expand the Interfaces folder to reveal our sole interface, IInteraction. If you're lost at this point, Figure 27.14 shows you where you should be in the Component Services tree view.

FIGURE 27.14

Component Services lists all interfaces for each COM+ Application components and will only allow you to mark as queued the interfaces that abide by certain rules.

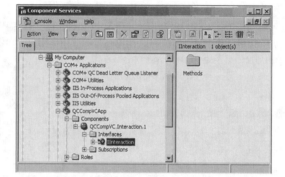

After you've selected the IInteraction interface, right-click it to display its context menu. From there, click the Properties menu option. When the IInteraction properties dialog appears, select the Queuing tab. As you can see in Figure 27.15, this dialog has a single check box control that allows you to specify whether you want this interface to be queued. Check the Queued option and click the OK button.

FIGURE 27.15

Any interface containing only unidirectional methods can be marked as queued using Component Services.

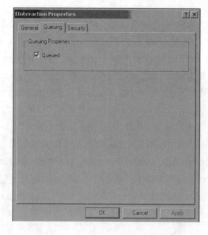

27

Note

If you select the properties for a given interface and find that the Queued check box is disabled, this can only mean one thing: at least one method in that interface has broken the rule of not using any of the following IDL attributes in its argument list: [out], [out,retval] or [in, out].

Another thing to note is that you cannot select which methods you want queued and which ones you do not within a single interface. In other words, either the entire interface (and all its defined methods) is queued or the interface is not queued. Therefore, if you have a component that consists of some methods that can be called in a queued manner and some, which cannot, simply split those methods into different interfaces. After all, the classic definition for COM interface is a "group of semantically related functions." In this case, the semantics would be governed by which methods can be queued.

Writing a Client Application in Visual C++

Now that you've finished with the server (component) side of things, it's time to write the client side. Because there's no admininstrator on the client side, this is even easier.

From the Visual C++ development environment, create a new project called QCClientVC. This project should be defined as a standard dialog-based application.

When you've created the project, open the project's main dialog resource template. Add an Edit Box that serves as the input mechanism for the message which will be sent to the queued component. When finished, your dialog should look similar to Figure 27.16.

FIGURE 27.16

The text entered in this dialog will be stored in a local MSMQ queue and then sent across the network to the component waiting on the server.

After you've

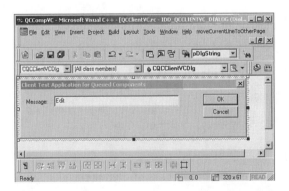

added the appropriate controls to the dialog template resource, add a DDX variable of type CString called m_strMessage. Then, add a message handler for the OK button. After you've done that, modify the CQCClientVCDlg::OnOk function so that when finished, it looks like the code in Listing 27.3.

LISTING 27.3   Visual C++ Client Code to Use a Queued Component

```cpp
void CQCClientVCDlg::OnOk()
{
 if (UpdateData(TRUE))
 {
  m_strMessage.TrimLeft();
  m_strMessage.TrimRight();

  if (0 < m_strMessage.GetLength())
  {
   IInteraction* pInteraction = NULL;
   HRESULT hr;

   BSTR bstrMessage;
   bstrMessage = m_strMessage.AllocSysString();

   ::CoInitialize(NULL);

   hr = ::CoGetObject(L"queue:/new:QCCompVC.Interaction.1",
    NULL,
    IID_IInteraction,
    (void**)&pInteraction);

   if (FAILED(hr))
   {
    if (MK_E_CONNECTMANUALLY == hr)
    {
     AfxMessageBox("Operation requires manual intervention");
    }
    else if (MK_E_EXCEEDEDDEADLINE == hr)
    {
     AfxMessageBox("Object creating timed out");
    }
    else if (MK_E_NEEDGENERIC == hr)
    {
     AfxMessageBox("Moniker needs to be generic");
    }
    else if (MK_E_UNAVAILABLE == hr)
    {
     AfxMessageBox("The request operation is unavailable");
    }
    else if (MK_E_SYNTAX == hr)
    {
```

LISTING 27.3   Continued

```
    AfxMessageBox("The display name param is invalid");
   }
   else if (MK_E_NOOBJECT == hr)
   {
    AfxMessageBox("Object could not be found");
   }
   else if (MK_E_INTERMEDIATEINTERFACENOTSUPPORTED == hr)
   {
    AfxMessageBox("Object does not support required interface");
   }
   else if (ERROR_NOT_AUTHENTICATED == hr)
   {
    AfxMessageBox("auth");
   }
   else
   {
    AfxMessageBox("Unknown error occurred");
   }

   return;
  }

  pInteraction->DisplayMessage(bstrMessage);
  pInteraction->Release();
  pInteraction = NULL;

  ::CoUninitialize();

  AfxMessageBox("Your message has been queued");
 }
 else
 {
  AfxMessageBox("Please enter a string to send to the queued component.");
 }
 }
}
```

Because some of this code is not very obvious, take a minute to walk through it to understand what is required on the client side.

The first thing the function does is to call UpdateData(FALSE) in order to retrieve the value that is entered on the dialog into the m_strMessage member variable. When that is done, a simple trimming of white space and verification that the string wasn't NULL takes place.

Now, we get to some basic COM stuff. A pointer to the IInteraction interface is declared as well as an HRESULT variable. After that is done, the m_strMessage member function, `AllocSysString` is called in order to convert from a `CString` to a `BSTR`. After COM is initialized in this thread (using `::CoInitialize`), the fun begins.

As you're aware of by now, you normally instantiate COM objects with a call to the `::CoCreateInstance` or `::CoCreateInstanceEx` functions or a call to a class factory's `CreateInstance` method. So what is this `::CoGetObject` function? It is used to create a connection to the component. Actually, this function creates and connects the client to a special Queued Component object called a Recorder. If you read the Queued Components Architecture section earlier in the chapter, you learned that this object acts as a proxy in the component's stead. However, the key issue here is that the client application code has absolutely no idea that it isn't talking directly to the component itself. Such is the beauty of the Queued Components service and the reason why the `::CoGetObject` function is used. This function acts as a layer of abstraction so that the client code doesn't have to worry about the details of how to connect to a component that might not even be available (because of being disconnected from the server) or how to deal with MSMQ (because this code might be used in a nondistributed environment one day). With Queued Components, you get the best of both worlds: a distributed solution for disconnected clients from a code base that works in both a distributed and a standalone environment.

Because this function is so instrumental in making this whole thing work, look at the `::CoGetObject` function a bit more closely. The first thing you probably notice is the strangely formatted string used as the first parameter. Actually, this string is really two parameters in one (delimited by a / character) and is called the component's *display string*.

```
queue:/new:QCCompVC.Interaction.1
```

The first part of the string (up to the / character) is called the *queue moniker*. A moniker is a COM+ object that takes a string argument and from that knows how to create and initialize another COM/COM+ object. As with all monikers, `ProgId` is associated with the queue moniker, and it is actually called—with the information after the colon being passed—an initialization string. Figure 27.17 shows an example Registry and the queue moniker entry in the `HKEY_CLASS_ROOT` husk.

We will jump a bit ahead of ourselves and ask what values could be passed to the queue moniker. The most oft-used parameter is the `ComputerName`. This value is how you specify where the component resides on your network. As an example, say that the component was installed on a server called MyBigBadNtServer. If that were the case, the line would read as follows:

```
queue:ComputerName=MyBigBadNtServer/new:QCCompVC.Interaction.1
```

FIGURE 27.17

All monikers have an entry in the Registry that enables the COM runtime to create the appropriate object.

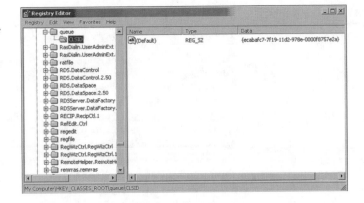

Now, when the queue moniker creates the queue object, it passes the value `ComputerName=MyBigBadNtServer`. It is then up to the queue object to know what to do with that information. What happens if you simply omit the queue moniker? Because the queue moniker is simply used to activate MSMQ, Windows 2000 would not know to use MSMQ and would attempt to create the component for you. If the component were available on the local machine, the code would work. If the component were only available on a remote machine through which Windows 2000 would need to use MSMQ, the call would fail. Table 27.1 contains the other parameters you should be familiar with regarding the use of queue monikers.

The second part of the component's display string is the new moniker. As you can probably guess from the context of the call, this moniker is used to create the specified component and to access the specified method.

TABLE 27.1 Queue Moniker Parameters and Descriptions

Parameter	Description
AppSpecific	This is very similar to the "window word" that can be passed to a newly created window. It is completely up to the component developer as to what information needs to be passed here. The only constraint you have is that the value must be of type unsigned integer.
AuthLevel	This value is used to specify the level of authentication that MSMQ is to use in verifying the message. Authenticated messages are digitally signed and require a registered certificate. NOTE: Although you can alter the authentication level for a COM+ application through Component Services, this parameter seems to be ignored.

TABLE 27.1 Continued

Parameter	Description
ComputerName	As you saw, this parameter is used to resolve to the actual server where the target component resides. If this parameter is omitted, Windows 2000 assumes that the component exists on the client (or local) machine.
Delivery	Used to determine which mode of delivery MSMQ is to use for the message (MQMSG_DELIVERY_RECOVERABLE or MQMSG_DELIVERY_EXPRESS).
EncryptAlgorith	This parameter enables the caller to specify the type of encryption algorithm being used. Valid entries are CALG_RC2 and CALG_RC4.
FormatName	Instructs MSMQ that a GUID is being used for the queue instead of the queue name. A MSMQ queue's GUID can be located by looking at its properties dialog from the Computer Management snap-in.
HashAlgorithm	Defines which hash algorithm is used to encrypt the message. Any of the following are valid: CALG_HMAC, CALG_MAC, CALG_MD2, CALG_MD4, CALG_MD5, CALG_SHA, CALG_SHA1, CALG_SHAMD5, CALG_SSL3, and CALG_TLS1PRF.
Journal	This specifies if a journal is to be used to track a message as it flows through a system. This value defaults to MQMSG_JOURNAL_NONE, which means no journal. You can track all messages by specifying MQMSG_JOURNAL. However, one really useful value is MQMSG_DEADLETTER, which allows you to track only messages that are sent to the dead letter queue.
Label	This value is for message tracking. For example, if you created a convention for labeling all your messages, it wouldn't be difficult to write an administrator application that could provide information on the types of messages being routed to the dead letter queue.
MaxTimeToReachQueue	As its name implies, this value allows you to specify (in seconds) the amount of time a message can take in reaching its destination. Aside from a numeric value, you can also use the values LONG_LIVED or INFINITE.
MaxTimeToReceive	This value is slightly different from MaxTimeToReachQueue. Although that value is only concerned with how long the message takes in reaching the queue, this value is concerned with how long it takes the message to be dequeued, or to be read out of the queue. Once again, the valid values are a numeric value indicating the time in seconds, LONG_LIVED or INFINITE.

TABLE 27.1   Continued

Parameter	Description
PathName	This parameter allows you to fully qualify a path to the server queue (specifying both computer name and queue name) in the format `<server name>/<queue name>`.
Priority	One of the most important values in any distributed system, this enables the application to prioritize the outgoing messages so that the server can be used as efficiently as possible. If you don't specify a value for this parameter, the Priority setting for the queue is used.
PrivLevel	Used to define the messages "privacy level." The valid values are MQMSG_PRIV_LEVEL_NONE, MQMSG_PRIV_LEVEL_BODY, MQMSG_PRIV_LEVEL_BODY_BASE, MQMSG_PRIV_LEVEL_BODY_ENHANCED.
QueueName	Explicitly tells MSMQ which queue to use. If you don't specify this parameter (which the demo doesn't), the queue associated with the server application is used. Specifying both the ComputerName and the QueueName parameters is the functional equivalent of using the PathName parameter.
Trace	This value determines if the message gets traced as it moves from the client to its destination (the server application). The valid values are MQMSG_TRACE_NONE and MQMSG_SEND_ROUTE_TO_REPORT_QUEUE.

27

QUEUED
COMPONENTS

After the `::CoGetObject` call, the function verifies that everything succeeded by checking the returned HRESULT structure. You can find a full list of the possible error types in the winerror.h header file.

If you get past the checking of the returned HRESULT structure, the function succeeded and the Queued Component Recorder object has been created. At this point, it can be used just as if you had a pointer to the actual object itself, which is exactly why the next call is to the IInteraction DisplayMessage method (passing to it the BSTR value converted earlier).

Finally, in the name of good housekeeping, the interface pointer is released and `::CoUninitialize` is called. If all went well, you will see a message box proclaiming, "Your message has been queued".

The last thing you need to do before building the demo test application is to include a couple of files at the top of the QCClientVCDlg.cpp file. These files are the QCCompVC.h header file (which defines the IInteraction interface) and the QCCompVC_i.c file (which defines the IID_IInteraction structure).

Testing the Component and Client Code

And now, we have arrived at the moment of truth. It's time to test the application. To test the application, simply run your client, type in the necessary information, and click OK. If you do that, you should see results similar to those shown in Figure 27.18.

FIGURE 27.18

If everything works correctly, the fact that the server application isn't running won't stop the client from functioning properly.

Tip

If you are receiving an error trying to send the message, the problem might be that you are running in a Workgroup installation. For security to work, you must be running on a Windows 2000 domain. The way around this problem is simple: From Component Services, right-click the COM+ application and select the Properties menu option. From there, click on the Security tab and set the Authentication Level for Calls to None.

After clicking OK and waiting a minute or two, you might be wondering where the message is from the server confirming that the message was received. The reason you don't see that message is that we haven't started the server application yet. First I wanted you to see that the client application would proceed along just fine without the server application/component even running.

At this point, switch to the Component Services and right-click your COM+ application. From the context menu, select the Start menu option. Depending on how impatient you were in getting your messages to display, you should now see something similar to what is shown in Figure 27.19

FIGURE 27.19

When the server application starts up, it begins to read in its queued messages and responds accordingly.

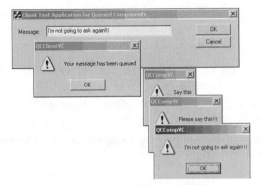

Exporting the COM+ Application

Up to now, we've worked almost exclusively on one machine (except when you learned how to use the queue moniker to resolve to a different computer name). In other words, you created the demo server application/component and installed it on the same machine as the client application. However, what happens when the client application gets moved or copied to another machine? The task is referred to as COM+ Application exporting and as you might suspect, Component Services has a tool for handling this obvious need.

To export a COM+ Application, simply select and right-click the desired COM+ application from the Component Services tree view. When the context menu is displayed, select the Export menu option. This action will invoke the COM Application Export Wizard. When the first page of this wizard is displayed, click the Next button. You should now see a page that enables you to specify where you want the exported application file to be created. Simply browse to the selected folder and enter the name of the installation file. As you can see in Figure 27.20, the demo uses the name QCCompInst.msi (where msi is the extension for a Microsoft Installation file). Another change you need to make to the page is the application type. Select the Application Proxy radio button so that requests for your component are directed to the server and not the local machine.

FIGURE 27.20

Installing a COM+ Application on another machine requires the use of the COM Application Export Wizard.

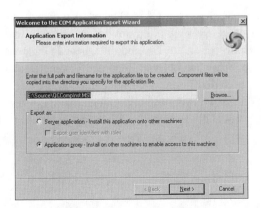

Now, click the Next button to create the installation file. This shouldn't take long because the demo application you've built is small. After the installation file is built, you will see a page confirming that fact. Click the Finish button to exit the wizard.

Go to the client machine where you want to install the COM+ Application. Assuming that you have either copied the installation file to a client machine or the client machine has access to the installation file (such as on a network), browse to the installation file in an Explorer window and right-click it. From the file's context menu, select the Install option. As shown in Figure 27.21, you will see a small dialog with a progress bar that shows the application being installed on the client machine.

FIGURE 27.21

In order to deploy your COM+ Applications to the client machines, create an installation application using the COM+ Application Export Wizard and then run that application on the target client.

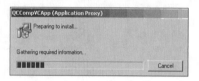

At this point, if you open the Component Services, you will see a new application called QCCompInst. The only thing to keep in mind here is that this is not the real application that exists on the server. Rather, it is a proxy that allows the client to function properly without the presence of the real server-side application. One key point to also make is that you will find your development cycle to be much easier if you completely test the component and client on one machine before deploying the application.

Summary

In this chapter, you began your quest for COM+ Queued Components knowledge by being introduced to a high-level overview of the service and when it would be applicable to use. You then went much deeper and discovered the Queued Components architecture and data flow involving the three main objects: Recorder, ListenerHelper and Player. After this information had been dispensed, you then learned how to write both the client and component side of a queued component arrangement. Finally, you discovered how to test your client and component and how to deploy your application to production clients.

INDEX

longevity, 398
PlaceOrder() function
example, 671-672
roots, 390, 399
state access functions, 670
**MTS Shared Property
Manager. See SPM**
Mtx.exe, 394
Mtxih.lib library, 384
multiple interfaces
cautions, 410
support, 353
multiple threads, 144
**multithreaded apartments
(MTAs), 61, 152, 161**
multitiered applications, 8
multitiered models, 37-39
constraints, 43
identifying components, 41-42
interfaces, 43
layers, 40
mutexes, 168-169
**MWSendMessage() function,
594**
**mymidlexperiment.h header
file, 268-271**

N

named pipes protocol, 283
names
applications, 737
nonsensical, 99
subscriptions, 709
TPs, 505
**Native Structured Storage
(NSS), 70**
NetDynamics, 21
Netscape, 21
**network cycles (DCOM),
203-204**
networks
application development, 561
client access restrictions, 358
Ethernet DLC links, 494
failures, 461
managing objects, 298
messaging, 560
downside, 562-563
system evolution, 562
*unifying dissimilar sys-
tems, 562*

MOM systems
administrative tools, 568
APIs, 567
monikers, 98
network authentication, 299
protocols, 13
security, 298-299
SIDs, 390
WinSock, 564
**net_start_msftpsvc com-
mand, 365**
**net_stop_iisadmin command,
365**
**neutral-threaded apartments,
60-61**
**New Subscription Wizard,
708-709**
**NewDllMain() function,
channel hooks, 533-534**
**NLB Service, load balancing
comparison, 537-538**
no-wait operations, 564
noise, filtering, 700
non-blocking I/O, 564
**non-generic composition
(monikers), 110**
nondurable state, 428
nonzero values, 349
**Not Supported transaction
setting, 455**
Notepad, 17
notification (event), 132
**NSS (Native Structured
Storage), 70**
**NT log, examining using
Event Viewer, 508**
**NT workstations, security,
299**
**NTLMSSP (NT LAN Manager
Security Service Provider),
298, 313**

O

objbase.h header, 606
object class
declaring, 284-285
defining, 285-289
**object oriented programming
(OOP), 50**
object pooling, 57
**object request brokers
(ORBs), 376**

object server, 285
Object Wizard (ATL), 155
object-bound state, 428
**Object-Oriented (OO) compo-
nent architecture, 548**
ObjectContext function, 459
**objects, 410. See also compo-
nents**
activities, 381
automation, 161
channel hooks
*DllCanUnloadNow() func-
tion, 533*
DllMain() function, 533
*load balancing issues,
532-534*
*NewDllMain() function,
533-534*
*ServerFillBuffer() function,
533*
client identity, 474
CLSID, 104
COM+
creating, 59
direct callers, 474
component software environment, 98
compound (IPersistStorage
interface), 75
connection point, 114
Context
*IObjectContext interface,
432, 435-436, 441*
MTS transactions, 670
context wrappers, 380
creating (MTS), 380
critical section, 166
deactivating, 400
destructors, 386
determining class and host
machine, 104
embedded, 108
event sinks, 114, 120
class declarations, 121
class definitions, 122
creating, 128
filenames, 98
happy flags, 399
IObjectControl interface, 433
*building COM+ compo-
nents with ATL, 435-436*
methods, 433-434

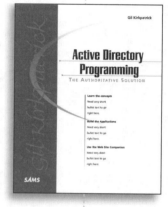

CD-ROM Installation

Windows 95/NT/2000 Installation Instructions

1. Insert the CD-ROM disc into your CD-ROM drive.
2. From the Windows 95/NT/2000 desktop, double-click the My Computer icon. Some features may be accessible by right-clicking on the CD icon from your My Computer menu.
3. Double-click the icon representing your CD-ROM drive.
4. Double-click the icon titled START.EXE to run the CD-ROM interface.

Note

If Windows 95/NT/2000 is installed on your computer, and you have the AutoPlay feature enabled, the START.EXE program starts automatically whenever you insert the disc into your CD-ROM drive.

Read This Before Opening This Software

By opening this package, you are agreeing to be bound by the following agreement:

You may not copy or redistribute the entire CD-ROM as a whole. Copying and redistribution of individual software programs on the CD-ROM is governed by terms set by individual copyright holders.

NOTE: This CD-ROM uses long and mixed-case filenames requiring the use of a protected-mode CD-ROM Driver.